THE OXFORD HANDBOOK OF

AMERICAN ECONOMIC HISTORY

VOLUME 1

THE OXFORD HANDBOOK OF

AMERICAN ECONOMIC HISTORY

VOLUME 1

Edited by

LOUIS P. CAIN

PRICE V. FISHBACK

and

PAUL W. RHODE

OXFORD

UNIVERSITY PRESS

OXFORD
UNIVERSITY PRESS

Oxford University Press is a department of the University of Oxford. It furthers
the University's objective of excellence in research, scholarship, and education
by publishing worldwide. Oxford is a registered trade mark of Oxford University
Press in the UK and certain other countries.

Published in the United States of America by Oxford University Press
198 Madison Avenue, New York, NY 10016, United States of America.

Library of Congress Cataloging-in-Publication Data
Names: Cain, Louis P., editor. | Fishback, Price Van Meter, editor. | Rhode, Paul Webb, editor.
Title: The Oxford handbook of American economic history / edited by Louis P. Cain, Price V. Fishback,
and Paul W. Rhode. Description: Oxford ; New York : Oxford University Press, [2018] |
Series: Oxford handbooks | Includes bibliographical references and index.
Identifiers: LCCN 2017052624 (print) |
LCCN 2017053491 (ebook) | ISBN 9780199983148 (online component) | ISBN 9780199947980 (updf) |
ISBN 9780199947973 (2-volume set : alk. paper) | ISBN 9780190882617 (volume 1 : alk. paper) |
ISBN 9780190882624 (volume 2 : alk. paper)
Subjects: LCSH: United States—Economic conditions.
Classification: LCC HC103 (ebook) | LCC HC103 .O98 2018 (print) | DDC 330.973—dc23
LC record available at https://lccn.loc.gov/2017052624

1 3 5 7 9 8 6 4 2
Printed by Sheridan Books, Inc., United States of America

CONTENTS

VOLUME 1

PART III. FACTORS OF PRODUCTION

Contributors

Samuel K. Allen is professor of economics at the Virginia Military Institute. His research in economic history explores workers' compensation insurance, labor laws, and public housing.

Jeremy Atack is professor emeritus and research professor of economics at Vanderbilt University. Prior to that he was at the University of Illinois. He is also a research associate with the National Bureau of Economic Research. He has been president of the Agricultural History Society, the Business History Conference, and the Economic History Association, and an editor of the *Journal of Economic History*.

Martha J. Bailey is professor in the Department of Economics and research professor at the Population Studies Center at the University of Michigan. She is also a research associate at the National Bureau of Economic Research, a research affiliate at CESifo, and an IZA Institute of Labor Economics research fellow. Her research focuses on issues in labor economics, demography, and health in the United States, within the long-run perspective of economic history.

Hoyt Bleakley is associate professor of economics at the University of Michigan and research associate professor at the Institute for Social Research. He studies health and education along the historical path of economic development.

Leah Boustan is professor of economics at Princeton University and a research associate at the National Bureau of Economic Research. She is the author of *Competition in the Promised Land: Black Migrants in Northern Cities and Labor Markets*.

Stephen Broadberry is professor of economic history at Nuffield College, University of Oxford. His books include *The Productivity Race: British Manufacturing in International Perspective, 1850–1990*; *Market Services and the Productivity Race, 1850–2000: British Performance in International Perspective*; the two-volume *Cambridge Economic History of Europe*, edited with Kevin O'Rourke; and (as coauthor) *British Economic Growth, 1270–1870*.

Devin Bunten is assistant professor of urban economics and housing at the Massachusetts Institute of Technology, in the Department of Urban Studies and Planning. Devin's work focuses on urban housing markets, including projects investigating zoning laws and gentrification.

Louis P. Cain is professor of economics emeritus at Loyola University Chicago and adjunct professor of economics at Northwestern University. He coauthored *The*

Children of Eve with Donald Paterson and *American Economic History* with the late Jonathan Hughes.

Robert L. Clark is the Stephen Zelnak Professor of Economics and Management, Innovation, and Entrepreneurship in the Poole College of Management at North Carolina State University. Clark and Lee Craig have written two books and a series of articles on the history of public pensions in the United States. Clark has also conducted research examining retirement decisions, the choice between defined benefit and defined contribution plans, and the role of supplementary retirement saving plans in the public sector.

Karen Clay is professor of economics and public policy at Carnegie Mellon University and a research associate of the National Bureau of Economic Research. She is the coauthor with Dan Berkowitz of *The Evolution of a Nation: How Geography and Law Shaped the American States.*

Lee A. Craig is alumni distinguished professor of economics in the Poole College of Management at North Carolina State University. His current research interests include the history and financing of pensions and social security; the impact of nutrition on long-run economic growth and the standard of living; and the history of the newspaper industry. His recent books include *Josephus Daniels: His Life and Times*, and, with Robert Clark, *A History of Public Sector Pensions in the United States* and *State and Local Retirement Plans in the United States.*

Stanley L. Engerman is emeritus professor of economics at the University of Rochester. Among the books he has coauthored is *Time on the Cross: The Economics of American Negro Slavery* (with Robert W. Fogel), and he is a coeditor of the four-volume *The Cambridge World History of Slavery* (with David Eltis and others).

Joseph P. Ferrie is professor of economics and history at Northwestern University and a research associate of the National Bureau of Economic Research. He has studied international migration into the United States, intergenerational mobility, and the impact of early life circumstances on later-life outcomes.

Daniel Fetter is assistant professor of economics at Wellesley College and a faculty research fellow at the National Bureau of Economic Research. He has published on the history of housing and housing policy in journals such as the *Journal of Economic History* and the *American Economic Journal: Economic Policy.*

Alexander J. Field is the Michel and Mary Orradre Professor of Economics at Santa Clara University, and served previously as executive director of the Economic History Association. He is the author of more than seventy scholarly articles as well as several books, including *A Great Leap Forward: 1930s Depression and U.S. Economic Growth*, which received the Alice Hanson Jones Prize.

Price V. Fishback is the Thomas R. Brown Professor of Economics at the University of Arizona, a research associate at the National Bureau of Economic Research, and executive director of the Economic History Association from 2012 to 2017. He is a co-author of *Government and the American Economy: A New History* and has won several awards for research and teaching from the Economic History Association and the Cliometrics Society.

Jonathan Fox is assistant professor of economics in the John F. Kennedy Institute for North American Studies at the Freie Universität, Berlin. His research has covered the history of public health programs in the United States and the consequences of different ecological environments on demographic outcomes.

Carola Frydman is professor of finance at the Kellogg School of Management at Northwestern University, and a research associate at the National Bureau of Economic Research. She works on business and financial history.

Rowena Gray is assistant professor of economics at the University of California, Merced. She specializes in the economic history of technological change and immigration in pre–World War II United States; her work has appeared in *Explorations in Economic History* and *Economics of Education Review*.

Michael R. Haines is the Banfi Vinters Professor of Economics at Colgate University and research associate at the National Bureau of Economic Research. He has been president of the Social Science History Association and vice president and program chair of the Economic History Association. He is coauthor of *Fatal Years: Child Mortality in Late Nineteenth Century America*, author of *Fertility and Occupation: Population Patterns in Industrialization*, and coeditor of *A Population History of North America*.

Owen Hearey is an associate with Analysis Group in Los Angeles. His research focuses on household residential choice, neighborhood composition, and local public goods.

Brad J. Hershbein is an economist at the W. E. Upjohn Institute for Employment Research, a labor studies research organization in Kalamazoo, Michigan, and a nonresident fellow in economic studies at the Brookings Institution.

Robert L. Hetzel was an economist with the Federal Reserve Bank of Richmond from 1975 until early 2018. He is the author of two books on the history of the Federal Reserve System: *The Monetary Policy of the Federal Reserve: A History*; and *The Great Recession: Market Failure or Policy Failure?*

Eric Hilt is professor of economics at Wellesley College, and a research associate of the National Bureau of Economic Research. His papers have been published in economic history, business history, and economics journals, and he has been the winner of the Arthur Cole Prize for the best paper in the *Journal of Economic History*, and the co-winner of the prize for the best paper in *Explorations in Economic History*.

Sok Chul Hong is associate professor of economics at Seoul National University. He is the coauthor of *The Changing Body: Health, Nutrition, and Human Development in the Western World since 1700*.

Douglas A. Irwin is professor of economics at Dartmouth College and a research associate of the National Bureau of Economic Research. His books include *Clashing over Commerce: A History of U.S. Trade Policy and Trade Policy Disaster: Lessons from the 1930s*.

Matthew Jaremski is associate professor of economics at Colgate University and is also a faculty research fellow at the National Bureau of Economic Research.

Taylor Jaworski is assistant professor of economics at the University of Colorado, Boulder, and faculty research fellow at the National Bureau of Economic Research.

Brooks Kaiser is professor in the Management and Economics of Resources and the Environment Group of the Department of Sociology, Environmental and Business Economics at the University of Southern Denmark and research fellow at the University of Hawaii Economic Research Organization. She is currently engaged in research on environmental and resource topics including historical energy transitions, threats to natural capital, and Arctic economic development.

Carl Kitchens is assistant professor of economics at Florida State University. He has published several academic articles that explore the impacts of electrification and the structure of the electric industry during the first half of the twentieth century.

Changkeun Lee is associate fellow at Korea Development Institute (KDI). A graduate of the University of Michigan, his research focuses on firm dynamics, productivity, and labor market. At KDI, he also engages in policy evaluation and government consultation.

Gary D. Libecap is professor at the Bren School of Environmental Science and Management and Department of Economics, University of California, Santa Barbara; research associate, National Bureau of Economic Research; and research fellow at the Hoover Institution Stanford. He examines the problems of open-access resources. Recent publications include *Environmental Markets: A Property Rights Approach*, with Terry L. Anderson, and "Addressing Global Environmental Externalities" in the *Journal of Economic Literature*.

Brendan Livingston is the director of Enrollment Management Analytics at the University of California, Davis.

Robert A. Margo is professor of economics at Boston University and a research associate of the National Bureau of Economic Research. His presidential address to the Economic History Association, "Obama, Katrina, and the Persistence of Racial Inequality," was published in the *Journal of Economic History*.

Robert A. McGuire is adjunct research professor of economics at The University of Akron. He specializes in historical economics, constitutional/legal political economy, and demographic/public health issues. He is the author of *We the People: A New Economic Interpretation of the United States Constitution*, co-author of *Parasites,*

Pathogens, and Progress: Diseases and Economic Development, and one of many coauthors of *Government and the American Economy: A New History.*

Petra Moser is associate professor of economics and Jules Backman Faculty Fellow at New York University Stern School of Business, and a faculty research fellow at National Bureau of Economic Research and the Centre for Economic Policy Research. Her work on the determinants of creativity and innovation has been honored with an NSF Career Grant, a fellowship at the Center for Advanced Studies in the Behavioral Science, and the Gerschenkron Dissertation Prize.

Suresh Naidu is associate professor of economics and public affairs at Columbia University. He works in the political economy of labor markets, economic history, and development.

Lee E. Ohanian is professor of economics at University of California, Los Angeles, and a senior fellow at the Hoover Institution at Stanford University. He has published extensively in the fields of economic growth and business cycles, and he is the author of "The Macroeconomics of War Finance in the United States."

Alan L. Olmstead is distinguished research professor at the University of California, Davis. His recent books coauthored with Paul W. Rhode include *Arresting Contagion: Science, Policy, and Conflicts over Animal Disease Control,* and *Creating Abundance: Biological Innovation and American Agricultural Development.* He is a fellow of the Cliometrics Society and of the Agricultural and Applied Economics Association.

John M. Parman is associate professor of economics at the College of William & Mary and a faculty research fellow at the National Bureau of Economic Research.

Roger L. Ransom is distinguished professor of history and economics, emeritus, at the University of California, Riverside. His books include: *One Kind of Freedom: The Economic Consequences of Emancipation* (with Richard Sutch); *Conflict and Compromise: The Political Economy of Slavery, Emancipation and the American Civil War;* and *The Confederate States of America: What Might Have Been.* He is a fellow of the Cliometric Society and past president of the Economic History Association.

Paul W. Rhode is the professor of economics at the University of Michigan, a research associate at the National Bureau of Economic Research, and former editor of the *Journal of Economic History.* He is coauthor (with Alan Olmstead) of *Creating Abundance: Biological Innovation in American Agricultural Development* and *Arresting Contagion: Science, Policy and Conflict over Animal Disease Control.*

Gary Richardson is professor in the Department of Economics at the University of California in Irvine and research associate at the National Bureau of Economic Research. He served as the official Historian of the Federal Reserve System. He has written extensively on the history of banking, central banking, and financial crises. He has also published on the political changes in England preceding the industrial revolution and on links between social, religious, and industrial change in medieval Europe.

Jonathan Rose is principal economist at the Board of Governors of the Federal Reserve System. He is the author, with Price V. Fishback and Kenneth Snowden, of *Well Worth Saving: How the New Deal Safeguarded Home Ownership*.

Peter L. Rousseau is professor of economics and history at Vanderbilt University, as well as the secretary-treasurer of the American Economic Association. He is a macro-economist and economic historian who studies the role of financial markets and institutions in growth and development. He is particularly interested in the monetary history of the United States and Europe and in how financial markets assist in spreading transformative technological changes through an economy.

Kenneth Snowden is professor of economics at the University of North Carolina Greensboro and a research associate at the National Bureau of Economic Research. He is also the coauthor of *Well Worth Saving: How the New Deal Safeguarded Home Ownership*, and the co-editor of *Housing and Mortgage Markets in Historical Perspective*.

Richard H. Steckel is Distinguished University Professor Emeritus at Ohio State University and a research associate at the National Bureau of Economic Research. He has been editor of *Explorations in Economic History* and is completing a manuscript on American slavery and its aftermath, entitled *A Dreadful Childhood: The Long Shadow of American Slavery*.

Melissa A. Thomasson is the Julian Lange Professor of Economics at Miami University. Her work on the economic history of health insurance and health care has been published in top journals, and she has received several grants and awards, including a grant from the National Science Foundation.

John Joseph Wallis is Mancur Olson Professor of Economics at the University of Maryland and research associate of the National Bureau of Economic Research. He works on the interaction of political and economic development. He is particularly interested in how patterns of economic institutions change over time and specifically how patterns of economic institutions interact with political institutions in a way that make both economic and political institutions sustainable over time.

Thomas Weiss is professor emeritus of economics at the University of Kansas, a research associate of the National Bureau of Economic Research, and a fellow of the CESifo Research Network. He is a past president of the Economic History Association and served as editor of the *Journal of Economic History*. He has published widely on topics in American economic history, including economic growth in colonial North America, industrialization in the antebellum South, the rise of the service sector, and most recently on the economic history of tourism.

Gavin Wright is the William Robertson Coe Professor of American Economic History Emeritus at Stanford University. He has written extensively on the role of natural resources in American economic development. His most recent book is *Sharing the Prize: The Economics of the Civil Rights Revolution in the American South*.

Noam Yuchtman is associate professor at the Haas School of Business and a research associate of the National Bureau of Economic Research. He has published articles on historical labor market institutions in leading academic journals, including the *American Economic Review* and the *Quarterly Journal of Economics*, and is a member of the editorial board of *Explorations in Economic History*.

INTRODUCTION

LOUIS P. CAIN, PRICE V. FISHBACK,
AND PAUL W. RHODE

AMERICAN economic history is the story of how a handful of struggling settlements on the Atlantic seaboard transitioned into the most successful economy in the world. The growth of that economy involved the production of an ever-larger quantity of goods and services by more and more people. Since output grew at a greater rate than did population, on average each person had command over more output; they grew better off over time. The nation and the economy also grew geographically, ultimately linking the Atlantic and Pacific Oceans and beyond. The US Constitution created a giant free trade zone into which the economy could grow. Over time, markets expanded to reach every corner of the nation.

The result can be seen in figure I.1, which documents the economic growth experienced by the American economy from the first census in 1790 to the end of the twentieth century as measured by the growth of real GDP per capita. Panel A graphs real GDP per capita in dollars. Panel B graphs the same series on a logarithmic scale; the slope displays the growth rate. The growth rate of GDP per capita for 1790–1840 was 0.67 percent per annum, and for 1841–2000 it was 1.89 percent per annum. At the former rate, income per person doubles every 108 years; at the later rate, it doubles every 38 years.

As the economy grew and developed, so did the methods used by economic historians to analyze the process. In the 1950s, a small group of American scholars adopted a new approach to investigating the economic past. That approach had roots dating back to the 1920s, but in the years following World War II, it was an element of a much wider transformation that affected history and the social sciences in general, economics in particular. It was driven by a more mathematical specification of economic theory, by the development of econometric methods, and, perhaps most important, by the coming of the computer. It also led to the unearthing or estimation of new sources of data. Ever more specific questions could be asked of a broader array of subjects. Furthermore, the data provided a laboratory where economic theory could be tested and economic policy alternatives analyzed.

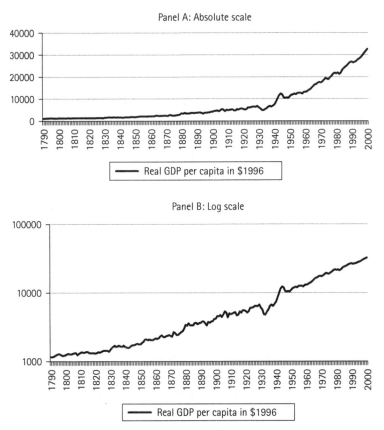

FIGURE I.1. Real GDP per capita, 1790–2000
Source: Carter et al. (2006, series Ca11).

World War II drew a large number of economists into government service and focused their attention on questions of "the long-term growth of national productive capabilities," as Moses Abramovitz (1989, *xii*) put it. In the immediate postwar years, there was widespread fear that the nation would revert to the depressed conditions of the 1930s. This led to a surge of interest in the economics of development and a resurgence of work on economic growth, which required both explanation and measurement. Economic historians such as Abramovitz and Simon Kuznets (1966) were among those who played major roles in that effort. Alexander Gerschenkron's (1952) model of "relative economic backwardness" linked economic growth to institutional structures and past development patterns. In brief, to understand where you were heading, you had to have an understanding of where you had been. Herbert Heaton (1965, 465) noted that in the mid-1950s economic historians were climbing onto the "Economic Growth Bandwagon."

Interest in economic history has sharply increased in recent years among the public, policymakers, and in the academy. For instance, the *New York Times* published fifty more articles using the term "economic history" from 2006 to 2010 as it did from either 2001 to 2005 or 1996 to 2000. Thomas Piketty's *Capital in the Twenty-First Century* (2014) topped the *New York Times* bestseller list for nonfiction. Economists trained as economic historians have assumed key positions setting economic policy. For example, Christina Romer was chair of the Council of Economic Advisers during Barack Obama's first term. The economic turmoil following the market collapse in 2008, calling forth comparisons with the Great Depression of the 1930s, is in part responsible for the surge in interest among the public and in policy circles. The turmoil also stimulated greater scholarly research into past financial crises, the multiplier effects of fiscal and monetary policy, the dynamics of the housing market, and international economic cooperation and conflict. Other pressing policy issues—including the impending retirement of the Baby Boom generation, the ongoing expansion of the health care sector, and the environmental challenges imposed by global climatic change—have further increased the demand for economic history research to provide long-run perspective.

Over and above these external forces, the emergence of new conceptual approaches, methods, and data sources within economic history have contributed to the increased vitality of the field. Understanding how, when, and through which mechanisms "history matters" has become a central concern. Further, it is almost impossible to assess the importance of a factor without supposing its absence in alternative circumstances, which has led economic historians to become explicit about their "counterfactual" hypotheses. In 1993, Robert Fogel and Douglass North were awarded the Nobel Memorial Prize in Economic Sciences for their work in promulgating this work. New work in "causal economic history" seeks to establish the direction of causation between changes in the structure and institutions in the American economy and changes in economic performance. Determining causation is made difficult because of the feedback effects between structure and performance. Often new policies were introduced to improve economic performance, but at the same time declines in economic performance led to the introduction of additional policies. These interactions make it difficult to untangle how effective the initial policy was. A variety of new methods have been developed to help resolve these issues, including the use of "natural experiments," "quasi-experiments," and historically informed "instrumental variables." The goal has been to find aspects of changes in policy that were not developed in response to economic performance to identify the causal relationships. As with many new techniques, these methods are constantly evolving. Economic historians, whether from economics or history departments, colleges of arts and sciences or business schools, use a variety of these methods.

In addition to these new approaches and methods, economic historians have benefited from the recent explosion of new data sources made available online. The five-volume *Historical Statistics of the United States*, millennial edition, which appeared in 2006, is a basic research tool for economic historians, and all its data can be downloaded http://hsus.cambridge.org/HSUSWeb/HSUSEntryServlet. The increased accessibility (in machine-searchable text) of newspapers, periodicals, reports of state and local governments and business organizations, and rare books now in the public domain promises to revolutionize studies of the US economy before 1922 (after which copyright restrictions may apply). The uses of geographic information system (GIS) and sophisticated mapping software have greatly improved our ability to investigate the effects of infrastructure expansion, environmental disasters, and other economic or social processes with a strong spatial dimension. New searchable patent databases, when subject to state-of-the-art analytical techniques, are transforming our understanding of invention and innovation. Similar advances, pushed by web-scraping software scripts and linking protocols, are occurring in research that matches individuals across different micro data sets. New panels constructed from such techniques have already informed path-breaking studies of life-cycle earning patterns, fertility behavior, migration, and intergenerational mobility. Another wave of eye-opening discoveries has begun to flow from the release of the full 1940 manuscript census, which contains individuals' names as well as the first complete data on education attainment and labor earnings.[1]

POPULATION AND HEALTH

Modern discussions of economic growth typically focus on the growth rate of real GDP per capita, the growth rate of a country's annual total output of final goods and services divided by the population of that country. For small changes, GDP growth will equal the sum of population growth and growth in real GDP per person. This is an important relationship to understand because real GDP per person is the customary measure of how well the typical individual is faring in the economy. In the limited resource world described by Thomas Malthus (1798) in which population grew faster than other resources, population growth could actually lead to declines in income per capita due to epidemics, wars, or other crises.

The United States has had an abundance of land and natural resources, ready access to capital, and impressive improvements in technology relative to other countries throughout its history. As a result, population growth has had a benign relationship with GDP per capita. The population has grown from 4 million people in 1790 to over 310 million today, while per capita incomes over the same period have grown from $1,100 to $50,000 (in 2009 purchasing power), or at a rate of 1.7 percent per year. Early in American history, population growth dominated per capita GDP growth in determining the total growth of real GDP, but the situation slowly shifted the other way. Between 1790 and 1820 most of the 4.3 percent rise in real GDP came from population growth of 3 percent per year, as per capita income growth was only 1.3 percent per year. The typical individual fared better in the late 1800s. Real GDP was growing slightly faster at 4.5 percent, but real GDP per capita grew 2.3 percent per year, while population growth slowed to 2.2 percent per year. In the thirty years before the Great Recession of 2008, real GDP growth slowed, primarily because population growth slowed to 1.1 percent per year while real GDP per capita still grew at 2 percent per year (Williamson 2016).

Like many other developed countries, the American population growth rates slowed as the United States experienced a demographic transition in which both the birth rate and the death rate fell, but the birth rate fell faster. The difference, known as the natural rate of increase, fell as a result. Unlike most other developed countries, however, the

United States has accepted large numbers of immigrants, and so population growth has remained robust (Cain and Paterson 2012).

High birth rates were one of the reasons that population growth was high before the Civil War in America relative to that in Europe. Blessed with abundant natural resources, American families married at earlier ages and had substantially more children than European families did. As the share of the population in agriculture declined and more people lived in cities, the benefits for families of having children to serve as workers declined and the opportunity costs for women of having children rose. Meanwhile, child survival rates rose, and parental preferences shifted toward having fewer children in whom more resources per child were invested. All four changes contributed to a long-run decline in the birth rate up to 1940. Following World War II, there was a baby boom in which the birth rate rose to a peak in the 1950s that approximated birth rates in the mid-1920s. The birth rate declined again thereafter in part due to development of "the pill," which gave women much more control over choices about having children. Some scholars have argued that the United States is experiencing a second fertility transition, but it is too early to tell whether the recent decrease in the fertility rate is distinct or simply a continuation of the first transition.

The United States also went through a mortality transition to substantially lower death rates. Infant death rates have plummeted over the past two centuries, while life expectancy at age twenty has increased. Death rates declined with increases in nutrition and the standard of living. In the late nineteenth and early twentieth centuries, better understanding of the germ theory of disease led many cities to improve sanitation—water, wastewater, and solid waste works. These changes and other public health programs that spread information about simple practices, like the washing of hands and better nutrition, led to substantial declines in mortality in urban areas. Economic historians have attempted to estimate the effectiveness of these systems and found that the social investments that financed them were justified.

The decline in death rates was accompanied by an epidemiological transition in which deaths due to the chronic diseases associated with the elderly became more common while those due to infectious diseases became less so. This transition meant that people were healthier over their longer lives. In addition to improving the quality of life, economists have found that better health led to higher income because healthy people are more productive.

After the late 1920s, advances in medical care began to play a larger role in improving health. There were tremendous technological improvements in medical treatment, including the introduction of sulfa drugs, penicillin, antibiotics, more vaccines, and a wide range of new surgical techniques. Access to these new treatments expanded with the rise of private and public health insurance. These dramatic improvements contributed to a sharp rise in health care spending from a relatively small share of GDP in the early 1900s to nearly 18 percent of GDP around 2015 with American governments paying roughly half the costs.

Even as the natural rate of increase in population (birth rate minus death rate) declined over time, growth rates in population did not decline as fast because significant numbers of people immigrated into the country. The immigration not only stimulated population growth; it also led to even faster growth in the labor force. Many immigrants were educated and trained in their home countries before moving to America during their prime working ages. They played important roles in building the nation's infrastructure and transforming its industrial sector, which expanded during booms and contracted during busts when immigrants returned home. Immigrants provided a flexible labor force that expanded to meet the increased labor demand during booms and contracted when demand fell. The "First Great Wave" (1800–1890) of migrants largely came from western and northern Europe. As the American economy continued to expand, a "Second Great Wave" (1890–1914) poured into the country from southern and eastern European countries. The immigrants discovered that the streets were not paved with gold, but the wages in America were substantially higher than at home. Despite the increases in supply associated with the influx of new workers, real wages continued to rise because the demand for workers rose even faster. World War I and immigration restrictions imposed by the federal government in the early 1920s slowed the flood somewhat until the 1960s. After 1965, migration flows expanded in new ways that have influenced the continuing political controversies over migration policy in the modern era.

The study of population growth and health has benefited from a broad range of new data sets and methods. The Integrated Public Use Microdata Series (IPUMS) hosted by the Minnesota Population Center provides enormous samples of individual households for each of the census years. In addition, a wide range of scholars have unearthed and digitized demographic data for many time periods and in many locations.

There has also been an expansion in the types of data that scholars have been using to study the welfare of Americans with the development of *anthropometric* history in the 1970s by Robert Fogel and his colleagues. Social scientists have gathered information on heights and weights of military personnel, slaves, prisoners, and a variety of other populations, and then made inferences about the nutrition and health of different populations. Although dominated by genes, the heights and weights of individuals are sensitive to diet, work effort, and disease, while income and its distribution affect the average height within a population. Scholars have found a wide range of evidence concerning the relative welfare of Americans, and they continue to find new records on heights, weights, skeletons, and consumption records that will continue to enrich our understanding of the health and welfare of populations.[2]

PRODUCTION AND STRUCTURAL CHANGE

American economic growth of output outpaced that of population, so real GDP per capita increased. That growth has been associated with substantial changes in the structure of production. Employment and economic activity has shifted from the primary sector (agriculture, forestry, and fisheries) to the secondary sector (manufacturing, mining, construction, transportation, and so on) and then to the tertiary sector (serv-ices). Figure I.2 reports the share of the labor force in each of these sectors at census years.

The sources of structural change are manifold. One set of sources arise from the de-mand side. The demand for food, according to Engel's Law, increases with rising incomes but at a slower rate. In economists' language, the income elasticity of food demand is less than one. On the one hand, this implies that in a growing (closed) economy, the agri-cultural sector will grow more slowly than the economy as a whole. On the other hand, the service sector is generally thought to produce "superior" goods; their income elas-ticity of demand exceeds one. This implies that as the income per capita rises, the service sector will grow disproportionately fast. A further set of sources for structural change arise from the supply side, from differential productivity growth. Goods and services experiencing more rapid productivity growth generally become cheaper. A "new good" might be considered the extreme case; the product was previously rare to the point of nonexistence, infinitely expensive, and now is available for consumption or use. In general, productivity growth means fewer resources are required to produce one unit of the good.

How differential productivity growth affects sectoral size—for example, its share of employment—depends on the interaction of supply and demand. If demand is highly responsive to price (the product is price elastic), then the sector will grow, and employ more resources, as technological progress makes its products cheaper. If demand is un-responsive to price (i.e., price inelastic), then the quantity demanded will not experience much growth with technological progress. The sector will feel pressure to release labor and other inputs, which can be economically painful. Factor returns in contracting sectors may fall behind those in expanding sectors. Structural change is often disruptive and challenges previously held beliefs about the normal order of things.

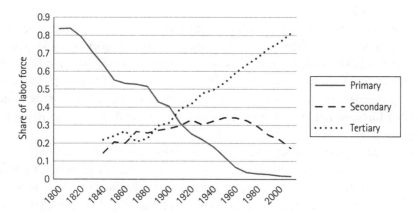

FIGURE I.2. Sector shares, 1800–2010

Sources: 1800–1900 (1930): Carter et al. (2006, series Ba 814–830); 1910–1990 (with 1930 interpolated): Carter et al. (2006, series Ba 652–659); 2000 and 2010: US Bureau of Labor Statistics, "Employment and Earnings Online," January 2011 issue, published March 2011, http://www.bls.gov/opub/ee/home.htm and http://www.bls.gov/cps/home.htm, Table 619.

The history of US agriculture represents an example of these forces at play. Technological changes including biological innovation and mechanization have allowed a smaller number of farmers to feed a growing population. In 1790, roughly 95 percent of the US population resided in rural areas and most worked on farms. By 2010, the farm share had fallen below 2 percent. The decline was especially pronounced in the twentieth century. There was what has been described as a "farm crisis" during the Great Depression of the 1930s, and the federal government responded with a number of policies that continue to impact farmers and consumers today.

Over the past two hundred years, industrial expansion has been the driving force in the economic development of most nations experiencing "modern economic growth." Industrial activity generally expanded faster than the economy as a whole. As a result, this sector grew to account for sizeable shares of output, employment, and trade. Manufacturing activities generally experienced faster rates of productivity growth than the economy as a whole, and its laborers were often paid higher wages. Manufacturing also contributed material and technology for military purposes. For these reasons, policymakers and the public have long viewed manufacturing as having greater importance than other activities. It is common to use the term "Industrial Revolution" for three major periods. The first (1810–1860) especially impacted the textile industry. It witnessed the development of many machines, new modes of power, and the rise of the factory. The second (1870–1920) was focused on the electrical and automotive industries; the third (1970–present) is the result of the electronics industry.

Growth accounting has decomposed the expansion of output into the portions attributable to productivity growth and to expansion in the factors of production. Although manufacturing output fell substantially during the Great Depression, the decade of the 1930s has been termed "a great leap forward" by Alex Field (2011), a leading scholar of manufacturing productivity growth. Manufacturing today is shaped by several key forces, such as globalization, the spread of information technologies, and deindustrialization.

The service sector, which includes a broad collection of heterogeneous activities, has grown to be the largest economic sector; it now employs over 80 percent of the American labor force. The growth of services began earlier and increased faster in the United States than in many other countries. The growth of this sector is related to other key changes, including the expansion of education, the entry of women into the paid labor force, variations in the extent of self-employment, and the changing role of foreign trade.

The sectoral shift in economic activity from agriculture to manufacturing and then to services was matched by structural shifts in the location of production from farms to factories to offices. Similarly, single proprietors working in small shops with family or a few hired laborers at the time of the American Revolution have grown into today's corporations. While proprietorships, partnerships, and corporations are not the only organizational forms available to business, they are the ones that have proven the most important. In particular, the corporation in the United States has grown from the common law model, which implied a special relationship with government (e.g., a bank or a bridge company) to today's large vertically integrated conglomerates serving global markets.

As the corporation evolved, the legal and institutional context of "big business" enterprises emerged. The resulting large capitalistic enterprises have become controversial not only as businesses but also for the executive compensation they offer. Compensation sharply declined during World War II, then fell more slowly in the late 1940s. These patterns are in line with the general decrease in wage inequality during the period that Claudia Goldin and Robert Margo (1992) call the "Great Compression." From the 1950s to the mid-1970s, executive compensation increased slowly (by less than 1 percent annually), but then accelerated beginning in the mid-1970s (growing about 10 percent per year in the 1990s). The expanding gap between the pay of corporate executives and that of the median employee has been an important contributor to rising income inequality in recent decades. The distribution of income depends crucially on the markets for the factors of production.

In recent years, there has been an explosion of interest in the economic history of income and wealth inequality and social mobility. The work of Thomas Piketty and Emmanuel Saez (2003) has highlighted the resurgence after the 1980s of the income shares of the top 10 and top 1 percent of Americans to the levels prevailing before World War II. Other important research (Long and Ferrie 2013; Lindert and Williamson 2016) is appearing in the area (fig. I.3). With new matching techniques, scholars are building samples to investigate intergenerational mobility rates. The area is very active, and many findings remain controversial. Interesting new work that will revise our understanding of the past appears regularly.

One related set of topics where economic historians have consolidated knowledge in the last three decades are trends in earnings ratios by gender and race. In path-breaking work, Claudia Goldin (1990) documented that in the early period (circa 1820), when agriculture dominated the US economy, the full-time earnings of women were about

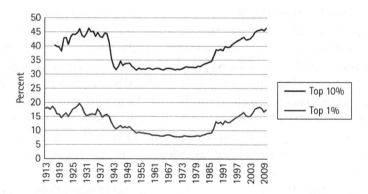

FIGURE I.3. Income shares of top earners, 1913–2009

Sources: Piketty (2003). (Longer updated version published in Atkinson and Piketty (2007), tables and figures updated to 2015 in Excel format, June 2016.)

30 percent of those of men. With the American industrial revolution, employment opportunities opened up where women could earn about one-half of what men were paid. Data improved over time, allowing Goldin (1990, 62, 64) to document the closing of the gender gap associated with the growth of the clerical sector. The earnings ratio rose from 0.46 in 1890 to 0.56 in 1930. The Great Depression and World War II witnessed a further closing of the gap, but the gap widened again in the 1950s. From the late 1950s through the early 1980s, as massive numbers of married women entered the paid labor force, the ratio of full-time female-to-male earnings was nearly constant at 60 percent. After the early 1980s, the ratio resumed its rise. The ratio climbed to just under 75 percent by 2000. The recent closure is explained in part by the continued growth in the educational attainment of women and stagnation or retreat in that of men. Goldin (2014, 1091) has called the convergence of the economic roles of women and men among the "grandest" social advances of the past century.

Economic historians have also devoted careful attention to documenting and analyzing racial income differences. The black–white income ratio in 1940, when reasonably good data first become available, was around 35 percent. The differences were due to: (1) the concentration of African Americans in low-earning regions and in lower-earning occupations, (2) lower levels of human capital (schooling), and (3) wage discrimination on the job. A lively debate rages about the relative importance of these causes. After World War II, the gap closed. In 1975, the black–white income ratio stood at around 62 percent. There has been a vigorous debate about the roles of gradually changing forces, such as the convergence in the stock of human capital per person, versus episodic (or rapidly changing) forces, such as the enactment of anti-discrimination policies. A part of the closure of the gap was surely due to the movement of African Americans out of low-paid employment in southern agriculture. In 1940, 75 percent of African Americans lived in the South, most in rural areas. In 1970, 47 percent of African Americans lived in the region. The change was associated with, first, a compositional shift of the African American population from the South, where their incomes were initially low relative to those of the region's whites, to African Americans living in the North, and, later, to a rise of black incomes in the South relative to all others. There was little change in the black–white income ratio within the North. As Leah Boustan (2016) convincingly argues, the large-scale movement of southern-born African Americans to the North after 1940 depressed the wages of northern-born African Americans. Since 1975, there has been little further change in the national black–white income ratio.

Changes before 1940 are less clearly understood largely because the national census did not ask income questions and scholars have to rely on smaller surveys separated in time. In 1870, immediately after emancipation, the income of African Americans was about one-quarter that of whites. This afforded African Americans a higher standard of living than that prevailing under slavery, but the main benefits from emancipation appear to have arisen from the freedom to allocate family labor. Robert Higgs (1977) made income estimates in 1870 and 1900 that suggest all of the closure of the racial income gap between 1870 and 1940 occurred in the late nineteenth century and that the early twentieth century witnessed a widening gap. This pattern fits a picture in which the spread of Jim Crow laws and disenfranchisement in the South set back African American economic progress. In important revisionist work, Robert Margo (2016) has re-estimated incomes by race in 1870 and 1900, revealing evidence for more continuous convergence.

FACTORS OF PRODUCTION

The output of goods and services in any economy is produced by combining the inputs of labor, capital, and natural resources. The existing technology, spirit of entrepreneurship, and methods of organizing production determine how these inputs can be combined into output. An increase in the amount of any input, holding the quantities of the other inputs constant, typically leads to more output. Therefore, total output in the economy can grow just by adding more laborers even while holding capital, land, and natural resources constant. All economies face the problem of diminishing returns, however, such that adding more workers with no change in the other factors, will eventually cause the increase in output from adding each extra laborer to get smaller. If labor expands relative to other inputs relatively quickly, it can lead to the negative consequences that Malthus so eloquently described in 1798.

The United States never really faced this Malthusian dilemma because abundant land and natural resources were available, and the structure of property rights and access to financial markets made it relatively easy to expand the amount of capital. Labor was relatively scarce and, as a result, the colonists had per capita incomes that were among the highest in the world from the beginning. Throughout American history, the number of workers has expanded with the population, yet access to natural resources, capital, new technologies, and methods of organization has expanded even faster. As a result, income per capita has grown.

The labor input is composed of human beings who are the decision-makers in the economy. It is not surprising, therefore, that labor is the input that receives the most attention in economic studies. In the nineteenth century, the labor force typically grew nearly twice as fast as the population as the ratio of children to adults fell and the United States welcomed immigrants. Since 1900, the labor force has grown only about 0.2 percentage points faster than population, as the rise of the share of women in the labor force has been offset by increased life spans and reductions in the number of elderly and males in the labor force. Similar patterns are present in trends in earnings, hours worked, unemployment, the occupational structure, and the demographic composition of the workforce.

A major thread of economic history research on the labor market has been devoted to the study of labor market institutions: slavery, indentured servitude, the rise and decline of unions, internal labor markets, and the broad range of labor regulations as they shifted between the local, state, and federal levels. During the colonial era a significant share of the population came to America as indentured servants or as slaves. Indentured servants from Europe signed contracts in which they chose to trade three to seven years of labor service in exchange for the cost of passage to the New World and payments of land and in-kind goods when the contract ended. The influx of indentures declined as increasing European wages and falling transport costs led to shorter indenture contracts. In contrast, African slaves were sold into slavery; they and their offspring became the property of their owner for life. Slavery was abolished in the northern colonies in the late 1700s, but it remained profitable and thrived in the South. There have been vigorous debates among economic historians about the quality of treatment received by the slaves and, once freed, the short- and long-run consequences of having lived as slaves for them and their ancestors. The abolition of slavery was a significant step forward in the promotion of economic freedom that was consistent with the ideals stated in the Declaration of Independence, Constitution, and the Bill of Rights.

As more people worked outside agriculture in the 1800s, many were hired by employers to work for wages in "at-will" relationships that allowed either side to end the relationship at any time. To gain a collective voice in the employment relationship, a number of workers sought to unionize. Between the 1870s and the early 1930s, most employers opposed these efforts and the ensuing tensions led to strikes and lockouts, some of which turned violent. Labor laws and court decisions set the rules for these interactions until the National Labor Relations Act of 1935 established a right to collective bargaining with an employer when a majority of workers voted to unionize. Private-sector unionization peaked in the 1950s and has declined since, while public-sector unionization has expanded.

Even before unions gained a stronger foothold, employers began establishing longer run relationships with their workers in "internal labor markets," in which workers had opportunities to move up the firm's occupational hierarchy as they gained more skills. In the early twentieth-century, employers and unions began to establish sickness and accident funds, a process that became more regulated with the enactment of workers' compensation laws. Since then, the benefits have expanded to include such items as life insurance, disability insurance, and pension plans. The pension plans promised payments of annual income that allow the employee to retire, typically around age sixty-five. In general, civilian workers in the public sector received such benefits before those in the private sector. Even today, workers in the public sector are more likely than private-sector workers to have pension coverage, and those pensions are typically more generous. Over the past decade, public-sector pension programs have run into trouble because many governments have promised their employees more in benefits than they have set aside to pay for them. Despite decades of knowing a "pension bomb" was about to explode, politicians ignored a problem that is likely to impact public finance for the foreseeable future.

What made it possible for wages and pensions to increase over time is, in part, increases in capital (both physical and human) that prevented diminishing returns to the increases in the amount of labor. The classical and early neoclassical economists viewed capital accumulation as the fundamental driver of growth. In contrast, capital accumulation is assigned a much smaller role by economists informed by twentieth-century growth accounting exercises and growth models developed by Solow and "New Growth" theorists. This now standard view assumes that certain features of the economy have been fixed over time: the rate of capital formation (i.e., the saving rate), the capital–output ratio, capital's share of income, and the rate of return on capital (i.e., the interest rate). There is reason to challenge the conventional thinking; the role of capital accumulation in economic growth is dynamic and has changed dramatically over the past two hundred years.

Much of the conventional literature focuses on physical capital (plant and equipment), but in the modern service-based economy, the acquisition of human capital has become more important than ever before. To understand the labor market today, it is crucial that one understand how American education evolved and contributed to the economy's growth. American primary and secondary education, largely supplied by the public sector at the local government level, has been unique among industrialized nations. Regional and racial differences in outcomes are a result of the manner in which education has been provided, and our school systems have been shown to play a pivotal role in perpetuating some of those differences and alleviating others. How education becomes "productive human capital" remains an open question. What Claudia Goldin and Lawrence Katz (2009) term "a race between education and technology" has important effects on the returns to education and the distribution of income.

A final factor helping to explain the high level of American wages and pensions is the abundance of natural resources. When describing how labor, capital, and natural resources are combined in analyses of production, there is sometimes a tendency to treat natural resources as fixed, but American resource abundance was not limited to some fixed endowment set by nature. As Gavin Wright (1990) argues, American natural resources have been "socially constructed" through responses to economic incentives, investments in transportation, and evolving technologies of exploration and extraction. During the nineteenth century, Americans adapted their technologies and consumption patterns toward wood from their abundant forests to an extent unmatched in the world at that time. The country's rise to world leadership in minerals was not based primarily on geological endowment, but on an accommodating legal environment and investments in knowledge about mining and minerals. The process continues, as the recent booms in American production of shale oil and natural gas demonstrate.

TECHNOLOGY AND URBANIZATION

A significant share of the growth in America's per capita income came from the development of new technology. Technology has played a major role in the American economy by allowing people and firms to recombine inputs in new ways, enhancing the productivity of each input, extending lives, improving the health of those still alive, and offering a broad array of new ways to enjoy life. As population expanded, improved technologies allowed people to live in larger groups in urban areas, and, in turn, urban living spawned new forms of technology. Urban living led to new arrangements for housing as people began to separate the location of where they lived from where they earned their living. Urbanization also led to new forms of leisure and entertainment, including professional spectator sports.

Economic historians have learned several major lessons about the development of technology. The relative abundance of labor, capital, and natural resources strongly influence the types of technology chosen. In the early nineteenth century, for example, Americans used more labor-saving and natural resource-using technologies. In particular, Americans chose technologies that involved much more wood per unit of output produced than in England because forests were still abundant in the United States, and wood, therefore, was a low-cost input.

As Zvi Griliches (1957) showed in his seminal work on the adoption of hybrid corn, the adoption of a new innovation, the introduction of a new invention to the market, tended to follow an S-shaped curve. When it first appeared, take-up rates were relatively slow. This was followed by a period of very rapid growth before the innovation eventually reached full usage. Further, the prior technology did not necessarily die out. Canals, for example, survived the introduction of the railroad for decades because canal owners found new uses for the canals and lowered freight rates to remain competitive. Continued progress in the prior technology often put a ceiling on the market share at the top of the "S" for the adoption of new technologies.

The incentive structure for invention also influenced innovation. Standard economic analysis suggests inventors will underinvest in inventive activity unless they can privately capture the social returns of their ideas. Patent laws prevent others from copying an inventor's ideas without permission. There has been a long-standing debate about the appropriate level of patent protection. Patents reward the inventor by providing monopoly returns for the life of the patent, but they are likely to slow innovation because of the higher prices a patent holder can charge. American government sought to find a middle ground by limiting a patent's life. An influential analysis by Kenneth Sokoloff and Zorina Khan (2001) adds that other distinctive features of American patent law—openness, low fees, priority for "the first and true inventor," and the ability to assign (sell) the patent—encouraged widespread participation in the inventive process. They also led to the development of a class of professional inventors who sold their output to business firms who then did the dirty work of innovation. In work with Naomi Lamoreaux, Sokoloff (1999) found the professionalization of invention became especially important as the physical and human capital requirements of invention rose over the late nineteenth and early twentieth centuries. Despite the potential gains of patenting, Petra Moser's (2012) study of the inventions exhibited at international technology fairs (e.g., the 1851 Crystal Palace World's Fair in London) shows that only a small share of inventions was patented. Inventors and companies have kept many processes secret for fear that releasing information while patenting could aid others in finding alternative ways to achieve the same end.

New technologies come in all shapes and sizes. Nathan Rosenberg (1982) emphasized that a large share of innovation and technological progress tends to come through small changes that accumulate in ways like grass grows. The changes are not easily seen day-by-day but are obvious a year later. Over the past seventy years, for example, the computer has developed from a room-size machine run by vacuum tubes to a more powerful hand-held device with access to huge amounts of information because of thousands of changes in electronics, circuitry, cooling, computer chips, electricity usage, and many other areas.

At the other end of the spectrum, Joseph Schumpeter (1942) emphasized the fundamental importance of innovation, introducing the "Great Inventions," to disrupting prevailing patterns of economic activity. Timothy Bresnahan and Manuel Trajtenberg (1995) offer a definition of General Purpose Technologies (GPTs), characterized by three features: (1) pervasiveness—a GPT eventually affects most sectors in the economy; (2) scope for improvement—a GPT becomes better over time; and (3) spillovers—a GPT spawns complementary innovations.

Two of the leading candidates for the appellation of Great Invention or GPT in American economic history are the railroad and electricity. Given the large size and low population density of the United States, transportation has always been a vital service connecting producers and consumers. Over time, technological change within specific modes of transportation and competition between water, land, and air modes of transportation have dramatically lowered shipping and travel costs—by over 90 percent in real terms. These changes have both created and diverted trade, promoting economic expansion. The railroad was the major link in this technological chain in the late nineteenth century. At one point in the 1950s, American historians considered the railroad to be a necessity for economic growth in the late 1800s. This view was altered by the simulations performed by Robert Fogel (1964) when he showed that the economy would have arrived at its 1890 output level only about two or three years later had the railroads not been invented. This finding should not be seen as denigrating the contributions of the railroads. Instead, it shows that the railroad was only one of many innovations that contributed to economic growth in an economy as large as the American economy.

The development of electricity and its impact on the economy has been a fruitful area of research over the past several years. First developed in the 1880s, electric power became widespread in urban areas by the 1920s; technological improvements in distribution and programs like the Rural Electrification Administration expanded access to most agricultural areas by 1950. The use of electricity improved manufacturing productivity by allowing companies to eliminate belts and shafts and thus place machinery closer together. The nature of electricity allowed firms to keep the factory cleaner and use less energy. The changes on the factory floor (and later in the office) led to major changes in the skills and organization of the labor force. At home, electricity enhanced household production in the form of refrigerators, dishwashers, vacuums, and washers and dryers, while opening the door to entertainment options such as radio, television, computers, and video games.

Some observers see the late nineteenth and early twentieth centuries as the greatest era of innovation (Smil 2005, 2006; Gordon 2016). Electric power is part of that era. Others (Kurzweil 2005; Brynjolfsson and McAfee 2014) argue the biggest changes are yet to come. One complication, as Paul David (1990) noted, is that it can take decades for the impact of a technological change to be fully realized. This is especially true for technologies such as electric power that operate through systems. David argues that, although electric power was developed in the late nineteenth century, it did not have important productivity effects until the interwar period (1919–1939). The transformations wrought by the micro-processor and personal computer were similarly delayed. The study of economic history provides insight into debates about the future of technological progress.

Technological change often was strongly intertwined with urbanization. New innovations in agriculture allowed more people to specialize in nonagricultural activities, and a broad array of technologies allowed large numbers of people to live safely and comfortably in a small area. Well into the nineteenth century, foreign immigrants and former farmers were attracted to cities in response to a rising urban wage premium as new manufacturing plants enhanced urban productivity. Although this premium fell after 1880, migrants remained attracted to cities as the public health investments improved the urban standard of living. Then, beginning in the 1920s and especially with the completion of the interstate highway system in the 1960s, the urban network began to change with the "rust belt" cities of the North and East losing relative to the "sunbelt" cities of the South and West. Those transportation changes combined with other technological changes and the drop in transportation costs made industry more footloose; employers began to look for places with more amenities. Within metropolises, both households and employers relocated to suburbs. Rising incomes and falling commuting costs explain much of this pattern, but crime and a city's racial composition are important push factors.

As rural dwellers moved to urban areas, they moved from homes on the farms where they worked to housing that was independent of their workplace. Homeownership rates in cities rose in the 1920s, fell in the 1930s, and then grew rapidly between 1940 and 1960, while the quality of the housing stock improved. Purchasing a home is the largest investment that most people make in their lifetime, and it typically requires the person to borrow to finance the purchase. Until the 1930s, most nonfarm home mortgage loans came through building societies, insurance companies, family and friends, or the prior owner. Thereafter institutional lenders gradually displaced individual lenders. Savings and Loans were the leading lenders from the late 1930s through the late 1980s; then a wide range of investors became involved when mortgages were combined into mortgage-backed securities and collateralized debt obligations in the 1990s and 2000s. Prior experiments with such securitization had taken place in the 1890s and 1920s. Starting with the New Deal, the federal government provided extensive subsidies to markets by purchasing troubled loans and refinancing them, providing loan guarantees, offering tax breaks on mortgage interest, and creating Fannie Mae and Freddie Mac to create secondary markets for mortgages.

As urban areas developed, people had more time for leisure and entertainment. A particularly popular and expanding form of entertainment has been professional spectator sports. Study of the economics of major team sports often captures the imagination of economics students because they have grown up as fans, and the data collected on professional sports can be used to examine a wide range of issues. The amount spent on spectator sports has risen rapidly over time with higher incomes, shorter work weeks, and the development of cable and satellite television. These changes coincided with shifts away from labor monopsony derived from reserve clauses to complex combinations of draft rights and free agency that have led to large-scale increases in players' salaries. The changes in race relations in American society are mirrored in the markets for labor and sports memorabilia, which have been used to measure the extent to which employers and consumers discriminate against black and Latin American players. Meanwhile, stadiums and arenas have become major public works projects in most cities, and there has been constant negotiation and renegotiation about the extent to which local and state governments should subsidize their construction.

GOVERNMENT AND ECONOMIC POLICY

Douglass North (1981) described economic history as the study of the "structure and performance of the economy through time." North emphasized that the structure of economies sets the incentives that determine the performance of economic actors, and, in turn, the economic actors often seek to change the structure of the economy. North joined John Wallis and Barry Weingast (2009) in suggesting that the vast majority of economies in history (and even today) were run by a relatively small number of elites who limited access to economic opportunity for the majority of the economy's participants. This is problematic for those economies because, as Daron Acemoglu and James Robinson (2012) show in *Why Nations Fail*, there is a strong association between high per capita incomes and better definition and enforcement of property rights, more unbiased rule of law, and better protection for individual freedoms. Building on a legal structure inherited from the British, the United States has long been a leader in all of these areas, starting with the US Constitution and Bill of Rights. The interactions within the governments that followed served to protect property rights and expand access to economic opportunities to a very broad range of the population.

One of the questions North, Wallis, and Weingast (2009) sought to address was: Why would the ruling elites be willing to relinquish their control and give the populace open access to the economy? The American experience was a grand experiment that illustrates the process. The political leaders who attended the constitutional convention were members of the economic elite of landowners, merchants, lawyers, and slave owners. The ocean separating the American colonies from Britain left the colonists relatively free. The Crown and Parliament did not exercise strong oversight of the colonists' economic affairs, and the abundance of land meant that a significant share of the population owned property. When colonists disliked a policy, it was often routinely violated. For example, high taxes on molasses in the 1730s led to extensive smuggling. In fact, the colonists revolted when Parliament sought to raise colonial taxes to levels still well below those paid in Britain and to tighten control over the economy.[3]

The Founders attending the 1787 Constitutional Convention and the first Congresses of the new Republic chose a wide range of basic rules for the economy that protected their own property rights, repaid the federal and state debts from the Revolutionary War, and established countervailing powers between the legislature, the executive, and the judiciary. Much of this activity was in their own self-interest, but their interests were also aligned with a large share of the population and matched the reasoning proposed by political philosophers such as Adam Smith and John Locke. There were flaws, such as the protections for slavery and limiting voting rights to property owners, but the decisions created economic opportunities for a wide range of the American public. Decisions made by the national, state, and local governments since that time have further expanded opportunity and political power for many in American society.

The Constitution and private property rights set the basic rules—the United States would have a market economy in which government would have a more limited role than in nearly every other society. Yet, national, state, and local representative governments made a wide range of decisions that strongly influenced economic activity and the rising standard of living. Governments at all levels played a variety of roles, including the enforcement of property rights, provision of defense from external threats, adjudication of disputes, regulation of various aspects of the economy, redistribution of incomes, and investments in public works (e.g., canals, roads, sanitation, and dams). Government spending at all levels rose from about 7.5 percent of GDP in 1902 to roughly 36 percent in the 2000s. The shares of government spending, taxation, and debt for the national, state, and local governments have also gone through major changes that can be divided into three distinct stages. Before 1850, state governments actively pursued policies to promote economic development; they were financed by revenues from state investments in, say, canals. Between 1850 and 1930, local governments became the most financially important level of government, developing and expanding schools, building public hospitals, laying down paved local road networks, and constructing sanitation facilities, among other activities. These were financed largely through property taxes. After 1930, the national government became the most active and largest level of government. It has been financed through income and payroll taxes, while developing an extensive network of grants to state and local governments.

One can see the same shifts between levels of government at the regulatory level, although the timing differed for different types of regulations. The Constitution originally limited the national government's power over the economy to international trade, national defense, the definition of the dollar, disposition of federal lands, and the maintenance of free trade within the United States. Most of the regulatory power over the economy was left to the states. Regulation of antitrust, safety, labor, railroads, food, and the environment originally developed at the state level or through common law court decisions, while poverty relief was commonly the purview of local governments with state governments playing an increasing role between 1920 and 1930. Between 1880 and 1920, the federal government expanded its regulatory authority over activities involved in interstate commerce—railroads, food safety, and antitrust. During the Great Depression and the New Deal, claims of a national emergency led to the expansion of the federal government's role in poverty and labor policy. During the early 1970s, there were additional expansions in federal regulation of the environment and workplace safety. However, there was a substantial movement to reduce regulations in banking, finance, and transportation.

Regulation of commercial banking is a particularly fascinating example. The banking system greases the wheels of commerce by creating loans that match savers with investors; it provides access to currency and demand deposits that lower transactions costs and allow more specialization. After 1792, states were not allowed to issue currency, but they were in a position to charter banks, and some states took ownership stakes in banks. Early banks were able to expand the amount of money available by making loans and putting into circulation their own paper notes that were backed by reserves of gold, silver and other assets. Originally, each bank obtained a charter through the state's legislative process, but in the 1820s states began passing "free banking" laws that allowed banks meeting the state's regulatory guidelines to open for business.

Until the early 1830s, the national government had an impact on the issuance of state banknotes because it deposited its funds in the First (1791–1811) and later the Second National Bank of the United States (1816–1836), which acted like central banks by following policies designed to keep state banknotes circulating at par value. During the Civil War, the national government began regulating banks and note issues when it created the National Banking System, issued its own "Greenback" notes during the Civil War, and drove many state banks out of operation by imposing a 10-percent tax on all state banknote issues. State banks began to reappear later in the century as new forms of deposit banking developed. In the late 1800s and early 1900s, there were occasional bank panics. Ultimately, a major panic in New York in 1907 led to the creation of the Federal Reserve System (the Fed) in 1913.

The Fed was expected to operate a universal and efficient payments system and promote a market for banks' short-term loans, known as banker's acceptances. Through discount window lending, it would create an "elastic currency" that would expand money and credit at seasonal peaks and more generally in response to the needs of business. Early Fed policy was strongly influenced by the "Real Bills Doctrine" and adherence to the international gold standard, which caused Fed leaders to fail to effectively use monetary policy to counteract the rise in bank failures and the sharp drop in output and prices between 1929 and 1933 during the Great Contraction. In the aftermath of this disaster, the federal government expanded its regulatory authority over banks, stock markets, and other financial sectors. In the modern era, the Fed, the Treasury, state governments, and several other national agencies play regulatory roles in the financial system. Following a period of deregulation beginning in the late 1970s, new legislation has led to new regulations in the aftermath of the Great Recession of the 2000s, regulations that are still being determined by the agencies administering the law.

The national government has maintained its authority throughout American history in two key areas: international trade policy and national defense. International trade has been a small but important part of the US economy, rising from about 6 percent of GDP in the late 1920s to around 14 percent in 2012. The Constitution gave Congress the authority to levy import duties, and these were a significant source of national government revenues before the income tax. The use of this power has been extremely controversial ever since, with the political debate revolving around whether tariffs on imports should be high or low. This debate has pitted export-oriented producers against domestic producers facing foreign competition. The vast majority of economists suggest the benefits to free trade and globalization for those who gain from greater trade exceed the costs to those who lose. After passage of the Smoot-Hawley Tariff Act of 1930, protectionism acquired a bad name, and the United States began to turn to reciprocal trade agreements with individual countries. This led to the formation of the General Agreement on Tariffs and Trade in 1947 and later agreements such as the North American Free Trade Agreement in 1993.

National defense, during peacetime, has accounted for roughly 3 to 5 percent of GDP in most years. However, major wars have always led to huge expansions in federal expenditures, taxes, national government debt, and inflation. The parabolic trajectory of production during wartime is similar for all major wars. Since one never knows how large a war one is about to fight, the first step is to work as hard as you can as fast as you can. Production rises. At some point, the needed amount of war material becomes known, and production slows to whatever pace is required. Then, as the end approaches, war production slows as the economy begins its reconversion to peacetime. In addition, most wars have led to forced savings, so the aftermath of the war is a buying spree that inevitably creates a sudden boom and collapse. The resulting upswing brings the return of normal peacetime conditions. *Panics + wars?*

Arguably the most important, and certainly the deadliest, war in American history was the Civil War in the early 1860s. The primary economic issue was slavery, and the war continued because the North refused to allow the United States to break apart. The largest change wrought by the war was the emancipation of four million slaves. Southern labor institutions changed, but the ex-slaves still struggled because they started with virtually no education and few resources. Their incomes grew substantially as they and their descendants gained more skills, more property, more education, and migrated *Jim Crow?* to new areas, but the low starting point still has an impact on relative black and white earnings today. The economic costs of the war, including the amounts spent by both sides and the deaths and injuries, have been estimated to be in the neighborhood of one year's GDP. Had that amount been used for a negotiated buyout (compensated emancipation), it could have paid the 1860 peak price to the owners for each slave, given each slave family 40 acres and a mule, and paid the slaves about one-fourth of a year's GDP in back pay. Compensation emancipation likely would have enhanced the economic welfare of ex-slaves and their descendants.

Of the two world wars of the twentieth century, World War II had much larger effects on the economy. The United States had just returned to its long-run growth trajectory as America entered the war, in part because of Allied demands for war materials. To fight the war, the federal government instituted many features of a command economy, devoted nearly 40 percent of the economy's resources to the production of military hard-ware, and pulled nearly 17 percent of the labor force into the armed forces. As a result, massive amounts of munitions were produced. The United States and its allies won the war, but both victories came at a cost. Many American saw their consumption limited by rationing; normal investment activity was sharply reduced; and there were signifi-cant losses of life and limb. World War II led to gains for women who showed that they could perform a larger range of industrial tasks and for minorities who often migrated to better opportunities after the hard times of the 1930s. Overall, the war decreased wage and wealth inequality.

Robert Higgs argues in *Crisis and Leviathan* (1987) that the crises of the two World Wars and the Great Depression contributed to large-scale expansions in the role of government in the American economy. The institutions created to manage World War I reappeared during the Great Depression and again in World War II. Each new crisis ratcheted up government's influence on economic activity during the crises. When the crises ended, government controls decreased, but not to pre-crisis levels.

The New Deal was the federal government's response to the Great Depression of the 1930s. The Roosevelt administration built an incredible array of public works and es-tablished a series of regulations, government insurance, and public assistance programs that are still in place today. Even though government spending expanded after 1929, the impact was stunted by a major increase in income tax rates and those on a wide variety of goods and services. When Roosevelt took office in 1933, monetary policy became more expansive once we left the gold standard. While government spending continued to increase during the New Deal, tax revenues were raised nearly as fast, so there was no true Keynesian attempt to stimulate the economy. In fact, attempts to balance the budget and an increase in reserve requirements to prevent inflation contributed to a second downturn in 1937–1938. The New Deal created dozens of programs to try to solve nu-merous specific problems. Recent research suggests that the most successful were the emergency relief and public works programs and the Home Owners' Loan Corporation. While these generally stopped the downturn, they did not lead to an economic upswing. The policies of the National Recovery Administration and the Agricultural Adjustment Administration are more controversial and may have done more harm than good.

The New Deal introduced a wide range of permanent changes in poverty and social insurance programs with the Social Security Act of 1935. These changes, and the attempts to provide more security since then (e.g., unemployment insurance, workers' compen-sation, and Medicare), have been a major part of the rise in government spending over the last one hundred years. The safety net from colonial times through the 1920s was composed of transfer programs run by local governments and private charities. State governments joined in by funding mothers' pensions and requiring workers' com-pensation after 1910. Beginning with the New Deal, the safety net grew much larger, dominated by social insurance programs run by different mixtures of the federal and state governments as well as private charities.

The federal government policies most commonly discussed in the press are fiscal and monetary policies targeted to smooth fluctuations in the macroeconomy and to limit inflation. The Employment Act of 1946 made macroeconomic policy a federal responsibility with a charge to "promote maximum employment, production, and purchasing power." Since then there have been extensive debates among macroeconomists about the success of monetary and fiscal policy. Early debates between Keynesians and Monetarists centered on whether fiscal or monetary policies were more effective. Once rational-expectations macroeconomists began to address issues relative to information and policy lags and the economy experienced a combination of high inflation and high unemployment in the 1970s, the debates centered on whether macroeconomic policy could do anything more than adjust inflation in the long run and raised the question of whether the macroeconomic policies were more likely to stabilize or destabilize the economy. Macroeconomists still address this issue today, but they use different tools. Real business cycle analysis uses dynamic structural models of the economy that simulate the impact of policies. Meanwhile, neo-Keynesians and other economists use econometric models to estimate the relationships between policies and outcomes.

With the Kennedy tax cut of 1964, and continuing after the Fed reduced money supply growth in the early 1980s following the "Great Inflation" of the late 1960s and 1970s, the United States experienced long expansions and short recessions through around 2007. Housing prices soared in the 2000s, fueled by a mixture of a bust in technology stocks around 2000, loosened Fed monetary policy, increases in sub-prime lending associated with government policy to expand homeownership, and incentives created by sales of loans to institutions that marketed mortgage-backed securities. The Great Recession of 2008–2009 ensued. The federal government appreciably expanded the deficit to 10 percent of GDP in 2009, and the Fed rapidly expanded open market operations, bought mortgage-backed securities, and offered credit to other firms. Since then, the Fed has kept short-term interest rates near zero, while the deficit has slowly declined. Economic growth has been slower than in previous recoveries. Even as the economy recovered, fears have been expressed that the United States has moved into a new era of slow growth, although many economists believe this is just a short-run malaise.

CONCLUSION

With the coming of the computer, economic historians have uncovered large amounts of new quantitative and narrative evidence that have advanced our understanding of the past and the modern world. Scholars young and old have explored new avenues for research that have revealed dimensions of the American economy that few had realized were important. They have described newly uncovered data, new methods for analyzing that data, and new avenues for research that will add to the richness of American economic history. We expect the coming decades to offer a rich cornucopia of new insights.

Notes

1. See the Economic History Association Symposium (2015). The US population is becoming increasingly diverse, and economic historians will need to employ categories and metrics that go beyond simple binary divisions such as native- and foreign-born, white and nonwhite.
2. For an example of such international comparisons, see the recent volume of surveys from around the world edited by Joerg Baten (2016) that includes many anthropometric comparisons.
3. For book-length summaries of the development of government in the United States, see Fishback et al. (2007) and Hughes (1991).

Bibliography

Abramovitz, Moses. (1989). *Thinking about Growth, and Other Essays on Economic Growth and Welfare.* New York: Cambridge University Press.

Acemoglu, Daron, and James Robinson. (2012). *Why Nations Fail: The Origins of Power, Prosperity, and Poverty.* New York: Crown.

Baten, Joerg, ed. (2016). *A History of the Global Economy: 1500 to the Present.* New York: Cambridge University Press.

Beard, Charles A. (1935 [1913]). *An Economic Interpretation of the Constitution of the United States.* New York: Macmillan.

Boldrin, Michele, and David K. Levine. (2008). *Against Intellectual Monopoly.* New York: Cambridge University Press.

Boustan, Leah. (2016). *Competition in the Promised Land: Black Migrants in Northern Cities and Labor Markets.* Princeton, NJ: Princeton University Press.

Bresnahan, Timothy F., and M. Trajtenberg. (1995). "General Purpose Technologies 'Engines of Growth'?" *Journal of Econometrics* 65(1): 83–108.

Brynjolfsson, Erik, and Andrew McAfee. (2014). *The Second Machine Age: Work, Progress and Prosperity in a Time of Brilliant Technologies.* New York: Norton.

Cain, Louis, and Donald Paterson. (2012). *The Children of Eve: Population and Well-Being in History.* Oxford: Wiley-Blackwell.

Carter, Susan B., Scott Sigmund Gartner, Michael R. Haines, Alan L. Olmstead, Richard Sutch, and Gavin Wright, eds. (2006). *Historical Statistics of the United States, Earliest Times to the Present.* Millennial ed. Cambridge: Cambridge University Press.

David, Paul A. (1990). "The Dynamo and the Computer: An Historical Perspective on the Modern Productivity Paradox." *American Economic Review, Papers and Proceedings* 80(2): 355–361.

EHA Symposium. (2015). "The Future of Economic History." *Journal of Economic History* 75(4): 1228–1257.

Field, Alexander J. (2011). *A Great Leap Forward: 1930s Depression and U.S. Economic Growth.* New Haven, CT: Yale University Press.

Fisback, Price, Robert Higgs, Gary Libecap, John Wallis, Stanley Engerman, Jeffrey Hummel, Sumner LaCroix et al. (2007). *Government and the American Economy: A New History.* Chicago: University of Chicago Press.

Fogel, Robert. (1964). *Railroads and American Economic Growth: Essays in Econometric History*. Baltimore, MD: Johns Hopkins University Press.

Gerschenkron, Alexander. (1952). *Economic Backwardness in Historical Perspective*. Cambridge, MA: Harvard University Press.

Goldin, Claudia. (1990). *Understanding the Gender Gap: An Economic History of American Women*. Chicago: University of Chicago Press.

Goldin, Claudia. (2014). "A Grand Gender Convergence: Its Last Chapter." *American Economic Review* 104(4): 1091–1119.

Goldin, Claudia, and Lawrence Katz. (2009). *The Race between Technology and Education*. Cambridge, MA: Harvard University Press.

Goldin, Claudia, and Robert Margo. (1992). "The Great Compression: The Wage Structure in the United States at Mid-Century." *Quarterly Journal of Economics* 107(1): 1–34.

Gordon, Robert J. (2016). *The Rise and Fall of American Growth: The U.S. Standard of Living since the Civil War*. Princeton, NJ: Princeton University Press.

Griliches, Zvi. (1957). "Hybrid Corn: An Exploration in the Economics of Technological Change." *Econometrica* 25(4): 501–522.

Heaton, Herbert. (1965). "Twenty-Five Years of the Economic History Association: A Reflective Evaluation." *Journal of Economic History* 25(4): 76–86.

Higgs, Robert. (1977). *Competition and Coercion: Blacks in the American Economy, 1865–1915*. New York: Cambridge University Press.

Higgs, Robert. (1987). *Crisis and Leviathan: Critical Episodes in the Growth of American Government*. New York: Oxford University Press.

Hughes, Jonathan R. T. (1991). *The Governmental Habit Redux: Economic Controls from Colonial Times to the Present*. Princeton, NJ: Princeton University Press.

Khan, B. Zorina, and Kenneth L. Sokoloff. (2001). "The Early Development of Intellectual Property Institutions in the United States." *Journal of Economic Perspectives* 15(3): 233–246.

Kurzweil, Ray. (2005). *The Singularity Is Near: When Humans Transcend Biology*. New York: Viking.

Kuznets, Simon. (1966). *Modern Economic Growth: Rate, Structure, and Spread*. New Haven, CT: Yale University Press.

Lamoreaux, Naomi R., and Kenneth L. Sokoloff. (1999). "Inventors, Firms, and the Market for Technology in the Late Nineteenth and Early Twentieth Centuries." In *Learning by Doing in Firms, Markets, and Nations*, edited by Naomi R. Lamoreaux, Daniel Raff, and Peter Temin, 19–60. Chicago: University of Chicago Press.

Lindert, Peter, and Jeffrey Williamson. (2016). *Unequal Gains: American Growth and Inequality since 1700*. Princeton, NJ: Princeton University Press.

Long, Jason, and Joseph Ferrie. (2013). "Intergenerational Occupational Mobility in Great Britain and the United States since 1850." *American Economic Review* 103(4): 1109–1137.

Malthus, Thomas. (1798). *An Essay on the Principle of Population; or, A View of Its Past and Present Effects on Human Happiness; with an Inquiry into Our Prospects Respecting the Future Removal or Mitigation of the Evils Which It Occasions*. 1st American edition—George Town: Published by J. Milligan, at J. March's bookstore, R. Chew Weightman, printer, 1809, was printed from the 3rd London edition: Printed for J. Johnson, by T. Bensley, 1806.

Margo, Robert. (2016). "Obama, Katrina, and the Persistence of Racial Inequality." *Journal of Economic History* 76(2): 301–341.

McGuire, Robert A., and Robert L. Ohsfeldt. (1984). "Economic Interests and the American Constitution: A Quantitative Rehabilitation of Charles A. Beard." *Journal of Economic History* 44(2): 509–519.

Mokyr, Joel, ed. (2003). *Oxford Encyclopaedia of Economic History*. New York: Oxford University Press.

Moser, Petra. (2012). "Innovation without Patents: Evidence from World Fairs." *Journal of Law and Economics* 55(1): 43–74.

North, Douglass. (1981). *Structure and Change in Economic History*. New York: Norton.

North, Douglass, John Joseph Wallis, and Barry R. Weingast. (2009). *Violence and Social Orders: A Conceptual Framework for Interpreting Recorded Human History*. New York: Cambridge University Press.

Piketty, Thomas. (2014). *Capital in the Twenty-First Century*. Trans. by Arthur Goldhammer. Cambridge, MA: Harvard University Press.

Piketty, Thomas, and Emmanuel Saez. (2003). "Income Inequality in the United States, 1913–1998." *Quarterly Journal of Economics* 118(1): 1–39.

Rosenberg, Nathan. (1982). *Inside the Black Box: Technology and Economics*. New York: Cambridge University Press.

Schumpeter, Joseph. (1942). *Capitalism, Socialism and Democracy*. New York: Harper and Brothers.

Smil, Vaclav. (2005). *Creating the Twentieth Century: Technical Innovations of 1867–1914 and Their Lasting Impact*. New York: Oxford University Press.

Smil, Vaclav. (2006). *Transforming the Twentieth Century: Technical Innovations and Their Consequences*. New York: Oxford University Press.

Williamson, Samuel H. (2016). "'What Was the U.S. GDP Then?" MeasuringWorth. Available at http://www.measuringworth.com/datasets/usgdp/result.php.

Wright, Gavin. (1990). "The Origins of American Industrial Success, 1879–1940." *American Economic Review* 80(4): 651–668.

PART I

POPULATION AND HEALTH

CHAPTER 1

....

DEMOGRAPHY IN AMERICAN ECONOMIC HISTORY

....

MICHAEL R. HAINES

In the two hundred years since the first federal census of the United States in 1790, the population of the United States increased from about 4 million to almost 309 million persons in 2010. This was predominantly due to natural increase, early driven by high birth rates and moderate mortality levels and later (after the Civil War) by declining death rates. In addition, over 76 million recorded legal immigrant arrivals (1819–2010) increased the growth rate. By the two decades prior to World War I, about one-third of the total increase originated in net migration, which has also been true since 1980. A number of unusual features characterized the American demographic transition. The fertility transition was early (dating from at least 1800) and from very high levels. The average woman had more than seven live births in 1800. The crude birth rate declined from about fifty-five in 1800 to about twenty-five in 1920 and about fourteen today. Much of this occurred prior to 1860 in an environment without widespread urbanization and industrialization in most of the nation. In the period 1947 to 1962, this was punctuated by a sharp upturn in birth rates known as the "Postwar Baby Boom." Mortality levels in the early nineteenth century were moderate, and death rates began their sustained decline only by the 1870s, long after the fertility transition had begun. This contrasts with the more usual stylization of the demographic transition in which mortality decline precedes or accompanies the fertility transition. Internal migration in the United States was also distinctive. Over most of the nineteenth century, flows followed east–west axes, although this began to weaken as rural–urban migration began to supplant westward rural migration in importance. Subsequently, migration flows have been marked by moves to the suburbs and to the states of the "sunbelt." International migration proceeded in waves and changed its character as the "new" migration from eastern and southern Europe replaced the "old" migration from western and northern Europe. In the last two decades of the twentieth century, this was replaced by large inflows from Latin America and parts of Asia.

In the late eighteenth century, Adam Smith commented on the rapid population growth, large family size, and early marriage in what was then British North America (1776, Book I, ch. 8, 70–71). These comments were reiterated by Thomas Robert Malthus in his well-known *Essay on the Principle of Population* (1798, 105). Although Malthus guessed at the rate of natural increase (implying a 2.8 percent per year rate of growth), he was not far off. During the second half of the eighteenth century, population growth (including migration) in what was to become the United States and Canada exceeded 3 percent per annum. In addition to notably high fertility, areas of North America, especially Canada, New England, and the northern Middle Atlantic region, also had a reputation as having more benign mortality conditions than those prevailing in much of Europe. These factors, combined with significant net in-migration in the early seventeenth century and after about 1720, led to the relatively high rates of population increase.

While this was true for the populations of European and African descent, it did not hold for the descendants of inhabitants indigenous to the continent at the time of contact with Europeans in the sixteenth century. Although the data are sketchy, it appears that the American Indian population of North America declined from more than 1 million persons circa 1650 down to about 250,000 by 1900. This was due to a variety of factors, including severe periodic epidemics, high baseline mortality, war, lower fertility (originating in traditional practice, disease, and socioeconomic disruption), and, underlying these, destruction of their economic base. There has been recovery since about 1900, which has accelerated in recent years. Some of the most recent growth has been, however, due to persons reidentifying themselves as American Indian. In general, this chapter will not deal with the demographic processes of the American Indian population and will concentrate on those originating in Europe, Africa, and elsewhere.

Every modern, economically developed nation has undergone a demographic transition from high to low levels of fertility and mortality. This was certainly true for the United States, which experienced a sustained fertility decline from at least about 1800 (see table 1.1). Around that time, the typical American woman had about seven or eight live births during her reproductive years, and the average person probably lived about thirty-five to forty years. But the American pattern was distinctive. First, the American fertility transition was underway from at least the beginning of the nineteenth century, and some evidence indicates that family size was declining in older settled areas from the late eighteenth century (see table 1.1). Other Western, developed nations, with the exception of France, began their sustained, irreversible decline in birth rates only in the late nineteenth or early twentieth centuries. It is perhaps not coincidental that both France and the United States experienced important political revolutions in the late eighteenth century and were then characterized by small-scale, owner-occupier agriculture. Second, it appears that fertility in America was in sustained decline long before mortality. This is in contrast to the stylized view of the demographic transition, in which the mortality decline precedes or occurs simultaneously with the fertility decline. Mortality in the United States did not stabilize and begin a consistent decline until about the 1870s. Third, these demographic processes were both influenced by the large volume of international net in-migration and also the significant internal population

Table 1.1 Fertility and Mortality in the United States, 1800–2008

Approx. Date	Birthrate[a] White	Black[f]	Child-Woman Ratio[b] White	Black	Total Fertility Rate[c] White	Black[f]	Expectation of Life[d] White	Black[f]	Infant Mortality Rate[e] White	Black[f]
1800	55.0		1,342		7.04					
1810	54.3		1,358		6.92					
1820	52.8		1,295	1,191	6.73					
1830	51.4		1,145	1,220	6.55					
1840	48.3		1,085	1,154	6.14					
1850	43.3	58.6[g]	892	1,087	5.42	7.90[g]	39.5	23.0	216.8	340.0
1860	41.4	55.0[h]	905	1,072	5.21	7.58[h]	43.6		181.3	
1870	38.3	55.4[i]	814	997	4.55	7.69[i]	45.2		175.5	
1880	35.2	51.9[j]	780	1,090	4.24	7.26[j]	40.5		214.8	
1890	31.5	48.1	685	930	3.87	6.56	46.8		150.7	
1900	30.1	44.4	666	845	3.56	5.61	51.8[k]	41.8[k]	110.8[k]	170.3
1910	29.2	38.5	631	736	3.42	4.61	54.6[l]	46.8[l]	96.5[l]	142.6
1920	26.9	35.0	604	608	3.17	3.64	57.4	47.0	82.1	131.7
1930	20.6	27.5	506	554	2.45	2.98	60.9	48.5	60.1	99.9
1940	18.6	26.7	419	513	2.22	2.87	64.9	53.9	43.2	73.8
1950	23.0	33.3	580	663	2.98	3.93	69.0	60.7	26.8	44.5
1960	22.7	32.1	717	895	3.53	4.52	70.7	63.9	22.9	43.2
1970	17.4	25.1	507	689	2.39	3.07	71.6	64.1	17.8	30.9
1980	15.1	21.3	300	367	1.77	2.18	74.5	68.5	10.9	22.2
2000	13.9	16.6			2.06	2.05	77.7	72.2	5.7	14.1
2008	13.9	16.6			2.07	2.13	78.4	74.3	5.6	13.2

Sources: Carter et al. (2006, Table Av1–10); US Bureau of the Census (2012).

[a] Births per 1,000 population per annum.
[b] Children aged 0–4 per 1,000 women aged 20–44, adjusted upward 47 percent for relative underenumeration of black children aged 0–4 for the censuses of 1820–1840.
[c] Total number of births per woman if she experienced the current period age-specific fertility rates throughout her life.
[d] Expectation of life at birth for both sexes combined.
[e] Infant deaths per 1,000 live births per annum.
[f] Black and other population for CBR (1920–1970), TFR (1940–1990), e(0) (1950–1960), IMR (1920–1970).
[g] Average for 1850–1859.
[h] Average for 1860–1869.
[i] Average for 1870–1879.
[j] Average for 1880–1884.
[k] Approximately 1895.
[l] Approximately 1904.

redistribution to frontier areas and to cities, towns, and (later) suburbs. Finally, the American fertility transition began from very high levels.

While the American case may be, in many respects, *sui generis*, it furnishes a long-term view of a completed demographic transition with accompanying urbanization. America was a demographic laboratory in which natives and migrants, different racial and ethnic groups, and varying occupational and socioeconomic strata experienced these significant behavioral changes in a fertile, land-abundant, resource-rich land.

SOURCES AND MATERIALS

A difficulty for the study of American historical demography is a lack of some types of data for the calculation of standard demographic measures. There were also a number of colonial censuses that have made estimates of total population size possible (McCusker 2006). A milestone in American demographic history was the institution of the federal decennial census in 1790 (Haines 2006a). Originally intended to provide the basis for allocating seats in the US House of Representatives, the published census grew from a modest one-volume compilation of spare aggregated statistics in 1790 to multiple-volume descriptions of the population, economy, and society by the late nineteenth century. Original manuscript returns exist for all dates except 1890, opening great analytical opportunities. Very usable samples of these manuscripts are available from the Integrated Public Use Microsample (IPUMS) website (http://www.ipums.org). These include samples matched across censuses with the complete count data. The complete count data for 1850, 1880, and 1900–1940 are now available. In addition, the Census Bureau now conducts an annual nationally representative sample, the American Community Survey. It began in 2001 and now is an approximate 1 percent sample. These are also available at the IPUMS website. The census has been the major source for the study of population growth, structure, and redistribution, as well as fertility prior to the twentieth century.

Vital registration (the recording of births, deaths, marriages, and divorces), on the other hand, did not cover the entire United States until 1933. Vital registration was left, however, to state and local governments and, in consequence, it was instituted unevenly. A variety of churches kept parish records of baptisms, burials, and marriages, and these have been used to construct demographic estimates for the colonial period, especially in New England and the Middle Atlantic region (Wells 1992). Although some cities (e.g., New York, Philadelphia) began vital registration earlier in the nineteenth century, the first state in the United States to do so was Massachusetts in 1842. An official Death Registration Area consisting of ten states and the District of Columbia was only successfully established in 1900, and data collection from all states was not completed until 1933. A parallel Birth Registration Area was only instituted in 1915 and was also complete by 1933. A digitized version of the vital statistics by state and county from 1915 to 1988 is now available at the Interuniversity Center for Political and Social Research (ICPSR) (www.icpsr.umich.edu). For an overview of vital statistics, see Haines (2006b).

The US census did collect mortality information with the censuses of 1850 to 1900, but there were significant problems with completeness. The data did improve over time, and, after 1880, census information was merged with state registration data. Nothing similar, unfortunately, was undertaken for birth data. One consequence of the lack of vital registration data before the early twentieth century has been a resort to special estimation techniques and indirect measures of fertility and mortality to gain insight into the demographic transition of the nineteenth century (see, e.g., Preston and Haines 1991). A summary of indirect estimation methods can be found in United Nations (1983).

International migration statistics are better than the vital data, although there are also serious shortcomings. For the United States, no official statistics exist prior to 1819, return migration was not counted until 1908, only immigrants through major ports were enumerated, and those crossing land borders were counted only for the period 1855–1885 and again after 1904.

The US census also provides, from 1850 to 1970, information on a person's place of birth and, after 1870, on the nativity of each person's parents. This was either state of birth for the native-born or country of birth for the foreign-born. These data permit study of international migration (e.g., the geographic distribution of the foreign-born) and also analysis of internal migration by providing cross-classification of the native-born by birth and current residence (from 1850 onward). Internal migration is a rather difficult issue because of lack of evidence on date of change of residence between birth and current residence. For the foreign-born, questions on duration of residence in the United States were asked in the censuses of 1890 to 1930, but a question was not asked of all inhabitants about duration of current residence until 1940 (when a question was asked concerning a person's place of residence five years prior to the census).

Overall, it seems that censuses in the mid-nineteenth century missed anywhere from 5 percent to 25 percent of the population. A careful analysis of the white population from 1880 to 1960 indicates overall under-enumeration of 6.1 percent in 1880, declining to 5.7 percent by 1920 and 2.1 percent by 1960 (Coale and Zelnik 1963). Similarly, collection of vital data also had deficiencies. A criterion for admission to the official United States Death Registration Area after 1900 and the Birth Registration Area after 1915 was only that registration be 90 percent complete. As late as 1935, it was estimated that birth registration was about 91 percent complete and only 80 percent complete for the nonwhite population.

Another source is the data from records of Union Army recruits, their places of origin, heights, pension records, and dates of death. These data have proven very useful in the historical study of health, morbidity, and mortality (see, e.g., Bleakley, Costa, and Lleras-Muney 2014).

Methods, Measurement, and Estimation

Demography, the study of human populations, depends heavily on measurement and estimation techniques. Most of the results presented here are simple tabulations or standard demographic rates. But a number of the newer findings arise from rather sophisticated techniques (see, e.g., Preston and Haines 1991, ch. 2; United Nations 1983). Estimation of better demographic information is of importance for research in economic history. Basic demographic structures and events, reflected in birth and death rates, population size and structure, growth rates, the composition and growth of the labor force, marriage rates and patterns, household composition, the levels and nature of migration flows, causes of death, urbanization and spatial population distribution, and so on determine the human capital of society as producers and consumers and also how that human capital reproduces, relocates, and depreciates. Demographic events are important both as indicators of social and economic change and as integral components of modern economic growth.

Most of the measures presented here are relatively straightforward, such as crude birth and death rates, rates of total and natural increase, and rates of net migration. These are presented in tables 1.1 and 1.2. Table 1.1 presents the expectation of life at birth for the white and black populations from 1850 onward. Another life table measure is the probability of an infant surviving from birth to the first birthday (exact age 1), which is presented here as the infant mortality rate (infant deaths per 1,000 live births per annum). Similarly, age-specific fertility rates can be summarized as the total fertility rate (TFR). Table 1.1 also provides a measure of fertility known as the child–woman ratio, which is the number of surviving children aged 0–4 per 1,000 women aged 20–44. It is a wholly census-based fertility rate, requiring no vital statistics. It is, in fact, the main direct source of information on fertility for the United States in the nineteenth century and is the basis for the early estimates of the crude birth rate and the total fertility rate also given in table 1.1. The child–woman ratio does have some serious drawbacks, since it deals with surviving children at the census and not actual births in the preceding five years. It also suffers from relative differences in under-enumeration of young children and adult women.

British North America Prior to 1790

For the period prior to the first US census in 1790, we have some limited information about vital rates and population characteristics. We know more about population size than other matters, especially because British colonial authorities carried out some enumerations (McCusker 2006). The non-American Indian population of British North America had increased to about 2.9 million (with about 2.3 million whites and about 600,000 blacks) in 1780. Of the white population, about 150,000 were living in

Table 1.2 Components of Population Growth, United States, 1790–2009 (Rates per 1,000 Mid–Period Population per Year)[a]

Period	Average Population (000s)	RTI	CBR	CDR	RNI[b]	RNM[b]	RNM as % of RTI
1790–1800	4,520	30.08			26.49	3.59	11.9
1800–1810	6,132	31.04			26.85	4.19	13.5
1810–1820	8,276	28.62			24.70	3.92	13.7
1820–1830	11,031	28.88			26.82	2.06	7.1
1830–1840	14,685	28.27			23.50	4.77	16.9
1840–1850	19,686	30.65			22.37	8.28	27.0
1850–1860	26,721	30.44			20.61	9.83	32.3
1860–1870	35,156	23.62			17.36	6.26	26.5
1870–1880	44,414	23.08	41.16	23.66	17.50	5.58	24.2
1880–1890	55,853	22.72	37.03	21.34	15.69	7.03	30.9
1890–1900	68,876	18.97	32.22	19.44	12.78	6.19	32.6
1900–1910	83,822	19.42	29.83	17.26	12.57	6.85	35.3
1910–1920	100,546	14.16	26.85	15.26	11.59	2.57	18.1
1920–1930	115,829	14.50	23.15	11.62	11.53	2.97	20.5
1930–1940	127,250	7.34	19.49	11.12	8.37	−1.03	−14.0
1940–1950	139,928	13.94	23.08	10.48	12.60	1.34	9.6
1950–1960	165,931	17.10	24.78	9.46	15.32	1.78	10.4
1960–1970	194,303	12.66	20.05	9.43	10.62	2.04	16.1
1970–1980	215,973	10.27	15.41	8.94	6.47	3.80	37.0
1980–1990	237,924	9.34	15.88	8.71	7.17	2.17	23.2
1990–2000	262,803	12.30	15.11	8.67	6.44	5.86	47.6[c]
2000–2009	307,439	8.50	12.48	7.31	5.16	3.34	39.3

Sources: Carter et al. (2006, Table Aa15–21); US Bureau of the Census (2012, Table 5).

[a] All rates are per 1,000 population per year. RTI = rate of total increase. CBR = crude birth rate (live births per 1,000 population per year. CDR = crude death rate (deaths per 1,000 population per year). RNI = rate of natural increase (= CBR − CDR). RNM = rate of net external migration.

[b] Rate of net migration calculated directly from net migrants 1790–1860. Gross migrants used for 1860–1870. For 1870–2000, RNM = RTI − RNI and thus is a residual. Prior to 1870, RNI is calculated as a residual (= RTI − RNM).

[c] Does not take into account results from the 2000 census.

Canada, 85 percent of these in French Canada. The slave population grew from a few in 1619 to almost 700,000 in 1790, both from the slave trade and from an excess of births over deaths.

For the future United States, birth rates were high with crude rates ranging from more than 40 live births per 1,000 population per annum to well more than 50. The crude birth rate for the United States as a whole has been estimated at more than 50 around 1800. Mortality was moderate for the era. Crude death rates varied from about 20 per 1,000 population per year to more than 40 (and even higher in crisis periods). Lower mortality was found, as a rule, in the colonies and states from Pennsylvania and New Jersey northward, and high mortality characterized the South. In the North, expectations of life at birth ranged all the way from the mid- to early twenties to possibly as high as forty. Based on available records and analysis done to date, we know a good deal about New England, somewhat less about the Middle Colonies and states, and least about the South (with the notable exception of the Chesapeake area) (Wells 1992).

Population Growth in the United States

As mentioned, the United States began its demographic transition from high to low levels of fertility and mortality from at least the beginning of the nineteenth century, if not earlier. Table 1.2 provides summary measures of population growth and its components by decades from 1790 to 2010. It is organized around the demographic balancing equation, which states that the decade rate of population growth or rate of total increase (RTI) equals the crude birth rate (CBR) minus the crude death rate (CDR) plus the rate of net migration (RNM):

$$RTI = CBR - CDR + RNM.$$

The difference between the birth rate and the death rate is the rate of natural increase (RNI):

$$CBR - CDR = RNI.$$

Several features of the American demographic transition can be discerned from tables 1.1 and 1.2. The United States experienced a truly remarkable population increase during its transition. From a modest 4 million inhabitants in 1790, the population grew to almost 309 million persons in 2010, an average annual growth rate of about 2 percent per year. In the early years of the republic, annual population growth rates were even higher, above 3 percent for the period 1790–1810 and again in the 1840s and 1850s. Such rapid growth is historically rather unusual and is comparable to the recent experience of some developing nations. The surge of growth in the 1840s and 1850s was particularly due to a significant increase in migration from abroad—the now familiar story of Irish, Germans, and others from Western and Northern Europe fleeing the great potato famine, the "Hungry Forties," and political upheaval and seeking better farming, business, and employment opportunities in the western hemisphere. Natural increase had been declining from the early 1800s, largely from decline in birth rates for both the white and black populations. Some of the decline in natural increase in the 1840s and 1850s was also likely due to rising mortality in those decades. Table 1.1 indicates, however, that mortality did decline steadily from the 1870s onward.

Another feature notable in table 1.2 is the dominant role played by natural increase in overall population growth. In the decades before 1840, less than one-sixth or one-seventh of total growth originated in net migration. With the surge in overseas migration after 1840, however, the share of net migration in total increase rose to a one-quarter or one-third. Notably, the share of labor force growth accounted for by migration was higher, since migration was selective of persons in the labor force ages. Nonetheless, despite declining birth rates, the American population grew rapidly in the nineteenth century, principally from an excess of births over deaths, although it must be recognized that the births to the foreign-born and their descendants made an important contribution. The surge in migration after 1840 can be recognized in the rise in the proportion of the population foreign-born from less than 10 percent in 1850 (the first census for which such data were available) to nearly 15 percent in 1890 and 1910 (table 1.3).

The effects of immigration restriction after World War I are apparent in the reduced rate of net migration after 1920. The Great Depression had a dramatic damping effect on both fertility and migration from abroad, resulting in the only decade of net out-migration since the first census in 1790. The post–World War II "baby boom" is apparent in the higher crude birth rates in the 1940s and 1950s. More recent changes in immigration regulations clearly affected the surge in net in-migrants, when 37 percent of population growth in the 1970s was due to this source, 47 percent in the 1990s, and 39 percent in the 2000s. These proportions were larger than those in the decades preceding both the Civil War and World War I.

Fertility and Nuptiality

The young republic was notable for its large families and early marriage. The total fertility rate in table 1.1 indicates an average number of births per woman of approximately seven in 1800, and the TFR was still more than five on the eve of the Civil War. While we know relatively little about marriage early in the nineteenth century, female age at first marriage was probably rather young, perhaps below 20. Males married on average several years older, and all but a relatively small proportion of both sexes eventually married. The federal census did not ask a question on marital status until 1880 and did not begin reporting results on this until 1890. A sample of seven New York state counties from the manuscripts of the census of 1865, for example, reveals an estimated age at first marriage of 23.8 years for females and 26.6 years for males. Percentages never married by the ages 45–54 were 7.4 percent for females and 5.9 percent for males, pointing to quite low levels of lifetime non-marriage. Although marriage age was probably higher in New York than in the nation as a whole and although marriage age had very likely risen by 1865, nuptiality was still rather extensive by European standards. By 1880, when

Table 1.3 Population by Race, Residence, Nativity, Age, and Sex, United States, 1790–2010 (Population in 000s)

Census Date	Total	% P.A. Growth	White	%	Black	%	Other	%	Urban	%	Foreign Born	%	Median Age	Sex Ratio[b]
1790	3,929	–	3,172	80.7	757	19.3	(NA)	[NA]	202	5.1	(NA)	–	(NA)	103.8
1800	5,308	3.01	4,306	81.1	1,002	18.9	(NA)	[NA]	322	6.1	(NA)	–	16.0[a]	104.0
1810	7,240	3.10	5,862	81.0	1,378	19.0	(NA)	[NA]	525	7.3	(NA)	–	16.0[a]	104.0
1820	9,639	2.86	7,867	81.6	1,772	18.4	(NA)	[NA]	693	7.2	(NA)	–	16.7	103.3
1830	12,866	2.89	10,537	81.9	2,329	18.1	(NA)	[NA]	1,127	8.8	(NA)	–	17.2	103.1
1840	17,070	2.83	14,196	83.2	2,874	16.8	(NA)	[NA]	1,845	10.8	(NA)	–	17.8	103.7
1850	23,192	3.06	19,553	84.3	3,639	15.7	(NA)	[NA]	3,544	15.3	2,245	9.7	18.9	104.3
1860	31,443	3.04	26,923	85.6	4,442	14.1	79	0.3	6,217	19.8	4,104	13.1	19.4	104.7
1870	39,819	2.36	33,589	84.4	4,880	12.3	89	0.2	9,902	24.9	5,567	14.0	20.2	102.2
1880	50,156	2.31	43,403	86.5	6,581	13.1	172	0.3	14,130	28.2	6,680	13.3	20.9	103.6
1890	62,948	2.27	55,101	87.5	7,489	11.9	358	0.6	22,106	35.1	9,250	14.7	22.0	105.0
1900	75,994	1.88	66,809	87.9	8,834	11.6	351	0.5	30,160	39.7	10,341	13.6	22.9	104.4
1910	91,972	1.91	81,732	88.9	9,828	10.7	413	0.4	41,999	45.7	13,516	14.7	24.1	106.0
1920	106,711	1.49	94,821	88.9	10,463	9.8	427	0.4	54,158	50.8	14,020	13.1	25.3	104.0
1930	122,755	1.40	110,287	89.8	11,891	9.7	597	0.5	68,955	56.2	14,283	11.6	26.5	102.5
1940	131,669	0.70	118,215	89.8	12,866	9.8	589	0.4	74,424	56.5	11,657	8.9	29.0	100.7
1950	150,697	1.35	134,942	89.5	15,042	10.0	713	0.5	96,468	64.0	10,431	6.9	30.2	98.6
1960	179,823	1.77	158,832	88.3	18,872	10.5	1,620	0.9	125,269	69.7	9,738	5.4	29.5	97.1
1970	203,302	1.23	178,098	87.6	22,580	11.1	2,883	1.4	149,325	73.4	9,619	4.7	28.1	94.8
1980	226,546	1.08	194,713	85.9	26,683	11.8	5,150	2.3	167,051	73.7	14,080	6.2	30.0	94.5
1990	248,710	0.93	208,704	83.9	30,483	12.3	9,523	3.8	187,053	75.2	21,632	8.7	32.8	95.1
2000	281,422	1.24	216,931	77.1	36,419	12.9	35,414	12.6	222,361	79.0	28,379	10.4	35.3	96.3
2010	308,746	0.92	223,553	72.4	38,929	12.6	47,164	15.0	249,253	80.7	39,956	12.9	37.2	96.7

Sources: Calculated from Carter et al. (2006, Part A, Chapter Aa, "Population Characteristics"); US Bureau of the Census (2012).

[a] White population.

[b] Males per 100 females.

the US census first asked a question on marital status, the average female age at first marriage was 23.0 years while that for males was 26.5 years. Age at marriage rose a bit up until 1890 and 1900 and thereafter began a longer term decline up to the 1950s. By 1960, age at marriage had fallen to 20.3 years for women and 23.4 years for men. Since the 1960s, there has been a sharp increase in the age at marriage for both men and women, especially in the black population, although this has not been accompanied by an increase in the proportions of the population at ages 45–54 who have never married. For a summary of marriage measures, see Haines (1996).

Similarly, in 1800 the United States was a nation of high fertility, but it then experienced a sustained decline in birth rates up until the 1940s when the baby boom interrupted this pattern. The unusual aspect of the American experience is that the reduction began before the nation was substantially urban or industrial. Both rural and urban birth rates declined in parallel. A decomposition of the fertility transition into the contributions of nuptiality and marital fertility found that, up to approximately 1850, half of the decline could be attributed to adjustments in marriage age and marriage incidence (Hacker 2003). Thereafter most of the decline originated in reductions of fertility within marriage. Even the fertility of the antebellum slave population showed signs of decline just prior to 1860, though family sizes for blacks were, on average, significantly larger than those for whites.

Such evidence as we have concerning fertility differentials by nativity (native-born versus foreign-born) points to relatively small differences at mid-century but generally higher fertility for the foreign-born thereafter. Birth rates of native-born women of foreign-born parentage were intermediate between those of native white women of native parentage and foreign-born white women, suggesting some assimilation to native-born white demographic patterns.

The inexorable decline of American birth rates continued apace after the Civil War. Since 1860 most of the decline originated in adjustments in fertility within marriage. Recent work data on children ever born (parity) from the 1900, 1910, and 1940 federal censuses show rapid reductions in marital fertility, especially among white urban women. In 1910, for example, over half of native-born white urban women aged 45–49 were estimated to have been effectively controlling fertility within marriage, and about one-quarter rural farm and non-farm women were doing the same. Among younger women (aged 15–34), the proportions were much higher, rising to more than 70 percent for native-born white urban women and over half for native-born white farm women. It could certainly be said that the "two child norm" was being established in the United States in this era.

One of the conclusions from this detailed study of fertility has been that the spacing of births from early in the childbearing years was, by the late nineteenth century, as important as the more conventional behavior of stopping before the biological end of the female reproductive span. The period after 1865 was further marked by reductions in fertility by residence and by race. For the rural and urban populations, relative differences in child–woman ratios did not disappear. Rural fertility remained higher than urban fertility, but absolute differences diminished as both types of resident progressively limited family size.

Fertility differences by race tended to converge after the middle of the nineteenth century. Whereas the black total fertility rate was 48 percent higher than that for whites in the 1850s, it was only 15 percent higher in 1920. The end of slavery, difficult conditions in the agrarian South, and increased urbanization of the black population all played roles in this. Differentials in birth rates by race have persisted up to the present and have actually widened somewhat after 1920, but the decline continued for both blacks and whites after the peak of the baby boom around 1960.

Finally, although we know rather less about the fertility of different socioeconomic status groups, the evidence points to smaller families among higher socioeconomic status groups, such as professionals, proprietors, clerks, and other white-collar workers. This was true, at least, from the middle of the nineteenth century onward. Among proprietors, however, an exception was owner-occupier farmers, who, throughout the century, typically had larger families than other groups. Unskilled workers (often characterized simply as laborers or farm laborers) tended to have fertility closer to that of farmers, while skilled and semiskilled manual workers and craftsmen occupied an intermediate position. These socioeconomic fertility differences may have widened over the course of the nineteenth century before they eventually narrowed (Haines 2000).

Fertility decline continued in the twentieth century, but it was punctuated by one of the most interesting demographic phenomena of modern times—the post–World War II baby boom. Birth rates reached a low point in the late 1930s, remained low during World War II, and rose dramatically until a peak in the early 1960s. Thereafter, birth rates fell to a low point in the middle of the 1970s, followed by a gradual rise to a plateau at about long-term replacement (i.e., a TFR of about 2.1). The white population is just about replacing itself, while the nonwhite population has fertility a bit above replacement. The decline in fertility after the early 1960s had multiple origins: greater access to contraception, increased education of women, and the decoupling of marriage and childbearing. Whether this constituted a "second demographic transition" is still a matter of debate (Bailey, Guldi, and Hershbein 2014). The basic trend to smaller families was already underway well before the 1950s.

The implication of the baby boom and subsequent "baby bust" are enormous. The large birth cohorts of 1946–1962 have influenced consumer spending, demand for housing, need for schools and higher education, savings behavior, voting patterns, and many other aspects of the society and economy. The smaller cohort born in the late 1960s and the 1970s posed new challenges. The smaller size of the bust generation relative to the boom generation has thrown into question long-standing formulas defining Social Security benefits and Medicare. When the "boomers" retire, the smaller succeeding cohorts must assume the burden of paying for these benefits.

There has been a dramatic increase in cohabitation recently, along with a significant rise in divorce. The proportion of the population living alone has also risen notably, particularly among the older population. One consequence of declining fertility has been an aging of the population. As table 1.3 shows, the median age of the American people rose from sixteen years in 1800 to more than twenty in 1870 and more than twenty-five in 1920. Today it stands at more than thirty-seven. The reason is that the age structure of the population, particularly the proportion of children, is most affected by fertility, which adds only to the base of the age pyramid. Mortality, in contrast, affects all ages. As fertility declines, so does the proportion of children and teenagers. The population ages. The implications of this are great, changing the society from one oriented toward children to one centered on adults and eventually the elderly. The implications are enormous. The future of the Social Security system and retirement in general is dominated by this concern: Will there be enough younger workers to pay for the retirement of older Americans well into the twenty-first century?

Explaining the American demographic transition poses a series of difficult issues. Conventional demographic transition theory has placed great reliance on the changes in child costs and benefits associated with structural changes accompanying modern economic growth, such as urbanization, industrialization, the rise in literacy and education, and increased employment of women outside the home. But, of course, the fertility transition began in the United States well before many of these structural changes became important. Consequently, a number of alternative explanations have been offered for the antebellum period. Some involve transfers from parents to children and means to provide for old age, such as the land availability hypothesis (Yasuba 1962; Forster and Tucker 1972; Easterlin 1976) and the child bargaining–local labor market hypothesis (Sundstrom and David 1988). Others involve the marriage market and the spreading idea of family limitation (Hacker 2003). The structural view seems to work much better after 1865, but the view which seems to tie things together best is the life cycle savings hypothesis of Franco Modigliani (Carter, Ransom, and Sutch 2004; Modigliani 1988).

Fertility of the black population can be described by child–woman ratios from 1820 and by the crude birth rate and the total fertility rate from the 1850s. Interestingly, from 1830, fertility decline also occurred for the black population, largely in the context of slavery, since 86 percent of the black population were slaves at that date. Also, despite the higher infant and child mortality among blacks, black child–woman ratios were higher than those for whites, pointing to even larger differential fertility for blacks. After the Civil War, the decline in black fertility was more similar in nature to the white fertility transition, influenced by urbanization, industrial development, growing shortage of good farmland, and changes in family norms.

In sum, the fertility transition in the United States was unusual. It began in a largely rural and agrarian nation long before most of the presently developed nations began their fertility transitions in the late nineteenth century. As the nineteenth century progressed, however, the more conventional socioeconomic variables had more explanatory power. These variables would include rising literacy and education, increased urbanization (with more expensive housing and crowding), more work by women and children outside the home, the spread of institutional restrictions like child labor laws and compulsory education statutes, the rising value of time as real wages and incomes increased, less reliance on children for support in old age, the improved status of women, and less available familial child care as smaller, urban nuclear families became dominant. There is also likely a role for declining infant and child mortality, at least after about 1880, which reduced the number of births necessary to achieve a desired number of children surviving to adulthood.

MORTALITY

We know less about the American mortality transition of the nineteenth century than we do about that for fertility. There are no ready census-based mortality measures like the child–woman ratio, and vital statistics were absent or incomplete for most areas up until the early twentieth century. We know the most about Massachusetts, which began statewide civil vital registration (the recording of births, deaths, and marriages) in 1842, but Massachusetts was not typical of the nation in the nineteenth century. It was more urban and industrial, had more immigrants, and had lower fertility. The federal census collected mortality information from 1850 to 1900, but the data were seriously flawed by incompleteness, biases, and uneven coverage. In consequence, there has been disagreement about trends, levels, and differentials in American mortality over the nineteenth century.

As mentioned, the official Death Registration Area was not formed until 1900, although there had been earlier attempts. In 1900, the Death Registration Area comprised ten states and the District of Columbia, covering 26 percent of the population. It only covered the entire United States from 1933 onward. Prior to 1900, official mortality data are limited to selected states and cities and to the imperfect mortality data of the census.

More recent work with genealogical data has concluded that adult mortality (on a period basis) was relatively stable after about 1800 and then rose in the 1840s and 1850s before commencing improvement after the Civil War (Pope 1992). This finding is quite unusual, since we have evidence of rising real income per capita and of significant economic growth during the 1840–1860 period. But income distribution may have worsened and urbanization and immigration may have had more deleterious effects than hitherto believed. Further, the disease environment may have shifted in an unfavorable direction. The decline in the heights of Civil War recruits from the birth cohorts of the 1820s to the early 1840s supports this view of declining health and economic well-being (see Steckel and Costa 1997).

Table 1.1 provides data on the expectation of life at birth and the infant mortality rate for the white population from 1850 onward. No information is given prior to 1850 because of the difficulty of finding comprehensive, comparable, and reliable mortality estimates (Preston and Haines 1991, ch. 2). The evidence in table 1.1 shows that both the expectation of life at birth and the infant mortality rate (and the crude death rate estimates in table 1.2) show sustained improvement in mortality only from about the 1870s onward. Serious fluctuations in mortality were less likely after the 1870s and this was integral in the process of the mortality transition. This also confirms one unusual aspect of the American demographic transition—fertility commenced its decline substantially before mortality. The new findings of rising mortality in the 1840s and 1850s support this contention that mortality in the United States was not substantially under control until after the Civil War.

What were the origins of the "epidemiologic transition" in the United States? A variety of factors affect mortality. In terms of cause of death, declines in infectious and parasitic diseases were a key. The factors may conveniently be grouped into ecobiological, public health, medical, and socioeconomic. These categories are not mutually exclusive, since, for example, economic growth can make resources available for public health projects and advances in medical science can inform the effectiveness of public health. Cancer and cardiovascular disease are now dominant. Ecobiological factors were not likely significant. While there may have been favorable changes in the etiology of a few specific diseases or conditions in the nineteenth century (notably scarlet fever and possibly diphtheria), reduced disease virulence or changes in transmission mechanisms were not apparent (Easterlin 1996).

The remaining factors, socioeconomic, medical, and public health, are often difficult to disentangle. For example, if the germ theory of disease (a medical and scientific advance of the later nineteenth century) contributed to better techniques of water filtration and purification in public health projects, then how should the roles of medicine versus public health be apportioned? Cutler and Miller (2005) have shown that public health projects, notably clean water and better sewerage disposal, played a central role in the twentieth-century mortality transition. But advances in medical science clearly informed public health activity, and improved living standards created greater resistance to infection and improved survivability. Progress in public health was not confined to water and sewer systems, though they were among the most effective weapons in the fight to prolong and enhance human life (Melosi 2000). Simply by reducing the incidence and exposure to disease in any way, overall health, net nutritional status, and resistance to disease were improved. Other areas of public health activity from the late nineteenth century onward included:

- vaccination against smallpox;
- use of diphtheria and tetanus antitoxins (from the 1890s);
- more extensive use of quarantine (as more diseases were identified as contagious);
- cleaning urban streets and public areas to reduce disease foci;
- physical examinations for schoolchildren;
- health education;
- improved child labor and workplace health and safety laws;
- legislation and enforcement efforts to reduce food adulteration and especially to obtain pure milk;
- measures to eliminate ineffective or dangerous medications (e.g., the Pure Food and Drug Act of 1906);
- increased knowledge of and education concerning nutrition;
- stricter licensing of physicians, nurses, and midwives;
- more rigorous medical education;

- building codes to improve heat, plumbing, and ventilation in housing;
- measures to alleviate air pollution in urban settings; and
- the creation of state and local boards of health to oversee and administer these programs.

One of the great events in human history has been the prolongation of life and reduction in mortality in the modern era, chiefly due to great declines in death from epidemic and endemic infectious disease. Americans and most people in the developed world no longer live with the kind of fear and fatalism that characterized a world in which sudden and pervasive death from disease was a fact of life. For the United States, most of this improvement took place since the late nineteenth century (see table 1.2).

During our period, both prior to and during the mortality transition, significant differentials in mortality existed—by sex, rural–urban residence, race, region, nativity (native-born versus foreign-born), and socioeconomic status. Male mortality usually exceeds female mortality at all ages. This was generally true in the United States in the nineteenth century. The relative differences were often smaller than in the mid- to late twentieth century, as a consequence of the hazards of childbearing and pervasive exposure to disease-causing organisms. It is clear that, before about 1920, urban mortality was much in excess of rural mortality; in general, the larger the city, the higher the death rate. A variety of circumstances contributed to the excess mortality of cities: greater density and crowding, leading to the more rapid spread of infection; a higher degree of contaminated water and food; garbage and carrion in streets and elsewhere not properly disposed of; larger inflows of foreign migrants, both new foci of infection and new victims; and also migrants from the countryside who had not been exposed to the harsher urban disease environment (Haines 2001; Preston and Haines 1991, 20–26). According to the Death Registration Area life tables for 1900/02, the expectation of life at birth was 48.2 years for white males overall—44 years in urban areas and 54 years in rural places. The comparable results for females were similar (51.1 years overall, 48 years for urban, 55 years for rural; Preston and Haines 1991, 36–39).

The black population of the United States certainly experienced higher death rates, both as slaves and then as a free population in the post-bellum period than did whites. Table 1.1 provides a breakdown of the expectation of life at birth and the infant mortality rate by race. As of 1920, when reasonably representative data are available for the black population in the official registration states, it is apparent that the mortality of blacks was substantially higher, despite their living in predominantly rural areas. For the 1890s, based on estimates using the 1900 census public use sample, the infant mortality rate was 111 infant deaths per 1,000 live births for the white population and 170 for the black population. The implied expectations of life at birth were 51.8 years for whites and 41.8 years for blacks (Preston and Haines 1991). The differential clearly had not disappeared by 1920, when the absolute difference in expectation of life at birth by race was 10.4 years and the black infant mortality rate was 60 percent higher than that for whites. Even in 2009, although some convergence had occurred, the difference in life expectancy was still 6.3 years and black infant mortality was 7.6 points higher than

white. The absolute difference had narrowed, but the relative difference in infant survival had actually worsened. Mortality is a sensitive indicator of socioeconomic well-
being, and, by that standard, the absolute improvement for the black population had
been considerable, although relative progress had been mixed. The historically disadvantaged status of the black population is apparent, since, despite a greater proportion
living in comparatively healthier rural areas, blacks still had substantially higher death
rates than whites.

The mortality and health of the antebellum slave population have more recently
been studied using plantation records and coastal shipping manifests (giving heights of
transported slaves). It has revealed very high mortality and very stunted stature among
slave infants and young children, pointing to poor health conditions. For example, the
infant mortality rate for slaves is estimated to have been as high as 340 infant deaths per
1,000 live births in comparison to 197 for the whole American population in 1860 (table
1.1). Death rates among slave children aged one to four were also very high, although
they began to move closer to those for whites for older ages. A hypothesis for the high
mortality and short stature of slave children is that they were not given much animal
protein in their diets until about age ten. In addition, pregnant and lactating women
were often kept hard at fieldwork, leading to lower birth weights and to less breast
feeding and earlier weaning. The better diets of adolescent and adult slaves brought their
mortality rates and stature closer to those for the white population.

Information on mortality differences between the native-born and foreign-born
populations is ambiguous. For the Death Registration Area life tables of 1900/02, life
expectancies at age 10 were rather similar by nativity: 51.6 years for native-born white
males and 49.1 years for foreign-born white males. The results for 1909/11 were 51.9
and 50.3 years, respectively. Differentials by nativity were converging and had largely
disappeared by the 1930s, since the higher mortality of the foreign-born was largely
due to lower socioeconomic status and a greater proportion in large cities. As socioeconomic attainment narrowed between the groups and as the rural–urban mortality
difference disappeared, the mortality penalty paid by the foreign-born also diminished
(Preston and Haines 1991, chs. 2 and 3).

Differences in survival probabilities also existed across socioeconomic groups, although here too the information is sketchy. Census mortality data for adult males reported by occupation in 1890 and 1900 and vital registration for 1908/10 show a rough
gradient with the lowest death rates among proprietors, clerical, and other white-
collar workers and the highest death rates among laborers and servants. Interestingly,
professionals did only about average. Farmers and clerks did well, as, surprisingly, did
workers in forestry and fisheries. The more rural environment for those in agriculture
and extractive industries undoubtedly helped. These results are echoed in estimates of
child mortality according to occupation of father from the 1900 census sample. Children
of white-collar workers, professionals, proprietors, and farmers did better than average,
while children of laborers (including agricultural laborers) had worse than average
survival chances. Again, the advantage to professionals, such as physicians, teachers,
and clergy, did not hold. An exception was race, where the black population was at a

disadvantage both within occupations and within rural–urban categories (Preston and Haines 1991, ch. 5).

There is some evidence from earlier in the nineteenth century that socioeconomic variables, such as wealth or income, occupation, and literacy, were less important in predicting mortality differentials. For the 1850s, for instance, survival probabilities differed little between the children of the poor and the wealthy. Rural–urban residence and region made more difference.

This had begun to change in the early twentieth century, however. Analysis of the 1910 census public use sample and published vital statistics from the Birth Registration Area in the 1920s has revealed, however, that the socioeconomic differentials widened in the United States as the new century progressed. Higher income and better educated groups more easily assimilated advice and improvements in child care, hygiene, and health practices and so were "leaders" in the mortality decline of the early twentieth century, much as the upper British socioeconomic status groups had been. Public health improvements led to a reduction in the level of mortality but did not lead to a reduction in relative differentials across class and occupation groups. Rural–urban differences did converge into the early twentieth century, but both relative and absolute mortality differences by race did not. The role of personal and household health behavior has been inadequately emphasized in the debate on the origins of the mortality transition. It was very likely central, although the precise contribution to differential child mortality is not easy to assess. For adults, the mortality gradient observed at the turn of the century from high mortality among laborers to intermediate levels among skilled manual workers to the most favorable mortality among white-collar workers persisted up to the middle of the twentieth century.

Overall, the mortality transition in the United States was a delayed event. Instead of a decline of death rates across the nineteenth century in parallel with the decline in birth rates, mortality exhibited an increase prior to the Civil War. The sustained decline only commenced nationally in the 1870s. A damping of year-to-year mortality fluctuations also took place after mid-century. In the nineteenth century, cities were definitely less healthy environments—the larger the city, the higher the mortality risk. The rural advantage was slowly eroded from late in the century, particularly due to the advance of urban public health, broadly defined. The mortality disadvantage of the black population persisted throughout the period considered here, although mortality levels improved for both whites and blacks. It is not easy to assign credit to various causal factors in the mortality transition, but the principal proximate cause was the control of both epidemic and endemic infectious diseases. By the later nineteenth century, public health certainly contributed much, with improvements in diet, housing, and standard of living also significant. The direct role of medical intervention was rather limited before the twentieth century but then increased as the germ theory of disease was accepted and better diagnosis and effective therapies were developed. Although difficult to assess, changes in personal health behavior must be assigned importance, particularly after the turn of the twentieth century.

MIGRATION

The United States was, and to a great extent remains, a nation of migrants. On the one hand, as seen in table 1.2, a large share (approximately 25 percent) of total population growth over the period 1790–1920 was due to migration from abroad. On the other hand, the slave population (which grew from about 700,000 in 1790 to almost 4 million in 1860) was not significantly augmented by the external slave trade. That was officially ended in 1808 by the Constitution. The slave population grew fundamentally by an excess of births over deaths.

Between 1819 and 1920, according to official statistics, more than 33.7 million migrants entered the United States from abroad. But, once here, both immigrants and the native-born continued to move—westward to the frontier, from rural to urban areas, and, more recently, to suburbia and to the sunbelt. Two migrations were driving internal migration—the movement from east to west and the movement from rural to urban areas. As table 1.3 demonstrates, urban population grew from about 5 percent of the total population in 1790 to 51 percent in 1920 and almost 81 percent in 2010 (which is probably an underestimate). The average annual growth rate over the 220 years since the first federal census was 3.3 percent for the urban population in contrast to only 1.3 percent per annum for rural dwellers. Since we have every indication the birth rates were lower and death rates higher in urban relative to rural areas, the more rapid growth of urban areas originated in population redistribution and not differences in natural increase. This rural to urban shift reflects, of course, labor market conditions as the economy changed its structure of opportunities from a rural, smallholder agriculture to an urban, industrial, and service-based economy made up predominantly of employees. This is certainly exemplified by the increase in the non-farm share of the labor force from 25.6 percent in 1800 to 44.2 percent in 1860 to 74.1 percent in 1920 and more than 99 percent today. A primary motive for migration in ordinary times is to take advantage of wage and income differences across space, which substitutes factor mobility for interregional trade in goods and services.

From 1850 onward, we are able to examine migration by place of birth and current residence. The proportion of the native-born population residing outside the state of birth ("lifetime" migrants) was relatively stable from the middle of the nineteenth century—23.3 percent of the white population in 1850, 23.5 percent in 1890, and 23.9 percent in 1920. The nonwhite population had lower rates of lifetime mobility in this period, about 15–20 percent until after 1920. Much of this interstate movement was on an east–west axis until the closing of the frontier at the end of the nineteenth century. A variety of explanations have been advanced for the migration along latitudes, but recently it has been shown that real and human capital invested in seed, livestock, implements, and farming techniques made movement along climate bands much more rational (Steckel 1983). This also provides a partial explanation for the greater preference of the bulk of the nineteenth-century immigrants from northern and western Europe for the Northeast and the Midwest—their human capital matched that climate band better. That was true for those going to rural areas, at least. The remainder of the explanation was largely the greater opportunities in the more rapidly urbanizing and industrializing North, as well as the tendency of migration streams, once established, to grow along familiar paths. Agrarian motives for migration diminished as the frontier closed in the late nineteenth century and as rural population growth slowed dramatically (to only 0.8 percent per year over the period 1890-1920). By late in the century, rural to urban flow assumed the dominant role. The major shift to a south to north movement only began on a large scale with the radical shifts in demand for labor accompanying World War I and the restriction, after 1921, of cheap immigrant labor. The shift to the sunbelt came even later, largely post-World War II. Changes in transportation technology, particularly the electric street railways and subways and later the automobile and motorized bus, led to a movement out of central cities and into suburban communities. This process was underway in parts of the Northeast by the end of the nineteenth century, but really accelerated after World War I, and again after 1945. This led to the ongoing process of suburbanization.

The urbanization process was accompanied by a filling out in the city size hierarchy. Large cities did tend to grow most rapidly. But the urban size hierarchy did not become distorted, as it has in some developing nations. That is, large cities did not grow such that medium and smaller urban places became unimportant, and this urban growth had powerful economic linkages. Considerable industrial output from the period after 1865 was devoted to providing infrastructure and materials to house, transport, and deliver public services to this massive population shift to towns and cities. Iron and steel for sewer and water pipe, bridges, rails, structural pieces, and nails; concrete, stone, brick, and asphalt for roads and structures; cut timber; transport equipment; glass, etc. were demanded in huge quantities to build the cities.

In discussions of migration to the United States over the long nineteenth century, the flood of immigrants from Europe usually takes center stage. It was dramatic and colorful as new arrivals added an ethnic flavor which pervades our culture today. Like internal migrants, the immigrants were most often motivated by economic concerns. The selectivity of international migration is partly the cause of the phenomenon seen in the last column of table 1.3. The sex ratio of the population (males per 100 females) was well above 100 in 1790 and increased in decades of highest immigration (the 1840s, 1850s, 1880s, and 1900s). Migration was selective of adult males in this case, as they were first to seek the opportunities. They clearly were raising the national average. The general decline of the sex ratio over time was, however, due to the aging of the population and declining fertility. More recently, however, the sex ratio has risen, partly due to increased migration flows from abroad. Waves of immigration were roughly synchronous with long swings in economic activity in the United States. It is also of importance to consider migration to the United States as one part of a global labor market that emerged in the second half of the nineteenth century. Even in times of relative prosperity in Europe, migrants left in increased numbers, since American labor market conditions were the dominant factor. An important exception was the great potato famine of the 1840s in Europe.

Average immigration increased from about 14,000 persons per year in the 1820s to almost 260,000 per year in the 1850s to approximately one million annually in the peak years 1911/14, an average growth of 4.9 percent per annum between the 1820s and 1911/14—very rapid indeed. More than one million migrants entered the United States in six of the fourteen years before World War I erupted in Europe in 1914. These magnitudes have not been exceeded for recorded, legal migration until very recently.

Another salient feature of immigration to America was the changing composition of the flows across the long nineteenth century. For the decades between 1821 and 1890, 82 percent of all immigrants originated in northern and western Europe and only 8 percent in central, eastern, and southern Europe. For the three decades 1891 to 1920, the situation had altered dramatically: only 25 percent of the migrants came from northern and western Europe and 64 percent from central, eastern, and southern Europe. This was termed by contemporaries as the shift from the "old" to the "new" immigration. This shift in composition, along with the strong upward trend in migration, spurred the formation of the US Immigration Commission of 1907/10 and probably to immigration restriction. Since the 1980s the composition of migrants has shifted to Latin America, Africa, and Asia.

There has been considerable nativist opposition to these migrants. The "Know Nothing" or American Party, which flourished in the 1840s and 1850s, proposed anti-alien and anti-Catholic legislation, particularly directed at the Irish. Similar groups arose in the 1870s and 1880s, including in California where hostility to Chinese immigration was strong. As the labor movement grew, there were calls for immigration restriction from that quarter, which is understandable, since the more rapid expansion in the supply of labor provided by immigrants restricted the growth of real wages, raised unemployment, and made labor organizing more difficult. The short-lived National Labor Union (1866–1872) advocated limits to immigration as well as repeal of the Contract Labor Law (1864). The latter allowed employers to advance the costs of passage to prospective immigrant workers. The American Federation of Labor (founded 1886) long campaigned for quotas on immigration. Nonetheless, between the Alien Act of 1798 (only briefly in force) and the Immigration Act of 1917, which imposed a literacy test, virtually nothing was done to restrict European immigration to the United States. Although migrants had to register with ships' masters (after 1819) and had to be screened for diseases, criminal records, or the possibility of becoming a public charge (after 1891), there was basically an "open door." A notable exception was the Chinese Exclusion Act of 1882 (renewed 1892 and made indefinite in 1902), directly aimed at cutting off the flow of East Asian migrants to the west coast. The literacy test imposed in 1917 over Woodrow Wilson's veto was merely a forerunner of the much more restrictive Emergency Immigration Act of 1921, which imposed quotas based on national origins. Immigration was limited annually to 3 percent of each nation's share of the American population in 1910. An even more narrow law was enacted in 1924, which reduced the annual quota per country to 2 percent of a nation's share of the US population in 1890, clearly favoring the nations of northern and western Europe at the expense of the areas of the "new" immigration. All immigration from East Asia was terminated. In 1929, the quotas were ultimately to be based on the census of 1920 but for a total not to exceed 150,000 per year, in contrast to the levels in excess of a million a year in the years just prior to World War I. The quota system basically came to an end gradually with the Hart-Cellar Act of 1965 and the Simpson-Mazolli Act of 1986. There has been a large upsurge of both documented and undocumented migration since the 1980s with the accompanying increase in nativist opposition.

CONCLUSIONS

This chapter has focused on the evolution of the American population over the period 1650 to the present. The discussion has perforce covered fertility, marriage, mortality, and both internal and international migration. The relatively rapid population growth since 1790 (averaging about 2 percent per year) was driven largely by high (though declining) birth rates and moderate levels of mortality, but immigration was also significant. About three-quarters of the growth was due to natural increase and about one-quarter to net in-migration. More than 34 million persons entered the United States between the 1790s and the end of World War I and an additional 42 million since 1920. The availability of a federal census every ten years since 1790 has made the tracing of the demographic history of the United States much easier. The availability of individual level data from the census, now promising to be complete counts of the population, will guide future research efforts. A great deal of work is underway matching individuals across censuses to examine issues such as social mobility. Other rich data sources include the Union Army recruits data on heights and mortality and health over time.

BIBLIOGRAPHY

Anderson, Margo J. (1988). *The American Census: A Social History*. New Haven, CT: Yale University Press.

Bailey, Martha J., Melanie Guldi, and Brad J. Hershbein. (2014). "Is There a Case for a 'Second Demographic Transition'? Three Distinctive Features of the Post-1960 US Fertility Decline." In *Human Capital in History: The American Record*, edited by Leah Platt Boustan, Carola Frydman, and Robert A. Margo, 273–312. Chicago: University of Chicago Press.

Bleakley, Hoyt, Dora Costa, and Adriana Lleras-Muney. (2014). "Health, Education, and Income in the United State, 1820–2000." In *Human Capital in History: The American Record*, edited by Leah Platt Boustan, Carola Frydman, and Robert A. Margo, 121–160. Chicago: University of Chicago Press.

Carter, Susan B., Roger L. Ransom, and Richard Sutch. (2004). "Family Matters: The Life-Cycle Transition and the Antebellum Fertility Decline." In *History Matters: Essays on Economic Growth, Technology, and Demographic Change*, edited by Timothy W. Guinnane, William A. Sundstrom, and Warren C. Whatley, 271–327. Stanford, CA: Stanford University Press.

Coale, Ansley J., and Melvin Zelnik. (1963). *New Estimates of Fertility and Population in the United States: A Study of Annual White Births from 1855 to 1900 and of Completeness of Enumeration in Census from 1880 to 1960*. Princeton, NJ: Princeton University Press.

Costa, Dora L., and Richard H. Steckel. (1997). "Long Term Trends in Health, Welfare, and Economic Growth in the United States." In *Health and Welfare during Industrialization*, edited by Richard H. Steckel and Roderick Floud, 47–89. Chicago: University of Chicago Press.

Cutler, David, and Grant Miller. (2005). "The Role of Public Health Improvements in Health Advances: The Twentieth Century United States." *Demography* 42(1): 1–22.

Easterlin, Richard A. (1976). "Population Change and Farm Settlement in the Northern United States." *Journal of Economic History* 36(1): 45–75.

Easterlin, Richard A. (1996). "The Nature and Causes of the Mortality Revolution." In *Growth Triumphant: The Twenty-first Century in Historical Perspective*, edited by Richard A. Easterlin, 69–82. Ann Arbor: University of Michigan Press.

Forster, Colin, and G. S. L. Tucker. (1972). *Economic Opportunity and Whiter American Fertility Ratios, 1800–1860*. New Haven, CT: Yale University Press.

Hacker, J. David. (2003). "Rethinking the 'Early' Decline in Marital Fertility in the United States." *Demography* 40(4): 605–620.

Haines, Michael R. (1996). "Long Term Marriage Patterns in the United States from Colonial Times to the Present." *The History of the Family: An International Quarterly* 1(1): 15–39.

Haines, Michael R. (2000). "The American Population, 1790–1920." In *The Cambridge Economic History of the United States*, edited by Stanley Engerman and Robert Gallman, Vol. 2, 143–205. New York: Cambridge University Press.

Haines, Michael R. (2001). "The Urban Mortality Transition in the United States: 1800–1940." *Annales de Demographie Historique* 1: 33–64.

Haines, Michael R., ed. (2006a). "Population." In *Historical Statistics of the United States*, edited by Susan B. Carter et al., Millennial ed., Vol. 1, 1–380. Cambridge: Cambridge University Press.

Haines, Michael R., ed. (2006b). "Vital Statistics." In *Historical Statistics of the United States*, edited by Susan B. Carter et al., Millennial ed., Vol. 1, 381–489. Cambridge: Cambridge University Press.

Haines, Michael R., and J. David Hacker. (2011). "Spatial Aspects of the American Fertility Transition in the Nineteenth Century." In *Navigating Space and Time in Historical Population Studies*, edited by Myron P. Gutmann, Glenn D. Deane, Emily R. Merchant, and Kenneth M. Sylvester, 37–63. New York: Oxford University Press.

Haines, Michael R., and Richard Steckel, eds. (2000). *A Population History of North America*. New York: Cambridge University Press.

Klein, Herbert S. (2004). *A Population History of the United States*. New York: Cambridge University Press.

Malthus, Thomas Robert. (1970 [1798]). *An Essay on the Principle of Population*. Edited with an introduction by Antony Flew. Baltimore, MD: Penguin Books.

McCusker, John J., ed. (2006). "Colonial Statistics." In *Historical Statistics of the United States*, edited by Susan B. Carter et al., Millennial ed., Vol. 5, 5-627–5-772. Cambridge: Cambridge University Press.

Melosi, Martin V. (2000). *The Sanitary City: Urban Infrastructure in America from Colonial Times to the Present*. Baltimore, MD: Johns Hopkins University Press.

Modigliani, Franco. (1988). "The Role of Intergenerational Transfers and Life Cycle Savings in the Accumulation of Wealth." *Journal of Economic Perspectives* 2(2): 15–40.

Pope, Clayne L. (1992). "Adult Mortality in America before 1900: A View from Family Histories." In *Strategic Factors in Nineteenth Century American Economic History: A Volume to Honor Robert W. Fogel*, edited by Claudia Goldin and Hugh Rockoff, 267–296. Chicago: University of Chicago Press.

Preston, Samuel H., and Michael R. Haines. (1991). *Fatal Years: Child Mortality in the Late Nineteenth-Century America*. Princeton, NJ: Princeton University Press.

Smith, Adam. (1937 [1776]). *An Enquiry into the Nature and Causes of the Wealth of Nations*. Edited by Edwin Cannan. New York: The Modern Library.

Steckel, Richard. (1983). "The Economic Foundations of East–West Migration during the 19th Century." *Explorations in Economic History* 20(1): 14–36.

Sundstrom, William A., and Paul A. David. (1988). "Old-Age Security Motives, Labor Markets, and Farm Family Fertility in Antebellum America." *Explorations in Economic History* 25(2): 164–197.

United Nations. (1983). *Manual X: Indirect Techniques for Demographic Estimation*. New York: United Nations. Available at http://www.un.org/esa/population/publications/ Manual_X/Manual_X.htm.

US Bureau of the Census. (2012). *Statistical Abstract of the United States 2012*. Washington, DC: Government Printing Office.

Wells, Robert V. (1992). "The Population of England's Colonies in America: Old English or New Americans?" *Population Studies* 46(1): 85–102.

Yasuba, Yasukichi. (1962). *Birth Rates of the White Population of the United States, 1800–1860: An Economic Analysis*. Baltimore, MD: Johns Hopkins University Press.

CHAPTER 2

HEALTH, DISEASE, AND SANITATION IN AMERICAN ECONOMIC HISTORY

HOYT BLEAKLEY, LOUIS P. CAIN,
AND SOK CHUL HONG

Tourists in Philadelphia who visit Benjamin Franklin's eighteenth-century home and printshop might make a stomach-churning discovery. At one spot in his courtyard, a circular stone denotes the location of Franklin's well from which his drinking water was drawn. Just a few paces away, another circular stone marks the location of his privy from the same period. How could Franklin, clearly a man of science and of the Enlightenment, have what seems to us an unenlightened approach to sanitation? While Franklin himself lived to the ripe old age of 85, the health outcomes of his time contrast with today's, as do the sanitary practices. Back then, perhaps one in four children died before becoming adults, and approximately 10 percent of Philadelphia's population perished in a yellow-fever epidemic a few years after Franklin's death. Changes in health outcomes and practices since Franklin's time are deeply related to other aspects of the economy.

The ultimate success of an economy critically depends on the health of its people. At an individual level, both the productivity and quality of life are related to health. How long one remains in the labor force and how long one lives are related to health. At an aggregate level, the public's health is an important economic policy issue whether it involves a new water treatment plant at the local level or the viability of Social Security, Medicare, and Medicaid at the national level. Since many diseases are borne by water or spread by organisms born in water (e.g., mosquitoes), sanitation (water supply, waste disposal, and drainage) has played a key role in protecting the public health. Understanding the determinants of good health and the economic benefits derived therefrom are important to understanding the performance of an economy. Historically, the United States has been a relatively healthier place to live and work than much of the rest of the world, but, with urbanization, maintaining the public health required considerable vigilance. In general, economic historians have not begun to explore the post–World War II world intensively. Their emphasis is on the decline of malnutrition and infectious disease.

LONG-TERM HEALTH TRENDS OF THE US POPULATION

Health is a subject that should be studied from a long-term perspective, both retrospectively and prospectively. The economic efficiency of health policies depends on how well we can predict health status in the future, and those predictions become more reliable and accurate if we extend our point of view into the more remote past. Over the past three centuries, human beings have enhanced their quality of life remarkably through improvements in nutrition, sanitation, and the disease environment (Floud et al. 2011). When viewed over shorter periods, these achievements may appear less dramatic. As Robert W. Fogel (1994) stressed, economic predictions that depend on transient circumstances may lead to a misunderstanding of current economic problems. For example, if our attention is limited to what has happened in the recent past, we might miss the significance of factors such as disease control and sanitation improvements.

There was a high risk of famine, disease, and death in colonial America, as was true throughout Europe in the years before the Industrial Revolution. Most people lived in a world described by Thomas Malthus. Nevertheless, it was suggested that colonial Americans were healthier and better nourished than their contemporaries in Europe. Adam Smith's *The Wealth of Nations* discussed this perception at some length. Fogel (1986) estimated life expectancy at age ten for native-born white males born in late eighteenth-century America to be about fifty-two years, six years more than his estimate of life expectancy at age ten for the British nobility of the same period. The average height of native-born American adults (a measure of their nutritional intake in childhood) was estimated to be around 172–173 cm (5 ft. 7¾ in.), while those of the United Kingdom and continental Europe were 165–169 cm (5 ft. 5¾ in.) and 163–167 cm (5 ft. 5 in.), respectively (see Fogel 1986; Floud, Wachter, and Gregory 1990). Lois Green Carr (1992) and James McWilliams (2005) emphasized two factors that account for colonial America's advantage: climate and soil conditions suitable for productive harvests and a low population density that could prevent contagion from infectious diseases.

Table 2.1 indicates that, since the colonial period, Americans have observed substantial improvements in three important health-related indicators (life expectancy, infant mortality, and height). For example, life expectancy at birth among whites, which has been reported since 1850, increased from 39.5 years in 1850 to 77.4 years in 2000. The average height of whites increased from 172.9 cm (5 ft. 5 in.) for the cohort born in 1800 to 177.4 cm (5 ft. 9¾ in.) for the one born in 1980. It is noteworthy that those

Table 2.1 Long-Term Trends of Health Indicators, 1710–2000

| Year | Life Expectancy (Years) | | | Infant Mortality | | Height (cm) | |
| | e (0) | | e (10) | (per 1,000 births) | | | |
	White	Black	White	White	Black	White	Black
1710						171.5	
1720			51.8			171.8	
1730			52.0			172.1	
1740			52.9			172.1	
1750			52.5			172.2	
1760			53.9			172.3	169.0
1770			54.8			172.8	169.5
1780			56.4			173.2	170.1
1790			56.7			172.9	169.8
1800			55.2			172.9	170.4
1810			52.3			173.0	170.3
1820			51.4			172.9	170.8
1830			51.0			173.5	170.1
1840			48.7			172.2	169.6
1850	39.5	23.0	45.5	216.8	340.0	171.1	
1860	43.6		47.1	181.3		170.6	
1870	45.2		48.5	175.6		171.2	
1880	40.5		46.7	214.8		169.5	
1890	46.8		48.7	150.6		169.1	
1900	49.6	41.8	50.6	119.8	170.3	170.0	
1910	54.6	46.2	51.3	96.5	142.6	172.1	173.8
1920	54.9	45.3	54.1	82.1	135.6	173.1	174.4
1930	61.4	48.1	55.0	60.1	99.5	175.8	175.2
1940	64.2	53.1	57.0	43.2	72.9	176.7	177.3
1950	69.1	60.8	59.0	26.8	43.9	177.3	177.9
1960	70.6	63.6	59.6	22.9	44.3	177.9	177.2
1970	71.7	64.1	59.8	17.8	32.6	177.4	177.6
1980	74.4	68.1		10.9	22.2		179.1
1990	76.1	69.1		7.6	18.0		
2000	77.4	71.7		5.8	14.6		

Source: Data and detailed information on sources are available from Carter et al. (2006), Vol. 1, Series Ab952, Ab955, Ab958 (crude death rate), Series Ab9–Ab10 (infant mortality), and Series Ab647 and Ab653 (life expectancy at birth).

improvements occurred for all races and that racial disparities have been substantially reduced over time.

Long-term trends in each of these series did not improve monotonically. For example, in the middle of the nineteenth century, when the US economy was growing rapidly, average health status as depicted by these data was countercyclical. Life expectancy at age ten was lower in 1850 than it had been at the start of the nineteenth century, and it did not recover to its former level until 1930–1940. The average adult height of whites declined by 4.4 cm (1¾ in.) between 1830 and 1890.

What caused these trends has been debated at length by American economic historians. John Komlos (1987) termed this the "antebellum puzzle" and argued that the decline—particularly of adult height—resulted from reduced caloric intake mainly due to the enormous mid-nineteenth-century European immigration to the United States. Robert Gallman (1996) raised several serious concerns about Komlos's argument; in particular, it was based on West Point cadets, which, at the time of the Civil War, excluded southerners who were taller on average than northerners.[1] Fogel (2000, 164–165) attributes the decline to a fall in net nutrition due to the spread of malaria and other diarrheal diseases. Michael Haines, Lee Craig, and Thomas Weiss (2003) emphasized the role of the disease environment promoted by urbanization and industrialization and the poor sanitation that existed throughout the nineteenth century. Recently, Roderick Floud et al. (2011) showed that both diet and energy consumption were the key determinants of health and economic productivity, but they suggested that frequent exposure to poor sanitary and infectious disease conditions better accounts for the trend of health indicators in the second-half of the nineteenth century.

Table 2.1 clearly shows that Americans' average health status has been improving since the turn of the twentieth century. Robert Fogel and Dora Costa (1997) argued that the interaction between technological advance and physiological improvement accounts for the long-term trends of human development. They noted that one's nutritional status, or net nutrition, is determined by a supply side (diet and caloric intake) and a demand side (energy consumption for combating infectious diseases). David Cutler and Grant Miller (2005) and the Centers for Disease Control (CDC) (1999) produced a four-component explanation for the twentieth-century trends, and, by implication, these contribute to an explanation for why the trend was countercyclical in the previous century. First, better personal sanitation was obtained through campaigns for improving individual hygiene such as washing hands and boiling drinking water. Second, regional eradication campaigns were conducted for two chronic infectious diseases: hookworm in the 1910s and malaria in the 1920s. Third, improved sanitation services became more widely supplied (e.g., drinking-water purification and sewage treatment). Fourth, advances in medical technology and knowledge (e.g., the shift from the miasmatic to the germ theory, antibiotics, and vaccination) came to play a key role in disease control. Joel Mokyr (1993) emphasized the evolutionary diffusion of public health techniques over the twentieth century to explain the decline in mortality rates and the emergence of a new demographic regime. Several economic historians have demonstrated that nutritional improvements (measured either by caloric or protein intake) are correlated with gains in income and health (Higgs 1971; Floud et al. 2011; Steckel 1995).

The result of these achievements and of the epidemiological transition can be seen clearly in figure 2.1 that displays the trend of cause-specific mortality rates for two infectious diseases (tuberculosis and influenza/pneumonia) and two chronic diseases (malignant (cancerous) or benign neoplasms and cardiovascular). Rampant infections and deaths from infections, which had been prevalent throughout the nineteenth century, began to improve in the early twentieth century. Since then, public health officials have refocused their attention from infectious to chronic diseases because, as figure 2.1 shows, death rates from some chronic diseases increased in the first decades of the twentieth century. Various studies have pointed out that health-related behaviors and their outcomes such as smoking and obesity induced such trends (McGinnis and Foege 1993; Mokdad et al. 2004). The downturn in the cardiovascular rate is largely the result of the increase in post–World War II medical research, as discussed by Kevin M. Murphy and Robert H. Topel (2003).

The most striking feature of figure 2.1 is the spike in the influenza death rate that occurred in 1918–1919, arguably the worst epidemic in US history. The definitive account of the epidemic is by Alfred Crosby (2003). Sometime in the late stage of World War I, the influenza virus arrived at a staging area for allied troops in France. It is not known exactly how it arrived, either from soldiers carrying a mild form of the virus from a

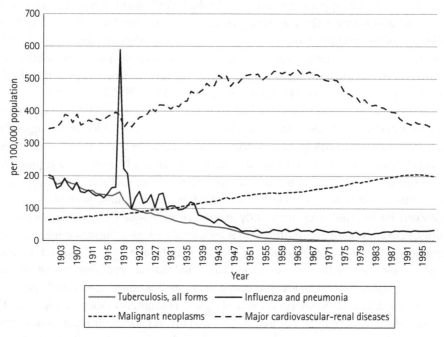

FIGURE 2.1. Death rate, by cause, 1900–1998

Source: Carter et al. (2006, series Ab 929, 937, 942, 939).

military base in Kansas or from Chinese construction workers brought to France. The flu spread rapidly among the troops who then brought it home at the war's end; it reached epidemic proportions in October 1918. The deaths were concentrated among the very young (less than twelve months) and young adults (twenty to forty years of age). Older members of the population did not experience elevated death rates from influenza suggesting that the virus was a mutation of an earlier one which gave them some immunity.

Control of Diseases and Economic Impacts

As John Duffy (1971) documented, various infectious diseases such as smallpox, yellow fever, and measles were prevalent across the United States from the colonial era up to the early twentieth century. All too often an outbreak of one of these diseases reached epidemic proportions, which would prove disastrous to people living in larger cities where the higher population density meant these contagious diseases could spread more easily. Charles E. Rosenberg (1962) reported that cholera outbreaks in 1832, 1849, and 1866 were especially serious; thousands died in New York City. Enoch Hale (1839) noted the contamination of water supplies spread typhoid, which could cause death on a large scale. Babies and children were the most susceptible. Anna Rochester (1923) pointed to the diarrhea caused by drinking contaminated milk in summer when the bacteria in the milk grew more rapidly; in the nineteenth century, these contributed to exceptionally high child mortality rates (one death out of five on average) and a low life expectancy at birth (about forty years) as reported by Samuel Preston and Michael Haines (1991).

In addition to these infections that had high mortality rates, Americans experienced less fatal infectious diseases such as hookworm and malaria, which had long-lasting impacts on lifetime health and economic outcomes. Hookworm was prevalent in hot, humid climates with sandy soils; the disease is transmitted from the soil through the skin. Prior to its eradication, it was quite prevalent in the southern states, perhaps a cause of the stereotypical lazy southerner. Children, in particular, were susceptible to hookworm because they were frequently barefoot, but the legacy of childhood exposure continued to adulthood even as infection rates waned with age. The incidence of malaria was related to temperature, rainfall, and elevation, but some types of malaria parasites could survive even in low temperatures. Thus, malaria was prevalent across most of the United States, especially less populated areas such as small towns and the countryside. As Garland Brinkley (1994) and Margaret Humphreys (2001) made clear, the diseases affected not only individuals' health and life but also their labor productivity. Consequently, manufacturing and, especially, agricultural output was diminished.

Unfortunately, the pathogen of those diseases was not clearly identified until the early twentieth century, when the germ theory was accepted. Some scientists in mid-nineteenth-century America such as Daniel Drake suspected that the incidence of malarial fevers was related to hot and humid climatic conditions, but the transmission of malaria by mosquitoes was not discovered until around the turn of the twentieth century (Levine 1964). In the absence of this knowledge, there were few effective measures of prevention and treatment. Duffy (1971) discussed that one of the most common and practical measures for preventing the spread of epidemics was to isolate those infected through quarantine at home or in a hospital or sanitarium.

Economic historians have estimated the impact of exposure to infectious diseases; this provides useful information for public health policy, especially contemporary problems with an international dimension. This research involves demography and public health, as well as economics, to examine such things as labor force participation, family income, educational attainment, the impact of chronic conditions, mortality, and life expectancy (see Bleakley 2010a). Historical studies have the advantage of combining useful research frameworks (e.g., a specific disease environment and its subsequent eradication) and longitudinal data (e.g., cohort methods and lifetime health records), which are less available for those alive today due to privacy concerns. This has enabled economic historians to identify how exposure to diseases could affect economic and health outcomes in the course of a lifetime, and how the impact changed over time.

A frequently used longitudinal database is the Union Army sample, which is comprised of nearly 40,000 veterans who enlisted in the army during the American Civil War. The data set was created as part of the Early Indicators of Later Work Levels, Disease and Death project led by Fogel and Costa; it is available at uadata.org. This is a longitudinal, life-cycle sample that combines various historical records such as regimental records, military and carded-medical records that show wartime experiences, postwar pension records, surgeon's certificates that recorded the detailed results of physical examinations for the purpose of pension, and 1850–1940 US federal census records. A series of studies based on this individual-level data have shown that infections or exposure to disease environments in ages as young as twenty significantly increased the onset of chronic conditions and scarring effects on mortality in ages as old as sixty (Costa 2000, 2003; Lee 2003; Cain and Hong 2009; Hong 2007, 2013). It also has been used to study early exposure to infectious diseases. Early exposure substantially lowered labor force participation and wealth accumulation in adulthood. This, in turn, suggests an impact on labor productivity (Costa 1996; Lee 2005; Hong 2011). These studies generate implications for understanding the significance of disease control historically as well as the economic dimensions of the aging process at an individual level.

Another line of research has addressed similar issues through the study of population cohorts. These have mainly used census samples like the IPUMS and relied on historical episodes of disease eradication and their regional variation to identify the economic benefits of disease control. Some of this work has focused on the eradication of malaria from the United States. Malaria, which was prevalent throughout most of the United States, began to retreat from the Midwest in the 1870s. According to Mark Boyd (1941), this was attributable to the increasing size of farms. However, the disease remained prevalent in the southern United States, and it frequently affected farm laborers. Hoyt

Bleakley (2010a) utilized malaria control in the 1920s to estimate the long-term impact of malaria on human capital accumulation. He compared cohorts who were born before and after the malaria-control campaign and found that those born after the campaign had greater income as adults.[2] The 1920s eradication campaign was the result of post-1900 scientific findings concerning the malaria pathogen (i.e., its transmission via mosquitoes). Consequently, the US Public Health Service and the Rockefeller Foundation's International Health Board made major investments in malaria eradication.[3] Bleakley estimated that perhaps 40 percent of the sizeable North–South gap in income could be attributed to these two diseases. Using the same methodology as Bleakley, Sok Chul Hong (2013) estimated that those born before the malaria eradication campaign had a higher probability of health problems that would limit their ability to work.

Utilizing cohort outcomes compiled from the 1960 IPUMS sample, Alan Barreca (2010) estimated that in-utero and post-natal exposure to malaria led to significantly lower levels of educational attainment and higher rates of poverty later in life. Barreca used the variation in malaria-promoting temperatures as an instrumental variable for malaria exposure. Similarly, Hong (2007) estimated a risk index for malarial fevers in mid-nineteenth-century America using environmental risk factors such as temperature, rainfall and elevation, and records on the incidence of malaria fevers from US fort data.

Three studies have examined the decline of malaria in the twentieth century. Alan Barreca, Price Fishback, and Shawn Kantor's (2012) investigation of the linkages between expenditures under the Agricultural Adjustment Act (AAA) in the 1930s, migration patterns, and changes in malaria deaths concluded that migration induced by the AAA played an important role. Carl Kitchens (2013a, 2013b) has concluded that public works constructed during the 1930s and 1940s by the TVA (Tennessee Valley Authority) and WPA (Works Projects Administration) helped account for the decline in malaria. In particular, the dams and reservoirs constructed by the TVA created large amounts of standing water in which the mosquitoes that carry malaria could breed. This contributed to a sharp increase in the malaria death rate. In response, the TVA developed a large anti-malaria program, while the WPA hired relief workers to undertake projects designed to reduce the rate. Parallel research was done for hookworm, which is known to cause substantial malnutrition, particularly among children. Garland Brinkley (1994) finds a negative conditional correlation between hookworm infection and agricultural income per capita at the level of US counties. Bleakley uses a cohort-study approach and the Rockefeller Sanitary Commission intervention of the 1910s to identify the economic effect of hookworm eradication; he finds that those born after the eradication campaign benefited through a substantial gain in adult income.[4]

While Nietzsche may have said that what does not kill us makes us strong, the empirical literature on health and income shows the importance of "scarring" effects of disease on health and income later in life. Scientists have proved that complications early in life can impair the function of body organs gradually over a lifetime and accelerate the process of aging through various mechanisms (e.g., disorders of the immune system, a reduction in nutritional status, secondary infections, and, particularly, accumulated inflammation; Crimmins and Finch 2006; Finch 2010). An increasing number of empirical studies have shown that childhood, as the period of physical growth, cognitive development, and human-capital investment, is a critical period whose conditions can influence later health and income, as the circular stones in Franklin's courtyard suggest (Conti and Heckman 2010; Heckman 2012). Melissa Thomasson and Price Fishback (2014) study the impact of state incomes for those born in and around the Great Depression on later disability and income.

This work is closely related to the advent of the fetal origins hypothesis, which seeks the origin of health and economic outcomes from in-utero conditions. The evidence supporting this hypothesis has accumulated in the epidemiological literature (see Almond and Currie 2011). The hypothesis, initially proposed by David J. Barker in 1992, suggests that various chronic conditions in adults, such as heart disease and type-2 diabetes, may be triggered by in-utero health conditions. Barker and other researchers have used such things as birth weight or a dummy variable for having been born with a low birth weight to measure in-utero health conditions. From an economic perspective, the hypothesis suggests any event that affects in-utero health can cause one's stock of human capital and lifetime economic productivity to deteriorate. Many economic studies have confirmed this hypothesis in historical settings, where panel data covering a considerable portion of life are available and various types of fetal shocks are observed. In addition, health shocks in-utero are considered as (relatively) exogenous in the historical era when medical and epidemiological knowledge was not advanced enough to control disease. Thus, the utilization of so-called natural experiments proved helpful in identifying the causality between health and economic outcomes.

A study of the Dutch famine (1944-1946) was among the earliest research investigating the fetal origins hypothesis in a historical framework (Stein et al. 1975). Further work found that those exposed to the famine in gestation were abnormally small at birth and that women exposed to the famine in-utero had more low-birth-weight infants than others, suggesting a transmission of this health shock over generations (Lumey 1998; Lumey and Stein 1997; Stein, Ravelli, and Lumey 1995). With respect to American history, Douglas Almond (2006) used a sample from the US census to show the cohort that spent its fetal years during the late 1918 influenza epidemic had poor outcomes in adulthood—in particular, higher rates of disability, lower levels of education, and lower socioeconomic status.

Weight at birth also has been used as a measure of fetal nutrition. In particular, low birth weight (less than 2,500 g) has been of great concern. It is well known that being born with low birth weight can delay children's physical growth and substantially increase the probability of having chronic conditions. The existing literature has identified socioeconomic, biological, and ecological factors that can cause low birth weight as summarized by Peter Ward (1993). Economic studies such as those by Sandra Black, Paul Devereux, and Kjell Salvanes (2007) and Heather Royer (2009) have linked low birth weight to adverse educational and labor-market outcomes. Claudia Goldin and Robert Margo (1989) and Costa (1998) produced pioneering studies based on lying-in hospital records that investigated the long-term trend of average birth weight and its relationship to the infant mortality rate.

THE EVOLUTION OF SANITATION STRATEGIES

Improvements in sanitation contributed to the control of many other infectious diseases. As urban historian Martin Melosi (2000) describes, sanitation systems progressed in a path-dependent fashion as each new sanitation problem and technological improvement led to a social investment.

Life is dependent on a supply of fresh water. When Europeans first established communities in North America, they were often surrounded by saltwater and had to dig wells and collect rain to obtain freshwater. As communities such as Boston and New York grew, they found it necessary to go several hundred miles into the mountains to get an ample supply of freshwater. The same would prove true for west coast communities such as Los Angeles and San Francisco. Once water was brought into a city, it was necessary to find a method to remove the wastewater, especially when the flush toilet became popular following the Civil War. This tied the problems of sewage disposal and drainage to that of water supply. A city's sanitation strategy must encompass all three.

The evolution of sanitation was gradual. As Duffy (1990) described in his synthetic history of US sanitation, there was little interest in public health for the first several centuries of colonization in North America. On the eve of the Civil War, an organized sanitary movement came into existence at the municipal level, buoyed by the statistical work of Edwin Chadwick in Britain and Lemuel Shattuck in Massachusetts. Duffy argued the expansion of government that resulted from the war plus a new philanthropic interest helped create what he termed the "new public health."[5] In addition, with the development of the germ theory in the late nineteenth century, cities became more scientific about their sanitation strategy. The germ theory led to the new techniques of bacteriology, which were employed to identify and prevent infectious diseases by municipal and state boards of health. It also led to new techniques of virology and parasitology.

As cities initiated new projects, data was collected and used in the design of future projects, in that and similar cities. In particular, *Engineering News*, edited by Moses N. Baker, was a weekly journal of "civil, mechanical, mining and electrical engineering." It contained articles, letters, and editorials on matters pertinent to all areas of sanitation. It facilitated an exchange of information between cities that encouraged improvements and eliminated costly mistakes. A good deal of this information is collected in Baker (1893), and the data have been used for historical research.[6] Additional data sources include two sanitation-related special reports in *General Statistics of Cities* (US Bureau of Census 1913, 1916). Almost a half century later, the US Public Health Service published several volumes on cities' water and waste facilities (e.g., USPHS, 1954, 1957). A particularly influential piece was Nelson Blake's (1956) book that reviewed the development of urban water supplies in four east coast cities (Boston, New York, Philadelphia, and Baltimore). More recently, Carl Smith (2013) has studied the water supply histories of Boston, Chicago, and Philadelphia.

With the coming of the New Deal and the World War II, both of which expanded the federal government's involvement in public health, the final major steps in the evolution of sanitation systems were taken. Duffy emphasized Titles V and VI of the Social Security Act, which significantly increased the federal funding of state health agencies.

THE EMERGENCE OF SANITATION SYSTEMS

Urban historians documented the growth of water supply, sewer, and solid waste disposal systems. In an essay entitled "Triumph and Failure," Stuart Galishoff (1980) discussed the acquisition of urban water supplies between 1850 and the 1930s. The triumph was that millions of urban dwellers possessed an abundant supply of pure water that was generally filtered and chlorinated; the failure was that pollution problems were generally ignored. Elsewhere in the same collection of essays, Joel Tarr, James McCurley, and Terry Yosie (1980) adopted a similar approach for sewers, almost all of which used waterways as the point of final discharge, increasing pollution. Tarr (1996) expanded upon the theme of increased urban pollution by focusing on water closets, wastewater technologies, and the politics of defining water-quality standards. McShane and Tarr (2007) discussed how horses polluted cities and contaminated water supplies. Price Fishback and Dieter Lauszus (1989) argued that, although coal towns were believed to supply a low level of services to their residents, the sanitation services supplied in the early 1920s were equivalent to that of similarly sized non-company towns; workers in towns that supplied fewer sanitation services understood that they should ask for higher wages.

Louis Cain (1978) investigated the delivery of sanitation in the unique case of Chicago. Unlike coastal cities, which were typically located on saltwater or rivers, many inland cities were located on freshwater lakes.[7] Such cities faced an interdependency problem in that the water resource (Lake Michigan in the case of Chicago) served as both water supply and wastewater receptacle. It did not take long to realize the latter was polluting the former. The site of Chicago was a glacial lakebed and that meant drainage was a problem. Residents complained about mud, but the flatness of the area complicated the installation of sewers. As a consequence, while cities such as New York and Boston devoted their energies to bringing water into the city, Chicago worried about how to get it out. In the 1850s, Chicago installed the first comprehensive sewer system in the United States (see Cain 1972). Given the flat terrain, for sewers to drain by gravity, the city had to pass an ordinance raising the level of the city. Most of the sewers emptied into the Chicago River, so the sewage was pushed out into Lake Michigan polluting the city's water supply. Consequently, a new water supply system was constructed during the Civil War with an intake two miles from shore. An important discovery was made during the dry summers of the 1850s. When water was pumped to maintain the summit level of the Illinois and

Michigan Canal, the flow of the Chicago River was reversed. This presented the city with the opportunity to separate water supply and wastewater disposal, and, in 1871, when the canal was dredged and its pumping capacity quadrupled, the reversal was made official. This has remained the city's strategy to this day. It is a strategy that depends on being adjacent to a low point on a divide between two drainage systems, an advantage not present in other lake cities given the height of the divide they would have to traverse (Cain 1974).

It can be argued such investments in a sanitation strategy contributed to urban growth. The turn of the twentieth century was a time of annexation and consolidation in American cities. On one hand, former suburban communities annexed themselves to central cities to tap into their comprehensive water and sewer systems. On the other hand, annexation stopped when it reach communities that were able to supply such services to their residents. Once the germ theory found general acceptance, sanitation capital was in high demand—and was highly effective. This is highlighted in the case of Chicago by Cain (1983). Letty Anderson (1988) described the diffusion of water supply systems in New England between 1870 and 1900.[8]

Martin Melosi (1981) focused on American attitudes toward and methods for removing solid waste. The United States continued to dump after the British had switched to incineration because the population in the United States was less dense and hauling the waste was less expensive. From a world in which garbage was treated as essentially "out of sight, out of mind," the development of the germ theory caused garbage to be considered a health problem in a similar manner to water supply and wastewater disposal. Reduction and incineration became the most common methods of disposal, but ever-increasing urban populations meant an ever-increasing supply of garbage. It was not until the mid-twentieth century that Americans began to consider ways to limit the production of solid wastes and to face the possibility of recycling in a serious manner.

DECLINING MORTALITY RATES

The primary advantage of sanitation improvements was manifest in a substantial decline of mortality rates during the late nineteenth and early twentieth centuries, the fastest rate of decline in American history. Edward Meeker (1971) was among the first to try to understand this change and the reasons behind it, a change that is now part of what is known as the demographic transition—the shift from a high birth and death regime to a low one. As life expectancy grew, mortality rates for the diseases of old age surpassed those of infectious diseases. By examining data on life expectancy, crude death rates, and disease-specific mortality, Meeker showed that the transition took place in the decade of the 1880s, that health improved very little before then and very rapidly thereafter. He argued that improvements in medical practice could only account for a small portion of the decline. He also noted that genetic changes played little role during his period. This meant that the explanation had to lie in improvements in public health practices and living levels. The former followed from the emergence of the germ theory, which rapidly gained acceptance in the 1880s and led to the investments in sanitation capital just discussed. The latter reflects improvements in diet and living conditions, which are in part attributable to those same investments. Meeker (1974) estimated social rates of return on the investments in public health projects between 1880 and 1910 and showed that they exceeded the market rate of return on capital.

Following Meeker, economic historians were active in researching the role of sanitation in the rapid decline of the mortality rate. The general conclusion is that this decline occurred concurrently with an epidemiological transition and the disappearance of the "urban mortality penalty." Throughout the nineteenth century, cities were unhealthy places in which to live, as many economic historians, Michael Haines (2001) in particular, documented. In the mid-nineteenth century, as railroads and steamships broadened the market and increased the commercialization of the economy, migrants from rural areas, as well as from abroad, increased the urban share of the population. And, in those pre-germ theory years, the logic of the miasmic theory of disease transmission made it difficult to suggest sanitation strategies to reduce the effects of the increase in urban density.

The mortality transition began with the first inklings of the germ theory in the 1870s. Robert Higgs (1973) estimated that urban mortality exceeded rural by 50 percent in the 1880s, but only by 21 percent in the 1910s. Looking at the final decade of the nineteenth century, Gretchen Condran and Eileen Crimmins-Gardner (1978) investigated death rates from specific diseases. They argued that the reductions in deaths attributable to typhoid and diarrhea, for example, were most likely due to the provision of waterworks and sewers, but the declines in diseases such as tuberculosis and diphtheria had a more tenuous relationship to the public health practices that were intended to combat them. Building upon Condran and Crimmins-Gardner, Haines argued that, with the acceptance of the germ theory in the 1880s, urban mortality began to decline faster than rural mortality, a phenomenon attributable to improvements in public works, public health, and ultimately medicine itself. By 1940, the transition was complete even though the urban share of the population continued to grow.

More recently, Cain and Hong (2009) found that, with respect to Union Army veterans, the urban mortality penalty was related to the size of the city. Even after controlling for life events and health insults at the individual level, the urban mortality penalty persisted. Among the hypotheses proffered to explain this finding is that rapid population growth taxed the ability of late nineteenth-century cities to expand their sanitation systems fast enough. Consequently, water and sewer systems were inadequate, especially when they began to be faced with industrial pollution.[9]

MEASURING THE BENEFIT OF A CLEAN WATER SUPPLY

Many studies have quantified the economic benefit of sanitation improvements, particularly water-purification systems, at the turn of the twentieth century. Cain and

Elyce Rotella (2001) linked the sanitation expenditures reported in *Financial Statistics of Cities* with mortality statistics reported in *Mortality Statistics of Cities* and estimated the marginal effect of expenditure for public health intervention in terms of the mortality rate. They examined both the operating and capital expenditures for water supply, wastewater, and solid waste disposal. They also found that mortality shocks from waterborne diseases like cholera and typhoid contributed to increased demand and expenditures on sanitation. In adopting the new technologies, they emphasized the role of demonstration effects and suggested that by lowering the cost of information about the ways that water and sewer technologies work, demonstration effects increased the willingness and ability to adopt new technologies.

Cutler and Miller (2005) studied the effectiveness of urban water supplies, arguing that, in major American cities, the causal influence of water purification (specifically filtration and chlorination) on mortality was quite large during the early twentieth century. Using what they argued was exogenous variation in both the timing and the location of the adoption of new technologies to identify these effects, they found that clean water was responsible for nearly half the total mortality reduction in those cities, as well as three-quarters of the infant mortality reduction and nearly two-thirds of the child mortality reduction. They also argued the phenomenon was not just limited to the largest cities (Cutler and Miller 2006). They looked at the development of urban water systems in the Progressive Era, a time when municipalities' access to capital was increasing substantially. As a result, the quantity of piped water in American cities began to grow at the turn of the twentieth century. While the largest cities expanded their works, perhaps more important, smaller cities made use of this greater access to capital markets to finance waterworks.

Cutler and Miller's results are consistent with those of Joseph Ferrie and Werner Troesken (2008) who looked at the problem directly. Using data from Chicago, the authors found support for the so-called Mills-Reincke phenomenon—for every death averted from a waterborne disease, more than one death is averted from other diseases.[10] Over their sample period, the crude death rate fell by 60 percent. They estimated that 35–56 percent of that fall can be attributed to water purification and the eradication of waterborne diseases. In particular, they pointed to the effects of typhoid fever that had a relatively low fatality rate but left survivors susceptible to infections such as tuberculosis and pneumonia. Thus, purifying water had both direct and indirect effects on morbidity and mortality. It directly reduced the risks associated with waterborne diseases and indirectly reduced the risks associated with other diseases by creating an overall healthier population. Ferrie and Troesken also concluded that the most important factor in reducing the death rate was water supply improvements, which in the case of Chicago included the steps taken to keep sewage out of Lake Michigan. The Mills-Reincke phenomenon also was asserted with respect to sewers (Schultz and McShane 1978; Schultz 1989).

Troesken examined two additional aspects of water supply improvements that are not part of the usual dialogue. First, Troesken (2004) tried to answer the puzzle that at the turn of the twentieth century, during a racist era in American history, life expectancy for blacks increased both relatively and absolutely. He found that the expansion of water and sewer works benefited all races, potentially a greater benefit for blacks than for whites. Concern about disease spillovers between the races led the whites to build works that would minimize this possibility, thereby benefiting those against whom they normally discriminated. Given that cities were not as residentially segregated then as they are now, it was difficult to exclude people. While black neighborhoods were not as well served as white ones, the difference was small, and the increase substantially reduced the impact of waterborne diseases, particularly yellow fever in the South. Second, Troesken (2006) emphasized the long-run problems introduced by the presence of lead in water mains. He presented a review of the extensive medical literature on the effects lead has on cardiovascular function, fetal health, pregnancy, and other health conditions. In 1900, according to Troesken's estimates, 85 percent of American cities used lead pipe in their water systems. He estimated that 25 percent of the infant mortality in Massachusetts was attributable to lead poisoning and that, in 1923, 10-12 percent of that state's population was suffering from some symptom of lead poisoning. Eliminating lead pipes from water supply systems was another sanitary improvement that reduced the death rate.

CONCLUSION

There has been a good deal of research that focuses on the causes and consequences of the long-run improvements in health. Although public water supplies and sewerage works helped initiate change, it was the acceptance of the germ theory of disease that provided a scientific base for an acceleration in health improvements. The work on the eradication of diseases such as hookworm and malaria have focused on rural areas, while sanitation improvements largely have been an urban phenomenon, given the expense of first installing water mains and sewers, then erecting the treatment facilities that characterize today's systems.

There are several lines of future research for which the initial steps are underway. One line that follows from the work done on panel data and specific cohorts is to extend the analysis across generations. There is some research being done on the health histories of fathers and sons, but the hope is to extend this to grandfathers as well (see Currie and Moretti 2007). The initial work has been limited to male lines because of the need to link people to the census. As desirable as health histories of mothers and daughters would be, name changes attributable to marriage make this is a more daunting prospect.

A second line will tie health history to institutional history. Troesken (2016) argues that, from colonial times, Americans preferred decentralized forms of governance that required private consent and voluntary action. These, in turn, have been argued to be contrary to public health needs, but Troesken shows that this is not always the case. Finally, the germ theory altered beliefs and led to an expansion of government involvement in public health. This ties his analysis to policy considerations directly, but also through such areas as property rights, which were critical to a city's ability to develop a system of water mains and sewers. The possible frictions are evident in the resistance to some forms of vaccination today; when are private rights trumped by public responsibilities?

A third potential line of future research reflects more micro-studies of individual diseases. For example, health economists have looked into the debates over DTP and polio vaccination, but such topics have evaded the longer term view of economic historians. As noted, work has been done on specific epidemics, such as the influenza epidemic of 1918, but less major outbreaks and the year-to-year progress of the disease in the United States has not been studied. We now know that those born during the influenza outbreak were different than those before or after. Less work has been done on related episodes. For example, the 1993 outbreak of the diarrheal disease cryptosporidiosis in Milwaukee is the largest documented waterborne disease outbreak in US history. The root cause of the epidemic was never identified, although it is known crypto-cysts from a sewage treatment plant two miles upstream in Lake Michigan passed through the filters of one of the city's water treatment plants. Over the course of two weeks, 403,000 Milwaukeeans fell ill (25 percent of the city's population and 50 percent of those served by that plant); 104 people died, largely the elderly and those with compromised immune systems. While it is probably still too soon to get the necessary data, one wonders if these known short-run effects tell the entire story.

All of these tie into one last line of future research. There is a good deal of debate on the limits of human life. How far into the future can the trends here identified be extrapolated? Will life expectancies continue to increase as they have over the past 125 years? Can we continue to postpone the onset of chronic disease, or have we already received the benefits of reduced cumulative disease in early life? Can we continue to conquer infectious disease? Will science and technology continue to enable us to stay ahead of nature? History tells us that pathogens will adjust. Will we?

NOTES

1. Komlos (1987) argued that the downward trend in adult height resulted from a substantial drop in pork consumption, which provided key nutrients to physical growth in childhood. His estimation of daily pork consumption was controversial. Gallman noted that Komlos underestimated average pork consumption because he did not consider the season when the census was surveyed.
2. Similar results are also estimated from cohort studies for other countries such as Colombia (Bleakley 2010b) and India (Cutler et al. 2010).
3. Malaria fevers were not completely eradicated in the 1920s. After the short-term success, there were fluctuations in malaria prevalence attributable to human migration and budget cuts for the campaign. Humphreys (2001) characterized the challenge of malaria control changing in the 1920s from "a one-armed man emptying the Great Lakes with spoon" to, in the 1930s, "kicking a dying dog." Thereafter, the prevalence and mortality rate of malaria declined, and the Center for Disease Control and Prevention announced its eradication in 1950. The use of DDT put the final nail in its coffin.

4. Bleakley (2007). Much of the literature on malaria, hookworm, and several other diseases is summarized in McGuire and Coelho (2011).
5. The legal aspects of public health control are discussed in Gostin (2008).
6. The *Engineering News* published a large variety of books with Baker as author or editor.
7. Cain (1977) explores the similar sanitation histories of cities located on freshwater lakes, saltwater, and what he characterizes as major and minor river cities. Major river cities are those that draw their water supply from the river, but minor river cities must supplement their river supply; both types use the river for wastewater disposal.
8. A technical discussion on this in the century before World War II can be found in Tarr and Dupuy, eds. (1988).
9. Similar results were found for French cities by Kesztenbaum and Rosenthal (2011).
10. At the St. Louis World's Fair of 1904, Allen Hazen, a leading advocate of water filtration, argued, "Where one death from typhoid fever had been avoided by the use of a better water, a certain number of deaths, probably two or three, from other causes have been avoided." Hiram Mills and Dr. J. J. Reincke of Hamburg, Germany, independently observed this phenomenon. The causal relationship has become known as "Hazen's Theorem" and the statistical regularity as the "Mills-Reincke phenomenon."

BIBLIOGRAPHY

Almond, D. (2006). "Is the 1918 Influenza Pandemic Over? Long-Term Effects of In-Utero Influenza Exposure in the Post-1940 U.S. Population." *Journal of Political Economy* 114(4): 672–712.

Almond, D., and J. Currie. (2011). "Killing Me Softly: The Fetal Origins Hypothesis." *Journal of Economic Perspectives* 25(3): 153–172.

Anderson, L. (1988). "Fire and Disease: The Development of Water Supply Systems in New England, 1870-1900." In *Technology and the Rise of the Networked City in Europe and America*, edited by J. Tarr and G. Dupuy, 135-156. Philadelphia: Temple University Press.

Baker, M. (1893). *Sewage Purification in America: A Description of the Municipal Sewage Purification Plants in the United States and Canada*. New York: Engineering News.

Barker, D. (1992). *Fetal Origins of Adult Disease*. London: British Medical Journal.

Barreca, A. (2010). "The Long-Term Economic Impact of In Utero and Postnatal Exposure to Malaria." *Journal of Human Resources* 45(4): 865–892.

Barreca, A., P. Fishback, and S. Kantor. (2012). "Agricultural Policy, Migration, and Malaria in the United States in the 1930s." *Explorations in Economic History* 49(4): 381–398.

Black, S., P. Devereux, and K. Salvanes. (2007). "From the Cradle to the Labor Market? The Effect of Birth Weight on Adult Outcomes." *Quarterly Journal of Economics* 122(1): 409–439.

Blake, N. M. (1956). *Water for the Cities: A History of the Urban Water Supply Problem in the United States*. Syracuse, NY: Syracuse University Press.

Bleakley, H. (2007). "Disease and Development: Evidence from Hookworm Eradication in the American South." *Quarterly Journal of Economics* 122(1): 73–117.

Bleakley, H. (2010a). "Health, Human Capital, and Development." *Annual Review of Economics* 2: 283–310.

Bleakley, H. (2010b). "Malaria Eradication in the Americas: A Retrospective Analysis of Childhood Exposure." *American Economic Journal: Applied Economics* 2(2): 1–45.

Boyd, M. (1941). "A Historical Sketch of the Prevalence of Malaria in North America." *American Journal of Tropical Medicine* 21: 223–244.

Brinkley, G. (1994). "The Decline in Southern Agricultural Output, 1860-1880." *Journal of Economic History* 57(1): 116–138.

Cain, L. (1972). "Raising and Watering a City: Ellis Sylvester Chesbrough and Chicago's First Sanitation System." *Technology and Culture* 13(3): 353–372.

Cain, L. (1974). "Unfouling the Public Nest: Chicago's Contested Sanitary Diversion of Lake Michigan Water." *Technology and Culture* 15(4): 594–613.

Cain, L. (1977). "An Economic History of Urban Location and Sanitation." *Research in Economic History* 2: 337–389.

Cain, L. (1978). *Sanitation Strategy for a Lakefront Metropolis: The Case of Chicago.* DeKalb: Northern Illinois University Press.

Cain, L. (1983). "To Annex or Not? A Tale of Two Towns: Evanston and Hyde Park." *Explorations in Economic History* 20(1): 58–72.

Cain, L., and S. C. Hong. (2009). "Survival in the 19th Century Cities: The Larger the City, the Smaller Your Chances." *Explorations in Economic History* 46(4): 450–463.

Cain, L., and E. Rotella. (2001). "Death and Spending: Did Urban Mortality Shocks Lead to Municipal Expenditure Increases?" *Annales de Démographie Historique* 101(1): 139–154.

Carr, L. (1992). "Emigration and the Standard of Living: The Seventeenth Century Chesapeake." *Journal of Economic History* 52(2): 271–291.

Carter, S., S. Gartner, M. Haines, A. Olmstead, R. Sutch, and G. Wright, eds. (2006). *Historical Statistics of the United States.* Millennial ed. Cambridge: Cambridge University Press.

Centers for Disease Control. (1999). "CDC on Infectious Diseases in the United States, 1900-99." *Population and Development Review* 25(3): 635–640.

Condran, G., and E. Crimmins-Gardner. (1978). "Public Health Measures and Mortality in U.S. Cities in the Late 19th Century." *Human Ecology* 6(1): 27–54.

Conti, G., and J. J. Heckman. (2010). "Understanding the Early Origins of the Education-Health Gradient: A Framework That Can Also Be Applied to Analyze Gene-Environment Interactions." *Perspectives on Psychological Science* 5(5): 585–605.

Costa, D. (1996). "Health and Labor Force Participation of Older Men, 1900-1991." *Journal of Economic History* 56(1): 62–89.

Costa, D. (1998). "Unequal at Birth: A Long-Term Comparison of Income and Birth Weight." *Journal of Economic History* 58(4): 987–1009.

Costa, D. (2000). "Understanding the Twentieth-Century Decline in Chronic Conditions among Older Men." *Demography* 37(1): 53–72.

Costa, D. (2003). "Understanding Mid-Life and Older Age Mortality Declines: Evidence from Union Army Veterans." *Journal of Econometrics* 112(1): 175–192.

Crimmins, E. M., and C. E. Finch. (2006). "Infection, Inflammation, Height, and Longevity." *Proceedings of the National Academy of Sciences of the United States of America* 103(2): 498–503.

Crosby, Alfred W. (2003). *America's Forgotten Pandemic: The Influenza of 1918.* 2nd ed. Cambridge: Cambridge University Press.

Currie, J., and E. Moretti. (2007). "Biology as Destiny? Short and Long-Run Determinants of Intergenerational Transmission of Birth Weight." *Journal of Labor Economics* 25(2): 231–264.

Cutler, D., W. Fung, M. Kremer, M. Singhal, and T. Vogl. (2010). "Early-Life Malaria Exposure and Adult Outcomes: Evidence from Malaria Eradication in India." *American Economic Journal: Applied Economics* 2(2): 72–94.

Cutler, D., and G. Miller. (2005). "The Role of Public Health Improvements in Health Advances: The Twentieth-Century United States." *Demography* 42(1): 1–22.

Cutler, D., and G. Miller. (2006). "Water, Water Everywhere: Municipal Finance and Water Supply in American Cities." In *Corruption and Reform: Lessons from America's History*, edited by E. Glaeser and C. Goldin, 153–184. Chicago: University of Chicago Press.

Duffy, J. (1971). *Epidemics in Colonial America*. Baton Rouge: Louisiana State University Press.

Duffy, J. (1990). *The Sanitarians: A History of American Public Health*. Urbana: University of Illinois Press.

Ferrie, J., and W. Troesken. (2008). "Water and Chicago's Mortality Transition, 1850–1925." *Explorations in Economic History* 45(1): 1–16.

Finch, C. E. (2010). "Evolution of the Human Lifespan and Diseases of Aging: Roles of Infection, Inflammation, and Nutrition." *Proceedings of the National Academy of Sciences of the United States of America* 108(Suppl. 1): 1718–1724.

Fishback, P., and D. Lauszus. (1989). "The Quality of Services in Company Towns: Sanitation in Coal during the 1920s." *Journal of Economic History* 49(1): 125–144.

Floud, R., R. Fogel, B. Harris, and S. C. Hong. (2011). *The Changing Body: Health, Nutrition, and Human Development in the Western World since 1700*. Cambridge: Cambridge University Press.

Floud, R., K. Wachter, and A. Gregory. (1990). *Height, Health and History: Nutritional Status in the United Kingdom, 1750–1980*. Cambridge: Cambridge University Press.

Fogel, R. (1986). "Nutrition and Decline in Mortality since 1700: Some Preliminary Findings." In *Long-Term Factors in American Economic Growth*, edited by S. Engerman and R. Gallman, 439–556. Chicago: University of Chicago Press.

Fogel, R. (1994). "Economic Growth, Population Theory, and Physiology: The Bearing of Long-Term Processes on the Making of Economic Policy." *American Economic Review* 84(3): 369–395.

Fogel, R. (2000). *The Fourth Great Awakening and the Future of Egalitarianism*. Chicago: University of Chicago Press.

Fogel, R., and D. Costa. (1997). "A Theory of Technophysio Evolution, with Some Implications for Forecasting Population, Health Care Costs and Pension Costs." *Demography* 34(1): 49–66.

Galishoff, S. (1980). "Triumph and Failure: The American Response to the Urban Water Supply Problem, 1860–1923." In *Pollution & Reform in American Cities, 1870–1930*, edited by M. Melosi, 35–57. Austin: University of Texas Press.

Gallman, R. (1996). "Dietary Change in Antebellum America." *Journal of Economic History* 56(1): 193–201.

Goldin, C., and R. Margo. (1989). "The Poor at Birth: Birth Weights and Infant Mortality at Philadelphia's Almshouse Hospital, 1848–1873." *Explorations in Economic History* 26(3): 360–379.

Gostin, L. O. (2008). *Public Health Law: Power, Duty, Restraint*. Revised and expanded. Berkeley and Los Angeles: University of California Press.

Haines, M. (1979). "The Use of Model Life Tables to Estimate Mortality for the United States in the Late-Nineteenth Century." *Demography* 16(2): 289–312.

Haines, M. (2001). "The Urban Mortality Transition in the United States, 1800–1940." *Annales de Démographie Historique* 101(1): 33–64.

Haines, M., L. Craig, and T. Weiss. (2003). "The Short and the Dead: Nutrition, Mortality, and the 'Antebellum Puzzle' in the United States." *Journal of Economic History* 63(2): 385–415.

Hale, E. (1839). *Observations on the Typhoid Fever of New England*. Boston: Whipple and Damrell, 9 Cornhill.

Heckman, J. J. (2012). "The Developmental Origins of Health." *Health Economics* 21(1): 24–29.

Higgs, Robert. (1971). *The Transformation of the American Economy, 1865–1914: An Essay in Interpretation*. New York: Wiley.

Higgs, Robert. (1973). "Mortality in Rural America." *Explorations in Economic History* 10(2): 177–195.

Hong, S. C. (2007). "The Burden of Early Exposure to Malaria in the United States, 1850–1860: Malnutrition and Immune Disorders." *Journal of Economic History* 67(4): 1001–1035.

Hong, S. C. (2011). "Malaria and Economic Productivity: A Longitudinal Analysis of the American Case." *Journal of Economic History* 71(3): 654–671.

Hong, S. C. (2013). "Malaria: An Early Indicator of Later Disease and Work Level." *Journal of Health Economics* 32(3): 612–632.

Humphreys, M. (2001). *Malaria: Poverty, Race, and Public Health in the United States*. Baltimore, MD: Johns Hopkins University Press.

Kesztenbaum, L., and J. Rosenthal. (2011). "The Health Cost of Living in a City: The Case of France at the End of the 19th Century." *Explorations in Economic History* 48(2): 207–225.

Kitchens, C. (2013a). "A Dam Problem: TVA's Fight against Malaria 1926–1951." *Journal of Economic History* 73(3): 694–724.

Kitchens, C. (2013b). "The Effects of the Works Progress Administration's Anti-Malaria Programs to Control Malaria: Georgia 1932–1947." *Explorations in Economic History* 50(4): 567–581.

Komlos, J. (1987). "The Height and Weight of West Point Cadets: Dietary Change in Antebellum America." *Journal of Economic History* 47(4): 897–927.

Lee, C. (2003). "Prior Exposure to Disease and Later Health and Mortality: Evidence from Civil War Medical Records." In *Health and Labor Force Participation over the Life Cycle: Evidence from the Past*, edited by D. Costa, 51–88. Chicago: University of Chicago Press.

Lee, C. (2005). "Wealth Accumulation and the Health of Union Army Veterans, 1860–1870." *Journal of Economic History* 65(2): 352–385.

Levine, Norman D., ed. (1964). *Malaria in the Interior Valley of North America: A Selection by Norman D. Levine from a Systematic Treatise, Historical, Etiological, and Practical, on the Principal Diseases of the Interior Valley of North America, As They Appear in the Caucasian, African, Indian, and Esquimaux Varieties of Its Population* (the treatise is that of Daniel Drake first published in 1850). Urbana: University of Illinois Press.

Lumey, L. H. (1998). "Reproductive Outcomes in Women Prenatally Exposed to Undernutrition: A Review of Findings from the Dutch Famine Birth Cohort." *Proceedings of the Nutrition Society* 57(1): 129–135.

Lumey, L. H., and A. D. Stein. (1997). "In Utero Exposure to Famine and Subsequent Fertility: The Dutch Famine Birth Cohort Study." *American Journal of Public Health* 87(12): 1962–1966.

McGinnis, J. M., and W. H. Foege. (1993). "Actual Causes of Death in the United States." *Journal of American Medical Association* 270(18): 2207–2212.

McGuire, R., and P. Coelho. 2011. *Parasites, Pathogens, and Progress: Diseases and Economic Development*. Cambridge, MA: MIT Press.

McShane, C., and J. Tarr. (2007). *The Horse in the City: Living Machines in the 19th Century*. Baltimore, MD: Johns Hopkins University Press.

McWilliams, J. (2005). *A Revolution in Eating: How the Quest for Food Shaped America.* New York: Columbia University Press.

Meeker, E. (1971–1972). "The Improving Health of the United States, 1850–1915." *Explorations in Economic History* 9(1): 353–373.

Meeker, E. (1974). "The Social Rate of Return on Investment in Public Health, 1880-1910." *Journal of Economic History* 34(3): 392–421.

Melosi, M. (1980). *Pollution & Reform in American Cities, 1870–1930.* Austin: University of Texas Press.

Melosi, M. (1981). *Garbage in the Cities: Refuse, Reform and the Environment, 1880–1980.* College Station: Texas A&M University Press

Melosi, M. (2000). *The Sanitary City: Urban Infrastructure in America from Colonial Times to the Present.* Baltimore, MD: Johns Hopkins University Press.

Mokdad, A. H., J. S. Marks, D. F. Stroup, and J. L. Gerberding. (2004). "Actual Causes of Death in the United States, 2000." *Journal of American Medical Association* 291(10): 1238–1245.

Mokyr, J. (1993). "Technological Progress and the Decline of European Mortality." *American Economic Review: Papers and Proceedings* 83(2): 324–330.

Murphy, K. M., and R. H. Topel. (2003). "The Economic Value of Medical Research." In *Measuring the Gains from Medical Research: An Economic Approach*, edited by K. M. Murphy and R. H. Topel, 41-73. Chicago: University of Chicago Press.

Preston, S. H., and M. Haines. (1991). *Fatal Years: Child Mortality in Late Nineteenth-Century America.* Princeton, NJ: Princeton University Press.

Rochester, A. (1923). *Infant Mortality.* Washington, DC: Government Printing Office.

Rosenberg, C. E. (1962). *The Cholera Years.* Chicago: University of Chicago Press.

Royer, H. (2009). "Separated at Girth: US Twin Estimates of the Effects of Birth Weight." *American Economic Journal: Applied Economics* 1(1): 49–85.

Schultz, S. K. (1989). *Constructing Urban Culture.* Philadelphia: Temple University Press.

Schultz, S. K., and C. McShane. (1978). "To Engineer the Metropolis: Sewers, Sanitation, and City Planning in Late-19th-Century America." *Journal of American History* 65(2): 389–411.

Smith, C. (2013). *City Water, City Life.* Chicago: University of Chicago Press.

Steckel, R. H. (1995). "Stature and the Standard of Living." *Journal of Economic Literature* 33(4): 1903–1940.

Stein, A., A. Ravelli, and L. H. Lumey. (1995). "Famine, Third-Trimester Pregnancy Weight Gain, and Intrauterine Growth." *Human Biology* 67(1): 135–150.

Stein, Z., M. Susser, G. Saenger, and F. Marolla. (1975). *Famine and Human Development: The Dutch Hunger Winter of 1944–1945.* New York: Oxford University Press.

Tarr, J. (1996). *The Search for the Ultimate Sink: Urban Pollution in Historical Perspective.* Akron, OH: University of Akron Press.

Tarr, J., and G. Dupuy, eds. (1988). *Technology and the Rise of the Networked City in Europe and America.* Philadelphia: Temple University Press.

Tarr, J., J. McCurley, and T. Yosie. (1980). "The Development and Impact of Urban Wastewater Technology: Changing Concepts of Water Quality Control, 1850-1930." In *Pollution & Reform in American Cities, 1870–1930*, edited by M. Melosi, 59-82. Austin: University of Texas Press.

Thomasson, M., and P. Fishback. (2014). "Hard Times in the Land of Plenty: The Effect on Income and Disability Later in Life for People Born during the Great Depression." *Explorations in Economic History* 54(4): 64–78.

Troesken, W. (2004). *Water, Race, and Disease.* Cambridge, MA: MIT Press.

Troesken, W. (2006). *The Great Lead Water Pipe Disaster*. Cambridge, MA: MIT Press.

Troesken, W. (2016). *The Pox of Liberty*. Chicago: University of Chicago Press.

US Bureau of Census. (1913). *General Statistics of Cities: 1909*. Washington, DC: Government Printing Office.

US Bureau of Census. (1916). *General Statistics of Cities: 1915*. Washington, DC: Government Printing Office.

US Public Health Service. (1954). *Inventory of Municipal and Industrial Waste Facilities in the United States, 1953*. Washington, DC: US Department of Health, Education, and Welfare, Public Health Service.

US Public Health Service. (1957). *Municipal Water Facilities, Communities of 25,000 Population and Over, Continental United States, as of December 31, 1954*. Washington, DC: US Department of Health, Education, and Welfare, Public Health Service.

Ward, W. P. (1993). *Birth Weight and Economic Growth: Women's Living Standards in the Industrializing West*. Chicago: University of Chicago Press.

CHAPTER 3

....

US FERTILITY RATES AND CHILDBEARING IN AMERICAN ECONOMIC HISTORY, 1800–2010

....

MARTHA J. BAILEY AND BRAD J. HERSHBEIN

OVER the past two centuries, the United States has witnessed dramatic changes in fertility rates and childbearing. Demand factors such as industrialization, urbanization, rising family incomes, public health improvements, and the growth in women's wages generally have reduced the benefits and raised the costs of having many children. Supply factors such as increases in infant and child survival and improvements in the technology of birth control and abortion have also altered parents' decisions about their childbearing.

This chapter discusses the long-run trends in US fertility rates and completed childbearing, both overall and by mothers' race/ethnicity and region, within three broad periods: the 1800 to 1930 decline in fertility rates, the 1930 to 1960 stabilization in fertility rates followed by the baby boom, and the post-1960 decline and subsequent stabilization in fertility rates. We discuss the determinants of childbearing in each period, including both economic and demographic explanations for these patterns. A final section weighs the evidence supporting the existence of *two* fertility transitions: a first transition driven by shifts in the demand for children and a second transition catalyzed by changes in supply side factors.

CHANGES IN US FERTILITY RATES, 1800–2010

....

The standard fertility rate timeseries (fig. 3.1) shows that American women reaching childbearing age around 1800 averaged around seven to eight live births during their reproductive years and that this number fell to between two and three children by 1930.

This decline also occurred in other industrialized countries and is considered part of a general demographic transition (Guinnane 2011). After the Great Depression, these patterns reversed, and the baby boom emerged. Between 1940 and 1960, the general fertility rate rose by around 60 percent, and cohort measures of completed fertility rates rose by 45 percent.[1] Note that this is more than a World War II phenomenon: fertility rates began increasing before mobilization, and they remained high for fifteen years after V-Day. After 1960, the decline in fertility rates resumed, and rates stabilized by the mid-1970s to around present-day levels. For the past twenty-five years, completed childbearing has hovered around two children, even as the timing of marriage, the timing of first birth, and the composition of parents have shifted in important ways.

These broad facts are well established, but the exact timing of the onset of fertility decline is disputed. Until recently, US (marital) fertility decline was believed to have begun in the late eighteenth century, almost seventy-five years before marital fertility rates began declining in most other nations (Binion 2001; Guinnane 2011; Haines 2000). This would make the United States distinctive, more similar to France—where marital fertility began declining *before* industrialization—than to England, Germany, or Italy, where marital fertility began declining *after* industrialization.

Less well known is that US fertility rates before 1880 are estimated using indirect methods and implicitly rely on assumptions about mortality rates, immigration, and the quality of census enumeration. These assumptions are important. Hacker (2003)

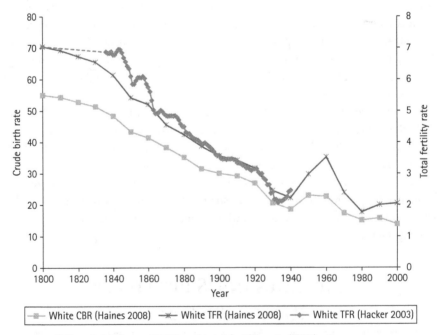

FIGURE 3.1. US crude birth rate (CBR) and total fertility rate (TFR), 1800–2000

Notes: The CBR is plotted on the left vertical axis and is measured as the number of births per 1,000 whites in the population. The TFR is plotted on the right vertical axis and measures the cumulative number of births a woman would be expected to have over her lifetime if she experienced the current period's age-specific birth rates.

Sources: Haines (2006, "Population," Table Av1–10, pp. 1–391). Also Hacker (2003).

shows that fertility rate estimates can change in important ways with the use of earlier census microdata (1860 and 1870) and alternative methods. Figure 3.1 presents Hacker's estimates, which account for *increasing* mortality rates in the early nineteenth century. Hacker's revised series shows that the fertility rates of the US white population declined *only slightly* (if at all) between 1800 and 1840. The Hacker series estimates that the total fertility rate of white women was around 6.95 in 1843 versus 7.04 in 1800. Hacker also shows that marital fertility rates began to decline in earnest after 1860. The implication of these revised numbers is that little of the decline in fertility rate occurred until after the Civil War (ca. 1865). In short, this revised series would make the US experience look less exceptional relative to other industrialized countries. The sensitivity of Hacker's estimates to earlier data and alternative assumptions remains an open research question.

An alternative method for examining changes in childbearing involves estimating co-hort fertility rates based on census questions. The 1900 and 1910 censuses, as well as most later twentieth-century censuses, asked ever-married women to report their number of live births. Answers to this question among women ages forty-one to seventy—who should have completed their childbearing—also suggest that the decline in fertility began in the mid- to later nineteenth century. Figure 3.2 plots this series against the

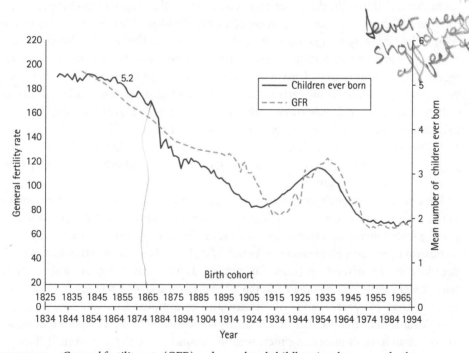

FIGURE 3.2. General fertility rate (GFR) and completed childbearing, by year and cohort

Notes: The general fertility rate (GFR) is plotted on the left vertical axis and is measured as the number of births per 1,000 women ages 15–44 in the population (lower *x*-axis). Before 1910, this series is for white women only. Mean live births is plotted on the right vertical axis and is the mean self-reported number of children ever born for each birth cohort as measured between the ages of 41 and 70. This series is plotted by birth cohort (upper *x*-axis).

Sources: Fertility rates are from the National Center for Health Statistics, http://www.cdc.gov/nchs/data/statab/t001x01.pdf. Mean live births are computed using the 1900, 1910, and 1940–1990 Decennial Census IPUMS samples (Ruggles et al. 2010) and the 1995–2010 June Current Population Surveys.

general fertility rate for reference. Women born around 1850 averaged about five births during their childbearing years, whereas women born twenty-five years later, in 1875, averaged 3.3 births over their lifetimes. This trend continued: women born in the early twentieth century averaged just 2.3 births over their lifetimes.

These census figures appear consistent with Hacker's argument and inconsistent with the early decline in the crude birth rate (CBR) or general fertility rate (GFR) time series: completed childbearing changed little before the Civil War among ever-married women (cohorts born before 1850, reaching childbearing age before the 1870s) and only modestly among women born between 1850 and the conclusion of the Civil War (reaching childbearing age after 1870). However, reductions in childbearing appear to have gained momentum among women born in the 1870s and persisted until the Great Depression (cohorts born around 1910).[2]

Figure 3.2 makes apparent that each generation of women in the late nineteenth and early twentieth centuries substituted toward fewer children. This reduction resulted primarily from improvements in spacing and stopping, rather than changes in the age at first marriage (Bailey, Guldi, and Hershbein 2014). The distribution in the number of children born shifted from nearly uniform for ever-married women born in 1850 (childbearing age in the 1870s) to highly concentrated over the next fifty years. For instance, figure 3.3(a) shows that two-thirds of ever-married women in the birth cohort of 1910 bore two or fewer children; a striking 23 percent remained childless. Consequently, US women born in the aughts (1900–1910) are commonly referred to as the "low-fertility cohorts."

The measurement of fertility rates in the twentieth century is more accurate and requires fewer assumptions. The voluntary adoption of national standards in vital statistics reporting by states in the early twentieth century facilitated the creation of national statistics on birth rates.[3] The entry of all states into the birth registration area (BRA) by 1933 enabled the federal government to publish statistics based on actual birth records rather than census enumeration and assumptions about mortality rates based on small geographic areas. Entry into the BRA was based on "tests" of whether at least 90 percent of a state's births were registered.

The availability of fairly complete birth registrations makes the size and duration of the baby boom much less controversial and even more impressive. This remarkable departure from longer-term trends was not a short-lived aberration reflecting postponed births from the Great Depression or World War II. The baby boom stretched over two decades and was driven by increases in completed childbearing (Rogers and O'Connell 1984; Ryder 1980). Between 1940 and 1960, the general and total fertility rates each rose by more than 50 percent, and cohort measures of completed fertility rose by 45 percent. Measured as the number of live births by cohort of women (reported at ages 41 to 70), completed childbearing increased by around one child per woman, from 2.3 to 3.3, between the low-fertility cohorts and the cohort of mothers born a generation later, around 1930. In a remarkable historical twist, women born in the mid-1930s had completed-fertility rates as high as their grandmothers born fifty years earlier (fig. 3.2).

The baby boom also reflected an increase in the fraction of women who ever had children. Figure 3.3(b) shows that, between the low-fertility cohorts and the mothers of the

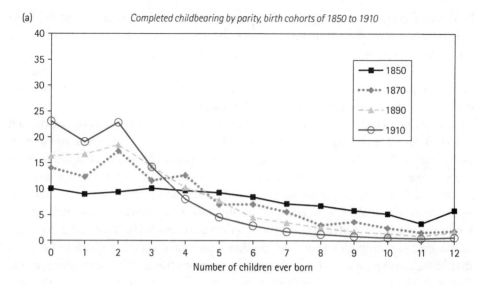

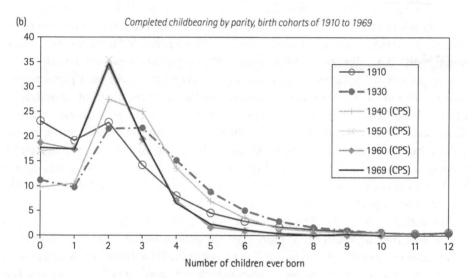

FIGURE 3.3. The distribution of children ever born, by cohort

Notes: These figures plot the percent of women ages 41–70 who report having each number of children. We include never-married women in the 1970 to 1990 censuses and June CPS when available so that figures include the recent rise in nonmarital childbearing. Children ever born is top-coded at 12 in the census and 10 in the CPS.

Sources: 1850 to 1930 cohorts use the 1900, 1910, 1940–1990 Decennial Censuses (Ruggles et al. 2010); 1940 to 1969 cohorts use the 1981–2010 June Current Population Surveys (CPS).

baby boom (1930s birth cohorts), childlessness among ever-married women fell from 23 percent to 8 percent, and the share of women having more than two children increased. The share of women ever marrying increased from around 90 percent to 95 percent, and the mean age at first marriage for the 1935 cohort was almost two years younger at 20.7 (Bailey, Guldi, and Hershbein 2014). In short, increases in the period fertility rates during the baby boom were achieved both by earlier and more universal marriage and by married women giving birth to more children. These changes were pervasive. Women born in different census regions, women living in both urban and rural areas, and women of different races and nativity experienced sharp upward changes in completed childbearing. Even the Amish experienced a dramatic baby boom (Bailey and Collins 2011).

Elevated fertility rates quickly subsided in the 1960s and early 1970s. Within roughly fifteen years of the baby boom's peak, US fertility rates had fallen to around replacement levels, and below those of the low-fertility cohorts born around the turn of the twentieth century. Importantly, this post-1960 decline represented different shifts in behavior than those accompanying prior declines in the nineteenth and early twentieth centuries. Figure 3.3(b) shows that the low-fertility cohorts achieved low fertility rates with many more women remaining unmarried and large increases in childlessness among those who did marry. In contrast, a much larger share of women reaching childbearing age after 1960 had exactly two children (35 percent versus 22 percent for the previous generation), with the distribution of childbearing collapsing around a two-child mode.

The current stabilization in childbearing was reached in the mid-1970s among women born in the late 1940s and in the 1950s. In fact, both the distribution and mode of completed childbearing have changed very little over the past quarter century; figure 3.3(b) shows nearly identical distributions in completed childbearing among cohorts born between 1950 and 1970. An additional feature worth noting is that childlessness among women born around 1970 is *lower* (at 16 percent) than it was among the low-fertility cohorts. Today's rates of childlessness are, however, higher than they were during the peak of the baby boom (10 percent).

Although broadly similar, these aggregate trends mask a great deal of heterogeneity in outcomes across racial and ethnic groups and geography. Figure 3.4(a) plots differences across time for both whites and nonwhites, as well as the US average.[4] In the early 1800s, childbearing was around 1.5 births per woman higher for nonwhites than for whites. This difference fell to roughly half that for women born in the mid-1870s, with an average racial gap of around 0.8 births. The difference narrowed some 50 percent further for cohorts born around the turn of the twentieth century, approaching 0.4 births per woman. After expanding briefly during the baby boom, the gap returned to its pre–baby boom level.

The US experience also differed a great deal across regions, with the more economically developed regions generally having lower fertility rates. Figure 3.4(b) shows that the Northeast had significantly lower completed fertility (about four and one-half births) for women born as early as the 1830s, whereas other, less economically developed regions averaged closer to six births per woman. The Midwest, however, had converged to lifetime childbearing averages that were similar to those in the Northeast by the turn of the twentieth century (women born around 1880); lifetime childbearing

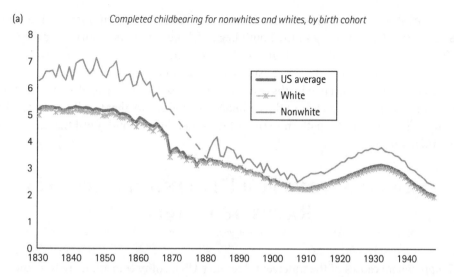

(a) *Completed childbearing for nonwhites and whites, by birth cohort*

Legend:
- US average
- White
- Nonwhite

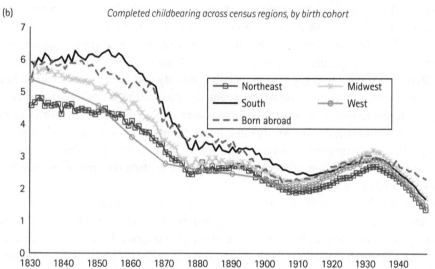

(b) *Completed childbearing across census regions, by birth cohort*

Legend:
- Northeast
- South
- Born abroad
- Midwest
- West

FIGURE 3.4. Completed childbearing across race/ethnicity group and geographic area

Notes: See Figure 3.2. Due to small sample sizes, points between 1870 and 1879 in panel (a) for nonwhites and before 1900 in panel (b) for the west are averaged into one cell. In panel (a), this average is plotted as 1874, and in panel (b) it is plotted by decade.

Sources: Fertility rates are from the National Center for Health Statistics, http://www.cdc.gov/nchs/data/statab/t001x01.pdf. Mean live births are computed using the 1900, 1910, and 1940–1990 Decennial Census IPUMS samples (Ruggles et al. 2010).

in the West was actually lower than in the Northeast for women born from around 1860 to 1870. Childbearing in the South began falling for women born after the Civil War and continued until around 1910. Today, differences in fertility rates across regions are very small relative to historical standards, and women born in all regions of the country average around two births over their lifetimes. Figure 3.4(b) also plots fertility rates for women born outside of the United States and shows that fertility rates for this group followed a similar pattern to those for women in the South until the turn of the twentieth century.

Explanations for Declining Fertility Rates, 1800–1960

The *proximate* causes of the nineteenth-century US fertility transition are well known. These fertility declines accompanied the disappearance of the Malthusian pattern of late marriage and the emergence of fertility control after the desired number of children had been reached. They took place in the absence of modern contraception and are widely believed to have been driven by changes in the demand for children due to industrialization, urbanization, increasing population density and land scarcity, public health improvements, rising educational attainment, and growth in women's market wages. All of these forces tended to raise incomes and increase the implicit "price" of having children, which gradually drove fertility rates down. A complementary demand-side model emphasizes how rising incomes tended to increase investments in children's health and education and to reduce fertility rates, a change that is often referred to as substitution between child quantity and quality.

In contrast, the Great Depression and the baby boom pose challenges to the simple demand-side narrative. As the economy entered the Depression, the downward trend in fertility rates changed little in pace. Even as per-capita disposable income plummeted by 23 percent between 1929 and 1932, the general fertility rate fell by a mere seven births per 1,000 women (55.9 to 48.6) between 1930 and 1933 (lagged one year because births occur nine months after pregnancies).[5] But the fertility rate had declined by about six births per 1,000 women (61.4 to 55.9) between 1927 and 1930 (Linder and Grove 1947). Thus, the speed of fertility decline barely budged from its earlier trend. Additionally, fertility rates stabilized—but did not appreciably grow—as the economy slowly rebounded between 1933 and 1938. This is surprising, given recent evidence on the strong relationship between fertility rates and unemployment (Currie and Schwandt 2014).

Another challenge lies in explaining the complete and rapid reversal of these trends. Between 1940 and 1960, the baby boom took place in the context of increasing wages, urbanization, and educational attainment—all trends associated with declining fertility rates before 1930. Adding to the apparent puzzle is that fertility trends again reversed as these trends in incomes, urbanization, educational attainment, and women's labor-force participation continued.

DEMOGRAPHIC EXPLANATIONS
FOR DECLINING FERTILITY RATES,
1800–1930

Much of the demographic literature has emphasized "demographic transition" theory as an explanation for the decline in nineteenth-century fertility rates. Based on the empirical observation that decreases in aggregate mortality rates were followed in many developed countries by declining birth rates, Notestein (1945) theorized a causal connection: high mortality rates *lead* married couples to have many births so that they can achieve their desired surviving family size. As mortality rates fall, couples have fewer births because fewer are necessary to achieve their desired family size. Interestingly, this story does not fit well with the US experience. Guinnane and others point out that the US fertility decline began *before* mortality rates began falling in the 1890s: "Fertility in the United States declined for decades before any noticeable decline in mortality" (Guinnane 2011, 599). This fact has provided additional motivation for claiming American exceptionalism.

The demographic literature has also focused on innovations in contraceptive methods, what economists might call the "supply side."[6] Generating systematic, empirical evidence on fertility control within marriage in the nineteenth and early twentieth centuries is difficult. Contraceptives and contraceptive practice were not often discussed openly and, therefore, were not well documented, except in special cases. As an alternative, historical demographers have studied "spacing" and "stopping" to identify effective contraceptive practice. For instance, being able to "stop" childbearing *before* one is no longer fecund is associated with highly effective contraceptive practice. Longer "spacing" between births, on the other hand, is generally associated with the consistent use of less-effective contraceptive practices.

For the sake of illustration, consider the following simple formula . Observe that the number of children one could expect to have, *n,* can be written as $n = \dfrac{E}{C+S}$ where *E* is the number of months a woman is at risk of becoming pregnant (the interval from first coitus to when one is no longer fecund), and *C* + *S* represents the average number of months between births. Fertility rates could be reduced by delaying marriage (and thus reducing *E,* the Malthusian recommendation, in a paradigm where nonmarital fertility is rare) or by greater spacing, either by increasing the length of the sterile period during pregnancy and after birth, *S,* or the length of the fecund interval, *C,* by using different contraceptive techniques. Extended breastfeeding offers one natural method for increasing *S,* and coitus interruptus (withdrawal) and reduced frequency of coitus offer others. Women in the nineteenth and early twentieth centuries likely used other contraceptive methods as well (including abortifacients), though prevalence is difficult to document. Lahey (2014a, 2014b) shows that anti-obscenity statutes regulating primitive, premodern contraceptive techniques are associated with *higher* fertility rates. This indirect evidence suggests that these early contraceptives, when not restricted by laws, may have helped couples control childbearing within marriage in the late nineteenth century.

Economic Explanations for Declining Fertility Rates, 1800–1930

The economics literature explains the nineteenth century's negative association between rising income and falling fertility rates with two complementary models: the opportunity cost and child-quality models.[7] The motivating questions in this literature relate to what led couples to desire fewer children (so that they used different contraceptive techniques or changed their sexual behaviors). The basic premise of both models is that children generate utility for parents, both because parents enjoy their children (children have "consumption value") and because children bring many other benefits to their parents (children have "production value") in addition to their costs. For instance, children might help with household chores, farm production, or care for parents in old age.

In standard economic formulations, parents weigh utility from children against their cost to the family. This cost includes both the costs of goods (such as food, clothing, and other necessities) as well as the opportunity costs (time of both parents away from other productive activities) of bearing and raising a child (Becker 1965). In this setting, benefits generated by children, such as their contribution to household production or their insurance value for parents in old age, can be modeled as reducing their net cost. Commensurately, the net cost of children rises if the value of these benefits falls or if bearing and raising children become more expensive. A key assumption of these models is that children are "normal" goods; that is, if parents' incomes increase, these models generally assume that parents want more ("high-quality") children.

In explaining the decline in fertility, the "opportunity cost" model emphasizes the importance of parents' incomes and implicit (or shadow) prices of children. The cost of raising children (net of their benefits) did not rise because food prices or clothing prices increased. On the contrary, rising productivity in manufacturing and agriculture tended to reduce the cost of clothing and feeding children (Atack, Bateman, and Margo 2008; Craig and Weiss 2000; Gallman 1972). But increasing agricultural productivity and industrialization mattered in another way: by increasing potential wages, these forces increased the opportunity cost of having children.[8] This could have been especially important to the extent that the value of women's time increased with industrialization.

Increasing population density and urbanization should also have powerful effects on childbearing through both income and opportunity-cost channels. Three-quarters of the US labor force worked on farms in 1800 (Weiss 1992). But as Americans settled the interior of the country, farmland became increasingly expensive and agriculture began mechanizing. Reductions in the demand for family labor to work on farms led to lower fertility rates as well. Consistent with this idea, Wanamaker (2012) shows that fertility rates among Southern white households that had small slave workforces in the antebellum period *rose* after 1865, when the emancipation of their slaves increased their need for family farm labor.

Moreover, employment opportunities increasingly drew the young to cities and away from farms. This reflects both the fact that parents had smaller farms to bequeath to their children and that children would earn less if they remained on farms (Easterlin 1976). Sundstrom and David (1988) argue that these forces may have reduced the likelihood that children cared for their parents in old age, which further reduced the benefits of children to parents. Steckel (1992) and Basso, Bodenhorn, and Cuberes (2014) show that fertility rates were lower in Northeastern counties with greater availability of banking and financial services, which enabled parents to save directly for retirement outside of their investments in children.

Industrialization and urbanization also altered the locus of production in ways that increased the opportunity cost of childbearing. Both trends imply that the place of work and place of residence became increasingly separate. Moving to a city meant that jobs were more often outside the home and difficult to combine with child supervision. If parents worked in factories or outside the home, parents would have to pay for child care—either directly or by forgoing work—both of which tended to increase the opportunity cost of childrearing. A second implication of urbanization is the rising cost of space. Because adding more children requires more space (or increases crowding), which is more expensive in cities, urbanization also raised the implicit price of childrearing (Simon and Tamura 2009).

The U-shape in women's labor force participation is also consistent with a rising opportunity cost of childbearing (Goldin 1990). Saxonhouse and Wright note that almost 60 percent of those employed in cotton textiles in the South in 1880 were women (Saxonhouse and Wright 1984, Table 1). Because many industries laid off women at marriage, industrialization may have also worked to limit completed childbearing by causing women to delay marriage, perhaps reducing the number of years exposed to the risk of childbearing (Goldin 1991).

The second model of the neoclassical school stresses the value of parental *enjoyment* of their children, or "child quality" (Becker and Lewis 1973; Willis 1973). Here, "quality" generally refers to the level of parents' investments in their children in terms of time or economic resources. In Becker and Lewis's canonical model of parental choice over child quantity and quality, an increase in household income is posited to induce substitution toward higher "quality" (but fewer) children. Consequently, increasing incomes (through rising productivity) leads parents to invest more in each child but perhaps have fewer children, which could also generate a negative association between income and fertility rates. Exogenous changes in the shadow price of child quality due to, for instance, improvements in public health could also lead parents to have fewer but healthier children. The neoclassical models allow both infant mortality and fertility rates to decline simultaneously or fertility rates to decline first (as was the case in the US), rather than in the sequence posited by demographic transition theory.

Evidence that parents invested more in their children is difficult to document empirically, but this model is consistent with other evidence. For instance, Moehling (1998) argues that the 75 percent decline in the employment of children ages ten to fifteen between 1880 and 1930 does not appear to be accounted for by changes in state labor legislation. Moreover, Stephens and Yang (2014) show that compulsory schooling laws explain very little of the shift in the quadrupling of American youth earning a high school diploma between 1910 and 1940.[9] One interpretation of these findings is that changes in parents' investments in children both increased children's human capital and also caused complementary changes in public infrastructure benefiting children. This might involve the building of schools and investment in public health.[10] Municipal sanitation, water filtration, and the expansion in water and sewer infrastructure, among other improvements, resulted in dramatic declines in infant and child mortality rates (Alsan and Goldin 2015; Cain and Rotella 2001; Cutler and Miller 2005; Ferrie and Troesken 2005; Troesken 2002). These investments continued with federal funding for maternity and child care through the 1922 Sheppard-Towner Act, which accounts for between one-tenth and one-fifth of the decline in infant mortality rates over the 1920s (Moehling and Thomasson 2014).

The quantity-quality model, therefore, suggests an important causal chain leading from reductions in fertility rates (or other changes in the implicit price of child quality), to increased investments in children and ultimately to faster economic growth; that is, dynamic versions of the quantity-quality model describe how economies transition from a "Malthusian" equilibrium of high fertility rates and slow growth to low fertility rates and rapid economic growth.[11] This literature provides important links between childbearing, investments in children, and the dynamics of the economy.

Economists, therefore, explain the nineteenth- and early twentieth-century declines in childbearing as driven by changes in demand. Falling fertility rates are a byproduct of rising costs (due to rising adult wages and productivity, as well as the separation of production from the home), diminishing returns (due to falling farm sizes and changes in children's care of their aging parents), and rising incomes (which induces greater investments in each child and a reduction in total number).

DEMOGRAPHIC AND ECONOMIC MODELS OF CHILDBEARING, 1930–1960

Explanations for changes in childbearing during the 1930–1960 period are more disputed. Two schools of thought have emerged: one emphasizing shifting preferences and the other stressing the neoclassical paradigm of relative prices and incomes. More recently, authors differ even *within* their schools of thought.

Richard Easterlin's "relative income hypothesis" represents one school of thought (Easterlin 1966, 1971, 1980). Easterlin's model provides a unified explanation for the low fertility rates during the Great Depression and the baby boom and bust. It emphasizes the importance of a cohort's perceived "earnings potential" relative to its "material aspirations" as a key input to adult preference formation. Children who grew up during the 1930s, according to the hypothesis, formed modest material aspirations due to the Great Depression. Rapid economic growth in the 1940s and 1950s, however, meant that this cohort's actual experience as young adults much surpassed these aspirations. When these cohorts realized they could achieve a higher standard of living than expected, they also decided to have more children. On the other hand, children growing up in the more affluent, postwar period of the late 1940s and 1950s had the reverse experience. Their preferences for material goods were shaped by the booming postwar economy, but they entered the labor market in the late 1960s and early 1970s when the US economy was struggling. Consequently, these cohorts had fewer children, which led to the post-1960 fertility decline. One advantage of this theory is that it integrates an explanation of fertility change over three decades. Problematic for this theory, however, is that fertility rates have not cycled since the baby boom despite sizable economic fluctuations.

Becker's neoclassical theory represents an alternative school of thought and emphasizes relative prices and incomes rather than preferences. In a dynamic reformulation of the static models of the 1960s and 1970s (including the opportunity cost and quantity-quality models discussed previously), Robert Barro and Becker stress how a one-time shock to the price of childbearing or childrearing could explain both low fertility rates during the Great Depression and the baby boom and bust. They are, however, noncommittal on the mechanism (Barro and Becker 1988, 1989).

Although the earlier neoclassical and Easterlin schools of thought in economics have moved closer together over time, a voluminous empirical literature has failed to reach consensus on the appropriate model (Sanderson 1976). In a comprehensive overview of studies of the Easterlin hypothesis, Pampel and Peters conclude that "different methods often result in conflicting findings" (1995, 165). Similarly, in their exhaustive review of tests of the neoclassical model, Hotz, Klerman, and Willis conclude that "the theory and econometric methods are much better developed than the empirical literature" (1997, 342).

Promising recent developments have extended both the theoretical and empirical literatures. In terms of theory, the Barro-Becker reformulation launched a new subfield in economics called "family macro." Papers in this new subfield generally model the long-run downward trend in childbearing (in the nineteenth and early twentieth centuries) as the increasing opportunity cost of childrearing. Although unified in their emphases on prices and incomes, recent variations on the Barro-Becker formulation claim that different price mechanisms explain the baby boom. Greenwood, Seshadri, and Vandenbroucke (2005) argue that increases in household productivity due to mechanization reduced the shadow price of having children. Doepke, Hazan, and Maoz (2015) claim that the flood of older women into labor markets during World War II depressed younger women's wages and therefore temporarily decreased the opportunity cost of childbearing. In response, younger women temporarily had more children until shifts in the demand for women's labor again raised the opportunity cost. Albanesi and Olivetti

(2016) assert that medical innovations that benefited the delivery of babies and artificial feeding (e.g., infant formula) reduced the price of childbearing and led to a temporary increase in childbearing. In a novel twist, they also argue that medical innovations contemporaneously altered parents' investments in girls' education (because these medical innovations raised their life expectancy), which increased the opportunity cost of childbearing for the next generation.

These theories illuminate how temporary shifts in the economy can influence a variety of outcomes for several generations. More problematic is that calibrations have difficulty predicting the baby boom *and* the speed of the post-1960 US fertility decline. Moreover, the proposed mechanisms are inherently difficult to test in empirical work. Two papers by Bailey and Collins (2011) and Lewis (2014) provide the only empirical tests of the electrification hypothesis. Using newly encoded, county-level data on appliance ownership and fertility for 1940, 1950, and 1960, Bailey and Collins show that the diffusion of modern household technologies—which began in earnest decades before the baby boom and continued afterward—does not align well with the burst in household productivity required to generate the baby boom. They also present regression evidence that measures of improved household productivity (such as electrification) are *negatively* correlated with fertility rates. Furthermore, the authors demonstrate that census data on completed fertility (the number of children ever born by ages forty-one to sixty) is negatively correlated with exposure to electrical service in early adulthood. Finally, Bailey and Collins show that the Old Order Amish—a group that on religious grounds strictly limited their use of modern appliances that increased household productivity—also had a relatively large and coincident baby boom. Lewis (2014) uses the expansion of the electrical grid between 1930 and 1960 to show that, consistent with electrification causing couples to substitute toward child quality, electrification caused decreases in both fertility and infant mortality rates.

This evidence provides a considerable challenge to arguments that modern household technology *necessarily* precipitated the US baby boom. It also challenges explanations that would not alter fertility rates among the Amish, including market wages for young women and the introduction of infant formula (Albanesi and Olivetti 2016; Doepke, Hazan, and Maoz 2015). In short, bursts in technologies boosting the productivity of women in the household do not appear, at least by themselves, to explain the baby boom. More theoretical and empirical research on the explanations for baby boom and bust is needed to vet existing theories and, perhaps, to develop new explanations.

THE BABY BUST AND CHILDBEARING AFTER 1960: CHANGES IN DEMAND, SUPPLY, OR BOTH?

Given that the baby boom interrupted the long-run decline in US fertility rates, it is sensible that the long-run decline eventually resumed. Yet the timing of this event is curious. By cause or coincidence, the end of the baby boom corresponded to revolutionary changes in contraception. The US Food and Drug Administration's approval of the first oral contraceptive in 1960, which became known as "the Pill," provided a more reliable and effective way to prevent pregnancy. The Pill required no attention or action at the time of intercourse and no cooperation or consent from male partners (Bailey 2006; Trussell 2004). And it was wildly popular: within five years of its release, almost one-quarter of married women had used the Pill (Bailey 2010).

Cursory empiricism attributed the post-1960 reduction in fertility rates to the causal role of the Pill. More rigorous survey research did as well. Ryder and Westoff (1971) heralded the 1960s as a period of "contraceptive revolution." In Westoff's Presidential Address to the Population Association of America, he argued that the effect of the Pill was so large that "the *entire* [emphasis added] decline in births within marriage across the decade of the 'sixties' can be attributed to the improvement in the control of fertility" (Westoff 1975, 579).[12] In the parlance of economics, the Pill presented a large shift in the supply of births.

An obvious counterargument is that the post-1960 fertility decline appears more like a reversion to trends before the baby boom—a decline typically attributed to the demand-side factors (as outlined in the previous sections). Becker's *Treatise on the Family* states plainly what became the dominant view in economics: "the 'contraceptive revolution' . . . ushered in by the Pill has probably not been a major cause of the sharp drop in fertility in recent decades" (1991, 143). But recent empirical work challenges this assertion with new causal evidence.

The challenge in testing these assertions about the role of the Pill and, more broadly, other supply-side developments (e.g., other modern contraceptives like the intrauterine device [IUD] or injectable or implantable contraceptives) is finding a credible empirical design. Theoretical reasoning argues that causal effects run in *both* directions. As Becker noted, women who desire fewer children are more likely to use the Pill. On the other hand, as Ryder and Westoff posit, users of the Pill are more likely to have fewer children due to lower failure rates.[13] In the United States, access to the Pill has never been intentionally randomly assigned to a representative set of locations or group of participants, making it difficult to quantify the magnitude of the causal channels running in either direction.[14]

Recent empirical studies, therefore, use natural experiments that effectively randomized the availability of the Pill across locations to shed light on this question. One paper uses state-level Comstock-era restrictions on the sale of contraceptives. Bailey (2010) shows that when the Pill was introduced, anti-obscenity statutes ("Comstock laws"), which had existed for almost three-quarters of a century, varied significantly in their language regarding the *sale* of contraceptives. These legal restrictions in twenty-four states affected the diffusion of oral contraception and reduced the speed of fertility declines in restrictive states from 1958 to 1965. After the *Griswold* Supreme Court decision invalidated these sales bans for married women, however, fertility rates in states with sales bans dropped sharply relative to those without these bans. There is little reason to expect the demand for children to change with this pattern, but it is clear that the supply of contraceptives did. Counterfactual estimates imply that, without sales bans, the marital fertility rate could have been 8 percent lower in states with sales bans and 4 percent lower in the United States as a whole. Bailey uses a back-of-the envelope calculation to show that as much as 40 percent of the decline in the marital fertility rate from 1955 to 1965 might be attributable to the Pill.

A second empirical test of the relevance of the Pill and other supply-side developments uses the county-level expansion of federally funded family-planning programs in the 1960s and early 1970s to quantify the effects of subsidized contraception on the childbearing of lower-income women. Beginning with the 1964 Economic Opportunity Act (EOA) and continuing with the passage of Title X ("Title Ten"), over 650 family-planning programs started or expanded in US communities from 1964 to 1973. Bailey (2012) uses the idiosyncratic timing of the EOA and Title X granting process at the county level to estimate the program's effects on fertility rates, using models that also account for the availability of abortion. The results show that family-planning programs, which reduced the cost of contraceptives and increased the availability of contraceptive-related services, led to substantial and sustained declines in fertility rates. The general fertility rate fell by roughly 2 percent within five years of the establishment of a federal family planning program and remained almost as low up to fifteen years after the program's inception. Assuming that these programs were used only by poor women, they imply a reduction in fertility rates among treated women of 20–30 percent within a decade—magnitudes large enough to account for half of the 1965 gap in childbearing between poor and nonpoor women. Follow-up work by Bailey, Malkova, and McLaren (forthcoming) shows that children born after these family-planning programs began were significantly less likely to grow up in poverty or to reside in households collecting public assistance. In summary, family-planning programs reduced birth rates among poor women and increased economic resources in childhood.

Changes on the supply side were not, however, independent of changes in the demand for children. A recent literature suggests that changes in contraceptive technology shifted the demand for children in meaningful ways. In particular, access to the Pill, as influenced by changes in state-level age-of-majority laws, altered young women's decisions to invest in their careers. Variation in access to the Pill between ages 18 and 21 shows that legal access to the Pill affected marital and birth timing and had broad effects on women's and men's education, career investments, and lifetime wage earnings.[15] Young women and men in states where the Pill was legal around age eighteen were more likely to enroll in and to complete college. Women in these states were also more likely to work for pay, invest in on-the-job training, and pursue nontraditional professional occupations. And as women aged, these investments paid off: Bailey, Hershbein, and Miller (2012) approximate that 30 percent of the convergence of the gender wage gap in the 1990s can be attributed to these changing investments made possible by the Pill. Ananat and Hungerman (2012) additionally show that access to contraception at younger ages improved the economic resources of children born to these women.

In summary, a variety of studies using different empirical strategies document the important role of the Pill and other supply-side developments in changing childbearing outcomes. Although the empirical literature has been silent on the role of different demand-side factors in the post-1960 period, it is clear that continued shifts in the demand for children due to rising wages and incomes are key to understanding the post-1960 period, as well as the longer-term narrative of the US fertility decline. In the absence of important shifts in the demand for children, the contraceptive revolution may have mattered little. Also key to the story is that shifts in supply and demand can have strong influences on one another. As Becker (1991) argued, shifts in the demand for children were integral to the funding and development of innovations in contraception. Importantly, changes in contraceptive technology appear to have influenced the demand for children in the last fifty years.

What Is the Case for a Second Demographic Transition?

A growing body of empirical work suggests that the Pill and other supply-side factors had quantitatively important effects on childbearing and women's careers. While internally valid, the short-term comparisons in these studies shed little light on how changes on the supply side may have had larger, general equilibrium consequences. For instance, they could have shifted attitudes, changed gender roles and women's bargaining power, and altered the culture of dating, cohabitation, and marriage. This means that recent empirical work documenting the short-term impact of the Pill is inherently silent on the bigger picture. We now weigh evidence related to whether the United States is in the midst of a *second* demographic transition, or SDT, and more broadly whether the same factors that led to the earlier fertility decline can satisfactorily explain the patterns observed in the post-1960 decline.

The concept of an SDT was introduced by Lesthaeghe and van de Kaa (1986), who hypothesized that the arrival of the contraceptive, sexual, and women's rights revolutions of the 1960s engendered a *distinct* demographic era—a period *exceptional* enough to be called a transition in its own right. The distinctive characteristics of the SDT, they argue, are persistently low fertility rates and high rates of childlessness, substantially delayed marriage and childbearing, increases in nonmarital cohabitation and childbearing, and high divorce rates. (Some formulations also invoke increases in women's labor-force participation.)

Other demographers have countered these claims. Cliquet argues that the SDT characteristics "already existed before the sixties [for Council of Europe member states]; in fact, most of them emerged with the . . . demographic transition around the turn of the [twentieth] century" (1991, 72). Others contend the SDT literature is ahistorical: "A graph truncated at [the 1950s and 1960s] gives a false impression of an inexorable downward slide coinciding with the onset of the [second demographic transition], while in fact in most countries the real decline was forty years earlier. The 1950s and the 1960s are a deceptive aberration in fertility history" (Coleman 2004, 18).

This critique of the SDT literature implicitly claims that the *same* forces (e.g., opportunity cost of childbearing, shadow price and income elasticity of child quality) drove fertility to decline in both periods. Under this hypothesis, the "right" test of recent exceptionalism is not an examination of the last fifty years, but rather the comparability of the early and later periods of fertility decline. By this metric, fertility rates are not much lower today than earlier in the twentieth century, nor did they decline much more quickly during the baby bust than they had some forty years earlier (Bailey, Guldi, and Hershbein 2014; see figs. 3.1 and 3.2 in this chapter). Although cohabitation rates have increased, age at first union (including both marriages and nonmarital cohabitations) is at its pre–baby boom level, as is age at first birth. Divorce rates are not appreciably different today from what their pre–baby boom trends would predict (Stevenson and Wolfers 2007).

Although this historical comparison of time series and trends appears inconsistent with the notion of an SDT, the current period is much more exceptional than is often credited. Generating time series spanning more than one hundred years of US history, Bailey, Guldi, and Hershbein (2014) show that the post-1960 fertility transition exhibits three features distinct from the nineteenth-century and early twentieth-century fertility decline.

Feature 1: The post-1960 period is distinguished by the emergence of a two-child norm, a reduction in the variance of completed childbearing, and a *reduction* in childlessness (see figs. 3.3a and 3.3b). Although women reaching childbearing age in the 1930s and 1970s had similar numbers of children on average, these cohorts achieved these means in very different ways. Most economic models simplify childbearing decisions to *how many* children to have and proxy for this theoretical concept in empirical work with the mean number of live births (or a measure of period fertility). This single moment of the childbearing distribution misses empirical regularities that enhance our understanding of the motivations and constraints that individuals faced over the twentieth century.

Consistent with demand-side explanations and patterns of increased spacing and stopping, the nineteenth-century and early twentieth-century fertility declines are associated with increasing variance in outcomes. That is, this period of fertility decline was characterized by high rates of childlessness, as well as still relatively high rates of women with high parity. On the other hand, consistent with supply-side models, the post-1960 fertility decline is associated with *reductions* in the variance in childbearing (Michael and Willis 1976). Rates both of childlessness and high parity (e.g., more than four live births) were relatively low.

Feature 2: The post-1960 period exhibits an unprecedented decoupling of marriage and motherhood. The age at first union (historically through marriage, more recently through cohabitation) and the age at first birth were strongly correlated in the early twentieth century, but this interrelationship began to disappear after 1960. Recent cohorts formed their first households at ages similar to cohorts born earlier in the century, but they more often cohabited before marriage and were more likely to switch partners. However, age at first union and age at first intercourse have become less predictive of motherhood timing, as many women give birth outside of marriage.

Feature 3: The post-1960 period has witnessed a transformation in the relationship between mothers' education and childbearing. When comparing relatively more- and less-educated women, completed childbearing, childlessness, and the likelihood of marriage are all much *more similar* today than in the early twentieth century. Despite these similarities, age at first household formation, age at first birth, and nonmarital childbearing diverged after 1960 by mothers' education, with more educated mothers more likely to delay household formation, motherhood, and childbearing within marriage.

These distinctive features should give pause to scholars who wish to argue that the fertility declines in the earlier and later parts of the twentieth century are part of the same, though interrupted, trend. After 1960, women were significantly more likely to have exactly two children and were less likely to remain childless. Patterns of completed childbearing and childlessness and the likelihood of eventual marriage are more similar across educational groups of mothers today than in the late nineteenth or early twentieth centuries. On the other hand, age at first union, age at first birth, and nonmarital childbearing have diverged sharply across educational groups. The decoupling of marriage and childbearing and the changing predictive importance of mothers' education hint that a larger demographic and economic transition is underway. The fact that these patterns have not yet stabilized suggests that the current fertility transition, perhaps part of a larger gender and cultural revolution, is still ongoing (Goldscheider 2012). Future research should invest more work into understanding how these changes may impact the longer-term evolution of families and childbearing.

CONCLUSION

Trends in fertility rates and the economic and demographic literature on the determinants of childbearing in three periods (1800–1930, 1930–1960, and 1960–2010) suggest that the first two periods of change in childbearing reflect demand-side factors. Fueled by economic development, the nineteenth- and early twentieth-century fertility decline reflected the rising cost of childbearing (due to rising adult wages and productivity, as well as the separation of production from the home), falling returns (due to falling farm sizes and changes in children's care of their aging parents), and rising incomes (which induced greater investments in each child and a reduction in total number). The explanation for the stabilization of fertility rates and then baby boom (1930–1960) is disputed, but changes in childbearing in this period also appear consistent with changes in the demand for children due to rising incomes and possibly large reductions in the relative prices of factors related to childbearing. The explanations for changes in childbearing in the post-1960 period, however, are still evolving, and likely reflect both demand factors and supply factors. Ultimately, it remains unclear whether the post-1960 supply-side changes are significant enough to constitute a *second* demographic transition or are simply the most recent stage in the ongoing *first* demographic transition (Lee and Reher 2011).

Notes

1. The general fertility rate is the number of live births for every 1,000 women of childbearing age (typically ages 15 through 44) in a given calendar year. Completed childbearing is a cohort measure and represents the average number of live births to women born in a certain year.

2. The census figures are unadjusted for differential survival of women by their number of children born and for unmarried childbearing. Figure 3.2 shows a sharp decline in completed fertility for women born in the late 1860s, but this decline coincides with seaming issues between the 1910 and 1940 censuses (the 1920 and 1930 censuses did not ask about completed childbearing). This means that estimates for cohorts born in the late 1860s are drawn from the 1910 census (when these women were in their forties). Estimates for cohorts born in the early 1870s are drawn from the 1940 census, when these women were in their sixties, and may reflect age-based mortality rates that are correlated with completed childbearing. Investigating this is a subject for future research.

3. See Shapiro (1950) for a detailed history on the development of the national vital statistics registration areas.

4. "Nonwhite" is an unsatisfactory category for racial and ethnic group, but it is the only classification that can be made consistently over such a long period.

5. The income data can be found at U.S. Bureau of Economic Analysis, National Income and Product Accounts: Table 7.1. The data were accessed in September 2015.

6. Economics models innovation in contraceptive technology as a reduction in the marginal cost of averting births (Michael and Willis 1976).

7. Opportunity cost model: Becker (1965); child-quality model: Becker and Lewis (1973).

8. This is defined as the amount of time required to bear and raise a child valued by the dollar equivalent of the relevant adult's marginal product in her most productive activity.

9. See Goldin (1998) for graduation rate estimates.

10. The building of schools is discussed in Goldin and Katz (2008).

11. See Becker, Murphy, and Tamura (1991) and Galor and Weil (2000). Galor and Weil call this "Unified Growth Theory." Their formulation endogenizes population growth and human capital investment decisions to explain the transition dynamics from a Malthusian equilibrium to a post-Malthusian system in which income grows while population is stable.

12. Economists have also noted the potential importance of the supply side (Easterlin 1975; Easterlin and Crimmins 1985; Easterlin, Pollack, and Wachter 1980; Hotz and Miller 1988; Michael and Willis 1976). For empirical papers on the role of greater access to reliable medical contraceptives, see Bailey (2006, 2010, 2012); Bailey, Hershbein, and Miller (2012); Goldin and Katz (2002); Guldi (2008); Kearney and Levine (2009).

13. Theoretical models suggest that women who use family-planning services are different in many ways from those who do not. Sah and Birchenall (2012) show why women who use family-planning services may be expected to differ in terms of their unobserved preferences as well as in the price associated with a conception. Theory also suggests that cross-sectional associations in childbearing and family planning may reflect both greater local demand for services and the effects of those services.

14. The earliest studies on this question used multivariate regressions to adjust estimates of the relationship between access to family planning (whether areas had a program or individuals used them) and fertility rates. These largely cross-sectional studies were limited by well-known omitted variables and endogeneity problems (see Rosenweig and

Wolpin 1986, and Hotz, Klerman, and Willis 1997) and it is not surprising that these studies led to mixed evidence on the effects of different types of family planning programs (see Mellor 1998 for a review). Recent studies use localized, randomized interventions that target teen pregnancies but generally conclude that these interventions had little effect (DiCenso et al. 2002 and Kearney and Levine 2015). See Bailey (2013) for a more detailed discussion of these studies.

15. See Bailey (2006, 2009); Bailey, Hershbein, and Miller (2012); Goldin and Katz (2002); Guldi (2008); Hock (2008). In a recent paper, Myers (2017) argues that the effects of changes in legal access to the Pill for younger women differs from Goldin and Katz's and Bailey's estimates when she changes the legal coding. While smaller, the magnitudes of her updated estimates are not statistically different from published estimates (Bailey, Guldi, and Hershbein 2013). Bailey et al. (2011) summarize the legal coding used in the different studies.

BIBLIOGRAPHY

Albanesi, S., and C. Olivetti. (2016). "Gender Roles and Medical Progress." *Journal of Political Economy* 124(3): 650–695.

Alsan, M., and C. Goldin. (2015). "Watersheds in Infant Mortality: The Role of Effective Water and Sewage Infrastructure, 1880 to 1915." NBER Working Paper No. 21263.

Ananat, E. O., and D. Hungerman. (2012). "The Power of the Pill for the Next Generation: Oral Contraception's Effects on Fertility, Abortion, and Maternal and Child Characteristics." *Review of Economics and Statistics* 94(1): 37–51.

Atack, J., F. Bateman, and R. A. Margo. (2008). "Steam Power, Establishment Size, and Labor Productivity Growth in Nineteenth Century American Manufacturing." *Explorations in Economic History* 45(2): 185–198.

Bailey, M. J. (2006). "More Power to the Pill: The Impact of Contraceptive Freedom on Women's Lifecycle Labor Supply." *Quarterly Journal of Economics* 121(1): 289–320.

Bailey, M. J. (2009). "More Power to the Pill: The Impact of Contraceptive Freedom on Women's Lifecycle Labor Supply: Erratum and Addendum." Available at http://www-personal.umich.edu/~baileymj/Bailey_Erratum.pdf.

Bailey, M. J. (2010). "'Momma's Got the Pill': How Anthony Comstock and Griswold v. Connecticut Shaped U.S. Childbearing." *American Economic Review* 100(1): 98–129.

Bailey, M. J. (2012). "Reexamining the Impact of U.S. Family Planning Programs on Fertility: Evidence from the War on Poverty and the Early Years of Title X." *American Economic Journal: Applied Economics* 4(2): 62–97.

Bailey, M. J. (2013). "Fifty Years of U.S. Family Planning: New Evidence on the Long-Run Effects of Increasing Access to Contraception." *Brookings Papers on Economic Activity* (Spring): 341–409.

Bailey, M. J., and W. J. Collins. (2011). "Did Improvements in Household Technology Cause the Baby Boom? Evidence from Electrification, Appliance Diffusion, and the Amish." *American Economic Journal: Macroeconomics* 3(2): 189–217.

Bailey, M. J., M. Guldi, A. Davido, and E. Buzuvis. (2011). "Laws and Policies Governing Contraceptive Access, 1960–1980." University of Michigan Working Paper.

Bailey, M. J., M. Guldi, and B. J. Hershbein. (2013). "Further Evidence on the Internal Validity of the Early Legal Access Research Design." *Journal of Policy Analysis and Management* 32(4): 899–904.

Bailey, M. J., M. Guldi, and B. J. Hershbein. (2014). "Is There a Case for a 'Second Demographic Transition': Three Distinctive Features of the Post-1960 U.S. Fertility Decline." In *Human Capital and History: The American Record*, edited by L. Boustan, C. Frydman, and R. A. Margo, 273–312. Cambridge, MA: National Bureau of Economics Research.

Bailey, M. J., B. J. Hershbein, and A. R. Miller. (2012). "The Opt-In Revolution? Contraception and the Gender Gap in Wages." *American Economic Journal: Applied Economics* 4(3): 225–254.

Bailey, M. J., O. Malkova, and Z. McLaren. (Forthcoming). "Do Family Planning Programs Increase Children's Opportunities? Evidence from the War on Poverty and the Early Years of Title X." *Journal of Human Resources.*

Barro, R. J., and G. S. Becker. (1989). "Fertility Choice in a Model of Economic Growth." *Econometrica* 57(2): 481–501.

Basso, A., H. Bodenhorn, and D. Cuberes. (2014). "Fertility and Financial Development: Evidence from US Counties in the 19th Century." NBER Working Paper No. 20491.

Becker, G., K. Murphy, and R. Tamura. (1991). "Economic Growth, Human Capital and Population Growth." *Journal of Political Economy* 98(5): S12–S137.

Becker, G. S. (1960). "An Economic Analysis of Fertility." In *Demographic and Economic Change in Developed Countries*, 208–230. Princeton, NJ: Princeton University Press.

Becker, G. S. (1965). "A Theory of the Allocation of Time." *Economic Journal* 75(299): 493–517.

Becker, G. S. (1991). *A Treatise on the Family (Enlarged Edition)*. Cambridge, MA: Harvard University Press.

Becker, G. S., and R. J. Barro. (1988). "A Reformulation of the Economic Theory of Fertility." *Quarterly Journal of Economics* 103(1): 1–25.

Becker, G. S., and H. G. Lewis. (1973). "On the Interaction between the Quantity and Quality of Children." *Journal of Political Economy* 81(2): S279–S288.

Binion, R. (2001). "Marianne in the Home: Political Revolution and Fertility Transition in France and the United States." *Population: An English Selection* 13(2): 165–188.

Cain, L. P., and E. J. Rotella. (2001). "Death and Spending: Urban Mortality and Municipal Expenditure on Sanitation." *Annales de Demographie Historique* 1: 139–154.

Cliquet, R. L. (1991). *The Second Demographic Transition: Fact or Fiction? Population Studies*, Vol. 23. Strasbourg: Council of Europe.

Coleman, D. (2004). "Why We Don't Have to Believe without Doubting in the 'Second Demographic Transition'—Some Agnostic Comments." *Vienna Yearbook of Population Research* 2: 11–24.

Craig, L. A., and T. Weiss. (2000). "Hours at Work and Total Factor Productivity Growth in Nineteenth Century U.S. Agriculture." In *Advances in Agricultural Economic History*, Vol. 1, 1–30. Stamford, CT: JAI Press.

Currie, J., and H. Schwandt. (2014). "Short- and Long-Term Effects of Unemployment on Fertility." *Proceedings of the National Academy of Sciences* 111(41): 14724–14739.

Cutler, D. M., and G. Miller. (2005). "The Role of Public Health Improvements in Health Advances: The 20th Century United States." *Demography* 42(1): 1–22.

DiCenso, A., G. Guyatt, A. Willan, and L. Griffith. (2002). "Interventions to Reduce Unintended Pregnancies among Adolescents: Systematic Review of Randomized Controlled Trials." *British Medical Journal* 324: 1426–1434.

Doepke, M., M. Hazan, and Y. D. Maoz. (2015). "The Baby Boom and World War II: A Macroeconomic Analysis." *Review of Economic Studies* 82(3): 1031–1073.

Easterlin, R. A. (1966). "Economic-Demographic Interactions and Long Swings in Economic Growth." *American Economic Review* 56(5): 1063–1104.

Easterlin, R. A. (1971). "Does Human Fertility Adjust to the Environment?" *Family Economic Behavior* 61(2): 399–407.

Easterlin, R. A. (1975). "An Economic Framework for Fertility Analysis." *Studies in Family Planning* 6(3): 54–63.

Easterlin, R. A. (1976). "Factors in the Decline of Farm Family Fertility in the United States: Some Preliminary Research Results." *Journal of American History* 63(3): 600–614.

Easterlin, R. A. (1980). *Birth and Fortune: The Impact of Numbers on Personal Welfare.* New York: Basic Books.

Easterlin, R. A., and E. M. Crimmins. (1985). *The Fertility Revolution: A Supply-Demand Analysis.* Chicago: University of Chicago Press.

Easterlin, R. A., R. A. Pollack, and M. L. Wachter. (1980). "Towards a More General Economic Model of Fertility Determination: Endogenous Preferences and Natural Fertility." In *Population and Economic Change in Less Developed Countries*, edited by R. A. Easterlin, 81–150. Chicago: University of Chicago Press.

Ferrie, J., and W. Troesken. (2005). "Death and the City: Chicago's Mortality Transition, 1850–1925." NBER Working Paper No. 11427.

Gallman, R. E. (1972). "Changes in Total U.S. Agricultural Factor Productivity in the Nineteenth Century." *Agricultural History* 46(1): 191–210.

Galor, O., and D. N. Weil. (2000). "Population, Technology, and Growth: From Malthusian Stagnation to the Demographic Transition and Beyond." *American Economic Review* 90(4): 806–828.

Goldin, C. (1990). *Understanding the Gender Gap: An Economic History of American Women.* New York: Cambridge University Press.

Goldin, C. (1991). "Marriage Bars: Discrimination against Married Women Workers from the 1920s to the 1950s." In *Favorites of Fortune: Technology, Growth, and Economic Development since the Industrial Revolution*, edited by H. Rosovsky, D. Landes, and P. Higonnet, 511–536. Cambridge, MA: Harvard University Press.

Goldin, C. (1998). "America's Graduation from High School: The Evolution and Spread of Secondary Schooling in the Twentieth Century." *Journal of Economic History* 58(2): 345–374.

Goldin, C., and L. F. Katz. (2002). "The Power of the Pill: Oral Contraceptives and Women's Career and Marriage Decisions." *Journal of Political Economy* 110(4): 730–770.

Goldin, C., and L. F. Katz. (2008). *The Race between Education and Technology.* Cambridge, MA: Belknap Press.

Goldscheider, F. (2012). "The Gender Revolution and the Second Demographic Transition: Understanding Recent Family Trends in Industrialized Societies." Keynote Address, 2012 European Population Conference, Stockholm, Sweden, June 13.

Greenwood, J., A. Seshadri, and G. Vandenbroucke. (2005). "The Baby Boom and Baby Bust." *American Economic Review* 95(1): 183–207.

Guinnane, T. W. (2011). "The Historical Fertility Transition: A Guide for Economists." *Journal of Economic Literature* 49(3): 589–614.

Guldi, M. (2008). "Fertility Effects of Abortion and Pill Access for Minors." *Demography* 45(4): 817–827.

Hacker, J. D. (2003). "Rethinking the 'Early' Decline of Marital Fertility in the United States." *Demography* 40(4): 605–620.

Haines, M. (2000). "The White Population of the United States, 1790–1920." In *A Population History of North America*, edited by M. R. Haines and R. H. Steckel, 305–369. New York: Cambridge University Press.

Haines, M. (2008). "Fertility and Mortality in the United States." *EH.Net Encyclopedia*, edited by R. Whaples. Available at http://eh.net/encyclopedia/fertility-and-mortality-in-the-united-states/.

Haines, Michael R. (2006). "Fertility and Mortality by Race: 1800–2000." In *Historical Statistics of the United States: Millennial Edition*, edited by Susan B. Carter, 1–391. New York: Cambridge University Press.

Hock, H. (2008). "The Pill and the College Attainment of American Women and Men." Florida State University Department of Economics Working Paper.

Hotz, V. J., J. A. Klerman, and R. J. Willis. (1997). "The Economics of Fertility in Developed Countries." In *Handbook of Population and Family Economics*, edited by M. R. Rosenzweig and O. Stark, Vol. 1A, 275–348. Amsterdam: Elsevier.

Hotz, V. J., and R. A. Miller. (1988). "An Empirical Analysis of Life Cycle Fertility and Female Labor Supply." *Econometrica* 56(1): 91–118.

Kearney, M. S., and P. B. Levine. (2009). "Subsidized Contraception, Fertility, and Sexual Behavior." *Review of Economics and Statistics* 91(1): 137–151.

Kearney, M. S., and P. B. Levine. (2015). "Media Influences on Social Outcomes: The Impact of MTV's 16 and Pregnant on Teen Childbearing." *American Economic Review* 105(12): 3597–3632.

Lahey, J. N. (2014a). "Birthing a Nation: The Effect of Fertility Control Access on the Nineteenth-Century Demographic Transition." *Journal of Economic History* 74(2): 482–508.

Lahey, J. N. (2014b). "The Effect of Anti-Abortion Legislation on Nineteenth Century Fertility." *Demography* 51(3): 939–948.

Lee, R. D., and D. S. Reher. (2011). "Introduction: The Landscape of Demographic Transition and Its Aftermath." *Population and Development Review* 37(1): 1–7.

Lesthaeghe, R. J., and D. J. van de Kaa. (1986). "Twee demografische transities." In *Bevolking, groei en krimp*, edited by R. Lesthaeghe and D. J. van de Kaa, 19–68. Deventer: Van Loghum Slaterus.

Lewis, J. (2014). "Fertility, Child Health, and the Diffusion of Electricity in the Home." Department of Economics, University of Montreal Working Paper.

Linder, F. E., and R. D. Grove. (1947). *Vital Statistics Rates in the United States 1900–1940.* Washington, DC: National Office of Vital Statistics.

Mellor, J. M. (1998). "The Effect of Family Planning Programs on the Fertility of Welfare Recipients: Evidence from Medicaid Claims." *Journal of Human Resources* 33: 866–895.

Michael, R. T., and R. J. Willis. (1976). "Contraception and Fertility: Household Production under Uncertainty." In *Household Production and Consumption*, edited by N. E. Terleckyj, 25–98. Cambridge, MA: National Bureau of Economic Research.

Moehling, C. M. (1998). "Work and Family: Intergenerational Support in American Families, 1880–1920." *Journal of Economic History* 58(2): 535–537.

Moehling, C. M., and M. A. Thomasson. (2014). "Saving Babies: The Impact of Public Education Programs on Infant Mortality." *Demography* 51(2): 367–386.

Myers, C. K. (2017). "The Power of Abortion Policy: Re-examining the Effects of Young Women's Access to Reproductive Control." *Journal of Political Economy* 125(6): 2178–2224.

National Center for Health Statistics. (2003). "Table 1-1: Live Births, Birth Rates, and Fertility Rates, by Race: United States, 1909–2000." Available at https://www.cdc.gov/nchs/data/statab/t001x01.pdf.

Notestein, F. W. (1945). "Population—The Long View." In *Food for the World*, edited by T. W. Schultz, 36–57. Chicago: University of Chicago Press.

Pampel, F. C., and H. E. Peters. (1995). "The Easterlin Effect." *Annual Review of Sociology* 21: 163–194.

Rogers, C. C., and M. O'Connell. (1984). "Childspacing among Birth Cohorts of American Women: 1905 to 1959." In *Current Population Reports*, Series P-20 No. 385. Washington, DC: Bureau of the Census.

Rosenweig, M. R., and K. Wolpin. (1986). "Evaluating the Effects of Optimally Distributed Public Programs: Child Health and Family Planning Interventions." *American Economic Review* 76(3): 470–482.

Ruggles, S., J. T. Alexander, R. Goeken, M. B. Schroeder, and M. Sobek. (2010). Integrated Public Use Microdata Series (Version 6.0) [Machine-readable database]. Minneapolis, University of Minnesota. Available at https://usa.ipums.org/usa/.

Ryder, N. B. (1980). "Components of Temporal Variations in American Fertility." In *Demographic Patterns in Developed Societies*, edited by R. W. Hiorns, 15–54. London: Taylor and Francis.

Ryder, N. B., and C. F. Westoff. (1971). *The Contraceptive Revolution*. Princeton, NJ: Princeton University Press.

Sah, R. K., and J. A. Birchenall. (2012). "Coituses and Contraceptive Reliability: Some Results on Behavior and Welfare." University of California at Santa Barbara Working Paper.

Sanderson, W. C. (1976). "On Two Schools of the Economics of Fertility." *Population and Development Review* 2(3–4): 469–477.

Saxonhouse, G., and G. Wright. (1984). "Two Forms of Cheap Labor in Textile History." In *Technique, Spirit and Form in the Making of the Modern Economies: Essays in Honor of William N. Parker. Research in Economic History Supp 3*, edited by G. Saxonhouse and G. Wright, 3–31. Greenwich, CT: JAI Press.

Shapiro, S. (1950). "Development of Birth Registration and Birth Statistics in the United States." *Population Studies* 4(1): 86–111.

Simon, C. J., and R. Tamura. (2009). "Do Higher Rents Discourage Fertility? Evidence from US Cities, 1940–2000." *Regional Science and Urban Economics* 39(1): 33–42.

Steckel, R. H. (1992). "The Fertility Transition in the United States: Tests of Alternative Hypotheses." In *Strategic Factors in Nineteenth Century American Economic History: A Volume to Honor Robert W. Fogel*, edited by C. Goldin and H. Rockoff, 351–374. Cambridge, MA: National Bureau of Economic Research.

Stephens, M., Jr., and D.-Y. Yang. (2014). "Compulsory Education and the Benefits of Schooling." *American Economic Review* 104(6): 1777–1792.

Stevenson, B., and J. Wolfers. (2007). "Marriage and Divorce: Changes and Their Driving Forces." *Journal of Economic Perspectives* 21(2): 27–52.

Sundstrom, W. A., and P. A. David. (1988). "Old-Age Security Motives, Labor Markets, and Farm Family Fertility in Antebellum American." *Explorations in Economic History* 25(2): 164–197.

Troesken, W. (2002). "The Limits of Jim Crow: Race and the Provision of Water and Sewerage Services in American Cities, 1880–1925." *Journal of Economic History* 62(3): 734–772.

Trussell, J. (2004). "Contraceptive Efficacy." In *Contraceptive Technology*, edited by R. A. Hatcher, J. Trussell, F. Stewart, A. Nelson, W. Cates, F. Guest, and D. Kowal, 18th rev. ed., 747–826. New York: Ardent Media.

U.S. Bureau of Economic Analysis. *National Income and Product Accounts*. Table 7.1, Selected Per Capita Product and Income Series in Current and Chained Dollars. Available at https://www.bea.gov/iTable/index_nipa.cfm. Accessed September 25, 2015.

U.S. Census Bureau. (1981–2010). *Current Population Surveys, June Supplement*. [Machine-readable data files]. Available at http://www.nber.org/data/current-population-survey-data.html.

Wanamaker, M. H. (2012). "Industrialization and Fertility in the Nineteenth Century: Evidence from South Carolina." *Journal of Economic History* 72(1): 168–196.

Weiss, T. (1992). "U.S. Labor Force Estimates and Economic Growth, 1800–1860." In *American Economic Growth and Standards of Living before the Civil War*, edited by R. E. Gallman and J. J. Wallis, 19–78. Chicago: University of Chicago Press.

Westoff, C. F. (1975). "The Yield of the Imperfect: The 1970 National Fertility Study." *Demography* 12(4): 573–580.

Willis, R. J. (1973). "A New Approach to the Economic Theory of Fertility Behavior." *Journal of Political Economy* 81(2): S14–S64.

CHAPTER 4

....

IMMIGRATION IN AMERICAN ECONOMIC HISTORY

....

JOSEPH P. FERRIE

THE economic history of immigration to the United States, like the country's experience of westward territorial expansion, industrialization, agricultural development, and political economy, is characterized by themes quite distinct from those seen in the longer established economies of Europe, Asia, and Africa. The American experience of immigration is instead similar to that of other settler economies in the Western Hemisphere and Australasia. Two major aspects of American immigration history have been studied extensively: (1) the causes and sources of immigration; and (2) the impact of immigration on the economy and on the immigrants themselves. United States immigration history can also be divided into four distinct eras: (1) the colonial period ("settler" migration); (2) 1800 through the 1880s (the "old" migration); (3) the 1880s through the early 1920s (the "new" migration); and (4) the post-1965 period.

Migration across Europe, Asia, and Africa had occurred throughout early human history in response to scarcity. The seventeenth century, however, witnessed something quite new: migration with the active encouragement of national governments pursuing mercantilist policies and in search of new resources in a process characterized by the explicit transplantation of economic ideas, attitudes, practices, and institutions. Though an indigenous population had been present in North America for more than 10,000 years before 1600, European settlers rapidly displaced them and transformed the New World to which they journeyed (Driver 2011). The majority of the European migrants in this era arrived as bound laborers: in exchange for their passage fare, they signed contracts that required them to serve a fixed number of years in the employment of the person who purchased their contract. The 1607 arrival of three ships at Jamestown in present-day Virginia opened the era of settler migration. This first colony was to be a money-making enterprise. The Virginia Company's plan was simple: raise funds as a joint stock company, recruit laborers in England, transport them to land across the Atlantic Ocean granted by the Crown, and profit from the sale of resources, such as gold, that the laborers sent back to England. The first three steps went well, but the last did not. The Company underestimated how harsh the settlers would find the new environment and overestimated the ease with which resources could be extracted and profitably returned to England. There was no gold, and it was another seven years after the initial settlement was nearly wiped out by starvation and disease before the first exports of tobacco were bound for England (Galenson 1981b; Smith 1947).

The Virginia Company's settlement at Jamestown never lived up to the hopes of its investors. It was nonetheless an important landmark in US economic history as the first example of significant immigration, and it set the template for much of the immigration that occurred over the following two centuries. That template involved bound labor: indentured servitude for whites and slavery for blacks. Indentured servitude accounted for as much as three-quarters of all white immigration to the thirteen British colonies, and slavery accounted for virtually all of the black labor that arrived from Africa or the West Indies. At the end of their term as servants, whites could receive a lump-sum payment in cash or land and begin their post-servitude careers with a modest stake.

Indentured servitude arose in the early decades of the Virginia Company's operations to solve a capital market failure. The colony needed settlers, and there were many English workers who would willingly travel to the colony, but the workers lacked the resources to finance the journey themselves. At the same time, no one would lend to an individual about to embark on a perilous voyage to a new life nearly four thousand miles away. The solution was for workers to sign contracts in which they bound themselves for a specified period of time to the owner of the contract in exchange for passage to the colonies. The contract length reflected the worker's projected productivity, with more productive workers getting shorter terms of service (Galenson 1981a). The length was set so that the worker's net product (above maintenance costs) over the life of the contract was equal to the roughly £7 cost of transporting the worker. When the now indentured servant reached the colonies, the contract was sold to anyone who had a demand for labor. The white indentured servants who came from England were drawn from all levels of that country's economic hierarchy. They came in roughly the proportions that they represented at home—equal shares of farmers, craftsmen, unskilled laborers, and individuals who had been young farm servants. Indentured servants also came from Ireland, Scotland, and Germany (Galenson 1978). Figure 4.1 shows estimates of net migration into the colonies before 1800 (Fogelman 1992).

Through 1700, roughly 160,000 immigrants arrived from Europe, followed by an additional 307,000 between 1700 and the American Revolution. Until the decade beginning in 1710, the colonies never received more than 30,000 net migrants over ten years. The volume of net white migration doubled from the 1680s to the 1710s, rose another 60 percent over the next two decades, and began a steep decline from its pre-1800 peak until the decade of the Revolution, when net white migration fell to a lower level than it had seen in the 1630s.

Immigrants in this early, pre-1800 period were drawn from just a small set of places in Europe—the British Isles and the northwestern part of Germany. These were among the first areas to experience two aspects of economic modernization—the consolidation of

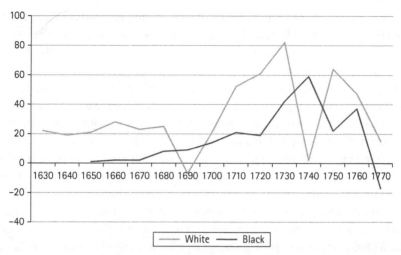

FIGURE 4.1. Net migration into the original thirteen colonies, 1630–1770 (thousands)
Source: Carter et al. (2006, Table Ad3–15). http://dx.doi.org/10.1017/ISBN-9780511132971.Ad1-89.

smallholdings in agriculture, and the shift in manufacturing from artisanal shops to factory floors. Together with growth in the population and the pressure it placed on wages and living standards, modernization on farms and in factories loosened the ties between people and places. The lure of the North American colonies then drew those whose future prospects at home were no longer bright.

The impact of settler migration through 1800 on the American colonies differed substantially by region. In the South, especially in the first decades after the establishment of Jamestown, population growth would have been negative in the absence of immigration. Even into the eighteenth century, immigration remained a substantial component of Southern population growth. In the Middle Colonies and New England, however, a generally healthier environment resulted in rapid population growth through high rates of fertility and low rates of mortality, so the role of immigration was more limited. For the immigrants themselves, immigration often represented a substantial improvement in their material standard of living and social status. For at least the early seventeenth century, former indentured servants, who came with nothing, were frequently able to rise into the class of property owners. Though some of this opportunity was foreclosed in the South as land prices rose, the Middle Atlantic colonies such as Pennsylvania remained places of substantial economic opportunity (Menard 1973).

THE FIRST GREAT WAVE, 1800–1890

Throughout the nineteenth and early twentieth centuries, two forces—modernization on farms and in factories and overall population growth—swept across Europe from the

northwest to the southeast. The mix of countries sending migrants to the United States
followed the path of those forces. Figure 4.2 shows the rise and decline of immigration
rates by European region of origin (Carter et al. 2006). "Old" origins are Britain, Ireland,
and Germany. "New" origins are Italy, Scandinavia, Greece, Poland, and Russia.

The impact of these forces on migration to the United States can be seen in the two
decades before the Civil War. This era witnessed the first great wave of European immigration to the United States. From 1820 (the first year for which reliable data are available) through the mid-1840s, the annual volume of immigration remained well below
100,000, or an immigration rate of 4–5 per thousand per United States population. But
the impact of modernization in farming and manufacturing was only part of the story
by the mid-1840s. Transportation costs were also falling dramatically as the transition
from sail to steam began in the 1850s. Immigration rose dramatically in 1847 following
the failure of the Irish potato crop in 1846 and the crop failures on the European continent in the following two years. Continental political turmoil in 1848 led to additional
departures. In 1850 alone, nearly 370,000 immigrants traveled to the United States. Over
the 1850s, the rate of immigration rose above 15 per thousand for the first, and only, time
in history. As had been the case in the nearly two centuries of European settlement before 1800, just three countries (Great Britain, Ireland, and Germany) accounted for
more than 90 percent of all arriving immigrants in the decades before the Civil War.
By the 1880s, modernization in farming and manufacturing had begun in Scandinavia.

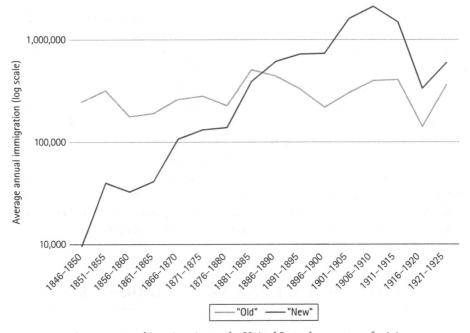

FIGURE 4.2. Average annual immigration to the United States by country of origin

Source: Carter et al. (2006, Table Ad25–50). http://dx.doi.org/10.1017/ISBN-9780511132971. Ad1-8910.1017/
ISBN-9780511132971.Ad1-89.

This decade saw a corresponding rise in the share of immigrants from Norway, Sweden, and Denmark.

The United States that these immigrants entered was still largely rural; in 1850, 83 percent of free native-born males between the ages of twenty and sixty-five lived in places with fewer than 2,500 inhabitants. Only 9 percent lived in places with populations greater than 10,000. Immigrants, in contrast, far more often settled in cities. More than 36 percent in 1850 lived in places with more than 10,000 inhabitants, while only 54 percent lived in rural places. Immigrants were also more prevalent in the Middle Atlantic states (43 percent) than natives (27 percent). They were only half as likely as natives to live in the South. In fact, immigrants after their arrival were so strongly drawn to a small set of large cities that half in 1850 lived in just three states: New York (27 percent), Pennsylvania (14 percent), and Ohio (9 percent) (Ferrie 1999).

The antebellum US economy was one in which economic activity was still primarily small-scale production on farms or in artisan's workshops: farmers were more than half of native-born males aged twenty to sixty-five in 1850. Another sixth were skilled workers. Just over a fifth were common laborers or servants, and only a tenth were in professional or commercial occupations. By contrast, in 1849, 28 percent of immigrants said at arrival that they were farmers, 23 percent said they were skilled workers, 46 percent said they were common laborers or servants, and 3 percent said they were in professional or commercial occupations (Ferrie 1999).

Though immigrants in this first great wave were highly concentrated geographically and more likely than natives to be unskilled laborers (particularly the Irish), they quickly moved away from their initial locations and advanced quickly to better jobs (though again, the Irish were exceptional in both case). In an economy characterized by high rates of geographic and occupational mobility, immigrants were clearly the most mobile (Ferrie 1995).

Immigrants in the great wave of antebellum migration were thought by many to have been trapped in Eastern city ghettos by poverty, ignorance, and prejudice (Handlin 1991). More recent research has found instead extremely high rates of mobility among a variety of immigrant groups (Ferrie 1999). Their high rates resulted in part from their lack of property and skill, giving them few ties to specific places and strong incentives to seek out opportunities at new locations. But greater immigrant geographic mobility holds even after controlling for wealth or occupation.

At their arrival on the docks of lower New York City, Boston, and Philadelphia, antebellum European immigrants faced an array of possibilities: they could remain where they arrived, or they could travel to any of a thousand places in the interior of the United States. Most who arrived between 1840 and 1850 left their port of arrival quickly. The exceptions were the poor, the Irish, and the commercial class. These stayed behind and remained only a few miles from where they first landed. Perhaps seven of every eight arrivals, though, moved on after no more than a few weeks and quickly moved to cities and towns where opportunities beckoned, with few stops between where they started and where they were found in 1850. The deliberateness with which they moved suggests that many had planned their journeys using the volume of information about opportunities in America available to them before their departure, either from formal (book, pamphlets, newspapers) or informal (family and friends who had gone before them) sources.

This era's immigrant flows were not monolithic. Settlement patterns differed by country of origin. As Ferrie shows, the British were partial to the Northeast, the Irish settled in both the East and West, and the Germans gravitated to the immigrant communities that arose in Western cities like Cincinnati, St. Louis, and Milwaukee. Scandinavians were drawn in large numbers to the farms of the Upper Midwest. Immigrants in this period who arrived at older ages with large families settled in the rural areas of the Western states. Perhaps they did so because they possessed the financial and human resources to take advantage of the West's unsettled farmland. Over the decade following their arrival, most immigrants continued to move, as more than half changed their county of residence, except for farmers and the Irish (the former unwilling, the latter perhaps unable to move) (Ferrie 1995).

A generation of research on the occupational mobility of immigrants to the United States in the first half of the nineteenth century concluded that upward occupational mobility was infrequent during the careers of first-generation immigrants. For example, less than a third of immigrants who began their careers in the United States as unskilled laborers in Newburyport, Boston, Poughkeepsie, and South Bend rose into the ranks of skilled or white-collar workers. This poor performance is inconsistent with the image of the United States, especially among immigrants themselves, as a place where economic advancement—particularly occupational mobility—was likely.

These studies focused solely on immigrants who remained in the same place for a decade or more, comparing the occupations of immigrants observed, for example, in 1850 Newburyport with their occupations in 1860 Newburyport. But such data will inevitably miss changes in occupation that occurred together with changes in location. As we have already noted, immigrants were among the most geographically mobile Americans in the nineteenth century. At the same time, these studies focus on mobility only after arrival in the United States, even though what may be most important to the immigrants themselves is the difference between their pre- and post-migration occupations.

Using data that follow immigrants from the European occupations they reported on the passenger ship lists describing them at arrival to US census manuscripts up to twenty years after they entered the United States, it is now possible to get a more accurate picture of immigrant occupational mobility. As was the case with geographic mobility, there are stark differences across countries of origin. Among those who arrived saying they were in skilled or white-collar jobs, for example, most Germans (more than 70 percent) were found in such occupations within a year of arrival. Most British were in less desirable jobs (such as unskilled laborer) within a year of arrival, but over their first ten years in the United States, most (again, more than 70 percent) had reacquired their pre-migration occupation. The Irish had even less success returning to such jobs immediately after arrival, and though they improved their occupations somewhat over their first ten years in the United States, fewer than half ever returned to their pre-migration occupations. Specific events in Europe (e.g., the Revolutions of 1848) had an impact on the characteristics of the immigrants who came in their wake and the success they had in reacquiring their pre-migration occupations. The German "Forty-Eighters," as they came to be known, were particularly successful at avoiding a fall in occupational status at their arrival (Ferrie 1997).

Another useful measure of the immigrant experience in the United States at this time is how quickly they were able to accumulate wealth. In his 1975 book, *Men and Wealth*—the most comprehensive analysis of nineteenth-century wealth holding— Soltow found that wealth rose with age but rose less rapidly at higher ages, there were marked differences in wealth between the native- and foreign-born, and differences by country of origin among the foreign-born. These differences might have resulted from differences in immigrants' time since arrival in the United States and their ability in the years after arrival to overcome barriers such as language, prejudice, and a lack of marketable skills. Subsequent work by Ferrie (1999) examined these mechanisms by following antebellum immigrants for up to twenty years after arrival.

There were indeed sharp differences in wealth holdings by country of origin in these data. In both 1850 and 1860, British immigrants were most likely to own real estate and owned the greatest average amounts. The Germans were less likely to own any real property in 1850, and they owned less on average than the British. These differences narrowed by 1860, with the Germans even surpassing the British in their average holdings of personal property. The Irish were least likely to own any property and owned smaller average amounts than the British or Germans, though these differences also narrowed between 1850 and 1860. Immigrants held less wealth on average than the native-born, but these disparities diminished as immigrants' length of residence increased.

European immigrants to the United States in the 1840s accumulated impressive amounts of wealth in the years after their arrival. In 1850, immigrants who had arrived in the 1840s owned $270 on average in real estate, a figure that had risen to more than $1,000 by 1860. With personal wealth included, immigrants held an average of $1,500 of wealth in 1860 after an average of fifteen years in the United States. Immigrants' wealth, like that of the native-born, increased with age, though immigrants' wealth did so more rapidly in percentage terms (Ferrie 1994).

Just as mid-nineteenth-century immigration had significant effects on the immigrants themselves, it also produced effects for the US population present before their arrival. As we noted earlier, immigrants at this time were distributed differently from the rest of the United States population in terms of both location and occupation. The arrival of so many immigrants in so short a time, and their concentration in a few locations and occupations, placed enormous pressure on some local labor markets. Circumstantial evidence—changes in the ethnic composition of the workforce in specific industries and places, the degradation of skilled work, the attitude toward immigration in the popular press, the rise of nativist political organizations, and the response of organized labor—suggests that immigration's impact was substantial in some circumstances.

The ethnic makeup of the labor force changed dramatically in some places where it has been possible to measure workers' nativity. In Lowell's textile mills, 90 percent of workers were native-born in 1849, but only 35 percent were native-born in 1855. A similarly rapid transformation of the labor force can be seen in other craft industries: carpentry, iron casting, shoemaking, tailoring, and cabinetmaking (see Ernst 1949; Hoagland 1913; Lazonick and Brush 1985; Ross 1985).

Labor historians have described the period preceding the Civil War as a time of "de-skilling"—"the general degradation of skill premiums by the downgrading of once highly skilled operations" (Fogel 1989, 358). An example of this process was the "Berkshire system" under which skilled ironworkers were gradually replaced by unskilled workers.

This process of displacement was most pronounced where changes in the manufacturing process allowed employers to replace skilled workers with semiskilled and unskilled workers. In these circumstances, the fact that it was immigrants displacing natives was probably less important than unskilled and semiskilled workers replacing skilled workers. Immigration merely hastened a process that would have occurred anyway, perhaps with rural workers' migration to cities if no immigration had taken place (Lane 1987).

The pressures that immigration placed on labor markets in the urban Northeast produced a substantial backlash in the 1850s. First, native workers increased their labor militancy: new labor organizations appeared between 1850 and 1854, and more than four hundred strikes took place in 1853 and 1854 (Commons et al. 1918; Fogel 1989). Second, support for nativist policies increased. A fringe philosophy previously now moved to center stage. The Order of the Star-Spangled Banner (popularly known as the "Know Nothings") capitalized on anti-immigrant, pro-temperance, and antislavery sentiment ignored by the two major political parties. By doing so, it grew from a few dozen members in 1852 to a national political organization boasting one million followers in just two years. The party "elected eight governors, more than one hundred congressmen, the mayors of Boston, Philadelphia, and Chicago, and thousands of other local officials" (Abinder 1992, ix). The Know Nothings claimed that immigration was impoverishing native-born labor:

> The effect of this immense influx of the laboring . . . immigrants, will inevitably depreciate the value of American labor. The price of labor depends upon the demand and supply, and it is indisputably true that for the last few years the supply has increased in a greater ratio than the demand, and consequently the value has been diminished, and . . . many, even among the native, who earn their livelihood by "the sweat of their brow," have been compelled to toil for barely sufficient to supply the actual necessaries of life. (Busey 1856, 78–79)

An analysis of data on immigrant flows and their effect on outcomes for natives reveals that the threat to the native-born was most acute among craftsmen in the urban Northeast. Surprisingly, among those who left in response to immigrants' arrival, that threat came not from similarly skilled British or German immigrants, but from largely unskilled Irish immigrants. Among those native-born craftsmen who remained in Northeastern cities, the British and Germans were a greater problem (Ferrie 1999).

THE SECOND GREAT WAVE, 1890–1924

Immigration to the United States changed dramatically in three ways by the end of the nineteenth century. The first change was in the origin countries represented by the new arrivals: as modernization in farming and manufacturing spread south and east across Europe, migration came for the first time from eastern Germany, Russia, Poland, and the Hapsburg Empire in the northeast of the continent and from Italy and Greece in the south (see fig. 4.2). The second change was the result of the significant fall in the cost of trans-Atlantic travel, as steamships custom-built for transporting migrants replaced cargo vessels under sail as migrants' principal mode of transportation. This made it easier both for migrants to travel in response to short-run disparities between economic conditions in the United States and in their home countries, and for migrants to plan to stay only a few years in the United States before returning home. Finally, this era of immigration witnessed a more widespread anti-immigration movement than either the era of settler migration or the first great wave of migration from the 1840s through the 1870s. The United States that immigrants entered in the second great wave differed in important ways from the one entered by immigrants who preceded them. By the end of the nineteenth century, the economy was increasingly urban (though it was not until 1920 that more than half of the population lived in places with 2,500 or more inhabitants), more industrial than agricultural, and populated by both the native-born and a large stock of immigrants from the old sending countries (Britain, Ireland, Germany, and Scandinavia) and their children. This was the setting within which the new wave of migrants, primarily from rural backgrounds, contemplated the journey to America.

What were the factors they weighed as they decided if and when to migrate? As in the first wave of migration, potential immigrants in the late nineteenth and early twentieth centuries were faced with wrenching structural change at home: modernization and consolidation in agriculture that squeezed small landholders and the rise of modern manufacturing that squeezed artisans. These developments loosened the bonds between potential immigrants and their home countries. Data on conditions in both origin countries and in the United States now allow us to say more about shorter-run forces that shaped migrants' decisions.

The countries that sent the largest fractions of their population to the United States in the second wave shared several characteristics. Population grew as birth rates rose and death rates fell. The growth, in turn, led to tighter labor markets two decades after each birth cohort's appearance as its members reached adulthood (what migration scholars have traditionally termed "push" factors), and gaps between per capita incomes at home and in the United States ("pull factors"). These developments in turn led to a distinctive "life cycle" in each country's immigration: countries only began sending immigrants after their economies achieved a threshold level (below which agricultural and industrial modernization had not yet occurred and poverty was a direct barrier to immigration). Then, as modernization arrived, migration rates rose dramatically. Finally, as they passed into a more mature phase of growth, their migration rates stabilized or even declined (Hatton and Williamson 1998).

The impact of the second wave of immigration on the native-born was a subject of intense debate in the first two decades of the twentieth century. Fears that the new immigrants were undermining wages and overwhelming the country's cities as they crowded into slums and ghettos, though voiced faintly in the 1850s, were by 1910 driving a national debate over whether too many immigrants were being admitted. The evidence reveals that, unlike the 1850s, the 1890s through the 1910s was indeed a period when negative effects from immigration could be seen in wages and urban living conditions (Goldin 1994; Hatton and Williamson 1998). Though immigration provided a net benefit to the United States economy, and an even larger net benefit after 1880 than before, that benefit was spread unequally across regions, industries, and classes (Neal and Uselding 1972). By the end of the 1910s, the balance of power in Congress had shifted away from the places deriving the largest net benefit, and the United States for the first time imposed across-the-board restrictions on immigration. These restrictions came in the form of a literacy test initially, and then in the 1920s in the form of a system of quotas based on each sending country's share in late nineteenth-century migration to the United States.

Something in the "absorptive capacity" of the US economy had changed between the first and second great immigration waves. Part of this change may be a result of the changing mix of source countries. The second wave brought migrants from vastly different backgrounds than had the first. These new arrivals were seen as not just different from prior arrivals, but also inferior to them: less intelligent, less assimilable, and less likely to move from the slums where they gathered. Compared to prior, primarily Protestant immigrants from northwestern Europe, the new arrivals from its south and east were more often Catholic, Orthodox, and Jewish. At the same time, many of these new arrivals were planning only a short sojourn in the United States—spending two or three years working for higher wages than they could earn at home, and then returning the places they had left with the resources to improve the circumstances of their families *in their home countries.*

This ability to come and go for short periods (sometimes for multiple short stays) was the result of the dramatic fall in passage fares. But that ability to come and go so easily may have been part of what generated the backlash that closed off immigration from the 1920s until the 1960s. Immigrants (primarily male) who were planning to return to their home countries behaved differently from those who came to the United States permanently. They eagerly took low-paying jobs with poor working conditions, as they were still earning more than if they had not migrated, and they had to endure those conditions for only a short time. They lived in overcrowded tenements in the poorest neighborhoods of the nation's largest cities, as they were intent on maximizing the savings they could bring back to Europe. They were reluctant to marry outside their ethnic groups or make many other US-specific investments (such as becoming polit-ically engaged or joining organized labor or civic organizations), because the returns to such investments were small over the short time horizon of their stay in the United States. In short, low passage fares made planned return migration so easy that these immigrants did not assimilate, widening the social and economic gaps between them and the native-born, and made it easy for nativists to characterize them as fundamen-tally different from prior immigrants, and a danger to the American economy.

These pre-planned return migrants were probably the majority of second-wave immigrants (they would have been rare in the first wave, when fares were high and journeys were dangerous and long). The evidence for these intentions can be seen in their demographic makeup: they were more likely to be young, unmarried males, with families left behind in Europe, than migrants had been previously. The rate of return migrants to new migrants is more than 0.5 for all major sending countries between 1900 and 1920 (except for Russia during 1900–1910) (Bandiera, Rasul, and Viarengo 2013). In this period, for each new arrival, more than half as many departures occurred.

These two-way migrant flows are interesting because they show migration in the second wave as something quite different from the permanent move it represented for most first-wave migrants. But it also fundamentally changes our view of the post-migration assimilation of immigrants for whom the move to the United States was in fact a permanent move.

Assimilation has conventionally been measured by the rate at which the earnings of immigrants converge with those of the native-born as immigrants' time in the United States increases. In a single cross section of data (say, the 1920 US Census of Population), this measure conflates two effects: (1) any actual "catch-up" achieved by immigrants; and (2) change over time in the earnings immediately following arrival across successive cohorts (perhaps because of change in the average skill level among successive arrival cohorts). For example, suppose Italian immigrants who arrived in 1900 made $500 at arrival and their earnings rose to $1,000 by 1920, but that the Italians who arrived in 1920 earned only $250 at arrival. The rate of earnings increase as time in the United States increases, measured with data only for 1920, will be ($1,000 – $200)/(20 – 0) = $40 per year since arrival. But we know that the 1900 arrivals increased their earnings by $500 over twenty years, or only $25 per year. The poor performance at arrival by the most re-cent arrivals makes the performance of the 1900 arrivals look better than it was. Early calculations of immigrant assimilation therefore overstated (understated) catch-up to native-born earnings if average immigrant earnings at arrival ("quality") declined (increased) over time. These duration and cohort effects can be successfully distin-guished if data from two or more cross sections can be analyzed together (Borjas 1995).

But the estimates of return migration described in the preceding make measuring assimilation even more complicated. Suppose return migration is not random, but is instead selective in terms of immigrant quality. Specifically, suppose that as time since arrival increases, the lowest-ability immigrants are most likely to return to their home countries. Under these circumstances, it is possible that there is no "catch-up" by immigrants who remain in the United States. Instead, their average quality increases with time since arrival as the lowest-quality migrants depart. Such patterns can be detected only by following the same immigrants over time.

Such an exercise reveals that for the 1900–1920 period, immigrants display no catch-up at all. Though some arrive with skills that result in earnings at arrival greater than the native-born, while some arrive with skills that result in earnings at arrival less than the native-born, immigrant earnings do not change in this period as time since arrival increases. The previously observed assimilation in earnings was driven entirely by a combination of declining average immigrant quality and selective return migration by the least successful immigrants. Any (dis)advantage relative to natives for immigrants from a particular origin persists into the second generation (Abramitzky, Boustan, and Eriksson 2014).

The "Great Pause," 1925–1965

Immigration dropped precipitously with the imposition of the quota system (see fig. 4.3). Though immigration shows a post–World War I rebound, even following the imposition of the literacy test in 1917, the quotas effectively ended the period of mass migration for good. The "old" sending countries (Britain, Ireland, Germany) continued to send immigrants, and the quota system was never binding on them, as the quotas were set according to each origin's share in the 1890 US population, which followed the period of greatest movement from these countries. But the "new" sending countries had, by definition, sent few immigrants to the United States by 1890, so their allocation of places for new arrivals under the quota system were in fact binding. The steady increase in immigration from 1943 to 1965 was

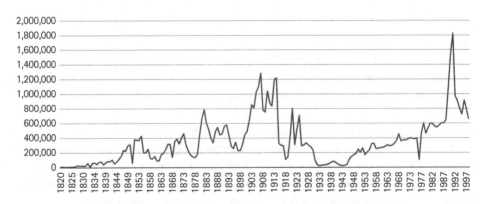

FIGURE 4.3.   Total immigrants into the United States, 1820–1997

Source: Carter et al. (2006, Table Ad1–2). http://dx.doi.org/10.1017/ISBN-9780511132971. Ad1-8910.1017/ISBN-9780511132971.Ad1-89.

driven primarily by arrivals from Latin America (especially Mexico), which were not capped under the quota system. It was during this "Great Pause" that migration by blacks from the South to the North increased sharply, as a response to the absence of a supply of unskilled and semiskilled Eastern and Southern Europeans in Northern US cities that continued to demand unskilled and semiskilled workers (Collins 1997).

POST-1965

Restrictions on immigration imposed by the United States in 1921 remained in place until 1965. Between 1920 and 1970, the share of the US population born outside the United States fell from 13.2 percent to 4.7 percent. With the passage of new legislation in 1965, immigration on a large scale resumed. The new immigration policy was designed to ease the process of family reunification. Over the forty years from 1970 to 2010, the fraction of foreign-born rose from 4.7 percent to 12.9 percent. As was the case in the nineteenth and early twentieth centuries, the source countries sending migrants to the United States changed as economic development's effects moved across the globe. By 2010, immigrants to the United States were coming primarily from Asia and Latin America. Together, these accounted for 60 percent of the US foreign-born population in 2010 (Ferrie and Hatton 2014).

Just as in the two great waves of migration that came in the years before 1921, the post-1965 immigration has had enormous consequences for both the immigrants themselves and the US economy they joined.

At arrival, post-1965 immigrants earned 10 percent less than comparable US-born workers (Chiswick 1978). But after thirteen years in the United States, they achieved earning parity with US-born workers, and after twenty years they exceeded them by 6 percent. Declining average immigrant quality slightly inflates these figures above the true rate of assimilation, but does not eliminate it (Borjas 1995). Much of this decline in quality has been the result of declining levels of education among more recent cohorts (Ferrie and Hatton 2014).

How immigrants affect the labor market prospects of US-born workers has been a topic of considerable debate since the 1980s. Some studies at the national level find that 1980–2000 immigration reduced earnings by 3 percent on average, but by nearly three times as much among those with less than a high school education (Borjas 2003). Other studies of local labor markets find essentially no effect, even among the least educated US-born workers (Card 1990).

As was the case in the years just before 1921, when the quota system was imposed, in the post-1965 period anti-immigration views have gained considerable traction. These post-1965 views, however, were initially driven by a phenomenon that, by definition, did not exist in the pre-1921 period—illegal immigration. By 2014, there were 11.3 million unauthorized immigrants present in the United States, just under half from Mexico. The adults in this population comprise just 5.1 percent of the total US labor force, but they are the majority of the workers in several industries (farm labor, food preparation, landscaping, and construction). The post-1965 anti-immigrant sentiment has been given additional impetus by the (largely mistaken) impression that today's immigrants are less likely to assimilate than immigrants from as recently as the 1970s and 1980s and by the uneven distribution of the costs and benefits of immigration (with the costs borne in states such as California, Florida, and Texas in education, social services, and health care, and many of the benefits, such as lower food prices, spread across the country).

By the early twenty-first century, attitudes toward immigration had evolved to the point that not just undocumented immigrants, but all immigrants, were seen by many as an increasing burden on the United States and that a "pause" in even normal, authorized immigration should be imposed. These attitudes ignore the important benefits that immigration continues to provide: new arrivals, especially those in skilled occupations, represent a substantial human capital transfer to the United States. Employers in health care, high tech, and agriculture rely on immigrants as a crucial supply of workers and actively lobby Congress for fewer restrictions on immigration. Immigrants also provide badly needed additions to the labor force at a time when the US population's "dependency ratio" (the number of children and elderly per worker) has risen as the population has aged, and they provide a disproportionate share of the nation's entrepreneurs and innovators (Fairlie and Meyer 1996). A comprehensive reform of the US immigration system should recognize these generalized benefits, but also identify and compensate those workers and regions that bear a disproportionate share of the costs of immigration.

Future Research

The study of immigration to the United States has been revolutionized by the recent availability of data on immigrants in their source countries that can then be linked to data on them after their arrival in the United States. For example, Abramitzky, Boustan, and Eriksson (2012) have followed thousands of Norwegian immigrants from their appearance in the Norwegian census until their later appearance in either a subsequent Norwegian census or the US census. With this information, they can assess the extent of immigrant self-selection (e.g., were migrants of higher or lower quality than the nonmigrants they left behind?). As more data become available in Europe, more work on this issue can be done.

New sources available for the United States (e.g., complete transcriptions of the censuses of population from 1850 to 1940) now make it possible to study immigrant enclaves down to the level of individual city blocks. This makes it possible to assess the impact of residence within these enclaves, how that impact differed by ethnicity, and how migrants selectively moved out of them as their time in the United States increased.

The issue of return migration to Europe, both in terms of its selectivity and its impact on the return migrants themselves and the friends and family they rejoined in Europe, can now be studied using the same sources described earlier that allow migrants traveling to the United States to be examined.

Immigrants' impact on the US labor market must contend with the possibility that the impact in a particular location is masked by the outmigration or decreased immigration of natives. The ability to follow native migrants and determine how they respond to the arrival of new immigrants allows us to account for this possibility.

BIBLIOGRAPHY

Abinder, T. (1992). *Nativism and Slavery: The Northern Know Nothings and the Politics of the 1850s*. New York: Oxford University Press.

Abramitzky, R., L. P. Boustan, and K. Eriksson. (2012). "Europe's Tired, Poor, Huddled Masses: Self-Selection and Economic Outcomes in the Age of Mass Migration." *American Economic Review* 102(5): 1832.

Abramitzky, Ran, Leah Platt Boustan, and Katherine Eriksson. (2014). "A Nation of Immigrants: Assimilation and Economic Outcomes in the Age of Mass Migration." *Journal of Political Economy* 122(3): 467–506.

Bandiera, Oriana, Imran Rasul, and Martina Viarengo. (2013). "The Making of Modern America: Migratory Flows in the Age of Mass Migration." *Journal of Development Economics* 102: 23–47.

Borjas, G. J. (1995). "Assimilation and Changes in Cohort Quality Revisited: What Happened to Immigrant Earnings in the 1980s?" *Journal of Labor Economics* 13: 201–245.

Borjas, G. J. (2003). "The Labor Demand Curve Is Downward Sloping: Reexamining the Impact of Immigration on the Labor Market." *Quarterly Journal of Economics* 118: 1335–1374.

Busey, S. S. (1856). *Immigration: Its Evils and Consequences*. New York: DeWitt and Davenport.

Card, David. (1990). "The Impact of the Mariel Boatlift on the Miami Labor Market." *Industrial & Labor Relations Review* 43(2): 245–257.

Carter, Susan B., Scott S. Gartner, Michael R. Haines, Alan L. Olmstead, Richard Sutch, and Gavin Wright. (2006). *Historical Statistics of the United States: Earliest Times to the Present: Millennial Edition*, 5 volumes. New York: Cambridge University Press.

Chiswick, B. R. (1978). "The Effect of Americanization on the Earnings of Foreign-Born Men." *Journal of Political Economy* 86: 897–921.

Collins, William J. (1997). "When the Tide Turned: Immigration and the Delay of the Great Black Migration." *Journal of Economic History* 57(3): 607–632.

Commons, J. R., D. J. Saposs, H. L. Sumner, E. B. Mittelman, H. E. Hoagland, J. B. Andrews, and S. G. Perlman. (1918). *History of Labour in the United States*, Vol. I. New York: Macmillan.

Driver, Harold E. (2011). *Indians of North America*. Chicago: University of Chicago Press.

Easterlin, Richard A. (1961). "Influences in European Overseas Emigration before World War I." *Economic Development and Cultural Change* 9(3): 331–351.

Ernst, R. (1949). *Immigrant Life in New York City, 1825–1863*. New York: King's Crown Press.

Fairlie, Robert W., and Bruce D. Meyer. (1996). "Ethnic and Racial Self-employment Differences and Possible Explanations." *Journal of Human Resources* 31(4): 757–793.

Ferrie, Joseph P. (1994). "The Wealth Accumulation of Antebellum European Immigrants to the US, 1840–60." *Journal of Economic History* 54(1): 1–33.

Ferrie, Joseph P. (1995). "The Geographic Mobility of Antebellum European Immigrants to the United States After Their Arrival at New York: 1840–1860." *Research in Economic History* 15: 99–148.

Ferrie, Joseph P. (1997). "The Entry into the US Labor Market of Antebellum European Immigrants, 1840–1860." *Explorations in Economic History* 34(3): 295–330.

Ferrie, Joseph P. (1999). *Yankeys Now: Immigrants in the Antebellum US 1840–1860*. Oxford: Oxford University Press.

Ferrie, Joseph P., and Timothy J. Hatton. (2014). "Two Centuries of International Migration." In *Handbook of the Economics of International Migration*, edited by Barry Chiswick and Paul Miller, 53–88. Amsterdam: Elsevier.

Fogel, R. W. (1989). *Without Consent or Contract: The Rise and Fall of American Slavery*. New York: Norton.

Fogleman, Aaron. (1992). "Migrations to the Thirteen British North American Colonies, 1700–1775: New Estimates." *Journal of Interdisciplinary History* 22(4): 691–709.

Galenson, David W. (1978). "'Middling People' or 'Common Sort'? The Social Origins of Some Early Americans Reexamined." *William and Mary Quarterly: A Magazine of Early American History* 35(3): 499–524.

Galenson, David W. (1981a). "The Market Evaluation of Human Capital: The Case of Indentured Servitude." *Journal of Political Economy* 89(3): 446–467.

Galenson, David W. (1981b). *White Servitude in Colonial America: An Economic Analysis*. Cambridge: Cambridge University Press.

Goldin, Claudia. (1994). "The Political Economy of Immigration Restriction in the United States, 1890 to 1921." In *The Regulated Economy: A Historical Approach to Political Economy*, edited by Claudia Goldin and Gary Libecap, 223–258. Chicago: University of Chicago Press.

Handlin, Oscar. (1991). *Boston's Immigrants, 1790–1880: A Study in Acculturation*. Cambridge, MA: Harvard University Press.

Hatton, T. J., and J. G. Williamson. (1998). *The Age of Mass Migration: Causes and Economic Impact*. New York: Oxford University Press.

Hoagland, H. E. (1913). "The Rise of the Iron Molders' International Union." *American Economic Review* III(1): 296–313.

Lane, A. T. (1987). *Solidarity or Survival? American Labor and European Immigrants, 1830–1924*. New York: Greenwood Press.

Lazonick, W., and T. Brush. (1985). "The 'Horndahl Effect' in Early United States Manufacturing." *Explorations in Economic History* XXII(1): 53–96.

Menard, Russell R. (1973). "From Servant to Freeholder: Status Mobility and Property Accumulation in Seventeenth-Century Maryland." *William and Mary Quarterly: A Magazine of Early American History* 30(1): 37–64.

Neal, Larry, and Paul Uselding. (1972). "Immigration: A Neglected Source of American Economic Growth: 1790 to 1912." *Oxford Economic Papers* 24(1): 68–88.

Ross, S. J. (1985). *Workers on the Edge: Work, Leisure, and Politics in Industrializing Cincinnati, 1788–1840*. New York: Columbia University Press.

Smith, Abbott Emerson. (1947). *Colonists in Bondage: White Servitude and Convict Labor in America, 1607–1776*. Chapel Hill: University of North Carolina Press.

Soltow, Lee. (1975). *Men and Wealth in the United States, 1850–1870*. New Haven, CT: Yale University Press.

....

CHAPTER 5

ANTHROPOMETRIC HISTORY
IN AMERICAN ECONOMIC
HISTORY

....

RICHARD H. STECKEL

ATTEMPTS to define and estimate the income of nations originated in England three centuries ago and eventually led to the system of national income accounts that gathered steam in the 1930s and became ubiquitous by the 1960s (Studenski 1958). Although economists recognize the great achievements of the accounts, research momentum has shifted to alternatives or supplements that address shortcomings in gross domestic product (GDP) as a welfare measure, or that indicate living standards in time periods or among groups for which conventional measures cannot be calculated. Height is an example now used extensively in the fields of economic history and economic development. Major applications in US history to be discussed in this chapter include long-term trends; the health of slaves; the health of Native Americans; and the study of inequality.

Many studies show that measures of health are positively correlated with income or wealth. Less well known are the relationship between height and conventional measures such as per capita income, and the ways that stature addresses certain conceptual inadequacies in GNP as a welfare measure. Height adeptly measures inequality in the form of nutritional deprivation; average height in the past century is sensitive not only to the level of income, but also to the distribution of income and the consumption of basic necessities by the poor. Unlike conventional measures of living, standards based on output, stature is a measure of consumption that incorporates or adjusts for individual nutritional needs over the course of childhood; it is a net measure that captures not only the supply of inputs to health but demands on those inputs. Moreover, heights are available in settings, such as eighteenth-century America, where income data are lacking (or of low quality) and for groups, such as slaves, for which income or wage concepts do not apply. Because growth occurs largely in childhood, stature also provides valuable insights into resource allocation within the family, an interesting phenomenon obscured from household-level data on income or earnings, much less aggregate statistics on output or inequality.

Although human biologists and physical anthropologists have known for some time that socioeconomic factors such as social class impinge on child growth and therefore adult height, a richer understanding of the relationship began to emerge when economists, historians, and other social scientists joined the conversation in the 1970s (Steckel 1998). The process began with the study of slave heights drawn from shipping manifests used in the coastwise trade (Trussell and Steckel 1978). Height-by-age profiles for girls showed that the peak of the adolescent growth spurt occurred around age 13.3 years, indicating that menarche occurred around age 15 on average and that these girls could have had children by age 16 to 16.5 years. Yet the average age at first birth was around 19.5 years, establishing that a period of abstinence was common.

Economic historians introduced new sources of data, added several useful concepts, and discovered numerous puzzles or apparent anomalies in the past that elucidated the contribution of socioeconomic factors to growth. Because the historical record encompasses a rich variety of human experiences, their efforts helped to illuminate intergenerational influences on body size, to measure the human capacity for growth following extreme deprivation, and to expand the knowledge of cultural conditions that are ultimately expressed through proximate influences on growth.

Some thirty-five years ago, economic historians formulated the concept of net nutrition (similar in meaning to nutritional status as used by nutritionists), which can be explained metaphorically by viewing the human body as a biological machine. Our machine operates on food as fuel (composed of protein, fat, micronutrients, and so forth), which it expends at idle times (resting in bed), while fighting infection, engaging in physical activity, and replacing worn-out cells (see Steckel 1995; Tanner 1978, 1981). Diseases may stunt growth by diverting nutritional intake to mobilize the immune system to combat infection, or by causing incomplete absorption of food that is eaten. Similarly, arduous physical activity or work places a substantial claim on the diet, which makes it possible to lose weight or even starve on 4,000 calories per day. For these reasons, average height reflects a population's history of net nutrition; growth of children occurs only if enough fuel is available after other expenditures needed for survival have been met. If better times follow a period of deprivation, growth may exceed that ordinarily found under good conditions. Catch-up (or compensatory) growth is an adaptive biological mechanism that complicates the study of child health using adult height because it can partially or completely erase the effects of deprivation. Between birth and maturity, a person may undergo several episodes of deprivation and recovery, thereby obscuring important fluctuations in the quality of life. Chronically poor net nutrition inevitably results in slow growth and stunting, which the National Center for Health Statistics formally defines as falling below the fifth percentile of modern height standards.

Readers unfamiliar with the methodology of anthropometric history should not be sidetracked by genetic issues. Genes are important determinants of individual heights, but genetic differences approximately cancel in comparisons of averages across most populations, and in these situations heights accurately reflects health status (Malcolm 1974).

EVIDENCE

Height data are available from numerous sources, as shown in figure 5.1. Military records are the most abundant source but hundreds of thousands of measurements are found in other locations. The superabundance of records, along with the fact that measurements are strewn over the past two and a half centuries, creates a valuable resource for the study of biological aspects of living standards.

Continuing with figure 5.1, one can see that stature has functional implications in the form of longevity (mortality), in that nutritionally stunted individuals tend to die younger (Fogel 2004). The precise biological reasons for this are unclear, but the empirical pattern is well established: in a relationship known as a Waaler curve (after the Norwegian scientists who assembled data on height and survival), an adult man's probability of death accelerates slowly for average adult male heights below 5'7" and rapidly below 5'3." Scientists speculate that major organ systems, such as the kidneys and cardiovascular system, are compromised if growth is stunted in utero. This process might also explain the relationship of height to morbidity and physical labor productivity.

In recent years, knowledge of the adverse cognitive effects of early childhood deprivation has diffused through the social sciences (Behrman et al. 2014). Children who suffered net nutritional insults in utero and/or in the first two years of life, a period when the brain matures, suffer cognitive deficits that are permanent. Therefore early life conditions may cast a long shadow on human opportunities, which may impact occupational choice, income, and societal inequality.

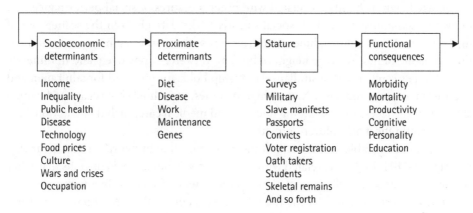

FIGURE 5.1. A flow diagram showing sources, determinants, and consequences of height
Source: Adapted from Steckel (1995, 1908).

Persico, Postlewaite, and Silverman (2004) suggested that boys who were taller in adolescence gain confidence, social skills, and related forms of human capital that serve them well in adult labor markets. The most recent strand of this research argues that taller people earn more because they have greater cognitive ability. Case and Paxson (2008) have challenged the Persico et al. mechanism linking height to higher wages, showing that people who were tall as adolescents were also tall and did well on cognitive tests in early childhood, before schooling could have selectively boosted their human capital. The benefits of robust physical growth in childhood extend into adulthood as reflected in better cognitive function, improved mental health, and ability to perform activities of daily living. This finding has several implications, including an explanation for why economic returns to height continue to be observed in wealthy countries. It also demonstrates the long reach into adulthood of early childhood conditions, suggesting that societies probably underinvest in prenatal and early childhood health and nutrition.

A 2015 paper by Schick and Steckel reconciles the competing views by recognizing that net nutrition, a major determinant of adult height, fosters both cognitive and noncognitive abilities. Using data from Britain's National Childhood Development Study (NCDS), they show that taller children have higher average cognitive and noncognitive test scores and that each aptitude accounts for a substantial and roughly equal portion of the height-earnings premium. Together, cognitive and noncognitive abilities explain the height premium.

If confirmed by other studies, the mechanisms outlined by Case and Paxson (2008) and by Schick and Steckel (2015) will have considerable influence on economic history, economic development, and our understanding of the sources of economic growth. It will bring nutritional status and height to the fore in comprehending rates of return to schooling, socioeconomic inequality that stems from cognitive deficits, and conceivably, rates of technological change. One could imagine dissertations on whether nutritional improvements helped trigger the Enlightenment, or whether increases in agricultural productivity, which preceded or accompanied industrialization in many countries, also contributed to economic growth via more effective decision-making.

Average height is highly correlated with other measures of social performance well known to economists and other social scientists. The data given in the scatter plot of figure 5.2 are drawn from eighteen countries across the world that have conducted national height studies. Average height of boys aged twelve is positively and nonlinearly related to per capita GDP (a similar relationship holds for girls and for adult men and adult women). In countries with very high incomes, most households can readily purchase all basic necessities, including housing and medical care, such that additional income has little effect on children's growth.

There is considerable scatter around the regression line in figure 5.2. It is clear that per capita GDP is highly correlated with average height, but it is also obvious that other conditions matter as well. One of these is the extent of income inequality within a country. To illustrate, consider the thought experiment of taking $1,000 per year from the richest family in a country and giving it to the poorest. Average height should increase. Why? The children of the rich are so well off that all their basic necessities

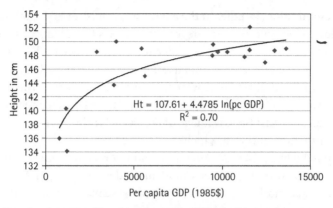

FIGURE 5.2. Per capita GDP and height at age twelve (boys)

Sources: Compiled from data in Eveleth and Tanner (1976, Appendix Tables 1, 25, 40, 57); Eveleth and Tanner (1990, Appendix Tables 1, 21, 33, 44, 56, 65); the Penn World Tables: http://pwt.econ.upenn.edu/php_site/pwt_index.php.

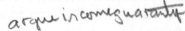

important for health and physical growth will still be met. Yet the poorest family is so impoverished (even in rich countries) that they will spend some and perhaps most of their additional income on food, clothing, shelter, medical care, and the like. Their children will therefore grow more than they would have otherwise.

Statistical analysis requires an empirical measure of inequality, which economists often quantify by a Gini coefficient that by definition has a range of 0 (perfect equality) to 1 (perfect inequality). Data for calculating a Gini are usually obtained from surveys, tax records, and so forth, and the process begins by ranking households from poorest to richest. Of course, neither extreme exists in reality; studies generally report values of 0.3 at the low end and 0.6 at the high end for inequality at the household level. Conspicuous among the former are rich European countries under governments of democratic socialism, and at the other end are developing countries with nontransparent governments having command over some valuable natural resources whose rewards are highly concentrated among a few families.

With this motivation, Steckel (1995) expanded the regression model to include other variables that affect stature, adding a Gini coefficient of household income to the regression of height on per capita GDP (see table 5.1). The coefficient of –14.34 displayed in the first column indicates that increasing the Gini coefficient from 0 to 1.0 would lower estimated average stature by 14.34 centimeters, or roughly 5.6 inches.

Values of the Gini close to 0 or to 1.0 do not exist; but a change from the lowest to the highest extreme (0.3 to 0.6) would reduce average stature by the change in the Gini coefficient (0.3) times the coefficient, or 0.3 x 14.34 = 4.3 centimeters, which is approximately 1.7 inches. Holding other variables constant, this is an effect equivalent to increasing per capita GDP from about $3 to $8 per day (annual GDP per capita from 1,095 to 2,920). Therefore inequality can have a powerful impact on stature and biological well-being.

Unfortunately for our analysis, numerous useful height studies are limited to specific groups such as students, the military, the rich, urban residents, and so forth. Is it possible to include these additional studies in the analysis? The answer is yes, by adding explanatory variables, called "dummy" or categorical variables that identify or control for the subgroup. These are listed in table 5.1 under the Gini coefficient. For example, urban residents were on average 0.81 centimeters taller than individuals found in national height studies, while rural residents were 1.35 centimeters shorter. The poor were particularly disadvantaged (coefficient of −6.29), while the rich were much better off (coefficient of 4.42). Note that the advantage of the rich over the poor is 6.29 + 4.42 = 10.71 centimeters, or slightly more than 4 inches.

A large gap in height existed between rich and poor adolescents, but few systematic differences existed across other groups. Students and military populations were slightly taller (but not statistically significant) and no systematic (statistically significant) difference in height existed between urban and rural populations. After controlling for income and the Gini, no systematic height differences existed across groups, with the exception of adolescents from Asian and Indo-Mediterranean countries. These results suggest that a large share of height differences across countries can be explained by environmental conditions correlated with income and inequality.

Long-Term Trends

Figure 5.3 reveals four distinctive periods of the American anthropometric experience: (1) The colonial period through the early 1800s, during which Americans were tall relative to Europeans; (2) American heights declined by 3–4 centimeters for half a century for cohorts born after 1830, a phenomenon whose initial phase is known as the "antebellum puzzle" because this trend contrasts with a period of industrialization and substantial economic growth; (3) American heights surged for births from 1880 to 1950; and (4) heights leveled off near the end of the twentieth century. Precise explanations are unavailable for these patterns but economic historians have constructed some plausible answers. Selectivity associated with volunteers as opposed to conscripts may have intruded into the data, confounding explanations. This point is particularly difficult to address, but comparisons with other sources do provide some comfort.

(1) A tall population: During the eighteenth century, heights of European men ranged from approximately 163 centimeters in France to 167 centimeters in Sweden, or roughly 5–7 centimeters below Americans (Koepke and Baten 2005). Why were Americans so tall? What were the sources of their net nutritional advantage? It seems clear that diet was one factor: good land was abundant and cheap, and this resource supported herds of horses and mules, which were used as draft animals to produce food. The land also supported other livestock such as cattle (used for draft power, milk, and meat), sheep, poultry, and goats. To this were added products familiar to European agriculture (small grains, fruits and vegetables, in addition to maize and potatoes from the Western Hemisphere. In other words, the diet was diverse and famines were unknown in colonial North America.

Table 5.1 Explaining Average Height by per Capita Income, Gini Coefficient, Place of Residence, Gender, Ethnic Group, and Age

Variable	Adolescents			Adults		
	Coeff.	t-Value	Sample Mean	Coeff.	t-Value	Sample Mean
Intercept	100.56	24.24		151.14	12.26	
Log Per Capita GDP	4.90	11.99	8.04	3.97	2.75	7.67
Gini Coefficient	−14.34	−2.84	0.41	−32.60	−4.00	0.43
Urban	0.81	1.16	0.21	−0.44	−0.31	0.13
Rural	−1.35	−1.95	0.11	−2.82	−1.49	0.03
Poor	−6.29	−5.17	0.05			
Rich	4.42	6.37	0.10			
Student				1.22	1.23	0.13
Military				2.02	1.56	0.13
Female	0.89	2.44	0.49	−11.41	−16.51	0.47
European Ancestry	−2.26	−2.32	0.29	−1.26	−0.70	0.09
African	2.83	1.89	0.05			
African Ancestry	−2.14	−1.69	0.05	−1.36	−0.74	0.13
Asian	−4.46	−4.39	0.25	−2.09	−0.98	−0.98
Indo-Mediterranean	2.51	2.04	0.25	4.09	1.25	1.25
Age 11	5.37	9.64	0.21			
Age 12	11.14	19.99	0.21			
Age 13	16.80	29.47	0.19			
Age 14	21.62	36.96	0.18			
R2	0.93				0.96	
Sample size	191					
Method		OLS				2SLS

Source: Steckel (1995, Table 3).
Notes: Definition of variables: Dependent variable = average height in centimeters. Income is measured in 1985 US dollars at international prices for the year that the height study was published. The mean of the dependent variable is 144.05 centimeters for adolescents and 163.69 centimeters for adults. The Gini coefficients are for households.

The omitted class refers to a national height study of Europeans. Age 10 is an excluded variable in the regression on adolescent height. Observations on "poor" and "rich" groups do not exist for the adults.

The countries represented for adolescents are Argentina, Australia, Egypt, France, Hong Kong, India, Japan, Republic of Korea, Malaysia, New Zealand, Spain, Sudan, Taiwan, Turkey, United States, Uruguay, and Yugoslavia. The countries represented for adults are Egypt, France, Hong Kong, India, Republic of Korea, New Zealand, Taiwan, Thailand, Turkey, United Kingdom, and the United States. Several countries have more than one height study.

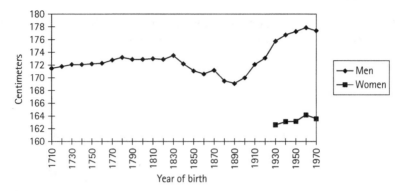

FIGURE 5.3. Height of native-born American men and women, by year of birth
Source: Steckel (2006, 2–502).

According to probate records studied by Alice Hanson Jones, the distribution of wealth was extraordinarily equal in colonial America, and other studies show that inequality dramatically increased into the twentieth century (Jones 1980; Steckel and Moehling 2001). The richest 1 percent of men in 1775 owned only 12.1 percent of the wealth compared with 29.0 percent in 1860 and 51 percent in 1929 (Saez and Zucman 2014; Soltow 1975). Even the poor had access to cheap land and could support themselves by working in agriculture. As a consequence, food was cheap relative to average incomes.

Low population density in colonial America impeded the transmission of communicable diseases. In 1800 a far larger share of population in Europe lived in cities and large towns (e.g., 19.2 percent in England and 12.2 percent in France) whereas 5.3 percent of Americans lived in places of 5,000 people or more (Barioch and Goetz 1986, Table 3). There were occasional epidemics of smallpox, which were devastating to Native Americans, and an epidemic of yellow fever occurred in Philadelphia in 1793, killing about 5,000 people in a city of 50,000, but epidemics of cholera did not occur until the 1830s (Patterson 1992). On the other hand, epidemics of smallpox were widespread in Europe, and the disease is estimated to have killed about 400,000 individuals per year in the eighteenth century (Koplow 2003).

(2) The antebellum puzzle: Initially, anthropometric historians skeptically viewed evidence of a nineteenth-century decline in heights since it clashed with well-established views on the economic prosperity of the era (Haines, Craig, and Weiss 2003; Komlos 1996). Steckel and Haurin (1982) discovered the mid-nineteenth-century downturn among the Ohio National Guard in 1981, but delayed publication until confirmation of a downturn in health was available and some reasonable explanations could be provided. Corroborating evidence was obtained from various sources, including height, weights, and mortality rates. West Point cadets lost approximately 1.4 centimeters in height between the cohorts of the 1820s and those of the 1860s, then recovered in the 1870s, a pattern of change that existed across regions and occupational groups (Komlos 1987). Their loss in height was less than that experienced by regular troops, possibly because

the cadets were raised in a higher socioeconomic stratum. A sample of heights taken from post–Civil War regular army troops further corroborates the decline its stature and its recovery in the last three decades of the nineteenth century (Craig, forthcoming).

Life expectancy at age ten followed a pattern similar to that of heights. After rising for most of the eighteenth century, life expectancy began to decline during the 1790s and continued to do so for the first half of the nineteenth century (Fogel 1986). Mortality rates for native-born adults calculated from genealogies also identify a loss in health during the first half of the nineteenth century. Life expectancy for men at age 20 declined from approximately 47 years at the beginning of the century to slightly less than 41 years in the 1850s. Among women the decline was steeper: from nearly 48 years in 1800–1809 to 37.1 years in the 1840s. Recovery to levels of the early 1800s was not attained until the end of the century (Pope 1992).

Not everyone agrees that the Antebellum Puzzle is genuine. Bodenhorn, Guinnane, and Mroz (2017) argue that sample selectivity, driven by improving labor market conditions associated with industrialization could have tempted taller individuals to forego the army, and instead work in the private sector. Others, however, find flaws in their statistical analysis and note among other things that civilian wages declined relative to military pay during the war (Komlos and A'Hearn 2017; Zimran 2017).

Evidence for the South suggests that the cycle in heights may have been a national phenomenon. Among slaves, the heights of children born after approximately 1830 declined by 2.5 to 7.5 centimeters in the two decades following (Steckel 1979b). The heights of slave women measured as adults declined by more than 1 centimeter over two decades for those born after 1810. In contrast, the heights of adult men rose by more than 1 centimeter over the same time period. Consistent with the trend for women and children, the infant mortality rate calculated from plantation records approximately doubled during the early 1800s, reached a peak in the 1830s, and then declined to its former level in the late 1850s. Data on the heights of Southern white men who signed amnesty oaths in the 1860s suggest that the loss in height extended beyond slaves. The average height of these men born before 1820 was approximately 1 centimeter above those born in the 1820s (Margo and Steckel 1992).

Economic historians have put forth several possible explanations for the height decline after 1830, including urbanization. Between 1830 and 1880, the share of the American population living in urban areas increased by 19.6 percentage points, and if urban men were 1.5 inches shorter than rural men, this shift would explain about 20 percent of the height decline, from 1830 to 1880 (Haines 2006, Table Aa22–35). Of course, other factors also contributed to the height decline, including the rise of public schools, which spread pathogens among children that caused diphtheria, whooping cough, and scarlet fever (Steckel 1995). Higher food prices and the Civil War were also relevant. The latter disrupted food production, and the widespread deployment of troops led to conditions that encouraged diseases to flourish, and close contact led to the spread of those diseases.

Growing inequality and business cycles emerged with industrialization of the 1830s, rendering the unemployed and the poor particularly vulnerable. American industrialization began first in the Northeast, and by the middle of the century the economy achieved modern economic growth, or sustained increases in real per capita income of 1.0 to 1.5 percent or more per year (Gallman 1996). This prosperity also registers in estimates of real wages, productivity improvements in agriculture and manufacturing, and increases in the capital stock per capita (Gallman 1992; Goldin and Margo 1992; Rothenberg 1992). Regional estimates of per capita income indicate that the Northeast was relatively prosperous in the mid-1800s, yet the military data show that this region had the lowest average height (Easterlin 1961). When the mid-nineteenth-century decline in height was first discovered around 1980, economic historians were initially skeptical; many favored alternative explanations, including sample selectivity and composition effects. The accumulation of a strong web of evidence since that time has persuaded many observers that a downturn and eventual recovery in health occurred (though its magnitude and timing are debatable), and a small industry has emerged to probe its dimensions, sources, and implications.

A height decline in the second quarter of the nineteenth century is clearly visible in the huge number of conscripts measured by the Union Army during the Civil War (Gould 1869, Chapter 5, Table 6). The downturn also appears in an independent source of evidence, Ohio National Guardsmen measured after the Civil War, and the temporal pattern in the height of Union Army troops remains after controlling for place of residence, occupation, and other factors (Margo and Steckel 1983; Steckel and Haurin 1982). West Point cadets fell in height among those born after approximately 1830, and data from regular army enlistments following the Civil War indicate that the decline continued for those born in the years immediately following the Civil War (see fig. 5.2; Komlos 1987).

Although the evidence collected to date is geographically thin for the next three decades, heights of the Ohio National Guard and of Citadel cadets reached a trough for those born in the 1880s or early 1890s, and data for World War II troops arranged by year of birth show the modern secular increase in height began around the turn of the century (Coclanis and Komlos 1995; Karpinos 1958; Steckel and Haurin 1982). Skeletal evidence also identifies the recovery underway at the turn of the twentieth century and suggests that a low point in height was probably reached among those born in the 1880s (Trotter and Gleser 1951). Moreover, mortality evidence from genealogies and from plantation records indicate that life expectancy deteriorated while heights declined during the antebellum period (Pope 1992; Steckel 1979). Although genetic drift cannot be ruled out as a factor in the height patterns, modern populations show little evidence of drift in height when living conditions are approximately constant. Moreover, we know that height is sensitive to the environment, and plausible explanations linked to changing environmental conditions are considered in the following.

Explanations should recognize that traditional national income accounting measures, real wage series, and average heights focus on different aspects of living standards. The first two emphasize market behavior and various imputations for productive activity, while average height reflects net nutrition and the distribution of income or wealth. Thus, a particular type of prosperity accompanied industrialization, while other aspects of the standard of living deteriorated. *Ceteris paribus*, the measured economic prosperity of the mid-1800s should have increased average height. The height decline suggests that other things must not have been equal. Specifically, nutritional liabilities (claims on nutrition or lower nutritional intake) that more than offset the advantages bestowed by higher incomes must have accompanied the economic prosperity.

(3) Recovery: Numerous explanations can be found for the secular growth in height that occurred from the late 1800s to the mid-twentieth century. Understanding of the germ theory of disease and the rise of the public health movement in the 1880s, with accompanying investments in purified water supplies, vaccinations, and sewage disposal, were crucial for preventing contagious diseases and improving health in the cities (Melosi 2000). Higher standards of personal hygiene and improved pre- and postnatal care led to better health for children (Duffy 1992; Preston and Haines 1991). Economic growth and higher incomes enabled families to purchase better diets, housing, and medical care. The emergence of antibiotics in the 1930s improved the chances of cures for diseases, while health insurance and public health programs increased access to modern medicine by the public (Brown 2005; Murray 2007).

(4) Leveling off: The growth in heights of native-born Americans slowed in the second half of the twentieth century and eventually stopped. Why? There are no definitive answers, but we do have numerous suspects. Growing income inequality has appeared since the early 1980s such that now the Gini coefficient of income is approximately as high as that reached in 1929, the peak in US history. More relevant for interpreting height trends, however, are reports on the trend in consumption inequality, which cast doubt on the power of this explanation. Meyer and Sullivan (2012) argue that a consumption-based poverty rate declined by 26.4 percentage points between 1960 and 2010. Second, the share of foreign-born, who tend to be relatively short, in the US population has risen dramatically in recent decades. Admittedly, the heights in figure 5.4 refer to native-born, but there are second- (and even third-) generation consequences of short height. Mothers who are small tend to have babies who are short as adults. The explanations are not entirely clear, but it is thought that intergenerational nutritional history affects metabolism and organ development of the fetus, leading also to short height. Third, there has been a growing share of the population that (until very recently under Obama Care) lacks health insurance. Even with health insurance, however, some families simply do not know how to use it to the advantage of their children.

SLAVERY

The extraordinary height-by-age profile of American slaves, given in tables 5.2 and 5.3, is one of the most arresting findings of the new anthropometric history. Falling below the 0.5 percentile of modern height standards, the young slave children were among the smallest ever measured. The typical child would have been cause for alarm in a modern pediatrician's office. Yet through compensatory or catch-up growth of nearly

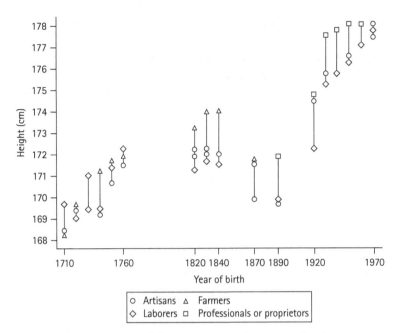

FIGURE 5.4. Mean height differentials by occupational class and birth cohort

Source: Costa and Steckel (1997, 55).

5 inches that began in adolescence, adult slaves reached approximately the 20th percentile of these standards (average of males and females). Slave adults exceeded the heights of Stuttgart aristocrats and the upper classes of Italy and fell less than one inch below Union troops who fought in the Civil War and cadets at England's Sandhurst military academy (Komlos 2007; Steckel 1986).

Two lines of debate have emerged over these findings: selectivity in the height-by-age profile induced by traders or by mortality, and explanations for the growth recovery of teenagers. Pritchett and Freudenberger (1992) pondered potential biases imposed on slave manifests by traders who selectively purchased "lemons" (short slaves) or, alternatively, who saw transportation cost advantages in exporting higher quality (taller) individuals. They compared heights reported on "certificates of good character" required by Louisiana law in 1829 with those on inward manifests to New Orleans, reporting that the extent of catch-up growth was probably understated by the manifests. Komlos and Alecke (1996) countered the theoretical and empirical basis of their conclusions, claiming that no upward bias existed, but that the average heights of children on the manifests were shorter than free black children in a Maryland sample. In subsequent work comparing the heights of children shipped by traders and nontraders, Pritchett (1997) reports that his estimates of upward bias diminished substantially with age, reinforcing the claim that the manifests understate catch-up growth.

Skeptics of height studies have noted correctly that selective mortality tends to eliminate short people from the height distribution. Does this weaken the claim that average

Table 5.2 Height by Age of Male Slaves

Age[a]	Mean	SD	N	Mean Percentile[b]	Fitted Height[c]	Point Velocity[d]	Fitted Percentile[b]
4	36.71	3.35	581	0.29	36.54	2.70	0.29
5	39.25	3.41	500	0.37	39.13	2.49	0.37
6	41.30	4.05	573	0.32	41.52	2.30	0.32
7	43.53	4.10	555	0.50	43.74	2.14	0.50
8	45.18	4.34	766	0.39	45.81	2.01	0.39
9	48.35	3.58	791	2.22	47.78	1.93	2.22
10	49.84	3.99	1,336	1.75	49.68	1.89	1.75
11	52.00	3.85	1,061	2.37	51.58	1.91	2.37
12	53.47	4.13	1,914	1.72	53.53	2.00	1.72
13	55.22	4.10	1,418	1.21	55.60	2.13	1.21
14	57.53	4.02	2,046	0.97	57.56	2.23	0.97
15	60.04	3.74	1,587	0.71	60.04	2.22	0.71
16	62.24	3.11	1,888	0.64	62.16	1.99	0.64
17	64.14	2.91	1,904	1.61	63.96	1.58	1.61
18	65.18	2.87	3,240	4.10	65.30	1.10	4.10
19	66.23	2.78	2,619	9.22	66.19	0.70	9.22
20	66.49	2.77	3,929	11.07	66.73	0.41	11.07
21	67.20	2.76	2,581	17.21	67.04	0.23	17.21
22	67.14	2.72	3,265	16.61	67.04		17.21

Source: Slave manifests in Steckel and Ziebarth (2016, Table 3).
[a]At last birthday; average age = age + 0.5.
[b]Calculated from Steckel (1996).
[c]From Preece-Baines model 1.
[d]First derivative of model 1 curve at average age.

height is a good measure of health? Does selective mortality create a negative correlation between average height and life expectancy, that is, short populations are healthier than tall ones (Riley 1994)? If so, the growth recovery observed among teenage slaves might have been exaggerated, if not created, by the selective death of the short. Bystanders to this discussion should know that population-wide physiological stress also reduces the height of survivors, and that the very tall are also more likely to die than individuals of typical height. Contrary to the selectivity hypothesis, average height and life expectancy are highly correlated at the national level (Steckel 1995). With regard to slave catch-up, in work yet to be published, Steckel undertook simulations showing that, under a wide range of model life tables, selective mortality explains less than 5 percent of the height gain after age ten.

Table 5.3 Height by Age of Female Slaves

Age[a]	Mean	SD	N	Mean Percentile[b]	Fitted Height[c]	Point Velocity[d]	Fitted Percentile[b]
4	36.66	3.40	577	0.44	36.44	2.75	0.31
5	39.06	3.40	556	0.61	39.06	2.50	0.61
6	41.28	4.05	692	0.94	41.45	2.28	1.17
7	43.33	4.08	650	1.21	43.65	2.11	1.72
8	45.23	4.48	918	1.33	45.70	2.00	2.09
9	48.39	3.75	919	3.90	47.66	1.95	2.13
10	49.75	4.23	1,288	1.81	49.62	1.98	1.62
11	51.98	4.09	1,143	1.28	51.65	2.10	0.94
12	53.36	4.30	1,836	0.33	53.83	2.24	0.54
13	55.94	4.12	1,544	0.65	56.10	2.27	0.77
14	58.22	3.72	2,179	2.44	58.06	2.06	2.12
15	60.07	3.28	2,213	7.90	60.05	1.52	7.80
16	61.34	2.71	3,105	14.38	61.29	0.97	13.90
17	62.15	2.60	2,486	18.04	62.03	0.55	16.73
18	62.36	2.68	3,676	18.26	62.44	0.28	19.11
19	62.75	2.79	1,578	23.07	62.64	0.14	21.62
20	62.55	2.88	2,885	20.45	62.74	0.07	22.92
21	62.78	2.83	797	23.43	62.79	0.03	23.55
22	62.74	2.87	1,538	22.87	62.79		23.55

Source: Slave manifests in Steckel and Ziebarth (2016, Table 4).
[a]Age at last birthday; average age = age + 0.5.
[b]Calculated from Steckel (1996).
[c]From Preece-Baines model 1.
[d]First derivative of model 1 curve at average age.

The Steckel (1986) paper argued that stunting from a poor diet was profitable, partly because humans are resilient and have a considerable capacity for catch-up growth if conditions improve before adolescence. A plausible model of planter decision-making supports the profitability argument by Rees and Komlos (2003). An alternative explanation hinges on reduced exposure to pathogens, specifically hookworm. Coelho and McGuire (2000) argue that young children were heavily exposed to this parasite around the plantation nurseries, but working teenagers largely escaped because they wore shoes and/or the infective larva were far less prevalent where they worked in the fields. Steckel (2000) notes that reduced hookworm exposure could be relevant, but intervention studies in developing countries report small growth recovery (about 0.3 centimeters) by infected children who underwent medical treatment, which is a tiny percent of the observed catch-up growth.

Steckel has coded and is now analyzing the entire collection of slave manifests available at the National Archives on nearly 125,000 individuals to prepare a book-length manuscript that will revisit this and many other topics in the health and nutrition of American slaves. Using these data, Steckel and Ziebarth (2016) divided the manifests into shippers who had a very high probability of being traders or a high likelihood of being nontraders. The differences in height-by-age of the two groups are barely detectable, and thus they conclude that trader selectivity could not have been an important source of measured catch-up growth.

NATIVE AMERICANS

Depictions of Native American life are arguably the most distorted and contradictory of any large ethnic group in American history. Several centuries ago, accounts of early explorers and missionaries merged with the primitivistic tradition of Western civilization to create an image of the noble savage who inhabited an ideal landscape and lived in harmony with nature and reason (e.g., see Berkhover 1988). During the westward movement the natives became "bad Indians," who then morphed into entertainers in Wild Bill Cody's Western shows. A few decades later, Western movies caricatured their habits, and by the end of the twentieth century many intellectuals saw aborigines as victims of Euro-American aggression.

Height data collected by Franz Boas and his assistants near the end of the century shed light on the health of Plains tribes who occupied a vast swath of land from northern Texas to southern Canada, an area much larger than most countries (Jantz 2003). At 172.6 centimeters on average, the men were taller than any national population for which evidence is available for the mid nineteenth-century (Prince and Steckel 2003; Steckel and Prince 2001). Komlos (2003) argued against the conclusion, reporting that some groups within the United States, such as rural residents of Georgia born in the 1820s, exceeded the average height of the Plains tribes. While true, Steckel and Prince (2001) qualified their comparison to the average height of countries whose individuals were born near the middle of the nineteenth century, when most of the people in the Boas sample were born. The chronological qualification is important because Euro-American heights declined for cohorts born after 1830. Plausibly, the Plains tribes were also taller prior to 1830, before epidemics and incursion by whites imposed physiological stress. In addition, if subgroups are the appropriate standard for comparison, at 176.7 centimeters the northern Cheyenne were also taller than any subgroup listed by Komlos.

In any event, perhaps the most interesting feature of the Plains data is the wide range of average heights across tribes (see table 5.4). Amounting to nearly 9 centimeters, this range exceeds by nearly 3 centimeters the growth in average height of Euro-Americans from the early 1700s to the present. Because the tribes had similar technologies and life ways, presumably ecological conditions and the differential pace of incursion by whites were relevant for their health.

Table 5.4 Mean Height in Centimeters of Adult Men

Tribe	Height	SD	N
Assiniboin	169.6	6.0	22
Blackfeet	172.0	5.3	58
Crow	173.6	6.7	227
Sioux	172.8	5.6	584
Arapaho	174.3	6.9	57
Cheyenne	176.7	5.6	29
Kiowa	170.4	5.7	73
Comanche	168.0	6.4	73
Total Sample	172.6	6.2	1,123

Source: Calculated from worksheets of Franz Boas for Native Americans born primarily from 1830 to 1872 (Jantz 2003).

The heights of Plains nomads followed an inverted U-shape by latitude, as demonstrated by the north-south arrangement of the tribal territories given in table 5.4. The heights were lower in southern latitudes (Oklahoma and Texas), peaked in the middle latitudes of Colorado, Kansas, and South Dakota, and were lower again on the far northern Plains and in southern Canada. This pattern was also found among Union Army soldiers born east of the Plains. To understand tribal differences, Steckel (2010) gathered evidence on new explanatory variables to the figure in the study of historical heights: proxies for effort prices in hunting and gathering food, including biomass, rainfall estimated from tree rings, and tribal area, as well as proximity to trails used by Western settlers and movement to reservations. He found that collectively these variables explain a substantial share of the systematic variation in average height across tribes.

INEQUALITY

Income or wealth inequality during industrialization have been staples in the literature of economic history (Lindert 2000; Williamson and Lindert 1980). In the case of England, where the debate has been most intense, groups are divided into "optimists" and "pessimists" according to their view of the fate of the working class during industrialization. Everyone agrees that the working class eventually fared well, but their status during the heart of change with respect to wages or income has been hotly contested. The dimensions of poverty of the working class aside, many scholars agree that income or wage inequality rose during industrialization, a phenomenon summarized by the "Kuznets curve," which depicts an inverted U between inequality and industrialization.

More recently, the discussion has extended to health inequality, whereby some researchers have asked whether a health Kuznets curve accompanied the more familiar curve denominated in monetary terms (Costa-Font, Hernandez Quevedo, and Sato 2013). In the case of the United States, the evidence presented indicates that, by all measures of health, those born in the nineteenth century fared much worse than those born in the twentieth, and those born in the mid-nineteenth century were worse off than those born in the first third of the century. Yet it is not enough to examine aggregate health. Although the impact of inequalities in health on aggregate production and output has not yet been incorporated in computable general equilibrium models, the intuition of economists has long been that long-run economic growth may be slowed if the health of a large fraction of the population is so poor that this fraction of the population is too unhealthy to increase its productivity and output. High mortality rates might also affect incentives to invest in human capital.

One way to establish changes in the distribution of health is to examine health differentials by occupational class. The data on heights provide the longest series on the distribution of health by occupational class. Figure 5.4 illustrates height differentials by occupational class for ten-year cohort intervals among white, native-born males aged twenty-five to forty-nine (Costa and Steckel 1997). Height differentials by occupational class narrowed from the cohort that was born in 1705–1714 to those born in 1745–1754 and 1755–1764 and then rose again to reach relatively high levels for the cohort that served in the Civil War. Height differentials by occupational class did not substantially narrow until the cohort born in 1935–1945. Evidence from the Ohio National Guard suggests that the range in heights was over 2 centimeters in the latter half of the nineteenth century (Steckel and Haurin 1982).

FUTURE RESEARCH

Because millions of stature measurements have been recorded, there is enormous potential for future research, a small selection of which is discussed in this section. A major task is to locate sources of evidence, which will usually involve matching stature records with other sources of information. One could examine the consequences of the Great Depression (and business cycles more generally) for child health as measured by stature. Data may be available from the following: records of military; voter registration; recruitment of firemen and policemen; prisons; and schools. For example, modern (twentieth-century) military personnel records are available at the National Personnel Records Center in St. Louis. Restrictions apply to files of soldiers who left the service less than seventy-two years ago. Econometric models could be estimated if statures could be arrange by year of birth within states, and then matched with economic indicators such as unemployment rates, per capita income, and government spending.

Labor economists have pondered the contribution of height, as a measure of health, to educational achievement. Studies now recognize that processes influencing physical growth in early childhood also benefit cognitive function and the development of personality traits that are productive in labor markets (Schick and Steckel 2015). One implication of this finding is that the returns to an additional year of schooling should be a positive function of stature, which is an idea that could be tested by matching wage data available in the 1940 census manuscript schedules with stature data obtained from military muster rolls or National Guard enlistment records.

If stature is a marker of health, then one might expect that taller individuals had lower rates of morbidity or illness. Sickness is difficult to measure with precision, but proxies are often used, such as days lost from work or school. The challenge is to obtain personnel records that contain both stature and days missed. When I was in grade school, the nurse recorded both. Presumably some school districts have retained these records, and under agreements of confidentiality, might make them available for research. This is a promising idea worth investigating.

BIBLIOGRAPHY

Barioch, P., and G. Goetz. (1986). "Factors of Urbanisation in the Nineteenth Century Developed Countries: A Descriptive and Econometric Analysis." *Urban Studies* 23: 285–305.

Behrman, J. R., J. Hoddinott, J. A. Maluccio, E. Soler-Hampejsek, E. L. Behrman, and R. Martorell. (2014). "What Determines Adult Cognitive Skills? Influences of Pre-school, School, and Post-school Experiences in Guatemala." *Latin American Economic Review* 23(1): 1–32.

Berkhofer, R. F. J. (1988). "White Conceptions of Indians." In *Handbook of North American Indians*, Vol. 4: *History of Indian-White Relations*, edited by W. E. Washburn, 522–547. Washington, DC: Smithsonian.

Bodenhorn, H., T. Guinnane, and T. Mroz. (2017). "Sample-Selection Biases and the Industrialization Puzzle." *Journal of Economic History* 77(1): 171–207.

Brown, K. (2005). *Penicillin Man: Alexander Fleming and the Antibiotic Revolution.* Gloucestershire, Sutton: Stroud.

Case, A., and C. Paxson. (2008). "Stature and Status: Height, Ability, and Labor Market Outcomes." *Journal of Political Economy* 116(3): 499–532.

Coclanis, P. A., and J. Komlos. (1995). "Nutrition and Economic Development in Post-Reconstruction South Carolina: An Anthropometric Approach." *Social Science History* 19(1): 91–115.

Coelho, P. R. P., and R. A. McGuire. (2000). "Diets versus Diseases: The Anthropometrics of Slave Children." *Journal of Economic History* 60(1): 232–246.

Costa, D. L., and R. H. Steckel. (1997). "Long-Term Trends in Health, Welfare, and Economic Growth in the United States." In *Health and Welfare during Industrialization*, edited by R. H. Steckel and R. Floud, 47–89. Chicago: University of Chicago Press.

Costa-Font, J., C. Hernandez Quevedo, and A. O. Sato. (2013). "A 'Health Kuznets' Curve'? Cross-Country and Longitudinal Evidence." CESifo Working Paper Series No. 4446, Munich.

Craig, L. A. (Forthcoming). "The Antebellum Puzzle." In *Oxford Handbook of Economics and Human Biology*, edited by J. Komlos and I. Kelly. Oxford: Oxford University Press.

Duffy, J. (1992). *The Sanitarians: A History of American Public Health*. Urbana: University of Illinois Press.

Easterlin, R. A. (1961). "Regional Income Trends, 1840–1950." In *American Economic History*, edited by S. Harris, 525–547. New York: McGraw-Hill.

Eveleth, P. B., and J. M. Tanner. (1990 [1976]). *Worldwide Variation in Human Growth*. Cambridge: Cambridge University Press.

Fogel, R. W. (1986). "Nutrition and the Decline in Mortality since 1700: Some Preliminary Findings." In *Long-Term Factors in American Economic Growth*, edited by S. L. Engerman and R. E. Gallman, 439–527. Chicago: University of Chicago Press.

Fogel, R. W. (2004). *The Escape from Hunger and Premature Death, 1700–2100*. Cambridge: Cambridge University Press.

Gallman, R. E. (1966). "Gross National Product in the United States, 1834–1909." In *Output, Employment, and Productivity in the United States after 1800*, edited by D. S. Brady, 1–90. Cambridge, MA: National Bureau of Economic Research.

Gallman, R. E. (1992). "American Economic Growth before the Civil War: The Testimony of the Capital Stock Estimates." In *American Economic Growth and Standards of Living before the Civil War*, edited by R. E. Gallman and J. J. Wallis, 79–120. Chicago: University of Chicago Press.

Goldin, C. D., and R. A. Margo. (1992). "Wages, Prices, and Labor Markets before the Civil War." In *Strategic Factors in Nineteenth Century American Economic History: A Volume to Honor Robert W. Fogel*, edited by C. D. Goldin and H. Rockoff, 67–104. Chicago: University of Chicago Press.

Gould, B. A. (1869). *Investigations in the Military and Anthropological Statistics of American Soldiers*. Cambridge: Riverside Press.

Haines, M. R. (2006). "Population Characteristics." In *Historical Statistics of the United States, Millennial Edition*, edited by S. B. Carter, S. S. Gartner, M. R. Haines et al., Vol. 1, 17–25. New York: Cambridge University Press.

Haines, M. R., L. A. Craig, and T. Weiss. (2003). "The Short and the Dead: Nutrition, Mortality, and the 'Antebellum Puzzle' in the United States." *Journal of Economic History* 63(2): 382–413.

Jantz, R. L. (2003). "The Anthropometric Legacy of Franz Boas." *Economics and Human Biology* 1(2): 277–284.

Jones, A. H. (1980). *Wealth of a Nation to Be: The American Colonies on the Eve of the Revolution*. New York: Columbia University Press.

Karpinos, B. D. (1958). "Height and Weight of Selective Service Registrants Processed for Military Service during World War II." *Human Biology* 30(4): 292–321.

Koepke, N., and J. Baten. (2005). "The Biological Standard of Living in Europe during the Last Two Millennia." *European Review of Economic History* 9(1): 61–95.

Komlos, J. (1987). "The Height and Weight of West Point Cadets: Dietary Change in Antebellum America." *Journal of Economic History* 47(4): 897–927.

Komlos, J. (1996). "Anomalies in Economic History: Toward a Resolution of the 'Antebellum Puzzle.'" *Journal of Economic History* 56(1): 202–214.

Komlos, J. (2003). "Access to Food and the Biological Standard of Living: Perspectives on the Nutritional Status of Native Americans." *American Economic Review* 93(1): 252–255.

Komlos, J. (2007). "On English Pygmies and Giants: The Physical Stature of English Youth in the Late-18th and Early-19th Centuries." *Research in Economic History* 25: 149–168.

Komlos, J., and B. A'Hearn. (2017). "Clarifications on a Puzzle: The Decline in Nutritional Status at the Onset of Modern Economic Growth in the U.S.A." Working Paper, University of Munich.

Komlos, J., and B. Alecke. (1996). "The Economics of Antebellum Slave Heights Reconsidered." *Journal of Interdisciplinary History* 26(3): 437–457.

Koplow, D. A. (2003). *Smallpox: The Fight to Eradicate a Global Scourge.* Berkeley: University of California Press.

Lindert, P. H. (2000). "When Did Inequality Rise in Britain and America?" *Journal of Income Distribution* 9(1): 11–25.

Malcolm, L. A. (1974). "Ecological Factors Relating to Child Growth and Nutritional Status." In *Nutrition and Malnutrition: Identification and Measurement*, edited by A. F. Roche and F. Falkner, 329–352. New York: Plenum Press.

Margo, R. A., and R. H. Steckel. (1983). "Height of Native-Born Whites during the Antebellum Period." *Journal of Economic History* 43(1): 167–174.

Margo, R. A., and R. H. Steckel. (1992). "The Nutrition and Health of Slaves and Antebellum Southern Whites." In *Without Consent or Contract: Conditions of Slave Life and the Transition to Freedom*, edited by R. W. Fogel and S. L. Engerman, Vol. 2, 508–521. New York: W. W. Norton.

Melosi, M. V. (2000). *The Sanitary City: Urban Infrastructure in America from Colonial Times to the Present.* Baltimore, MD: Johns Hopkins University Press.

Meyer, B. D., and J. X. Sullivan. (2012). "Winning the War: Poverty from the Great Society to the Great Recession." *Brookings Papers on Economic Activity* 45(2 Fall): 133–183.

Murray, J. E. (2007). *Origins of American Health Insurance: A History of Industrial Sickness Funds.* New Haven, CT: Yale University Press.

Patterson, K. D. (1992). "Yellow Fever Epidemics and Mortality in the United States, 1693–1905." *Social Science & Medicine* 34(8): 855–865.

Persico, N., A. Postlewaite, and D. Silverman. (2004). "The Effect of Adolescent Experience on Labor Market Outcomes: The Case of Height." *Journal of Political Economy* 112(5): 1019–1053.

Pope, C. L. (1992). "Adult Mortality in America before 1900: A View from Family Histories." In *Strategic Factors in Nineteenth Century American Economic Growth*, edited by C. Goldin and H. Rockoff, 267–296. Chicago: University of Chicago Press.

Preston, S. H., and M. R. Haines. (1991). *Fatal Years: Child Mortality in Late Nineteenth-Century America.* Princeton, NJ: Princeton University Press.

Prince, J. M., and R. H. Steckel. (2003). "Nutritional Success on the Great Plains: Nineteenth-Century Equestrian Nomads." *Journal of Interdisciplinary History* 33(3): 353–384.

Pritchett, J. B. (1997). "The Interregional Slave Trade and the Selection of Slaves for the New Orleans Market." *Journal of Interdisciplinary History* 28(1): 57–85.

Pritchett, J. B., and H. Freudenberger. (1992). "A Peculiar Sample: The Selection of Slaves for the New Orleans Market." *Journal of Economic History* 52(1): 109–127.

Rees, R., J. Komlos, N. V. Long, and U. Woitek. (2003). "Optimal Food Allocation in a Slave Economy." *Journal of Population Economics* 16(1): 21–36.

Riley, J. C. (1994). "Height, Nutrition, and Mortality Risk Reconsidered." *Journal of Interdisciplinary History* 24(3): 465–492.

Rothenberg, W. B. (1992). "The Productivity Consequences of Market Integration: Agriculture in Massachusetts, 1771–1801." In *American Economic Growth and Standards of Living before the Civil War*, edited by R. E. Gallman and J. J. Wallis, 311–344. Chicago: University of Chicago Press.

Saez, E., and G. Zucman. (2014). "Wealth Inequality in the United States since 1913: Evidence from Capitalized Income Tax Data." NBER Working Paper Series. Cambridge, MA: National Bureau of Economic Research.

Schick, A., and R. H. Steckel. (2015). "Height, Human Capital, and Earnings: The Contributions of Cognitive and Noncognitive Ability." *Journal of Human Capital* 9(1): 94–115.

Soltow, L. (1975). *Men and Wealth in the United States, 1850–1870*. New Haven, CT: Yale University Press.

Steckel, R. H. (1979a). "A Dreadful Childhood: The Excess Mortality of American Slaves." *Social Science History* 10(4): 427–465.

Steckel, R. H. (1979b). "Slave Height Profiles from Coastwise Manifests." *Explorations in Economic History* 16(4): 363–380.

Steckel, R. H. (1986). "A Peculiar Population: The Nutrition, Health, and Mortality of American Slaves from Childhood to Maturity." *Journal of Economic History* 46(3): 721–741.

Steckel, R. H. (1995). "Stature and the Standard of Living." *Journal of Economic Literature* 33(4): 1903–1940.

Steckel, R. H. (1998). "Strategic Ideas in the Rise of the New Anthropometric History and Their Implications for Interdisciplinary Research." *Journal of Economic History* 58(3): 803–821.

Steckel, R. H. (2000). "Diets versus Diseases in the Anthropometrics of Slave Children: A Reply." *Journal of Economic History* 60(1): 247–259.

Steckel, R. H. (2006). "Health, Nutrition and Physical Well-Being." In *Historical Statistics of the United States, Millennial Edition*, edited by S. B. Carter, S. S. Gartner, M. R. Haines et al., Vol. 3, 499–620. New York: Cambridge University Press.

Steckel, R. H. (2010). "Inequality Amidst Nutritional Abundance: Native Americans on the Great Plains." *Journal of Economic History* 70(2): 265–286.

Steckel, R. H., and D. R. Haurin. (1982). *Height, Nutrition, and Mortality in Ohio, 1870–1900*. Columbus: Ohio State University.

Steckel, R. H., and C. M. Moehling. (2001). "Rising Inequality: Trends in the Distribution of Wealth in Industrializing New England." *Journal of Economic History* 61(1): 160–183.

Steckel, R. H., and J. M. Prince. (2001). "Tallest in the World: Native Americans of the Great Plains in the Nineteenth Century." *American Economic Review* 91(1): 287–294.

Steckel, R. H., and N. Ziebarth. (2016). "Trader Selectivity and Measured Catch-up Growth of American Slaves." *Journal of Economic History* 76(1): 109–138.

Studenski, P. (1958). *The Income of Nations; Theory, Measurement, and Analysis: Past and Present; A Study in Applied Economics and Statistics*. New York: New York University Press.

Tanner, J. M. (1978). *Fetus into Man: Physical Growth from Conception to Maturity*. Cambridge, MA: Harvard University Press.

Tanner, J. M. (1981). *A History of the Study of Human Growth*. Cambridge: Cambridge University Press.

Trotter, M., and G. C. Gleser. (1951). "Trends in Stature of American Whites and Negroes Born between 1840 and 1924." *American Journal of Physical Anthropology* 9(4): 427–440.

Trussell, J., and R. H. Steckel. (1978). "The Age of Slaves at Menarche and Their First Birth." *Journal of Interdisciplinary History* 8: 477–505.

Williamson, J. G., and P. H. Lindert. (1980). "Long-Term Trends in American Wealth Inequality." In *Modeling the Distribution and Intergenerational Transmission of Wealth*, edited by J. Smith, 9–94. Chicago: University of Chicago Press.

Zimran, A. (2017). "Does Sample-Selection Bias Explain the Antebellum Puzzle? Evidence from Military Enlistment in the Nineteenth-Century United States." Working Paper, Vanderbilt University.

CHAPTER 6

....

HEALTH POLICY IN AMERICAN ECONOMIC HISTORY

....

MELISSA A. THOMASSON

THE late nineteenth century witnessed the beginning of a strong, downward trend in mortality in the United States. Estimated to be 22 deaths per 1,000 in 1850, the crude death rate fell to 18 by 1900 and 11 by 1940 (Meeker 1972; US Census Bureau 1941; US Census Office 1902). Life expectancy at birth increased from 47 years in 1900 to 68 years by 1950. Figures 6.1 and 6.2 show changes in life expectancy and infant mortality over time. Accompanying this decline in mortality was a transition from infectious disease mortality to chronic disease mortality; by 1915, mortality from the chronic diseases associated with old age surpassed that of infectious disease (Haines 2001; Meeker 1972). Most of the early declines in mortality resulted from gains in public health; medical care was relatively ineffective in terms of treatment, and healthcare spending was low. In real terms, per capita spending on actual health care was only $134 in 1900 (Craig 2006, 3–232). However, as the twentieth century progressed, the share of the economy devoted to health care increased. By 2011, the healthcare sector in the United States employed 10.6 percent of workers. Health spending accounted for 17.9 percent of gross domestic product (GDP), with federal, state, and local governments financing 45 percent of expenditures.[1]

Economists and others have been identifying and measuring the factors that contributed to these gains in health and to the growth of the healthcare sector over the twentieth century. Most work falls under one of several strands of research. Public health efforts, innovations in medical technology, and the rise of social insurance and health insurance all play important roles in explaining the decline in mortality, the improvement in health in the United States over the twentieth century, and the growth in the healthcare sector.

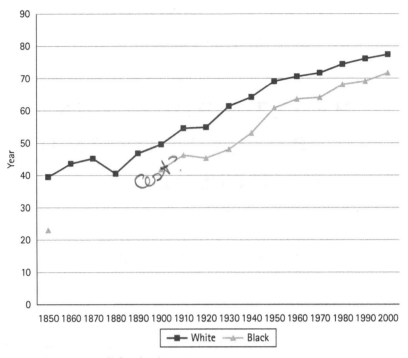

FIGURE 6.1. Expectation of life at birth, 1850–2000

Source: Data are from Haines (2006, Table Ab1–10, "Fertility and Mortality, by Race: 1800–2000). http://dx.doi.org/
10.1017/ISBN-9780511132971.Ca1-2610.1017/ISBN-9780511132971.Ca1-26.

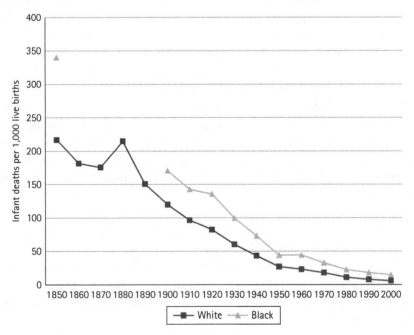

FIGURE 6.2. Infant mortality per 1,000 live births, 1850–2000

Source: Data are from Haines (2006, Table Ab1–10, "Fertility and Mortality, by Race: 1800–2000"). http://dx.doi.org/
10.1017/ISBN-9780511132971.Ca1-2610.1017/ISBN-9780511132971.Ca1-26.

PUBLIC HEALTH EFFORTS

The decline in mortality that occurred in the late nineteenth and early twentieth centuries occurred despite the fact that medical technology was very rudimentary. In the very early twentieth century, even the best-trained physicians could only diagnose illness and educate patients on hygiene and health-promoting behaviors. Their ability to treat patients was limited in that most weapons in the medical arsenal had yet to be developed. Thus, reductions in mortality in the early part of the century can be largely attributed to the increasing availability of clean water, sewer systems, and improved sanitation. Other health-improving efforts involved the eradication of hookworm and malaria, public health education initiatives, and the fortification of food with iron.

Research has shown that much of the decline in mortality over the early twentieth century can be attributed to public health interventions such as water filtration, sanitation, sewer and refuse systems, and food inspection. Water purification and delivery played a key role in the decline of mortality. Several studies analyze the impact of clean water on mortality. David Cutler and Grant Miller (2005) use a difference-in-difference approach to examine the impact of water filtration and chlorination on mortality across cities, and find that these technologies together accounted for nearly half of the mortality reduction in major cities, 75 percent of the decrease in infant mortality, and two-thirds of the decrease in child mortality. Werner Troesken (2004) finds that the expansion of public water and sewer service caused the near elimination of deaths from typhoid and other waterborne diseases.

Access to clean water not only reduced deaths from waterborne illnesses, but also, according to the Mills-Reincke hypothesis, may have reduced mortality from nonwaterborne diseases (Sedgwick and MacNutt 1910). Mills-Reincke refers to the separate observations by Hiram F. Mills and J. J. Reincke that nontyphoid death rates from gastroenteritis, tuberculosis, pneumonia, influenza, bronchitis, heart disease, and kidney disease fell after water filtration systems were introduced. Joseph P. Ferrie and Werner Troesken (2008) analyze the impact of water filtration and chlorination on the health of people living in the city of Chicago between 1870 and 1925, and find that clean water reduced mortality associated with waterborne diseases such as typhoid and diarrhea, but also reduced deaths exclusive of these diseases one year later, a finding consistent with the Mills-Reincke hypothesis.

In addition to water purification, scholars have identified a number of other factors related to public health that have contributed to the mortality decline. While the delivery of clean water reduced mortality, Troesken shows that cities that used lead water pipes may have unintentionally increased infant mortality depending on the age of the pipe and the acidity of the municipal water supply (Troesken 2006, 2008). The effect could be large; Troesken finds lead resulted in increases of 25–50 percent for infant mortality and stillbirths in 1900 for the average Massachusetts town. As cities abandoned lead water pipes in the early 1900s, the deleterious effects of lead exposure on infant mortality were reduced, although a lack of data makes it difficult to estimate the size of the reduction (Troesken 2006, 2008).

Non-water related improvements in public health also reduced mortality. For example, Joshua Lewis uses variation in the timing of power plant construction to show that electrification accounts for between 25 and 30 percent of the reduction in infant mortality over the period 1930–1960 (Lewis 2013). While public works projects such as sewers and electric grids represented large interventions, numerous other public health interventions may have also resulted in declining mortality. Early in the twentieth century, the federal government played only a minor role in public health, so that most public health initiatives occurred at the state and local levels (Preston and Haines 1991, 21). State and local public health departments operated to reduce mortality in a variety of ways, including street cleaning, refuse collection, distribution of diphtheria antitoxin, and food and milk inspection (Condran and Crimmins-Gardner 1978; Meckel 1990).[2] States also operated hospitals and sanitaria early in the twentieth century. Alex Hollingsworth (2013) finds that in pre-antibiotic North Carolina, access to sanitaria reduced tuberculosis death rates for whites.

The effectiveness of these activities at the state and local level is hard to quantify, but several sources of data report information on state and local health-related spending in broad categories. *Bureau of Labor Statistics Bulletins* 24, 30, 36, and 42 provide data on municipal finances for 1899–1902, and *Census Bulletin* 20 provides similar information for 1902–1903. *Statistics of Cities* reports annual data on municipal-level health-related expenditures for cities over 30,000 between 1905 and 1908. *Financial Statistics of Cities* provides similar information for the years 1909–1913, 1915–1919, and 1921–1930. The specific categories that are related to health include information on health conservation and sanitation cost payments; health conservation and sanitation outlays; charities, corrections, and hospital cost payments; and charities, corrections, and hospital outlays. At the state level, *Financial Statistics of States* provides similar information to that of *Financial Statistics of Cities* beginning in 1915.[3] These reports include the category of payments for "Conservation of Health, and Sanitation" that include the following subcategories: General supervision; Vital statistics; Prevention and treatment of communicable diseases (for Tuberculosis and "All Other"); Conservation of child life; Food regulation and inspection; Regulation of professional occupations; and Other health and sanitation.[4]

Several papers use these state and local data on expenditures to examine government spending on hospitals and on health outcomes. Price Fishback, Samuel Allen, Jonathan Fox, and Brendan Livingston (2010) note that state and local governments contributed public funds for hospital care, with a mean per capita expenditure of $10.79 (1990 dollars) in 1923 and $13.87 in 1930. Louis P. Cain and Elyce Rotella (2001) focus on the impact of public sanitation spending by examining data from forty-eight US cities. They find that expenditures on sewers and refuse collection had a large effect on reducing death rates from typhoid, dysentery, and diarrhea.

Another paper that uses data from *Financial Statistics of Cities* was published by Grant Miller in 2008. Miller uses these data to analyze how suffrage may have impacted child survival. He finds that women's enfranchisement led to large shifts in public spending on hygiene campaigns that resulted in a decrease in child mortality. One limitation of the *Financial Statistics* data is that they fail to provide details about the types of activities on which states and municipalities may have spent money. Different types of spending may have had different effects on health outcomes. For example, Carolyn Moehling and Melissa A. Thomasson (2014) use data on the various activities states conducted under the auspices of the Sheppard-Towner program, which gave matching funds to states to engage in infant and child public health initiatives. Their results indicate that monies spent on interventions that provided one-on-one care, such as nurse visits and health centers, reduced infant deaths more than impersonal activities such as classes and conferences.

The effectiveness of these public health education campaigns is also supported in work by Fishback, Werner Troesken, Trevor Kollmann, Michael Haines, Paul W. Rhode and Melissa Thomasson (2011), who show that strong positive relationship between temperature and mortality over the period 1930–1940 disappears when measures of illiteracy, access to radios, and access to magazines are incorporated into the analysis. These findings suggest that access to information may have played an important role in mortality declines throughout the twentieth century, although more work needs to be done in this area.

Eliminating environmental pathogens in the early to mid-twentieth century also contributed to improvements in public health. Among these, the eradication of malaria and hookworm represented major public health achievements, particularly in the South, where up to 30 percent of the population was infected with malaria in the early 1900s (Kitchens 2013a). Malaria can cause death, and even those who avoid death can suffer from stunted physical stature and impaired cognitive development (Bleakley 2010; Hong 2007). Research indicates that several New Deal agencies and programs contributed to the decline of malaria. Alan Barreca, Price Fishback, and Shawn Kantor (2012) find that the Agricultural Adjustment Act (AAA) indirectly lowered malaria rates in the South. By paying farmers to take land out of cultivation, the AAA resulted in out-migration of farm laborers away from mosquito breeding grounds (Humphreys 2001). Barreca, Fishback, and Kantor estimate that this out-migration accounts for about 10 percent of the decline in malaria between 1930 and 1940. In two papers, Carl Kitchens (2103a, 2013b) examines the impact of other New Deal projects on malaria. Using county-level panel data from Alabama and Tennessee, Kitchens (2013b) shows that the construction of dams under the Tennessee Valley Authority (TVA) created a vast increase in coastline suited for mosquito breeding. Despite subsequent efforts of the TVA to control mosquitos, Kitchens calculates that the TVA led to a significant increase in loss of life due to malaria that reduced the fiscal benefit of dam construction by 24 percent.

While Kitchen's work suggests that the fiscal benefits associated with the TVA were substantially mitigated by the extra cost of lost life due to malaria, his other paper (2013a) shows how another New Deal agency engaged in projects that significantly reduced malaria mortality. Specifically, Kitchens uses county-level data from Georgia between 1932 and 1941, and demonstrates that drainage projects constructed under the auspices of the Works Progress Administration (WPA) explain over 40 percent of the observed reduction in malaria during the period.

Hoyt Bleakley (2007) studies the eradication of another predominantly Southern parasite: hookworm. Hookworm, a parasite transmitted through contaminated soil, lodges in the intestine of a victim. While rarely fatal, symptoms include lethargy and anemia, making it difficult for children to attend school and to cognitively focus. Moreover, Garland Brinkley (1997) shows that the sharp decline in Southern agricultural output after the Civil War can be attributed to increased rates of hookworm infection. The Rockefeller Sanitary Commission (RSC) estimated in 1910 that 40 percent of Southern schoolchildren were affected with hookworm. The RSC engaged in an eradication campaign, involving sending healthcare workers to dispense de-worming medication. Bleakley's results indicate that children living in areas with greater rates of hookworm infection prior to the RSC's campaign showed greater gains in school enrollment, attendance, and literacy than those living in areas with lower rates of infection. According to Bleakley, eliminating hookworm may have closed about half the literacy gap between the North and the South, and reduced the income gap by up to 20 percent.

Eliminating hookworm generated significant improvements in school enrollment because hookworm infection led to nutritional insufficiency (Bleakley 2007). As several economic historians have shown, nutritional improvements (measured by caloric and/or protein intake) are correlated with gains in both income and health (Fogel 1994; Floud et al. 2011; Higgs 1971; Steckel 1995).

A paper by Gregory Niemesh (2015) adds to this literature by demonstrating the impact that government policies that affect diet can have on health. Niemesh examines the impact of the first federal requirement to fortify bread with iron in 1943. Iron deficiency in infants and children causes developmental delays and behavioral problems, and reduces productive capacity in adults. By leveraging pretreatment variation in iron consumption, Niemesh finds that the law led to increases in income and educational attainment in areas with lower levels of iron consumption prior to the mandate. In other work, James Feyrer, Dimitra Politi, and David N. Weil (2013) similarly examine the impact of salt iodization in the United States in the 1920s on later cognitive outcomes. Their findings suggest that iodized salt raised IQ for those who were most deficient, but also increased thyroid-related deaths, particularly among older individuals.

MEDICAL TECHNOLOGY, DOCTORS, AND HOSPITALS

At the turn of the twentieth century, the role of doctors and hospitals in reducing mortality was limited. Only a few vaccines or successful treatments for illness existed. While Jenner published his work on the effectiveness of a vaccine for smallpox in 1799, it was not until 1885 that Pasteur and Roux developed another effective vaccine, for rabies (Lehrer 1979). But, increasing acceptance of the germ theory of disease led to dramatic discoveries in bacteriology by the late nineteenth century (Preston and Haines 1991, 7). Among these was the discovery of the diphtheria antitoxin, which prevented death from diphtheria infection if administered early in the course of illness. The antitoxin first became available in the United States in the late fall of 1894 (Hammonds 1999, 88).

However, even when treatments were available, they were not necessarily applied. Much medical care was ineffective (Higgs 1971). Preston and Haines note that diphtheria accounted for between 11 and 14 percent of deaths in 1900 among children aged 1 to 14, "despite the availability of diphtheria antitoxin since the mid 1890s" (Preston and Haines 1991, 6). A 1907 report published by the Indiana State Board of Health echoes their findings, lamenting that "[t]he prophylactic use of antitoxin is not practiced to the degree it should be. If it were used in all outbreaks for immunizing, the number of cases would be greatly diminished" (State of Indiana 1907, 7). Why did the diphtheria antitoxin not readily diffuse? It could have been that few physicians kept up to date on medical knowledge. For the most part, physician training was poor; a few of the best schools required a baccalaureate degree for admission and had a rigorous curriculum, but most had low standards and similarly low expectations. State licensing regulations were also lax (Moehling, Thomasson, and Treber 2013).

This situation changed rapidly. One of the defining characteristics of the healthcare sector during the twentieth century was the rapid pace of advance in medical technology and the rise of the medical-industrial complex. By the time Abraham Flexner wrote his highly critical report on the state of medical education in 1910, changes in physician training were well underway. Medical schools increased standards for admission, lengthened their periods of instruction, added rigorous courses in the basic sciences as well as clinical instruction, and built modern laboratories to encourage research by faculty and students. Perhaps most important, medical schools also formed alliances with hospitals, creating partnerships that cemented the system of clinically based teaching and academic research that today form the basis of the medical-industrial complex in the United States.

As physician training moved to hospitals, so did patients. While only 5 percent of births occurred in hospitals in 1900, half of all births and 75 percent of urban births occurred in hospitals by 1935 (Wertz and Wertz 1977, 133). The initial improvement in training and a shift to hospital-based procedures may not have improved health outcomes initially. Thomasson and Treber (2008) show that while the medicalization of childbirth did not initially reduce maternal mortality, it did lower mortality once sulfa drugs became available in 1937. Sulfa provided physicians with their first effective treatment against a range of bacterial infections. Jayachandran, Lleras-Muney, and Smith (2010) show that in addition to reducing maternal mortality, sulfa use also reduced deaths from pneumonia and scarlet fever. They estimate that sulfa reduced overall mortality from two to three percent, and added 0.4 to 0.7 years of life expectancy. Continued advances in medical technology, such as penicillin in 1942 and a vaccine for polio in 1955, undoubtedly further reduced mortality, but little research has been done in these areas. Cutler and Meara (2004) note that infectious disease mortality was extremely low by 1960, and argue that reductions in mortality since 1960 have been driven by medical interventions that have lowered cardiovascular disease mortality and reductions in neonatal infant mortality.

HEALTH INSURANCE

The first organized effort to implement compulsory health insurance occurred in 1915 when, following compulsory health insurance initiatives in Germany and Great Britain, the American Association for Labor Legislation (AALL) proposed a plan calling for comprehensive medical benefits and disability benefits for low-income workers. Under the plan, local mutual insurance companies would manage premium contributions shared by employers, workers, and the state. Employers and workers would each contribute 40 percent of the plan's premium, while the state would contribute the remaining 20 percent (Chasse 1994, 1067). While model bills were introduced in several state legislatures, California was the only state in which there was a referendum on state-provided health insurance. Voters defeated the bill 358,324 to 133,858 (Costa 1995).

The proposal's defeat occurred because consumers did not feel a need for either medical or disability benefits. Early in the twentieth century, actual insurance for health expenditures did not exist. Demand was nonexistent; the low state of medical technology and correspondingly low medical expenditures obviated the need for health insurance. On the supply side, commercial insurance companies did not offer health insurance because of what they perceived to be an insurmountable problem of adverse selection (Thomasson 2002). Even though consumers did not perceive a need for health insurance, about one-third of them in 1916 had "sickness" (disability) insurance to protect against wages lost due to illness (Murray 2007, 42). Workers obtained insurance through fraternal societies, mutual benefit organizations, industrial sickness funds organized by employers, trade unions, and commercial casualty firms (State of Illinois 1919, 164). As John E. Murray (2007) notes, the ability of establishment funds, trade unions, and fraternal organizations to meet workers' needs for accident and sickness insurance prevented the AALL's proposals for compulsory health insurance from gaining any traction.

While states did not mandate health insurance coverage in the 1910s, they acted to encourage its growth in the late 1920s and 1930s. During this period, the prepayment plans that later became known as Blue Cross and Blue Shield developed. These plans were initially formed as single hospital plans that offered limited benefits for a fixed, prepaid fee. States encouraged their development by enacting enabling legislation that granted the Blues nonprofit, tax-exempt status, and did not require the usual capital and reserve requirements faced by insurance companies. Without the enabling legislation, the Blues would have had to either meet reserve requirements or be subject to assessment liability.

Thomasson (2002) shows that states that passed the legislation sold about 16 percent more accident and health insurance than states that did not.

The success of Blue Cross and Blue Shield in avoiding issues with adverse selection led commercial insurance companies to enter the industry. About 12.3 million Americans (9 percent) had private health insurance coverage in 1940, but this number grew quickly during the 1940s. A 1942 ruling under the War Stabilization Act allowed firms to offer employees health insurance even though they could not raise wages. In 1943, an administrative tax court ruled (a ruling that was later codified in the Internal Revenue Code of 1954) that employer contributions to health insurance premiums were exempt from employee taxable income—which increased the mean value of coverage by 9.5 percent. Coupled with major medical advances such as sulfa and penicillin, the number of people covered by health insurance rose to nearly 75 percent of the population by 1957 (Thomasson 2002, 2003). With effective new technologies, demand for medical care increased, and expenditures rose as well. Medical expenditures per capita in real 1935 dollars more than doubled between 1935 and 1955, rising from $22.65 to $54.06 (Steckel 2006, Vol. 2, 511).

Government Intervention

Outside of funding public health education initiatives such as Sheppard-Towner, the federal government did not become directly involved in health policy until the Great Depression.[5] Infant mortality has trended downward throughout the mortality transition, except in 1933 and 1934. Federal relief spending during the New Deal may have impacted health outcomes because it acted as a safety net for the unemployed and poor. Price Fishback, Michael R. Haines, and Shawn Kantor find that federal relief spending reduced infant deaths, suicides, deaths from infectious diseases, and diarrheal deaths (Fishback, Haines, and Kantor 2007). Each $2 million spent on relief reduced infant deaths, deaths from suicide, and deaths from diarrhea by 1, and reduced deaths from infectious disease by 2.4 (Fishback and Wallis 2013).

While proponents argued for national health insurance as a component of the 1935 Social Security Act, the bill passed only when the proposal was stricken from the bill. Nevertheless, included in the bill were funds paid to states on a matching basis for "... maternal and infant care, the rehabilitation of crippled children, general public health work, and aid for dependent children under age sixteen" (Starr 1982, 270). Under the 1950 amendments to the Social Security Act, the federal government provided matching funds to states to pay doctors and hospitals for providing medical care to welfare recipients.

A second attempt to implement universal health insurance failed in the 1940s after the American Medical Association (AMA) spent $1.5 million to lobby against it (Shi and Singh 2008, 103). Nevertheless, the federal government became involved in two large initiatives during the decade. In 1943, Congress established the Emergency Maternal and Infant Care Program (EMIC), to provide maternal and infant care to the wives and infants of enlisted men in the lower four pay grades, which continued until 1946. More research into the effects of this program needs to be done; while the narrowing gap between black and white infant mortality during this period has been documented, we do not yet have a solid understanding of what drove this closure (Collins and Thomasson 2004).

In 1946, Congress passed the Hospital Survey and Construction Act, better known as the Hill-Burton program. Over the period 1947–1971, federal, state, and local governments spent $12.8 billion on nonprofit and public hospital construction and modernization. In total, 344,453 new hospital beds were added under the program, accounting for about half of the existing beds in the United States (Hill-Burton Project Register 1971; US Department of Health Education and Welfare 1966). Under the Act, federal funds could be used to construct racially separate facilities until 1963, when the Supreme Court ruled that the "separate but equal clause" under Hill-Burton was unconstitutional (Quadagno 2005, 84). While Title VI of the Civil Rights Act affirmed the inability of hospitals to racially discriminate against patients, it was not until 1966, when the federal government could withhold Medicare funding from noncomplying hospitals, that racial discrimination effectively ended. Douglas V. Almond, Kenneth Y. Chay, and Michael Greenstone (2006) examine the impact of hospital desegregation in Mississippi, and conclude that when Hill-Burton facilities were made available to blacks, black post-neonatal infant mortality declined immediately. Overall, they estimate that the program prevented the deaths of 25,000 black infants between 1965 and 2002. More researchers need to examine Hill-Burton. Its scale alone shaped the hospital industry, and may have affected health on a wide scale.

In 1960, most Americans were covered by insurance through work, but it was difficult for the elderly to obtain health insurance coverage. Under the Kerr-Mills bill, which became law in 1960, the vendor payments to providers that were part of the 1950 amendments to Social Security were extended to include elderly persons who were not entitled to welfare but nevertheless needed help to pay medical bills (US Social Security Administration 2011, Chapter 4). While earlier proposals to enact universal coverage met with great resistance, the election of John F. Kennedy in 1960 helped set into motion the program that would eventually become Medicare. A report published in 1964 by a special Committee on Aging in the US Senate found that only 25 percent of Americans over the age of sixty-five were adequately insured (US Senate Report 1964, 4–5). Political support for federally sponsored insurance coverage for the aged grew, and in 1965, Medicare was enacted into law, providing hospital insurance (Part A) and voluntary supplemental medical insurance (Part B).

The impact of Medicare on the elderly, on the healthcare industry, and on the economy is large by any measure. Amy Finkelstein and Robin McKnight (2008) find that the implementation of Medicare had no effect on the mortality of the elderly, but did reduce their out-of-pocket financial risk, generating welfare gains that are equal to about 40 percent of the cost of Medicare. Finkelstein (2007) attributes 37 percent of the rise of real hospital expenditures between 1965 and 1970 to Medicare, due to new hospital entry and the expansion of existing hospitals. She calculates that about half of the rise of medical expenditures between 1950 and 1990 can be attributed to Medicare.

Medicaid was also implemented in 1965 to cover other populations in need of assistance with medical bills. Unlike Medicare, which was wholly funded by the federal government and provided the same benefits to all enrollees, Medicaid was enacted as a means-tested, federal-state program to provide medical benefits originally to recipients of public assistance, although legislative changes over the years have expanded eligibility. Under the Medicaid program, the federal government specified minimum standards for eligibility and benefits, although states have the option to offer more generous levels of coverage or broaden the eligibility requirements (Gruber 2000). Research into the impact on Medicaid has leveraged exogenous changes in eligibility, or randomized design, to examine the impact of the program on health. A study conducted by Janet Currie and Jonathan Gruber (1996) indicates that a 30 percentage point increase in the number of women eligible reduced infant mortality by 8.5 percent, although they find that targeted increases in eligibility were more effective than broad increases in eligibility. More recently, the Oregon Health Study group used a randomized study design to analyze the impact of extending Medicaid to uninsured individuals. Their results suggest that increased access to Medicaid by low-income, able-bodied people in Oregon led to increased access to and utilization of healthcare services and reduced financial stress, but had no impact on blood pressure, cholesterol levels, or glycated hemoglobin over the two-year period of the study (Oregon Health Study Group 2013).

Conclusions and Areas for Future Research

The contributions of economic historians and others offer a better understanding of health policy in the United States over the course of the twentieth century. Excellent contributions have demonstrated the tremendous role in public health infrastructure and education in reducing mortality. Improvements in physician training and major advances in medical technology also reduced mortality and morbidity. Efforts to improve access to health care developed as the demand for more advanced medical technologies increased. Economists have studied the rise of private insurance and the effect of public insurance programs, such as Medicare and Medicaid, on outcomes and expenditures.

Despite these efforts, there remains an enormous amount of work to be done in the area. Areas ripe for future research include detailed studies about the political economy of Medicare and Medicaid (especially since Medicaid varies so much at the state level), as well as the effect of medical vendor payments on health, the effect of the EMIC program on infant mortality and maternal care, the impact of the Hill-Burton program, and the overall contribution of medical care to the mortality transition. In addition, much work remains to be done in other areas, for example, on the impact of the Pure Food and Drugs Act of 1906, the development of the Food and Drug Administration, as well as the origins and impacts of "sin" taxes on cigarettes and alcohol.

Notes

1. Data on national health expenditures and sources of financing are from Centers for Medicare and Medicaid Services, "National Health Expenditures 2011 Highlights." Available online at http://www.cms.gov/Research-Statistics-Data-and-Systems/Statistics-Trends-and-Reports/NationalHealthExpendData/downloads/highlights.pdf. Health care sector employment calculations are from Richard Henderson, Table 2.7, "Employment and Output by Industry," January 2012 *Monthly Labor Review*. Available online at http://www.bls.gov/emp/ep_table_207.htm. Workers in the health care sector in this calculation include those who work in ambulatory healthcare services, outpatient and laboratory services, hospitals, offices of private practitioners, nursing and residential care facilities, and home healthcare services. Social assistance workers are not included.
2. Mokyr and Stein (1996) note that by 1905, thirty-two states had laws preventing the adulteration of milk. The effectiveness of these laws on improving public health is hard to measure. While milk adulteration may have posed a health risk, microbiological contamination posed an even bigger risk, but pasteurization was rarely required. Even in New York, only 15 percent of the milk supply was pasteurized by 1911 (Preston and Haines 1991).
3. While Financial Statistics of States begins being reported in 1915, Lott and Kenny (1999) and Miller (2008) use data collected by Richard E. Sylla, John B. Legler, and John Wallis and reported in *State and Local Government: Sources and Uses of Funds: Twentieth Century Statistics* (ICPSR Study 6304).
4. Unfortunately, the Census Bureau did not collect data for 1920, and only some states provided data for 1921. In 1922, the Census Bureau published data on cost payments for conservation of health and sanitation, but did provide data on cost payments for the conservation of child life. The Census Bureau defines "cost payments" as "payments for governmental costs or for their expenses, interest, outlays, less amounts which have been returned or are to be returned by reason of error or otherwise."
5. Perhaps the first federal policy that directly affected human health was the Pure Food and Drugs Act of 1906, which prevented the manufacture, sale, or transportation of adulterated foods, drugs, and medicines (see Law 2003 and Law and Libecap 2006 for a thorough discussion of the origins of state pure food regulation and the Pure Food and Drugs Act). Indirectly, federal actions in the late nineteenth century did affect human health. Alan L. Olmstead and Paul W. Rhode (2013) note that the federal government indirectly became involved in health policy by involving itself in combating lifestock diseases as early as 1884, many of which could be transmitted to humans. Moreover, the regulation set a template for disease eradication that would become the model for later federal policies specifically aimed at human health. Werner Troesken (2013) offers an insightful examination of federal versus state government involvement in health.

Bibliography

Almond, D. V., K. Y. Chay, and M. Greenstone. (2006). "Civil Rights, the War on Poverty, and Black-White Convergence in Infant Mortality in the Rural South and Mississippi." MIT Department of Economics Working Paper No. 070-04.

Barreca, A. I., P. V. Fishback, and S. Kantor. (2012). "Agricultural Policy, Migration, and Malaria in the United States in the 1930s." *Explorations in Economic History* 49: 381–398. doi: 10.1016/j.eeh.2012.05.003.

Bleakley, H. (2007). "Disease and Development: Evidence from Hookworm Eradication in the American South." *Quarterly Journal of Economics* 122(1): 73–117.

Bleakley, H. (2010). "Malaria Eradication in the Americas: A Retrospective Analysis of Childhood Exposure." *American Economic Journal: Applied Economics* 2(2): 1–45.

Brinkley, Garland L. (1997). "The Decline in Southern Agricultural Output, 1860–1880." *Journal of Economic History* 57(1): 116–138.

Cain, L. P., and E. J. Rotella. (2001). "Death and Spending: Urban Mortality and Municipal Expenditure on Sanitation." *Annales de demographie historique* 1(101): 193–154.

Chasse, D. J. (1994). "The American Association for Labor Legislation and the Institutionalist Tradition in National Health Insurance." *Journal of Economic Issues* 28(4): 1063–1090.

Collins, W. J., and M. A. Thomasson. (2004). "The Declining Contribution of Socioeconomic Disparities to the Racial Gap in Infant Mortality Rates." *Southern Economic Journal* 70(4): 746–776.

Condran, G., and E. Crimmins-Gardner. (1978). "Public Health Measures and Mortality in U.S. Cities in the Late Nineteenth Century." *Human Ecology* 6(1): 27–54.

Costa, D. L. (1995). "The Political Economy of State Provided Health Insurance in the Progressive Era: Evidence from California." National Bureau of Economic Research Working Paper No. 5328.

Craig, L. A. (2006). "Consumer Expenditures." In *Historical Statistics of the United States, Earliest Times to the Present: Millennial Edition*, edited by S. B. Carter, S. S. Gartner, M. R. Haines, A. L. Olmstead, R. Sutch, and G. Wright, 3-225–3-229. New York: Cambridge University Press.

Currie, J., and J. Gruber. (1996). "Saving Babies: The Efficacy and Cost of Recent Changes in the Medicaid Eligibility of Pregnant Women." *Journal of Political Economy* 104(6): 1263–1296.

Cutler, D., and E. Meara. (2004). "Changes in the Age Distribution of Mortality Over the 20th Century." National Bureau of Economic Research Working Paper No. 8556.

Cutler, D. M., and G. Miller. (2005). "The Role of Public Health Improvements in Health Advances: The Twentieth-Century United States." *Demography* 42(1): 1–22.

Emery, G., and J. C. H. Emery. (1999). *A Young Man's Benefit: The Independent Order of Odd Fellows and Sickness Insurance in the United States and Canada*. Montreal: McGill-Queen's University Press.

Emery, J. C. H. (1996). "Risky Business? Nonactuarial Pricing Practices and the Financial Viability of Fraternal Sickness Insurers." *Explorations in Economic History* 33(2 April): 195–226.

Ferrie, J. P., and W. Troesken. (2008). "Water and Chicago's Mortality Transition, 1850–1925." *Explorations in Economic History* 45: 1–16. doi:10.1016/j.eeh.2007.06.001.

Feyrer, J., D. Politi, and D. N. Weil. (2013). "The Cognitive Effects of Micronutrient Deficiency: Evidence from Salt Iodization in the United States." National Bureau of Economic Research Working Paper No. 19233.

Finkelstein, A. (2007). "The Aggregate Effects of Health Insurance: Evidence from the Introduction of Medicare." *Quarterly Journal of Economics* 122(1): 1–37.

Finkelstein, A., and R. McKnight. (2008). "What Did Medicare Do? The Initial Impact of Medicare on Mortality and Out of Pocket Medical Spending." *Journal of Public Economics* 92: 1644–1688.

Fishback, P. V., S. Allen, J. Fox, and B. Livingston. (2010). "A Patchwork Safety Net: A Survey of Cliometric Studies of Income Maintenance Programs in the United States in the First Half of the Twentieth Century." *Journal of Economic Surveys* 24(5): 895–940.

Fishback, P. V., M. R. Haines, and S. Kantor. (2007). "Births, Deaths, and New Deal Relief during the Great Depression." *Review of Economics and Statistics* 89(1): 1–14.

Fishback, P. V., W. Troesken, T. Kollman, M. Haines, P. W. Rhode, and M. A. Thomasson. (2011). "Information and the Impact of Climate and Weather on Mortality Rates During the Great Depression." In *The Economics of Climate Change: Adaptations Past and Present*, edited by Gary D. Libecap and Richard H. Steckel, 131–168. Chicago: University of Chicago Press.

Fishback, P. V., and J. J. Wallis. (2013). "What's New about the New Deal?" In *The Great Depression of the 1930s: Lessons for Today*, edited by Nicholas Crafts and Peter Fearon, 290–327. Oxford: Oxford University Press.

Floud, R., R. Fogel, B. Harris, and S. C. Hong. (2011). *The Changing Body: Health, Nutrition, and Human Development in the Western World since 1700*. Cambridge: Cambridge University Press.

Fogel, R. W. (1994). "Economic Growth, Population Theory, and Physiology: The Bearing of Long-Term Processes on the Making of Economic Policy." *American Economic Review* 84(3): 369–395.

Gruber, J. B. (2000) "Medicaid." National Bureau of Economic Research Working Paper No. 7829.

Haines, M. R. (2001). "The Urban Mortality Transition in the United States, 1800–1940." *Annales de demographie historique* 1(101): 33–64.

Haines, M. R. (2006). "Vital Statistics." In *Historical Statistics of the United States, Earliest Times to the Present: Millennial Edition*, edited by Susan B. Carter, Scott Sigmund Gartner, Michael R. Haines, Alan L. Olmstead, Richard Sutch, and Gavin Wright, 1-381–1-390. New York: Cambridge University Press.

Hammonds, E. M. (1999). *Childhood's Deadly Scourge: The Campaign to Control Diphtheria in New York City, 1880–1930*. Baltimore, MD: Johns Hopkins University Press.

Higgs, R. (1971). *The Transformation of the American Economy, 1865–1914: An Essay in Interpretation*. New York: John Wiley.

Hollingsworth, A. (2013). "The Impact of Sanitaria on Pulmonary Tuberculosis Mortality: Evidence from North Carolina, 1932–1940." Unpublished Working Paper.

Hong, S. (2007). "The Health and Economic Burden of Malaria: The American Case." PhD diss., University of Chicago.

Humphreys, M. (2001). *Malaria: Poverty, Race, and Public Health in the United States*. Baltimore, MD: Johns Hopkins University Press.

Jayachandran, S., A. Lleras-Muney, and K. V. Smith. (2010). "Modern Medicine and the Twentieth Century Decline in Mortality: Evidence on the Impact of Sulfa Drugs." *American Economic Journal: Applied Economics* 2(2): 118–146.

Kitchens, C. (2013a). "The Effects of the Works Progress Administrations Anti-Malaria Programs in Georgia 1932–1947." *Explorations in Economic History* 50: 567–581. doi: 10.1016/j.eeh.2013.08.003.

Kitchens, C. (2013b). "A Damn Problem: TVA's Fight against Malaria, 1926–1951." *Journal of Economic History* 73(3): 694–724. doi: 10.1017/S0022050713000582.

Law, M. T. (2003). "The Origins of State Pure Food Regulation." *Journal of Economic History* 63(4): 1103–1130.

Law, M. T., and G. D. Libecap. (2006). "The Determinants of Progressive Era Reform: The Pure Food and Drugs Act of 1906." In *Corruption and Reform: Lessons from America's Economic History*, edited by Edward L. Glaeser and Claudia Goldin, 319–342. Chicago: University of Chicago Press.

Lehrer, S. (1979). *Explorers of the Body*. Garden City, NY: Doubleday.

Lewis, J. (2013). "Fertility, Child Health, and the Diffusion of Electricity into the Home." Working Paper, University of Toronto Department of Economics.

Lott, J., and L. Kenny. (1999). "Did Women's Suffrage Change the Size and Scope of Government?" *Journal of Political Economy* 107: 1163–1198.

Meckel, Richard A. (1990). *Save the Babies: American Public Health Reform and the Prevention of Infant Mortality, 1850–1929*. Baltimore, MD: Johns Hopkins University Press.

Meeker, E. (1972). "The Improving Health of the United States, 1850–1915." *Explorations in Economic History* 9(4): 353–374.

Miller, G. (2008). "Women's Suffrage, Political Responsiveness, and Child Survival in American History." *Quarterly Journal of Economics* 123(3): 863–904. doi: 10.1162/qjec.2007.123.3.863.

Moehling, C., M. A. Niemesh, G. T. Thomasson, and J. Treber. (2017). "The Swan Song of the Country Doctor: Flexner and the Economics of the Practice of Medicine." Manuscript, 1–36.

Moehling, C., and M. A. Thomasson. (2014). "Saving Babies: The Impact of Public Health Education Programs on Infant Mortality." *Demography* 51(2): 367–386.

Mokyr, J., and R. Stein. (1996). "Science, Health and Household Technology: The Effect of the Pasteur Revolution on Consumer Demand." In *The Economics of New Goods*, edited by Timothy F. Bresnahan and Robert J. Gordon, 143–206. Chicago: University of Chicago Press.

Murray, J. E. (2007). *Origins of American Health Insurance: A History of Industrial Sickness Funds*. New Haven, CT: Yale University Press.

Niemesh, G. (2015). "Ironing Out Deficiencies: Evidence from the United States on the Economic Effects of Iron Deficiency." *Journal of Human Resources* 50(4): 919–958.

Olmstead, A. L., and P. W. Rhode. (2013). "Arresting Cognation: Science, Policy, and Conflicts over Animal Disease Control." Manuscript.

Oregon Health Study Group (K. Baicker, S. Taubman, H. Allen, M. Bernstein, J. Gruber, J. Newhouse, E. Schneider, B. Wright, A. Zaslavsky, and A. N. Finkelstein). (2013). "The Oregon Experiment—Effects of Medicaid on Clinical Outcomes." *New England Journal of Medicine* 368: 1713–1722. doi: 10.1056/NEJMsa1212321.

Preston, S., and M. Haines. (1991). *Fatal Years: Child Mortality in Late Nineteenth-Century America*. Princeton, NJ: Princeton University Press.

Quadagno, J. (2005). *One Nation, Uninsured: Why the U.S. Has No National Health Insurance*. New York: Oxford University Press.

Sedgwick, W. T., and J. S. MacNutt. (1910). "On the Mills-Reincke Phenomenon and Hazen's Theorem Concerning the Decrease in Mortality from Diseases Other Than Typhoid Following the Purification of Public Water Supplies." *Journal of Infectious Diseases* 7: 564–589.

Shi, L., and D. A. Singh. (2008). *Delivering Health Care in America: A Systems Approach*. 4th ed. Sudbury, MA: Jones and Bartlett.

Starr, Paul. (1982). *The Social Transformation of American Medicine*. New York: Basic Books.

State Board of Health of Indiana. (1907). *Twenty-fifth Annual Report of the State Board of Health of Indiana*. Indianapolis.

State of Illinois. (1919). *Report of the Health Insurance Commission of the State of Illinois, 1919*. Springfield.

Steckel, R. H. (1995). "Stature and the Standard of Living." *Journal of Economic Literature* 33: 1903–1940.

Steckel, R. H. (2006). "Health." In *Historical Statistics of the United States, Earliest Times to the Present: Millennial Edition*, edited by S. B. Carter, S. S. Gartner, M. R. Haines, A. L. Olmstead, R. Sutch, and G. Wright, 2-499–2-508. New York: Cambridge University Press.

Sylla, R. E., J. B. Legler, and J. Wallis. (1991). *Sources and Uses of Funds in State and Local Governments, 1790–1915*: [United States]. New York: New York University; Athens, GA: University of Georgia; and College Park, MD: University of Maryland [producers]. Ann Arbor, MI: Inter-university Consortium for Political and Social Research [distributor], 1993. doi:10.3886/ICPSR09729.v1.

Thomasson, M. A. (2002). "From Sickness to Health: The Twentieth Century Development of U.S. Health Insurance." *Explorations in Economic History* 39(3): 233–253.

Thomasson, M. A. (2003). "The Importance of Group Coverage: How Tax Policy Shaped U.S. Health Insurance." *American Economic Review* 93(4): 1373–1384.

Thomasson, M. A., and J. Treber. (2008). "From Home to Hospital: The Evolution of Childbirth in the United States, 1928–1940." *Explorations in Economic History* 45(1): 76–99.

Troesken, W. (2004). *Water, Race, and Disease*. Cambridge, MA: MIT Press.

Troesken, W. (2006). *The Great Lead Water Pipe Disaster*. Cambridge, MA: MIT Press.

Troesken, W. (2008). "Lead Water Pipes and Infant Mortality at the Turn of the Twentieth Century." *Journal of Human Resources* 43(3): 554–575.

Troesken, W. (2014). "The Pox of Liberty: How the Constitution Left Americans Rich, Free and Prone to Infection." Manuscript.

US Bureau of Labor Statistics. (1899–1902). *Bureau of Labor Statistics Bulletin* 24, 30, 36, and 42. Washington, DC: US Government Printing Office.

US Census Bureau. (1904). *Census Bulletin* 20. Washington, DC: US Government Printing Office.

US Census Bureau. (1941). *Sixteenth Census of the United States, 1940*. Washington, DC: US Government Printing Office.

US Census Office. (1902). *Twelfth Census of the United States, 1900*. Washington, DC: US Government Printing Office.

US Congress. Senate. Special Committee on Aging. (1964). "Blue Cross and Private Health Insurance Coverage of Older Americans." 88th Congress, 2d. Sess. Washington, DC: US Government Printing Office.

US Department of Health, Education and Welfare. (1966). *Hill-Burton Program 1946–1966*. Washington, DC: US Government Printing Office.

Wertz, R. W., and D. C. Wertz. (1977). *Lying-in: A History of Childbirth in America*. New Haven, CT: Yale University Press.

PART II

PRODUCTION
AND STRUCTURAL
CHANGE

CHAPTER 7

....

AGRICULTURE IN AMERICAN ECONOMIC HISTORY

....

ALAN L. OLMSTEAD AND PAUL W. RHODE

THROUGHOUT human history, a dominant concern has been how to produce enough
food and fiber to feed and clothe the population. In 1790, roughly 95 percent of the US
population resided in rural areas, and most worked on farms. The nineteenth and twentieth centuries witnessed a continual decline in the share of the US workforce engaged in
agriculture. In 2010, about 1.6 percent of the civilian labor force worked on farms (Carter
et al. 2006, Series Aa31; US President 2012, 361). The story of how an ever shrinking percentage of the workforce could provide the raw materials to feed and clothe the nation
and provide a bounty of exports is largely a saga of how scientific advances and a stream
of new technologies transformed the agricultural landscape. In the United States, the
cultivation of vast sections of new land and the diffusion of new technologies fundamentally changed agricultural constraints and dramatically reduced the real price of
most farm products.

AGRICULTURAL EXPANSION

....

In the 1893 speech that launched his career to preeminence in the American history profession, Frederick Jackson Turner famously announced the "Closing of the Frontier" at
the World's Columbian Exposition in Chicago. For Turner, the availability of new land
resources had provided a "safety value" that reduced class conflict in the United States
and provided the "material forces that gave vitality to Western democracy" (Turner
1903, 92; 1921, 63, 281). Turner's pronouncement, based on population density statistics
from the 1890 census, proved premature, at least from the perspective of the agricultural sector. The nation's farmland stock continued to grow into the 1920s and 1930s. But
Turner's main point was correct: the outward push of the frontier occurring after the
1890s paled in comparison to what had come before. The change in cropland harvested

tells the story. The total stock of land devoted to crops in United States in 1800 was, according to the best estimates, around 10–11 million acres (Gallman 1972, 199).[1] By 1850, the number had grown to 80 million acres. By 1900, over 283 million acres were devoted to crops—more than twenty-five times the area in crops in 1800. Such a rapid rate of growth was extraordinary and clearly unsustainable.

This rapid expansion shaped the American economy, society, politics, and culture in myriad ways, some that Turner noted and others that he did not. It left a legacy of conquest, as indigenous peoples were subjugated and displaced in the drive to acquire their lands. The outward expansion also contributed to traditions of social rootlessness and of limitless sprawl. But the opportunity to acquire farmlands cheaply also encouraged economic mobility, greater equality in the regions without slavery, and more generally an atmosphere of a "people of plenty." Apart from the first chaotic years of European settlement, the United States and its colonial antecedents never experienced a general famine. This is true of few other regions of the world.

The expansion involved a great shift in the location of agricultural activity. In 1800, the nation's agricultural center, as measured by the mean latitude and longitude of the county-level distribution of the farm labor force, was in Fairfax County, Virginia (near Washington, DC). In 1850, the center was located in Martin County, Kentucky, on the (West) Virginia border. By 1900, the agricultural center had shifted some 300 miles to the west into Gallatin County, Illinois, moving roughly six miles per year over this half-century.[2] In this period, there was little northerly shift in the *center* of agricultural activity. The movement west continued into the twentieth century, albeit at a slower pace. Tracking movement of the center is informative, but it is also important to investigate changes in the fringes of the geographical distribution of the farm labor stock to gauge the shift in the frontier. For this purpose, we can focus on changes in the longitude dividing the location of the westernmost 10 percent of the labor force from the more eastern 90 percent. In 1800, the line was just west of 82 degrees longitude (think of a line running north-south through central Ohio); in 1850, it ran just east of 91 degrees (near the Mississippi River); and in 1900, the 90 percent line lay midway between 97 and 98 degrees of longitude (well into the Great Plains). These changing margins of production defined the western expansion of commercial agriculture.

SHIFTING FRONTIERS
AND BIOLOGICAL LEARNING

The lore of westward movement as ingrained in American culture and myth depicts rugged and daring settlers venturing out onto new lands in the search of a new livelihood and independence. Vast tracks of land were there for the taking. There were many challenges—building a new capital stock (houses, barns, fences, and water supplies), creating new states and political institutions, extending the transportation infrastructure, and sometimes confronting understandably hostile indigenous populations. But settlement also invariably involved overcoming fundamental scientific barriers—learning how to grow crops in an alien environment. Agricultural production is location specific, subject to growing conditions that varied across regions and even nearby farms. The new lands in the continent's interior typically possessed more arid and variable climates than those from which the settlers came. And the learning process did not stop once the settlers got their start because, as areas matured, farmers often adopted more intensive agricultural regimes, requiring additional experimentation. We can profitably explore the processes by analyzing the changing location and climatic conditions faced by the producers of America's three great nineteenth-century staples—wheat, corn, and cotton.

Wheat was the most important settler crop in the westward expansion in the northern United States (and Canada). Circa 1800, wheat culture was centered in the Chesapeake and Mid-Atlantic states (as diseases limited the crop in many parts of New England and the Lower South.) The best estimate is that the United States produced just under 26 million bushels in 1800 (Gallman 1972, 199).[3] With the push of the agricultural frontier over the Appalachia Mountains, wheat culture entered a vast new territory for expansion. From 1839 to 1929, US wheat production increased nearly ten times, rising from roughly 85 million to 801 million bushels. During this ninety-year span the geographical center of US wheat output shifted 967 miles from near Wheeling, (West) Virginia, to the Iowa/Nebraska borderlands. The changes in the geographic center of wheat production reflected enormous shifts in the range of growing conditions. According to Mark Carleton, a prominent agronomist, the regions of North America producing wheat in the early twentieth century were as "different from each other as though they lay in different continents" (Carleton 1900, 9). Table 7.1 displays the main features of the changing geographic distribution of the US wheat crop across latitudes, longitudes, annual mean temperature and precipitation, and January mean temperature for four selected years—1839, 1899, 1929, and 2002. It also shows the median (the 50th percentile) as well as the lower and upper deciles (the 10th and 90th percentiles). For example, the 90th percentile by longitude shows the dividing line where 90 percent of production was grown east of that longitude and 10 percent to the west. Looking at the fringes of production, the tails of the distribution, offers a good sense of what was possible and how this changed over time.

The top panel of table 7.1 shows the distribution of wheat production by longitude. It indicates a steady westward shift in the median location. The rapid movement in the most westward frontier (at and above the 90 percent line) captures the takeoff of wheat culture in California. The panel of latitude indicates that the median always lies in or near a band between 40 to 41 degrees north (roughly speaking, the latitude of New York City). But the northernmost 10 percent of production moved nearly 5 degrees (or about 335 miles) between 1839 and 1929. Most of this movement took place in the nineteenth century. The changes in the median annual and January temperatures were small. But the range of temperature conditions greatly widened, with production moving into both hotter and colder areas. The movement into more frigid zones was most pronounced.

Table 7.1 Distribution of US Wheat Production

Attribute		Percent of Production	1839	1899	1929	2002
Longitude	East	10	76.02	81.49	84.23	86.04
Degrees		50	80.65	95.69	99.33	99.00
	West	90	87.02	117.25	116.91	117.25
Latitude	South	10	35.19	36.84	36.39	35.19
Degrees		50	39.95	41.17	40.50	40.84
	North	90	42.94	46.88	47.65	48.21
Annual	Driest	10	33.2	18.0	13.9	11.8
precipitation	(inches)	50	39.0	29.2	22.0	21.0
	Wettest	90	47.0	42.6	38.7	42.0
Annual	Coldest	10	47.8	41.0	40.9	40.2
temperature	(°F)	50	52.6	50.4	51.6	51.3
	Hottest	90	58.7	59.8	57.9	61.2
January	Coldest	10	23.6	7.5	8.3	5.9
temperature	(°F)	50	30.1	26.8	27.8	27.8
	Hottest	90	38.5	38.7	36.0	40.5
Output	M/bu.		85	659	801	1,577
Acreage	Million		N/A	52.6	62.6	45.5
Yield	bu/acre		N/A	12.5	12.8	34.6

Sources: Olmstead and Rhode (2011b, 174–175); Carter et al. (2006, Series Da 730, 731); USDA (2004, Table 34).

Between 1839 and 1929 the average annual temperature of the coldest 10 percent of production (the 10 percent line) dropped nearly 7°F, and for the January temperature, the coldest 10 percent fell by over 15°F. The most pronounced changes occurred in the distribution of production by annual precipitation. In 1929, median production took place in a drier environment than virtually anything recorded in 1839. In 1929 the marginal fringe with less than fifteen inches of rain produced as much wheat as was grown in the entire United States in 1839, when the wheat areas' median precipitation was about 40 inches, and almost no wheat was produced in areas with less than 30 inches. The varieties of wheat adapted to the Eastern states or Western Europe simply would not prosper on the Western prairie, Great Plains, or Inland Empire of the Pacific Northwest. The farmers who tried to grow the eastern varieties in the early years of settlement typically met with ruin.

The successful spread of wheat cultivation to the Great Plains was dependent on the introduction of hard red winter and hard red spring wheats that were entirely new to the American continent.[4] The first important hard spring wheat was Red Fife. According to the standard account, David and Jane Fife saved and increased the seed stock from a single plant grown on their Ontario, Canada, farm in 1842. Red Fife was the first hard spring wheat grown in North America and became the basis for the development of the northern wheat belt. Another notable breakthrough was the introduction of a hard red winter variety "Turkey" which was suitable to the southern wheat belt. Here the standard account credits German Mennonites, who migrated to Kansas from southern Russia, with its introduction in 1873. By 1919, Turkey-type wheat accounted for over 80 percent of wheat acreage in Kansas and Nebraska and almost 70 percent in Oklahoma and Colorado. Agronomists also contributed important new varieties. Following seed-gathering expeditions in the Russian Empire, Mark Carleton imported several durum varieties to the northern plains and hardy winter wheats to the southern grain belt around 1900. Fledgling scientific laboratories and extension farms yielded other important varieties. A key twentieth-century innovation was Marquis, bred by Charles Saunders of Canada and introduced to the United States in 1912–1913. Offering a sense of its superior performance, by 1919 its range stretched from Washington State to northern Illinois (Olmstead and Rhode 2008, 25–37).

When possible, grain growers prefer to plant winter wheat instead of spring wheat. Winter wheat offers higher yields and is less subject to pest damage, but suffers from winterkill in colder climates. Biological innovation expanded the range in which winter wheat was feasible. In 1869, the "spring wheat–winter wheat" frontier ran southeast from Chicago, through northern Missouri, and then swept to the southwest into southeastern Kansas. By 1929, this frontier had shifted to the north and west, to incorporate much of Illinois, most of Iowa and Nebraska, and almost all of Kansas. The new winter wheat area accounted for almost 30 percent of total US production in 1929 (Olmstead and Rhode 2008, 37–38). This and other advances based on the introduction, selection, and breeding of new wheat varieties significantly enhanced the productivity of American farmers.

As with wheat, US corn production expanded and shifted dramatically. Circa 1800, production by European Americans and African Americans was concentrated along the Atlantic seaboard. Gallman estimates their total crop was 135 million bushels (1972, 199). By 1839, production had nearly tripled to 378 million bushels. The expansion had just begun; in the 1920s, the corn crop was about seven times larger than in 1839. Between 1839 and 1929, the geographic center of corn production moved from the vicinity of Richmond, Kentucky, to near Hannibal, Missouri, about 425 miles to the west-northwest. The "Corn Belt" shifted from Kentucky and Tennessee into the Midwest (Hudson 1994). Table 7.2 shows the changing distribution of US corn production by location and climatic conditions. The panel on longitude captures the westward movement in corn production—the median location shifted by about 6 degrees (over 330 miles) between 1839 and 1929. The median latitude shifted 2.5 degrees (roughly 200 miles) to the north. There were significant changes in climatic conditions. In the ninety years after 1939, the median annual temperature under which corn was grown fell by almost 5°F, and the median annual precipitation fell by almost nine inches.

As with wheat, varietal changes in maize helped make these geographic and climate shifts possible. The Corn Belt Dent varieties that came to dominate in the

Table 7.2 Distribution of US Corn Production

Attribute		Percent of Production	1839	1899	1929	2002
Longitude	East	10	76.70	82.64	83.00	85.70
Degrees		50	84.54	90.75	92.05	92.68
	West	90	90.12	97.25	97.86	98.73
Latitude	South	10	33.31	34.71	34.40	37.79
Degrees		50	37.78	40.10	40.48	41.38
	North	90	40.58	42.63	43.29	44.42
Annual	Driest	10	36.9	27.9	25.1	22.1
precipitation	(inches)	50	43.9	36.0	34.8	32.4
	Wettest	90	53.3	47.3	48.4	40.5
Annual	Coldest	10	50.9	47.7	46.4	44.5
temperature	(°F)	50	56.3	52.5	51.5	49.9
	Hottest	90	63.3	61.4	61.8	56.1
January	Coldest	10	26.7	18.8	16.3	12.9
temperature	(°F)	50	35.1	26.9	26.2	22.7
	Hottest	90	45.4	41.7	42.4	33.2
Output	M/bu.		378	2666	2131	8613
Acreage	Million		N/A	94.9	83.2	68.2
Yield	bu/acre		N/A	28.1	25.6	126.2

Sources: Olmstead and Rhode (2011b, 182–183); Carter et al. (2006, Series Da708, 709); USDA (2004, Table 34).

Midwest differed from those grown further east. Yankee farmers typically planted Flint corns, a set of early-maturing varieties that produced one or more long, cylindrical ears with smooth, hard kernels. Southern farmers typically planted higher-yielding, later-maturing Dent corns, which produced several rounded ears with softer, dimpled kernels. In the places where migration flows from New England and from Virginia/Kentucky overlapped, the northern Flints crossed with the southern Dents. The resulting Corn Belt Dents combined the higher yields of the Dents with the earlier maturation and greater hardiness of the Flints. Such crosses occurred accidentally thousands of times during the Midwest's settlement. But the process of corn improvement was not just the product of serendipity—breeders such as John Lorain, Christopher and Jacob Leaming (father and son), and Robert Reid systematically developed key varieties of open-pollinated corn. Of special significance was the work of Andrew Boss, C. P. Bull, and Willet Hays at the University of Minnesota who developed Yellow Dent Minnesota No. 13 and No. 23. These early-ripening varieties reduced the necessary growing season by over one month, allowing farmers to grow corn much further north than previously possible. Between 1869 and 1929, it became feasible for farmers in much of Michigan, Wisconsin, Minnesota, and South Dakota, and parts of other states, to convert from wheat to corn production when this move made economic sense. Just as the spring-winter wheat frontier shifted north, the corn-wheat frontier also moved into more frigid areas. The construction of the famous Corn Palace at Mitchell, South Dakota, in 1892 celebrated this northern shift of the corn frontier. Without biological innovation, this movement would not have been possible (Olmstead and Rhode 2008, 71–75, 80–86).

Upland cotton similarly required extensive adaptation as its culture spread across the southern United States. According to J. O. Ware, a leading cotton researcher, the varieties that became the basis for the South's development were a distinctly "Dixie product." In its native environment in Central America, upland cotton was a frost-intolerant, perennial shrub with short-day photoperiod response. These traits meant that many of the varieties first introduced to the United States did not mature properly. Success required finding a mutation/cross or a variety with the appropriate characteristics. Green seed cottons, available in the early 1790s, gave the Southern industry its start. Improved varieties, mostly notably "Petit Gulf," which was introduced and spread in the early 1830s, provided another great boost. This disease-resistant, easy-to-pick, large-bolled cotton variety was especially adapted to the Mississippi River valley and encouraged a westward shift of production. Further changes led to the development of the cluster cottons and semi-cluster cottons of the late antebellum period. These all represented biological innovations that substantially raised labor productivity. The postbellum period also witnessed the development or importation/acclimation of new varieties suited to addressing new environmental challenges. Among the emerging challenges were survival on the harsh and windy Texas plains, problems with new pests such as the boll weevil (which entered the United States from Mexico in 1892 and swept across the traditional cotton belt by 1920), and adjustments to the irrigated agricultural practices of the Southwest (Olmstead and Rhode 2008, 126).

Cotton culture, which had been concentrated on the South Carolina/Georgia coast around 1800, moved west rapidly over the early nineteenth century. By 1859, the center of cotton production had crossed the Mississippi-Alabama border. In contrast, the center of wheat production did not reach this far west until the 1880s. After 1859, the pace of cotton's westward shift slowed, and the geographic center of production remained within the boundaries of the state of Mississippi for at least the next sixty years. The quantity of cotton output grew over seven times between 1859 and 1929.[5] In the early twentieth century, the geographical fringes of production moved to western lands in Arizona and Central California, with hotter and significantly drier climates. This is particularly evident in table 7.3, which for 2002 shows that the driest 10 percent of production occurred in areas with about one-fifth as much rainfall as the median area of production received in 1839. To facilitate this movement into arid regions, breeders discovered and improved upon hardy varieties, and growers developed new cultural patterns.

Table 7.3 Distribution of US Cotton Production

Attribute		Percent of Production	1839	1899	1929	2002
Longitude	East	10	81.11	81.34	81.98	83.58
Degrees		50	87.63	90.24	90.82	91.85
	West	90	91.54	97.12	99.54	118.88
Latitude	South	10	30.88	30.61	31.22	31.27
Degrees		50	32.76	32.95	33.6	33.96
	North	90	34.98	35.07	35.62	36.32
Annual	Driest	10	45.4	34.0	23.4	10.2
precipitation	(inches)	50	51.8	49.0	47.7	45.4
	Wettest	90	57.0	54.4	54.0	52.3
Annual	Coldest	10	60.9	61.0	60.0	58.9
temperature	(°F)	50	64.1	64.1	63.4	62.3
	Hottest	90	66.8	67.5	66.9	67.6
January	Coldest	10	41.2	40.9	38.9	38.3
temperature	(°F)	50	46.2	45.4	43.8	43.7
	Hottest	90	50.9	50.0	49.9	51.2
Output	M. Bales		1.98	9.54	14.57	17.14
Acreage	Million		N/A	24.28	43.23	12.47
Yield	Bales/acre		N/A	0.39	0.34	1.37

Sources: Olmstead and Rhode (2011b, 188–189); Carter et al. (2006, Series Da766, 767); USDA (2004, Table 34).

✳MECHANIZATION

Mechanization joined biological innovation in contributing to the growth of US farm output and productivity over the nineteenth and early twentieth centuries. American inventors supplied farmers with a marvelous array of labor-saving devices. Among the most significant early innovations were the steel moldboard plow, the grain thresher, and the mechanical reaper. When first introduced in the 1830s, the thresher and reaper were nothing short of revolutionary. Cyrus McCormick, the principal inventor of the reaper, began known as the "man who made bread cheap." (The reaper's close cousin, the mechanical mower invented by Obed Hussey, eased the hay harvest.) The reaper (especially after a series of improvements) vastly reduced the need for harvest labor and encouraged the expansion of small grain acreage per farm. It also induced western settlement, as the machine method proved better suited to the flat and open terrains of the Midwest and Great Plains than to the rockier and enclosed lands of the East. The technology of early grain machines served as platforms for further invention and refinement, eventually cumulating in the marriage of the reaper and thresher in the giant combined harvesters of the late nineteenth century. These early combines were powered by forty or so mules or horses and were at the time one of the wonders of the world. Reflecting the importance of geographical forces, they were first mass-produced and adopted in California, where the large farms and arid climate were conducive to their deployment (Olmstead and Rhode 2014).

Mechanization, in general, involved replacing hand tools and human power with machinery driven by draft power (first from animals and later from fossil fuels and electricity). The shift increased the amount of land one worker could plant and harvest and often also raised yields per acre by allowing more thorough and timely work. Mechanization increased farm productivity and changed the nature of farm work. In 1900, the typical American farm worker produced twice as much total output and over three times as much crop output as a worker in 1800 (Weiss 1993, 335).

Many conventional accounts equate mechanization with labor saving and increased acreage per worker and equate biological innovation (improved seeds, better fertilizers, etc.) with increased yields per acre. The reality is more complicated. Some new seed varieties, such as Petit Gulf cottons, allowed for higher labor productivity by opening the boll wide and allowing slaves to pick about four times as much cotton per day in 1860 as in 1810. Conversely, some new machines (such as Eli Whitney's saw gin of 1793) were labor saving at the farm level because even with the early primitive models, one laborer could do the work of a hundred people picking out seeds by hand. The gin gave planters an incentive to plant more—a lot more—cotton. Thus it induced agricultural development to follow a far more labor-using path at the economy-wide level than was otherwise possible. The net result was the use of far more labor in the cotton enterprise.

An analysis of the impact of the gasoline tractor illustrates the issues involved. The first tractors of the 1900s and 1910s were behemoths suitable for such tasks as plowing, harrowing, and belt-work. Among the scores of innovations that increased the machine's appeal was the 1924 introduction of the general-purpose tractor, which could pull cultivating implements through fields of growing crops. Around the same time, the power takeoff became available, enabling the transfer of power from the engine directly to implements under tow. The stock of tractors increased from about one thousand machines in 1910, to 246,000 in 1920, and to 920,000 in 1930. The machine's spread led to the displacement of horses and mules. The tractor greatly increased the amount of power available to farmers and saved considerable labor that had been devoted to caring for animals. Thus, the tractor was an important labor-saving innovation. However, the machine reduced the amount of land needed to grow feed for draft stock, eventually releasing about one-quarter of US cropland to produce food and fiber for human consumption. Thus, at the level of the agricultural sector as a whole and for individual farmers, the tractor also proved to be a major land-saving innovation (Olmstead and Rhode 2008, 372–384).[6] This case was not an exception—many other machines saved both labor and land, just as many biological innovations saved both factors of production.

AGRICULTURAL GROWTH AND
THE AGGREGATE ECONOMY

One notable feature of American economic development over the nineteenth and early twentieth centuries is that the agricultural sector continued to expand even as the country industrialized. While its relative share of the economy declined, the agricultural sector grew enormously in absolute terms. Information from *Historical Statistics of the United States* helps illustrate these changes (Carter et al. 2006, Series Ba 821, Ba 829, and Ba 830). The farm labor force increased from 1.3 million workers in 1800 to 4.9 million in 1850 and then to 10.4 million in 1900. To provide a sense of the importance of the agricultural sector, over the same period, the US manufacturing labor force rose from a fewer than one hundred thousand in 1800 to 1.5 million in 1850 and to 5.9 million in 1900. The farm sector's share of the total labor force fell from 74 percent in 1800 to 60 percent in 1850 and then to 36 percent in 1900. Although the agricultural sector experienced a relative decline, the number of farms and the farm population continued to grow in absolute terms into the 1920s and 1930s (see fig. 7.1, based on Carter et al. 2006, Series Da 1, Da 4, Da 14, Da 16, Da 612). The combination of agricultural expansion and rapid industrialization was a rarity in countries experiencing modern economic growth.

The relationship between the development of agricultural and nonagricultural sectors in the United States was been debated since the earliest days of the Republic. The 1790s began with a set of heated policy debates between Thomas Jefferson and Alexander Hamilton over the inherent value of agricultural/rural development versus industrial/commercial/urban development, over the political and social roles of the family farm,

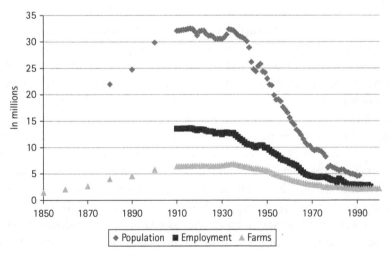

FIGURE 7.1. Farm population, employment, and number of units
Source: Carter et al. (2006, Da 1, Da 4, Da 14, Da 16, Da 612).

and over the desirability of using federal government policies to promote the welfare of one sector at the expense of the other. Jefferson saw land-owning yeoman farmers as the Republic's "most valuable citizens," writing, "I think our governments will remain virtuous for many centuries; as long as they are chiefly agricultural; and this will be as long as there shall be vacant lands in any part of America. When they get piled upon one another in large cities, as in Europe, they will become corrupt as in Europe" (Jefferson 1953, 426; 1955, 433). The Jefferson-Hamilton policy debates raged over whether the public lands should be sold off rapidly in small parcels at low prices to actual settlers, or slowly in large parcels at high prices to huge land developers/speculators; whether to impose protective tariffs to tax consumers/farmers to promote industrialization; whether to charter federal-sponsored financial institutions to provide short-term trade credit to merchants only, or to also extend long-term mortgages to farmers; among other issues. These debates continued throughout the nineteenth century, coming to a head in the Populist Revolt led by William Jennings Bryan in the 1890s.

There was a related debate over linkages connecting the agricultural and nonagricultural sectors. Benjamin Franklin saw the agricultural and nonagricultural sectors as inherently competitive; Alexander Hamilton disagreed. In Hamilton's view, the two sectors were complementary (and hence government policies that promoted industry ultimately benefited agriculture as well) (Meyer 2003, 1–6). According to his 1791 Report on Manufactures, "the *aggregate* prosperity of manufactures, and the *aggregate* prosperity of Agriculture are intimately connected" (Hamilton 1964, 164). A prosperous commercially oriented agricultural sector encouraged industry by providing larger markets for manufactured products, and by supplying inexpensive raw materials for processing, as well as cheap food for industrial workers. Local manufacturing development created a larger market for agricultural products, subject to fewer "injurious interruptions" than foreign trade. The key was that American agriculture took a commercially oriented path (rather than one based on self-sufficiency). By Hamilton's reckoning, the competition for labor was muted because manufacturing could employ women and children who were underutilized on the farm, as well as attract new migrants from abroad.

Benjamin Franklin countered,

> Manufactures are founded in poverty. It is the number of poor without land in a country, and who must work for others at low wages or starve, that enables undertakers to carry on a manufacture.. ... But no man, who can have a piece of land of his own, sufficient by his labor to subsist his family in plenty, is poor enough to be a manufacturer, and work for a master. Hence while there is land enough in America for our people, there can never be manufactures to any amount or value. (Franklin 1760, 18).

Franklin's position is consistent with a textbook neoclassical trade model where industry and agriculture compete for the nation's fixed stock of labor and sell their products in a large international market.

The main issues in this debate are whether the economy is open or closed to trade and whether the supply of labor is fixed and fully employed (Matsuyama 1992). If an economy is open to trade, then the links between agricultural and industrial development in that economy are weaker—for example, the industrial sector can draw on imports to sustain its population. Agricultural advances in an open economy characterized by comparative advantage in the agricultural sector can slow the economy's industrial development. The American South after the invention and diffusion of the cotton gin offers a prominent example. In a closed economy, the situation is different. If food demand follows Engel's Law—as income rises, the share spent on food falls—then a revolution in agricultural productivity can free up resources, raise income and nonfood demand, and thereby promote industrialization. These are among the potential channels affecting whether industrial growth occurred *in spite of* agricultural growth or *because of* and/or *along with* agricultural growth.

Franklin himself had noted another channel whereby the changes within the rural areas reduced the competition between agriculture and other activities. In early America, where land was readily available, the rate of natural population increase was very high. The age of first marriage was low, marriage was virtually universal, and fertility was high. As a result, in any given area, the rapidly growing labor pool eventually pressed against the land constraint. As land became scarcer locally, some chose to migrate away to newly opened agricultural areas or to towns and cities to take up nonagricultural occupations. The rate of natural increase in rural areas tended to fall over time but remained above the economy-wide average and typically above required replacement rates (Craig 1993; Easterlin 1976; Franklin 1755; Smith 1980).

The relationships linking agriculture to other sectors have long been of concern to economists interested in development and growth. Many cross-country studies have recently highlighted how variations in the size and performance of the agricultural sector account for most of the variations in the overall performance (per capita income, productivity, and so on) across nations and regions (Caselli 2005, 719–727; Restuccia, Tang, and Zhu 2008). Productivity and income per worker tend to be lower in the agricultural sector than in the nonagricultural sector. Hence, nations or regions with large workforce shares in agriculture tend to have lower overall productivity and income per worker. Cross-country studies have also shown that the performance of the agricultural sector tends to vary much more across nations and regions than the performance of the nonagricultural sector. Areas that are poor tend to have the agricultural sectors with the lowest productivity and income per worker. Achieving higher economy-wide per capita income is associated with improving the performance of the agricultural sector and contracting its shares of the labor force and population. A rapid movement out of farming does not require "anti-agricultural" policies. As John W. Mellor noted, "the faster agriculture grows, the faster its relative size declines" (1995, 1). Most studies of the United States in the post-1870 period find the patterns of regional growth conform to these more global observations.

The observation that measured output (income) per worker is lower in the agricultural sector than in the nonagricultural sector is hardly news; rather, it lies at the core

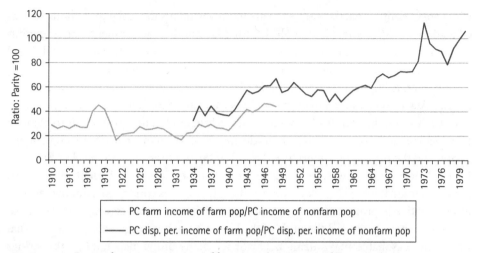

FIGURE 7.2. Ratio of per capita income of farm population to nonfarm population

Notes: The "Farm Income Series," available from 1910 to 1949, excludes the income of the farm population from nonfarm sources other than government payments. The "Disposable Personal Income Series," available after 1934, includes all nonfarm income of the farm population.

Sources: USDA, *Farm Income Situation* (July–August 1949, 10); (July 1974, 50); the disposable personal income series spliced after 1974 to USDA, *Agricultural Statistics* (1981, 418).

of Simon Kuznets's investigations of the "development gap." Figure 7.2 shows the ratio of per capita income of the farm population relative to that of the nonfarm population. In the 1930s, the ratio stood around 40 percent. The low relative agricultural income reflected the lower labor productivity in that sector. This represented a classic case of resources not having moved fast enough out of a traditional sector (and perhaps a preference by some for a rural lifestyle). After 1940, the gap began to close due to the rapid exodus of labor out of agriculture and the increasing rate of technological change within the sector. By the 1970s, per capita farm and nonfarm incomes were nearly equal. Many have bemoaned the decline in the agricultural population for social and nostalgic reasons, but it is unlikely that the rapid rise in agricultural incomes could have been possible without these changes. An international perspective reinforces this conclusion.

A related set of issues of great interest focuses on what structure of agriculture best promotes economic growth. The common view confirmed in many historical and con-temporary studies is that where farming involves very large-scale operations owned by a small elite and using disempowered, unskilled labor, long-run growth will be stymied. By contrast, where agriculture involves family farms made up of relatively homoge-nous populations, growth and development will be more likely. The underlying argu-ment deals largely with the different political economy of societies with dramatically contrasting income and wealth distributions. This is a dynamic argument rather than an assertion that one or another type of agricultural landholding pattern is inherently more efficient at any point in time than the other. The egalitarian regions associated with family farms and homogeneous populations are far more likely to foster societies with widespread political participation and greater investments in local public goods such as education, transportation, and public health. Many of these investments can be conducive to technological and social innovations, which can be disruptive to the established order. These societies are also more likely to foster the growth of local urban centers, which generate important spinoffs for development (Acemoglu and Robinson 2012, 74–80, 243; Atack and Bateman 1987, 37–101; Engerman and Sokoloff 2011, 9–30).

In US history, the contrast between the American South and North tends to confirm these general notions. Southern planters during the slave regime failed to invest in public goods, and the plantations internalized many of the functions that in the New England, Mid-Atlantic, and Midwestern states led to urban development (Wright 1986, 19–28; 2006, 55–70). After the Civil War, some of these tendencies continued. Landowners had little incentive to promote the education of poor laborers and sharecroppers—to do so would only have increased the odds of the laborers leaving for greener pastures. What was likely reasonable maximizing behavior for many individuals holding the strings of political power was detrimental to the larger society's development. In the North, even many small farmers and certainly many residents of villages, towns, and smaller cities voted to tax themselves to pay for public education and other collective goods. Education (and human capital formation more generally) has been a driving engine of economic growth around the world, and by the mid-nineteenth century many Northern regions were clearly on course for developing the world's premier broad-based public schooling system. As appealing as this argument on the effect of the relative distribution of land, wealth, and power on economic development is, there are counter examples. One can point to cases where the small-scale individual proprietors adopted a conservative peasant orientation and avoided risk, change, or market engagement.

Another counterexample to "the small-farms are good for development" paradigm can arise in very dynamic societies. In California, very large estates emerged from the legacy of Mexican and Spanish land grants, railroad land grants, the control of water access, and the like. Gradually, many of the large estates were broken up by market forces as California's agriculture intensified, but many remained—especially in parts of the Central valley (the San Joaquin and Sacramento valleys) and the Salinas valley. A snapshot taken at any number of historical dates would show a handful of wealthy landowners and a large number of itinerant laborers and their families. This is the picture made popular in John Steinbeck's *Grapes of Wrath*. But before Steinbeck's Great Depression dust bowl migrants of the 1930s, Chinese, Japanese, Sikh, Filipino, Armenian, various southern European, and Mexican immigrants replaced one another to fill this niche at the bottom of the agricultural ladder. Since the 1930s, Mexican immigrants and workers of Mexican descent have largely occupied the lower rungs of the ladder. Critics of California's historic labor arrangements and landholding patterns point to squalid conditions and the inability of the immigrants to move up the *agricultural ladder* to become renters and eventually independent owners. This critique misses the tremendous economic and social mobility that in fact has occurred as past cohorts and their descendants moved up the *occupational ladder*.

Agricultural labor offered immigrants, many of whom had little facility with the English language and little understanding of American society, a stepping stone into the larger robust economy. Hard work, high savings rates, and the availability of public education worked wonders: few of the descendants of the earlier generations of agricultural laborers toil in the fields today. Some of those separated by a few generations from the original immigrants are in fact landowners, but most have moved into urban blue- and white-collar professions with skills, educational levels, and incomes on par with citizens who are descendants from earlier waves of northern European migrants. Over the span of decades, agricultural labor in California has not been a dead-end pursuit creating a permanent class of peasant laborers, but this result is dependent on the existence of a growing nonagricultural economy.

STRUCTURAL TRANSFORMATION
AND GOVERNMENT POLICY

Since 1970, the American economy has experienced a fundamental transformation from an industrial to an information- and service-based economy. The earlier shift of the American economy away from its agricultural base offers an important example of a structural transition, illustrating the significant societal impacts and policy responses accompanying in such major changes. The size of the US farm sector plateaued during the 1910–1940 period (see fig. 7.1). The farm population ranged between 30.5 and 32.5 million persons and the number of farms between 6.4 and 6.8 million units. Even the "hard times on the farm" of the 1920s and 1930s did not cause the sector to contract. After World War II, US agriculture entered a period of rapid transformation. Between 1945 and 1960, some 15 million people left the farm sector. By 1960, about 16 million people lived on the nation's 4 million farms. By 2000, the numbers were further reduced, with fewer than 5 million people (less than 2 percent of the US population) residing on the nation's 2 million farms. Figure 7.1 offers a long-run perspective on the size of the farm population, farm employment, and the number of farms. The rapid declines starting around 1940 represent a dramatic break from the historical pattern.

Among the drivers in the structural transformation was rapid technological change within agriculture. Mechanization continued apace, allowing for increasing the land-labor ratio, greater farm size, and more output per farm worker. In addition, new knowledge about genetics and chemistry, along with the maturation of the publicly funded Agricultural Research System, led to the so-called biological revolution from the 1930s on. This was associated with the first significant widespread wave of increasing national average yields per acre of the major staple crops.[7] Yields were pushed higher by the use of improved seeds, such as hybrid corn, and the greater application of farm chemicals, especially of nitrogen-based fertilizers. The federal-state Agricultural Research System contributed greatly to the development and diffusion of these new technologies. The origins of this research-and-extension system date back to establishment of the state land grant college system and the US Department of Agriculture (USDA) in 1862, of a dedicated animal health service (the Bureau of Animal Industry) in 1884, of the agricultural experiment station system in 1887, and of the cooperative extension service in 1914. After some delays, the effects of the system began to kick up, yielding very high payoffs.

These government-funded research investments helped address the problem that bio-agricultural advances were often public goods. Their creation yielded spillovers that individual private inventors found hard to capture. Hybrid corn, the poster child of the biological revolution, represents something of an exception. The basic scientific knowledge was generated in the public research system, specifically from the development in 1918 of the double-cross method by Edward East and Donald Jones of the Connecticut Experiment Station. But private firms, most notably Pioneer (founded by Henry A. Wallace in 1924) and DeKalb (which originated from the DeKalb County Illinois Soil Improvement Association, established in 1912) successfully commercialized the technology (Olmstead and Rhode 2008, 65–67). These firms could appropriate the returns from their investments in intellectual property because farmers could not gain the benefits of the improved seed without buying fresh stock every year. Pioneer and DeKalb became leading firms in the biological and later "bio-tech" revolutions. The hybridization method could be extended to sorghum and a few other crops, but not to most agricultural products. And efforts to create intellectual property through the passage of the 1930 Plant Patent Act, which covered asexually reproduced plant materials (such as plants reproduced by cuttings rather than seeds), had little initial impact on agriculture. Until the most recent period, the public sector contributed most of the investment in agricultural research and extension. Overall, these investments yielded a high rate of return to the nation (Alston et al. 2010, 271–311, 353–408).

Another key change in the post–World War II period was the decision to reinstate the prewar price and acreage-based regulations, and thus reject returning to the free market conditions that had existed before the 1930s. The New Deal measures had been suspended during World War II, but after the war, farm organizations and their political leaders lobbied effectively against returning to the free market regime or even adopting policies to insure against income variability. Federal farm support programs, which were originally justified as emergency measures, proved very difficult to eliminate as Jefferson's once resourceful farmers became dependent on government handouts. Farmers lost a large measure of control over what to grow and on how much land. In return, they received higher prices and direct subsidies and largely retained control over how to grow their crops, including taking measures to increase yields on the allotted acreage.

Agricultural prices and incomes had long been highly volatile. And farmers have long complained, but the federal government began to respond only in the 1920s and 1930s. America's World War I experience with government control of the economy created a model and helped legitimize interventionist policies. Shortages during World War I led to high crop prices and soaring land values. The post-1920 bust left the US agricultural sector with overcapacity and a large debt overhang. Hard times had hit the farm. The leaders of increasingly powerful farm organizations sought relief through the creation of cooperatives to impose "orderly marketing" schemes and via government-sponsored trade interventions. Their main initiative was the McNary-Haugen plan to separate the domestic and export markets through tariffs. The federal government would buy at high "parity" prices any output that did not clear in the domestic market at artificially set high prices and dump the surplus abroad at the lower world prices. In 1927 and 1928, the McNary-Haugen bills passed the Republican-led Congress but were vetoed by President Coolidge, who deemed the measures un-American. His successor, Herbert Hoover, responded to the worsening farm crisis by establishing the Federal Farm Board to buy and store commodities in order to raise prices. This scheme backfired because after the Board's initial funding dried up, it was forced to sell off its hoards into the depressed markets, pushing prices lower still. These unsuccessful first steps did not diminish the calls for government market interventions (Benedict 1953, 194–198, 216–266).

The agricultural situation was grave in March 1933, when Franklin D. Roosevelt assumed the presidency. The Agricultural Adjustment Act (AAA) became the foundation for his farm relief program. The ultimate goal was to raise the purchasing power of most agricultural products to the 1909–1914 parity ratio of agricultural-to-manufacturing prices by restricting production. Seven "basic" commodities (wheat, cotton, rice, field corn, hogs, tobacco, and dairy products) were originally eligible for production controls (eight other commodities were added by 1935). Under the Commodity Credit Corporation, farmers could pledge their crops as collateral (at generous evaluations) for "nonrecourse loans" and could contract with the government to remove cropland from cultivation in return for a "benefit payment." The "loans" were often little more than a subterfuge for outright government purchases, because if commodity prices failed to increase, farmers could keep the loan payment and the government would obtain ownership of the crop. The AAA proved a bureaucratic nightmare. The slaughter of six million baby pigs and the plowing under of crops during a period of widespread hunger was highly controversial. The displacement of black sharecroppers and laborers was also of great concern (Rasmussen and Baker 1979; De Pew, Fishback, and Rhode 2013). The US Supreme Court declared the first AAA unconstitutional in early 1936. Citing environment disasters such as the Dust Bowl drought, Congress reinstated many of the same acreage programs under the Soil Conservation Act (1936) and the Second Agricultural Adjustment Act (1938). These and other measures were upheld by the Supreme Court. The New Deal also added other crops; created marketing control boards for specialty crops; and subsidized credit, crop insurance, and exports. The federal government also passed legislation that allowed farmers to renegotiate contracts and reacquire farmsteads lost to banks—forcing lenders to renegotiate contracts set a precedent for similar measures proposed in response to the financial crisis and downturn beginning in 2007.

Pressure to increase output during World War II led to a removal of acreage restrictions. But the Second AAA (together with the 1949 Farm Act) became the organic legislation for many postwar farm-support programs. The decision to reinstate the farm programs after World War II offers an example of Robert Higgs's ratchet effect. Policies

fulldiss too

started in response to a crisis can persist long after the emergency conditions are gone (Higgs 1987, 82–83). In 1949, USDA Secretary Charles F. Brannan proposed replacing price subsidies with direct income payments and setting a maximum amount any one farmer could receive. The Brannan plan would have been economically more efficient than price and acreage controls, but his proposals failed because large commercial farmers opposed limits on subsidies and feared that income-support payments would attract more public scrutiny than the less visible price supports.

High price supports led to unsustainable accumulations of surplus stocks through the 1950s and early 1960s. In the early 1960s, there was a significant shift away from commodity loans and stockpiling toward voluntary acreage diversion programs and direct price-support payments. There have been numerous later program changes to adapt to unintended or undesired consequences. In the late 1970s and early 1980s, high support prices led to a renewed buildup of agricultural stocks. This led to Ronald Reagan's Payment in Kind (PIK) experiment of 1983. PIK allowed farmers to withdraw additional acreage in exchange for title to commodities in government stockpiles. The result was one of the largest and most expensive farm programs in US history, idling 20 percent of US cropland at the cost of $78 billion dollars.

Figure 7.3 plots the value of the stock of crops held by the federal government and the number of cropland acres idled. The wild gyrations of both series suggest the difficulty in stabilizing agricultural markets. As government stocks accumulated, the programs were adjusted to idle more land, leading to a fall in output and a decline in government stocks. But these program adjustments involved large and ultimately unsustainable expenses. The long history of government attempts to stabilize agricultural prices and control production has for the most part proved an inefficient and costly exercise

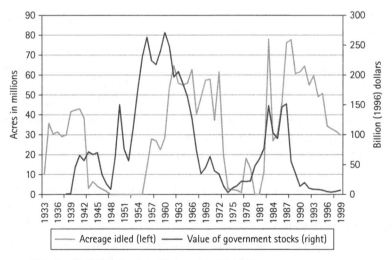

FIGURE 7.3. Cropland idled and value of government stocks

Note: The nominal value of government stocks is converted into real (1996) purchasing power using the GDP deflator.

Source: Carter et al. (2006, Da 1453, Da 1412, Ca 13).

in government regulation. The farm policies were responses not only to the crises of the 1920s and 1930s, but also to the long-run problem of structural transformation, with the number of farmers remaining high and their incomes low. The policies were not designed to provide a root-cause solution to the long-run problem, but rather to transfer resources from the nonfarm sector to the farm sector. The persistence of farm programs illustrates how a small concentrated interest group can often out-lobby a much larger but more diffuse interest. As a general rule, poor countries with large shares of their populations in agriculture tend to tax their farmers. But, as countries get richer and the relative size of the agricultural population shrinks, policies tend to flip and farmers begin receiving subsidies (Gardner 2002, 213–249).

The transition of labor out of agriculture has not affected all groups equally, and has had important consequence both outside and inside the agricultural sector. One of the most socially significant trends was a decline in the number of nonwhite farm operators, especially in the South. The count of nonwhite Southern farm operators fell from 882,000 in 1940 to fewer than 48,000 in 1974. The African American population, which had been predominately rural and Southern, relocated to urban areas across the nation. This shift created enormous challenges for both the migrants and the receiving areas and altered existing political alignments (Alston and Ferrie 1999, 119–142; Wright 1986, 245–527). Pre–World War I emigrants entered an economy offering many backbreaking jobs in manufacturing and mining for low-skilled workers. Recent cohorts of low-skilled Hispanics and Southern African Americans have migrated into a nonagricultural economy that demands more education and that offers far fewer manual jobs in nonagricultural pursuits. This puts a high premium on the new entrants to obtain human capital. The flip side of the falling number of farms since 1940 has been a major change in farm size and structure. Because the number of farms decreased much more sharply than the agricultural land base between 1940 and 2007, the average size of farms in the United States increased from 175 to 418 acres. The share of farms with 1,000 or more acres rose from less than 2 percent of the total number of units in 1940 to about 8 percent in 2007; their share of US farmland increased from 34 percent to 68 percent over the same period.[8] Another feature of the agricultural transformation has been a change in where many farmers chose to live and where many farm residents chose to work. The share of farm operators who live off their farms increased from 5 percent in 1940 to 19 percent in 1999.[9] In addition, many residents of farms have often taken up nonfarm employment.

But what is notable is that US farmers have not greatly changed their use of hired farm labor. In 1910, nonpaid or family workers accounted for 75 percent of total employees. In the mid-1990s, family workers still made up about 70 percent of the total. There is substantial regional variation, with the specialty crop producers on the coasts depending heavily on hired labor and Midwestern farms remaining mostly family-run operations. Because farming requires detailed local knowledge, quick response to emergent situations, and effective supervision of a dispersed workforce, a decentralized family form of management offers many advantages. In activities such as livestock-raising operations, significant economies of scale led to a more concentrated industrial-type structure. But even with the spread of the corporate form of business organization in farming, such factory farming is not likely to become a dominant feature of American agriculture.

CONCLUSION

Studies in American agricultural history offer valuable insights into many important contemporary issues and promising future research directions, including the adaptation to global climatic changes, the impact of genetically modified organisms, the maintenance of food security, the role of agricultural sector in general economic development, and many other topics.

One new direction of exploration seeks to learn lessons regarding past adaptation to climatic challenges and past responses to environment disasters (e.g., the Dust Bowl, great floods) and instances of resource depletion. Recent work in this area has been conducted by scholars including Cunfer (2005), Libecap and Steckel (2011), and Hornbeck (2012; see also Hornbeck and Naidu 2014; Olmstead and Rhode 2011a, 2011b), among others. Scholars also are seeking to understand how societies deal with market failures and collective action problems related to contagious diseases, invasive species, and pest threats. Examples of recent work in this area include Lange, Olmstead, and Rhode (2009), Olmstead and Rhode (2015), and others.

Economic historians, agricultural economists, and students of technology are engaging in exciting new work to investigate the effects of intellectual property rights on the creation of biological knowledge and the importance of public and private investments in agricultural research. Work includes Moser and Rhode (2012) and the important contribution by Alston et al. (2010). Other recent work delves into the origins, impacts, and persistence of federal farm programs, especially to scrutinize how, in a democratic political process, a small fraction of the population tilts government policies in its favor.[10]

Another area of ongoing research relates to understanding how the structure and dynamics of the agricultural sector affect the growth and development of the broader economy. One active research vein that shows no sign of running out explores how the initial distribution of land and labor resources in the agricultural sector influences the formation of economic and political institutions and how these institutions in turn shape the long-run course of economic development. Work in this area includes Wright (2006), Engerman and Sokoloff (2011), Berkowitz and Clay (2011), and Acemoglu and Robinson (2012). A final area of active research investigates how structural change in the allocation of labor (and other mobile resources) between the agricultural and nonagricultural sectors interacts with the regional/sectorial gaps in productivity and earnings to generate (or account for) aggregate income growth. The well-documented American case shows that the movement of resources from low- to high-productivity regions and sectors has been a major source of GDP growth as conventionally measured. The US experience informs investigations into the development process of other countries.[11]

Notes

1. As a point of reference, an acre is 43,560 square feet, which is slightly smaller than the playing area of an American football field (300 feet long times 160 feet wide). There are 640 acres in a square mile.
2. Based on data from Craig and Weiss (1998) linked to county centroids from US Department of Health and Human Services, Health Resources and Services Administration, Bureau of Health Professions Resource File. ICPSR 9075.
3. Estimates by Towne and Rasmussen (1960, 294) of wheat output entering gross product are broadly consistent with Gallman's figure.
4. Winter wheat is planted in early fall and harvested in the early summer, hence it is in the field over the winter. Spring wheat is planted in the spring and harvested in mid- to late summer.
5. Towne and Rasmussen (1960, 308) estimated cotton production expanded 23-fold between 1800 and 1840.
6. It is important to clarify the absolute versus relative uses of the terms in factor-saving. In an absolute sense, a technology can be both labor and land saving, with both the labor-to-net-output and the land-to-net-output ratios falling. In a relative sense, the technology will be called labor saving if the labor falls faster than land.
7. For the changes in yields of wheat, corn, and cotton, see the bottom rows of tables 7.1–7.3.
8. http://www.agcensus.usda.gov/Publications/2007/Full_Report/Volume_1,_Chapter_1_US/st99_1_009_010.pdf.
9. http://www.agcensus.usda.gov/Publications/1997/Agricultural_Economics_and_Land_Ownership/Quick_Facts/1999 Agricultural Economics and Land Ownership Survey (AELOS).
10. Leads to pertinent literature can be found in Gardner (2002), Libecap (1998), and Fishback and coauthors (see De Pew, Fishback, and Rhode 2013).
11. Entree into the relevant literature may be found in Caselli and Coleman (2001) and Restuccia, Tang, and Zhu (2008).

Bibliography

Acemoglu, Daron, and James A. Robinson. (2012). *Why Nations Fail: The Origins of Power, Prosperity, and Poverty.* New York: Crown Business.

Alston, Julian M., Matthew A. Andersen, Jennifer S. James, and Philip G. Pardey. (2010). *Persistence Pays: U.S. Agricultural Productivity Growth and the Benefits from Public R&D Spending.* New York: Springer.

Alston, Lee J., and Joseph P. Ferrie. (1999). *Southern Paternalism and the American Welfare State: Economics, Politics, and Institutions in the South, 1865–1965.* New York: Cambridge University Press.

Atack, Jeremy, and Fred Bateman. (1987). *To Their Own Soil: Agriculture in the Antebellum North.* Ames: Iowa State University Press.

Benedict, Murray R. (1953). *Farm Policies of the United States, 1790–1950: A Study of Their Origins and Development.* New York: Twentieth Century Fund.

Berkowitz, Daniel, and Karen Clay. (2011). *The Evolution of a Nation: How Geography and Law Shaped the American States.* Princeton, NJ: Princeton University Press.

Carleton, Mark A. (1900). "The Basis for the Improvement of American Wheats." *USDA Division of Vegetable Physiology and Pathology Bulletin* 24.

Carter, Susan, Scott S. Gartner, Michael R. Haines, Alan L. Olmstead, Richard Sutch, and Gavin Wright. (2006). *Historical Statistics of the United States: Millennial Edition.* New York: Cambridge University Press.

Caselli, Francesco. (2005). "Accounting for Cross-Country Income Differences." In *Handbook of Economic Growth*, edited by Philippe Aghion and Steven N. Durlauf, Vol. 1A, 680–741. Amsterdam: Elsevier.

Caselli, Francesco, and Wilbur J. Coleman. (2001). "The U.S. Structural Transformation and Regional Convergence: A Re-Interpretation." *Journal of Political Economy* 109(3): 584–616.

Craig, Lee A. (1993). *To Sow One Acre More: Childbearing and Farm Productivity in the Antebellum North.* Baltimore, MD: Johns Hopkins University Press.

Craig, Lee A., and Thomas Weiss. (1996). "Rural Agricultural Workforce by County, 1800–1900." Available at http://eh.net/databases/agriculture/.

Cunfer, Geoff. (2005). *On the Great Plains: Agriculture and Environment.* College Station: Texas A&M University Press.

De Pew, Briggs, Price Fishback, and Paul W. Rhode. (2013). "New Deal or No Deal in the Cotton South: The Effect of the AAA on the Agricultural Labor Structure." *Explorations in Economic History* 50(4): 466–486.

Easterlin, Richard. (1976). "Population Change and Farm Settlement in the Northern United States." *Journal of Economic History* 31(1): 45–75.

Engerman, Stanley, and Kenneth Sokoloff. (2011). *Economic Development in the Americas since 1500: Endowment and Institutions.* New York: Cambridge University Press.

Franklin, Benjamin. (1755 [1751]). *Observations Concerning the Increase of Mankind, Peopling of Countries, etc.* Boston: Kneeland.

Franklin, Benjamin. (1760). *The Interests of Great Britain Considered with Regard to Her Colonies and the Acquisitions of Canada and Guadaloupe.* London: T. Becket.

Gallman, Robert E. (1972). "Changes in Total U.S. Agricultural Factor Productivity in the Nineteenth Century." *Agricultural History* 46(1): 191–210.

Gardner, Bruce L. (2002). *American Agriculture in the Twentieth Century: How It Flourished and What It Cost.* Cambridge, MA: Harvard University Press.

Hamilton, Alexander. (1964). "Report on the Subject of Manufactures, Communicated to the House of Representatives, December 5, 1791." In *Reports of Alexander Hamilton*, edited by Jacob Cooke, 115–205. New York: Harper & Row.

Higgs, Robert. (1987). *Crisis and Leviathan: Critical Episodes in the Growth of American Government.* New York: Oxford University Press.

Hornbeck, Richard. (2012). "The Enduring Impact of the American Dust Bowl: Short- and Long-Run Adjustments to Environmental Catastrophe." *American Economic Review* 102(4): 1477–1507.

Hornbeck, Richard, and Suresh Naidu. (2014). "When the Levee Breaks: Black Migration and Economic Development in the American South." *American Economic Review* 104(3): 963–990.

Hudson, John C. (1994). *Making the Corn Belt: A Geographic History of Middle-Western Agriculture*. Bloomington: Indiana University Press.

Jefferson, Thomas. (1953). "Letter to John Jay, 23 Aug. 1785." In *Papers of Thomas Jefferson*, Vol. 8: *25 February to 31 October 1785*, edited by Julian P. Boyd and Kaveh Azar, 426–426. Princeton, NJ: Princeton University Press.

Jefferson, Thomas. (1955). "Letter to James Madison, 20 Dec. 1787." In *Papers of Thomas Jefferson*, Vol. 12: *7 August 1787 to 31 March 1788*, edited by Julian P. Boyd, 438–443. Princeton, NJ: Princeton University Press.

Lange, Fabian, Alan L. Olmstead, and Paul W. Rhode. (2009). "The Impact of the Boll Weevil, 1892–1932." *Journal of Economic History* 69(3): 685–718.

Libecap, Gary D. (1998). "The Great Depression and the Regulating State: Federal Government Regulation of Agriculture: 1884–1970." In *The Defining Moment: The Great Depression and the American Economy in the Twentieth Century*, edited by Michael D. Bordo, Claudia Goldin, and Eugene N. White, 181–224. Chicago: University of Chicago Press.

Libecap, Gary D., and Richard H. Steckel, eds. (2011). *Climate Change Past and Present: Uncertainty and Adaptation*. Chicago: University of Chicago Press.

Matsuyama, Kiminori. (1992). "Agricultural Productivity, Comparative Advantage, and Economic Growth." *Journal of Economic Theory* 58(2): 317–343.

Mellor, John W., ed. (1995). *Agriculture on the Road to Industrialization*. Baltimore, MD: Johns Hopkins University Press.

Meyer, David R. (2003). *Roots of American Industrialization*. Baltimore, MD: Johns Hopkins University Press.

Moser, Petra, and Paul W. Rhode. (2012). "Did Plant Patents Create the American Rose?" In *The Rate and Direction of Inventive Activity Revisited*, edited by Joshua Lerner and Scott Stern, 413–442. Chicago: University of Chicago Press.

Olmstead, Alan L., and Paul W. Rhode. (2003). "The Evolution of California Agriculture, 1850–2000." In *California Agriculture: Dimensions and Issues*, edited by Jerome B. Siebert, 1–28. Berkeley: University of California Press.

Olmstead, Alan L., and Paul W. Rhode. (2008). *Creating Abundance: Biological Innovation and American Agricultural Development*. New York: Cambridge University Press.

Olmstead, Alan L., and Paul W. Rhode. (2011a). "Adapting North American Wheat Production to Climatic Challenges, 1839–2009." *Proceedings of National Academy of Sciences* 108(2): 480–485.

Olmstead, Alan L., and Paul W. Rhode. (2011b). "Responding to Climatic Challenges: Lessons from U.S. Agricultural Development." In *Climate Change Past and Present: Uncertainty and Adaptation*, edited by Gary D. Libecap and Richard H. Steckel, 169–194. Chicago: University of Chicago Press.

Olmstead, Alan L., and Paul W. Rhode. (2014). "Agricultural Mechanization." In *Encyclopedia of Agriculture and Food Systems*, edited by Neal K. Van Alfen, 168078. Amsterdam: Elsevier.

Olmstead, Alan L., and Paul W. Rhode. (2015). *Arresting Contagion: Science, Policy, and Conflicts over Animal Disease Control*. Cambridge, MA: Harvard University Press.

Rasmussen, Wayne, and Gladys L. Baker. (1979). *Price-Support and Adjustment Programs from 1933 through 1978: A Short History*. Washington, DC: USDA.

Restuccia, Diego, Dennis Tao Yang, and Xiaodong Zhu. (2008). "Agriculture and Aggregate Productivity: A Quantitative Cross-Country Analysis." *Journal of Monetary Economics* 55(2): 234–250.

Smith, Daniel S. (1980). "A Malthusian-Frontier Interpretation of US Demographic History before c. 1815." In *Urbanization in the Americas: The Background in Comparative Perspective*, edited by Woodrow W. Borah, Jorge E. Hardoy, and Gilbert A. Stelter, 15–24. Ottawa: National Museum of Man.

Thorbecke, Erik, ed. (1969). *The Role of Agriculture in Economic Development; A Conference of the Universities–National Bureau Committee for Economic Research.* New York: Columbia University Press.

Towne, Marvin W., and Wayne D. Rasmussen. (1960). "Farm Gross Product and Gross Investment in the Nineteenth Century." In *Studies in Income and Wealth,* Vol. 24: *Trends in the American Economy in the Nineteenth Century,* edited by William Parker, 255–312. Princeton, NJ: Princeton University Press.

Turner, Frederick J. (1903). "Contributions of the West to American Democracy." *Atlantic Monthly* 91(January): 83–89.

Turner, Frederick J. (1921). *The Frontier in American History.* New York: Henry Holt.

USDA. (1974). *Farm Income Situation* (July–Aug. 1947, July 1974). Washington, DC: Government Printing Office.

USDA. (1981). *Agricultural Statistics.* Washington, DC: Government Printing Office.

USDA. (1999). *Agricultural Economics and Land Ownership Survey* (AELOS). Available at   www.agcensus.usda.gov/Publications/1997/Agricultural_Economics_and_Land_Ownership/Quick_Facts/1999.

USDA. (2004). *Census of Agriculture 2002, United States: Summary and State Data,* Vol. 1: *Geographic Area Series.* Washington, DC: Government Printing Office.

USDA. (2009). *Census of Agriculture 2007.* Available at www.agcensus.usda.gov/Publications/2007/Full_Report/Volume_1,_Chapter_1_US/st99_1_009_010.pdf.

US Department of Health and Human Services, Health Resources and Services Administration, Bureau of Health Professions Resource File. (1994). ICPSR 9075.

US President. (2012). *Economic Report of the President.* Washington, DC: Government Printing Office.

Weiss, Thomas. (1993). "Long Term Changes in US Agricultural Output per Worker, 1800–1900." *Economic History Review* 66(2): 324–341.

Wright, Gavin. (1986). *Old South, New South: Revolutions in the Southern Economic Since the Civil War.* New York: Basic Books.

Wright, Gavin. (2006). *Slavery and American Economic Development.* Baton Rouge: Louisiana State University Press.

CHAPTER 8

··

MANUFACTURING GROWTH AND STRUCTURAL CHANGE IN AMERICAN ECONOMIC HISTORY

··

CHANGKEUN LEE AND PAUL W. RHODE

OVER much of the past two centuries, industrialization was the driving force in the economic development of most nations experiencing "modern economic growth." Industrial activity generally expanded faster than the economy as a whole, and the sector grew to account for sizable (though rarely dominant) shares of output and employment. Manufactured products usually represented an even larger fraction of goods entering international trade, and hence were a key component in the balance of payments. Manufacturing had importance for national interests in other ways, providing materials and technologies for the military. Manufacturing activities generally experienced faster rates of productivity growth than the economy as a whole and often paid labor and other factors of production higher returns than the agricultural and service sectors. For these reasons, manufacturing had long been valued more highly than other economic activities, and policymakers often sought to promote the development of this "strategic" sector at the expense of other productive activities, consumers, taxpayers, and the environment. And for the same reasons, trends toward deindustrialization in the second half of the twentieth century have been viewed with alarm.

Even when the manufacturing sector was not the single largest employer or the economy's principal "engine of growth," it acted as a bellwether regarding the general state of the economy. The condition of the manufacturing sector reflected the major forces (input supplies, output demands, technological shocks) impinging on the overall economy. The sector has also been more subject to macro-economic shocks than the resource extraction or service sectors. Manufacturing activities are more standardized and easier to measure and compare over time and space and, as a result, the sector often serves as the benchmark case for economic analysis.

Since the 1960s, the role of manufacturing in the US economy has changed. As figure 8.1 shows, the sector's share of employment stopped rising and has started to

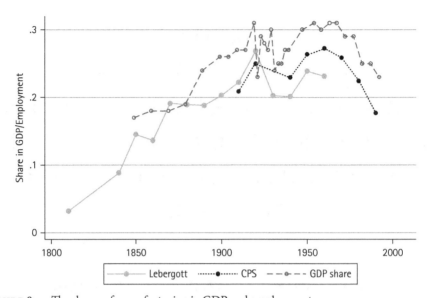

FIGURE 8.1. The shares of manufacturing in GDP and employment

Sources: (GDP share) GDP from series Historical Statistics, Ca10 and total value added from our data set; (Employment) Historical Statistics, series Ba814 and Ba821, and Current Population Survey.

decline. After the mid-1980s, the number of jobs has fallen in absolute terms, with the contraction accelerating since 2000. The number of manufacturing employees in early 2014 was equal to the number before the country entered the World War II, at a time when total employment in all activities was one-quarter its current size.[1] The sector's share of gross domestic product (GDP) has followed a more complicated process. It falls when measured in current prices, but holds steady when one uses constant prices. The process of deindustrialization has been associated with changes in the rate and direction of technological progress, shifts in product demand, and the globalization and outsourcing of production.

The discussion of American manufacturing can be organized around three industrial revolutions. Table 8.1 highlights the timing and key differences between the first, second, and third industrial revolutions. The first industrial revolution took place in the United States between roughly 1810 and 1860, one generation after it occurred in Great Britain. This epochal period saw the mechanization of textile production, the application of fossil fuels to the metal industries, and the advent of the factory system. The second industrial revolution occurred between 1870 and 1920 simultaneously in the United States, Britain, and other countries on the European continent. It saw advances associated with chemicals, electrical equipment, and the internal combustion engines. At the end of the period, the United States had become the leading industrial nation in the world. The third industrial revolution, tied to information technology (IT), began in the 1970s and is continuing today. It is linked to the globalization of production and deindustrialization in the traditional manufacturing heartland. The "industrial revolutions"

Table 8.1 The Three Industrial Revolutions

	First	Second	Third
Timing	US 1810–1860	1870–1920	1970–
	UK 1780–1830	.	.
Technological base	Tinkering	Engineering	Formal science
Products	Iron	Steel, electrical machinery,	Integrated circuits,
	Textiles	chemicals, automobiles	computers/mobile phones
Power	Steam engine,	Electric dynamo,	Lithium battery
	water wheel	internal combustion engine	
Newly cheap inputs	Cotton,	Steel, coal,	Information,
	coal, and iron	petroleum	silicon chips
Organization	Factory	Modern business enterprise	Global supply chain
	Family firm	Clerical sector	
Finance	Kinship networks	Investment banks	Venture capital
	Retained earnings	Equity markets	IPOs

framework allows one to review growth and structural change in the manufacturing sector over the past two centuries. As emerging industries brought new products and more efficient production methods into being, resources were reallocated toward newer and more productive activities, and overall productivity grew.[2]

DEFINITIONS AND DATA

Manufacturing is the process that transforms raw materials and components into intermediate and final products. The goods made and technologies employed in these activities have dramatically changed over time, leading to problems in defining the sector precisely. In the period since 1850, the US Census Office, which conducted a separate Censuses of Manufactures, has refined the lines of demarcation to keep up with the changing economy. It will be important to bear these revisions in mind when making comparisons over time.

Changes made in 1904 and 1923 are illustrative. Before 1904, the census enumerated establishments with an annual product of $500 or more. Thereafter, it was "confined to manufacturing establishments conducted under what is known as the factory system" (US Bureau of the Census 1907). This led to the omission of establishments engaged in custom trade or services.[3] The classification system continued to change over time. In 1923, the size cutoff went up from $500 to $5,000. The modern SIC (Standard Industry Classification) system was created in 1947 and revised in 1972 and 1987. To adapt to the changes in IT and business services and to harmonize statistics internationally, the Census Bureau adopted the NAICS (North American Industry Classification System) in 1997.

The evolution of the US manufacturing can be investigated by using a new data set compiled from the Censuses of Manufactures of three-digit 1972-SIC industries defined as consistently as possible over the period since 1849.[4] This allows us to chart the growth in the size of a consistently defined manufacturing sector and to document structural changes such as the growth in establishment size and shifts across different activities.

THE FIRST INDUSTRIAL REVOLUTION

Early manufacturing growth in the United States largely involved imitating the techniques and practices from Great Britain, the pioneer in the first industrial revolution. American manufacturers copied the British in (1) their substitution of machinery for handicraft skills, in activities such as textiles: (2) the widespread applications of inanimate power sources (water wheels and steam engines); and (3) the mass utilization of cheap materials, especially iron made using coked coal. In these activities, Americans generally followed the British with a lag of one or more generations. In many cases, Americans copied selectively, adopting specific techniques better suited to the nation's distinctive resource endowment and product markets. In a handful of cases, Americans created technologies in pace with the British or made important advances on top of what the British had accomplished. As examples, the invention of a high-pressure steam engine by Oliver Evans of Philadelphia in the 1790s was roughly simultaneous with the efforts by Richard Trevithick in Wales, and the refinements by Francis Cabot Lowell and Paul Moody of the Boston Associates of Cartwright's power loom improved its commercial viability. In addition to imitating British production technologies, American manufacturers also copied British organizational changes such as the factory. The factory, for reasons discussed in the following, slowly became the dominant form in the US industrial sector.

In the early nineteenth century, American manufacturers made two crucial innovations relative to British practice, innovations that opened the way for the country's distinctive path in the subsequent periods. The first was the integrated firm, as exemplified by the Boston Manufacturing Company (BMC). This corporation, chartered by the Boston Associates with an initial capital stock of $100,000 in 1813—more than ten times the size of other US textile firms of the period—combined cloth weaving, yarn spinning, and all of the prior operations under the same roof (Dalzell 1987, 26–27).[5] Both the formation of a joint-stock company and the extent of vertical integration differed from the British way of doing business. The model of the BMC provided several of the threads contributing to the development of what Alfred D. Chandler called modern business enterprise in 1977. These large-scale national corporations, which came to dominate key sectors of the US industrial economy circa 1900, were managed by a hierarchy of salaried executives who coordinated the flow of resources between the multiple operating units, that is, its multiple plants or product lines.

The second major innovation was the development of the American system of interchangeable parts. Here the pioneer was Eli Whitney, who garnered an early federal contract to make muskets using precision manufacturing with newly invented machine tools. Operatives constructed complex mechanisms that were made in Britain by craft workers skilled at filing and fitting. Armory practice developed into the "American System of Manufacturing," a name bestowed by British observers of the US exhibit at the 1851 Crystal Palace Fair near London. This system involved, in the words of Eugene Ferguson, "the sequential series of operations carried out on successive special-purpose machines that produce interchangeable parts" (Hounsell 1984, 15). It was employed in the antebellum period to produce firearms, tools, and clocks, and then watches (1860s), typewriters and sewing machines (1870s), and bicycles (1880s). It led in turn to the advent of "mass production" and use of the moving assembly line in the automobile industry and beyond. Lively debates rage over the importance of economic profit-seeking versus engineering enthusiasm in driving the development process, over the roles of the public and private sectors, and over the dates at which true interchangeability became technically and commercially viable.

Industrialization posed many problems for the early American Republic, including how having large forces of dependent hired laborers was consistent with the country's political and social values. Opinion leaders were especially suspicious of the evolving British factory system, especially its associations with the workhouse and impoverished wage-workers. Both for cultural and economic reasons, adoption of this mode of production proceeded slowly. A factory, according to pioneering American social scientist Carroll D. Wright, was defined as a "establishment where several workmen are collected for the purpose of obtaining greater and cheaper conveniences for labor than they could procure individually at their homes; for producing results by their combined efforts which they could not accomplish separately; and for preventing the loss occasioned by carrying the articles for place to place . . ." (Wright 1882, 1). The core principle was of *association*: "each laborer, working separately . . . directs his producing powers to effect a common result . . . ." (Wright 1882, 1). Many scholars would add to the organization's definition the use of supervision—what is known as "factory discipline"—and the application of extensive specialization or the division of labor (Berg 1994). To make these concepts operational using the available statistical evidence, a "factory" is commonly specified as a manufacturing establishment utilizing a power source (water or steam) and employing a number of wage earners (the lower cutoff is often around fifteen).

At the beginning of the nineteenth century, virtually all US manufacturing production occurred in artisanal shops where a highly skilled craft worker, using hand tools and perhaps aided by one or two assistants, would perform all of the operations to make a product. Only in a handful of textile mills, such as Samuel Slater's plant at Pawtucket, Rhode Island, merited the title "factory." As the evidence in table 8.2 shows, as late as 1850, less than one in twenty (4.5 percent) of American manufacturing establishments employed sixteen or more workers and used either water or steam power. Such

Table 8.2 Percentage Distribution of Manufacturing Activity by Scale and Power, 1850 and 1880

		1850		1880	
	Scale	No Power	Power	No Power	Power
Establishments	Small	61.0	29.2	59.6	26.4
	Large	5.3	4.5	5.7	8.3
Workers	Small	28.2	12.7	16.8	9.3
	Large	26.0	33.2	24.5	49.4
Value Added	Small	21.0	22.4	11.3	14.2
	Large	32.7	23.9	35.9	38.6

Source: Atack, Bateman, and Margo (2005, 593).
Notes: Small scale is 15 or fewer employees; large scale is 16 or more. Power includes the use of steam or water power.

establishments accounted for 33.2 percent of all workers and produced 23.9 percent of all value added (Atack, Bateman, and Margo 2005, 593).

Kenneth Sokoloff argued that early manufacturers could achieve large gains in labor productivity without mechanizing or increasing capital per worker by instead expanding the scale of operations and more fully exploiting the division of labor (Sokoloff 1984, 1986). Comparing data for manufacturing operations in the Northeastern United States from the censuses of 1820 and 1850, he finds that nonmechanized industries saw the number of workers per establishment increase by roughly two-thirds. This growth in scale was equal to that in the typical mechanized industries, though below the nearly tripling in scale occurring in the cotton textile sector. Higher scale was associated with higher labor productivity. In the 1820 cross section, Sokoloff estimated that establishments with sixteen or more workers produced 35 percent more per worker than establishments with one to five workers; those with six to fifteen workers produced 30 percent more.[6] Examining changes between 1820 and 1850, Solokoff found that the increases in labor productivity in nonmechanized industries were on par with that in mechanized industries and that these increases were primarily due to total factor productivity growth rather than to capital deepening.

Claudia Goldin and Kenneth Sokoloff (1982, 1984) also show that expanding to a very large scale in this period involved employing increasing fractions of women and children. Women in the Northeast could earn relatively more (compared with men) in manufacturing than in agriculture. But this source of labor proved only a temporary solution to the US industrial labor problem. The employment of immigrant workers, after the European troubles of the 1840s, and the increasing concentration of industrial activity in urban areas proved a more permanent solution. Over this entire period, increasing scale was associated with decreasing skill levels. But the inverse association of scale and skill was not complete. As Claudia Goldin and Lawrence Katz (2010, 123–124) argue, the larger-scale establishment had to employ highly skilled mechanics to adjust and maintain the capital equipment. Robert Zevin (1971) argued that skilled mechanics were initially so rare that their scarcity represented a binding constraint on the expansion of the factory system.

The rise of the factory came in the train of broader forces. Jeremy Atack, Fred Bateman, and Robert Margo (2008) show that the large-scale establishments adopted steam engines more quickly; labor productivity rose with establishment size faster in operations using steam than in those using water or hand power. The diffusion of steam power did not begin in US manufacturing until the 1840s; only in 1870 did steam horse-power capacity equal that of water. Jeremy Atack, Michael Haines, and Robert Margo (2011) demonstrated that the spread of the large-scale industrial plants was also causally linked with the diffusion of the railroad. Such transportation improvement allowed the expanded output to be sold in wider markets and raw materials to be assembled more swiftly and cheaply. Urbanization and immigration also played roles.

As the data in table 8.2 indicate, by 1880 the shares of establishments employing sixteen or more workers and an inanimate power source had nearly doubled to 8.3 percent of all manufacturing units. These factories accounted for almost one-half (49.4 percent) of all workers and nearly four-tenths (38.6 percent) of manufacturing value added. The shift was accompanied by an increase in the capital intensity of industrial production. Between 1850 and 1880, the ratio of the real capital stock to worker rose by over 75 percent, and the ratio of the real capital stock to output rose by over 50 percent

These developments did not solve the social problems that opinion leaders in early America associated with factories. By 1880, the manufacturing labor force was differentially drawn from the foreign-born population and was disproportionally located in urban areas. The nation's manufacturing activity became concentrated in the Northeast and the eastern Midwest, in what became known as the Core Industrial Belt and later the Rust Belt. And when industrial wage workers began to out-earn farm owners in the late nineteenth century, the social divisions and political conflicts only became more intense.

The young American Republic faced another set of problems in its early industrialization process. The United States was land abundant and labor scarce. Its apparent comparative advantage was in agriculture and other forms of resource extraction, rather than in manufacturing. Its nascent industries faced competition from more mature rivals in lower-wage countries, most notably in the industrial leader, Britain. To meet these challenges, US manufacturers sought out pockets of underemployed labor—the women and children who came to work in the textile mills—and they lobbied for high protective tariffs. The latter policies created intense domestic divisions. While the Northeast shifted into manufacturing, the American South continued thorough the antebellum period and most of the early postbellum period to specialize in agriculture. Agrarians correctly saw the tariffs as taxes disproportionately burdening their sector.

John Habakkuk (1962) suggested that American manufacturers met the challenges of industrializing in the land-abundant and labor-scarce setting in a different, more creative way. Based on a comparison of British and US practices, Habakkuk asserted that Americans developed and adopted technological innovations that economized on their scarce labor by applying more capital. Habakkuk went beyond the standard factor substitution argument regarding technique choice in a static production function given input prices. He asserted that the technological advances changing the US production function were directed to the invention and diffusion of labor-saving machines. He linked the purported labor-saving, capital-using biases in US innovation to its scarcity of labor and abundance of land. Going further, he claimed that the rate of technological change in the United States was faster than in Britain. Earlier authors, including John Hicks (1932) and Erwin Rothbard (1946), had sketched out parts of this induced innovation argument, but Habakkuk's hypothesis was more complete and controversial.

A number of scholars took issue with Habakkuk at a general level. They asserted that innovators would seek to save on every factor (all are scarce at the margin) and that the inducement argument assumes that innovators possess prior knowledge concerning how to generate specific new technologies. Other scholars, most notably Paul David, labored to disentangle the numerous different and potentially conflicting factual and theoretical claims knotted up in Habakkuk's magnum opus (David 1975, 19–91). Peter Temin (1966) had perceptively noted that early America was not only labor scarce, but also capital scarce; this observation complicates induced innovation logic for adopting new labor-saving machinery. The work of Robert Gallman (1986) and Alexander Field (1983, 1985) called into question the common conflation of the manufacturing capital stock with machinery. In the nineteenth century, most manufacturing capital was composed of structures and goods-in-process; only a small fraction was equipment. Field further argued that the high interest rates do help explain the cheaper construction of buildings and the more rapid rates of capital usage and wear-and-tear. Such faster rates of depreciation could account for higher rates of gross investment and a younger (more up-to-date) capital stock in America.

Based on studies of the machine tool industry and of armory practice, Edward Ames and Nathan Rosenberg (1968) asserted that in mid-nineteenth-century America, natural resources were complements to the new technologies that replaced skilled labor with a combination of capital and unskilled labor. The Ames-Rosenberg channel through which resource abundance affected technological choice was different from Habakkuk's, but the effects were similar. John James and Jonathan Skinner (1985) have argued that the so-called labor scarcity paradox can be resolved when one distinguishes between the handful of activities associated with the "American System of Manufacturing" and the rest of the US industrial sector. Advancing what became the most accepted viewpoint, Paul David (1975) argued that Britain and the United States were on distinctive paths of development, each suited initially to its own factor endowments and product markets and each making progress through undirected, largely random learning-by-doing processes. The "dumb luck" of being on the faster innovation path associated with larger-scale production of more homogeneous products accounts for America's rise to technological leadership. In the past decade, the induced innovation debate has sprung back to life with the theoretical work of Daron Acemoglu (and coauthors) (2008) on "directed technological change" and the empirical claims of Robert Allen (2009) locating the origin of the British industrial revolution in that country's relatively high wages (below the United States, but well above global averages), large pool of technically competent workers, and low coal prices. One can expect more research in this area in the near future.

GROWTH AND STRUCTURAL CHANGE
OVER THE LONG RUN

Debates over early industrialization are intense both due to the inherent interest of the questions involved and because the fragmentary data admit many interpretations. The picture becomes somewhat clearer after 1849, when the US Census Office began to enumerate manufacturing activities more comprehensively. One cannot take the published data as given, due to frequent shifts in data definitions and industrial categories. To define the manufacturing sector in a consistent way, it is necessary to place specific industries into appropriate three-digit SIC categories.

Figure 8.2 graphs measures of manufacturing activity, including the number of establishments, production workers, the real wage bill, and real value added from 1849 to 1992. The statistics are from the Census of Manufactures and were

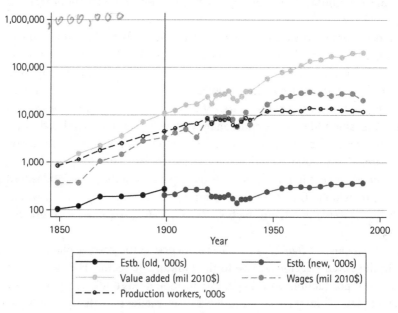

FIGURE 8.2. Measures of manufacturing activity in the United States, 1849–1992

Note: Used GDP deflator for value added and the BLS's CPI series for wages.

Source: Compiled from Census of Manufactures.

compiled from industry-level data selected to maintain consistency (i.e., to elimi-nate nonmanufacturing activities such as mining and blacksmithing from the early years). The series are graphed on a log scale, so that changes over time measure percentage rates of growth, and the changing relative levels of the series show the changing ratios. The bottom series shows that the number of establishment ex-panded substantially over the 1849 to 1899 period, rising 2.6-fold. Thereafter, growth in the number of establishments was much slower. The next highest series shows that the number of production workers grew even more rapidly between 1849 and 1899—increasing 5.4-fold—and continued to expand through the 1900s and 1910s. In 1919, the average number of production workers per establishment was 31.3, up from 16.4 in 1899 and 8.1 in 1849. The total number of production workers fluctuated sharply in the interwar era—the availability of the census on a biennial basis draws out these variations—but the trend was flat. Growth re-emerged in the World War II period. The series on wages and value added exhibit even faster and more sustained expansion over the 1849 to 1967 period. Over this long period, real value added grew at an average rate of 4.3 percent per annum, real wages at 3.9 percent, and the number of production workers at 2.4 percent. Labor productivity and compensation were rising. Since 1967, the wage bill has remained flat and the number of produc-tion workers has declined. The share of wages in manufacturing value added had been stable over the late nineteenth and early twentieth centuries, as evident in the close co-movements of the top two series in figure 8.2. The share began to decline, as shown by the emerging gap, after the 1960s. The early growth, maturation, and slow decline of the manufacturing sector have been accompanied by important structural changes.

The most common dividing line used to analyze shifts in the industrial structure is the dichotomy between durable and nondurable goods. (The formal division is whether the products last more or less than three years.) Durable goods production is tradition-ally thought to characterize a more mature or advanced economic structure.[7] The top panel of figure 8.3 traces out the shares of the durable goods industries of production workers and value added in the entire manufacturing sector. Given that the durable and nondurable goods dichotomy is exhaustive, the remaining shares are the nondurable goods shares. The graph shows that the durable goods shares in general have gone up from about 40 percent in the 1850s to about 60 percent in the 1980s, and stayed around 55 percent thereafter. The short-run variations such as the Great Depression are also noteworthy. Durable goods production was typically associated with greater cyclical volatility.

The bottom panel of figure 8.3 provides evidence on the average plant sizes and labor shares in the durable sector relative to the nondurable sector. The average number of durable goods production workers per establishment was under unity in 1850, meaning the average plant of durable goods producers was smaller than that of nondurable goods producers then. However, the average plant size of the durable goods producers rose faster than that of the nondurable goods producers, hitting nearly a ratio of two in the 1920s. Since then, the average plant size in the two sectors converged. In the same vein,

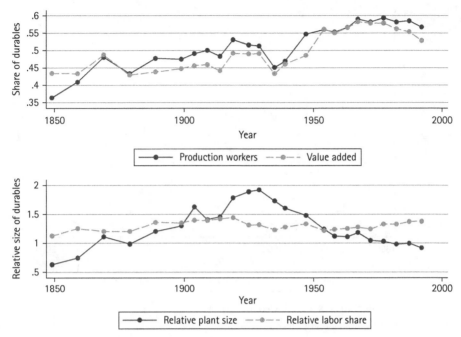

FIGURE 8.3. Ratio of durables sector to nondurables sector

Source: Compiled from Census of Manufactures.

the dashed line presents the relative labor share of the durable producing sector, where labor share is defined as the total wage payments to production workers as a ratio to the value added in each sector.

Nathan Rosenberg (1982) and Gavin Wright (1990) have both argued that a major source of US industrial leadership was derived from exploiting its resource base.[8] A large fraction of early American manufacturing was composed of grain mills, lumber mills, distilleries, meat-packing houses, and other activities that added value to natural resources. Many of these activities were located in rural and semi-rural areas to be close to the supply of materials. Even in industries such as the integrated textile mills of New England, production utilized greater unit volumes of material inputs (cheaper cotton) than was common in Britain. Figure 8.4 graphs the changing production worker and value added shares of the resource-based industries.[9] The value added share is generally higher than the production worker share, indicating the "raw" labor productivity was higher in the resource industries than in the nonresource industries. The pattern is especially evident in the period before World War I and re-emerges in the 1930s and 1940s. Over the twentieth century, the US manufacturing sector shifted away from resource-based industries.

Another key dividing line is between manufacturing activities producing consumer and capital goods. Alfred D. Chandler (1972) noted that early factory production in the United States was concentrated in making consumer goods such as cotton textiles. The production of boots and shoes, which moved from artisanal shops to nonmechanized

FIGURE 8.4. Shares of the resource-based industries

Source: Compiled from Census of Manufactures as described in Rhode (2001).

manufactories over the 1820–1850 period, also figured largely among industries of the date. Chandler argues that the fabrication of capital goods and of metal products in general was uncommon during the country's first phrase of industrialization and expanded only after the discovery and exploitation of suitable coal resources (first of anthracite coal in eastern Pennsylvania and then of bituminous seams in western Pennsylvania, Ohio, and West Virginia). Heavy industry became important in the second phrase.

In his classic work, *The Growth of Industrial Economies*, W. G. Hoffman has argued that this shift was more general. Across the world, the typical pattern of industrialization "has been characterized by a steady increase of the share of the net output of the capital-goods industries." Earlier industrialization tended to concentrate on producing consumer goods, but over time output and employment "in all countries" shifted into capital-goods industries (Hoffman 1958, 16, 145).[10] As the evidence in figure 8.5 reveals, the US experience largely fits the Hoffman predictions, with the share of industrial activity devoted to capital goods production steadily rising to a plateau in the 1960s.

Of particular interest is the evolution of the metal-based capital goods sector. This collection of sectors includes primary and fabricated metals, electrical and non-electrical machinery, and transportation equipment (that is, major SIC groups 33–37). Over the 1859 to 1958 period, the metal-based sector's share of total value added climbed from 24 percent to 43 percent and of production workers doubled from 21 percent to 42 percent.

FIGURE 8.5. Shares of capital goods industries

Source: Compiled from Census of Manufactures as described in Rhode (2001).

THE SECOND INDUSTRIAL REVOLUTION

Between the Civil War and World War I, US manufacturing experienced a second industrial revolution. The sector's growth accelerated as movement toward higher capital-labor ratio and greater scale accelerated. These changes helped propel the United States to become the global industrial leader by about 1900.

One of the industries that led the second revolution was the steel industry, which produced a major new input for other industries. The diffusion of Bessemer and open-hearth blast furnaces increased the productivity of steel production and lowered its price dramatically, serving the growing demand of the machinery, transportation equipment, and construction sectors. Petroleum-based fuels supplemented coal and provided byproducts such as lubricants used for increasing the operating speed of plants.

The second industrial revolution also witnessed important changes in business organization, as the pursuit of the economies of scale and scope gave rise to the modern business enterprise (MBE). Chandler (1977, 1990) offered a sophisticated examination of the long evolution in this new business form. As transportation and communication costs fell, a large national market emerged in North America. At the same time, technologies allowing large-scale production emerged. These two forces created a new competitive environment that hastened the marriage of mass production and mass distribution. Distributers retained power in the traditional industries, while mass producers discovered reasons to coordinate the whole flow from production to distribution themselves in new, more capital-intensive industries. Producers of perishable goods (dressed meat), sophisticated goods that required after-sale contact (the sewing machine), and high-volume goods (tobacco, soap, canning) all found advantages in setting up the distribution networks suitable to their own products.

Since the 1880s, vertical and horizontal integration led to the creation of large enterprises. The pursuit of higher "throughput" (fuller capacity utilization) drove greater integration of production. Vertical integration assured input supplies and output markets, cut transactions costs, and reduced holdups in cases of asset specificity. Greater optimal size of production facilitated horizontal integration to realize the economies of scale. Table 8.3 lists industries having most Chandlerian MBEs. The table shows that steel and petroleum refining are good examples, where both horizontal and vertical integration took place. The MBE form arose to systematize the control and coordination of business processes. Middle managers ran everyday operations, while top management devised long-term strategies, including financial planning, product diversification, and a search for overseas markets. Also, as an effort to solve information overload problems and excessive bureaucratization within firms, multidivisional structures developed. General Motors and du Pont were leaders in this process.

European scholars often attributed their continent's lagging productivity levels to differences in business organization. European competitors were often either small-scale family-run firms, as in Britain, or bank-financed, tariff-protected cartels, as in Germany. They did not move as rapidly to adopt the MBE form as did firms in the United States. This led to concern in Europe as recently as the mid-1960s, when J. J. Servan-Schreiber

Table 8.3 Top Industries in Number of Chandlerian MBEs

SIC	Industry	Number of Chandlerian MBE		
		1917	1930	1948
291	Petroleum refining	21	25	22
331	Blast furnace and basic steel product/steel rolling and finishing	21	15	14
371	Motor vehicles and equipment	12	12	16
333	Primary nonferrous metal	10	8	8
374	Railroad equipment	9	7	6
201	Meat products	6	5	6
210	Tobacco products	6	5	5
286	Industrial organic chemicals	6	6	6
352	Farm machinery and equipment	6	5	5

Sources: Chandler (1977). The numbers indicate the number of industrial enterprises listed in Chandler (1977, Appendix A).

(1968) argued that US multinationals were taking over the European economy. Stephen Broadberry (2006, 355) asserted that the source of the high American productivity from the "*industrialisation* of market services in the United States, which involved the transition from a customised, low-volume, high-margin approach to business organised on the basis of networks to a more standardised, high-volume, low-margin business with hierarchical management . . . with mass production in manufacturing." He estimated that the relative US/UK labor productivity in industry rose in the second half of the nineteenth century to nearly two, and the differential stayed around that level throughout the most of twentieth century. The differential in total factor productivity has been smaller than that, but still between 1.5 and 2.

The emergence of large firms had implications for industrial structure and market power. Forming a "trust" was a means to limit entry and maintain market dominance of the incumbents. The Whiskey trust, for example, attempted to use exclusive dealing agreements as a tool of vertical restraints. Its efforts failed due to the low entry costs of new competitors and enforcement of new antitrust laws (Clay and Troesken 2002; Troesken 1998). The motivation for such strategic behavior was stronger in industries where firms made huge investments in fixed costs.[11] The Panic of 1893 imperiled firms producing goods subject to unstable demand, leading to collusion and eventually the Great Merger Movement from 1895 to 1905. Naomi Lamoreaux (1998) explained that the business strategies seeking greater stability in fluctuating markets led to consolidations such as International Harvester, Otis Elevator, and Standard Oil. These consolidations made their efforts to sustain prices and prevent new entries. However, Lamoreaux found that consolidations failed to maintain the market dominance in the long run. Keeping prices high and deterring entry at the same time was not an easy task. In addition, the federal government adopted antitrust policies to curb the concentration of economic power and to set out rules of "fair competition." The courts ruled many pools and cartels illegal, and dissolved trusts in industries such as petroleum refining and tobacco.

The structural transformation of the American industry culminated after the end of the World War I. Electric power became the most important power source, letting businesses more easily choose the location of production sites based on the access to markets and cheap inputs, rather than the proximity to coal or water power. Electrification also improved productivity of plants, by providing illumination and allowing greater flexibility in redesigning factory floors to take advantage of straight-line production principles. Paul David (1990, 359) pointed out that the faster growth of total factor productivity in the 1920s "did not exhausted the full productivity ramifications of the dynamo revolution." It took time for more plants to adjust the factory and work designs to fully realize the potential of the electric power in the 1930s.

The automobile industry was the most symbolic and glamorous sector of the interwar period. During this period, it became one of the largest US industries in terms of output and employment. But the significance of the auto industry was greater, because it gave birth to the assembly line, a main driver of the so-called American Century. There have been many attempts to locate the technological origin of the assembly line, but David Nye (2013) convincingly answers this question from an evolutionary perspective.

He notes that a manufacturing process that "looks like an assembly line" can be found as early as in the 1880s in meat slaughtering. However, Henry Ford's assembly line of 1913 was special because of its accomplishments: the subdivision of labor, interchangeable parts, single-function machines, the sequential ordering of machines, and the movement to work to worker by belts and slides. Most of all, Ford's assembly line successfully combined all these in a systematic way.[12] Electrification played an important role in building such systems, because it improved factory layout and the use of space that enhanced the flow of materials and parts. Productivity gains from mass production lowered the price of cars and allowed the automobile firms and their ilk to pay high wages so that their workers could buy the product. Nye emphasized this macro virtuous cycle where the development of mass production and mass consumption provided positive feedback to each other.

Although many contemporary observers saw mass production as the most advanced mode of production, flexible specialization was still an alternative in the United States, and the techniques persisted longer in Europe.[13] In the United States, although mass production captured the popular imagination as the modern way to manufacture, a large fraction of US industrial firms continued to employ custom production methods. By examining plant-level information from the census, Timothy Bresnahan and Daniel Raff (1991) show that such craft plants persisted to 1929, although a majority of them failed to survive during the Great Depression. Philip Scranton (1997) offers a broader perspective by categorizing all industries into those using routinized production methods and those using specialized methods. This dichotomy corresponds well to Chandler's categorization of industrial activities into those dominated by the "modern" versus "traditional" business enterprise (Chandler 1990, 638–657).

Figure 8.6 compares shares of thee-digit manufacturing activities that Scranton classified as employing specialized and routinized techniques circa 1909 (panels a and b) and 1923 (panels c and d). The shares of the routinized and specialized activities do not sum to one because (1) roughly one-third of the three-digit industries used "mixed" practices and were not allocated to either category, and (2) some industries did not exist in 1909 or 1929, or were not included on his list. Overall, the figure supports Scranton's claim that the specialized sector always accounted for a significant share of manufacturing activity. The routinized activities increased in importance over the nineteenth century both in terms of output and employment. The specialized industries increased in importance until the first decade of the twentieth century, and then their shares stabilized. However, the evaluation of routinized industries' importance depends on the definition year.

Figure 8.7 graphs the relative labor productivity of specialized industries to routinized industries. The relative productivity never exceeds one and shows a long-term decline trend, which implies that productivity grew faster in the twentieth century among the routinized industries, where the mass production technique was frequently used. However, note a reversal around the 1970s, when traditional sector started losing competitiveness and industry turned to more flexible production technologies.

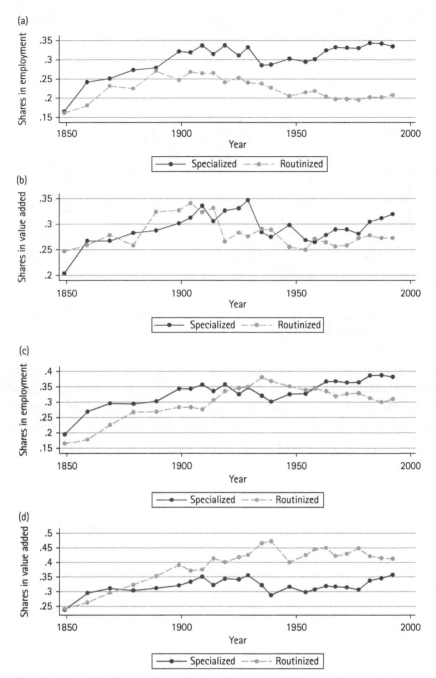

FIGURE 8.6. (a) and (b) Shares of specialized and routinized industries, by 1909 definition

Source: Compiled from Census of Manufactures as described in Rhode (2001).

(c) and (d) Shares of specialized and routinized industries, by 1923 definition

Source: Compiled from Census of Manufactures as described in Rhode (2001).

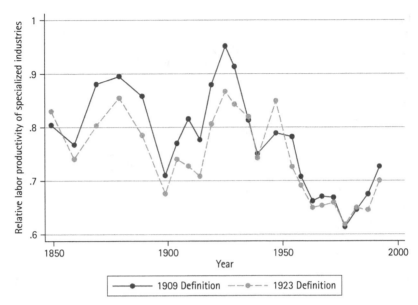

FIGURE 8.7. Labor productivity of specialized industries relative to routinized industries
Source: Based on data in Figure 8.6.

Modern business enterprises required many middle managers to control the integrated production process and its operation. Figure 8.8 presents evidence of the growing importance of nonproduction workers. When the Census of Manufactures started counting the number of nonproduction workers (salary earners) in 1899,

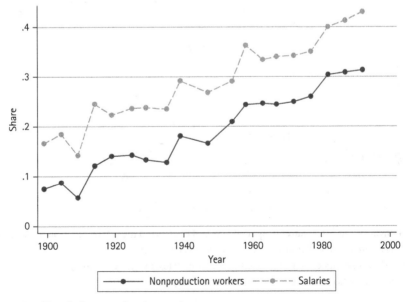

FIGURE 8.8. Trend of nonproduction workers
Source: Compiled from Census of Manufactures.

their share in total employment was just 10 percent. But the share rose steadily over throughout the twentieth century, reaching around 30 percent of employment in the early 1990s. Salary earners received higher average annual compensation than wage earners did, so their share of the labor bill was even higher. Investigating occupational data from the Census of Population, IPUMS, Katz and Margo find the "white collar" share trended upward.

The determinants of this skill premium have attracted research attention, and skill-biased technological change has been the usual suspect. Goldin and Katz (1998) find strong evidence of capital-skill complementarity during the 1910s and 1920; industries where the new technologies spread more extensively (as measured by use if purchased electricity) employed more educated production workers and paid higher wage premia. Rowena Gray (2013) extends their analysis to study the impacts of electrification on occupational skill content. She finds that electrification increased the demand for clerical, numerical, planning, and interpersonal skills, and "hollowed out" workers in the middle of the distribution. Goldin and Katz (2010) document how the changing demand in industry and widening education opportunities interplayed and how that contributed to the high human capital of the United States in the twentieth century.

The Third Industrial Revolution

During World War II, US manufacturing, especially its mass production sector, became the "Great Arsenal for Democracy." To arm several million soldiers of the United States and allied nations, American industry quickly shifted into military production mode, conversing peacetime factories and building many new production sites. War production exploded. Aircraft production illustrates the production miracle. Before the war, annual production never exceeded a few thousand planes of all types. In 1942, production of combat aircraft reached about 24,900 units, but output more than doubled to 54,100 in 1943 and 74,100 in 1944. During the same period, Germany could produce only 11,600 in 1942, 19,300 in 1943, and 34,100 in 1944 (Harrison 1998, table 1.6). Despite lack of experience in producing aircraft, mass production firms shifted over. For example, the Willow Run Bomber Plant built by Ford initially suffered from slow production and low quality, as Ford had been out of aircraft production for about two decades, but by 1943 it managed to produce one B-24 bomber per hour.

World War II had lasting impacts on the postwar industrial sectors. High productivity association with mass production not only differentiated the war's winners and the losers. It also impressed the allied nations and led them to adopt American techniques as part of their reconstruction efforts. David Nye noted that "the Marshal Plan institutionalized the drive toward European mass production" (2013, 138). The spread of mass production with additional progress such as automation was a strong driving force for the postwar economic miracle in Europe and Japan. Firms in these areas, equipped with more flexible production methods, would soon challenge US industrial leadership.

The war also laid the foundation of the IT industry from the development in electronic technology such as radar, avionics, calculators, and cipher/decipher machines. Although it took some decades for electronic computers to be utilized commercially and the military remained the largest and more sophisticated customer, the logical structure of the computer was well established by John von Neumann, and the development of related hardware such as transistors and integrated circuit by private-sector companies was underway in the 1940s and 1950s. The experiences in World War II and the Cold War also induced greater government support for research and development (R&D) and science-based education.

By the early 1970s, American leadership in manufacturing productivity was under threat. Challenges from overseas competitors intensified and the deindustrialization began. The old champions, notably the auto and steel industries, began to experience decline. They were locked in long-term collective bargaining relationships with powerful unions, continued to use in old mass-production technologies, and failed to adapt to new requirements for lower energy use and more flexible modes of production (Smil 2013).

American automakers kept the old ways of making a limited number of models per production line and maximizing the utilization rates, while the Japanese counterparts began their invasion with lower prices, greater variety within the smaller number of lines, and higher quality. All these were made possible by their "lean production system" that emphasized quality control, continuous improvement (*Kaizen*) and harmonious labor-management relations. To many observers, the need for shift to a better technology was obvious, but path dependence hindered the major US firms from adopting the new methods. Industrial relations were an important source of path dependence, because unionized labor opposed the lean production system as it meant more intensified work, less idle time, and less job security for workers. To enforce lean production in this situation, American managers had to take on greater risks than their Japanese counterparts. The lean system could be adopted only after Japanese producers opened plants on the American soil, either alone or jointly with American producers, and pressured domestic firms. These new lean plants showed higher productivity than traditional mass production plants with higher capital-labor ratio. This was a consequence of more flexible use of labor. The new plants gradually replaced the old-type plants; this reallocation led to higher aggregate productivity between 1982 and 1996 (Van Biesebroeck 2003).

Steel followed similar steps. Over the late 1940s through early 1960s, the large US steel companies continued to invest in huge open-hearth furnaces and ingot production or separate rolling mills, when new basic oxygen furnaces and continuous casting showed greater efficiencies. Bureaucracies of managers, unionism, and protectionism from political pressures reduced the incentives facing the steel giants to adopt new technologies.[14] As in the auto industry, it was the smaller and more nimble firms that moved to the technological frontier. Aggregate productivity change between 1963 and 2003 came from the replacement of old vertically integrated production system with a new technology (mini-mills) and competition pressure on existing plants by the new firms' entry (Allan Collard-Wexler and Jan de Loecker 2013).

Bronwyn Hall (1994) and Chandler (1994) provide a more aggregate-level perspective by arguing that the strongest international pressures on American manufacturing came in low-tech industries and stable-tech industries with long investment horizons. Firms in industries with long horizons faced difficulties during high and uncertain inflation rates of the 1970s and high real interest rates and managerial flux (associated with leveraged buyouts) of the 1980s and early 1990s. High-tech industries and stable-tech sectors with short investment horizons were initially better able to survive in the increasingly global market.[15]

INFORMATION TECHNOLOGY AND THE THIRD INDUSTRIAL REVOLUTION

The IT sector commonly refers to computers and telecommunication devices that are used for the collection, analysis, and dissemination of information. James Cortada (2004) surveyed how digital technologies (computer hardware and software) developed and how IT transformed every aspect of manufacturing. Computer-assisted inventory control, numerically controlled (NC) machines, automation, and quality management increased efficiency and precision in production. The impact was especially great at auto and steel firms that adopted the appropriate business strategies. More integral and hierarchical management became possible in process-oriented industries such as petroleum and pharmaceuticals. The use of computers had more fundamental impacts on research and development, because computer-aided design and manufacturing (CAD/CAM) facilitated constant design changes and made possible more complex designs for autos and aircrafts.[16]

Computing power is the fundamental factor that determines the quality of the processes and the equipment used. William Nordhaus (2007) provides direct measures of performance that are comparable over machines at different times. He shows that since World War II, computing power exponentially increased and that price declined even faster when evaluated by performance, rather than the standard official statistics. His results imply that the computer may have had larger impacts on productivity than previously thought. Since computers and other network devices were also used extensively for services that could have improved productivity in manufacturing, the rise of IT deserves to be called a "revolution."

Despite the common word usage, the definition of IT does not need to be limited to computer-related industries. Marc Porat (1977) defines the IT sector broadly to include older means of collecting, processing, and distributing information such as paper, printing, and publishing. His definition is historically relevant, enabling us to measure the amount of produced inputs devoted to such information activities.[17] Figure 8.9 shows the IT shares of manufacturing activity in value added and employment after 1939 according to Porat's definition. The IT sector's shares continuously rose from the end of

FIGURE 8.9. The shares of IT industries

Source: Compiled from Census of Manufactures as described in Rhode (2001).

World War II, with a remarkable leap between 1977 and 1982 when personal computers (PC) were increasingly used in offices. The size and relative growth of employment were not as fast as those of output. "Jobless growth" was still one of the characteristics the "new economy," or the IT-led productivity resurgence in the late 1990s and the first decade of the 2000s.

Scholars offer contrasting views about the productivity impacts of IT (Byrne, Oliner, and Sichel 2013). Paul David (1990) evaluated the potential of computers, noting the negligible marginal costs of information exchange might have the unexpected effect of generating information overload. He also argued that complementary changes in organization were required for the potential of the new technology to be fully realized. Robert Gordon (2016) advanced a more skeptical view, arguing that the productivity growth is limited to computer production and related durables sector. He also claims that computers have the feature of diminishing returns and that the Internet increased consumer welfare but failed to raise productivity. Gordon's observation was made before the advent of new information technologies that add value directly to production processes. Baily and Bosworth (2014) give a list of emerging technologies that influence manufacturing directly: industrial robots and automation, additive manufacturing, advanced design, direct interconnections over the Internet among machines and locations, materials science, and biotechnology.[18] Although how much of their potential will be realized into measured productivity is an open question, their examples show at least how computers and the Internet can increase the efficiency of production in various ways.

Information technology has spread worldwide, which may serve to strengthen or re-verse the trend of global production and offshoring (Cortada 2012). The trend toward offshoring in search for cheap labor started in the 1970s, but the introduction of the enterprise resource planning (ERP) systems in the 1990s and the global supply chain management system accelerated the separation of core design and strategy units and manufacturing. Developing countries supplied initially cheap, then educated and higher skilled labor and improving infrastructure. This trend is more prominent among giant IT firms such as Intel and Apple, which do not maintain major US production sites. Information technology journals and news websites have often analyzed the cost struc-ture of the iPhone, and the breakdown by manufacturer's country shows the importance of Korean, Japanese, and Taiwanese suppliers in the global production of Apple elec-tronics (Hessendahl 2013; "Slicing an Apple" 2011). However, there is a possibility that new technologies may favor re-shoring. Heavier use of robots makes the international wage differential less salient, and additive manufacturing promotes individualized pro-duction by those who have 3D printers, which are not affordable in many of developing countries ("Reshoring Manufacturing" 2013).

CONCLUSION

There are several directions for future research. The induced innovation debate has sprung back to life with the theoretical and empirical work on "directed technological change." One can expect more research in this area in the near future. Current research is also going beyond use of the Census of Manufactures to investigate the nature of technological change, the importance of economies of scale, and the complementarity of skills and capital at a more detailed level, using data on specific production opera-tions. The hope is to open the black box to better distinguish between the productivity advances associated with the division of labor, the adoption of machinery, and increases in scale. The role of government policy in affecting and guiding structural shifts, espe-cially the course of deindustrialization, will be the subject of continuing research.

There is intense ongoing debate about the future of productivity growth.[19] Opinions range from extreme optimism to deep pessimism. By the optimistic account of Ray Kurzweil (2005), we are nearing a "technological singularity" where artificial intelli-gence will create self-generating IT advances. By way of contrast, in Robert Gordon's influential account (2016), we have exhausted opportunities for innovation equal to those of the past, especially relative those from the second industrial revolution. In the more complicated "Race against the Machine" vision of Erik Brynjolfsson and Andrew McAfee (2013), IT-based innovations will continue rapidly, but will lead to the tech-nological displacement of human workers and rising income inequality. Examination of economic performance during the three industrial revolutions considered in this chapter provides the leading examples shaping these debates.

Additional issues of interest include the sources and impact of productivity advances in manufacturing and their role in the aggregate economy, the impact of trade policies, the effects of the patent system and other measures to capture gains from innovation, the diffusion of electricity and other energy sources in the economy, the geographic location (region, metropolitan/nonmetro mix) of economic activities, and the relationship between industry and agriculture.

NOTES

1. Figure 8.1 suggests higher shares of manufacturing in GDP for the post–World War II period than the BEA series that are commonly used. Both the NBER-CES database that was used in constructing our data set and the Historical Statistics present greater size of value added than the BEA, and the differences could be explained partly by these two facts: (1) Adjustment for changes in finished goods and in-process inventory made for the NBER-CES data set might have been noisy. (2) According to the December 2005 issue of *Survey of Current Business*, the BEA estimates for 1947–1986 were ones extrapolated backward from the estimates for 1987–1997, to reflect the revisions. This might have led to an underestimation.

2. Lucas (1993, 270) argued that for sustained learning to occur and ensure economic growth, "it is necessary that workers and managers continue to take on tasks that are new to them, to continue to move up what Grossman and Helpman call the 'quality ladder.'" Productivity growth would diminish until a new product or method that entails learning.

3. Our data set excludes industries later defined as custom trade or services. But for the period before 1899, we could not exclude activities at custom *establishments* in industries containing a mix of factories and custom trade. This limitation prevents us from closing the gap between the old and new system as shown in figure 8.2. The summary report of the 1904 Census present the revised statistics of 1899, letting us compare the differences due to the change.

4. We supplement this with the NBER-CES Manufacturing Industry Database by Bartelsman and Gray from 1963 to 1992. For documentation see Becker, Gray, and Marvakov (2013), which is based on Bartelsman and Gray's (1996) original technical paper.

5. The capital stock was slated to rise in installments up to a total of $400,000, which as a share of GDP is equivalent to nearly $6.2 billion in 2010 dollars.

6. Sokoloff imputes entrepreneurial labor, which he argues is underreported. The differences are much smaller without this adjustment.

7. The durables sector includes the following major groups: 24 Lumber, 25 Furniture, 32 Stone/Glass/Clay, 33 Primary Metals, 34 Fabricated Metals, 35 Machinery, Non-electrical, 36 Electrical Equipment, 37 Transportation Equipment, 38 Instruments, and 39 Misc. Manufacturing. The nondurables sector includes: 20 Food, 21 Tobacco, 22 Textiles, 23 Apparel, 26 Paper, 27 Printing and Publishing, 28 Chemicals, 29 Petroleum and Coal, 30 Rubber and Plastics, and 31 Leather.

8. See also Ames and Rosenberg (1968). Wright (1990) found the United States excelled in resource-intensive industries such as iron and steel, petroleum, cooper products, cotton, motor vehicles. His analysis of trade data indicates that the nation's revealed comparative

advantage was based on natural resources and that this pattern grew stronger over the 1889 to 1929 period when the United States became the world's industrial leader.

9. The definition of the resources sector is taken from Maskus (1983), 2–3, 78. It includes the following three-digit sectors: 201–209, 211–213, 241–245, 249, 261–263, 266, 291, 293, 295, 299, 311, 313, 324–325, 327–328, 333, 335–336; 245 and 293 were added at the authors' discretion.

10. According to Hoffman, the consumer goods industries include major SIC groups 20, 21, 22, 23, 25, 31 and capital goods industries include 28, 33, 34, 35, 36, 37. There is an intermediate category.

11. Anthony O'Brien (1988) argues the increase in scale preceded the Great Merger Wave. Using a sample of 171 consistently defined industries, he shows that the size of the average manufacturing plant increased two-and-one-half times between 1869 and 1929 and that "almost two-thirds of the increase in factory size" took place by 1889 (O'Brien 1988, 645).

12. The first chapter of Nye (2013) traces the origin of assembly line. The third chapter discusses the public reception of mass production. His book builds on Hounshell (1984), which discusses how the American manufacturing system developed to Ford's mass production system.

13. Drawing on the work of Michael Piore and Charles Sabel (1984), and Tolliday and Jonathan Zeitlin (1991), Stephen Broadberry (1997, 1) developed the contrast between the two industrial paradigms: "With mass production, standardized products are produced with special purpose machinery, requiring a relatively unskilled shopfloor labour force, whilst with flexible production, customized products are produced with general purpose machinery, requiring a highly skilled shopfloor labour force."

14. Paul Tiffany (1984) argues that the postwar administrations' lenient policy toward foreign steelmakers was one of the factors for the decline of steel.

15. Chandler (1994) divides industries into three categories: high-tech, stable-tech, and low-tech. The high-tech industries have high R&D expenditures and develop new products. These include pharmaceuticals (except soaps), electronics, aerospace, electrical equipment, and instruments. The low-tech industries spend little on R&D and compete through marketing. These sectors include food (SIC 20), textiles (22), and lumber and wood products (SIC 24). The stable-tech industries made a stable set of products, subject to small improvements. Hall further subdivides the stable-tech industries between those with long and short investment horizons. The stable tech industries with long horizons include chemicals, petroleum, primary metals, machinery, and automobiles (except parts). Those with short horizons include rubber and plastics, stone-clay-glass, fabricated metals.

16. For general history of computer and neighboring industries, there are several good books. For semiconductors, see Langlois (2002); for the Internet, Abbate (1999); for software, Mowery (1999). Mowery and Nelson (1999) includes chapters for the development of other industries. For the prehistory of the computer industry, see Cortada (1993).

17. According to Porat (1977), the most relevant three-digit SIC manufacturing industries belonging to the IT sector were 252, 253, 262, 264, 271–279, 357, 365–367, 381–383, 386–387, and 395.

18. A special report by *The Economist* provides a similar, useful survey ("A Third Industrial Revolution" 2002).

19. Baily, Manyika, and Gupta (2013) and Gordon (2013) in the same issue of *International Productivity Monitor* give a digest of the contrasting views.

BIBLIOGRAPHY

Abbate, Janet. (1999). *Inventing the Internet.* Cambridge, MA: MIT Press.

Acemoglu, Daron. (2008). *Introduction to Modern Economic Growth.* Princeton, NJ: Princeton University Press.

Allen, Robert C. (2009). *The British Industrial Revolution in Global Perspective.* New York: Cambridge University Press.

Ames, Edward, and Nathan Rosenberg. (1968). "The Enfield Arsenal in Theory and History." *Economic Journal* 78(312): 827–842.

Atack, Jeremy, Fred Bateman, and Robert A. Margo. (2005). "Capital Deepening and the Rise of the Factory: The American Experience during the Nineteenth Century." *Economic History Review* 58(3): 586–595.

Atack, Jeremy, Fred Bateman, and Robert A. Margo. (2008). "Steam Power, Establishment Size, and Labor Productivity Growth in Nineteenth Century American Manufacturing." *Explorations in Economic History* 45(1): 185–198.

Atack, Jeremy, Michael Haines, and Robert Margo. (2011). "Railroads and the Rise of the Factory in the United States, 1850–1870." In *Economic Evolution and Revolution in Historical Time*, edited by Paul Rhode, Joshua Rosenbloom, David Weiman, 162–179. Stanford, CA: Stanford University Press.

Baily, Martin Neil, and Barry P. Bosworth. (2014). "U.S. Manufacturing: Understanding its Past and its Potential Future." *Journal of Economic Perspectives* 28(1): 3–26.

Baily, Martin Neil, James Manyika, and Shalabh Gupta. (2013). "U.S. Productivity Growth: An Optimistic Perspective." *International Productivity Monitor* 25(Spring): 3–12.

Bartelsman, Eric J., and Wayne Gray. (1996). "The NBER Productivity Database." NBER Technical Working Paper No. 205.

Becker, Randy, Wayne Gray, and Jordan Marvakov. (2013, February). "NBER-CES Manufacturing Industry Database: Technical Notes." Available at http://www.nber.org/nberces/nberces5809/nberces_5809_technical_notes.pdf.

Berg, Maxine. (1994). "Factories, Workshops, and Industrial Organization." In *The Economic History of Britain since 1700*, Vol. 1: *1700–1860*, edited by Roderick Floud and Donald McCloskey, 2nd ed., 123–150. New York: Cambridge University Press.

Bresnahan, Timothy F., and Daniel M. G. Raff. (1991). "Intra-Industry Heterogeneity and the Great Depression: The American Motor Vehicles Industry, 1929–1935." *Journal of Economic History* 51(2): 317–331.

Broadberry, Stephen. (2006). *Market Services and the Productivity Races, 1850–2000: Britain in International Perspective.* New York: Cambridge University Press.

Broadberry, Stephen N. (1997). *The Productivity Race: British Manufacturing in International Perspective, 1850–1990.* Cambridge: Cambridge University Press.

Brynjolfsson, Erik, and Andrew McAfee. (2013). *The Second Machine Age: Work, Progress, and Prosperity in a Time of Brilliant Technologies.* New York: W. W. Norton.

Byrne, David, Stephen Oliner, and Daniel Sichel. (2013). "Is the Information Technology Revolution Over?" Finance and Economics Discussion Series, Federal Reserve Board Working Paper, Washington, DC.

Chandler, Alfred D., Jr. (1972). "Anthracite Coal and the Beginnings of the Industrial Revolution in the United States." *Business History Review* 46(2): 141–181.

Chandler, Alfred D., Jr. (1977). *The Visible Hand: The Managerial Revolution in American Business.* Cambridge, MA: Belknap Press.

Chandler, Alfred D., Jr. (1990). *Scale and Scope: The Dynamics of Industrial Capitalism*. Cambridge, MA: Harvard University Press.

Chandler, Alfred D., Jr. (1994). "The Competitive Performance of U.S. Industrial Enterprises since the Second World War." *Business History Review* 68(1): 1–72.

Collard-Wexler, Allan, and Jan de Loecker. (2015). "Reallocation and Technology: Evidence from the U.S. Steel Industry." *American Economic Review* 105(1): 131–71.

Cortada, James W. (1993). *Before the Computer: IBM, NCR, Burroughs, and Remington Rand and the Industry They Created, 1865–1956*. Princeton, NJ: Princeton University Press.

Cortada, James W. (2004). *The Digital Hand*, Vol. I: *How Computers Changed the Work of American Manufacturing, Transportation, and Retail Industries*. New York: Oxford University Press.

Cortada, James W. (2012). *The Digital Flood: The Diffusion of Information Technology across the U.S., Europe, and Asia*. New York: Oxford University Press.

Dalzell, Robert F., Jr. (1987). *Enterprising Elite: The Boston Associates and the World They Made*. Cambridge, MA: Harvard University Press.

David, Paul A. (1975). *Technical Choice, Innovation and Economic Growth*. New York: Cambridge University Press.

David, Paul A. (1990). "The Dynamo and the Computer: An Historical Perspective on the Modern Productivity Paradox." *American Economic Review P&P* 80(2): 355–361.

Field, Alexander. (1983). "Land Abundance, Interest/Profit Rates, and Nineteenth-Century American and British Technology." *Journal of Economic History* 43(2): 405–431.

Field, Alexander. (1985). "On the Unimportance of Machinery." *Explorations in Economic History* 22(4): 378–401.

Gallman, Robert E. (1986). "The United States Capital Stock in the Nineteenth Century." In *American Economic Growth and Standard of Living before the Civil War*, edited by Stanley Engerman and Robert E. Gallman, 185–206. Chicago: University of Chicago Press.

Goldin, Claudia, and Lawrence F. Katz. (1988). "The Origins of Technology-Skill Complementarity." *Quarterly Journal of Economics* 113(3): 688–732.

Goldin, Claudia, and Lawrence F. Katz. (2010). *The Race between Technology and Education*. Cambridge, MA: Belknap Press.

Goldin, Claudia, and Kenneth Sokoloff. (1982). "Women, Children, and Industrialization in the Early Republic: Evidence from the Manufacturing Censuses." *Journal of Economic History* 42(4): 741–774.

Goldin, Claudia, and Kenneth Sokoloff. (1984). "The Relative Productivity Hypotheses of Industrialization: The American Case, 1820 to 1850." *Quarterly Journal of Economics* 99(3): 461–488.

Gordon, Robert J. (2013). "U.S. Productivity Growth: The Slowdown Has Returned After a Temporary Revival." *International Productivity Monitor* 25(Spring): 13–19.

Gordon, Robert J. (2016). *The Rise and Fall of American Growth: The U.S. Standard of Living since the Civil War*. Princeton, NJ: Princeton University Press.

Gray, Rowena. (2013). "Taking Technology to Task: The Skill Content of Technological Change in Early Twentieth Century United States." *Explorations in Economic History* 50(3): 351–367.

Grossman, Gene, and Elhanan Helpman. (1991). *Innovation and Growth in the Global Economy*. Cambridge, MA: MIT Press.

Habakkuk, H. J. (1962). *American and British Technology in the Nineteenth Century: The Search for Labor-Saving Innovation*. Cambridge: Cambridge University Press.

Hall, Bronwyn. (1994). "Corporate Restructuring and Investment Horizons in the United States, 1976–1987." *Business History Review* 68(1): 110–143.

Harrison, Mark. (1998). "The Economics of World War II: An Overview." In *The Economics of World War II: Six Great Powers in International Comparison*, edited by Mark Harrison, 1–44. Cambridge: Cambridge University Press.

Hessendahl, Arik. (2013). "Teardown Shows iPhone 5S Costs at Least $199 to Build, $173 for the 5C." *All Things D.* Available at http://allthingsd.com/20130924/teardown-analysis-shows-iphone-5s-costs-at-least-199-to-build-173-for-the-5c/.

Hicks, John. (1932). *The Theory of Wages.* London: Macmillan.

Hoffman, W. G. (1958). *The Growth of Industrial Economies.* Manchester, UK: Manchester University Press.

Hoke, Donald R. (1990). *Ingenious Yankees: The Rise of the American System of Manufactures in the Private Sector.* New York: Columbia University Press.

Hounshell, David A. (1984). *From the American System to Mass Production, 1800–1932.* Baltimore, MD: Johns Hopkins University Press.

James, John A., and Jonathan S. Skinner. (1985). "The Resolution of the Labor-Scarcity Paradox." *Journal of Economic History* 45(3): 513–540.

Katz, Lawrence F., and Robert A. Margo. (2013). "Technical Change and the Relative Demand for Skilled Labor: The United States in Historical Perspective." NBER Working Paper No. 18752.

Kurzweil, Raymond. (2005). *The Singularity Is Near: When Humans Transcend Biology.* New York: Viking.

Lamoreaux, Naomi. (1988). *The Great Merger Movement in American Business, 1895–1904.* New York: Cambridge University Press.

Langlois, Richard N. (2002). "Digital Technology and Economic Growth: the History of Semiconductors and Computers." In *Technological Innovation and Economic Performance*, edited by Benn Steil, David Victor, and Richard R. Nelson, 265–284. Princeton, NJ: Princeton University Press for the Council on Foreign Relations.

Lucas, Robert E., Jr. (1993). "Making Miracles." *Econometrica* 61(2): 251–272.

Maskus, Keith E. (1983). *Changing Structure of Comparative Advantage in American Manufacturing.* Ann Arbor, MI: UMI Research Press.

Mowery, David. (1999). "The Computer Software Industry." In *Sources of Industrial Leadership*, edited by David Mowery and Richard Nelson, 133–168. New York: Cambridge University Press.

Mowery, David, and Richard Nelson. (1999). *Sources of Industrial Leadership.* New York: Cambridge University Press.

Nordhaus, William D. (2007). "Two Centuries of Productivity Growth in Computing." *Journal of Economic History* 67(1): 128–159.

Nye, David E. (2013). *America's Assembly Line.* Cambridge, MA: MIT Press.

O'Brien, Anthony P. (1988). "Factory Size, Economies of Scale, and the Great Merger Wave of 1898–1902." *Journal of Economic History* 48(3): 639–649.

Piore, Michael, and Charles Sabel. (1984). *The Second Industrial Divide: Possibilities for Prosperity.* New York: Basic Books.

Porat, Marc Uri. (1977). *The Information Economy: Sources and Methods for Measuring the Primary Information Sector.* OT Special Publication 77–12 (1) US Department of Commerce, Office of Telecommunications.

"Reshoring Manufacturing: Coming Home." (2013). *The Economist*, January 17, digital edition.

Rosenberg, Nathan. (1982). *Inside the Black Box: Technology and Economics*. New York: Cambridge University Press.

Rothbard, Erwin. (1946). "Causes of the Superior Efficiency of U.S.A. Industry Compared with British Industry." *Economic Journal* 56(223): 383–390.

Scranton, Philip. (1997). *Endless Novelty: Specialty Production and American Industrialization, 1865–1925*. Princeton, NJ: Princeton University Press.

Servan-Schreiber, Jean Jacques. (1968). *American Challenge*. London: Hamish Hamilton.

"Slicing an Apple." (2011). *The Economist*, August 10, digital edition.

Smil, Vaclav. (2013). *Made in the USA*. Cambridge, MA: MIT Press.

Smith, Merritt R. (1977). *Harpers Ferry Armory and the New Technology: The Challenge of Change*. Ithaca, NY: Cornell University Press.

Sokoloff, Kenneth. (1984). "Was the Transition from the Artisanal Shop to the Nonmechanized Factory Associated with Gains in Efficiency? Evidence from the U.S. Manufacturing Censuses of 1820 and 1850." *Explorations in Economic History* 21(4): 351–382.

Sokoloff, Kenneth. (1986). "Productivity Growth in Manufacturing during Early Industrialization: Evidence from the American Northeast, 1820–1860." In *Long-Term Factors in American Economic Growth, Studies in Income and Wealth*, edited by Stanley Engerman and Robert Gallman, Vol. 51, 679–736. Chicago: University of Chicago Press.

Temin, Peter. (1966). "Labor Scarcity and the Problem of American Industrial Efficiency in the 1850s." *Journal of Economic History* 36(3): 277–298.

"A Third Industrial Revolution." (2012). *The Economist*, April 21, digital edition.

Tiffany, Paul. (1984). "The Roots of Decline: Business-Government Relations in the American Steel Industry, 1945–1960." *Journal of Economic History* 44(2): 407–419.

Tolliday, Steven, and Jonathan Zeitlin. (1991). *Between Fordism and Flexibility: The Automobile Industry and Its Workers*. London: Bloomsbury Academic.

Troesken, Werner. (1998). "Exclusive Dealing and the Whiskey Trust, 1890–1895." *Journal of Economic History* 58(3): 755–778.

Troesken, Werner, and Karen Clay. (2002). "Strategic Behavior in Whiskey Distilling, 1887–1895." *Journal of Economic History* 62(3): 999–1023.

US Bureau of the Census. (1907). *Census of Manufacturers: 1905, Part. 1*. Washington, DC: Government Printing Office, xxi.

van Biesbroeck, Johannes. (2003). "Productivity Dynamics with Technology Choice: An Application to Automobile Assembly." *Review of Economic Studies* 70(1): 167–198.

Wright, Carroll D. (1882). "Report on the Factory System of the United States." In US Census Office, *Tenth Census of the United States: Manufactures, 1880*. Washington, DC: Government Printing Office.

Wright, Gavin. (1990). "Origins of American Industrial Success, 1879–1940." *American Economic Review* 80(4): 651–668.

Zevin, Robert. (1971). "The Growth of Cotton Textile Production after 1815." In *The Reinterpretations of American Economic History*, edited by Robert W. Fogel and Stanley L. Engerman, 122–147. New York: Harper & Row.

CHAPTER 9

MANUFACTURING PRODUCTIVITY GROWTH IN AMERICAN ECONOMIC HISTORY

ALEXANDER J. FIELD

THERE are two main productivity concepts in economics. The first, and more commonly encountered, is labor productivity. Labor productivity is the ratio of output (Y) to labor input (N), measured as the number of employees, or the number of labor hours. Labor productivity means output per hour, and the growth rate of labor productivity is the difference between the growth rate of output (y) and the growth rate of hours (n). Labor productivity growth is critical in understanding improvement in the material standard of living, as measured by per capita output. Output per employee hour is not the same as output per capita—they have different denominators and may grow at different rates because of changes in labor force participation or the number of hours worked. But over the long run, it is impossible to have a sustained increase in output per capita without a sustained increase in output per hour. That is one reason we pay so much attention to labor productivity.

The second and less familiar concept is total factor productivity (TFP), which is the ratio of output to a combined measure reflecting both capital and labor inputs. We commonly assume that labor (N) and capital (K) input combine in generating output (Y) according to the Cobb-Douglas functional form, with β representing capital's share in national income:

$$Y = AK^{\beta}N^{1-\beta}$$

In this case, (A) is the level measure of total factor productivity: the ratio of output Y to the combined input measure ($K^\beta N^{1-\beta}$):

$$A = \frac{Y}{K^\beta N^{1-\beta}}$$

Differentiating both sides of this equation with respect to time, we have the growth of total factor productivity (a) as the difference between the growth in output (y) and a weighted average of the growth of capital services (k) and labor hours (n), the weights corresponding to the shares of factors in national income (typically about 25–40 percent for capital—the higher share is applicable to the end of the twentieth century and the beginning of the twenty-first—and the remainder for labor), with lowercase letters corresponding to continuously compounded rates of change.

$$a = y - \beta k - (1-\beta)n$$

When, measuring between business cycle peaks, output grows more than a combined measure of the two key inputs, we can interpret the difference as a rough measure of the growth in capacity due to technological and organizational advance.

Since the end of the Civil War, the US economy has grown at a long-term rate of a little more than 3 percent per year. Again, taking a very long view, this can be decomposed into a long-term rate of population growth, and thus labor force, and thus hours, of roughly 1 percent per year, combined with a growth rate of output per hour (labor productivity) of about 2 percent per year (this is due to the identity y = n + (y – n), where n is growth in hours and y – n is growth in output per hour).

The growth of manufacturing productivity is an important aspect of the broader history of advance in the entire economy. It is, however, by no means the whole story. Other important sectors have mattered: transportation, communication, wholesale and retail distribution, and of course agriculture and the other extractive industries. Advances in sectors outside of manufacturing have affected productivity growth within it, and vice versa.

IMPROVEMENTS IN MANUFACTURING PRODUCTIVITY FROM COLONIAL TIMES TO THE TWENTIETH CENTURY

During the eighteenth and nineteenth centuries, the locus of manufacturing moved from individual homes (whether organized within a family economy or by merchant-entrepreneurs in putting-out systems) to specialized structures—factories—exhibiting varying degrees of mechanization and the use of inanimate power sources. Not all industries went through the same sequence of stages, but a common aspect of transitions was that each was associated with an increase in output per unit of input. Several factors contributed to this. Moving from simple home production to putting out (production within the home, but workers specialized in specific tasks as entrepreneurs coordinated movements of raw materials and subassemblies among different houses) allowed greater division of labor. In *The Wealth of Nations*, Adam Smith granted that repeating the same task over and over might make workers stupid and mean, but he also stressed that doing so could improve productivity by allowing the worker to become more proficient at a particular task, save the time otherwise spent moving from one task to the other, and perceive ways in which he or she might improve the production process (Rosenberg 1965).

Boots and shoes, a manufacturing industry that began in New England, went through all of these stages (Hazard 1913). Other sectors largely skipped putting out or production in nonmechanized factories. Cotton textiles, for example, transitioned from home spinning and weaving to limited putting out to mechanized water-driven factories for spinning and eventually, starting in the 1820s, integrated mills performing both spinning and weaving (Field 1978). Eighteenth- and nineteenth-century mechanized manufacturing increased output per hour and total factor productivity by exploiting inanimate sources of power: water and wind, and eventually steam, by the use of imported or newly developed machinery, and by exploiting technological and organizational innovations in transportation and communication that enabled all-weather, all-year operation of larger plants.

A major obstacle to improving TFP in manufacturing during the nineteenth century was intermittent operation. During snow and mud season, much of the country's transportation infrastructure was inoperative. Communication was slow, generally limited to the speed of a fast horse. Depending on the nature of the industry—the impact of these handicaps varied—factories could not be assured a steady supply of raw materials, nor could they always ship their output easily to final users. Even during the summer, factories could be forced to shut down due to inadequate water flows, both because this affected the availability of a source to drive the prime mover, and because it could impede passage along canals or rivers. Labor productivity in antebellum manufacturing grew rapidly, but there was not a significant growth advantage for highly mechanized or capital-intensive industries (Sokoloff 1986). In that regard, the large integrated textile mills of Lowell and Lawrence, Massachusetts, or Manchester, New Hampshire, to which much historical attention has been paid, were the exception rather than the rule prior to the Civil War.

The second industrial revolution of the postbellum period saw the development of large-scale heavy industry (integrated steel mills, petroleum refineries, cigarette manufacturing, large slaughtering plants), requiring innovations in transportation and communication (in particular the railroad and the telegraph), the invention of new machinery and industrial processes in manufacturing itself, and a new organizational form (what Alfred Chandler in 1977 called modern business enterprise) that could manage large-scale units.

The railroad and the telegraph provided reliable all-weather transportation and communication, which made it possible for the first time, in certain industries, to operate large-scale factories with heavy fixed capital installations on a more or less full-time basis. The steam engine, beyond its indirect effects on manufacturing through use in locomotives, made factory location more flexible and reduced vulnerability to the weather (and water flows) in terms of access to inanimate power. The first big businesses in the United States were railroad and communication companies (examples: the Pennsylvania Railroad and Western Union). These were followed by large mail-order houses (Sears Roebuck, Montgomery Ward) and department stores (like Macy's) that adopted the multidivisional organizational form that first appeared in transport and communication. Finally, we see Chandler's modern business enterprise in a select group of industrial firms in sectors such as iron and steel (Carnegie), petroleum refining (Standard Oil), cigarette manufacture (American Tobacco), and hog and beef slaughtering (Swift) (Chandler 1977; Field 1987). Still, there is evidence of substantial part-time operation in manufacturing as late as 1880, a reminder that the penetration of large-scale capital intensive manufacturing varied by sector, and that a broad range of manufacturing establishment sizes coexisted (Atack, Bateman, and Margo 2002).

By the 1880s, one could say that the commanding heights of the manufacturing economy were occupied by large-scale enterprises exploiting inanimate sources of power and elaborate power transmission and machinery installations. But the apotheosis of manufacturing productivity growth would not take place until three decades later. During the 1920s (1919–1929) manufacturing TFP grew at a continuously compounded rate of over 5 percent per year (Kendrick 1961). There had been nothing like it prior to that decade, and there has been nothing quite like it since.

THE MANUFACTURING REVOLUTION
OF THE 1920S

The fundamental cause of record-breaking TFP growth in that decade was a revolution in factory design and the distribution of power within it, associated with a shift from steam (or in a few cases, still, water) power to electric power. Because of square-cube relationships involving cost savings associated with larger boilers and pistons, a single large steam engine as prime mover had, in prior years, almost always been the economically attractive option for a fixed installation. In a steam-powered factory, motive force was generated centrally and distributed to work stations by means of a mechanical system of leather belts, pulleys, and rotating horizontal shafts. The economics of factory design required balancing the increased cost per square foot of multistory designs with the imperative to minimize the sum of runs from the prime mover to individual stations, so as to keep a lid on the substantial power losses attributable to friction when mechanical transmission was used.

The fact that power-driven factories in the nineteenth century were typically two, three, four, or five stories tall was not generally the result of high urban land values.

This was obviously so in the case of water power, which dominated mechanized factories in the antebellum period. The early textile cities, such as Lowell and Lawrence, Massachusetts, were greenfield sites.[1] Water held on tenaciously in New England (in 1900 over 35 percent of the horsepower in the region was still generated by these means), but steam came to predominate elsewhere in the country, a development facilitated by advances in high-pressure engineering and the development of large, powerful, and energy-efficient engines such as the Corliss (Atack, Bateman, and Weiss 1980; Rosenberg and Trajtenberg 2001). The prime mover in a steam-powered factory was typically housed in its own room, with a leather belt, often several feet wide and several hundred feet long, connecting the flywheel to the main drive shaft. Although use of steam power allowed location of new factories closer to existing supplies of labor and transport facilities, the basic design of a plant remained fundamentally unchanged, and its height was driven by the same considerations involving the internal distribution of power as had dictated its profile in the age of water.

Thus for both water- and steam-powered plants, the multistory factory building of the nineteenth century was the result of a different economic imperative than that which pushed up the height of commercial office structures in central business districts. The most persuasive evidence for this is what happened in the twentieth century. With electrification, and the eventual elimination of the old internal system for distributing power, factories went predominantly single story, even though the population of the United States was larger and more concentrated, so in principle, land was scarcer (more flexible surface transportation, associated with the diffusion of the internal combustion engine and related infrastructure, also played a role in this transition). To a very considerable degree, multistory factory construction in the nineteenth century reflected an engineering solution to the problem of distributing power mechanically from a central prime mover.

Edison began selling electric power to the public from his Pearl Street station in New York City in 1882. The initial market was upscale residential illumination. Subsequently, power was sold to street car and cable car companies for traction. The first factory electrification (for power rather than illumination) involved simply replacing one large prime mover with another. The steam engine was removed and an electric engine substituted—but there were no changes in the mechanisms for distributing power internally—and mechanically—within the factory. It took several decades for factory designers and electrical engineers fully to appreciate how, using a few large power-generating plants and a multitude of smaller electric motors, they could dispense with the onsite prime mover *and* the apparatus for mechanically distributing power, replacing the latter with a network of relatively cheap and flexible electric wires. An intermediate step (group drive) involved use of medium-sized motors to turn somewhat shorter drive shafts, which in turn supplied power to groups of machines (Devine 1983).

The change in the way in which power was distributed removed a straightjacket from factory design, allowing one-story layouts and a reconfiguration of internal work flow that went hand in hand with the diffusion of assembly-line techniques in such industries as transport equipment and electrical machinery. There are many features distinguishing twentieth-century factory buildings from those constructed in the nineteenth, but the most salient is that the twentieth-century structure, like Ford's River Rouge facility, is single storied, whereas the nineteenth-century factory was not. Single-storied buildings had lower construction costs per square foot, but there were other advantages, particularly in industries based on mechanical or electrical engineering that required the assembly of many parts. The best way to engineer an assembly line, except in the few instances where gravity can be harnessed to particularly good effect, it to keep it on a single level. A bonus was reduced risk of fire. Multistory factories with mechanical power distribution required openings between floors so that power could be transferred across drive shafts on different floors. These openings created natural avenues through which fire could spread, entailing higher fire insurance premiums and/or the costs of enclosures to mitigate the risk (Devine 1983, 361).

Electrical internal power distribution and the use of small electric motors made all floor areas of the factory—not just those close to an overhead shaft—of roughly equivalent economic value. In the steam-powered factory there was prime real estate near the overhead shafts and there were "dead" areas that could be used only for storage. Such areas could now also be used for stages of the manufacturing process. The dismantling or elimination of the mechanical system for distributing power internally, which had required brackets and rotating drive shafts hanging from the ceiling, made it much easier to install overhead cranes for moving subassemblies. The possibility of using portable tools powered by electricity was another contributor to productivity advance. Finally, new single-storied buildings could utilize skylights for illumination and ventilation—a rare feature in a nineteenth-century factory.

It was during the 1920s that much of this transition took place, and the decade is unique in the history of US manufacturing. The growth rates of TFP in manufacturing were extremely high, and this was true across the board at the two-digit level (see Field 2011, table 2.2).[2] The profits associated with this transition played a major role in fueling the stock market boom between 1925 and 1929.

As a result of this revolution in factory design, layout, and internal power distribution, the level of TFP in US manufacturing was higher in all subsequent periods. But one of the lessons learned from analysis of the Solow growth model is that it is far easier to raise the trajectory of levels of productivity in a sector or economy than it is to permanently increase productivity growth rates. Of course, whenever levels increase, there will be a transition in which the rate of growth will accelerate. But the higher rates, whether due to a higher saving rate or to the availability of new technologies, usually cannot be sustained.

And so it was in this case. American manufacturing could not hope to sustain a rate of increase of TFP of over 5 percent per year in perpetuity from the electrification/assembly-line/one-story transition. Eventually, as old factories were reconfigured, and as new factories replaced old, there would be fewer and fewer opportunities to reap additional gains. As Devine shows, the transition from steam to electric power, which began around the turn of the century, and accelerated after World War I, was largely complete by the end of the 1920s. By 1929, electricity was responsible for driving about 79 percent of total capacity within US manufacturing (Field 2011, 349).

The decades following the 1920s have seen productivity growth rates in manufacturing trend generally downward, as has the share of overall TFP advance in the economy accounted for by the sector. Gavin Wright argued forcefully in his presidential address to the Economic History Association that it is time that we think of the entire twentieth century, including (and in his mind especially) the period after World War II, as an appropriate venue for research in economic history. While much useful work will continue to be done on the nineteenth century, there are rich opportunities to explore the data of the last century with the tools, perspectives, and aesthetics of an economic historian (Wright 1999).

The focus here is on TFP, rather than the more commonly studied labor productivity; the former is conceptually one of the two contributors to the latter. Keep in mind that the factors driving the growth of output and output per hour, though related, are not identical. The growth of output over a particular time period is decomposable into the contributions made by the growth of hours (n), the growth of the services of physical capital (k), and the growth in the power and efficacy of the recipes (a), whereby these inputs are combined to generate output (total factor productivity):

$$y = a + \beta k + (1 - \beta) n$$

The growth of output per hour, in contrast, is the sum of TFP growth (a) and capital's share (β) times the rate of capital deepening. The growth of total factor productivity is one of two influences on the growth of labor productivity. The contribution from total factor productivity, representing in a very broad sense the benefits we get from technological and organizational progress (Solow called this "manna from heaven"), and a contribution attributable to saving and accumulation, or capital deepening, a process that results in members of the labor force cooperating with larger quantities of physical capital. Capital deepening (rises in the capital-labor ratio) by itself makes workers more productive. Ditch diggers using backhoes will move more cubic meters of earth per hour than those using shovels or hand tools. Moving from hand tools to backhoes (capital deepening) makes workers more productive, even if it is not reflective of any change in the available book of blueprints. This decomposition is reflected in the following equation, a rearrangement of the fundamental growth accounting equation:

$$y - n = a + \beta(k - n)$$

Total factor productivity growth therefore helps explain the growth of both output and output per hour. Here is a striking illustration of how important it can be. Between 1929 and 1941, labor hours in the US private nonfarm economy (PNE) were effectively unchanged. Because of population growth, the labor force was larger in 1941, but the unemployment rate in 1941 was still several times what it had been in 1929, so total hours were about the same. Capital input by some measures had declined. For practical purposes, we can say that private-sector inputs, conventionally measured, grew not at all between 1929 and 1941. No matter how we weight the growth rates of the two inputs, we will get combined private-sector input growth close to zero. But real output was between 33 and 40 percent higher in 1941 as compared with 1929.[3] The difference between growth of inputs of zero and a growth of output of somewhere between 2.3 and 2.8 percent per year over the twelve-year period reflected improvement in total factor productivity. Since the growth of both labor hours and physical capital in the private sector was close to nil between 1929 and 1941, there was no capital-deepening (increase in the capital-labor ratio) over these years. Therefore, during this unusual period, virtually all of the increase in both output and output per hour is attributable to growth in total factor productivity.

Manufacturing's Contribution: Historical Perspective

The relevant output measure when one is considering an individual sector like manufacturing is not gross sales but value added. Value added is the difference between gross sales and purchased inputs, including energy, materials, and subassemblies, and services other than those provided by employees.[4] Value added represents a sector or firm's contribution to gross domestic product (GDP). Purchased materials include the contributions of other sectors or firms. Safeway's contribution to GDP is not its gross sales, since that would inappropriately credit the supermarket chain with the value added by its suppliers. Since wage and salary payments as well as those to owners of capital are made out of the flow of net revenue generated by value added, value added also represents a sector or firm's contribution to gross domestic income (GDI). It is because this equality must be true for every individual economic unit that in the aggregate, Gross Domestic Product must, subject to a statistical discrepancy, equal Gross Domestic Income.

Value added in manufacturing peaked at about a third of the private nonfarm economy during World War II, averaging a little over 30 percent of the economy in the 1940s, 1950s, and 1960s. Its share declined thereafter, and today it generates a smaller fraction of national income, and employs a smaller fraction of the labor force, than it did in 1869.[5] It is important to focus not only on the growth of manufacturing productivity per se, but also on the sector's contribution to productivity advance in the larger aggregates, which depends on both the sectoral productivity growth rate and on the relative size of the sector during a particular epoch.

Table 9.1 summarizes TFP growth in the manufacturing sector and the private nonfarm economy in the United States from 1919 to 2015, as well as the former's contribution to the latter (the PNE comprises about three-fourths of total output; the most important exclusions are government and agriculture). Manufacturing's TFP growth was faster than the PNE average during the interwar period, especially so between 1919 and 1929, and between 1995 and 2005, but by a much smaller margin. It was

Table 9.1 Manufacturing's Contribution to PNE TFP Growth Rate, 1919–2015

Years	PNE TFP Growth (%)	Manu. TFP Growth (%)	Manu. Share of PNE	Percentage Points Contrib. to PNE TFP Growth	Manu. Share of PNE TFP Growth
1919–1929	2.02	5.12	0.257	1.32	0.65
1929–1941	3.18	3.89	0.268	1.04	0.33
1941–1948	2.70	.24	0.363	0.09	0.03
1948–1973	1.88	1.49	0.334	0.50	0.26
1973–1995	0.40	0.68	0.253	0.17	0.41
1995–2005	1.72	1.78	0.187	0.33	0.19
2005–2015	.48	−.12	0.154	−.02	−.04

Notes and sources: Growth rates are annual, continuously compounded. TFP: 1919–1929: Kendrick (1961, Tables A–XXIII, D1, and D2). 1929–1941 and 1941–1948: PNE TFP calculations are based on Kendrick (1961) for labor input, the BEA for capital input, and the newer chain-weighted indexes of output from the BEA and include a cyclical adjustment for 1941. Manufacturing TFP calculations begin with Kendrick for output and labor input and the BEA for capital input. See text for description of adjustments. 1948–1995: data are from US Department of Labor (2004, 2018b). 1995–2015: http://www.bls.gov, accessed March 9, 2018. Manufacturing share of PNE: Kendrick (1961); US Department of Commerce (2018a, b); accessed March 9, 2018.

also higher during the dark ages (1973–1995), although both rates were quite low then. In contrast, sectoral productivity growth in manufacturing lagged the PNE average during the golden age (1948–1973) and between 2005 and 2015. The TFP growth in the sector was broadest and most uniformly high during the 1920s, but advance was higher across the Depression years than during any subsequent period, including 1995–2005. Within the manufacturing sector, the locus of advance was narrower during the 1930s than the 1920s, and narrower still during the period of the information technology (IT) productivity boom.

What particularly distinguished the interwar period from 1995 to 2005 was a combination of strong forward movement in both labor and capital productivity. Although labor productivity growth in manufacturing between 1995 and 2005 was stronger than during any period save the 1920s (see table 9.2), capital productivity deteriorated. That's because the advance was fueled by very large increases in information technology (IT) capital (computers, routers, fiber optic cable, etc.), the measured increase of which has been augmented by the use of hedonic methods to account for claimed quality improvements.

Table 9.1 also reports manufacturing's varying contributions over time to overall PNE TFP growth. The calculations are based on multiplying the sectoral productivity rate by the average ratio of manufacturing value added to PNE value added during the relevant

Table 9.2 Manufacturing's Contribution to PNE Labor Productivity Growth Rates, 1919–2015

Years	PNE LP Growth (%)	Manu. LP Growth (%)	Manu. Share of PNE	Percentage Points Contrib. to PNE LP Growth	Manu. Share of PNE LP Growth
1919–1929	2.27	5.45	0.257	1.40	.62
1929–1941	3.03	3.34	0.268	.89	.29
1941–1948	3.27	1.68	0.363	.61	.19
1949–1973	2.85	2.51	0.334	.84	.30
1973–1995	1.45	2.61	0.253	.66	.46
1995–2005	2.92	4.63	0.187	.87	.30
2005–2015	1.31	1.27	0.154	.20	.15

Notes and sources: Growth rates are annual, continuously compounded. 1919–1929: Kendrick (1961, Tables A–XXIII, D1 and D2). 1929–1948: see text. 1948–1995: US Department of Labor (2004); US Department of Commerce (2013a). 1995–2015: US Department of Labor (2018b), accessed March 9, 2018.

time period.[6] This produces a percentage point contribution which, considered in relation to overall PNE TFP growth rates, provides a rough measure of manufacturing's relative contribution to growth in the latter.

Calculations of PNE TFP for 1929–1941 and 1941–1948 differ from those drawn directly from Kendrick (1961) because they use the newer chain-weighted indexes of output and include a cyclical adjustment for 1941 (for details, see Field 2013). Unadjusted data from Kendrick yield 1929–1941 PNE TFP growth of 2.31 percent per year, and 1.29 percent between 1941 and 1948 (Field 2003; 2011, Chapter 1). The cyclical adjustment for the level of TFP in 1941 raises the TFP growth rate for 1929–1941 but lowers it for 1941–1948. The use of chained index methods generates faster growth in output and perforce faster TFP growth over both periods.

One can make a comparable adjustment in manufacturing TFP growth rates over the two periods. Begin with manufacturing output from Kendrick, hours from Kendrick, and manufacturing capital (structures and equipment) from the Bureau of Economic Analysis's (BEA's) Fixed Asset Table 4.2, line 19. From this, generate TFP level calculations (A) using the Cobb-Douglas specification and an assumed capital share of .31:

$$A = \frac{Y}{\left(K^{.31} * N^{.69}\right)}$$

where Y is output, K is fixed capital, and N is labor hours.

Taking natural logs of these levels, and differencing them, use the same technique employed in Field (2011, 2013) to make a cyclical adjustment to PNE TFP growth rates for 1929–1941 and 1941–1948. Regress the log differences of TFP levels (which represent continuously compounded growth rates of TFP from one year to the next) against the change in the civilian unemployment rate, which yields the following results (t statistics in parentheses):

Dep. Var.	Years	n	Constant	ΔUR	R^2
1.1 Δln (MANUTFP)	1929–1941	12	.0360	−.0153	.666
			(2.41)	(−4.47)	

The regression can be interpreted in this way: the estimated trend growth rate of TFP in manufacturing between 1929 and 1941 was about 3.6 percent per year, but overlaid on this was a strong cyclicality effect. Every 1 percentage point increase in the unemployment rate from one year to the next chopped about 1.5 percentage points off the annual manufacturing TFP growth rate. Every 1 percentage point drop in the unemployment rate did the reverse, adding about 1.5 percentage points to the TFP growth rate. As is the case with the PNE, big increases in the output gap and the unemployment rate reduced the growth rate of sectoral TFP, and where the increases were large enough, drove it into negative territory.

One can then ask what the level of manufacturing TFP would have been in 1941 if the output gap had closed—in other words, if the unemployment rate had been 3.8 percent, as it was in 1948, 6.1 percentage points lower than it actually was in 1941.[7] Based on the regression coefficient on the change in the unemployment rate, we can estimate that this would have added (−6.1 × −.0153) = .093 to the log of the level of 1941 manufacturing TFP. This cyclical adjustment yields manufacturing TFP growth at 3.52 percent per year between 1929 and 1941, rather than the 2.74 rate one would calculate from the cyclically unadjusted data.

Recall, however, that we are using Kendrick's measures of manufacturing output, which are not based on chained indexes. The BEA does not provide chained index estimates of manufacturing value added prior to 1947. If we are willing to make the assumption that moving to chained index methods would add proportionately as much to manufacturing output growth as it does to PNE output growth, we can proceed. Any increment to manufacturing output growth will, of course, flow directly to manufacturing TFP growth, since the latter is estimated as the difference between output growth and a weighted average of input growth. From Kendrick, PNE output growth between 1929 and 1941 is 2.33 percent per year. Using 1996 chained dollars, PNE output growth over the same period is 2.70 percent per year, a difference of .37 percentage points per year. Adding a similar amount—.37 percentage points per year—to the manufacturing TFP growth rate yields 3.89 percent per year.

For 1941–1948, TFP growth in manufacturing using the Kendrick data for output and hours and the BEA data for capital, and including a cyclical adjustment for 1941, is – 1.71 percent per year. Make the same assumption—that chained index methods would add to the growth rate of manufacturing output the same growth increment in percentage points as they do to the PNE output measure. The PNE output growth between 1941 and 1948 according to Kendrick is 3.51 percent per year. Using 1996 chained dollars, it is 5.47 percent per year, a difference of 1.95 percentage points per year (Carter et al. 2006, Series Ca142). When added to the –1.71 percent calculated using the cyclically adjusted measure of TFP growth in manufacturing, TFP growth for the sector moves into slightly positive territory (.24 percent per year).

Table 9.1 shows that during 1919–1929 approximately two-thirds of PNE TFP growth can be attributed to the manufacturing sector, whereas between 1929 and 1941 this portion drops to about a third. Across the war years (1941–1948), TFP growth in manufacturing was barely positive, as we have just discussed, due principally to the disruptions associated with war mobilization and demobilization and the huge amount of capital that was injected into the sector in that process.

Between 1948 and 1973, the golden age, manufacturing TFP advance remained below economy-wide levels, but still contributed 26 percent of PNE TFP growth: .50 percentage points out of 1.88 percent per year. In the dark ages (1973–1995), a period in which TFP growth in manufacturing and just about everywhere else plummeted, the sector contributed just .14 percentage points out of annual PNE growth of .40 percent per year, a little over 40 percent of the dismal economy-wide achievement.

The calculation of manufacturing's share of the PNE from 1948 onward is based on the ratio of manufacturing value added to PNE value added, averaged over the relevant time period. (Value added for the PNE is from table 1.3.5 of the BEA's online NIPA accounts. Manufacturing value added can be found in Value Added by Industry in the GDP by Industry and Input-Output portion of the site.)

Such data are not available prior to 1947. Volume 2 of the 2001 print version of the *National Income and Product Accounts of the United States, 1929–47*, table 6.1a, contains information beginning in 1929 on industry contributions to national income. The estimates of manufacturing's share prior to 1947 are constructed by dividing manufacturing (line 7) by private industry (line 1) less agriculture, forestry and fisheries (line 4). For a variety of reasons, including differences in the degree to which the PNE has been successfully approximated in the denominator, this approach yields a share about 3 percentage points higher for 1948 than the share calculated using the sources described for 1948 and thereafter. I reduce the shares for the earlier years so that the earlier year series can be spliced at 1948, and then average the adjusted shares for 1941–1948 and 1929–1941.

For 1919–1929, I calculate the ratio of Kendrick's index of manufacturing output (table D-I) to his index of PNE output (table A-XXIII), adjust this series so that it can be spliced at the 1929 value calculated using the national income data, and then average across the ten-year period.

Compared to earlier work (e.g., Field 2011, Chapter 5), table 9.1 contains several refinements. It includes estimates of manufacturing TFP growth (not just PNE TFP growth) that feature cyclicality adjustments for 1941 and take into account that chained index estimates of output grow more rapidly during the interwar period. It incorporates the effects of recent revisions in the Bureau of Labor Statistics estimates of TFP growth, allowing us to push estimates into the twenty-first century. And it applies an improved and more consistent methodology in calculating manufacturing's share.

Labor Productivity

TFP growth is important in its own right, as a rough measure of the technological and organizational progress that contributes to economic growth. It is also a key determinant of labor productivity growth, which is influenced as well by capital deepening, the relative importance of these two factors varying across different time periods. First, let us consider the broader economy. For the PNE, output per hour grew 2.67 percent per year between 1929 and 1941, and 3.60 percent between 1941 and 1948. These calculations use chained index output measures from the BEA and labor input (unadjusted) from Kendrick, and they are before a cyclical adjustment to reflect the fact that 1941 was not a year of full employment.[8]

How should we make that adjustment? Labor productivity growth is the sum of TFP growth and capital's share times the rate of capital deepening. In posing a counterfactual of no output gap in 1941 (3.8 percent unemployment instead of the actual 9.9 percent), we need to consider two effects that might partially have counterbalanced each other. On the one hand, the level of TFP in 1941 would likely have been higher. On the other hand, the capital-labor ratio would likely have been lower, because labor input would have grown much more rapidly than capital as the economy approached potential from below. That dynamic is reflected in the positive coefficients on the change in the unemployment rate in regressions 1.2 and 1.3. When the unemployment rate shrinks, K/N grows more slowly (or even declines), and this effect is particularly pronounced in manufacturing.

Dep. Var.	Years	n	Constant	ΔUR	R^2
1.2 Δln (PNE K/N)	1929–1941	12	−.009	+ .0197	.969
			(−1.87)	(17.81)	

Dep. Var.	Years	n	Constant	ΔUR	R^2
1.3 Δln (MANU K/N)	1929–1941	12	−.023	+ .0327	.893
			(−1.45)	(9.137)	

For the PNE, procyclical TFP growth would have added .0631 (–6.1 × –.01035) to the 1941 level of labor productivity.[9] The second effect (countercyclical capital deepening) would have been partially offsetting, adding –.0372 = .31 × –6.1 × .0197 (the terms on the right-hand side are capital's share, the posited difference in the unemployment rate in percentage points, and the cyclicality coefficient from regression 1.2). Summing the two effects yields .0258 to be added to the natural log of 1941 PNE labor productivity. This adjustment leaves us with 3.03 percent PNE labor productivity growth between 1929 and 1941 and 3.27 percent between 1941 and 1948.

Now let's consider the manufacturing sector alone. According to Kendrick, manufacturing output per hour grew 2.61 percent per year between 1929 and 1941 and 2.37 percent between 1941 and 1948 (Kendrick 1961, table D-1). Adjusting for TFP procyclicality adds .0933 to the 1941 log level of manufacturing labor productivity (see regression 1.1 and discussion in the preceding paragraphs). Adjusting for K/L countercyclicality subtracts .0618. This is derived from regression 1.3 (–.0618 = .31 × –6.1 × .0327.[10] The net effect is +.0315. Incorporating both adjustments yields manufacturing labor productivity growth of 2.87 percent between 1929 and 1941 and –.25 percent between 1941 and 1948. Finally, making the same assumption as in the TFP calculations about the effect of switching to chained index measures of output— that the increase in manufacturing value added growth would be proportionate to the increase in PNE output growth resulting from the switch—we get to 3.34 percent per year for manufacturing labor productivity growth for the years 1929–1941, and 1.68 percent per year between 1941 and 1948.

In the 1920s (1919–1929) and in the 1930s (1929–1941), the proportions of PNE labor productivity growth contributed by manufacturing (62 and 29 percent) are similar to those made by the sector for TFP growth in the PNE (65 and 33 percent). Rates of capital deepening in the sector and in the PNE were similar in the 1920s and then again in the 1930s (though the rates of each of these metrics differed substantially between the two periods). During the World War II period, manufacturing's contribution to PNE productivity growth was low in absolute terms, but higher for labor productivity (19 percent) than for TFP (3 percent), in part because the rate of capital deepening in manufacturing was high during 1941–1948 relative to other sectors. Capital deepening meant that manufacturing's labor productivity growth rate—1.68 percent—though lower than that for the PNE overall—was much higher than its TFP growth rate (.25 percent per year).

For 1995–2005, the manufacturing labor productivity growth rate was much higher than its TFP growth rate (4.62 vs. 1.78). This is reflective of the fact that capital-deepening within the sector (as opposed to TFP growth) was a major contributor to labor productivity growth. There's a difference between how much (expressed as shares) manufacturing contributed: 19 percent of PNE TFP growth as compared with 30 percent of PNE labor productivity growth.

HISTORICAL PERSPECTIVE

What underlay the differences in manufacturing's absolute and relative contributions to productivity growth over these different intervals? The peak TFP and labor productivity advance in manufacturing in the 1920s resulted from transformative organizational and technological progress involving both new products (especially the automobile and electrical appliances) and a revolution in factory organization and design in which the traditional methods of internally distributing power through metal shafts and leather belts were replaced with electrical wires and small electric motors. But outside of manufacturing, there was less progress. Thus we have two-thirds of PNE TFP advance during that period coming out of manufacturing, and almost the same fraction of PNE labor productivity growth. Capital-deepening within manufacturing during the 1920s was not a major contributor to the sector's labor productivity growth—indeed, the critical new innovations were often capital-saving, particularly of the services of structures.

Because a high fraction of the manufacturing sector was already electrified by 1929, the puzzle is not so much why manufacturing TFP growth declined from 5.12 percent per year (1919–1929) to 3.89 percent per year between 1929 and 1941 as why it did not fall further. There are two considerations that help explain why. The first reflects the residual influences—the tail end—of the electrification transition. In some cases, as Bresnahan and Raff (1991) have shown for the automobile industry, some older and less productive plants that had persisted in operation during the boom period of the 1920s simply shut down, as the economy went into recession between 1929 and 1933, and it was the remaining (and higher productivity) facilities that supplied output as the economy recovered. Some of the more marginally productive facilities were never brought back.

But the second and more important influence involved the maturing of a privately funded research and development (R&D) system that had begun with Edison at Menlo Park and reached maturity during the 1930s. Both R&D employment and spending soared during the Depression years, and as Margo (1991) has shown, scientists and engineers were largely protected from the risk of unemployment that fell so heavily on other job groups.

Thus one must use a light touch in contextualizing trends in manufacturing TFP during the interwar period. In the decades after 1929, TFP growth in manufacturing was substantially lower and less uniform across two-digit industries than it had been in the 1920s. Nevertheless, by any standard of comparison other than that of the 1920s, TFP growth in manufacturing during the Depression years was high.

What made the 1930s (1929–1941) so unusual was the combination of still rapid advance in manufacturing with the effects of spillovers in transportation and distribution resulting from the build-out of the surface road network. Total factor productivity (TFP) growth within manufacturing slowed compared to its unparalleled record in the 1920s, though it remained world class by any standard of comparison other than the 1920s. And the sector grew slightly in relative importance, so its weight was larger. Nevertheless, of greater significance to overall PNE TFP growth during this period was the organizational and technological transformation of transportation and distribution (wholesale and retail trade) made possible by street, highway, bridge, and tunnel construction.

During the 1920s the expansion of car and truck production outpaced the modernization of the road network. Developing an infrastructure suitable for a transportation system rolling increasingly on rubber tires required overcoming political disputes about where the new US route system would be located. These obstacles were largely resolved by November 1926, and if one looks at the data on street and highway improvements from then until the beginning of World War II, the effects of the Depression appear modest and short lived, mostly affecting the years 1933, 1934, and 1935. In contrast, the building of private structures remained depressed throughout the decade.

The growth of public infrastructure resulted in large productivity gains in distribution and in transportation, where a striking complementarity developed between the rail system and the growing trucking industry. Together, the gains in manufacturing, transportation, distribution, and smaller sectors such as communication meant that the technological and organizational contribution to the growth of capacity across the Depression years was larger than in other periods of US history, and also substantially more diversified in its sectoral origins.

Although World War II provided a massive fiscal and monetary stimulus that eliminated the remnants of Depression-era unemployment, it was, on balance, disruptive of the forward pace of technological progress in the private sector. Military initiatives such as the Manhattan Project diverted scientific and engineering talent away from the private sector. And the economy was forced through wrenching changes as the military economy quickly expanded and then almost as rapidly shrank. The industrial buildup between mid-1942 and October 1943 was heavily unbalanced, focused on a small number of war-related sectors, such as other transportation equipment, iron and steel, chemicals, and electrical equipment. From 1944 onward, there was an almost equally rapid unwinding of the war economy. While the fiscal effect of war spending provided the final boost to bring the economy out of the Depression, the war experience, which involved in total perhaps forty months of serious war mobilization, with the peak effort lasting sixteen months, had a more muted and ultimately retardative effect on the growth of capacity, particularly in manufacturing. It was the expansion of potential output during the Depression, largely unappreciated because it took place against a backdrop of double-digit unemployment, that laid the foundation both for successful war mobilization and for the golden age that followed.

The golden age (1948–1973) experienced a quarter century of sustained growth in the material standard of living. Much of this resulted from the revival of more "normal" patterns of physical capital accumulation (the acquisition of new structures and equipment), a process that had been disrupted by financial crisis during the Depression and distorted during the war. Organizational and technological progress per se proceeded at a respectable rate, but one that was more moderate than had been experienced during the Depression years. Growth of TFP in manufacturing recovered from its war year doldrums, but continued to slow in comparison with the prewar period (this was also true for labor productivity). Strong advance within such sectors as transportation and distribution persisted. Both the declining influence of progress within manufacturing (compared especially with the 1920s) and the significance of the continued transition within transport and distribution reflected trends whose origins are to be found in the interwar years.

The golden-age decline in PNE TFP growth as compared with the Depression years is almost entirely accounted for by manufacturing. The sector had enjoyed unprecedented gains in the 1920s based on electrification and new products, and somewhat weaker although still strong R&D–based advance during the 1930s. During World War II, manufacturing benefited from, but was also bloated and distorted by, the increase in military procurement and the injection of GOCO (government owned, contractor operated) capital. American industry nevertheless emerged from the conflict in a position of world dominance. Technical frontiers had been expanded by a host of new product and process innovations during the 1930s, and some of this potential had begun to be realized prior to the war. In other cases, such as television, all of the development work had been done prewar, and the product was poised for rapid exploitation with the ending of controls after V-J (Victory over Japan) day.

With European and Japanese manufacturing hobbled by war damage, US manufacturing faced extraordinary global opportunities in helping to rebuild foreign industries and in satisfying their domestic markets while this took place. Continued high levels of military spending during the Korean and Cold Wars meant a stream of direct orders for defense contractors and a stimulus to and stabilization of aggregate demand for the rest of the economy.

This was the environment in which the manufacturing corporations described in John Kenneth Galbraith's *New Industrial State* (1971) consolidated their distinguishing characteristics. Galbraith described them as islands of planned economy within an ostensibly market-based system. Many corporations offered something equivalent to lifetime employment security. Through marketing and planned obsolescence, the disruptive force of technological change, what Schumpeter called "creative destruction," had largely been domesticated, at least for a time. Whereas large corporations had funded research leading to a number of important innovations during the 1930s, many critics now argued that these behemoths had become obstacles to transformative innovation, too concerned about the prospect of devaluing rent-yielding income streams from existing technologies. Disruptions to the rank order of the largest US industrial corporations during this quarter-century were remarkably few. And the overall rate of TFP growth within manufacturing fell by more than 2.5 percentage points compared with the 1930s, and more than 3.5 percentage points compared with the 1920s (the drop-off was less severe in labor productivity, principally due to the contribution of the high rate of postwar capital accumulation).

The view of the quarter-century following 1948 as one of more moderate innovative advance within manufacturing is consistent with the enumerations of basic innovations by Schmookler (1966), Mensch (1979), and Kleinknecht (1987). All of their series show

disruptions
innovations

peaks in the 1930s, particularly its second half. Kleinknecht's analysis, which runs through 1969, shows a big peak in total and product innovations in the 1930s, although process innovations peak in the 1950s. Schmookler's data, which run through 1959, shows a peak of forty-eight basic innovations in the 1935–1939 period, dwindling to zero in 1955–1959 (Schmookler 1966).

A consideration of PNE TFP growth in the United States during the golden age (1948–1973) raises two related questions: On the one hand, why was it so strong, and on the other hand, why were TFP growth rates lower than they were during the Depression years (1929–1941)? A continuing downward trend in TFP growth within manufacturing and its declining share after World War II help provide answers to the latter question. A persisting productivity windfall associated with the build-out of the surface road infrastructure helps answer the former question. We can also understand the retardation of productivity growth after 1973 as in part the consequence of the decline in infrastructure spending following the completion of the Interstate Highway System.

The causes of the slowdown in productivity growth during the "dark ages" (1973 through 1989 or 1995) remain an enigma. The retardation was broad based: the continued slippage in the manufacturing TFP growth rate can account for only about a sixth of the TFP slowdown in the PNE. The decrease in non-defense R&D spending likely played a role. Another influence was the conclusion of the build-out of the surface road infrastructure marked by the completion of the Interstate Highway System. Continued road construction would not necessarily have avoided retardation: by the early 1970s, the low-hanging fruit had largely been harvested. Nevertheless, exhaustion of potential gains from such infrastructural investments does help us understand why productivity growth slowed after 1973.

The economic and productivity history of the twentieth century up through 1995 can thus be thought of as a tale of two transitions. The first involved the electrification and reconfiguration of the American factory, a development that had its roots in the 1880s but blossomed only in the 1920s, producing enormously high rates of TFP growth in manufacturing during that decade. The TFP growth rates in manufacturing then trended generally downward for most of the remainder of the century. The second transition, involving the movement of goods, peaked later. From the late 1920s through the early 1970s, trucking expanded its share of interstate ton mileage, while the rail sector shrunk, specializing as it did.

The IT boom, which ran from 1995 to 2005, offered a respite from the doldrums into which productivity growth had fallen between 1973 and the mid-1990s. It was dramatic and has changed our lives. But from a historical perspective, advance was narrowly concentrated in the manufacturing sectors producing IT products such as computers, cell phones, and routers, as well, at least initially, in a few IT-intensive using sectors such as retailing and securities trading. Compared to the Great Depression, the locus of revolutionary change was not as broad, and its overall impact on the growth of economic capacity has been more modest.

CONCLUSION

As we step back from the subperiods, and consider the 1919–1973 years as a long swing characterized by exceptionally high TFP and labor productivity growth, we should appreciate the extent to which developments in the postwar period—both the declining influence of advance within manufacturing (compared especially with the 1920s) and the significance of the continued transition within transport and distribution—reflect the extension of trends already evident during the interwar years. In doing so, we can move beyond the inclination to treat the golden age sui generis, and see within it the unfolding of developments that, although temporarily disrupted by the war, had their origins in the interwar years.

The resurgence of TFP growth in the IT boom after 1995, reflected in the 1995–2005 growth rates, was almost entirely driven by advance within manufacturing, and within the sector by advance in durables production, almost all of which occurred in the old SIC 35 and 36 categories: the sectors producing the computers, routers, and cell phones that lay at the heart of the boom. The PNE TFP advance in both the 1920s and 1995–2005 was largely a story of developments in manufacturing, but during the 1920s, TFP growth could be seen across the board at the two-digit level, whereas in the 1990s, forward movement was much more narrowly concentrated within the sector. It is notable that although IT breakthroughs did in a very real sense give the 1990s its character, there is no single innovation or set of innovations that we can speak of as having given its character to the technological and organization advance of the 1930s. That does not mean that progress was less significant during that period. Indeed, the opposite was true. The twelve-year period (1929–1941) during which TFP growth in the PNE exceeded 3 percent per year was and remains historically unprecedented. It was the expansion of potential and, eventually, actual output, disguised by a decade of double-digit unemployment, that laid the foundation for the successful prosecution of World War II, as well as the quarter century of sustained living standard improvement (1948–1973) that followed.

NOTES

1. Greenfield in the sense that they were built on sites which were not previously industrial or urban.
2. The Standard Industrial Classification (SIC) system was officially used for the study of manufacturing in the United States until 1997. The SIC has now been supplanted by the North American Industrial Classification System, but SIC codes are still commonly used in historical work.
3. The higher estimate results from the use of new chained index methods of calculating the growth of real outputs. The problem that chain index methods address is that real output growth calculated using beginning year prices will not be the same as if it is calculated using end-period prices. This is the essence of the index number problem. The chain index

method calculates growth between two years using initial year prices and then using end-year prices and taking a geometric average of the two. A geometric average multiplies the two growth rates together and takes the square root of the product.

4. It is also possible to use gross sales as the output measure, as does the Bureau of Economic Analysis with its KLEMS methodology, but in this case these purchased materials or services must be included along with labor and the services of physical capital as inputs.

5. The labor force is a subset of the population that includes those working and those actively seeking work.

6. The average is of the initial and end year ratios.

7. For 1941 I use Lebergott (1964) rather than Darby (1976) unemployment, which includes as employed those in programs such as the Civilian Conservation Corps or the Works Project Administration. I am doubtful that reductions in calculated unemployment resulting from including as employed those in workfare were likely to be associated with the same cyclical changes in measured TFP as were reductions caused by increased private sector employment.

8. BEA chained output indexes for GDP adjusted to approximate those applicable to the private nonfarm economy. For details, see Field (2013); Kendrick (1961, table A-XXIII).

9. −.01035 is the coefficient on the change in the unemployment rate in a regression identical to regression 1.1 except that the dependent variable is the change in the log level of PNE rather than manufacturing TFP; see Field (2010).

10. The right-hand terms reflect capital's share, the posited difference in the unemployment rate in percentage points, and the coefficient in regression 1.3 reflecting the change in the log of the manufacturing capital-labor ratio on the change in the unemployment rate. Manufacturing capital is from the Bureau of Economic Analysis Fixed Asset Table 4.2, and manufacturing hours are from Kendrick (1961, table D-1).

BIBLIOGRAPHY

Atack, Jeremy, Fred Bateman, and Robert Margo. (2002). "Part-Year Operation in Nineteenth-Century American Manufacturing: Evidence from the 1870 and 1880 Censuses." *Journal of Economic History* 62(September): 792–809.

Atack, Jeremy, Fred Bateman, and Thomas Weiss. (1980). "The Regional Diffusion and Adoption of the Steam Engine in American Manufacturing." *Journal of Economic History* 40(June): 281–308.

Bresnahan, Timothy F., and Daniel M. G. Raff. (1991). "Intra-Industry Heterogeneity and the Great Depression: The American Motor Vehicles Industry, 1929–1935." *Journal of Economic History* 51(June): 317–331.

Carter, Susan B., Scott Sigmund Gartner, Michael R. Haines, Alan L. Olmstead, Richard Sutch, and Gavin Wright, eds. (2006). *Historical Statistics of the United States*. Millennial edition. New York: Cambridge University Press.

Chandler, Alfred. (1977). *The Visible Hand: The Managerial Revolution in American Business*. Cambridge, MA: Harvard University Press.

Darby, Michael R. (1976). "Three-and-a-Half Million U.S. Employees Have Been Mislaid: Or, an Explanation of Unemployment, 1934–1941." *Journal of Political Economy* 84(February): 1–16.

Devine, Warren. (1983). "From Shaft to Wires: Historical Perspective on Electrification." *Journal of Economic History* 43(June): 347–372.

Field, Alexander J. (1978). "Sectoral Shift in Antebellum Massachusetts: A Reconsideration." *Explorations in Economic History* 15(April): 146–171.

Field, Alexander J. (1987). "Modern Business Enterprise as a Capital-Saving Innovation." *Journal of Economic History* 47(June): 473–485.

Field, Alexander J. (2003). "The Most Technologically Progressive Decade of the Century." *American Economic Review* 93(September): 1399–1413.

Field, Alexander J. (2010). "The Procyclical Behavior of Total Factor Productivity in the United States, 1890–2004." *Journal of Economics History* 70(June): 326–350.

Field, Alexander J. (2011). *A Great Leap Forward: 1930s Depression and U.S. Economic Growth.* New Haven, CT: Yale University Press.

Field, Alexander J. (2013). "Economic Growth and Recovery in the United States, 1929–1941." In *The Great Depression of the 1930s: Lessons for Today*, edited by Nicholas Crafts and Peter Fearon, 358–394. Oxford: Oxford University Press.

Galbraith, John Kenneth. (1971). *The New Industrial State.* 2nd ed. Boston: Houghton Mifflin.

Hazard, Blanche E. (1913). "The Organization of the Boot and Shoe Industry in Massachusetts in 1875." *Quarterly Journal of Economics* 27(February): 236–262.

Kendrick, John. (1961). *Productivity Trends in the United States.* Princeton, NJ: Princeton University Press.

Kleinknecht, Alfred. (1987). *Innovation Patterns in Crisis and Prosperity: Schumpeter's Long Cycle Reconsidered.* New York: St. Martin's Press.

Lebergott, Stanley. (1964). *Manpower in Economic Growth: The American Record Since 1800.* New York: McGraw Hill.

Margo, Robert. (1991). "The Microeconomics of Depression Unemployment." *Journal of Economic History* 51(June): 331–341.

Mensch, Gerhard. (1979). *Stalemate in Technology: Innovations Overcome the Depression.* Cambridge: Ballinger.

Rosenberg, Nathan. (1965). "Adam Smith on the Division of Labor: Two Views or One." *Economica* New Series 32(May): 127–139.

Rosenberg, Nathan, and Manuel Trajtenberg. (2001). "A General Purpose Technology at Work: The Corliss Steam Engine in the Late 19th Century U.S." NBER Working Paper No. 8485.

Schmookler, Jacob. (1966). *Invention and Economic Growth.* Cambridge: Cambridge University Press.

Sokoloff, Kenneth. (1986). "Productivity Growth in Manufacturing during Early Industrialization." In *Long Term Factors in American Economic Growth*, edited by Stanley L. Engerman and Robert E. Gallman, 679–736. Chicago: University of Chicago Press.

US Department of Commerce, Bureau of Economic Analysis. (2001). *The National Income and Product Accounts of the United States, 1929–1997.* Washington, DC: Government Printing Office.

US Department of Commerce, Bureau of Economic Analysis. (2018a). "National Income and Product Accounts: Domestic Product and Income Tables." Available at http://www.bea.gov.

US Department of Commerce, Bureau of Economic Analysis. (2018b). "National Income and Product Accounts: Fixed Asset Tables." Available at http://www.bea.gov.

US Department of Labor, Bureau of Labor Statistics. (2004). "Multifactor Productivity in U.S. Manufacturing and in 20 Manufacturing Industries." Available at https://www.bls.gov/mfp/tables.htm, Superseded Historical SIC Measures for Manufacturing Sector and 2-digit SIC Manufacturing Industries, 1949–2001.

US Department of Labor, Bureau of Labor Statistics. (2018a). "Net Multifactor Productivity and Cost, 1948–2016." Available at https://www.bls.gov/mfp/tables.htm, Historical Multifactor Productivity Measures (SIC 1948-87 linked to NAICS 1987–2016).

US Department of Labor, Bureau of Labor Statistics. (2018b). Multifactor and Labor Productivity tables. Available at http://www.bls.gov.

Wright, Gavin. (1999). "The Civil Rights Revolution as Economic History." *Journal of Economic History* 59 (June): 267–289.

CHAPTER 10

··

SERVICES IN AMERICAN ECONOMIC HISTORY

··

STEPHEN BROADBERRY, LOUIS P. CAIN, AND THOMAS WEISS

By the turn of the twenty-first century, Walmart was not only the leading private employer in the United States, it was the leading private employer in the world. In fact, whether measured as just the United States or the entire world, seven of the top ten private employers were in the service sector. This came as something of a surprise to generations used to thinking of "big business" in terms of manufacturing. At the time of the first US Census, that of 1790, farmers made up 90 percent of the labor force. In the nineteenth century, agriculture and industry employed between one-half and three-quarters of the labor force. Today, services account for more than four-fifths of the labor force. Despite its relative importance, the service sector was rather neglected until recently, although there are some early studies of the sector on a worldwide basis (Fisher 1935; Clark 1957; Kuznets 1966, 1971). Economic historians have lavished much more attention on agriculture and industry, particularly when dealing with topics such as economic growth and productivity performance.

Recent work has shown that the United States forged to world productivity leadership between the late nineteenth and mid-twentieth centuries largely through what Broadberry (2006) refers to as the "industrialization" of services (i.e., the adoption of large-scale methods to produce services for a mass market). Other countries began to catch up only after World War II. Trends in the proximate determinants of performance include investment in physical and human capital, as well as the more fundamental determinants such as competition and the institutional framework.

There are a number of reasons for the rise of the service sector, but the most important is simply that as people got richer, they spent a growing share of their incomes on services, an income elasticity of demand greater than one. This is an extension of Engel's Law, named after the nineteenth-century economist who first documented the negative relationship between income and the share of food expenditures in household budgets. A change in the relative importance of industry vis-à-vis agriculture, similar to the rise of services, occurred earlier in history and provoked concerns about the sustainability of incomes if too many people worked in what were perceived as unproductive activities. Just as the policy proposals of the Physiocrats (a school of eighteenth-century French economists who believed government policy should not interfere with the economy) seem at best quixotic today, the concerns of those urging a rebalancing of the economy to counter "deindustrialization" (the rise of services) will in the fullness of time seem misplaced. Being a rich economy today requires high productivity in services above all else.

China?.

DEFINING THE SERVICE SECTOR

Defining services is not a simple matter. Generally speaking, the industries involved are directly concerned with enhancing the quality of life through service and indirectly with the production and distribution of food and goods. The term covers a wide variety of loosely related activities. Thomas Weiss noted in his introduction to the services chapter of *Historical Statistics of the United States* that a portion of these industries is singled out in the national income accounts as *service industries* (2006, 4-1061). Included are a wide variety of services such as hotels and other lodging places; personal services, such as barbering; business services, such as advertising and secretarial services; amusement and recreation services; health, legal, and educational services; services provided by those employed in private households, and a residual of other miscellaneous services.[1]

These are all final services, those that are not resold. A more complete *service sector* would also include intermediate services, such as transportation, retail trade, and finance, that are listed separately in the national accounts. Weiss (2006) discussed the definitional difficulties presented by the heterogeneous nature of service sector industries.[2]

Once defined, the service sector can be measured in different ways. The most common measures reflect the size of labor force and the value of output, and the size of the sector is slightly different depending on which measure is chosen. Further, these have been measured in different ways at different times in US history. In the US data, the labor force measure was defined as "gainful workers" in the nineteenth century and "persons engaged" in the twentieth century; the value of output, "value added" in the nineteenth century and "national income originating in" since. Given that questions of interest often involve the share of services relative to agriculture and manufacturing, the unit of measure will not matter if the same measure is used for each of the three sectors. For other potential questions (e.g., international comparisons), the unit of measure is dictated by the need to have a common unit across countries. It is important to be aware of what measure is employed.

THE RISE OF THE SERVICE SECTOR

Over time, regardless of definition or measure, the share of services in the American economy has increased. The changing share of services in economic activity can be seen in figure 10.1.

This growth is not unique to the United States; it is observable in most developed and many developing nations. There are many patterns, and the pattern and timing may differ depending on whether labor force or output is used as the measure. Regardless, the growing share of services appears to be a general phenomenon with few exceptions.

The first thing to note about the rise of the service sector is that it started long ago. The earliest year for which data are available is 1839, when occupational data were first reported in the 1840 census. Even then, the sector was quite large, more so for output than labor, as shown in figure 10.1. Over time, the sector increased its share of both output and the labor force, with the increase in the latter being noticeably greater. One of the leading students of the service sector, Victor Fuchs, noted in his 1968 study, *The Service Economy*, that in the years immediately following World War II, the United States had become "the world's first service economy," which he defined as the service share of the labor force having passed 50 percent.

One reason why this occurred first in the United States is that US incomes rose faster and earlier than other countries, thus increasing the demand for services. It was not because the United States had a preference for services in comparison to other countries (Weiss 1984). A second reason, which Fuchs argued was the main reason for the increase in the share of workers in services, was the relatively slower growth of productivity in

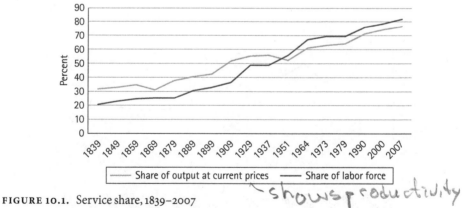

FIGURE 10.1. Service share, 1839–2007 ~shows productivity

Note: The value of shelter services has been excluded from both service output and national income because there is no labor force associated with the annual production of shelter services and its inclusion would distort the comparison of relative output per worker.

Sources: 1839–1899: Gallman and Weiss (1969); 1869–1929: Broadberry (2006); Kendrick (1961); US Department of Commerce (1983). 1929–1979: Broadberry (2006); US Department of Commerce (1983). 1979–2007: EU KLEMS database (O'Mahony and Timmer 2009).

service production than in goods production (Fuchs 1968). This relative growth of productivity in services is indicated by the time path of the labor productivity of services
in figure 10.2, which is obtained by dividing the share of output by the share of labor.
A figure above 1.00 indicates higher output per person employed in services than in the
economy as a whole. In the late nineteenth century, income per person was much lower
in agriculture, which continued to employ a large share of the labor force. Income per
person employed was therefore much higher in services than in the economy as a whole.
However, income per person employed was also relatively high in US manufacturing, so
as workers moved out of agriculture, incomes in services moved toward the average for
the economy as a whole. By the post–World War II period, when services accounted for
more than half of all employment, service sector incomes were no longer above average.

It is worth noting that because productivity growth has been faster in the production of agricultural and industrial goods than in the provision of services, the price of
goods has fallen relative to the price of services. As service prices rose relative to other
prices, this slowed the growth of the services share, so one should view the progress in
figure 10.2 as a net effect.

William Baumol referred to this phenomenon of slower productivity growth and
faster increases in prices as "the cost disease of the service sector" (Baumol 1967; see
also Baumol, Blackman, and Wolff 1992). Although Baumol's "cost disease" sounds
worrisome, there are reasons to be more optimistic. First, Baumol and Bowen (1966)
argued that, in fact, Beethoven string quartets take exactly the same amount of time to
perform today as when they were composed! While their example was drawn from the
performing arts, its conclusion was assumed to apply to services defined more broadly.
However, not all service production functions are as constrained as that for classical
music. Moreover, if one measures the contribution of a single performance not in terms
of the time it takes to perform a piece, or by the number of people performing, but by the

FIGURE 10.2. Labor productivity of services, 1839–2007

Sources: 1839–1899: Gallman and Weiss (1969); 1869–1929: Broadberry (2006); Kendrick (1961);
US Department of Commerce (1983). 1929–1979: Broadberry (2006); US Department of Commerce (1983).
1979–2007: EU KLEMS database (O'Mahony and Timmer 2009).

number of people listening, then productivity growth can be observed as concert halls grow larger and concerts are recorded so that large numbers of people can enjoy it via both audio and visual recordings. While this is not how productivity has been measured in the national accounts, it does suggest the possibility that there may have been more productivity growth than calculated. Bakker (2008) has examined such measurement issues in relation to other entertainment industries, and considerable attention has been devoted to appropriate ways of measuring output in other service sectors.[3]

Second, since a considerable amount of research and development (R&D) is a service activity, services clearly play a crucial role in innovation and productivity growth. Whereas the basic cost disease model predicts that a shift of labor toward services will lower overall productivity growth, Baumol's (2002) model with an R&D sector incorporates the possibility that it could boost overall productivity growth. This is due to the "Oulton theorem," which examines the case where the service sector produces intermediate rather than final outputs (Oulton 2001). So long as productivity growth in the relatively stagnant service sector is positive, it has a further positive effect through the use of the intermediate outputs in the more dynamic final goods sector. Hence the growing share of services has continued to be consistent with positive productivity growth in the economy as a whole.

As suggested earlier, the rapid increase in services has caused some nervous concerns, among which are the slower growth of productivity in services and "deindustriali-zation," the term coined to describe the decline of the manufacturing share and usu-ally described as a post–World War II phenomenon. The perceived result is a decline in overall US productivity, slower growth of the entire economy, and, consequently, a decline in the US standard of living. A high-wage blue-collar worker whose job on an assembly line has been replaced by a robot is likely to have faced income decline, but, as figure 10.1 reveals, the share of the service sector has been on the increase since the mid-nineteenth century, a period of rapid growth for the American economy. It was supported by the rise in productivity in both the primary sector (agriculture, mining, fishing, forestry) and the secondary sector (manufacturing, raw-materials processing).

In a more abstract sense, the jobs of blue-collar assembly-line workers have been replaced by robot designers, programmers, and the like. The new jobs reflect an invest-ment in skills and education. Often they reflect greater specialization and a finer divi-sion of labor. All of these are expected to increase productivity, to lower costs. Thus, for the economy as a whole, the growth of services should reflect a move toward a more pro-ductive, more efficient, economy, even though the transition involves hardship for some workers and some neighborhoods in industrialized cities.

The Nineteenth Century

As figure 10.1 highlights, from the time we first get data in the 1840 census, the service sector was surprisingly large; as Gallman and Weiss (1969) report, that sector produced

32 percent of the nation's output and employed 20 percent of its labor force. Sixty years later, at the turn of the twentieth century, the percentages were 43 and 33, respectively. Some components grew rapidly from the first, reflecting the overall growth of the economy, but as a whole, service sector output grew at about the same rate as industrial output. To a large extent, this reflects the fact that intermediate services, the industries that served other industries, were the dominant part of the service sector throughout the nineteenth century. Trade and transportation accounted for about half the sector's output for the entire period from 1840 to 1900. As manufacturing output increased and agricultural goods moved over longer distances, these intermediate service industries, essential to the production and marketing of those goods, grew at about the same pace. The output of some services, for which output per worker was relatively low in 1840, grew faster than that of manufacturing. This suggests that, early on, the income elasticity of demand for services was an important factor behind the growth of the sector, notably the growth of education after the Civil War; the decision to offer mass elementary schooling funded by local governments meant that the United States had more educated youth than any other country by the mid-nineteenth century.

When the service sector is measured using the labor force, a somewhat different picture emerges. The service labor force increased even faster than output. It had to, because labor productivity growth in services was slower than in the whole economy. Early in the century, intermediate services, which produced most of the output, employed a much smaller share of the labor force. Transport, trade, and finance accounted for two-thirds of the sector's output in 1840, but employed less than 30 percent of the labor force. The reason for this discrepancy is that output per worker in these industries, and especially in finance, was way above average. On the other hand, personal service, including slave labor before the Civil War, had a relatively small average output per worker, so it required a large labor force to produce the output, a much larger share of employment than output. Indeed, personal service employed more than half of the sector's labor force in 1840, but this declined to where it was less than 30 percent at the century's end.

THE TWENTIETH CENTURY

The twentieth century witnessed a continuation of the trends that had begun back before the Civil War, which again can be seen in figure 10.1. Both output and the labor force increased, with the latter increasing faster than the former. What is different about the twentieth century is the industries leading those upward trends. Another difference is that services had become such a large part of the economy by mid-century, whether measured by output or labor force, as to generate concern about "deindustrialization."

During the period between the two world wars, output in the service sector continued to grow at about the same rate as the economy as a whole. However, employment in services grew more rapidly than in the rest of the economy because labor productivity in services continued to grow more slowly than in the economy as a whole. Productivity growth in transport-communications remained strong, but this was offset by low (or no) productivity growth in the rest of the sector. After World War II, services output grew faster than agricultural and manufacturing output. However, labor productivity growth in services continued to be considerably slower than in the rest of the economy, as the labor input continued to increase rapidly in services, while it declined in agriculture and increased only slowly in manufacturing.

In 1947, the measured output of the service industries (narrowly defined) was roughly two-thirds that of retail trade, but, by the end of the century, the former was 250 percent of the latter (see Weiss 2006, 4-1065). This can be explained by the large increases in health and business services, as can be seen in figure 10.3. The story is even more dramatic when told with labor force statistics. Between 1929 and 1996, employment in the service industries increased by 460 percent, but employment in business services increased by more than 3,000 percent. While the falling share of personal services can be seen in figure 10.3, the share of "all other" services was also falling. "All other" services was the dominant category in 1929, accounting for 56 percent of employment. The overwhelming majority of jobs in that category (seven-eighths) were people employed in private households as butlers, maids, cooks, laundresses, and the like, people who were being displaced by technology as the electrification of homes, the emergence of supermarkets, and many other changes meant that middle- and upper middle-class homes didn't need a large and increasingly expensive labor force. By 1997, the share of all other services had halved from what it had been in 1929, and those employed in private households were but a sixth of the total.

After 1990, output continued to grow more rapidly in services than in manufacturing. The reverse was true with respect to labor productivity growth, with the exception of transportation-communications. The most rapid labor productivity growth occurred in distribution, as the ICT (information and communications technology) revolution at last broke free from what had been coined the Solow paradox. Economist Robert Solow

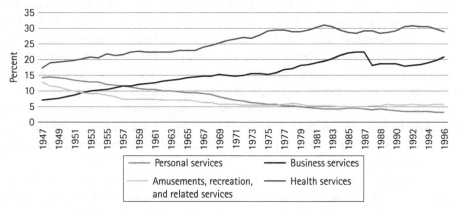

FIGURE 10.3. Gross product of selected services as a percent of total gross services, 1947–1996
Source: Carter et al. (2006, series Dh37, 38, 39, 42, and 43).

famously quipped, "You can see the computer age everywhere but in the productivity statistics." By 1990, computers began to appear in the productivity statistics.[4]

Education was an important factor throughout the twentieth century. The United States continued to have the most educated youth until the end of the century, which Claudia Goldin (2001) termed the "human-capital century." In the first half of the twentieth century, the increase in the supply of labor was tied to the expansion of high schools; in the second half, to the expansion of universities. Most of that expansion was tax supported. Goldin and Lawrence Katz document what they term the "Great Transformation" in American education, the period between 1910 and 1940, when the high school movement made education available to far more teenagers than was true in most other countries. This was a time when the demand for young people in manufacturing was declining and the demand for white-collar labor was increasing. By the 1920s, the demand for more educated blue-collar workers was also increasing. This increase in the demand for education caused the rate of return to education to fall in the first half of the twentieth century and to increase in the second. Goldin and Katz attribute this to "a race between education (the supply of skill) and skill-biased technological change (the demand for skill)" (Goldin and Katz 2008, 291).

The importance of employment growth in the service sector is enhanced by considering that the greatest single change in the composition of the labor force in the twentieth century was the extent of female participation. In 2004, 57 percent of those employed in the service sector were women, and, of all women in the labor force, almost 90 percent were in the service sector. In *Understanding the Gender Gap*, Goldin calculates the labor force participation of married women over the past two centuries and finds a U-shaped relationship. There was a reduction in the late nineteenth century as wage work became more common. In 1900, only 18 percent of the *employed* (that is, wage-earning) labor force was female. By the end of the twentieth century, that proportion had more than doubled. Goldin places the bottom of the U just after World War I.

It was thought that women entered the labor market, exited to have families, and then re-entered. Goldin argues that, in the 1920s and 1930s, the date of exit was marriage, not pregnancy. There was very little re-entry; those who exited were unlikely to return. Few women remained in the labor force their entire working lives, but Goldin finds a high rate of work experience among married women still working. Only 5 percent of married women officially were in the labor force in 1890, compared with nearly 60 percent today, but this comparison is somewhat misleading as the 1890 figure excludes farm wives, boardinghouse keepers, and the like. It is clear that, whether on the farm or in their husbands' artisanal shops, married women were active participants. With industrialization, as the relative number of farm households fell and a separation developed between home and urban workplace, the participation of married women workers shrank, while that of young single women grew.[5]

After 1890, the share of white women working in the clerical and professional sectors began to expand, although for several decades personal service remained the single most important occupation for both white and black women. The relative importance of personal service began to decline for a number of reasons, especially as work formerly done in the home was either transferred to businesses (e.g., a commercial laundry doing the work once performed by a servant) or to new inventions and innovations within the home (e.g., a washing machine doing the work once performed by a servant at a tub). An electric iron, for example, eliminated the specialized knowledge required to operate its predecessor and made it possible for middle-class families to do the work themselves (Katzman 1981; Kwolek-Folland 2007). In 1870, half of all wage-earning women were in domestic service, cleaning houses, cooking meals, and doing laundry, but by 1900 only 30 percent did so (Lebergott 1966; Stigler 1946; Weiss 1999). Although the absolute number of domestic servants would continue to rise, it did so slowly, and the proportion of wage-earning women in domestic service fell, especially for white women.[6] By 1920, almost half of wage-earning women worked as teachers or in a shop or office (Katzman 1981).

Clerical employments provided maximum flexibility for women who were increasingly able to leave home. As capital goods replaced brute strength, as education replaced on-the-job training, and as the market expanded, we would expect a narrowing of "the gender gap"—the difference between the wages received by males and females. The work of Elyce Rotella (1981b) shows that the rise of female clerical workers, from 2.5 percent of all clerical workers in 1870 to 52.5 percent in 1930, was the result of the mechanization of office work, which also worked to separate office skills from management functions. Although the move toward white-collar work extended the period of women's employment, most did not stay long enough to receive promotions. Both men and women started at about the same salary, the men starting as "mail boys" or messengers; however, the men stayed longer and enjoyed promotion to positions with significantly higher salaries. Occupational segregation barred women from some positions and men from others. Since women were expected to leave the workplace sooner rather than later, firms chose neither to invest in training for them nor to place them in positions with opportunities for promotion. They remained in jobs that involved no promotion, like those in the secretarial pool, or that involved limited promotion up a much shorter ladder than that enjoyed by men. The difference in long-term prospects produced evidence of "wage discrimination" even as the gender gap narrowed.

An important component of the labor force that has been influenced by the growth of services is self-employment. Given that capital requirements are relatively lower in services than in other sectors of the economy, the costs of entry into self-employment in services is less. The growth of services provided an opportunity for people to enter self-employment. As Victor Fuchs (1968) pointed out, the fact that many of these employments involved person-to-person interactions and/or few economies of scale (e.g., barbers and beauticians) made self-employment more attractive. Indeed, three times as many people identified themselves as self-employed in 1997 as did so in 1929, four times as many in finance, insurance, and real estate alone. That said, the overall trend in self-employed service industries and, especially, retail trade has been down. Supermarkets and big box stores (e.g., Walmart) have been replacing self-employed "mom-and-pop" shops since the Great Depression.

One last aspect of the growth of services in the United States that deserves mention is the increase in their importance in foreign trade. For decades (maybe a century), the balance of trade literature emphasized the trade in goods, neglecting services, and perhaps rightly so, as services did not amount to more than 10 percent of all US exports (see fig. 10.4). During World War II, the export and import of services dramatically rose. Following the war, service exports rose until the beginning of the "great inflation" of the late 1960s and 1970s, almost reaching 30 percent; then it fell before beginning a new surge that brought it to 30 percent by the end of the twentieth century. It has remained near 30 percent in the early twenty-first century. The largest category of service exports is "other private services," which includes business, professional, and technical services, insurance services, and financial services. On the other hand, beginning in the late 1950s and early 1960s, service imports began to fall from nearly 35 percent of the total to closer to 15 percent at the end of the century, where it has remained. Because service exports have been rising faster than the export of goods, and because service exports exceed service imports, they contribute favorably to the US balance of trade.

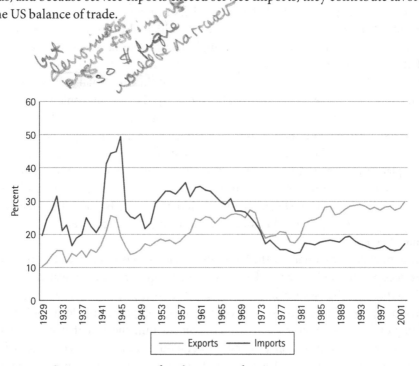

FIGURE 10.4. Services as a percent of total exports and imports

Source: Carter et al. (2006, series Ee376, 378, 379, and 381).

THE ROLE OF SERVICES IN AMERICA'S CHANGING COMPARATIVE PRODUCTIVITY PERFORMANCE

In *The Productivity Race*, Broadberry (1997b) argued that there was little change in the comparative productivity performance of US, UK, and German manufacturing between the mid-nineteenth century and the late twentieth century. Using data derived from Broadberry (1997b), he found that, in both 1870 and 1990, US labor productivity in manufacturing was about twice the British level, while German labor productivity in manufacturing was about the same as in Britain (Broadberry 1997a). He also noted that value added per employee varied between manufacturing and the rest of the economy, and that the size of the manufacturing sector differed across countries and over time. This meant that it was still possible for manufacturing to have contributed to the US overtaking of Britain at the whole economy level between 1870 and 1914 through the greater structural shift away from agriculture and into manufacturing in the United States. Nevertheless, the central message of *The Productivity Race* was that to understand the forging ahead of American productivity and living standards since the mid-nineteenth century, it is necessary to understand what happened in services.

Broadberry (2006) has focused on America's comparative productivity performance in services, focusing in particular on market services (i.e., those services provided through the market by the private sector rather than tax-financed services provided largely by the state).[7] To begin, the comparative productivity trends in services are established and fitted into the patterns for the whole economy. What emerges is that comparative productivity trends in services, unlike those in manufacturing, do mirror comparative productivity trends in the whole economy. In table 10.1, the United Kingdom is treated as the *numeraire* country, with UK labor productivity taking a value of 100 in all sectors in all years. Thus, for example, the first row says that in about 1870, the United States had labor productivity in industry that was 53.6 percent higher than in the United Kingdom, but in services, US labor productivity was only 85.9 percent of the UK level. Thus, services help explain why the United States had lower overall labor productivity than Britain at this time.

However, the United States overtook Britain in both services and the whole economy before World War I and continued to forge ahead until after World War II, when Britain slowly began to narrow the gap. Further, looking at table 10.2, it is clear that Britain's loss of labor productivity leadership in services was not due to trends in governmental services, where it is difficult to measure output independently of inputs. Rather, it reflected US overtaking in private or market services, including transport and communications, distribution and finance.

Table 10.1 Comparative US/UK Labor Productivity Levels by Sector, 1869/1871 to 2007 (UK = 100)

	Agriculture	Industry	Services	Aggregate Economy
1869/1871	86.9	153.6	85.9	89.8
1889/1891	102.1	164.1	84.2	94.1
1909/1911	103.2	193.2	107.4	117.7
1919/1920	128.0	198.0	118.9	133.3
1929	109.7	222.7	121.2	139.4
1937	103.3	190.6	120.0	132.6
1950	126.0	243.5	140.8	166.9
1973	131.2	214.8	137.4	152.3
1990	151.1	163.0	129.6	133.0
2007	196.4	166.2	125.1	127.7

Sources: Derived from Broadberry (1997a), updated using the EU KLEMS database (O'Mahony and Timmer 2009).
Note: Benchmark estimates of comparative productivity levels for 1937 are projected to other years using time series for output and employment from historical national accounting sources.

Table 10.2 Comparative US/UK Labor Productivity Levels in Market Services, 1869/1871 to 2007 (UK = 100)

	Transport and Communications	Distribution	Finance, Professional, and Personal Services
1869/1871	110.0	66.9	64.1
1889/1891	167.1	97.0	53.2
1909/1911	217.4	120.0	77.9
1919/1920	250.6	109.0	103.6
1929	231.5	121.9	101.5
1937	283.4	119.8	96.1
1950	348.4	135.2	111.5
1973	303.3	149.6	118.0
1990	270.5	166.0	101.0
2007	228.1	198.3	87.7

Sources: Derived from Broadberry (1997a), updated using the EU KLEMS database (O'Mahony and Timmer 2009).

Broadberry (2006) provides a framework to explain this comparative productivity performance in services. The central theme concerns what he refers to as the "industrialization" of market services, the adoption of high-volume, low-margin methods to produce industrialized or mass-market services. As with the related introduction of "mass production" in manufacturing, the industrialization of services led to sustained growth of labor productivity. However, the gains from the introduction of the technology and organization of industrialized service provision varied by sector and over time. Understanding the differential spread of industrialized service provision in the United States, Britain, and other countries is crucial to understanding the patterns of comparative productivity performance in services. A more disaggregated picture of comparative productivity performance within market services helps to put the general argument more firmly in its historical context.

Explaining America's Comparative Productivity Performance in Services

Comparative labor productivity figures have already been set out in table 10.1 for the economy as a whole and for a three-sector breakdown into agriculture, industry, and services. Whereas around 1870, US aggregate labor productivity was approximately 90 percent of the British level, by 1990 this had risen to 133 percent. Turning to the sectoral breakdown, it is clear that this owed little to developments in industry, where the US/UK comparative labor productivity level changed little between 1870 and 1990. Furthermore, although comparative labor productivity in agriculture changed in the right direction and by a substantial amount, it is important to remember that whereas agriculture accounted for 50 percent of US employment in 1870, it accounted for less than 3 percent in 1990. The most important development in understanding America's rise to overall labor productivity leadership was thus the United States overtaking the United Kingdom in services.

Table 10.2 provides a breakdown of the comparative labor productivity performance of services, focusing attention on the key market service sectors. The United States caught up with and overtook Britain in distribution and financial services, and forged further ahead in transport and communications.

The "industrialization" of services involved the transition from a world of customized, low-volume, high-margin business organized on the basis of networks to a world of standardized, high-volume, low-margin business with hierarchical management (Broadberry and Ghosal 2002, 2005). This transformation from the world of the "counting house" to the world of the "modern office" depended on technologies to improve communications and information processing, including the telegraph, telephone, calculating machines, typewriters, duplicators, and vertical filing systems (see Yates

1989 and Rotella 1981a). The transition began in the United States and spread with a lag to Britain and other European countries.

Chandler (1977, 1980) described the origins of service sector industrialization in the United States. To assess the significance of these developments, it is important to understand the basis of the earlier British dominance in international commerce. British service sector firms had been highly successful during the nineteenth century, playing a key international role in shipping, distribution, and finance. This British success was based largely on external rather than internal economies of scale, with the City of London providing the largest agglomeration of commercial activity in the world, but based on a large number of small firms, rather than a small number of giant firms. This large scale of the overall activity facilitated specialization, and each firm could benefit from the proximity of other specialized firms, as in a classic Marshallian district (Marshall 1920). Since asymmetric information was endemic in this type of activity, it was important to be able to deter opportunistic behavior. As a result, trade often took place within networks of agents who could trust each other. As Greif (2000) shows, for individuals to be able to enter into mutually beneficial relationships, they have to be able to commit to fulfilling their contractual obligations, and merchant networks can be seen as a way of mitigating this "fundamental problem of exchange."

From the late nineteenth century, however, the United States began to displace Britain as the productivity leader in services, with the emergence of large firms reaping internal economies of scale. The process started on the US railroads (Chandler 1977, 81–121). Unlike turnpikes or canals, railroads required centralized operation, since steam locomotives moved much faster than horse-drawn carriages or barges and operated on a single track. As the length of the track that a railroad operated extended beyond what could be managed personally by a single superintendent, the railroad was divided into geographic divisions, and each division was further subdivided by function and managerial hierarchies appeared (Chandler 1980, 16). By the beginning of the twentieth century, the modern corporate form had spread to other parts of the transportation and communications sector, including steamship lines, urban traction systems, and the telegraph and telephone systems (Chandler 1977, 189–203).

These changes in transportation and communications were accompanied by the emergence of modern business enterprise in distribution, with commodity dealers who bought directly from farmers and sold directly to processors, replacing commission merchants in the distribution of agricultural produce, and with full-time wholesalers replacing commission merchants in the marketing of manufactures (Chandler 1980, 19–20). Nevertheless, distribution was slower to industrialize than transport and communications. For one thing, there were limits to the degree of centralization and standardization that consumers found acceptable in retailing, particularly given the relatively low levels of population density and the distances involved in the United States (Cain and Haddock 2005; Field 1996, 27; Hall, Knapp, and Winsten 1961, 131–138). And, second, as Field notes, there were restraints on competition, which acted to support small retail outlets (1996, 25–27). In particular, resale price maintenance retained an ambiguous legal status until 1975 and limited price competition, making it easier for small independent retailers to survive (see McCraw 1996). In addition, state legislation aimed at supporting the independent retailers applied escalating tax rates to businesses with two or more retail outlets (Perkins 1999, 119–120; Tedlow 1996, 214–226).

American finance was relatively slow to industrialize, partly because of the regulatory environment. Dealing first with the nature of the business, there are obvious dangers in adopting a high-volume, impersonal, standardized approach to banking and finance, since asymmetric information and trust are very important in this sector (see Lamoreaux 1994; Stiglitz and Weiss 1981). Although simple routines have been developed for assessing risks on relatively small transactions, reputation and personal contact have often remained important on large transactions. Hence, it is not surprising that low-volume, high-margin business has continued to be important in financial services, particularly in international finance, where networks of personal contacts can be more important than modern business enterprise in generating high value added (Jones 1993). Nevertheless, it seems clear that the industrialization of banking and finance in the United States has also been limited by regulation. In particular, regulations prevented the growth of interstate banking, keeping concentration in US banking relatively low (White 2000, 749). Calomiris (1995) also cites the Glass-Steagall Act and regulation Q as helping to keep American banks small by keeping apart commercial and investment banking and by setting a ceiling on interest rates that could be paid on bank deposits.

The British response involved patterns of large-scale company formation that were similar to those in the United States, but with a delay in the adoption of modern office technology and hence a delay in the increase of productivity. Campbell-Kelly (1992, 1994, 1998) points to an apparent resistance to modern office technology in Britain (see also Broadberry and Ghosal 2002, 977–983). The Post Office Savings Bank, for example, did without calculating machines before 1914 by maintaining its interest rate at 2.5 percent, which corresponded to a halfpenny per pound per month. Complicated calculations were avoided by paying the interest only on whole pounds for whole months and making the calculation only at the end of the year. Typewriters were also resisted by using hundreds of preprinted letters responding to all conceivable inquiries.

To reap the benefits of the industrialization of services, it is necessary to make the required investments in physical and human capital. Sectoral data on physical capital are available for services only on a very limited basis before World War II, particularly on an internationally comparable basis. The comparative total factor productivity (TFP) data in table 10.3, when compared with the comparative labor productivity data in table 10.1, suggest some role for physical capital in explaining the US rise to labor productivity leadership, but still leave substantial TFP gaps that require explanation.

Turning to human capital, it is important to consider both education and vocational training, and to distinguish between a university degree and an intermediate vocational training degree (Prais 1995, 17). Dealing first with formal education, table 10.4 presents data on enrollments in primary, secondary, and higher education per 1,000 population under the age of twenty. The United States had a general educational advantage over Britain for most of the nineteenth century, with the laggard Britain achieving universal primary education only toward the end of the century. Between the wars, the United

Table 10.3 Comparative US/UK Total Factor Productivity
Levels by Sector, 1869/1871 to 2007 (UK = 100)

	Agriculture	Industry	Services	Aggregate Economy
1869/1871	99.5	154.2	86.5	95.2
1889/1891	123.0	139.6	64.3	83.3
1909/1911	118.7	150.9	71.6	90.5
1919/1920	133.1	158.3	92.1	108.2
1929	118.0	187.8	92.0	112.7
1937	119.2	161.2	89.1	105.9
1950	132.6	217.6	110.2	138.1
1973	125.9	202.2	120.6	137.4
1990	138.8	157.3	119.8	125.3
2007	184.2	167.9	115.7	122.0

Sources: Derived from Broadberry (1997a, 1998), updated using the EU KLEMS database (O'Mahony and Timmer 2009).

States moved to universal secondary (high school) education, which was only achieved in Britain after World War II. At this point, the United States moved to mass higher education, a point arrived at in Britain and other European countries only in very recent years. There may be a general advantage arising from high levels of education that goes beyond the specific knowledge taught in class, with pupils learning social skills, teamwork, and flexibility (see Goldin 2001). This appears to be what Abramovitz (1986) had in mind when seeing education as a key measurable indicator of the "social capabilities" of nations.

However, the apparent British disadvantage in formal education for much of the twentieth century was offset by a much greater provision of vocational training than in the United States (Broadberry 2004). Britain led in the provision of higher level training through membership in professional organizations, particularly before World War II, and many of these professionals worked in the service sector. As Broadberry documents, Britain had an early lead in the provision of qualified higher level accountants. It also had an advantage in the provision of intermediate level training through apprenticeship (Broadberry 2003, 112, 118). Although this was initially focused on industry, it was extended into the service sector, particularly after World War II. However, it should be noted that continental European countries such as Germany developed an even greater advantage in intermediate-level vocational qualifications in services.

Putting together the different types of human-capital formation, it is unlikely that the United States had a substantial overall human-capital advantage over Britain before World War II, especially in services. But reliance on vocational rather than general education meant that Britain's strengths were in traditional, rather than "industrialized,"

Table 10.4 Enrollments in Primary, Secondary, and
Higher Education per 1,000 Population
under Age Twenty

A. United States

	Primary	Primary and Secondary	Primary, Secondary, and Higher
1870	390.6	394.8	
1890	492.5	502.8	
1910	475.6	502.4	
1930	479.2	578.8	601.9
1950	409.6	534.8	586.8
1970	443.0	630.4	741.9
1990	479.2	653.1	845.7
2010	465.1	656.9	904.1

B. Britain

	Primary	Primary and Secondary	Primary, Secondary, and Higher
1871	118.6		
1891	285.8		
1911	374.1	385.2	387.9
1931	380.6	412.3	416.6
1951	323.1	487.5	496.2
1971	337.4	595.4	621.4
1991	343.5	628.7	727.6
2011	343.7	655.7	808.6

Sources: Derived from Broadberry and Ghosal (2002, 986); Broadberry
(2004, 59); updated from US Department of Commerce, Statistical Abstract
of the United States; UK Department of Education, Education and Training
Statistics for the United Kingdom.

mechanized mass market, services. However, after World War II, any higher level advantage that Britain had enjoyed over the United States in services from the large number of qualified members of professional associations was offset by the spread of mass higher education in the United States.

So far, the focus has been on the proximate causes of the changing comparative productivity performance in services, highlighting relatively high rates of accumulation of physical and human capital in the United States. This, however, merely raises the issue of why rates of accumulation were higher in the United States than in Britain, and points to an examination of competition and the institutional framework. To see the importance of these factors, consider first why changing comparative productivity in services has contributed more than changing comparative productivity in industry to the explanation of changing comparative productivity performance overall. The reason for this is that services have typically been more sheltered from competitive pressures than industry. Although there have also been periods when protection and regulatory policies have slowed down the exit of inefficient firms in industry, in the long run, competitive forces have acted more effectively in industry than in services. In much of the service sector, competition from providers located abroad is impossible, while in other parts, firms typically have to obtain licenses to operate and are required to submit to a high degree of official regulation. In these heavily regulated sectors, collusion between providers has been common. Whereas British manufacturers that failed to keep up with productivity growth abroad were ultimately replaced by imports, there was no such possibility of replacing the bulk of Britain's service providers. Hence poor performance by service sector firms tends to show up in the productivity figures, while poor performance by industrial firms tends to show up in the sectoral composition of economic activity. Exports of both manufactures and services were more important for Britain than the United States, as the British economy has always been much more open. In 1870, British exports of goods were 22 percent of GDP, while exports of services were 7.1 percent. In the United States, the corresponding figures were 5.6 and 1.0 percent. Thus, increased international competition accentuated the impact.

Different institutional frameworks affect the incentives to accumulate and innovate. Whereas US governments have generally taken a strongly procompetitive stance since the emergence of large-scale modern business enterprise in the late nineteenth century, British and European governments generally have been more equivocal. Before World War II, cartels were widely accepted in Britain, where policy can at times be described as protrust rather than antitrust, particularly during the interwar period (Broadberry and Crafts 1990; Lucas 1937). After World War II, a corporatist postwar settlement in Britain continued to tolerate anticompetitive behavior in product and factor markets, which affected the incentives for accumulation of physical and human capital (see Bean and Crafts 1996; Eichengreen 1996). Although Britain was closing the productivity gap, particularly the labor productivity gap, with the United States from 1950, the pace of catching up was slow compared with other European countries; thus Britain fell behind other continental economies until the end of the 1970s. British performance then began to improve markedly during the 1980s as the postwar settlement was discarded in favor of a more American-style, market-oriented, less regulated regime under the governments of Margaret Thatcher (Crafts 2012).

After 1990, the ICT revolution affected comparative productivity performance in services. Whereas technological change during most of the twentieth century tended to favor standardization and hierarchical organization, the ICT revolution has tended to favor customization and networks, while preserving the high volume and high productivity of industrialized services. In earlier periods, the trend toward standardization and hierarchy occurred unevenly between sectors, and similarly, the information revolution has had an uneven impact on different sectors. To the extent that these changes tap into social capabilities that have remained strong in Britain, this should lead to an expectation of improved relative performance. To some extent, this expectation has been borne out, with Britain beginning to catch up with continental European countries during the 1990s. However, with the new technology coming largely from the United States, Anglo-American productivity gaps have been slow to narrow.

As Brynjolfsson and Hitt note, a fall of more than 99.9 percent in the cost of automated information processing since the 1960s has had a dramatic impact on efficient work practices, restoring autonomy to individual workers (Brynjolfsson and Hitt 2000, 26). However, this has happened within an "industrialized" environment of high-volume and low-margin provision of services. In the "New Economy," many routine tasks have been automated, most workers perform their own clerical tasks using personal computers and email, and most workers have access through the use of networked computers and the Internet to information that was previously only available centrally. It is in the technology-intensive service sectors that the impact has been greatest. However, as with the earlier innovations favoring standardization and hierarchical forms of organization, conditions have varied between sectors, affecting the pace at which the new ICT technologies have been adopted. Bresnahan, Brynjolfsson, and Hitt (2002) argue that investment in information technology has been greater in organizations that are decentralized and that have a greater investment in human capital, while Brynjolfsson et al. (1994) argue that greater levels of investment in information technology are also associated with smaller firms and less vertical integration.

POTENTIAL FUTURE RESEARCH

There are several questions that have been, and are likely to continue to be, studied. Victor Fuchs (1968) was among the first to raise the question of whether deindustrialization, the rise of services, would prove a problem for the US economy. This appears to be a question destined to be raised again and again. The "productivity crisis" of the 1970s and 1980s called attention to Baumol's "cost disease" and contributed to worries about deindustrialization (see Inman 1985; Kutscher and Personick 1986; Urquhart 1984). Those worries have not dissipated. Much of the ensuing discussion has made it appear that the shift toward services is a recent change, but it has been ongoing for at least a century. The industrial revolution was as much a movement toward services as toward manufacturing. By the 1970s, the agricultural sector had become so small that the continued expansion of the service sector had to come largely at the expense of manufacturing. While all three sectors are growing absolutely in terms of the value of output or numbers of people employed, that tends to get lost in a discussion based on percentages, on relative growth rates. Baumol, Blackman, and Wolff (1992) noted that the slower productivity growth of the 1970s and 1980s could be considered normal growth from the point of view of the past century, while that of the post–World War II years was much faster than normal. The role of services in the growth performance of the US economy will remain an important question.

Baumol and Bowen's (1996) comment that it is almost impossible to increase productivity in the arts raises the question of what is the appropriate measure of output for any given service industry? The heterogeneity of the service sector, however, means that while there are segments with slow productivity growth, there are also segments with rapid productivity growth (e.g., consider the efficiencies the Internet has introduced to many services). Since measured productivity growth in the service sector has been and likely always will be slower than other sectors, given the service sector has been a growing share of economic activity, it has been believed that the sector imparted a downward push in the aggregate economic growth rate. Some of this, however, may be attributable to measurement error. The tie between productivity improvement and the difficulties in measuring output in service-producing industries is another area for much future research.

A particular source of measurement error—one that could lead to underestimating the value of some services—stems from the somewhat artificial division that is usually made for those goods and services. For example, the purpose of purchasing a pair of soccer boots or golf clubs, recreational goods, is to make use of the local soccer field or golf course that produces recreational services. Durable recreational goods help produce recreational services in the same sense that a house produces housing services. Further, many of the facilities that help provide such services are offered for what is often a subsidized price, which is adopted to make the service available to people who otherwise might not be able to afford it. This means that as more people have had access to such services, it is reasonable to argue that the standard of living has increased for all Americans (Costa 1999).

It seems likely that there will be much more research tying services to income, in general, and the standard of living, in particular. The shift toward services is a reflection, at least in part, of the fact many services are luxury goods with an income elasticity of demand greater than one. Since the end of World War II, services' share of GDP has doubled. Firms such as Walmart now sell goods with far more services embodied in them than firms a half century ago. Services are not, as was once thought, "a luxury that cannot be afforded" (Costa 1997, 22). That quote referred to the consumption of passive activities (e.g., motion pictures and sports events). Today, any discussion of services is more likely to be about education, health care, and other services that are increasingly considered to be "rights" of all Americans.

Notes

1. The national income and product accounts (NIPA) are produced by the Bureau of Economic Analysis of the Department of Commerce and are accessible at www.bea.gov. The exact definition of "services-producing industries" can be found be found in the NIPA glossary (www.bea.gov/national/pdf/glossary.pdf) on p. 27.

2. One such issue is created by the decision a nonservice-sector firm makes to hire, say, business services in the market or bring them inside the firm. Accounting, legal, and other such services produced inside the firm will appear in national accounts as part of the industry including the nonservice firm; see Stanback et al. (1981).

3. Gorman (1969) on banking and Reder (1969) on medical care attempt to capture what could be defined as productivity improvements; see also Fuchs (1968).

4. "We'd Better Watch Out," *New York Times Book Review*, July 12, 1987, p. 36.

5. The only nonservice sector to employ a significant number of women was factory employment, where more than four million were employed. By the middle of the nineteenth century, especially in places like Massachusetts, women working in factories accounted for a third of all employed white women. Women provided a pool of relatively cheap manufacturing labor; see Alice Kessler-Harris (1982).

6. Stigler (1946) argues that the decline in domestic servant employment in the 1910s shown in census data is partly spurious.

7. In Europe, large parts of health and education are provided by the state as nonmarket services, which affect the way that output is monitored, and hence has an impact on productivity comparisons.

BIBLIOGRAPHY

Abramovitz, M. (1986). "Catching Up, Forging Ahead and Falling Behind." *Journal of Economic History* 46: 385–406.

Bakker, G. (2008). *Entertainment Industrialised: The Emergence of the International Film Industry, 1890–1940*. Cambridge, MA: Cambridge University Press.

Baumol, W. J. (1967). "The Macroeconomics of Unbalanced Growth." *American Economic Review* 57: 415–426.

Baumol, W. J. (2002). "Services as Leaders and the Leader of the Services." In *Productivity, Innovation and Knowledge in Services: New Economic and Socio-economic Approaches*, edited by J. Gadrey and F. Gallouj, 147–163. Aldershot, UK: Edward Elgar.

Baumol, W. J., S. A. B. Blackman, and E. N. Wolff. (1992). *Productivity and American Leadership*. Cambridge, MA: MIT Press.

Baumol, W. J., and W. G. Bowen. (1966). *Performing Arts—The Economic Dilemma: A Study of Problems Common to Theater, Opera, Music and Dance*. New York: Twentieth Century Fund.

Bean, C., and N. F. R. Crafts. (1996). "British Economic Growth since 1945: Relative Economic Decline . . . and Renaissance?" In *Economic Growth in Europe since 1945*, edited by N. F. R. Crafts and G. Toniolo, 131–172. Cambridge, MA: Cambridge University Press.

Bresnahan, T., E. Brynjolfsson, and L. Hitt. (2002). "Information Technology, Workplace Organization, and the Demand for Skilled Labor: Firm-Level Evidence." *Quarterly Journal of Economics* 117: 339–376.

Broadberry, S. N. (1997a). "Forging Ahead, Falling Behind and Catching-Up: A Sectoral Analysis of Anglo-American Productivity Differences, 1870–1990." *Research in Economic History* 17: 1–37.

Broadberry, S. N. (1997b). *The Productivity Race: British Manufacturing in International Perspective, 1850–1990*. Cambridge, MA: Cambridge University Press.

Broadberry, S. N. (1998). "How Did the United States and Germany Overtake Britain? A Sectoral Analysis of Comparative Productivity Levels, 1870–1990." *Journal of Economic History* 58: 375–407.

Broadberry, S. N. (2003). "Human Capital and Productivity Performance: Britain, the United States and Germany, 1870–1990." In *The Economic Future in Historical Perspective*, edited by P. A. David and M. Thomas, 103–134. Oxford: Oxford University Press.

Broadberry, S. N. (2004). "Human Capital and Skills." In *The Cambridge Economic History of Modern Britain*, Vol. 2: *Economic Maturity, 1860–1939*, edited by R. Floud and P. Johnson, 56–73. Cambridge, MA: Cambridge University Press.

Broadberry, S. N. (2006). *Market Services and the Productivity Race, 1850–2000: Britain in International Perspective*. Cambridge, MA: Cambridge University Press.

Broadberry, S. N., and N. F. R. Crafts. (1990). "The Impact of the Depression of the 1930s on Productive Potential in the United Kingdom." *European Economic Review* 34: 599–607.

Broadberry, S. N., and S. Ghosal. (2002). "From the Counting House to the Modern Office: Explaining Anglo-American Productivity Differences in Services, 1870–1990." *Journal of Economic History* 62: 967–998.

Broadberry, S. N., and S. Ghosal. (2005). "Technology, Organisation and Productivity Performance in Services: Lessons from Britain and the United States since 1870." *Structural Change and Economic Dynamics* 16: 437–466.

Brynjolfsson, E., and L. M. Hitt. (2000). "Beyond Computation: Information Technology, Organizational Transformation and Business Performance." *Journal of Economic Perspectives* 14(4): 23–48.

Brynjolfsson, E., T. Malone, V. Gurbaxani, and A. Kambil. (1994). "Does Information Technology Lead to Smaller Firms?" *Management Science* 40: 1628–1644.

Cain, L., and D. Haddock. (2005). "Similar Economic Histories: Different Industrial Structures: Transatlantic Contrasts in the Evolution of Professional Sports Leagues." *Journal of Economic History* 65: 1116–1147.

Calomiris, C. W. (1995). "The Costs of Rejecting Universal Banking: American Finance in the German Mirror, 1870–1914." In *Coordination and Information: Historical Perspectives on the Organization of Enterprise*, edited by N. R. Lamoreaux and D. M. G. Raff, 257–321. Chicago: University of Chicago Press.

Campbell-Kelly, M. (1992). "Large-Scale Data Processing in the Prudential, 1850–1930." *Accounting, Business and Financial History* 2: 117–139.

Campbell-Kelly, M. (1994). "The Railway Clearing House and Victorian Data Processing." In *Information Acumen: The Understanding and Use of Knowledge in Modern Business*, edited by L. Bud-Frierman, 51–74. London: Routledge.

Campbell-Kelly, M. (1998). "Data Processing and Technological Change: The Post Office Savings Bank, 1861–1930." *Technology and Culture* 39: 1–32.

Carter, S. B., S. S. Gartner, M. R. Haines, A. L. Olmstead, R. Sutch, and G. Wright, eds. (2006). *Historical Statistics of the United States*. New York: Cambridge University Press.

Chandler, A. D., Jr. (1977). *The Visible Hand: The Managerial Revolution in American Business*. Cambridge, MA: Harvard University Press.

Chandler, A. D., Jr. (1980). "The United States: Seedbed of Managerial Capitalism." In *Managerial Hierarchies: Comparative Perspectives on the Rise of the Modern Industrial Enterprise*, edited by A. D. Chandler, Jr., and H. Daems, 9–40. Cambridge, MA: Harvard University Press.

Clark, C. (1957). *The Conditions of Economic Progress*. 3rd ed. London: Macmillan.

Costa, D. (1997). "Less of a Luxury: The Rise of Recreation since 1888." National Bureau of Economic Research, Working Paper No. 6054.

Costa, D. (1999). "American Living Standards: Evidence from Recreational Expenditures." National Bureau of Economic Research, Working Paper No. 7148.

Crafts, N. F. R. (2012). "British Economic Decline Revisited: The Role of Competition." *Explorations in Economic History* 49: 17–29.

Eichengreen, B. (1996). "Institutions and Economic Growth: Europe after World War II." In *Economic Growth in Europe since 1945*, edited by N. F. R. Crafts and G. Toniolo, 38–72. Cambridge, MA: Cambridge University Press.

Field, A. J. (1996). "The Relative Productivity of American Distribution, 1869–1992." *Research in Economic History* 16: 1–37.

Fisher, A. G. B. (1935). *The Clash of Progress and Security*. London: Macmillan.

Fuchs, V. R. (1968). *The Service Economy*. New York: Columbia University Press.

Fuchs, V. R., ed. (1969). *Production and Productivity in the Service Industries*. Cambridge, MA: National Bureau of Economic Research.

Gallman, R., and T. Weiss. (1969). "The Service Industries in the Nineteenth Century." In *Production and Productivity in the Service Industries*, edited by Victor R. Fuchs, 287–352. Cambridge, MA: National Bureau of Economic Research.

Goldin, C. (1990). *Understanding the Gender Gap: An Economic History of American Women*. New York: Oxford University Press.

Goldin, C. (2001). "The Human-Capital Century and American Leadership: Virtues of the Past." *Journal of Economic History* 61: 263–292.

Goldin, C., and L. Katz. (2008). The *Race between Education and Technology*. Cambridge, MA: Harvard University Press.

Gorman, J. A. (1969). "Alternative Measures of the Real Output and Productivity of Commercial Banks." In *Production and Productivity in the Service Industries*, edited by Victor R. Fuchs, 155–195. Cambridge, MA: National Bureau of Economic Research.

Greif, A. (2000). "The Fundamental Problem of Exchange: A Research Agenda in Historical, Institutional Analysis." *European Review of Economic History* 4: 251–284.

Hall, M., J. Knapp, and C. Winsten. (1961). *Distribution in Great Britain and North America: A Study in Structure and Productivity*. Oxford: Oxford University Press.

Inman, R., ed. (1985). *Managing the Service Economy: Problems and Prospects*. Cambridge, MA: Cambridge University Press.

Jones, G. (1993). *British Multinational Banking, 1830–1990*. Oxford: Oxford University Press.

Katzman, D. M. (1981). *Seven Days a Week: Women and Domestic Service in Industrializing America*. Champaign-Urbana: University of Illinois Press.

Kendrick, J. W. (1961) *Productivity Trends in the United States*. Princeton, NJ: Princeton University Press, National Bureau for Economic Research.

Kessler-Harris, A. (1982). *Out to Work: A History of Wage-Earning Women in the United States*. New York: Oxford University Press.

Kutscher, R., and V. Personick. (1986). "Deindustrialization and the Shift to Services." *Monthly Labor Review* 109(June): 3–13.

Kuznets, S. (1966). *Modern Economic Growth: Rate, Structure, and Spread*. New Haven, CT: Yale University Press.

Kuznets, S. (1971). The *Economic Growth of Nations*. Cambridge, MA: Harvard University Press.

Kwolek-Folland, A. (2007). "Gender, the Service Sector, and U.S. Business History." *Business History Review* 81(Autumn): 429–450.

Lamoreaux, N. (1994). *Insider Lending: Banks, Personal Connections, and Economic Development in Industrial New England*. Cambridge, MA: Cambridge University Press.

Lebergott, S. (1966). "Labor Force and Employment, 1800–1960." In *Output, Employment and Productivity in the United States after 1800*, edited by Dorothy Brady, 117–210. New York: National Bureau of Economic Research.

Lucas, A. F. (1937). *Industrial Reconstruction and the Control of Competition: The British Experiments*. London: Longmans.

Maddison, A. (1995). *Monitoring the World Economy, 1820–1992*. Paris: Development Centre of the Organisation for Economic Co-operation and Development.

Marshall, A. (1920). *Principles of Economics*. 8th ed. London: Macmillan.

McCraw, T. (1996). "Competition and 'Fair Trade': History and Theory." *Research in Economic History* 16: 185–239.

O'Mahony, M., and W. de Boer. (2002). "Britain's Relative Productivity Performance: Has Anything Changed?" *National Institute Economic Review* 179: 38–43.

O'Mahony, M., and M. Timmer. (2009). "Output, Input and Productivity Measures at the Industry Level: The EU KLEMS Database." *Economic Journal* 119: F374–F403.

Oulton, N. (2001). "Must the Growth Rate Decline? Baumol's Unbalanced Growth Revisited." *Oxford Economic Papers* 53: 605–627.

Perkins, E. J. (1999). *Wall Street to Main Street: Charles Merrill and Middle-Class Investors*. Cambridge, MA: Cambridge University Press.

Prais, S. J. (1995). *Productivity, Education and Training: An International Perspective*. Cambridge, MA: Cambridge University Press.

Reder, M. W. (1969). "Some Problems in the Measurement of Productivity in the Medical Care Industry." In *Production and Productivity in the Service Industry*, edited by Victor Fuchs, 95–131. Cambridge, MA: National Bureau of Economic Research.

Rotella, E. J. (1981a). *From Home to Office: U.S. Women at Work, 1870–1930*. Ann Arbor, MI: UMI Research Press.

Rotella, E. J. (1981b). "The Transformation of the American Office: Changes in Employment and Technology." *Journal of Economic History* XLI: 51–57.

Stanback, T. M., Jr., P. J. Bears, T. J. Noyelle, and R. A. Karasek. (1981). *Services: The New Economy*. Montclair, NJ: Allanheld, Osmun.

Stigler, G. (1946). "Domestic Servants in the United States, 1900 to 1940." National Bureau of Economic Research Occasional Paper No. 24, April.

Stiglitz, J., and A. Weiss. (1981). "Credit Rationing in Markets with Imperfect Information." *American Economic Review* 71: 393–410.

Tedlow, R. S. (1996). *New and Improved: The Story of Mass Marketing in America*. Boston: Harvard Business School.

UK Department of Education. (Various years). *Education and Training Statistics for the United Kingdom*. London: HMSO.

Urquhart, M. (1984). "The Employment Shift to Services: Where Did It Come From?" *Monthly Labor Review* 107 (April): 15–22.

US Department of Commerce. (1983). *National Income and Product Accounts of the United States, 1929–1982*. Washington, DC: Government Printing Office.

US Department of Commerce. (Various years). *Statistical Abstract of the United States*. Washington, DC: Government Printing Office.

Weiss, T. (1984). "The Nineteenth Century Origins of the American Service Industry Workforce." *Essays in Economic and Business History* 3: 48–67.

Weiss, T. (1999). "Estimates of White and Non-White Gainful Workers in the United States by Age Group and Sex, 1800 to 1900." *Historical Methods* 32(1): 21–36.

Weiss, T. (2006). "Introduction to Services." In *Historical Statistics of the United States*, edited by S. B. Carter, S. S. Gartner, M. R. Haines, A. L. Olmstead, R. Sutch, and G. Wright, 4-1061–4-1068. New York: Cambridge University Press.

White, E. N. (2000). "Banking and Finance in the Twentieth Century." In *The Cambridge Economic History of the United States*, Vol. III: *The Twentieth Century*, edited by S. L. Engerman and R. E. Gallman, 743–802. Cambridge, MA: National Bureau for Economic Research.

Yates, J. (1989). *Control through Communication: The Rise of System in American Management*. Baltimore, MD: Johns Hopkins University Press.

CHAPTER 11

....

BUSINESS ORGANIZATION IN AMERICAN ECONOMIC HISTORY

....

ERIC HILT

In the decades that followed the Revolution, the American economy experienced a dramatic transformation. Whereas economic life in the colonies had been dominated by agriculture and commerce, in the early national period the economy began to industrialize. This process continued throughout the nineteenth century, and by 1890, the value of American industrial output was threefold greater than the value of its agricultural output. By 1914, American industrial output was nearly as great as that of Great Britain, Germany, and France combined, and real income per capita in the United States was slightly higher than that of Great Britain.

Facts such as these are well known. Less well known are the changes in the organization of firms that underpinned the development and industrialization of the American economy. As the work of Davis (1917) makes clear, at the time of the Revolution, few large-scale business enterprises of any kind existed in the United States: there was just one insurance corporation, no banks, and what little manufacturing was being done was mostly conducted in artisanal shops. During the subsequent decades, large-scale manufacturing enterprises began to emerge, as did firms engaged in the provision of financial services and the creation of transportation infrastructure (see Clark 1916; Gillingham 1933; Hammond 1957; Klein and Majewski 1992; Ware 1931). The rapid proliferation and growth of businesses eventually began to produce some very large enterprises, such as railroads, but also much greater numbers of small and medium-sized firms. Many were organized as corporations, a form that the American states made increasingly accessible (Sylla and Wright 2013). However, the partnership remained quite important in most sectors, and new organizational forms such as the limited partnership and the "partnership association" were made available as well.

In choosing an organizational form and capitalizing their firms, entrepreneurs confronted a range of problems. Overcoming adverse selection and attracting investments from outsiders was of course a significant issue. But also important were incentive problems that might be faced by the managers to whom day-to-day operations might be delegated; the potential for conflicts among the owners, or for a controlling owner to utilize the resources of the firm for his own benefit; and, of course, the risk of financial losses and how they would be borne. Early entrepreneurs configured the rights of their firms' investors and creditors to address these problems, but in doing so, they were constrained by the menu of available organizational forms, and the features of those organizational forms that the law made accessible to them.

Over time, new forms of economic activity emerged, as technological innovation created new goods and new production techniques. In addition, declines in the cost of transportation and communication contributed to greater economic integration, and expanded potential markets for firms. However, exploiting those new opportunities required entrepreneurs to address a new series of information and incentive problems, and to create businesses capable of surmounting them (see Lamoreaux, Raff, and Temin 2003). The organizational and contractual means available to address those problems changed as well, as legal doctrines relative to business enterprise evolved, and new managerial technologies, such as sophisticated accounting and control systems, were developed.

To analyze the history of American business organizations is to trace two parallel processes of evolution: the changing needs of entrepreneurs and investors, on the one hand, and the changing legal and institutional environment, on the other. Over successive generations, as economic activity evolved, entrepreneurs confronted new problems, and they developed mechanisms to address those problems within the existing institutional framework. Those mechanisms, however, were not necessarily optimal, or even adequate. A learning process occurred, among entrepreneurs, as well as among legislators and jurists. Prominent failures and successes changed subsequent behavior on the part of all three. In extreme cases, waves of scandals shattered investors' faith in the management of large-scale enterprises, and in the legal and institutional framework that existed to protect their rights. The resolutions of such episodes sometimes produced new laws, and sometimes produced other institutional changes beyond the law.

Another force behind these processes of evolution was politics. The governments of the American states used the law to promote economic development, and granted corporate charters to large numbers of enterprises. In the early nineteenth century, a corporation could only be created by a special act of the state—essentially, the government had to pass a law granting a corporate charter to a business—and it was necessary for corporations to be chartered by the state within which they operated (Henderson 1918; Hurst 1970). However, control over access to the corporate form led to serious problems of corruption, and political factions within state governments sometimes rationed charters in profitable industries such as banking in order to perpetuate their influence. This led reform movements to push for the adoption of general incorporation statutes, which facilitated open access to the corporate form through a simple registration procedure. The reform impulse also contributed to efforts to authorize the use of new organizational forms that had some corporate characteristics, such as the limited partnership. The terms of a state's general incorporation statutes (if it had one), and its statutes authorizing the use of other organizational forms, were important determinants of the degree of flexibility enjoyed by entrepreneurs in organizing their firms.

This chapter presents the history of the organization of American enterprise, up to the twentieth century and the emergence of large, vertically integrated conglomerates. It begins with a synopsis of the early origins of large-scale firms and the use of the corporate form. It then presents a discussion of the alternative organizational forms that were available to entrepreneurs in the American states, and the significance of those legal innovations. Finally, it presents a discussion of the rise of what became known as "big business" in the late nineteenth century, and the legal and institutional context within which those enterprises began to emerge. The discussion of each is focused on the changing nature of the problems faced by entrepreneurs, and the changing legal and institutional environment in which they operated.

Among the most influential scholarship on the history of business enterprises has been that of Alfred Chandler. Chandler's work chronicles the emergence of industrial conglomerates, and emphasizes the efficiency gains achieved by these firms. However, Chandler's work has been criticized as exaggerating the role of vertically integrated firms in the early twentieth-century economy (Scranton 1997). More important, economic changes that occurred around the time of the publication of Chandler's work have partly undermined the dominant position of many large industrial conglomerates (see Lamoreaux, Raff, and Temin 2003).

More recent work on the history of American business enterprises has focused on the importance of firms' legal forms of organization, and on the conflicts that may arise both between firms' managers and their outside investors, and among a firm's different owners. This research has renewed interest in the questions pursued in Berle and Means's *The Modern Corporation and Private Property* (1932). Berle and Means's work influenced the development of a literature focusing on incentive conflicts among corporate managers.[1]

Less well known is the historical narrative of Berle and Means, which presents an account of the evolution of the business corporation. Berle and Means argue that the American business corporation was once a well-governed institution, partly due to the active participation of the state in its creation, and partly due to its small size and the active participation of its owners. They then argue that the changes in corporation law that occurred over the nineteenth century, and the emergence of firms of unprecedented scale with thousands of completely passive shareholders, together caused ownership to become separated from control in the early twentieth century. In their view, firms like AT&T, which had half a million shareholders at the time they were writing, were fundamentally different than corporations from earlier eras: the owners of the firm, none of whom held more than a tiny fraction of the company's equity, were no longer the dominant or controlling force in its governance.

Most of the literature on the history of corporate governance has accepted Berle and Means's characterization of the evolution of the business corporation (see, for example, Coffee 2001; Dodd 1938; Hovenkamp 1991). But the early history of American corporations has not been well documented, and the arguments of Berle and Means may have been accepted simply because they seemed appealing and persuasive in light of what is known about corporate governance in the twentieth century. Recent work on the governance of early corporations has challenged Berle and Means's characterization of early corporate governance (Hilt 2008).

Another major strand of this literature has focused on the common-law origins of the American legal system, and its legacy. In a highly influential work, La Porta et al. (1998) argue that the advanced state of economic and financial development of the American economy is due in part to its adoption of the common law. An enormous literature on the consequences of "legal origins" followed (see La Porta, Lopez-de-Silanes, and Shleifer 2008 for a survey). The advantages of the common law have been held to include its flexibility, and the efficiency with which its courts adjudicate disputes and revise doctrines in response to the real-world needs of businesses. However, recent work comparing the menu of organizational forms offered by countries with different legal systems, and the response of courts to innovations in organizational forms, have identified a relative *in*flexibility of the American common law toward new organizational forms (see, e.g., Guinnane et al. 2007; Lamoreaux 2014; Lamoreaux and Rosenthal 2005).

The influence of the common law on the development of American enterprise may be somewhat overstated in the legal origins literature. For example, in contrast to other areas of the law, the United States did not inherit a well-developed set of judicial precedents relating to business corporations from England (Gower 1956; Harris 2000). The enterprise law that developed here was largely an American creation, which was shaped and modified in response to local circumstances and experience. Legislators in many states even drew on civil law institutions, such as the limited partnership, or created new organizational forms such as the "partnership association" out of whole cloth. The creativity and energy of American legislators was responsible for the character and quality of American business law as much as any courts, a fact that is difficult to reconcile with some of the claims made within the literature on legal origins.

Early Industrialization and the Corporation

In the years following the Revolution, the elite merchants and lawyers who controlled the federal and state governments began to create business corporations to facilitate economic development. Many of these enterprises created transportation infrastructure or provided access to water; others were insurance companies or banks; and a few pursued large-scale manufacturing. Some of these corporations were unsuccessful, but many, particularly the banks, enjoyed immediate and lasting success. These included the largest businesses that had ever existed in North America, and they fundamentally reshaped the development of the American economy.

But they also provoked intense rancor, and divided American politics. The reasons for the opposition of those who would eventually come to call themselves Republicans or Democratic-Republicans are manifold, but the most important relate to the legal status of the corporation. Corporate charters conferred exclusive legal privileges on the businesses they created, which could range from limited liability for investors, to franchises from the state to engage in particular activities. Businesses without a corporate charter could not obtain these privileges; by controlling access to corporate charters, the government effectively controlled entry into many industries, or at least held the power to create firms with particular advantages. And the elite political figures who created these corporations, who came to be called Federalists, did not hesitate to use this control for personal financial gain for themselves and their allies. For example, Hilt and Valentine (2012) document that the wealthiest class of owners of New York's early corporations were in fact political officeholders, and included the governor, prominent jurists, and many state senators. Republican critics of corporations derided them as "monopolies," not just in the sense of market power, but also meaning something dangerous and menacing toward democracy and access to opportunity.

Over time, American politics became more democratic, the Federalists' control over governments in many states broke down, and the Republicans gained power. However, once in office, the party of anticorporate rhetoric presided over the greatest wave of business incorporations the world had ever seen. "If they could not extirpate monopoly," wrote Bray Hammond (1957, 146), the Republicans "could at least reduce its inequities by seizing a share of its rewards." In many economic sectors, particularly those in which incumbent firms or other interests were not acutely threatened by new entry, petitions for charters were granted quite liberally. By 1830, around 4,500 business corporations had been created in the United States (see Davis 1917; Kessler 1940; Sylla and Wright 2013).

Many of the earliest corporations were quite large, and were initially conceived to be local monopolies. Their capitalizations required them to raise large sums from investors, which inevitably led them to seek subscriptions from individuals with little or no connection to their founders, many of whom would remain entirely passive as owners. The most important problem faced in the governance of such enterprises was the danger that a controlling shareholder could use the resources of the firm for his own benefit, or would otherwise act in ways that were contrary to the interests of the other investors. Although ownership data from this era are quite scarce, a large sample of corporations from the 1820s reveals that many early corporations were indeed dominated by large shareholders (Hilt 2008).

Offering some assurance to outside investors that their interests would be protected was a critical objective in many early corporations. And many corporate charters from the early nineteenth century contain provisions intended to offer such protections. For example, some offered "graduated voting rights" to shareholders, which decreased the votes per share to which an investor was entitled as the number of shares they held increased, and thereby enhanced the relative influence of small investors when in the presence of large shareholders. A substantial literature has analyzed the purpose and effects of these voting rights: on their political significance, see Dunlavy (2004, 2006); on their effects among nineteenth-century American banks, see Bodenhorn (2012); Hansmann and Pargendler (2010) analyze their effects on consumers; and Hilt (2013b) presents a synthesis of the different viewpoints. Early corporate charters also sometimes imposed requirements that the firms submit annual reports to the state or to shareholders, and regulated the size and sometimes also the composition of the board of directors.

Evidence from surviving lists of shareholders also indicates that early investors often resided in the same location as the corporation, and sometimes had business ties to the corporation. Although different motives could explain these patterns, it seems likely that they helped resolve information problems related to investment, in particular the conflicts between insiders and outsiders that were so acute among many firms. Detailed ownership data do survive from individual firms, from firms located in particular locations or operating in particular industries.[2]

In the early nineteenth century, trading activity in corporate stock began to develop, and the shares of a few dozen corporations were listed on securities exchanges, along with some bonds of federal state and local governments (Martin 1886; Werner and Smith 1991). The public corporations traded in New York included some well-governed and successful urban banks, and, in an expansion of credit and speculative activity in the mid-1820s, the shares of a number of insurance corporations. Some of these latter corporations had defied banking regulations and issued bank-note-like instruments to finance their lending (Hilt 2009a, 2009b). These firms are noteworthy not only for the aggressiveness with which they conducted their financial operations, but also for the degree to which their managers were able to profit personally from their utilization of their resources. When an economic downturn began, and investors began to regard the liabilities of those firms with suspicion, a panic broke out, and several firms faced runs. The failure of a number of prominent financial institutions in 1826 led to waves of criminal prosecutions, private litigation, and extensive legal reforms. A consensus emerged that the legal and institutional framework in place to protect the interests of investors in public companies, particularly financial institutions or "moneyed incorporations," was inadequate, and a number of changes were made in response. New legal protections for investors were produced, through significant changes to New York's corporation laws.

In addition to this evolution in the regulations imposed on corporations, the legal institutions governing the creation of corporations also changed significantly, particularly in the mid-nineteenth century. Beginning in the mid-1840s, a solution to the problems created by the special privileges granted to corporations was found in "general incorporation" statutes. Under general laws, incorporation became a routine administrative procedure, outside the realm of political influence. However, early general statutes often did not grant entrepreneurs much freedom in the configuration of their enterprises, but instead created an organizational template that corporations were required to adopt. Entrepreneurs wishing to incorporate a firm that did not conform to the template, for example with a greater capitalization than permitted, would still need to petition for a charter.

General incorporation statutes typically only applied to one class of corporation. Many states first enacted them only for manufacturing firms, and then gradually added legislation for other categories of firms such as banks (the so-called free banking laws), insurance companies, or railroads. But gradually, over the course of the nineteenth century, virtually every state introduced general statutes for most classes of corporations. These statutes are the precursors to the corporation laws that currently prevail in the American states.[3]

The Partnership and Alternative Organizational Forms

Some early businesses had no choice but to adopt the corporate form. This was true for firms that needed special franchises from the state, for example to engage in banking or to create transportation infrastructure. But the vast majority of entrepreneurs, at least those sufficiently well connected to gain access to a corporate charter, could choose whether to incorporate their business or to adopt some other organizational form. And many of them instead chose to organize their firms as partnerships, a form that required no authorization from the state.

The corporate form gave firms a number of characteristics that were difficult to obtain otherwise. These generally included limited liability for the owners, transferability of shares, legal personality, and the "locking-in" of capital.[4] The first of these, limited liability, is often regarded as synonymous with the corporate form, and one might imagine that it was the principal reason to incorporate. Yet many early corporations were explicitly denied limited liability; the state of Massachusetts, a prolific creator of early business corporations, imposed unlimited personal liability on shareholders of manufacturing corporations until 1830 (see Handlin and Handlin 1945). This suggests that attributes other than limited liability were sought among early incorporators. The other attributes of corporations, particularly the transferability of shares, were likely desirable for firms seeking to obtain investments from large numbers of passive shareholders.

For firms that did not need to raise large sums from outside shareholders, and particularly for firms in which the human capital of a few individuals was critically important for its success, the partnership was often preferred. This was frequently true for firms engaged in the provision of services, such as wholesale and retail mercantile firms, private bankers, and law firms, but the partnership also remained popular within the manufacturing sector as well. As there is no registration requirement for partnerships within a common-law legal system, it is not possible to obtain counts of partnerships from public records. Early city directories, however, list large numbers of partnerships in those sectors (see, e.g., Hilt and O'Banion 2009; Lamoreaux 1997).

In a partnership, the members of the firm all share in its profits, and bear unlimited personal responsibility for its debts.[5] The partners also hold discretion over the admission of any new members—a membership stake is not transferable or divisible. These characteristics help provide strong incentives for the members to perform their roles well, and help ensure that only highly productive new members are admitted to the firm. Corporations attempting to compete with partnerships may therefore face a "lemons problem" (see Kingston 2007).

But these same characteristics were unattractive to passive investors, and the partnership form generally could not accommodate investments from anyone but full partners, bearing unlimited personal liability, and holding nontransferable stakes. The resulting inability to raise capital from passive investors represented a significant constraint for some firms that otherwise would have preferred the partnership form. Experimentation with the corporate form in industries in which the partnership was generally optimal did occur; the statute books of many states include some charters granted to mercantile firms, agricultural firms, and maritime enterprises, to name a few. These efforts generally did not meet with success (see Hilt 2006).

In other circumstances, the corporate form was preferred, but some of its characteristics created problems. This was particularly true for company founders who wished to retain control over their enterprise, or to avoid disclosing sensitive information in annual reports, or to prevent the owners of a competing firm from acquiring control or gaining access to strategic information by purchasing its shares. The shares of corporations were usually freely transferable, so any shareholder could sell her or his stake to a rival firm without the consent of the founders. And shareholders were entitled to access the company's books, as well as vote in director elections. Entrepreneurs seeking to avoid these characteristics of the corporation for their enterprises were forced to use the partnership form. But they did so at the cost of facing substantial difficulties in attempting to raise capital from passive investors, and losing other corporate characteristics.

Over time, some American legislators developed innovative solutions to these problems in order to better meet the needs of entrepreneurs. The limitations of the partnership form were addressed in part through the introduction of a form previously unknown to the common law, the limited partnership. Limited partnerships were like ordinary partnerships except that they could have a new class of partner, known as a special partner, who was granted limited liability. The special partners were required to be passive investors, and were forbidden from participating in the management of the firm. But the form of the limited partnership created a mechanism for investments from outsiders in firms organized as partnerships.

The limited partnership form likely originated in twelfth-century Italy, and was among the organizational forms included in the 1807 commercial code of France. The earliest American limited partnership statutes were in fact adapted from the language of the French code. The first and most influential of these statues was New York's, which was enacted in 1822 (*Laws of New York*, 1822, Chapter 244). By the late 1880s, limited partnerships were authorized in all but three of the then-existing states and territories

(Bates 1886). These statutes required that the founders file a registration certificate with basic information about the firm with a government agency, and that the contents of the certificate be publicized in a local newspaper.

The limitations of the corporate form were addressed to varying degrees in different states' corporation laws; some states offered entrepreneurs considerable flexibility in the configuration of their enterprises. But beginning in the mid-nineteenth century, a few states began to offer entrepreneurs an organizational form that was a hybrid of a corporation and a partnership. This form, which was sometimes called a "partnership association" in the statutes, would later be called the limited liability company (LLC). These were like corporations, in that the investors had limited liability, but they were also like partnerships, in that the members of the firms could exercise discretion over the admission of new members. Transferability of shares, which was fundamental to the corporate form, could be regulated or blocked by the members.[6]

The earliest state to authorize the use of the partnership association was Michigan, whose 1846 statute referred to them as "private associations" (*Laws of Michigan*, 1846, no. 148). Eventually, a few other states authorized the use of the form, including Pennsylvania (1874), New Jersey (1880), and Ohio (1881), but the form was apparently not adopted by other states during the nineteenth century.

The innovative nature of these new organizational forms resulted in a source of uncertainty in their implementation: the stance the courts would take toward firms that adopted them. This was a particularly important concern with regard to the limited partnership. Partly because the form represented a radical departure from the common-law doctrine of personal liability in partnerships, limited partnership statutes declared that special partners would be made general partners with unlimited liability if the firm failed to adhere to any of the provisions of the law. Much of the prior literature on limited partnerships has argued that common-law judges tended to side with creditors who tried to use any minor deviation from the terms of the statutes to strip special partners of their limited liability (see, e.g., Warren 1929). Some scholarship has concluded that as a result, the form was not widely adopted (Howard 1934).

However, the stance taken by the courts toward these firms varied across states, and perhaps also over time. In the state of New York, for example, jurists appear to have been reasonably generous in their interpretation of the limited-partnership statute.[7] And indeed, research on the use of the form in New York City, where the economic sectors in which the partnership form dominated were quite well developed, found that the limited partnership was used extensively, with more than a thousand created through the 1850s (Hilt and O'Banion 2009). However, the experience with the form in New York City may not have been representative of other major cities; more research on the topic is needed.

In the case of the partnership association or LLC, even less is known about the frequency with which the form was adopted. Pennsylvania's 1874 statute was utilized by some prominent firms, such as Carnegie Steel. However, at times the state's courts took a particularly hostile approach toward the form, which reduced its utility. This problem was compounded by the fact that in 1897, a court in the state of Massachusetts, which did not have a partnership association law, held that a partnership association organized under Pennsylvania's law was in fact an ordinary partnership with unlimited liability for its members (see Lamoreaux 2014).

A final organizational form that may have found frequent use during this period is the unincorporated joint-stock company. These were firms that sought to obtain corporate-like characteristics through private contracting, rather than through the grant of a corporate charter from the state. Essentially, the founders would write a contract specifying the structure and characteristics of their new enterprise, declare themselves a "company," and commence operations.[8] Historians have documented the existence of numerous American unincorporated joint-stock companies, particularly in the eighteenth century when corporate charters were relatively difficult to obtain (Davis 1917). Some have even claimed that the unincorporated joint stock company was more important in many respects than the corporation itself (Livermore 1939). However, unincorporated companies were most commonly used for businesses that would have been characterized as "joint adventures"— investments or speculative transactions undertaken jointly by several investors, such as investments in land, or maritime voyages. There is far less evidence of its use among more complex business enterprises, in which the corporate form would have offered greater advantages. Moreover, any claims among these firms to limited liability for their investors may have been vulnerable to challenges from creditors; as with limited partnerships and partnership associations, the stance that the courts would take toward these enterprises was likely a significant source of uncertainty. One legal treatise, citing a number of cases, stated that in an unincorporated company "each member is liable" for debts "no matter what the private arrangements among the members may be" (Rowley 1916, II: 1419).

THE SECOND HALF OF THE NINETEENTH CENTURY: RAILROADS, "BIG BUSINESS," AND BANKERS

During the second half of the nineteenth century, most of the American states and territories adopted general incorporation statutes for many types of businesses. The corporate form became increasingly accessible, and was quite frequently used by businesses of all sizes. By 1900 there were more than thirty-seven thousand manufacturing corporations in the United States, many of which were relatively small. Systematic data on the organization form of manufacturing firms was first collected in 1900 the federal Census of Manufactures (Census of Manufactures 1905, Part 1, tables 8 and 9). A comparative study of the use of the form in 1910 found that corporations were unusually common in the United States, and their average size relative to those of other countries was unusually small (Hannah 2014).

But this era also witnessed the emergence of a number of extraordinarily large business enterprises, particularly within the railroad industry. The regional railroad systems that were assembled from the merger of smaller railroads, along with the transcontinentals chartered by the federal government, created many corporations whose individual capitalization was equivalent to around 40 percent of the *total* capitalization of all manufacturing companies traded on the Boston Stock Exchange, which was then the most important market for such securities (see Atack and Rousseau 1999).

The growing influence of these firms in ordinary Americans' lives, and the market power they enjoyed over routes where there was no competition from water transportation or other railroads, led to calls for regulation of railroad rate setting. After a halting series of efforts to regulate railroads at the state level, the Interstate Commerce Commission (ICC) was created by the federal government in 1887 to serve that purpose (see Ely 2001). Although the railroads initially resisted the ICC with some success, its creation marked one of the earliest significant efforts on the part of the federal government to regulate businesses, and it was subsequently strengthened by the Hepburn Act of 1906 and the Mann-Elkins Act of 1910.

In addition to transforming domestic transportation and communication, the railroads had a significant impact on financial markets. The construction of a major railroad required enormous sums, which were raised by selling securities through investment banks, both domestically and overseas. Given the relative opacity of railroad operations to early investors, and the resulting information asymmetries between railroad insiders and investors, some historians have argued that the "pecking order" theory of capital structure dictated that railroads rely most heavily on debt, and they indeed often did so (Baskin 1988). Railroads also had excellent collateral in the form of land and equipment, which enabled them to issue debt in the form of mortgage bonds on more favorable terms than firms in other industries. Despite the heavy reliance on debt, railroad equities also gradually became widely held, and dominated trading on the stock market in New York, although these issues were regarded as highly speculative.

Railroads faced a range of unprecedented challenges in running their operations, and were great innovators in developing managerial and accounting systems to address those challenges (Chandler 1977). But the governance problems they faced were equally significant, and perhaps even more difficult to resolve. Railroad insiders found ample opportunities to enrich themselves at the expense of the other investors, by paying themselves exorbitant salaries, engaging in insider trading, or issuing themselves shares of stock in exchange for worthless securities (see Lamoreaux and Rosenthal 2006, 126–127). The transcontinentals, which received subsidies from the federal government, offered their founders even more lucrative strategies for self-enrichment. The directors of the Union Pacific created their own construction company, Crédit Mobilier of America, and hired it to build the line, while also distributing Crédit Mobilier shares to important Congressmen (White 2012).

When exposed, scandals in the management of railroads produced outrage among securities holders. Yet some of the worst manipulations undertaken by those men seemed to violate no law, or in extreme cases, railroad insiders used their political influence to manipulate the law so as to sanction what they had done. The legal system was at times no match for the "railroad barons," and seemed incapable of protecting the interests of securities holders. Adams and Adams (1871) present a detailed narrative of several noteworthy and audacious railroad scandals, and the legal manipulations undertaken by railroad insiders.

Although efforts were made to strengthen the law in response to these episodes, some of the most important changes they produced were not legal. A relatively small number of investment banks had developed the capacity to distribute the large bond issues of railroads, and such scandals infuriated their clients, and threatened their ability to raise capital for the industry. The partners of some of these firms began to take an activist role in the management of railroads, often by holding board seats. This enabled them to monitor the managers, and to offer investors the assurance that they would represent the interests of the railroads' securities holders in the conduct of the business. Particularly following the Panic of 1893, which resulted in a wave of bankruptcies in the industry, investment bankers became heavily involved in the reorganization and governance of railroads (Carosso 1970). The power of bankers was certainly not absolute; efforts to withhold capital from wayward railroad managers who engaged in rate wars or threatened incumbent firms with construction along their lines were not successful. Nonetheless, their influence on management likely curbed the most egregious behavior among railroad executives.

The increasing integration of the economy created by the development of the railroad network made possible the emergence of large-scale manufacturing firms that could potentially distribute their products nationwide. Yet in spite of the Constitution's prohibition against internal tariffs or customs barriers, many states acted to protect local firms through licensing and inspection laws that discriminated against out-of-state competitors. As McCurdy (1978) makes clear, it took the emergence of large firms, which stood to realize significant gains if such barriers were removed, to actually pursue the costly legal challenges to states' protectionist measures. In this sense, large industrial corporations were instrumental in creating a nationally integrated market.

Greater levels of economic integration presented a new set of problems for many producers, in the form of increased competition. In the face of price wars and unstable market conditions, firms in many industries attempted to form cartels by establishing what were called "pools," often through trade associations. In the 1880s, pools were created among the producers of cotton bagging, metal pipes, and in the distilling industry, among others (Ripley 1916). Yet such arrangements were often subject to cheating among the members, and were legally unenforceable—even before they were explicitly prohibited under Sherman Act of 1890 (see Freyer 1992).

Given the problems associated with cartels, in some industries competitors sought to merge. However, many states' corporation laws often presented significant barriers to the acquisition of one corporation's capital stock by another, or to the ownership of property by an out-of-state corporation. Standard Oil developed an innovative solution to this problem, by using the legal form of the trust (hence the term "antitrust"). The trust was used to facilitate combinations in the distilling industry, and in sugar refining. However, later court decisions held these trusts to be illegal (Ripley 1916).

Ultimately a solution to this problem was offered by the state of New Jersey, which hoped to use its corporation statutes as a major source of revenue. In a series of revisions to its corporation laws enacted in the late 1880s and early 1890s, New Jersey granted businesses incorporated in the state the right to hold stock in other corporations—that is, to act as "holding companies." New Jersey also granted its corporations the right to operate in other states; they only needed to establish an office in New Jersey in order to be officially domiciled there (Grandy 1989). In effect, any business could incorporate in New Jersey and utilize the liberal terms of its statutes. A handful of other states quickly moved to emulate New Jersey's statutes and compete for incorporations, with the state of Delaware copying New Jersey's statutes verbatim.

Corporate promoters were quick to take up the newly liberalized statutes. But the impetus to merge was strengthened by the Supreme Court's *E. C. Knight* decision of 1895, which held that a merger of competitors in manufacturing did not violate antitrust laws, even if it absorbed virtually all of the capacity of an industry, since manufacturing was not "commerce." In response, an enormous wave of mergers occurred, which has been denoted the Great Merger Movement. Between 1895 and 1904, more than 1,800 firms were absorbed into mergers, many of which controlled more than 70 percent of their industry's markets (Lamoreaux 1985). As a share of gross domestic product (GDP), this was the largest merger wave in American history. It died down partly in response to the Roosevelt administration's more aggressive pursuit of antitrust cases, in particular the 1904 *Northern Securities* case, which held that a merger of competing railroads violated the Sherman Act.

Many of these mergers, particularly those operating in industries in which there were few barriers to entry, ultimately performed poorly (Dewing 1914). Nonetheless, the Great Merger Movement produced a number of successful firms, and resulted in unprecedented changes in the structure of American business. As was the case in the railroad industries, financiers were frequently represented on the boards of these new enterprises, to help reassure the holders of their securities that management would represent their interests.

THE TWENTIETH CENTURY

The end of the nineteenth century and the beginning of the twentieth witnessed the emergence of large industrial corporations that became vertically integrated. Firms producing new goods, or operating at enormous scale, could no longer rely on traditional supply networks for raw materials, or urban wholesalers for distributing their products; Porter presents numerous illustrations of these problems driving firms to integrate vertically (Porter 2006). In Chandler's formulation, firms replaced the "invisible hand" of market transactions for raw material supplies and for distributing their products with a "visible hand" of a vertically integrated organization that coordinated those functions internally through a managerial bureaucracy (Chandler 1977). Williamson (1981) developed a more formal analysis of the forces that led to this integration, based on the theory of transactions costs. Williamson notes that the asset specificity problem, which arises when an asset is specialized to a single user, and therefore increases the governance costs of market transactions, and the demand externality problem, which arises when the actions taken by a retailer can affect a product's reputation and its sales by other retailers, can be addressed through backward and forward integration—the replacement of market transactions by expanding the boundaries of the firm to encompass all stages of production and distribution. The emergence of vertically integrated manufacturing firms can therefore be seen as a means to minimize transactions costs.

Beginning in the first two decades of the twentieth century, some of these firms began to diversify horizontally, often through acquisitions. Whereas the Great Merger Movement generally consisted of consolidations within a single industry, these acquisitions enabled large firms to diversify into new products and new industries, although they initially tended to be ones that were related to their existing operations. Thus, beginning with firms such as General Motors and Du Pont, industrial conglomerates were born. Chandler (1962) argues that this horizontal diversification ultimately required firms to change their internal organization to a "multidivisional form," as the centralized control structure, or "unitary form," of most firms was ill-suited to coordinating production in multiple markets and industries. Williamson (1975) presents a transactions-cost analysis justifying the multidivisional form's efficiency in the context of a diversified firm.

Although these new industrial conglomerates may have created organizational structures that were well-suited to the challenges they faced, some contemporary economists held that their scale and diffuse ownership insulated them from accountability to their shareholders, and enabled their management to engage in various forms of self-enrichment at the shareholders' expense (Ripley 1915, 1927). The governance of major corporations was examined in detail by Berle and Means (1932), who documented the ownership structures of the 200 largest companies of their time. Berle and Means present a typology of "control structures": private ownership, majority control, minority control, control by legal device, and management control. Their data indicate that many firms were in fact controlled by large shareholders— just as public companies often were in the 1820s (Hilt 2008). They also argue, however, that 32.5 percent of their firms had no significant shareholders, and were therefore subject to management control. Berle and Means do not, however, document any serious consequences associated with this separation of ownership from control, and indeed Adolph Berle (1959) later developed a favorable view of "power without property," in which corporations were run by a kind of "non-statist civil service" of salaried administrators.

Berle and Means also documented the existence of some pyramidal business structures in the early 1930s, which resembled somewhat the "business groups" familiar in other countries today (La Porta, Lopez-de-Silanes, and Shleifer 1999). However, they were almost never created among industrial corporations (Bonbright and Means 1932). Instead, they were used among railroads, and to a much greater extent, among public utilities. For utilities, the complex holding company structures that emerged in the 1920s were created principally in response to local utilities regulation and public service commissions. Thus, to the extent pyramidal structures did emerge in the United States, they were mostly used for industry-specific purposes. Broad, diversified business groups that encompass manufacturing firms and financial institutions, such as those of Asia today, do not seem to have been present (see also Cheffins and Bank 2010).

One element of the governance of major corporations that was not considered by Berle and Means, and yet was the subject of intense public controversy, was the role of financiers. In 1912 the House of Representatives authorized an investigation of the "money trust"—the concentration of control over access to finance among a small number of New York institutions—by a committee headed by Representative Arsène P. Pujo. The committee collected extensive data and documented the nearly ubiquitous presence of prominent financiers on the boards of major nonfinancial corporations. In a series of essays published as the book *Other Peoples' Money and How the Bankers Use It*, Louis Brandeis (1914) used the committee's finding to argue that the control of a small group of elite financiers over access to credit, and over the operations of many important corporations, enabled them to cartelize much of the economy, and enrich themselves at the expense of the shareholders in those companies. These views became quite influential among the public, and in government: several provisions of the Clayton Antitrust Act of 1914 reflected the spirit of the committee's findings.

However, research by financial historians has challenged the Brandeis-Pujo view of the role of investment bankers in the economy (Carosso 1970; Morrison and Wilhelm 2007; O'Sullivan 2015). Econometric analyses by De Long (1991), Ramirez (1995), and Cantillo Simon (1998) all found positive effects of the presence of J. P. Morgan partners on a firm's board. Frydman and Hilt (2017) used a provision of the Clayton Act that prohibited securities underwriters from holding board seats with their client railroads to estimate the effects of banker directorships, and found that the effects were positive. Although their positions as banker-directors created potential conflicts of interest, they also enabled financiers to monitor management and help resolve problems associated with asymmetric information. And as influential "independent" directors, they could also potentially help address problems related to the separation of ownership from control.

The Great Depression and the New Deal fundamentally changed many of the institutions relating to the governance of American corporations, and the organization of the economy. During the 1920s, the rate at which ordinary Americans held financial assets grew rapidly, and the numbers of shareholders of the largest public firms rose into the hundreds of thousands. And a rapid run-up of stock prices beginning in 1927 seemed to herald the beginning of a new era of prosperity (White 2006). The stock market crash of 1929 shattered investors' confidence in financial markets in general, and in the institutions that distributed corporate securities in particular. This led to another congressional investigation of financiers, the Pecora hearings, which produced a number of embarrassing revelations about prominent financiers. Ultimately, the New Deal included a series of new regulations on financiers and financial markets. The Glass-Steagall Act of 1933 prohibited investment banks from engaging in deposit banking or holding directorships with commercial banks. The Securities Exchange Act of 1934 created the first federal securities regulations, and a new agency, the Securities and Exchange Commission, to enforce those regulations. Together, these changes had significant effects on the returns earned by investors on new issues, the governance mechanisms chosen by firms, and likely diminished the role of financiers in corporate governance (Avedian, Cronqvist, and Weidenmier 2015; Simon 1989).

Other new regulations included the Public Utility Holding Company Act of 1935, which was intended to break apart the pyramidal holding company structures that had been created among public utilities, and the Investment Company Act of 1940, which, among other things, restricted the role that mutual funds or other such intermediaries could play in corporate governance (Roe 1994). A new era of regulated and routinized corporate finance was to prevail (Seligman 1982).

Other New Deal policies promoted labor unions, cartelized industries, and established new regulatory commissions. Some of these changes, coupled with the effects of the financial collapse, which differentially impacted smaller and lesser-known firms, may have strengthened the position of large industrial conglomerates in the economy (Bernanke 1983). Over subsequent decades, many such firms continued to expand, and there was something of a "merger mania" that peaked in the 1960s. Careful empirical research has shown that the shareholders of acquirers benefited from these diversification acquisitions (Matsusaka 1993). The market clearly believed that these acquisitions were beneficial.

And yet, beginning in the late 1970s or 1980s, the dominant position of conglomerates began to end. The stock market applied significant discounts to diversified firms (Lang and Stulz 1994). New merger waves aimed at undoing the earlier shifts toward conglomeration and a return to specialization occurred, and firms began to divest unrelated businesses (Kaplan and Weisbach 1992). And new generations of highly specialized and entrepreneurial technology companies became the source of dynamism in the economy.

What accounts for the decline in industrial conglomerates? Increased competition from international firms offering innovative, high-quality products certainly challenged many large American firms, whose bureaucratic managerial structures were seemingly incapable of adapting. But more important, those organizations were created to minimize problems related to transactions costs, and technological changes and innovations in business practice made it possible to address those problems without expanding the boundaries of the firm (Lamoreaux, Raff, and Temin 2003). Vertical integration and conglomeration was no longer necessary, and their limitations began to exceed their advantages.

CONCLUSION AND TOPICS
FOR FUTURE RESEARCH

The discussion in this chapter has characterized the development of business organizations in American history, and has traced out two parallel processes of evolution. Over time, changes in the economic environment presented entrepreneurs with new problems. And simultaneously, the legal and institutional environment evolved, which changed the range of potential solutions available to entrepreneurs.

The problems and solutions found in some eras were unique. For example, the emergence of greater levels of competition among firms in different industries, a product of greater economic integration beginning in the second half of the nineteenth century, combined with a legal environment that seemed to tolerate horizontal mergers, led to an unprecedented wave of consolidation within industries. Once the legal environment changed, as the Roosevelt administration began to pursue stricter antitrust enforcement, the Great Merger Movement died down.

Other problems seem to have always have been present, although the solutions found differed over time. For example, agency problems between controlling insiders and outside investors were an issue for large-scale enterprises in the eighteenth, nineteenth, and early twentieth centuries. They were so ubiquitous that one might consider them an inherent problem. Over time, the solutions utilized to address the problem varied. In the eighteenth and early nineteenth centuries, corporations attempted to address it using graduated voting rights for shareholders. In the late nineteenth century, railroads began to address the problem using the participation of financiers in their governance. During the New Deal, federal securities laws were imposed, which were intended to create new legal mechanisms to address the problem.

A number of interesting questions are raised by the analysis of this chapter, which might serve as productive topics for future research. One question that is quite general in nature is this: To what extent and in what way do legal constraints matter for businesses? That is, if existing statutes do not offer entrepreneurs an appropriate mechanism for addressing a particular problem, is the legal system sufficiently flexible for them to develop their own solutions? For example, if a state was extremely restrictive in granting access to the corporate form, or if its laws imposed extremely restrictive constraints on the ways business organizations could be configured, were fewer firms created? In theory, entrepreneurs could "contract around" such limitations of existing law and, for example, create an unincorporated joint stock company with whatever characteristics they desired. But how well such organizations' claims to limited liability or other attributes normally reserved to corporations would have withstood challenges in the courts is unclear. One promising strategy for investigating this question might be to evaluate the impacts of significant changes in states' laws, particularly if they were implemented in response to political pressures unrelated to prevailing business conditions. If the law truly matters, then sharp changes in the law should be reflected in the rate at which businesses were created or in the survival rates or profitability of businesses.

A second question is more comparative in nature, and relates to unique patterns in the organization of American businesses. Whereas firms in many countries become affiliated together in "business groups" that are often family controlled, this does not seem to have been present in the United States. This is a topic that has aroused some recent controversy; using a particularly broad definition of "business groups," Kandel et al. (2013) argue that they were in fact present up through the mid-twentieth century. The claims of Kandel et al. contradict some of the arguments of Bonbright and Means (1932), as well as Cheffins and Bank (2010). Careful evaluation of these authors' evidence, and perhaps the presentation of new, comprehensive data on the subject, would be quite valuable. But putting aside this debate, if it is indeed the case that business groups were not important phenomena in the United States, an interesting question is, why? For example, why didn't the Rockefellers, whose Standard Oil controlled close to 90 percent of petroleum-refining capacity in the United States, use their enormous incomes to knit together a network of affiliated companies, which might have included banks, railroads, manufacturing and mining firms, and so on?   *opportunities with — later with France*

Finally, the decline of many of America's conglomerates merits further research. An *company ownership* enormous empirical literature developed particularly in the 1990s, which analyzed their valuations and measured the "diversification discount." Yet there has been relatively little work on the deeper causes of their demise. The work of Chandler (1977) and Williamson (1981) held that these organizations were created to minimize transactions costs, and Lamoreaux, Raff, and Temin (2003) have argued that the changing economic environment made available new techniques to address those transactions costs. But much more detailed analysis is necessary in order to fully understand these developments. A careful study of the demise of the conglomerates might shed new light on the forces that led to their creation, and whether the Williamson (1981) analysis was indeed correct.

NOTES

1. Prominent contributions include Baumol (1959), Williamson (1964), and Jensen and Meckling (1976). Some of the analysis of this literature stands somewhat at odds with the conclusions of Chandler (1977).
2. See, for example, Davis (1958) on New England textile corporations; Majewski (1996) on transportation companies; Wright (1999) and Bodenhorn (2012) on banks; Khan (2015) on the corporations of Maine; Hilt and Valentine (2012) on the corporations of New York; and Majewski (2006) on corporations from Pennsylvania.
3. Chronologies of these laws and analyses of their contents are presented in Hamill (1999) and Hilt (2015).
4. A thorough discussion of corporate attributes in the context of modern law is presented in Kraakman et al. (2004).

5. Another feature of partnerships is that their assets may not be fully protected from the demands of the partners' creditors; on the concept of entity shielding, see Hansmann, Kraakman, and Squire (2006).
6. A discussion of the advantages of the form is presented in Guinnane et al. (2007).
7. For example, the state's courts rejected the claims of a creditor that an error in the spelling of the name of the partners in the publication of the certificate was sufficient to strip the special partners of their limited liability. See *Bowen v. Argall*, 24 Wend. 496 (N.Y. 1840).
8. British unincorporated companies, which were quite common given the difficulty of obtaining corporate status, often vested their assets in trustees through a deed of settlement. A trust enabled the firm to obtain some corporate-like characteristics, but also had some important shortcomings (see Freeman, Robin, and Taylor 2012; Harris 2000). The frequency with which American unincorporated companies used the trust form has not been documented.

BIBLIOGRAPHY

Adams, Charles F., and Henry Adams. (1871). *Chapters of Erie, and Other Essays*. Boston: James R. Osgood.

Allen, F., and R. Michaely. (2003). "Payout Policy." In *Handbook of the Economics of Finance*, edited by G. Constantinides, M. Harris, and R. Stulz, 337–429. Amsterdam: North Holland.

Angell, Joseph K., and Samuel Ames. (1832). *A Treatise on the Law of Private Corporations Aggregate*. Boston: Hilliard, Gray, Little & Wilkins.

Atack, Jeremy, and Peter L. Rousseau. (1999). "Business Activity and the Boston Stock Market." *Explorations in Economic History* 36(2): 144–179.

Avedian, Arevik, Henrik Cronqvist, and Marc D. Weidenmier. (2015). "Corporate Governance and the Creation of the SEC." Working Paper.

Ayer, J. C. (1863). *Some of the Usages and Abuses in Our Manufacturing Companies*. Lowell: C. M. Langley.

Baskin, Jonathan B. (1988). "The Development of Corporate Financial Markets in Britain and the United States, 1600–1914: Overcoming Asymmetric Information." *Business History Review* 62: 199–237.

Baskin, Jonathan B., and Paul J. Miranti. (1997). *A History of Corporate Finance*. New York: Cambridge University Press.

Bates, Clement. (1886). *The Law of Limited Partnership*. Boston: Little, Brown.

Baumol, William. (1959). *Business Behavior, Value, and Growth*. New York: Macmillan.

Bebchuck, Lucian A., and Assaf Hamdani. (2002). "Vigorous Race or Leisurely Walk: Reconsidering Competition over Corporate Charters." *Yale Law Journal* 112: 553–615.

Becht, Marco, and J. Bradford Delong. (2005). "Why Has There Been So Little Blockholding in America?" In *A History of Corporate Governance around the World*, edited by R. K. Morck, 613–660. Chicago: University of Chicago Press.

Benmelech, Efraim. (2009). "Asset Salability and Debt Maturity: Evidence from Nineteenth-Century American Railroads." *Review of Financial Studies* 22(4): 1545–1584.

Benmelech, Efraim, and Tobias Moskowitz. (2010). "The Political Economy of Financial Regulation: Evidence from U.S. State Usury Laws in the 19th Century." *Journal of Finance* 65: 1029–1073.

Berle, Adolf A. (1959). *Power Without Property: A New Development in American Political Economy*. New York: Harcourt, Brace.

Berle, Adolf A., and Gardiner C. Means. (1932). *The Modern Corporation and Private Property*. New York: Harcourt, Brace.

Bernanke, Ben. (1983). "Nonmonetary Effects of the Financial Crisis in the Propagation of the Great Depression." *American Economic Review* 73(3): 257–276.

Bodenhorn, Howard. (2006). "Bank Chartering and Political Corruption in Antebellum New York: Free Banking as Reform." In *Corruption and Reform: Lesson's from America's Economic History*, edited by E. L. Glaeser and C. D. Goldin, 231–257. Chicago: University of Chicago Press.

Bodenhorn, Howard. (2011). "Federal and State Commercial Banking Policy in the Federalist Era and Beyond." In *Founding Choices: American Economic Policy in the 1790s*, edited by D. Irwin and R. Sylla, 151–176. Chicago: University of Chicago Press.

Bodenhorn, Howard. (2012). "Voting Rights, Share Concentration and Leverage in Nineteenth-Century U.S. Banks." NBER Working Paper Series, No. 17808.

Bodenhorn, Howard. (2013). "Large Block Shareholders, Institutional Investors, Boards of Directors and Bank Value in the Nineteenth Century." NBER Working Paper Series, No. 18955.

Bonbright, James C., and Gardiner C. Means. (1932). *The Holding Company: Its Public Significance and Its Regulation*. New York: McGraw-Hill.

Boyle, A. J. (1965). "The Minority Shareholder in the Nineteenth Century: A Study in Anglo-American Legal History." *Modern Law Review* 28(3): 317–329.

Braggion, Fabio, and Lyndon Moore. (2011). "Dividend Policies in and Unregulated Market: The London Stock Exchange, 1895–1905." *Review of Financial Studies* 24(9): 2935–2973.

Braggion, Fabio, and Lyndon Moore. (2013). "The Economic Benefits of Political Connections in Late Victorian Britain." *Journal of Economic History* 73(1): 142–176.

Brandeis, Louis D. (1914). *Other People's Money and How the Bankers Use it*. New York: Frederick A Stokes.

Cadman, John W. (1949). *The Corporation in New Jersey: Business and Politics, 1781–1895*. Cambridge, MA: Harvard University Press.

Cantillo Simon, Miguel. (1998). "The Rise and Fall of Bank Control in the United States: 1890–1939." *American Economic Review* 88(5): 1077–1093.

Carosso, Vincent. (1970). *Investment Banking in America*. Cambridge, MA: Harvard University Press.

Carosso, Vincent. (1987). *The Morgans: Private International Bankers, 1854–1913*. Cambridge, MA: Harvard University Press.

Census of Manufactures. (1905). "Department of Commerce and Labor, Bureau of the Census." *Manufactures 1905, Part 1: United States by Industries*. Washington, DC: Government Printing Office.

Chandler, Alfred. (1962). *Strategy and Structure: Chapters in the History of the American Industrial Enterprise*. Cambridge, MA: MIT Press.

Chandler, Alfred. (1977). *The Visible Hand: The Managerial Revolution in American Business*. Cambridge, MA: Harvard University Press.

Chandler, Alfred. (1990). *Scale and Scope: The Dynamics of Industrial Capitalism*. Cambridge, MA: Harvard University Press.

Cheffins, Brian R., and Steven A. Bank. (2010). "The Corporate Pyramid Fable." *Business History Review* 84: 435–458.

Claessens, Stijn, and B. Burcin Yurtoglu. (2013). "Corporate Governance in Emerging Markets." *Emerging Markets Review* 15: 1–33.

Clark, Victor S. (1916). *History of Manufactures in the United States, 1607–1860*. Washington, DC: The Carnegie Institution.

Coffee, John C. (2001). "The Rise of Dispersed Ownership: The Roles of Law and the State in the Separation of Ownership and Control." *Yale Law Journal* 111(1): 1–82.

David, Paul. (1967). "New Light on a Statistical Dark Age." *American Economic Review* 57(2): 294–306.

Davis, Joseph S. (1917). *Essays in the Earlier History of Corporations*. Cambridge, MA: Harvard University Press.

Davis, Lance E. (1958). "Stock Ownership in the Early New England Textile Industry." *Business History Review* 32: 204–222.

Davis, Lance E. (1963). "Capital Immobilities and Finance Capitalism: A Study of Economic Evolution in the United States, 1820–1920." *Explorations in Entrepreneurial History* 2(I): 88–105.

Delong, J. Bradford. (1991). "Did J. P. Morgan's Men Add Value? A Historical Perspective on Financial Capitalism." In *Inside the Business Enterprise*, edited by Peter Temin, 205–236. Chicago: University of Chicago Press.

Dewing, Arthur S. (1914). *Corporate Promotions and Reorganizations*. Cambridge, MA: Harvard University Press.

Dodd, Edwin M. (1938). *Lectures on the Growth of Corporate Structure in the United States with Special Reference to Governmental Regulation*. Cleveland: Cleveland Bar Association.

Dodd, Edwin M. (1954). *American Business Corporations until 1860*. Cambridge, MA: Harvard University Press.

Dunlavy, Colleen A. (2004). "From Citizens to Plutocrats: Nineteenth-Century Shareholder Voting Rights and Theories of the Corporation." In *Constructing Corporate America: History, Politics Culture*, edited by K. Lipartito and D. Sicilia, 66–87. Oxford: Oxford University Press.

Dunlavy, Colleen A. (2006). "Social Conceptions of the Corporation: Insights from the History of Shareholder Voting Rights." *Washington & Lee Law Review* 63: 1347–1387.

Ely, James W. (2001). *Railroads and American Law*. Lawrence: University of Kansas.

Engerman, Stanley L., and Kenneth L. Sokoloff. (2002). "Factor Endowments, Inequality, and Paths of Development among New World Economies." NBER Working Paper No. 9259.

Evans, George H. (1948). *Business Incorporations in the United States, 1800–1943*. New York: National Bureau of Economic Research.

Franks, Julian, Colin Mayer, and Stefano Rossi. (2009). "Ownership: Evolution and Regulation." *Review of Financial Studies* 22(10): 4009–4050.

Freeman, Mark, Robin Pearson, and James Taylor. (2012). *Shareholder Democracies? Corporate Governance in Britain and Ireland before 1850*. Chicago: University of Chicago.

Freyer, Tony. (1992). *Regulating Big Business: Antitrust in Great Britain and America, 1880–1990*. Cambridge: Cambridge University Press.

Frydman, Carola, and Eric Hilt. (2017). "Investment Banks as Corporate Monitors in the Early 20th Century United States." *American Economic Review* 107(7): 1938–1970.

Gillingham, Harrold E. (1933). *Marine Insurance in Philadelphia 1721–1800*. Philadelphia: Patterson and White.

Glaeser, Edward, and Andrei Shleifer. (2003). "Rise of the Regulatory State." *Journal of Economic Literature* 41(2): 401–425.

Gompers, Paul, Ishii, Joy, and Andrew Metrick. (2010). "Extreme Governance: An Analysis of Dual-Class Firms in the U.S." *Review of Financial Studies* 23: 1051–1088.

Goodrich, Carter. (1960). *Government Promotion of American Canals and Railroads.* New York: Columbia University Press.

Gower, L. C. B. (1956). "Some Contrasts between British and American Corporation Law." *Harvard Law Review* 69(8): 1369–1402.

Grandy, Christopher. (1989). "New Jersey Corporate Chartermongering, 1875–1929." *Journal of Economic History* 49(3): 677–692.

Guinnane, Timothy, Ron Harris, Naomi Lamoreaux, and Jean-Laurent Rosenthal. (2007). "Putting the Corporation in Its Place." *Enterprise & Society* 8(3): 687–729.

Hamill, Susan Pace. (1999). "From Special Privilege to General Utility: A Continuation of Willard Hurst's Study of Corporations." *American University Law Review* 49: 81–177.

Hammond, Bray. (1957). *Banks and Politics in America from the Revolution to the Civil War.* Princeton, NJ: Princeton University Press.

Handlin, Oscar, and Mary Flug Handlin. (1945). "Origins of the American Business Corporation." *Journal of Economic History* 5(1): 1–23.

Handlin, Oscar, and Mary Flug Handlin. (1969). *Commonwealth: A Study of the Role of Government in the American Economy: Massachusetts, 1774–1861.* Cambridge, MA: Belknap Press.

Hannah, Leslie. (2010). "The 'Divorce' of Ownership from Control from 1900 Onwards: Calibrating Imagined Global Trends." *Business History* 49(4): 404–438.

Hannah, Leslie. (2014). "A Global Corporate Census: Publicly Traded and Close Companies in 1910." *Economic History Review* 68(2): 548–573.

Hansmann, Henry, Reinier Kraakman, and Richard Squire. (2006). "Law and the Rise of the Firm." *Harvard Law Review* 119: 1335–1403.

Hansmann, Henry, and Mariana Pargendler. (2010). "Voting Restrictions in 19th Century Corporations: Investor Protection or Consumer Protection?" Working Paper, Yale Law School.

Harris, Ron. (2000). *Industrializing English Law: Entrepreneurship and Business Organization, 1720–1844.* New York: Cambridge University Press.

Hartz, Louis. (1948). *Economic Policy and Democratic Thought: Pennsylvania, 1776–1860.* Cambridge, MA: Harvard University Press.

Henderson, Gerard C. (1918). *The Position of Foreign Corporations in American Constitutional Law.* Cambridge, MA: Harvard University Press.

Hilt, Eric. (2006). "Incentives in Corporations: Evidence from the American Whaling Industry." *Journal of Law and Economics* 49: 197–227.

Hilt, Eric. (2008). "When Did Ownership Separate from Control? Corporate Governance in the Early Nineteenth Century." *Journal of Economic History* 68: 645–685.

Hilt, Eric. (2009a). "Rogue Finance: The Life and Fire Insurance Company and the Panic of 1826." *Business History Review* 83: 87–112.

Hilt, Eric. (2009b). "Wall Street's First Corporate Governance Crisis: The Conspiracy Trials of 1826." NBER Working Paper Series, No. 14892.

Hilt, Eric. (2013a). "Corporate Governance and the Development of Manufacturing Enterprises in New England." Working Paper, Wellesley College.

Hilt, Eric. (2013b). "Shareholder Voting Rights in Early American Corporations." *Business History* 55(4): 620–635.

Hilt, Eric. (2015). "Corporation Law and the Shift toward Open Access in the Antebellum United States." NBER Working Paper Series, No. 21195.

Hilt, Eric, and Katharine O'Banion. (2009). "The Limited Partnership in New York, 1822–1858: Partnerships without Kinship." *Journal of Economic History* 69(3): 615–645.

Hilt, Eric, and Jacqueline Valentine. (2012). "Democratic Dividends: Politics, Wealth and Stockholding in New York, 1790–1826." *Journal of Economic History* 72: 332–363.

Holderness, Clifford G., Randall S. Kroszner, and Dennis P. Sheehan. (1999). "Were the Good Old Days That Good? Changes in Managerial Stock Ownership since the Great Depression." *Journal of Finance* 54: 435–469.

Horwitz, Morton. (1977). *The Transformation of American Law, 1780–1860.* Cambridge, MA: Harvard University Press.

Hovenkamp, Herbert. (1991). *Enterprise and American Law, 1836–1937.* Cambridge, MA: Harvard University Press.

Howard, Stanley E. (1934). "The Limited Partnership in New Jersey." *Journal of Business of the University of Chicago* 7(4): 296–317.

Huebner, Solomon. (1903). "The Distribution of Stockholdings in American Railways." *Annals of the American Academy of Political Science* 22(3): 63–78.

Hurst, James W. (1945). *Law and the Conditions of Freedom in the Nineteenth-Century United States.* Madison: University of Wisconsin Press.

Hurst, James W. (1970). *The Legitimacy of the Business Corporation in the Law of the United States, 1780–1970.* Charlottesville: University of Virginia Press.

Jensen, Michael, and William Meckling. (1976). "Theory of the Firm: Managerial Behavior, Agency Costs, and Ownership Structure." *Journal of Financial Economics* 3: 305–360.

Kandel, Eugene, Konstantin Kosenko, Randall Morck, and Yishay Yafeh. (2013). "Business Groups in the United States: A Revised History of Corporate Ownership, Pyramids and Regulation, 1930–1950." NBER Working Paper Series, No. 19691.

Kaplan, Stephen, and Michael Weisbach. (1992). "The Success of Acquisitions: Evidence from Divestitures." *Journal of Finance* 47(1): 107–138.

Kehl, Donald. (1939). "The Origin and Early Development of American Dividend Law." *Harvard Law Review* 53(1): 36–67.

Kessler, William C. (1940). "A Statistical Study of the New York General Incorporation Act of 1811." *Journal of Political Economy* 48: 877–882.

Kessler, William C. (1948). "Incorporation in New England: A Statistical Study, 1800–1875." *Journal of Economic History* 8: 43–62.

Khan, B. Zorina. (2015). "Related Investing: Corporate Ownership and the Dynamics of Capital Mobilization during Early Industrialization." Working Paper.

Kingston, Christopher. (2007). "Marine Insurance in Britain and America, 1720–1844: A Comparative Institutional Analysis." *Journal of Economic History* 67(2): 379–409.

Kingston, Christopher. (2011). "Marine Insurance in Philadelphia during the Quasi-War with France, 1795–1801." *Journal of Economic History* 71(1): 162–184.

Klein, Daniel B., and John Majewski. (1992). "Economy, Community and Law: The Turnpike Movement in New York, 1797–1845." *Law & Society Review* 26(3): 469–512.

Kraakman, Reinier, Paul Davies, Henry Hansmann, Gerad Hertig, Klaus Hopt, Hideki Kanada, and Edward Rock. (2004). *The Anatomy of Corporate Law.* New York: Oxford University Press.

Kroszner, Randall S., and Raghuram G. Rajan. (1997). "Organization Structure and Credibility: Evidence from Commercial Bank Securities Activities before the Glass-Steagall Act." *Journal of Monetary Economics* 39(4): 475–516.

Kroszner, Randall S., and Philip E. Strahan. (2001). "Bankers on Boards: Monitoring, Conflicts of Interest, and Lender Liability." *Journal of Financial Economics* 62(3): 415–452.

Lamoreaux, Naomi. (1985). *The Great Merger Movement in American Business, 1895–1904*. New York: Cambridge University Press.

Lamoreaux, Naomi. (1996). *Insider Lending: Banks, Personal Connections and Economic Development in Industrial New England*. New York: Cambridge University Press.

Lamoreaux, Naomi R. (1997). "The Partnership Form of Organization: Its Popularity in Early Nineteenth-Century Boston." In *Entrepreneurs: The Boston Business Community, 1750–1850*, edited by C. E. Wright and K. P. Viens. Boston: Massachusetts Historical Society.

Lamoreaux, Naomi. (2009). "Scylla or Charybdis? Historical Reflections on Two Basic Problems of Corporate Governance." *Business History Review* 83: 9–34.

Lamoreaux, Naomi. (2014). "Revisiting American Exceptionalism: Democracy and the Regulation of Corporate Governance in Nineteenth-Century Pennsylvania." NBER Working Paper Series, No. 20231.

Lamoreaux, Naomi, and Christopher Glaisek. (1991). "Vehicles of Privilege or Mobility? Banks in Providence, Rhode Island during the Age of Jackson." *Business History Review* 65: 502–527.

Lamoreaux, Naomi, Daniel Raff, and Peter Temin. (2003). "Beyond Markets and Hierarchies: Toward a New Synthesis in American Business History." *American Historical Review* 108(2): 404–433.

Lamoreaux, Naomi, and Jean-Laurent Rosenthal. (2005). "Legal Regime and Business's Organizational Choice: A Comparison of France and the United States during the Era of Industrialization." *American Law and Economics Review* 7: 28–61.

Lamoreaux, Naomi, and Jean-Laurent Rosenthal. (2006). "Corporate Governance and Minority Shareholders in the United States before the Great Depression." In *Corruption and Reform: Lessons from America's Economic History*, edited by E. L. Glaeser and C. D. Goldin, 125–152. Chicago: University of Chicago Press.

Lang, Harry, and Rene Stulz. (1994). "Tobin's Q, Corporate Diversification, and Firm Performance." *Journal of Political Economy* 102: 1248–1280.

La Porta, Rafael, Florencio Lopez-de-Silanes, and Andrei Shleifer. (1999). "Corporate Ownership around the World." *Journal of Finance* 54(2): 471–517.

La Porta, Rafael, Florencio Lopez-de-Silanes, and Andrei Shleifer. (2008). "The Economic Consequences of Legal Origins." *Journal of Economic Literature* 46(2): 285–332.

La Porta, Rafael, Florencio Lopez-de-Silanes, Andrei Shleifer, and Robert W. Vishny. (1997). "Legal Determinants of External Finance." *Journal of Finance* 52: 1131–1150.

La Porta, Rafael, Florencio Lopez-de-Silanez, Andrei Shleifer, and Robert W. Vishny. (1998). "Law and Finance." *Journal of Political Economy*, 106: 1113–1155.

Larcom, Russel C. (1937). *The Delaware Corporation*. Baltimore, MD: Johns Hopkins University Press.

Livermore, Shaw. (1939). *Early American Land Companies: Their Influence on Corporate Development*. New York: Commonwealth Fund.

Mahoney, Paul G. (2003). "The Origins of Blue-Sky Laws: A Test of Competing Hypotheses." *Journal of Law and Economics* 46: 229–251.

Maier, Pauline. (1993). "The Revolutionary Origins of the American Corporation." *William & Mary Quarterly* L(1): 51–84.

Majewski, John. (1996). "Who Financed the Transportation Revolution? Regional Divergence and Internal Improvements in Antebellum Pennsylvania and Virginia." *Journal of Economic History* 56: 763–788.

Majewski, John. (2006). "Toward a Social History of the Corporation: Shareholding in Pennsylvania, 1800–1840." In *The Economy of Early America: Historical Perspectives and New Directions*, edited by C. Matson, 294–316. Philadelphia: University of Pennsylvania.

Martin, Albro. (1971). *Enterprise Denied: Origins and Decline of the American Railroads, 1897–1917.* New York: Columbia University Press.

Martin, Joseph G. (1886). *Martin's Boston Stock Market*. Boston: Author.

Matsusaka, John G. (1993). "Takeover Motives during the Conglomerate Merger Wave." *RAND Journal of Economics* 24(3): 357–379.

McCraw, Thomas K. (1984). *Prophets of Regulation*. Cambridge, MA: Belknap Press.

McCurdy, Charles. (1978). "American Law and the Marketing Structure of the Large Corporation, 18751890." *Journal of Economic History* 38(3): 631–649.

McGouldrick, Paul F. (1968). *New England Textiles in the Nineteenth Century*. Cambridge, MA: Harvard University Press.

Mitchell, Lawrence E. (2007). *The Speculation Economy: How Finance Triumphed over Industry*. San Francisco: Berrett-Koehler.

Moody, John. (1904). *The Truth about the Trusts*. New York: Moody.

Morck, Randall. (2005a). "How to Eliminate Pyramidal Business Groups: The Double Taxation of Inter-corporate Dividends and Other Incisive Uses of Tax Policy." In *Tax Policy and the Economy*, edited by J. Poterba, 19: 135–179. Cambridge, MA: MIT Press.

Morck, Randall, ed. (2005b). *A History of Corporate Governance around the World*. Chicago: University of Chicago Press.

Morck, Randall. (2011). "Finance and Governance in Developing Countries." NBER Working Paper No. 16870.

Morck, Randall, and Bernard Yeung. (2005). "Dividend Taxation and Corporate Governance." *Journal of Economic Perspectives* 19(3): 163–180. Cambridge, MA: MIT Press.

Morrison, Alan D., and William J. Wilhelm. (2007). *Investment Banking: Institutions, Politics and Law*. Oxford: Oxford University Press.

Musacchio, Aldo. (2009). *Experiments in Financial Democracy: Corporate Governance and Financial Development in Brazil, 1882–1950*. New York: Cambridge University Press.

Nevins, Allen, and Milton H. Thomas, eds. (1952). *The Diary of George Templeton Strong*, 4 vols. New York: Macmillan.

North, Douglass C., John J. Wallis, and Barry R. Weingast. (2009). *Violence and Social Orders: A Conceptual Framework for Interpreting Recorded Human History*. New York: Cambridge.

O'Sullivan, Mary. (2015). "Too Much Ado about Morgan's Men: The U.S. Securities Markets, 1908–1914." Working Paper.

Pak, Susie J. (2013). *Gentlemen Bankers: The World of J. P. Morgan*. Cambridge, MA: Harvard University Press.

Porter, Glenn. (2006). *The Rise of Big Business, 1860–1920*. New York: John Wiley & Sons.

Porter, Glenn, and Harold C. Livesay. (1971). *Merchants and Manufacturers: Studies in the Changing Structure of Nineteenth-Century Marketing*. Baltimore, MD: Johns Hopkins University Press.

Pujo Committee. House Committee on Banking and Currency. (1913). *Money Trust Investigation*. Washington, DC: Government Printing Office.

Rajan, Raghuram G., and Luigi Zingales. (2003). "The Great Reversals: The Politics of Financial Development in the 20th Century." *Journal of Financial Economics* 69: 5–50.

Ramirez, Carlos D. (1995). "Did J. P. Morgan's Men Add Liquidity? Corporate Investment, Cash Flow, and Financial Structure at the Turn of the Twentieth Century." *Journal of Finance* 50(2): 661–678.

Ratner, David L. (1970). "The Government of Business Corporations: Critical Reflections on the Rule of One Share, One Vote." *Cornell Law Review* 56: 1–56.

Redlich, Fritz. (1951). *The Molding of American Banking: Men and Ideas.* New York: Hafner.

Ripley, William Z. (1915). *Railroads: Finance and Organization.* New York: Longmans.

Ripley, William Z. (1916). *Trusts, Pools, and Corporations.* New York: Ginn.

Ripley, William Z. (1927). *Main Street and Wall Street.* Boston: Little Brown.

Roe, Mark. (1994). *Strong Managers, Weak Owners: The Political Roots of American Corporate Finance.* Princeton, NJ: Princeton University Press.

Rowley, Scott. (1916). *The Modern Law of Partnership.* Indianapolis: Bobbs-Merrill.

Scott, William R. (1912). *The Constitution and Finance of English, Scottish, and Irish Joint-Stock Companies to 1720.* Cambridge, England: The University Press.

Scranton, Philip. (1983). *Proprietary Capitalism: The Textile Manufacture at Philadelphia, 1800–1885.* New York: Cambridge University Press.

Scranton, Philip. (1997). *Endless Novelty: Specialty Production and American Industrialization, 1865–1925.* Princeton, NJ: Princeton University Press.

Seavoy, Ronald E. (1982). *The Origins of the American Business Corporation, 1784–1855.* Westport, CT: Greenview Press.

Seligman, Joel. (1976). "A Brief History of Delaware's General Corporation Law of 1899." *Delaware Journal of Corporate Law* 1(2): 249–287.

Seligman, Joel. (1982). *The Transformation of Wall Street: A History of the Securities and Exchange Commission and Modern Corporate Finance.* Boston: Houghton Mifflin.

Simon, Carol J. (1989). "The Effect of the 1933 Securities Act on Investor Information and the Performance of New Issues." *American Economic Review* 79(3): 295–318.

Strouse, Jean. (2000). *Morgan: American Financier.* New York: HarperPerrenial.

Sylla, Richard, and Robert E. Wright. (2013). "Corporation Formation in the Antebellum United States in Comparative Context." *Business History* 55(4): 653–669.

Troubat, Francis J. (1853). *The Law of Commandatary and Limited Partnerships in the United States.* Philadelphia: James Kay, Jun, & Brother.

Villalonga, Belen, and Raphael Amit. (2009). "How Are U.S. Family Firms Controlled?" *Review of Financial Studies* 22(8): 3047–3091.

Wallis, John. (2003). "Market-Augmenting Government? States and Corporations in Nineteenth-Century America." In *Market-Augmenting Government*, edited by O. Azfar and C. Cadwell, 223–265. Ann Arbor: University of Michigan Press.

Wallis, John. (2006). "The Concept of Systematic Corruption in American History." In *Corruption and Reform: Lesson's from America's Economic History*, edited by E. L. Glaeser and C. D. Goldin, 23–62. Chicago: University of Chicago Press, 2006.

Ware, Caroline F. (1931). *The Early New England Cotton Manufacture.* New York: Houghton Mifflin.

Warren, Edward H. (1929). *Corporate Advantages without Incorporation.* New York: Baker, Voorhis.

Warshow, H. T. (1924). "The Distribution of Corporate Ownership in the United States." *Quarterly Journal of Economics* 39(1): 15–38.

Werner, Walter. (1986). "Corporate Law in Search of Its Future." *Columbia Law Review* 81: 1610–1666.

Werner, Walter, and Steven T. Smith. (1991). *Wall Street*. New York: Columbia University Press.

White, Eugene N. (2006). "Bubbles and Busts: The 1990s in the Mirror of the 1920s." NBER Working Paper Series, No. 12138.

White, Richard. (2012). *Railroaded: The Transcontinentals and the Making of Modern America*. New York: W. W. Norton.

Williamson, Oliver. (1964). *The Economics of Discretionary Behavior: Managerial Objectives in a Theory of the Firm*. Englewood Cliffs, NJ: Prentice Hall.

Williamson, Oliver. (1975). *Markets and Hierarchies: Analysis and Antitrust Implications*. New York: Macmillan.

Williamson, Oliver. (1981). "The Modern Corporation: Origins, Evolution, Attributes." *Journal of Economic Literature* 19(4): 1537–1568.

Wright, Robert E. (1999). "Bank Ownership and Lending Patterns in New York and Pennsylvania, 1781–1831." *Business History Review* 73: 40–60.

Wright, Robert E. (2002). *The Wealth of Nations Rediscovered: Integration and Expansion in American Financial Markets, 1780–1850*. New York: Cambridge University Press.

Wright, Robert E. (2013). *Corporation Nation*. Philadelphia: University of Pennsylvania Press.

CHAPTER 12

....

EXECUTIVE COMPENSATION IN AMERICAN ECONOMIC HISTORY

....

CAROLA FRYDMAN

EVER since the rise of large corporations at the turn of the twentieth century, top executives have composed a small but central part of the American labor force. Their decisions affect the fortunes of some of the largest enterprises in the economy. By influencing managerial decisions, compensation contracts can have a meaningful impact on firm outcomes and, more generally, on economic growth. While the careers and compensation of top managers have received much attention in recent decades, our understanding of the long-run trends in executive pay is more limited.[1]

The history of executive compensation is intimately related to the rise of big business. Until the mid-nineteenth century, production took place in small business units, where there was often little or no distinction between owners, managers, and workers. The development of railroads, the first modern business enterprises, brought about the professionalization of managers, among many other changes. The building of large railroad systems in the 1880s and 1890s required full-time salaried managers at the top who could develop strategies for their firms' long-term growth, including establishing alliances with other railroads, and making allocation and investment decisions. But these managers' ability to act independently was often curtailed by active boards that, representing large owners or financing interests, did not always shy away from intervening in managerial decisions.

From 1895 to 1904, the American economy experienced a radical process of industrial "trustification" that transformed the organization of manufacturing and the ownership of corporations. During this period, a vast number of manufacturing firms combined to form large consolidated corporations, many of which dominated their industries (Lamoreaux 1988). These behemoths often integrated backward into the supply of inputs, and forward into distribution, marketing, and financing. The increased scale and scope of industrial businesses required a team of professional top managers—individuals who, much as modern executives, were not entrepreneurs, and who often held little or no stock ownership in the company (Chandler 1977).

The formation of large businesses brought about an increased separation of corporate ownership from corporate control, which in turn gave incentives to chief executives and other top managers to make decisions that maximized their own welfare, even if these actions were costly to shareholders (Berle and Means 1932). In the early 1920s, the widespread use of the multidivisional form of organization made decision-making even more decentralized, and increased the importance of managers below the chief executive officer (CEO) rank. The separation of ownership from control, and the existence of a decentralized hierarchy of top and middle managers with control rights gave rise to the typical principal-agent problem. As they are today, compensation contracts emerged as one plausible mechanism to incentivize managers, and therefore to alleviate the agency problem.

Relatively little is known about the level and structure of executive compensation prior to the 1930s. For the most part, the pay of top managers was a closely guarded secret. Thus, the historical evidence on executive salaries available for this period is relatively scattered, based on court cases, survey data, or anecdotes—any glimpses they give us into the pay of top managers hardly can be argued to be representative. More systematic revelations regarding the level of pay first occurred during World War I, when railroad corporations became managed by the federal government and the exorbitant salaries of railroad officers were exposed. Public scrutiny intensified during the 1920s, when the compensation of railroad and banking executives were published in the popular press. By the early 1930s, the controversy surrounding the level of pay had extended to executives in all kinds of businesses. As the economy slipped into the Great Depression, the nation became increasingly troubled by the lavish stipends and bonuses awarded to the leaders of large public corporations. Prompted by these concerns, the Reconstruction Finance Corporation, the Federal Trade Commission, and several other government agencies began to request information on the compensation of officials in firms under their respective jurisdictions. Finally, the creation of the Securities and Exchange Commission (SEC) in 1934 made the disclosure of executive compensation mandatory for all publicly traded firms. It was only then that a comprehensive and systematic analysis into executive compensation could properly begin.

EXECUTIVE COMPENSATION FROM 1936 TO THE PRESENT

Since 1935, American publicly traded companies have disclosed the compensation of their highest paid executives in 10-K filings and proxy statements (DEF 14A SEC forms). Disclosure requirements have changed substantially over time; the number of executives and the forms of pay that are reported has grown, and the information contained in proxy statements has become more detailed. For example, firms were not required to report perquisites until the late 1970s, and the actuarial value of pension benefits was first included in these statements in 2006. In 2006, the accounting standards also began to require the reporting of the estimated fair value of stock options and equity-based compensation. These changes in reporting regimes make comparisons over time for some forms of pay—particularly, for equity-based pay and incentive bonuses—more difficult. Yet salaries, bonuses, equity holdings, and stock options can be tracked in a relatively consistent manner. And despite these limitations, proxy statements are the best primary source of information on the compensation of top executives.

Frydman and Saks (2010b) present the longest consistent time series evidence on executive pay available to date. Utilizing the historical collection of annual proxy statements and 10-K forms at Baker Library, they construct a consistent data set containing detailed information on the compensation of the five highest paid executives in the fifty largest firms in 1940, 1960, and 1990—a total of 101 firms—from 1936 to 2005. This sample is broadly representative of the largest three hundred publicly traded corporations in each year. It does not, however, cover small firms, and it presents very limited industry variation. The micro-data can be accessed at the authors' websites.

Researchers focusing on recent decades will find Standard and Poors' Execucomp database, available at the Wharton Research Data Services (https://wrds-web.wharton. upenn.edu/wrds/), particularly useful. Execucomp provides data collected from the proxy statements for up to nine executives in the Standard & Poor's (S&P) 500 firms for 1992 and 1993 and, starting in 1994, for all companies included in the S&P 500, S&P MidCap 400, S&P SmallCap 600 indices, as well as some additional firms—covering roughly 1,800 companies each year.

Besides these two publicly available data sets, other researchers working on executive compensation have constructed and analyzed data based on various primary sources. Hall and Liebman (1998) utilize proxy statements to analyze the compensation and equity holdings of chief executives for roughly 500 firms from 1980 to 1994, effectively extending the coverage of Execucomp for CEOs for more than a decade. Frydman and Molloy (2012) utilize reports based on proxy statements published by the National Industrial Conference Board during 1940s—the only period of great compression in executive pay—to study changes in salaries and bonuses for about 250 firms of various sizes. Other useful data sources for historical research include the Forbes compensation surveys for the 1970–1991 period, which report the realized pay for the CEOs of the largest 800 firms in the economy, and the Work Projects Administration data, which contain information on the salary and bonus paid to the highest paid executives based on proxy statements for about 800 large corporations from 1934 to 1938 (see Jensen and Murphy 1990).

It is important to note that the available data sources only provide a consistent view of the long-run changes in the level and structure of executive pay for large, publicly traded corporations. Very little is known about the remuneration of those managing small or privately held firms in the United States, both in recent years and in the past. The analysis of the historical trends is therefore focused on the compensation of the managers of large, publicly traded corporations.

Much of the debate on executive pay in recent years has centered on whether executives are paid too much, and whether they are properly incentivized. Therefore, it is necessary to start by describing the long-run changes in the level and the structure of pay, and in the incentives that managers receive through their compensation contracts. To provide a long-run view, the discussion in this chapter is primarily based on the Frydman-Saks data. For consistency, the analysis is based on the three highest-paid executives in the sample—consisting primarily of presidents, chairmen, CEOs, executive vice presidents, and other top officers.[2]

Much of the literature on executive pay focuses on the "ex-ante" grant-date value of compensation, which approximates the cost to the company at the time that the remuneration is awarded. This measure of pay is appropriate, for example, to analyze the role of corporate governance in determining executive compensation. While calculating this estimated, ex-ante value of compensation over the long run is straightforward for some forms of pay, for other types of pay (such as deferred bonuses or long-term incentive plans) historical proxy statements often report the cash payments received by an executive in a given year for bonuses awarded in prior years. For these forms of pay, one is forced to use the realized payments. The grant value of employee stock options can be measured using the Black-Scholes formula. To calculate this value, some of the inputs for this formula sometimes need to be imputed.

Another measure of pay is the actual or realized value of compensation, which measures the value that the executive takes home in a given year. This measure is appropriate, for example, to calculate the managers' elasticity of taxable income—that is, the percent change in taxable pay for a 1 percent change in the effective income tax rate. While it is often possible to estimate the realized value from exercised stock options, proxy statements do not always provide a measure of the amount received from deferred bonuses that are contingent on reaching certain performance targets, or the value of payouts from vested restricted stock.

Finally, the academic literature often ignores that risk-averse and undiversified executives will value riskier forms of compensation less than what these types of pay cost to their firms. Appropriately adjusting each form of pay for the risk premium of executives is nontrivial, and it is generally sensitive to the choice of models and parameters.[3]

The total annual compensation can be defined as the sum of salaries, current bonuses, value of cash or stock paid out from long-term incentive payments, and the Black-Scholes value of stock option grants. Using the Frydman-Saks data, table 12.1 presents the evolution of annual compensation for the three highest-paid executives in large American publicly traded corporations calculated over five- to ten-year intervals from 1936 to 2005. It begins by analyzing the change in the median level of pay. Since the Frydman-Saks sample is broadly representative of the largest three hundred publicly traded corporations in each year, the trends in median compensation can be interpreted as describing the evolution of pay for the typical executive of the 150th largest publicly traded firm in the economy.

Table 12.1 Level and Structure of Total Compensation by Percentile and CEO Status, 1936–2005

	1936–1939	1940–1945	1946–1949	1950–1959	1960–1969	1970–1979	1980–1989	1990–1999	2000–2005
Panel A: Level of Total Compensation (Millions of Year 2000 Dollars)									
Three highest-paid officers									
10th percentile	0.36	0.4	0.36	0.39	0.45	0.47	0.57	0.91	1.31
25th percentile	0.53	0.59	0.53	0.55	0.60	0.64	0.85	1.35	2.19
50th percentile	0.85	0.80	0.72	0.77	0.83	0.93	1.33	2.36	4.08
75th percentile	1.24	1.15	1.01	1.09	1.18	1.31	2.05	4.43	9.42
90th percentile	1.80	1.59	1.53	1.63	1.66	1.84	3.18	8.29	16.9
Average	0.97	0.95	0.85	0.94	0.99	1.09	1.74	4.35	7.63
Median CEO	1.11	1.07	0.90	0.97	0.99	1.17	1.81	4.09	9.20
Median other top officers	0.74	0.70	0.65	0.67	0.74	0.82	1.12	1.89	3.02
Within-firm ratio of CEO to other top officers	1.50	1.48	1.38	1.43	1.29	1.42	1.58	2.00	2.58
Panel B: Structure of Compensation									
Average long-term pay / Total compensation									
CEOs	0.00	0.01	0.01	0.03	0.06	0.05	0.07	0.15	0.23
Other top officers	0.00	0.01	0.01	0.03	0.05	0.05	0.07	0.15	0.22
Average stock option grants / Total compensation									
CEOs	0.00	0.00	0.00	0.04	0.07	0.11	0.19	0.32	0.37
Other top officers	0.00	0.00	0.00	0.03	0.05	0.10	0.17	0.27	0.31
Panel C: Stock Holdings									
Median fractional stock holdings	0.118	0.045	0.034	0.035	0.037	0.023	0.019	0.030	0.028

Source: Frydman and Saks (2010b).

Notes: Based on the three highest-paid officers in the largest 50 firms in 1940, 1960, and 1990 in the Frydman–Saks data. Total compensation is the sum of salaries, bonuses, long-term bonus payments, and the Black–Scholes value of stock option grants. Long-term pay is payouts from prior long-term bonus awards. In firms where the title CEO is not used, the CEO is identified as the president. Other top officers include any executive among the three highest-paid who is not the CEO. The within–firm ratio is the median across firms of the ratio of the CEO's total compensation to the average pay of the two other highest-paid officers. Median executive to average worker wages is the average across years of the ratio of the pay of the median top executive in each year in the decade to the wages of the average worker in that year from the National Income and Product Accounts. Fractional stock holdings are the shares held by executives relative to the total number of shares outstanding at the 50th percentile, multiplied by 100. Dollar values are in inflation–adjusted 2000 dollars.

Panel A of table 12.1 reveals a J-shaped pattern in executive compensation over the 1936–2005 period. The real value of median total pay experienced a sharp decline during World War II, which continued, though at a slower rate, in the late 1940s. Frydman and Molloy (2012) suggest that a strengthening in the power of labor unions may have been partly responsible for the compression in pay during the 1940s. Executive pay increased slowly from the early 1950s to the mid-1970s at an average rate of about 0.8 percent per year. The pace of growth accelerated quickly from the mid-1970s to until almost the end of the sample in 2005. The increase in compensation over this period was most pronounced in the 1990s, when growth rates reached more than 10 percent per year.

The high levels of CEO pay have continued in recent years, despite the economic downturns (and the concomitant reductions in compensation) of the first decade of the 2000s. Analyzing the trends in pay from 1992 to 2011, Murphy shows that the grant-date compensation for the median CEO in S&P 500 firms bottomed out at $7.4 million (measured in year 2011 US dollars) in 2009. By 2011, median CEO pay had reached $9.0 million, almost back to the peak level of $9.3 million experienced in 2006, and more than three times the value of median compensation in 1992 (Murphy 2013). Moreover, the pay of the chief executives of SmallCap 600 and MidCap 400 S&P firms increased almost steadily over this period, from a median level of $1.5 million in 1992 to just above $3 million in 2011.

Thus far, the median has been selected as the statistic to describe the aggregate changes in compensation. Because executive pay is highly skewed, using averages amplifies the changes in pay. For example, median executive pay grew by 380 percent from the late 1930s to the early 2000s, while the increase in average pay was a much steeper 687 percent over the same period. Focusing on medians is therefore important if the goal is to analyze the experience of the typical manager, particularly during periods of rapid growth in pay or when comparing the remuneration of top executives to the wages of workers.

Table 12.1 also shows that the distribution of compensation has exhibited a relatively similar pattern to the changes in median pay over time. However, the decrease in the real value of pay in the 1940s, and its rapid increase since the 1980s, were both more pronounced at the top end of the distribution. In recent decades, the rise in the compensation of the highest-paid executives has been so rapid that inequality among executives has increased noticeably. Whereas the ratio of total pay at the ninetieth to the fiftieth percentile fluctuated between 1.8 and 2.4 from 1936 to 1980, this gap rose to more than 3.5 by 2005. A similar pattern is evidenced within firms, as described by the total pay of the CEO relative to the average compensation of the other two highest-paid officers in the firm. This ratio hovered around 1.4 until the 1970s, but it has risen steadily since then. By the end of the sample in the middle of the first decade of the 2000s, CEOs earned about 2.6 times more than the other two top executives in their firm. This pattern suggests that the returns to being the main decision-maker in large corporations have increased significantly since the 1980s.

Top executives have been among the highest income earners in the economy throughout the past century, so it is perhaps not surprising that the trends in executive pay relative to other workers have been similar to the evolution of income inequality at the top of the income distribution. Figure 12.1 presents the long-run changes in top income and wage inequality in the economy, based on the influential work of Piketty and Saez (2003), and contrasts it with the earnings disparities between executives and workers from 1936 to 2005. The square line in figure 12.1, measured against the right axis, presents the fraction of total income (excluding capital gains) that accrued to the taxpayers at the top 0.1 percent of the distribution.[4] According to this measure, income inequality has followed a U-shaped pattern over the twentieth century. The top 0.1 percent of income earners received 6.7 percent of the total income in 1936, but this fraction declined rapidly during the 1940s, and it was less than 2 percent in the early 1970s. Since then, the concentration of income at the top experienced a relentless increase, and it surpassed its prewar levels by the end of the sample period. The disparities in labor earnings at the top of the distribution, however, followed a J-shaped pattern over time. The triangle line in figure 12.1 displays the share of the top 0.1 wage income group. These tax units accounted for 4.53 percent of the wage income at the end of the sample in 2005, almost twice more than their level in the late 1930s.

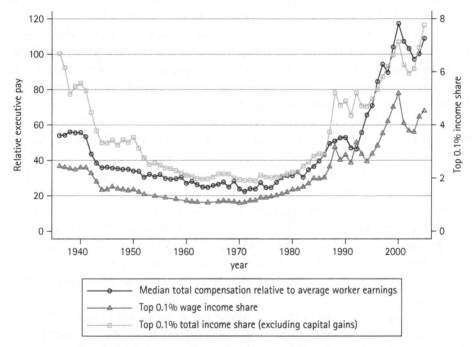

FIGURE 12.1. Trends in relative executive pay and income inequality, 1936–2005

Notes: The circle line, displayed on the left axis, presents the ratio of median total pay for the three highest-paid officers in the Frydman-Saks data relative to average worker earnings in the economy. Average worker earnings are the wages and salaries per full-time equivalent employee obtained from Table 6.6 of the National Income and Product Accounts. The right axis presents two measures of income inequality. The square line displays the share of total income (excluding capital gains) accrued to the top 0.1 percent of the distribution, based on column (5) of Table A1 in Piketty and Saez (2003; online version updated on June 2015). The triangle line presents the top 0.1 percent wage income share, as reported in column (6) of Table B2 in Piketty and Saez (2003; online version updated on June 2015).

Sources: Frydman and Saks (2010b); Piketty and Saez (2003).

These remarkable changes in income inequality over time are also evidenced when contrasting the pay of top executives with those of workers. The circle line in figure 12.1 (with its scale displayed on the left axis) presents the ratio of median executive pay in the Frydman-Saks data to the earnings of the average worker in the economy. This measure of labor income inequality also followed a J-shaped pattern over the twentieth century: a rapid decline in executive-to-worker earnings in the 1940s was followed by a smaller but steady contraction up to the 1970s; inequality then increased at a rapid pace from the 1980s to the end of the sample. In the first five years of the 2000s, the median executive earned about 106 times more than the average worker in the economy, about double the level of inequality in the pre–War World II period. While this approach focuses on median executive compensation to calculate this relative pay measure, the academic literature and the popular press often use the mean level of CEO pay instead. But the distribution of executive pay has become much more skewed since the 1980s. Focusing on the compensation for the average executive therefore results in a much more exacerbated increase in inequality. Since average executive pay may be less informative of the experience for the typical top manager, a ratio based on median executive pay may reflect more accurately the overall changes in the dispersion in pay between executives and workers.

In sum, the trends in income inequality at the top and in relative executive pay have been relatively similar since the 1930s. It is important to note that comparisons between these two sources of data should be interpreted cautiously; the Piketty-Saez information is based on the incomes of tax units, while the compensation data represent the pay earned by individuals.[5] Moreover, both sources focus exclusively on the changes in income inequality at the very top of the distribution.[6]

Panel B of table 12.1 presents the evolution of the major components of executive compensation, using again the Frydman-Saks data. Total compensation is divided into three main forms of pay: salaries and current bonuses, payments from long-term incentive plans, and the grant value of stock options. From 1936 to the 1950s, the pay of top executives was composed mainly of salaries and annual bonuses. As they are today, these bonuses were typically nondiscretionary, tied to one or more measures of accounting performance, and paid in either cash or stock. Payments from long-term incentive plans were paid out over several years, again with payment in either cash or stock. These long-term rewards started to make a noticeable impact on the level of pay in the 1960s, and became sizable toward the end of the sample, primarily due to the increasing use of restricted stock plans.

The most striking change in the structure of pay is the surge in stock option compensation since the 1980s. By tying remuneration directly to share price, stock options give executives an incentive to increase shareholder value. The use of stock options was negligible until 1950, when the Revenue Act established that the payoffs from certain types of employee stock options (called "restricted" options) could be taxed at the capital gains rate rather than at the much higher labor income tax rate that was prevalent at that time. Although many firms quickly adopted restricted stock option plans, the frequency of option grants remained too small to have much of an impact on median pay levels until the late 1970s.

During the 1980s and especially the 1990s, stock options surged to become the largest component of executive pay, particularly for chief executive officers. Option compensation comprised about 20 percent of CEO pay in the 1980s but rose to about 37 percent on average in the early 2000s. The rapid expansion in stock option use during the 1990s coincided with an increased awareness of the value of providing incentives by linking CEO pay to share prices following Jensen and Murphy's seminal paper of 1990. The use of employee stock options has declined during the last decade, perhaps due to the stock market downturn of 2000–2001 and the introduction of mandatory option expensing in 2005. But the importance of equity-based pay in compensation packages has remained strong since the popularity of restricted stock grants increased over time as the use of stock options dwindled. In 2011, stock awards accounted for 33 percent of the median total pay for the CEOs of S&P 500 companies, whereas the value of stock options granted represented only 16 percent of their pay. While the value of other components of pay has increased over time, the majority of the overall rise in CEO pay since the 1980s is explained by the increase in equity-based pay, in the form of stock options and restricted stock awards.

Although most of the analysis of executive pay has focused on salaries, bonuses, and stock options, executives are remunerated with various other forms of pay, including, among others, perquisites, signing bonuses, pension benefits, and termination payments. These important components of pay packages have received less attention because of a lack of data. In recent years, a series of improvements to disclosure rules introduced by the Securities and Exchange Commission (SEC) have shed new light on these pay components. For example, Murphy (2013) documents that these forms of "other compensation" accounted for about 7 percent of the total pay for the median CEO of S&P 500 corporations in 2011. While there is little hope of providing information of similar quality for earlier periods, it may still be possible to improve our understanding of the long-run trends for some of these forms of pay (in particular, for pensions) with careful use of historical primary sources.

Since the use of equity-based pay is widespread, executives typically hold a nonnegligible portion of their firms' shares outstanding. Historically, some top executives also had high ownership stakes because they belonged to the firms' founding family. Fractional equity ownership is not, strictly speaking, a form of compensation—an executive's current stock of his firm's shares is typically much higher than those awarded in his current paycheck, and he may have acquired those shares in ways other than direct compensation. However, equity stakes do play a significant role in determining managerial incentives. Thus, Panel C of table 12.1 presents the evolution of the fractional ownership for the median executive in the sample. Equity holdings relative to the firm's total number of shares outstanding have mostly declined over the century, with most of the contraction occurring during World War II. By 2005, median fractional stock holdings were about one-third of their peak level in the 1930s, when the median executive in the sample held about 0.1 percent of the shares outstanding of the firm that he managed.

Ever since the separation of corporate ownership from corporate control, the principal-agent problem between shareholders and executives has been a central concern for proper corporate governance (Berle and Means 1932). If managers are self-interested and if shareholders cannot perfectly monitor them, executives are likely to pursue their own well-being at the expense of shareholder value. One mechanism to alleviate this agency problem is to design compensation contracts to align the incentives of managers with those of shareholders.

Economic theory suggests that optimal contracts should be tied to the measures that are the most informative about an executive's contribution to the value of the firm. Since this ideal performance measure is not observable, compensation contracts in practice link the wealth of executives to the firms' stock price or to accounting measures of firm performance, in the hopes that these measures capture important aspects of the executives' impact on firm value. Empirically, the quantitatively most important linkage between executive wealth and shareholder value are changes in the value of the managers' portfolio of firm equity and stock options to changes in the market value of their firms. Top executives also receive incentives from bonuses based on accounting measures of firm performance, and from the threat of dismissal for poor performance.

The literature on managerial incentives first began to quantify the relationship between CEO compensation and firm performance in the 1950s. Early studies focused, without reaching a satisfactory conclusion, on identifying the measure of firm size or performance (e.g., sales, profits, or market capitalization) that best explains differences in the level of pay across firms. More recently, studies on this topic have quantified the degree of incentives provided by compensation contracts by relating changes in executive pay to stock price performance—what is generally called pay-to-performance. Hall and Liebman (1998) established that revaluations of the portfolio of stock and stock options account for most of the correlation between shareholder and executive wealth, and Frydman and Saks (2010b) showed that this relationship has been strong throughout most of the twentieth century.

The literature has used a variety of metrics to quantify incentives, without reaching a consensus on the "right" measure. More recently, several theoretical studies have proposed that the appropriate measure of incentives depends on how CEO behavior affects firm value. The current consensus suggests that incentives should be measured by the dollar change in CEO wealth for each dollar change in firm value when the marginal product of CEO actions are independent of the value of the firm. This specification is therefore appropriate for activities such as perk consumption (e.g., purchasing a corporate jet) that have the same dollar impact regardless of the initial size of the firm. Instead, when CEO actions have a multiplicative effect on firm value, as is the case for corporate reorganizations, the dollar change in CEO wealth for a percentage change in firm value most accurately measures incentives. Finally, when CEO effort has a multiplicative effect on both utility and firm value, incentives are most appropriately measured by the percentage change in CEO wealth that arises from a percentage change in firm value (often scaled by annual pay to avoid this measure to be trivially close to one).[7]

In sum, the theoretical literature suggests that the correct measure of incentives depends on modeling choices. In practice, CEOs engage in a wide variety of activities that scale and do not scale with the size of the firms that they manage, or with their utility. Thus, recent empirical studies on the degree of pay-to-performance present each of the measures corresponding to these various models. Two important considerations regarding these empirical measures are therefore worth mentioning. First, since it is arguably impossible to know the distribution of tasks across these different types of activities for each individual, it is difficult to determine whether an executive is well incentivized overall. Second, determining whether observed compensation contracts optimally address the agency problem between shareholders and CEOs is difficult. Thus, the optimal level of pay-to-performance depends on a host of parameters that are unobservable, such as the executive's risk aversion or the noise-to-signal ratio in the performance measure. Studies sometimes portray a stronger link between executive and shareholder wealth as evidence for a move toward optimality, but it is important to keep in mind that increases in pay-to-performance could actually be detrimental for shareholder value if the initial level of incentives exposed a risk-averse manager to too much volatility in her pay.

With these caveats in mind, table 12.2 uses the Frydman-Saks data to present the long-run evolution in the various measures of incentives. Column 1 of table 12.2 shows the dollar change in wealth for a dollar change in firm value, based solely on changes in executive wealth that are driven by revaluations of stock and option holdings. According to this measure, the incentives of the median executive in the sample declined sharply in the 1940s, recovered in the next two decades, and shrank again in the 1970s. This measure increased rapidly since the 1980s, but it had not regained its pre–World War II level by the end of the sample in 2005. Column 2 reports instead the median dollar change in wealth for a 1 percent change in firm value. Although this measure follows a similar pattern of ups and downs, it paints a different picture of the strength of incentives toward the end of the sample period. Executives have had increasingly more equity at stake for a percent change in shareholder wealth in every decade since the 1960s than at any other point in the sample. According to this measure, incentives were twelve times larger in the 2000–2005 period than at the beginning of the sample in the late 1930s. Finally, column 3 presents an estimate of the elasticity of changes in executive wealth for a moderate improvement in firm performance, where this moderate change is defined as a movement from the median rate of return (8.4 percent) to the seventieth percentile rate of return (22.7 percent) in the sample. The change in executive wealth is scaled by the sum of total compensation and the change in executive wealth at median firm performance. Using this definition, the elasticity of executive wealth to firm value ranged between 1 and 4 in most decades, confirming that managerial incentives were not always small prior to the 1980s.

Explaining CEO Pay: Theories

The rapid surge in CEO pay since the 1980s has sparked a contentious, and still unresolved, debate about the determinants of executive compensation. While the academic

Table 12.2 Managerial Incentives from Stock and Option Holdings, 1936–2005

	Dollar Gain for $1,000 Increase in Firm Value	Dollar Gain for 1% Increase in Firm Value	Elasticity of Changes in Wealth (Median to 70th Percentile in Returns)
	(1)	(2)	(3)
1936–1940	1.350	18,670	2.0
1941–1949	0.399	6,814	0.64
1950–1959	0.452	13,975	1.60
1960–1969	0.675	38,978	3.54
1970–1979	0.470	21,743	2.03
1980–1989	0.551	34,679	1.92
1990–1999	0.946	120,342	3.66
2000–2005	1.080	227,881	4.12

Sources: Frydman and Saks (2010b); Frydman and Jenter (2010).
Notes: Based on the three-highest paid executives in the 50 largest firms in 1940, 1960, and 1990 in the Frydman-Saks data. Columns present the median across all executives in each decade. Column 1 shows the executives' fractional equity ownership ((number of shares held + number of options held * average option delta) / (number of shares outstanding)) multiplied by $1,000. Column 2 presents the product of the executive's fractional equity ownership and the firm's equity market capitalization. Column 3 presents the elasticity of changes in managerial wealth for a change in firm performance from median rate of return to the 70th percentile in returns. Dollar values are in inflation-adjusted 2,000 dollars.

literature has considered many plausible explanations, two main theories have gathered the most attention. First, the level and composition of compensation are often viewed as the outcome of a competitive labor market for managerial talent that optimally assigns executives to firms. According to this "efficient contracting" hypothesis, managerial incentives are set to maximize firm value, and the recent growth in CEO pay is the efficient result of an increase in the demand for scarce managerial talent caused by an expansion in the scale and scope of firms. Based on seminal work by Rosen (1981, 1982), theoretical models in this area are founded on the intuition that higher CEO talent is more valuable in larger firms. Therefore, larger firms should offer higher levels of pay to attract more able CEOs if the labor market for managers is competitive and frictionless (Gabaix and Landier 2008). Edmans and Gabaix (2015) survey a wide range of assignment models, and show that the empirical predictions of these frameworks depend critically on the modeling assumptions.

In contrast to the efficient contracting hypothesis, other scholars view the high levels of CEO pay as the result of weak corporate governance and acquiescent corporate boards that allow executives to (at least partly) set their own pay and extract excessive compensation (often called rents) from the firms they manage (see, e.g.,

Bebchuk and Fried 2003). Thus, this view portrays the current high remuneration levels as inefficient. Moreover, the "rent extraction" hypothesis argues that CEOs are more likely to extract rents in forms of pay that are more difficult to observe or to value, such as stock options or stealth compensation (including, e.g., pensions, perquisites, and severance pay). This theory has certainly influenced academic research and policy discussion, and many features of executive pay do point to important inefficiencies in pay. However, there has been only limited development of careful models of managerial rent extraction, and consequently there is a lack of specific empirical predictions based on theory with which to test this hypothesis, and to contrast it with the predictions from the efficient contracting view.

Although these two opposing explanations receive the majority of the attention, they both face limitations in explaining the various features of executive pay in the data. Many other alternative explanations for the rise in CEO pay have emerged in recent years. Murphy and Zábojník (2010) and Frydman (2015) link the trends in compensation to changes in the nature of the job of top executives that have, for example, increased the demand for general managerial skills over time (though the transformation in skills appears to have been more slow-moving than that of compensation). Piketty, Saez, and Stantcheva (2014) argue that executives have more incentives to bargain with boards over their pay when tax rates on their labor income are lower, thereby creating a negative relationship between CEO pay and tax rates. Alternatively, it may be possible that the widespread adoption of high-powered incentives since the late 1980s may have caused the sharp increase in the total level of pay during this period, as a way to compensate risk-averse executives for the increased volatility in their pay. However, one would then have to ask what caused the increased use of equity-based pay in the first place, and why the forms of pay utilized to provide incentives have changed at specific points in time.

Indeed, Murphy (2013) notes that most of the explanations commonly offered to account for the total level of pay are relatively mute about the stark changes in the structure of executive compensation that have occurred over time. Instead, he argues, government intervention, in the form of disclosure requirements, tax policies, accounting rules, and legislation, has been a major driver of the trends in executive pay over time. These political factors have often come into play after instances of perceived abuses in compensation, following recessions or financial crises, and at times in which managerial pay is deemed excessive (e.g., when compared to the pay of workers).

Finally, the remarkably similar trends in relative executive pay and income inequality described in the preceding suggest that the changes in executive compensation over time may also be driven by factors that have contributed to the evolution of disparities in pay more generally. These factors include, among others, skilled-biased technological change (Autor, Katz, and Kearney 2008), "globalization" (Williamson 1997), and changes in social norms and labor market institutions (Levy and Temin 2007).

Explaining CEO Pay:
Empirical Evidence

Each of the main theories is supported or contradicted by empirical evidence.[8] Theories of optimal contracting receive strong support from the correlated increase in firm value and CEO pay since the 1980s. Using specific assumptions about the distribution of CEO talent, Gabaix and Landier (2008) show that a competitive assignment model predicts a one-for-one move between the size of the typical firm in the economy and CEO pay. Indeed, a calibration of their model reveals that the growth in median market values can fully account for the increase in total CEO pay in S&P 500 firms from 1980 to 2003. More recently, they have shown that aggregate changes in firm value and CEO compensation tracked each other fairly well throughout the financial crisis and economic recovery experienced from 2007 to 2011.

Several studies have questioned the estimated correlation between firm size and CEO pay, as well as its interpretation. Critics emphasize, among other points, that the strong correlation between these two variables does not imply that their relationship is causal; indeed, their association could be driven by a third omitted variable, including CEOs' ability to extract rents. For the purposes of economic historians, however, a more important observation is that the relationship between aggregate executive pay and firm value was almost nonexistent from the 1940s to the 1970s. Understanding the factors that drove the changes in these empirical patterns over time remains an open question.

The rent extraction view of CEO compensation has received much public attention, in part because of specific cases of egregious abuses of compensation practices. A persuasive explanation, however, should be able to account for the pay of the typical executive. Moreover, optimal contracting theories can sometimes justify the use of forms of pay often argued to be evidence for rent extraction. For example, large severance payments awarded to ousted CEOs following poor performance can be thought of as an ex-ante commitment necessary to incentivize an outsider executive to switch corporations in a competitive labor market. Various other widespread practices, such as CEOs hedging exposures to the value of their own firm created by equity-based pay, stock option backdating, and "pay-for-luck" (that is, the fact that CEOs tend to be rewarded for lucky events beyond their control but are not equally penalized for similar unlucky events), are a bit more immune to this criticism.

It is not entirely clear, however, that managers' ability to extract rents can explain the long-run changes in executive pay. Indeed, most available indicators of corporate governance, such as the independence of corporate boards, were weaker earlier in the century when pay levels were lower, and have actually strengthened in the past four decades, a period of exceptional high levels in CEO pay. However, proxies for corporate governance are imperfect, and it is ultimately difficult to quantitatively assess how it has changed over time. But even if the available indicators accurately represent the true changes in governance, it is still possible that other changes have interacted with governance to contribute to the rapid growth in compensation in recent years. For example, social norms against unequal pay and institutions (such as labor unions) that limited extreme pay outcomes weakened over this period.

Changes in the progressiveness of the tax system may also have contributed to the high levels of executive pay. Labor income tax rates were extremely high until 1969, when the pay of top managers was not (relatively speaking) much higher than the wages of the average worker. The rise in CEO pay since then coincided with significantly lower levels in the top marginal tax rates on labor income, which may have given high income earners an incentive to bargain for higher pay (Piketty, Saez, and Stantcheva 2014). If this explanation is correct, then the response to changes in tax rates must be relatively slow moving. For example, the top marginal tax rate on labor income was constant for most of the 1990s, when the pay of top executives experienced the fastest recorded growth rates. Moreover, Frydman and Molloy (2011) show that the elasticity of executive pay to changes in tax rates is remarkably low in the short and medium run.

While some of these theories explain the trends in the level of executive pay reasonably well, they do not offer equally convincing explanations for the changes in the composition of pay packages. As suggested by Murphy (2003), the features of compensation contracts do appear to respond to specific government interventions, such as changes in tax policy, accounting rules, and disclosure requirements. For example, the use of stock options became widespread following the Revenue Act of 1950, which increased the tax advantages of restricted options relative to other forms of pay (Frydman and Molloy 2011). More recently, firms have substituted restricted stock grants for stock options, perhaps as a consequence of the mandate to expense stock options starting in 2005. Yet the structure of pay has also evolved at times of limited government intervention, and it is not entirely clear why the level of compensation should respond to these political forces (unless these interventions also affect other factors, such as the outside options of executives or their bargaining power). Corporate boards acting in the best interest of shareholders should ideally replace one form of pay for another in response to regulatory changes, while trying to minimize the wage bill of the firm. In the absence of other forces, political factors may not be sufficient to explain the changes in pay levels over time.

What emerges from a critical assessment of the literature is that none of the proposed theories is fully consistent with the available evidence. Moreover, the rent extraction and the optimal contracting explanations are often cast as competing hypotheses—much of the current work tries to demonstrate that various characteristics of real-world compensation contracts are consistent with either rent extraction or optimal contracting. But theoretical models do not offer clear testable predictions that differ between these two approaches, and so ultimately the approach of the current literature is not very productive. More important, the various explanations are not mutually exclusive. For example, a competitive labor market could contribute to inefficiently high levels of pay to attract managerial talent if a subset of firms overpays their executives.

Most empirical studies of the determinants of executive compensation have focused on establishing correlations with various industry, firm, and manager characteristics. The level of pay and incentives tend to be positively correlated with firm size, performance, and growth opportunities, and negatively correlated with firm volatility. Moreover, CEOs receive higher levels of pay if they are hired from outside the firm, and if they are also the chairmen of the board of directors. Recent studies have used modern econometric techniques to decompose the variation in executive pay into five groups of determinants: firm observable time-variant characteristics, manager observable time-variant characteristics, firm unobservable time-invariant characteristics (i.e., firm fixed effects), manager unobservable time-invariant characteristics (i.e., manager fixed effects), and time effects (i.e., year fixed effects), utilizing data from 1992 to the present. Interestingly, manager fixed effects explain a much larger fraction of the variation in pay levels and in incentives than any of the other four groups of determinants. Whether managerial fixed effects were equally important in the past remains an open question.

Recent studies have started to make progress in understanding the causal effects of various forces on the level of pay and incentives, for example by examining exogenous changes in the contracting environment, industry deregulations, shocks to exchange rates and output prices, and regulatory changes to board composition. Economic history may provide a valuable laboratory to advance our knowledge in this area given the many legislative changes introduced to regulate executive pay over time.[9] Another fruitful and largely unexplored avenue of research is the use of structural estimation to assess the ability of theoretical models to match historical data (Frydman and Papanikolaou 2016).

Conclusions and Future Research

Although the contemporaneous literature on executive compensation is quite extensive, researchers have mostly focused on the evolution of pay since the 1980s. Except for a handful of studies, this topic remains largely unexplored by economic historians. Yet some of the most significant changes in the structure and the level of top manager pay occurred during earlier time periods. Moreover, the large number of regulatory changes experienced over time may allow economic historians to exploit these sources of "natural experiments" to provide more convincing answers to the effects that various forces have on managerial contracts. In particular, any progress on the causal effect of pay-to-performance on firm outcomes and on managerial risk-taking decisions would be welcome.

The long-run trends in the level of executive pay give rise to some important unanswered questions. While there is some evidence linking the compression in compensation during the 1940s to a weakening of labor unions, we know much less about the factors that led to the stark changes in the structure of CEO pay, and the rapid increase in the growth rate in total pay, since the 1980s. Moreover, the lack of growth in executive pay at a time of rapid growth in firm size during the 1950s and 1960s remains an open challenge.

While the available data provide a consistent view of the changes in executive pay since the 1930s, they have some important limitations. In particular, the Frydman-Saks data do not allow studying changes in executive pay and their determinants across different industries. Moreover, relatively little is known about the compensation of top managers in smaller firms, and in private corporations, throughout the twentieth century. Finally, there is a dearth of systematic information prior to the 1930s. Primary sources from corporate archives may be a useful resource to expand the available historical information and provide valuable new insights on the compensation and careers of an important part of the American labor force over the long run.

NOTES

1. Useful surveys summarizing various theoretical, empirical, and historical aspects of the extensive literature on executive compensation can be found in Murphy (1999), Frydman and Jenter (2010), Wells (2012), Murphy (2012), Murphy (2013), and Edmans and Gabaix (2015).
2. For further details on these data, see Frydman and Saks (2010a, 2010b).
3. For most of the description, the chapter focuses on the measure of pay that best proxies the grant-date value of compensation in a consistent manner over the long run. For a more detailed discussion on the differences between grant-date pay, realized pay, and risk-adjusted pay, see Murphy (2013).
4. The analysis focuses on the shares of the top 0.1 percent because the majority of the executives in the Frydman-Saks data earned incomes above the thresholds that define this fractile for most of the sample period. See Piketty and Saez (2003) for a thorough description of the evolution in income inequality within the top decile from 1913 to the present, and for robustness of the documented patterns to alternative income measures.
5. These two measures of inequality have likely become less comparable over time. The increase in female labor force participation over the last century has led to a reduction in the share of the tax unit income earned by the primary earner over time.
6. For a discussion of the patterns and potential causes of the long-run changes in American income inequality more broadly, see Goldin and Katz (2008) and Lindert and Williamson (2016).
7. See Edmans and Gabaix (2015) for an insightful review of these (and some alternative) models.
8. Since the empirical literature on executive compensation is quite extensive, many important findings cannot be covered. Researchers interested in this area could refer to the surveys by, among others, Murphy (1999), Frydman and Jenter (2010), and Murphy (2013) for further guidance.
9. See Murphy (2012) for a thorough description of this legislative history.

BIBLIOGRAPHY

Autor, David H., Lawrence F. Katz, and Melissa S. Kearney. (2008). "Trends in U.S. Wage Inequality: Revising the Revisinists." *Review of Economics and Statistics* 90(2): 300–323.

Bebchuk, L. A., and J. M. Fried. (2003). "Executive Compensation as an Agency Problem." *Journal of Economic Perspectives* 17(Summer): 71–92.

Berle Jr., Adolf A., and Gardiner C. Means. (1932). *The Modern Corporation and Private Property*. New York: Macmillan.

Chandler, Alfred D. (1977). *The Visible Hand: The Managerial Revolution in American Business*. Cambridge, MA: Belknap Press.

Frydman, Carola. (2015). "Rising Through the Ranks: The Evolution of the Market for Corporate Executives, 1936–2003." *Management Science*, forthcoming.

Frydman, Carola, and Dirk Jenter. (2010). "CEO Compensation." *Annual Review of Financial Economics* 2: 75–102.

Frydman, Carola, and Raven Molloy. (2011). "The Effect of Tax Policy on Executive Compensation: Evidence from Postwar Reforms." *Journal of Public Economics* 95: 1425–1437.

Frydman, Carola, and Raven Molloy. (2012). "Pay Cuts for the Boss: Executive Compensation in the 1940s." *Journal of Economic History* 72: 225–251.

Frydman, Carola, and Dimitris Papanikolaou. (2016). "In Search of Ideas: Technological Innovation and Executive Pay Inequality." *Journal of Financial Economics*, forthcoming.

Frydman, Carola, and Raven E. Saks. (2010a). "Data Appendix—Executive Compensation: A New View from a Long-Term Perspective, 1936–2005." Manuscript.

Frydman, Carola, and Raven E. Saks. (2010b). "Executive Compensation: A New View from a Long-Term Perspective, 1936–2005." *Review of Financial Studies* 23: 2099–2138.

Gabaix, Xavier, and Alex Edmans. (2015). "Executive Compensation: A Modern Primer." *Journal of Economic Literature* 54: 1232–1287.

Gabaix, Xavier, and Augustin Landier. (2008). "Why Has CEO Pay Increased So Much?" *Quarterly Journal of Economics* 123: 49–100.

Goldin, Claudia, and Lawrence F. Katz. (2008). *The Race between Education and Technology*. Cambridge, MA: Harvard University Press.

Hall, Brian J., and Jeffrey B. Liebman. (1998). "Are CEOs Really Paid Like Bureaucrats?" *Quarterly Journal of Economics* 113: 653–691.

Jensen, M. C., and Kevin J. Murphy. (1990). "Performance Pay and Top-Management Incentives." *Journal of Political Economy* 98(2): 225–264.

Lamoreaux, Naomi R. (1988). *The Great Merger Movement in American Business, 1895–1904*. New York: Cambridge University Press.

Levy, Frank, and Peter Temin. (2007). "Inequality and Institutions in 20th Century America." NBER Working Paper No. 13106.

Lewellen, Wilbur G. (1968). *Executive Compensation in Large Industrial Companies*. New York: National Bureau of Economic Research.

Lindert, Peter H., and Jeffrey G. Williamson. (2016). *Unequal Gains: American Growth and Inequality since 1700*. Princeton, NJ: Princeton University Press.

Murphy, Kevin J. (1999). "Executive Compensation." In *Handbook of Labor Economics*, edited by O. Ashenfelter and D. Card, Chapter 38, 2485–2563. Dordrecht: Elsevier Science.

Murphy, Kevin J. (2012). "The Politics of Pay: A Legislative History of Executive Compensation." In *The Research Handbook on Executive Pay*, edited by J. Hill and R. Thomas, Chapter 1, 11–40. Cheltenham, UK: Edward Elgar.

Murphy, Kevin J. (2013). "Executive Compensation: Where We Are, and How We Got There." In *Handbook of the Economics of Finance*, edited by George Constantinides, Milton Harris, and René Stulz, Chapter 4, 211–356. Dordrecht: Elsevier Science.

Murphy, Kevin J., and Jan Zábojník. (2010). "Managerial Capital and the Market for CEOs." Working Paper.

Piketty, Thomas, and Emmanuel Saez. (2003). "Income Inequality in the United States, 1913–1998." *Quarterly Journal of Economics* 118(1): 1–39.

Piketty, Thomas, Emmanuel Saez, and Stefanie Stantcheva. (2014). "Optimal Taxation of Top Labor Incomes: A Tale of Three Elasticities." *American Economic Journal: Economic Policy* 6(1): 230–271.

Rosen, Sherwin. (1981). "The Economics of Superstars." *American Economic Review* 71: 845–858.

Rosen, Sherwin. (1982). "Authority, Control and the Distribution of Earnings." *Bell Journal of Economics* 13: 311–323.

Wells, Harwell. (2012). "U.S. Executive Compensation in Historical Perspective." In Research *Handbook on Executive Pay*, edited by R. S. Thomas and J. G. Hill, Chapter 2, 41–57. Cheltenham, UK: Edward Elgar.

Williamson, Jeffrey G. (1997). "Globalization and Inequality, Past and Present." *The World Bank Observer* 12(2): 117–135.

PART III

FACTORS OF PRODUCTION

CHAPTER 13

THE LABOR FORCE IN AMERICAN ECONOMIC HISTORY

ROBERT A. MARGO

CAPITAL, natural resources, and labor are the three "factors of production" in classical economics. Income per capita is the product of output per worker—average labor productivity—and the number of workers per person—the aggregate labor force participation rate. Average labor productivity, in turn, is a function of complementary inputs—capital and natural resources—per worker and the state of technology—total factor productivity. There is a direct connection, therefore, between the average standard of living, measured by per capita income, and the labor force—the productivity of the average worker, and the size of the labor force relative to population.

SOURCES OF INFORMATION

The most fundamental source of information on the American labor force is the federal census, taken every ten years since 1790. The pre-1850 censuses are relatively limited in economic data; however, enough information exists that, with reasonable assumptions, it is possible to estimate the size of the labor force beginning in the early nineteenth century. Beginning with the 1850 census, information on occupation was recorded at the individual level, and in 1910, on industry. A question on unemployment was first included in 1880 and subsequently was refined; more general questions on employment status made their first appearance in 1910. The experience of the Great Depression greatly increased the demand for information about the labor force. In this regard, the 1940 census was a watershed document. Not only did it contain new, detailed questions about labor force status at the time the census was taken, it was also the first to ask questions about weeks worked during the census year, wage and salary earnings, and educational attainment.

Although the census is indispensable for establishing long-run trends, it provides no evidence on short-run movements. For this purpose, the Current Population Survey (CPS) is taken every month. The CPS is a random sample with similar labor information to the census. The CPS began to be taken regularly after World War II. More recently, the Census Bureau has established the American Community Survey (ACS), which is taken on an annual basis, and is intended to supplement the decennial census. Other specialized surveys that are widely used to study labor force outcomes are the Panel Study of Income Dynamics (PSID) and the National Longitudinal Surveys (NLS).

Government data on wages are scarce for the pre–Civil War period. Among the handful of government sources for the pre–Civil War period are estimates of average earnings of manufacturing workers, which can be constructed from information in the federal censuses of manufacturing; and estimates of wages for selected occupations reported in the 1850 and 1860 federal censuses of social statistics. Most scholars have relied on archival information derived from account books or payroll records. The most extensive collection of payroll information by far pertains to civilian employees of the US Army; these form the basis of the wage series produced by Margo (2000b) for the period 1820–1860. During the second half of the nineteenth century, the collection of wage information became more frequent. State governments established bureaus of labor and industrial statistics, which periodically surveyed firms or workers about wages and working conditions. In the late nineteenth century, the federal government conducted two especially important surveys, the *Weeks* and *Aldrich* reports. Both contain extensive retrospective information on wages in manufacturing establishments in existence when the surveys were taken.

Established in the late nineteenth century, the US Bureau of Labor Statistics (BLS) soon became an essential source of regular wage information, initially through specialized surveys and later, in 1932, through the establishment of a monthly canvassing of employment and earnings that survives to this day (as the Current Employment Survey, or CES). The BLS also has conducted "Area Wage Surveys" for many years, which provide information on differences in wages by occupation across metropolitan areas.

Researchers wishing to use the federal data will find convenient links at the Census Bureau (www.census.gov) and BLS (www.bls.gov) websites. Especially useful are the public-use "micro-data" (PUMS) versions of the census and CPS data; these are random samples from the original records. Census samples exist for all census years starting in 1850 through 2010 (except 1890, because the original records were mostly destroyed in a fire). CPS samples are available from the early 1960s to the present, whereas public-use ACS samples begin in 2007. The IPUMS project at the University of Minnesota (www.ipums.umn.edu) is an excellent, "one-stop shopping" source for census micro-data. The IPUMS website is constantly updated, with new samples added regularly. These include, for example, samples in which individuals are linked across census years (e.g., 1850–1880) and also "complete count" (100 percent) datasets which contain all of the surviving records for a given census year, from which scholars can construct their own linked samples. These linked samples offer unprecedented opportunities to study how labor force outcomes vary across individuals as they age, or across generations.

It is well beyond the scope of this survey to discuss methods of analyzing labor force data. In brief, scholars used a variety of techniques from simple averages (to produce estimates of labor force participation) to more elaborate regression analyses and applications of econometrics (e.g., in estimating the impact of educational attainment on a person's earnings). For detailed discussion of historical and modern labor force data, researchers should consult the online *BLS Handbook of Methods* (http://www.bls.gov/opub/hom/) and its companion, *BLS Handbook of Labor Statistics*.

THE LABOR FORCE, 1800–PRESENT

It is useful to begin by reviewing how the labor force is measured. From 1940 to the present, estimates of the labor force are based on the survey week method. According to this measure, a person is in the labor force if he or she is employed or is actively seeking work if unemployed during the survey week. Individuals are "out of the labor force" if they do not hold a job and are not actively seeking work. For the period from 1870 to 1930, the labor force is based on the so-called gainful worker definition. A gainful worker is one who reported an occupation to the census, such as "carpenter" or "house servant." Census enumerators were supposed to record a gainful occupation if the person spent the majority of his or her time engaged in it. Although the direct evidence is limited, most economic historians believe that the two methods would generally give similar estimates of labor force activity for adult males prior to World War II (because adult males were almost always employed or seeking work), but this is far from the case for children or female workers.

For the census years 1850–1870, the gainful worker statistics are deficient in whole or part for child labor, women, and slaves, and adjustments must be made to correct for these. Prior to 1850, direct evidence on labor force activity, occupations or otherwise, is limited, and labor force estimates are based on assumptions about participation rates that vary by race, gender, and age (Weiss 1999).

The total labor force and the aggregate labor force participation rate (labor force divided by population of all ages) are shown in table 13.1 for census years from 1800 to 2010. At the turn of the nineteenth century, the total labor force consisted of 1.7 million persons, or about 32 percent of the population. A century later, the labor force was 29.1 million strong, and the labor force participation rate had increased to 38 percent. In 2010 there were 154 million Americans in the labor force, approximately half of the population.

In the long run (1800–2010), the labor force grew at an average annual rate of 2.1 percent per year, which was about 0.2 percent faster per year than the population. The labor force in total grew more quickly in the nineteenth century (2.9 percent per year) than in the twentieth century (1.5 percent), but per capita the growth rate was slightly higher in

Table 13.1 The Labor Force in the United States, 1800–2010

	Labor Force (in 1,000s)	Per 1,000 Population, All Ages
1800	1,713	323
1810	2,337	323
1820	3,163	328
1830	4,272	332
1840	5,778	338
1850	8,193	353
1860	11,293	359
1870	13,752	345
1880	18,089	361
1890	23,701	376
1900	29,483	387
1910	37,873	411
1920	42,345	399
1930	49,343	401
1940	56,168	425
1950	62,208	411
1960	69,628	388
1970	82,771	405 [604]
1980	106,940	472 [638]
1990	125,840	506 [665]
2000	140,863	501 [671]
2010	153,889	497 [647]
Average Annual Rate of Growth, 1800–2010	2.11%	0.21%
Average Annual Rate of Growth, 1800–1900	2.88%	0.18%
Average Annual Rate of Growth, 1900–2010	1.50%	0.24%

Notes and sources: Labor Force: 1800–1900: computed by summing male (white and nonwhite) and female (white and nonwhite) figures from Weiss (1999, Table 1, 22). 1910–1940: Weir (1992, Table D3, 341–343), spliced to Weiss and to Carter (2006, Series Ba479, 2–85). The splicing procedure is as follows. First, the ratio of Weiss's labor force estimate to Weir's is computed for 1900; call this R(1900). Next, the ratio of Carter's to Weir's estimates is computed for 1950; call this R(1950). The analogous ratios for 1910, 1920, 1930, and 1940 are linearly interpolated between R(1900) and R(1950); call these R(1910), R(1920), R(1930) and R(194). The labor force estimates for 1910–1940 are Weir's figures multiplied by the relevant ratio (e.g., the 1920 labor force estimate is Weir's figure for 1920 multiplied by R(1920). Carter (1910, Statistical Abstract 2012, Table 586). Population (all ages) is from the decennial census. Figures in brackets [ ] give the size of the labor force expressed per 1,000 persons in the noninstitutionalized civilian population age 16 and over; the "noninstitutionalized civilian" population excludes persons who are incarcerated or in other types of institutions (e.g., mental health) or in the military. Average annual rate of growth is the coefficient of time trend from regression of ln (labor force) or ln (labor force per 1,000 persons).

the twentieth century (0.24 percent per year) than in the nineteenth (0.18 percent per year). Significant differences in growth rates across decades are also apparent—for example, the labor force grew relatively quickly compared with population from 1840 to 1860, and also after 1970.

Secular change in the aggregate labor force participation rate reflects many causal factors. Fertility has declined in the long run, and consequently there are relatively fewer children per adult today than in the past. The decrease in the "dependency ratio" is associated with a rise in the aggregate participation rate because adults are more likely to be in the labor force than children. During the second half of the twentieth century, there has been a substantial rise in the labor force participation of married women. Immigration has waxed and waned over American history; during periods in which the foreign-born share has been rising, such as in recent decades, labor force growth is buoyed because immigrants tend to have higher labor force participation than the native born. Offsetting these factors have been long-term decreases in child labor; increased longevity and reductions in labor force participation among the elderly (retirement); and, in recent decades, decreases in labor force participation among prime-age adult males.[1]

"Composition" refers to demographic—age, gender, and so on—features of the labor force, rather than occupations. There have been substantial changes in labor force composition over time. In the nineteenth century, the most salient compositional feature was legal status—slave or free. Among adult men, labor force participation rates were essentially the same for slaves and free workers, but participation rates were much higher among slaves for young children and, especially, women. In the aftermath of the Civil War, participation rates declined for African Americans living in the South, and the reductions were largest for women and children (Ransom and Sutch 1977; Weiss 1999).

In the twentieth century, there have been four major changes in labor force composition. First, the incidence of child labor has declined dramatically. This decline primarily reflects decreases in the relative demand for child labor and in their relative supply, rather than the impact of compulsory education or child labor laws restricting their employment. Second, there has been a substantial decline in labor force participation among the elderly, usually referred to as the rise in "retirement." There are substantial disagreements among economic historians about whether the rise in retirement was gradual or whether it accelerated after the establishment of Social Security in the 1930s. Third, in recent decades there have been decreases in labor force participation among middle-aged and somewhat older men who, conventionally, are thought to be too young to retire. Fourth, and most important, while single adult women throughout the twentieth century have had relatively high participation rates, there has been a very substantial rise in the labor force participation rate of married women, primarily since World War II. This increase has been attributed to shifts in economic structure that have favored women (and thus have increased the relative demand for their labor), rising investment in human capital, technical progress in "home production" that frees up time for market work, and reduced childbearing.

In addition to changes in the number of persons working, there has been change on the "intensive" margin—namely, hours worked. These changes have occurred in hours worked per day, the number of days worked per week, and weeks worked per year.[2] For the nineteenth-century United States, most of what is known about hours worked pertains to the manufacturing sector. In the early 1830s, the average work week in manufacturing was about sixty-nine hours; this declined to about sixty-two hours on the eve of the Civil War. Weekly hours continued to trend downward for the remainder of the century but slowly—in 1900, the typical work week was fifty-nine hours.

The decline in weekly hours in the nineteenth century occurred because of reductions in hours per day rather than days per week. Hours per day were just shy of 11.5 in the early 1830s, declining to 10.5 by 1860. By 1880 the average worker in manufacturing labored 10 hours per day. Daily hours varied across industries, location, and season of the year (Atack and Bateman 1992).

The decline in daily and weekly hours does not mean that annual hours also fell. On the contrary, annual hours rose in manufacturing as an increased share of manufacturing establishments operated on a full-year basis (Atack, Bateman, and Margo 2002). Although the evidence is not as detailed, it is likely that annual hours also increased in agriculture in the nineteenth century. The causes of the changes in hours in the nineteenth century are complex. Some of the changes can be attributed to technology—for example, improved indoor heating and lighting enabled manufacturers in colder climates to remain in operation during the winter months. Improved transportation facilitated the integration of goods and raw materials markets, making it less likely that firms would shut down because of supply or product market interruptions. Larger establishments used more fixed capital per worker and had an incentive, therefore, to remain in operation more continuously. A portion, likely very small, of the decline may be attributed to the efforts of organized labor and to the passage of legislation regulating maximum daily hours.

Weekly hours continued to decline in the twentieth century. Weekly hours fell from an average of sixty in 1900 to approximately fifty by World War I. The decline continued through the 1920s and 1930s, particularly in the latter decade—the Great Depression— when employers adopted work-sharing as a means of preventing further layoffs. Hours temporarily spiked during World War II, but by the early postwar years were back to forty. Since World War II the trend has had a very gentle downward slope, settling just below forty hours as the standard workweek.

The modern definition of the labor force includes workers who are "unemployed"— individuals who lack a job but are actively seeking one. In an economy in which self-employment is common—such as the mid-nineteenth-century United States in which the majority of workers were engaged in agriculture—unemployment is a nebulous concept. However, over the course of American economic history, the shares of workers who are self-employed or who are employers of other workers have declined; most members of the labor force, in other words, are employees. Except for a very small fraction of workers covered by contracts that ensure employment in most situations—for example, tenured faculty members in research universities—most workers are employed "at will" and can lose their jobs, either temporarily or permanently. If, while jobless, they seek work elsewhere, they are still in the labor force, albeit unemployed. The overall unemployment rate, therefore, can be thought of as a function of the rate at which workers lose their jobs—the probability of becoming unemployed—and the probability that, conditional on searching for work, an unemployed individual is re-employed.

The 1880 census was the first to attempt to measure unemployment but the data are thought to be poor in quality and have remained largely unanalyzed. Much better data were collected in the 1890–1910 censuses; analysis of the 1900 and 1910 data reveals that the incidence of unemployment—the probability that a worker would become unemployed at some time during a given year—was much higher than today, but the duration of unemployment—and thus the chances of regaining work—was much shorter (Margo 1990). The federal response at the onset of the Great Depression was much hampered by the lack of reliable economic data, including unemployment. The 1940 census was the first modern census to collect unemployment statistics using the survey week method. Since the late 1940s, unemployment data are collected very frequently, primarily by the CPS.

Although reliable annual data on unemployment rates exist for the post–World War II period, the same cannot be said for the period before 1940. Unemployment rates before 1940 have been estimated using the identity that the labor force is the sum of employed and unemployed persons. This method requires annual estimates of the labor force and employment, however, and any errors in these will be magnified in the unemployment rate estimates. Lebergott (1964) followed this method to generate an annual unemployment series beginning in 1890, but his estimates have been criticized by Romer (1986), who argues that Lebergott's methods produce a series that is excessively volatile. A separate issue is the treatment of persons with so-called "work relief" jobs in the 1930s. These were counted as unemployed by Lebergott, following the practice in the 1940 census, but Darby (1976) has argued that such persons should be counted as employed (Lebergott 1964; Margo 1993; Romer 1986).

Since World War II, the unemployment rate has shown relatively little tendency to drift upward or downward. That said, there are differences in unemployment within the labor force that have proven to be remarkably stubborn. The most important difference pertains to youth and race: youth unemployment is much higher than adult unemployment, and the unemployment rate for African American adult males is roughly twice that for adult white males. Such gaps tend to widen in recessions and narrow in booms, as do analogous gaps between more- and less-educated workers.

Occupations

The occupations of American workers have changed dramatically over time. Table 13.2 presents distributions for the United States for 1850, 1900, 1950, and 2000. These distributions are meant to be comprehensive—for example, prior to the Civil

Table 13.2 Occupation Distributions for the United States, 1850–2000

Panel A: Tasks

	1850	1900	1950	2000
White Collar	6.9%	17.1%	37.5%	61.8%
Professional-Technical	2.3	4.3	8.9	23.4
Manager	3.1	5.7	9.0	14.2
Clerical/Sales	1.5	7.2	19.6	24.2
Skilled Blue Collar	11.6	11.0	14.0	9.8
Operative/Unskilled/Service	28.7	36.4	36.8	27.1
Agriculture	52.7	35.3	11.7	1.2
Operator/Supervisory	23.9	20.0	7.7	0.6
Farm Laborer	28.8	15.5	4.1	0.6

Panel B: Skill Groups

	1850	1900	1950	2000
High Skill	5.4	10.0	17.9	37.6
Middle Skill	37.1	38.3	41.3	34.6
Low Skill	57.5	51.9	40.8	27.6

Source: Katz and Margo (2015, 37).
Notes: High skill: prof/man/tech. Middle skill: skilled blue collar + agricultural operator/supervisory + clerical/sales. Low skill: operator/unskilled/service + farm laborer.

War, they include slaves and for all years for which the issue is quantitatively relevant, they include child labor (ages 10–15). The distributions are shown in "one-digit" form, meaning that the occupation categories are the broadest possible. The basic data are taken from the IPUMS samples of the US federal census, to which are made a series of adjustments.[3]

Panel A of table 13.2 shows the distributions in terms of the occupational tasks performed. The numbers highlighted in bold-face add up to 100 percent (and thus are occupational shares). The most dramatic changes are the decline in the share of workers in agriculture and the rise in the share of white-collar workers. Although occupation information prior to 1850 is limited, there is no doubt that the decline in the farm share started much earlier than 1850; the best current estimate is that approximately three-quarters of the labor force in 1800 was engaged in agriculture.

Because agriculture was such a large share of the economy, the explanation of the shift of labor off the farm is necessarily a "general-equilibrium" one, reflecting causal factors occurring on the farm, as well as the structure of demand for farm and nonfarm goods. Broadly speaking, technical progress increased labor productivity both on and off the farm. However, the domestic demand for agricultural goods tended to be relatively inelastic with respect to price and income, whereas the opposite (relatively elastic) was true of the demand for nonfarm goods. Improvements in agricultural technology, as a result, tended to drive down the value of the marginal product of labor in agriculture, encouraging workers to leave the farm. Conversely, improvements in technology in the nonfarm sector increased the value of the marginal product of workers off the farm, pulling workers into nonagricultural occupations.

As Panel A shows, as workers shifted out of agriculture during the second half of the nineteenth century, both the white-collar and operative/unskilled/service shares expanded, while there was little change in the share of skilled blue-collar labor in the aggregate economy from 1850 to 1900. The stability in the skilled blue-collar share reflects two influences. In manufacturing, a growing sector after 1850, both the white-collar and operative/unskilled shares were increasing, while the share of blue-collar workers fell. This reflects what labor historians call "de-skilling"—a shift away from the traditional, artisan shop form of manufacturing toward the factory system. This shift increased the use of less skilled workers through division of labor, but also expanded the use of white-collar workers, because the firms were larger in size and more complex to manage. Outside of manufacturing, use of skilled blue-collar labor was growing, as the construction sector expanded. Between 1900 and 1950, labor continued to shift strongly out of agriculture, white-collar occupations grew dramatically, the skilled blue-collar share rose modestly, and the operative/unskilled/service share remained stable. From 1950 to the present, the white-collar share continued to increase, while the other occupation groups declined in proportion, especially agriculture, which, as of the turn of the twenty-first century, comprises just 1.2 percent of the labor force.

Panel B of table 13.2 offers a different perspective on changes in the occupational structure, from the standpoint of skills. Three categories are specified: high skill, middle skill, and low skill. High-skill jobs are those that required considerable training, native ability, or especially over time, increased education attainment. Middle-skill jobs required less training or schooling, while low-skill jobs required little training or education compared with the other two categories.

The share of high-skill jobs expanded steadily over time, while the share of low-skill jobs increased. The share of middle-skill jobs expanded slightly from 1850 to 1950, but has declined since the mid-twentieth century. As Katz and Margo (2015) discuss, these shifts reflect, in part, a relentless feature of economic growth in the United States—capital deepening. Over time, capital has become cheaper relative to labor, and capital per worker has increased substantially. On net in the aggregate, capital has been complementary to skilled labor, even in the nineteenth century, when technology was less complex. Effectively, technical change has increased the relative demand for skilled labor. This is particularly true in the long run for high-skill labor; it was also true for middle-skill jobs up through the first half of the twentieth century, but in the past several decades, middle-skill jobs have also declined as a share of the labor force, along with the secular decrease in low-skill jobs.

WAGES AND WAGE STRUCTURE

A wage rate is a payment for the use of labor services, and thus is stated in terms of a unit of time—for example, dollars per hour. Historically, it was common for workers to be paid partly in terms of money and partly in terms of "in-kind compensation," or goods or services (e.g., "room and board"). Such compensation can also take the form of desirable work characteristics or arrangements—a flexible time schedule, a corner office. Ideally, a historical wage series should incorporate in-kind compensation, but this is not always possible.

Fundamentally, changes in wages over time reflect shifts in the demand for labor relative to supply. Growth in labor productivity, whether through technical change, physical capital deepening (more physical capital per worker), or investments in human capital (e.g., schooling or health) will tend to raise real wages over time ("real" in this context refers to adjusting for changes in the price level, by dividing "nominal" or wages in current dollars by a suitable price index).

The phrase "wage structure" refers to differences in wages across groups of workers. The grouping should serve a useful comparative purpose—for example, highly educated or skilled workers versus less educated or less skilled workers, men compared with women, African Americans versus other racial groups. Overall wage inequality can be "decomposed" (divided) into differences in wages across groups versus differences among workers within groups. By its very nature, within-group inequality is difficult to explain—it could be due to hard-to-measure attributes of workers ("ability," "perseverance") or it could simply reflect random forces ("luck").

Margo (2006) provides a variety of long run series of real wages.[4] As a rough rule of thumb, real wages have increased on average by about 1.5 percent per year, or approximately doubling every half century. In this regard, growth has been more rapid in the twentieth century than in the nineteenth, and it is also apparent that year-to-year fluctuations in growth or volatility have decreased over time. That said, there clearly have been lengthy periods of time during which real wages for unskilled workers have been stagnant or even falling (compare the recent past with the early 1970s).

What about differences across occupations? Although much work is ongoing, economic historians have begun to unravel the history of the American wage structure. Arguably, the key feature that has emerged concerns the relative wages of educated, white-collar labor. During the nineteenth century, wages of white-collar labor appear to have grown more quickly than wages of skilled blue-collar or unskilled labor. Because the share of white-collar workers in the labor force was rising (see table 13.2), it follows that the demand for white-collar labor relative to other occupations must have been rising in the 1800s. Because white-collar workers were undoubtedly better educated on average, this suggests (but does not prove) that the demand for educated labor was increasing relative to supply in the nineteenth century. Conversely, white-collar wages—and more

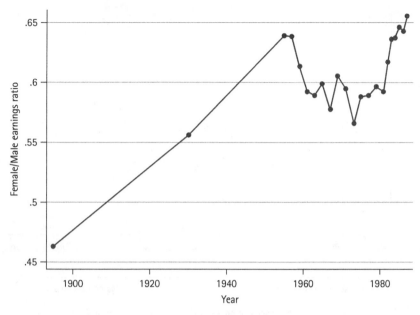

FIGURE 13.1. Female/male earnings ratio, 1890–1990
Source: Goldin (1990, Tables 3.1, 3.2).

generally, those of well-educated (high school or higher) workers—were declining relative to other occupations during the first half of the twentieth century, remaining more
or less stable from 1950 to 1970. Since 1970 the "returns to schooling" have risen sharply,
again signaling that the relative demand for educated workers has increased compared
with their relative supply.

Other key features of changes in wage structure are demographic, regional, and industrial. The wages of women rose relative to adult men during the first half of the nineteenth century, as women entered the expanding manufacturing sector, and the gender
gap has also declined since World War II (see fig. 13.1) (Goldin 1990; Goldin and Sokoloff
1982). Historically, too, the incomes of African Americans have fallen short of those of
whites, but the racial gap has narrowed substantially from the end of the Civil War to the
present, particularly between 1940 and 1980 (see fig. 13.2). A vast literature in economics
and economic history has debated the various factors responsible for narrowing gender
and racial differences, including changes in the quantity and quality of schooling; the integration of regional labor markets; the structure of the economy; attitudes of employers;
and antidiscrimination legislation (Donohue and Heckman 1991; Goldin 1990; Margo
2016; Smith and Welch 1989). Historically, there were large regional differences in
wages, but these have lessened substantially over time as regional economies have become more integrated. Historically as well, there were large differences in wages across
industries, but somewhat surprisingly these have been more stable over time than regional variation (Allen 1995).

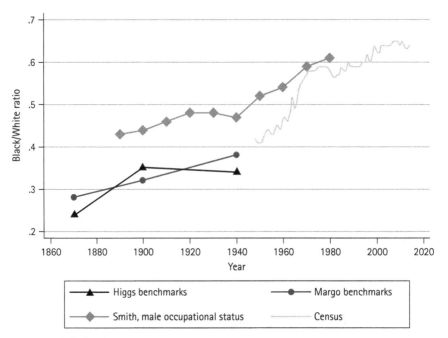

FIGURE 13.2. Black-white income ratios, 1870–present

Sources: Margo (2016, 330–334). Higgs Benchmarks, Margo Benchmarks, Census: Black/white ratio of per capita income. Higgs benchmarks: estimates prepared by Robert Higgs for ca. 1870, 1900, and 1940; see Margo (2016, 330–334). Margo benchmarks: estimates prepared by Robert Margo for 1870, 1900, and 1940; see Margo (2016, 330–334). Census: from US census data, 1948–2012; see Margo (2016, 334). Smith, Male Occupational Status: Smith (1984, 695).

LABOR MARKET INSTITUTIONS, UNIONS, AND REGULATION

The institutional framework is an inextricable part of the fabric of economic growth. Formal and informal institutions have shaped the size and structure of the American labor force and the economic outcomes experienced by American workers since the beginning of the republic.

Historically, the most important shift in institutions is surely that from various forms of "bound" labor to "free" labor. "Bound" labor indicates the institutions of indentured servitude and servitude (Carter 2006, 9–10). Such institutions have emerged quite frequently in "settler" economies in which land is abundant, labor is initially scarce, and transport costs to the settler economy from more populated regions are high.

Indentured servants were a common sight in colonial America. Indentured servants were contractually bound to a particular employer for a period of time. Aside from the length of indenture, the contracts often specified other features of the employment relationship, such as whether the employer was required to provide training or so-called freedom dues at the end of the contract. Among economic historians the generally accepted explanation for indentured servitude is that it enabled workers in the Old World, mostly young, to migrate to the New World by providing a mechanism for financing the cost of passage. This cost was a large fraction of per capita income in the Old World, and it was thus very unlikely that prospective migrants could finance the costs of passage on their own. Ship captains were the intermediary, providing passage that was financed by employers in, say, Pennsylvania, who were then repaid by the net profit (the difference between the marginal product of labor less the costs of maintaining the servant plus the annualized costs of dues at the end of the contract) obtained by employer.

To a first approximation, the cost of passage was the same for all indentured servants at a point in time, and thus variations in the length of indenture serve as a type of "price" that equilibrated the market. Servants with higher expected labor productivity served shorter terms; shorter terms, as well, characterized contracts in certain locations in British America, such as the Caribbean, which had high relative mortality among European settlers. Although the institution of indentured servitude persisted after the Revolution, it was already declining in the eighteenth century and essentially disappeared in the early nineteenth century. The reasons were simple—real incomes had increased in the Old World, while the cost of passage across the Atlantic had plummeted. Prospective migrants no longer needed a long-term contract to finance the cost of passage.

Indentured servitude died out without any help from government, but American slavery was another matter. The Atlantic trade supplied African slaves to New World economies in North and South America and the Caribbean. Over time, slavery displaced indentured servitude as the dominant form of bound labor. Although slaves were present throughout colonial America, their numbers diminished sharply in the North in the early nineteenth centuries as owners manumitted their chattel and as states abolished the institution on moral grounds. In the South, however, slavery persisted and even thrived, as the economics of staple crop production—sugar, tobacco, rice, and especially cotton—favored the use of slave labor. Slavery as it was practiced in the antebellum South was a highly profitable institution (Fogel 1989). Slave plantations were carefully managed businesses, often well ahead of Northern enterprises in accounting and other management practices. There is no evidence that on the eve of the American Civil War, slavery would have disappeared on economic grounds, as had happened for indentured servitude. It took a protracted and bloody civil war, vastly more costly in resources than the market value of slaves in 1860, to end the "Peculiar Institution" in the United States. Even so, the South's loss led to a sharp reduction in per capita income that persisted for many decades, manifested in the case of the labor market in the form of a large gap in wages between the South and the rest of the nation.

Although unions of crafts workers existed in colonial America, the modern origins of the labor movement can be dated to the 1820s and 1830s. During these decades there were spirited if sporadic attempts at union organizing, political action, and work stoppages—that is, strikes. Activity tended to be pro-cyclical, rising during booms but declining during recessions. Union activity picked up pace considerably in the North during the middle of the Civil War, in response to rising prices and falling real wages. By the early 1870s, the numbers of union members had swelled to several hundred thousand. Growth in unions continued in the late nineteenth century, as some organizations went national, such as the Knights of Labor and the American Federation of Labor. Labor strife increased, sometimes culminating in violence, such as the infamous bombing incident at a rally of the Knights in Chicago in May 1886. But growth in union membership continued apace, and by the eve of World War I, approximately 16 percent of industrial workers in the United States were unionized, a 13 percentage point increase from the level in 1880.

As a percentage of the nonfarm labor force and in absolute numbers, union members continued to grow during the first half of the twentieth. Union density (that is, the percent union) reached a peak in the mid-1940s, while in absolute numbers, union membership peaked in the mid- to late 1970s. Union density began to decline in the 1950s, while absolute numbers shrunk from the 1980s to the present. Although some of the rise and decline can be attributed to shifts in industry and worker composition, much is explained by shifts in public and private sentiments toward unions, as well as the ability of employers to successfully oppose union organizing. By far the most successful union advances after World War II have been in the public sector, particularly at the federal level, but even public sector unionization has been in retreat, particularly during the "Great Recession" beginning in 2008.

The ostensible purpose of unions is to improve the wages and working conditions of union members directly, and indirectly, those of nonunion members (the idea is that employers will raise wages of nonunion members preemptively to stem off union organizing). Although there is considerable uncertainty about the size of the effects, most economists agree that unions do raise wages of union members, typically more for less-skilled workers—thus, in addition to having a higher average wage, the union wage distribution is compressed relative to the nonwage distribution. While there may be some spillovers to the rest of the workforce, most economists believe that the spillovers can explain, at best, only a small fraction of long-run growth in real wages.[5]

LABOR MARKET REGULATIONS

When economists speak of a "free" labor market today, the sense of "free" is only partly the opposite of "slavery," discussed previously. "Free" here means "unfettered"—a labor market dominated by "employment at will" on both the demand and supply sides. But even if "unfettered" is more a matter of degree than kind, the degree has changed markedly over time (Fishback 1998). Today's labor market in the United States is subject to a vast array of government regulations issued and enforced at all levels of government— local, state, and federal.

Most of these regulations are the outcome of twentieth-century politics. However, the nineteenth century was not without important government interventions. The most important, of course, are those dealing with slavery, the Thirteenth and Fourteenth Amendments to the US Constitution being the pinnacle. The Thirteenth Amendment, adopted in December 1865, abolished slavery and involuntary servitude (the exception to the latter as punishment for crimes). The Fourteenth Amendment was adopted in July 1868. Its "due process" and "equal protection" clauses form the legal basis for the extension of the original Bill of Rights to the states and the precedent for the outlawing of racial and gender discrimination much later in the twentieth century.

Aside from these Amendments, the most important nineteenth-century government regulations aimed at labor markets were various types of "protective" legislation. Here, "protective" means legislation aimed at a specific population group. The key examples are child labor, compulsory schooling, and "maximum hours" laws. Compulsory schooling laws required children to attend school until a certain age, while child labor laws prevented the employment of young children. New England was at the forefront of both types of legislation, and by the late nineteenth century, many states in the North had followed suit. The South, however, was a laggard, not adopting such laws until well into the twentieth century.

Most economic historians believe that nineteenth-century compulsory schooling and child labor laws had a positive effect on school attendance rates, but the effects were small (Margo 2000a, 240). In retrospect this is not surprising because political support for such laws was generally strongest where child labor was relatively unimportant and where parental interest in schooling for children was greatest. In addition, enforcement of such laws was typically weak at the time. By contrast, twentieth-century laws of the same type have been more effective, but even so, it would be a mistake to attribute long-term trends in child schooling and employment to the impact of such regulations, rather than decreases in the relative demand for child labor and increases in the relative demand for educated labor. Maximum hours laws attempted to reduce the length of the working day, ostensibly for women, but in fact for all workers. First passed in New Hampshire and Massachusetts in the late 1840s, by the end of century thirteen states had enacted laws restricting hours. Except in Massachusetts, where the law appears to have been enforced to some extent, the laws seemed to have little effect, and yet as noted earlier, hours of work per day did decline over the nineteenth century.

Labor market regulations in the twentieth century are far too numerous to discuss here. Although an oversimplification, arguably the most important have been occupational health and safety, minimum wage laws, unemployment insurance, and antidiscrimination legislation. Occupational health and safety regulations pertain to working conditions and are intended to safeguard worker health. These regulations have their origins in factory inspection statutes adopted in the nineteenth century and expanded significantly in the twentieth century, especially since World War II. Although there were minimum wage and unemployment insurance statutes at the state level in the early twentieth century, federal regulations were not adopted until the Great Depression. Minimum wage laws set floors on wage rates, while unemployment insurance provides compensation to workers who are laid off for some period of time. Although minimum wages in theory can cause unemployment to rise, in practice the effects seem to be small, perhaps because minimum wages in the continental United States have never been set high enough to have such effects. In macroeconomic terms, unemployment insurance is an "automatic stabilizer" in that consumption of unemployed workers can be maintained even when current income falls due to unemployment; there may also be some efficiency gains if unemployed workers wait for a good match, rather than take the first job that comes along. Antidiscrimination legislation seeks to prohibit discrimination on the basis of race, gender, ethnicity, and more recently, sexual orientation. Although some cities and states passed antidiscrimination ordinances aimed at policing racial discrimination in the aftermath of World War II, fundamental civil rights legislation of this type is a product of the 1960s. Labor economists and economic historians attribute a significant portion of the narrowing of black-white income differences in the late 1960s and early 1970s to the effects of antidiscrimination legislation (Donohue and Heckman 1991).

DIRECTIONS FOR FUTURE RESEARCH

Although economic historians have largely mapped out the major issues on the evolution of the American labor force, many important issues remain to be probed, particularly for the nineteenth century. It is useful to group these issues into those pertaining to labor force quantities—such as the participation rate, hours worked, unemployment—versus wages.

"Benchmark" (census year) estimates of the labor force and its composition for the 1850 to 1900 are reasonably solid, but those for the pre-1850 rest on a series of assumptions about labor force participation rates, for which further refinement would be welcome. However, the most important remaining issue for the nineteenth century is the absence of reliable annual estimates. Given the available evidence, it may prove to be impossible to construct such estimates, but educated guesses of shifts in labor force size and composition over shorter periods could significantly enhance our understanding of nineteenth-century business cycles ("panics," as they were called). Our knowledge of trends in average hours worked, as well as the distribution of hours worked across individuals, is also very limited for the nineteenth century. As noted earlier, much remains to be learned about the history of unemployment prior to the 1930s.

The shift of labor out of agriculture was fundamental to long-run economic growth in the United States. Educational choices across generations were a key feature of this shift. As the demand for educated, skilled labor increased over time relative to farm labor, farm children invested in schooling, leaving agriculture when they reached adulthood. This process of intergenerational occupational choice is poorly understood, but might be illuminated by analyzing linked census samples, such as those produced by the IPUMS project at the University of Minnesota.[6]

Although there have been significant advances in recent years in tracing the history of wages in the United States, much remains to be discovered. In particular, relatively little is known about the economic returns to schooling before the twentieth century. As discussed earlier, on the basis of changes in occupational wages, it seems reasonable to conclude that the relative demand for educated labor grew more rapidly than supply during the nineteenth century, but unraveling the precise role played by formal schooling in occupational choice in the nineteenth century is an important task for future research.

Notes

1. For further discussion and detailed statistics, see Margo (2000a), Goldin (2000), and Carter (2006).
2. See Sundstrom (2006) for detailed statistics.
3. For further details on the construction of the occupation distributions, see Katz and Margo (2015).
4. See also http://www.measuringworth.com/uswage/.
5. For further discussion and statistics on unions in American history, see Rosenbloom (2006).
6. See table 13.2 and Katz and Margo (2015) for evidence on broad changes in occupations over time.

Bibliography

Allen, Steven. (1995). "Updated Notes on the Inter-Industry Wage Structure." *Industrial and Labor Relations Review* 48: 305–320.

Atack, Jeremy, and Fred Bateman. (1992). "How Long Was the Workday in 1880." *Journal of Economic History* 52: 129–160.

Atack, Jeremy, Fred Bateman, and Robert A. Margo. (2002). "Part-Year Operation in Nineteenth Century Manufacturing: Evidence from the 1870 and 1880 Censuses." *Journal of Economic History* 62: 792–809.

Carter, Susan. (2006). "Labor." In *Historical Statistics of the United States, Earliest Time to the Present, Millennial Edition, Part B: Work and Welfare*, edited by S. B. Carter, S. S. Gartner, M. R. Haines, A. L. Olmstead, R. Sutch, and G. Wright, Vol. 2, 3–35. New York: Cambridge University Press.

Darby, Michael. (1976). "Three-and-a-Half Million US Employees Have Been Mislaid: Or, an Explanation of Unemployment, 1934–1941." *Journal of Political Economy* 84: 1–16.

Donohue, John, and James J. Heckman. (1991). "Continuous versus Episodic Change: The Impact of Affirmative Action and Civil Rights Policy on the Economic Status of Black Americans." *Journal of Economic Literature* 29: 1603–1643.

Fishback, Price V. (1998). "Operations of 'Unfettered' Labor Markets: Exit and Voice in American Labor Markets at the Turn of the Century." *Journal of Economic Literature* 36: 722–765.

Fogel, Robert W. (1989). *Without Consent or Contract: The Rise and Fall of American Slavery*. New York: W. W. Norton.

Goldin, Claudia. (1990). *Understanding the Gender Gap: An Economic History of American Women*. New York: Oxford University Press.

Goldin, Claudia. (2000). "Labor Markets in the Twentieth Century." In *The Cambridge Economic History of the United States*, edited by S. L. Engerman and R. Gallman, Vol. 3, 549–624. New York: Cambridge University Press.

Goldin, Claudia, and Kenneth L. Sokoloff. (1982). "Women, Children, and Industrialization in the Early Republic: Evidence from the Manufacturing Censuses." *Journal of Economic History* 42: 741–774.

Katz, Lawrence F., and Robert A. Margo. (2015). "Technical Change and the Relative Demand for Skilled Labor: The United States in Historical Perspective." In *Human Capital in History: The American Record*, edited by L. P. Boustan, C. Frydman, and R. A. Margo, 15–57. Chicago: University of Chicago Press.

Lebergott, Stanley. (1964). *Manpower in Economic Growth: The American Record.* New York: McGraw-Hill.

Margo, Robert A. (1990). "The Incidence and Duration of Unemployment: Some Long-Term Comparisons." *Economics Letters* 32: 217–220.

Margo, Robert A. (1993). "Employment and Unemployment in the 1930s." *Journal of Economic Perspectives* 7: 41–59.

Margo, Robert A. (2000a). "The Labor Force in the Nineteenth Century." In *The Cambridge Economic History of the United States*, Vol. II: *The Long Nineteenth Century*, edited by S. L. Engerman and Robert E. Gallman, 207–243. New York: Cambridge University Press.

Margo, Robert A. (2000b). *Wages and Labor Markets in the United States, 1820 to 1860.* Chicago: University of Chicago Press.

Margo, Robert A. (2006). "Wages and Wage Inequality." In *Historical Statistics of the United States, Earliest Time to the Present, Millennial Edition, Part B: Work and Welfare*, edited by S. B. Carter, S. S. Gartner, M. R. Haines, A. L. Olmstead, R. Sutch, and G. Wright, Vol. 2, 40–46. New York: Cambridge University Press.

Margo, Robert A. (2016). "Obama, Katrina, and the Persistence of Racial Inequality." *Journal of Economic History* 76: 301–341.

Ransom, Roger, and Richard Sutch. (1977). *One Kind of Freedom: The Economic Consequences of Emancipation.* New York: Cambridge University Press.

Romer, Christina. (1986). "Spurious Volatility in Historical Unemployment Data." *Journal of Political Economy* 94: 1–37.

Rosenbloom, Joshua. (2006). "Labor Unions." In *Historical Statistics of the United States, Earliest Time to the Present, Millennial Edition, Part B: Work and Welfare*, edited by S. B. Carter, S. S. Gartner, M. R. Haines, A. L. Olmstead, R. Sutch, and G. Wright, Vol. 2, 54–59. New York: Cambridge University Press.

Smith, James. (1984). "Race and Human Capital." *American Economic Review* 74: 685–698.

Smith, James, and Finis Welch. (1989). "Black Economic Progress after Myrdal." *Journal of Economic Literature* 27: 519–564.

Sundstrom, William. (2006). "Hours and Working Conditions." In *Historical Statistics of the United States, Earliest Time to the Present, Millennial Edition, Part B: Work and Welfare*, edited by S. B. Carter, S. S. Gartner, M. R. Haines, A. L. Olmstead, R. Sutch, and G. Wright, Vol. 2, 46–54. New York: Cambridge University Press.

Weiss, Thomas. (1999). "Estimates of White and Non-White Gainful Workers in the United States by Age Group, Race, and Sex: Decennial Census Years, 1800–1900." *Historical Methods* 32: 21–35.

....

CHAPTER 14

LABOR MARKET INSTITUTIONS IN THE GILDED AGE OF AMERICAN ECONOMIC HISTORY

....

SURESH NAIDU AND NOAM YUCHTMAN

THE nineteenth century was an era of historically high and increasing economic ine-quality in the United States, and an important dimension of this inequality was between capital and labor. In figure 14.1, one can see that the wealth-to-income ratio was high by historical standards in the late nineteenth century until World War I; the concentra-tion of wealth was also increasing, with the top 1 percent of households' share of wealth growing from around 20 percent in the mid-nineteenth century to over 40 percent in the early twentieth century.

Did labor market institutions contribute to late nineteenth- and early twentieth-century inequality? On the one hand, institutions were a central concern of early twentieth-century economists such as John R. Commons and of a large literature in the "new" labor history, examining the working class and the causes of Gilded Age labor conflict (Brody 1960; Commons 1918; Montgomery 1987). On the other hand, economic historians such as Fishback (1998) and Goldin (2000) have argued that markets played a more important role than the institutionalists suggested. Thus, one might believe that inequality was primarily a product of market outcomes. Indeed, the late nineteenth-century Northern United States is sometimes viewed as an archetypal laissez-faire economy: markets, and particularly the labor market, *were* in fact largely unregulated institutional spaces. Especially in the cities, the free exchange of labor appears to have been close to a textbook labor market.

An economist casually observing late nineteenth-century American labor markets might view the absence of regulation as an indication that a perfectly competitive labor market was at work. However, the absence of labor market regulation does not imply the absence of market imperfections or frictions. Nor does it imply that labor market

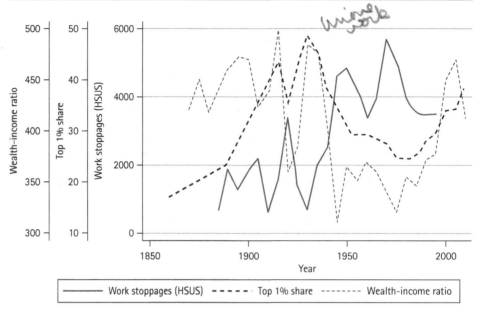

FIGURE 14.1. Economic inequality and labor market conflict in the nineteenth and twentieth centuries

Note and sources: Figure shows the wealth to income ratio in the United States (from Piketty and Zucman 2014); the share of wealth held by the top 1% of households (from Roine and Waldenstrom 2015; Saez and Zucman 2016); and the number of work stoppages per year (series Ba4954 from the *Historical Statistics of the United States*, 2006).

institutions were irrelevant to the determination of wages and the distribution of income. Interestingly, in figure 14.1, one can see a negative association between work stoppages—strikes, which reflect workers' attempts to increase their share of any rents in the labor market—and economic inequality in the late nineteenth and early twentieth centuries.

Labor market institutions and labor conflict indeed played an important role in shaping economic outcomes in the late nineteenth and early twentieth centuries, but this chapter takes a somewhat different approach from the institutional economists and labor historians. This perspective is influenced by modern research in labor economics, which highlights the importance of frictions in the labor market and bargaining over rents between workers and employers, as well as by political economy and law and economics research on strikes, conflict, and the importance of the judiciary. There is evidence that there existed frictions and rents in the nineteenth-century (Northern) American labor market; moreover, conflict over the distribution of rents in the labor market—and the institutions that resolved them—played an active role in determining labor market outcomes.

New evidence suggests rents in the labor market: when urban, industrial firms experienced (plausibly exogenous) positive output price shocks, their employees earned wage premia, relative to other employees with similar skills in the very same labor market. The existence of wage rents that were not competed away contributes new evidence to a rich, but mixed, historical literature on frictions in the US labor market in the nineteenth century.[1]

Fishback (1998) discusses a set of institutions that arose in response to nineteenth-century labor market frictions, arguing that they reduced transaction costs. This analysis complements Fishback's discussion of labor market institutions in the nineteenth century, focusing on institutions meant not to reduce transaction costs, but to determine the distribution of rents that were bargained over—sometimes battled over—by employers and employees. This chapter focuses on labor strikes, and the institutions—the police, militias, and especially the courts—that employers used to combat them. Worker strikes and employers' attempts to squash strikes with legal injunctions represented institutional determinants of the distribution of rents, rather than simply institutions that reduced transaction costs.

The chapter presents evidence on strikes in the late nineteenth century: the rising frequency of strikes across time (using data from the *Historical Statistics of the United States*); the increase in the number of labor-related events involving violence (from Turchin 2012); and the number of deaths arising from labor conflict (again, from Turchin 2012). Next, it examines the impact of strikes on employee wages in the late nineteenth century; controlling for a variety of firm characteristics, strikes were correlated with higher wages.[2] The chapter also presents evidence on the determinants of strikes' outcomes, finding that a crucial determinant of strikes' outcomes was the ability of employers to hire replacement workers. That is, the distribution of labor market rents—going to incumbent workers, or going to employers and to replacement workers—was at the crux of labor market conflict in the late nineteenth century.

Next, the chapter presents evidence on the legal institutions—in particular, judicial labor injunctions—that supported employers' efforts to suppress worker strikes in the late nineteenth and early twentieth centuries. Labor injunctions were legal requests made by employers to judges to end a labor strike and force employees to return to work (a substitute for hiring replacement workers that might be especially desirable when the latter option was costly). Injunctions also broke up picketing or other activities that prevented replacement workers from continuing work. The present authors used the legal databases LexisNexis and Westlaw to identify all reported cases involving a legal injunction used as a remedy in a labor dispute between 1875 and 1930. One can see a sharp rise in the use of injunctions in the late nineteenth and early twentieth centuries; this analysis builds on Currie and Ferrie (2000), who examine the effects of the legal "rules of the game" on labor market outcomes, and follows Orren (1991) in pointing to the crucial role played by the judicial branch in establishing the rules of the game in the nineteenth-century labor market.[3]

This analysis suggests that economic historians ought to devote more attention to the de facto labor market institutions that determine the distribution of rents within the labor relationship, as well as to the courts that often set the rules of the bargaining game. The present authors also believe that this study of labor market institutions in the Gilded Age has lessons beyond the historical setting studied, especially in light of contemporary scholarship documenting recent increases in income and wealth inequality—the possible rise of a second Gilded Age (refer again to fig. 14.1) (Piketty 2014). A first lesson of history and recent scholarship is that high levels of inequality can be associated with wasteful (sometimes violent) social conflict (Esteban and Ray 2011), or wasteful expenditures to deter and suppress this conflict (Bowles and Jayadev 2006). Second, while contemporary policy proposals aimed at reducing inequality often focus on income taxation and redistribution, the present examination of the nineteenth-century labor market institutions suggests the importance of policies affecting the distribution of rents within the labor contract. Increasing workers' bargaining power, changing the distribution of rents between high- and low-skill workers and between workers and firm owners, could play an important role in reducing contemporary inequality. ─────

Frictions and Rents in Nineteenth-Century American Labor Markets

Economic historians have found that supply and demand were important drivers of the level and distribution of wages in the late nineteenth and early twentieth centuries. Fishback, reviewing the literature on the nineteenth century American labor market, writes,

> Turn-of-the-century America offers an unusual empirical opportunity to expand our understanding of the operation of largely unregulated labor markets. The American experience between 1890 and 1930 illustrates the roles of exit and voice in determining worker welfare in the absence of unemployment insurance, social security, wage and hour regulations, the National Labor Relations Board, anti-discrimination laws, and many other modern regulatory influences. (Fishback 1998, 722)

Fishback continues,

> Turnover rates were higher in the early 1900s than in the modern era and there were strong signs of labor market integration between most regions of the United States. The South, which some consider isolated, offered numerous opportunities for workers to raise their earnings near levels in the North through migration within the region. The combination of competition among employers and the use by workers of both exit and collective action served to limit the extent to which employers could earn monopsonistic rents from their workers in the long run. (Fishback 1998, 723)

Yet, labor historians and economic historians, including Fishback, also find evidence of significant frictions, rents to be bargained and fought over, and the existence of institutions that fundamentally shaped labor market outcomes. There are disagreements, however, about how much these factors interfered with the operations of supply and demand in labor markets.

From one perspective, the primary determinants of employment and wage patterns are supply and demand, and these were surely important drivers of the level and distribution of wages. Both labor supply and demand certainly changed in important ways in the late nineteenth century. On the supply side, of paramount importance were the massive inflows of immigrants, which increased the supply of labor in the late nineteenth century (see Abramitzky, Boustan, and Eriksson 2012). Expanded schooling—the establishment of common schools, then the expansion of secondary schooling—was undoubtedly important, too, in shaping the distribution of earnings (Goldin and Katz 2008).

On the labor demand side, the nineteenth-century United States saw the rise of the large corporation (Chandler 1977) and rapid technical change (Atack, Bateman, and Margo 2008). Goldin and Katz (1998) and Katz and Margo (2014) explore the effects of factory production and the introduction of new technology on the demand for workers with differing skill levels. They find increased demand for skilled labor coming from complementarities with new technologies, such as electrification in the early twentieth century, as well as a "hollowing out" of the occupational distribution, with nineteenth-century manufacturing crowding out traditional artisans, and substituting the labor of low-skill workers and high-skill, white-collar workers.

Increased productivity was (at least partially) reflected in workers' wages in the late nineteenth and early twentieth centuries, with unskilled workers' real wages rising slowly, but steadily, from 1860 to 1918 (see fig. 14.2). Were the higher wages earned commensurate with changes in workers' marginal products? The mapping from worker

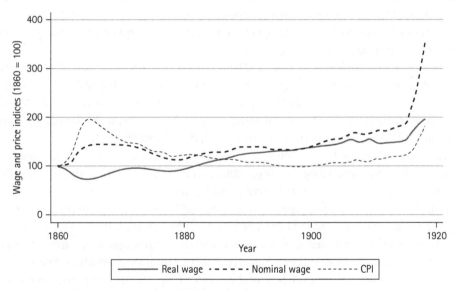

FIGURE 14.2. Real and nominal unskilled workers' wages, 1860–1918

Note: Figure shows the evolution of unskilled workers' nominal wage, price level, and unskilled workers' real wage indices (1860 = 100) from 1860 to 1918.

Source: All data come from Historical Statistics of the United States (2006): the nominal wage index is series Ba4218 and the price index is series Cc2 (the real wage is their ratio).

productivity to wages might not have been so simple: in addition to supply and demand, labor market outcomes may have been shaped by frictions, the distribution of rents that were bargained and fought over, and the functioning of labor market institutions.

Indeed, economic historians have collected a wide range of evidence on the imperfections in nineteenth century labor markets, despite the lack of regulatory interference. One obvious labor market friction was simply imperfect worker mobility. Rosenbloom, using census earnings data, suggests that "although labor market integration was proceeding on a regional level, this process did not extend to the national level" (1996, 652). While Rosenbloom focused on geographic wage dispersion, he also points to other frictions: recruitment costs meant that employer search depended on recruiting through social networks; wages, he notes, did not adjust to reflect variation in local amenities, such as infant mortality.

Recent work reveals substantial *firm*-specific wage premia, even in contemporary labor markets (Card et al. 2016). One source of these premia is employee investment in firm-specific human capital, which produces rents within the employment contract to be bargained over between employees and (incumbent) employers (Jäger 2016). Sundstrom (1988) presents evidence that firms in the nineteenth-century United States relied on internal promotion to fill skilled positions, which suggests that workers acquired valuable firm-specific skills on the job. Long tenures for employees also point to an important role for firm-specific human capital (see Carter and Savoca 1990; Sundstrom 1988; see also Jacoby and Sharma 1992, for an alternative perspective). Another literature has looked explicitly at monopsony in the nineteenth-century labor market. Fishback and Boal (1995)examine monopsony in nineteenth-century coal mining, and find some evidence of monopsony power, though they emphasize relatively low rates of "exploitation" (i.e., gaps between wages and marginal product) and high rates of worker mobility across employers.[4]

Zevin (1975) and Vedder, Gallaway, and Klingaman (1978) present evidence suggesting some degree of employer monopsony power among urban textile mills in the nineteenth century. There is no doubt that nineteenth-century labor markets were affected by search frictions, and there existed some rents in the employment relationship—yet the extent of the imperfection remains very much the subject of debate.[5]

The present authors take a different approach to studying frictions in nineteenth-century labor markets, using the 1850–1880 national samples from the nineteenth-century Census of Manufacturing (collected by Jeremy Atack, Fred Bateman, and Thomas Weiss) to test for firm-specific wage premia.[6] To do so, we examine the relationship between firms' value added per worker and employee wages. While it would not be surprising if the value added of firms were correlated with wages across markets, in a perfectly competitive market there should be little variation in wages across firms in the same industry, within the same labor market, at a single point in time, particularly once skill and worker characteristics are accounted for.[7]

A series of papers by Jeremy Atack, Fred Bateman, and Robert Margo have used these data to document patterns in the manufacturing sector in the late nineteenth century.[8] The work closest to the approach taken in this chapter is Atack, Bateman, and Margo

Table 14.1 Summary Statistics: Census of Manufacturing

Variable	Mean	SD	n
Labor (Raw)	11.322	41.853	8,305
Monthly average wage (1% Winsorized)	26.777	16.306	8,305
Capital	8,312.277	36,168.466	8,305
Value added per unit labor	755.068	1,254.086	8,305
Rural	0.788	0.409	8,305
Output 1 price	50.45	275.307	3,570
Fraction men	0.954	0.146	8,305
Skill premium	1.91	0.755	2,711

Source: Data come from the 1850–1880 national samples of the Census of Manufacturing collected by Jeremy Atack, Fred Bateman, and Thomas Weiss.

(2004), in which the authors look at patterns of wage dispersion between 1850 and 1880. They find that, *ceteris paribus,* larger firms had lower wages, as firms adopting modern production methods had a lower demand for skill. In addition, they find that wage dispersion was increasing over this period, as the increasingly important larger firms employed lower wage workers. Katz and Margo (2014) argue that rather than strict "deskilling," the nineteenth century saw a "hollowing out" of the labor market, as middle-skill jobs disappeared.

Table 14.1 provides summary statistics from the Manufacturing Census data, showing the size of a firm's workforce; average monthly wages, constructed following Atack, Bateman, and Margo (2004); value added per worker; output prices; and information on the gender and skill composition of a firm's workforce. This analysis begins simply by documenting correlations in the raw data between firms' value added per worker and firms' average wages. The left-hand panel of figure 14.3 shows a scatterplot of wages against firm value added per worker, along with the best-fit linear relationship. One can see that, unconditionally, higher value added firms paid higher wages.

Of course, higher value added firms may differ from lower value added firms in a variety of ways, and wages may differ across these firms for a variety of reasons other than labor market imperfections. To more directly examine differences in wages across firms that ought to be competing in the same labor market, the relationship between value added and wages conditional on city × industry × year is examined. The right-hand panel of figure 14.3 shows a scatterplot of wage residuals (conditioning out the city × industry × year fixed effects) against value added per worker residuals. One can still see a strong positive relationship between firm value added and wages—even looking within the same city, within the same industry, within the same year.

Next the robustness of the relationship between wages and value added is examined, estimating a series of regressions, first regressing log average wages on log value added

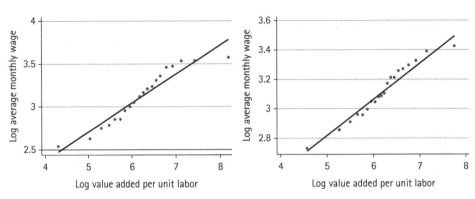

FIGURE 14.3. Relationship between firms' wages and value added

Notes: Figure shows binned scatterplots of firms' log average wages against log value added per worker. Left-hand panel shows unconditional values. Right-hand panel absorbs city × industry × year fixed effects and plots residuals.

Source: Firm-level data on wages and value added per worker are from the national sample of the Census of Manufacturing 1850–1880 collected by Jeremy Atack, Fred Bateman, and Thomas Weiss.

per worker, conditional on city × year fixed effects. The motivation behind this specification is that cities are natural labor markets, and systematic firm-level variation in wages conditional on these fixed effects provides a first indication that there is not a single market wage facing all firms. Thus the following model is estimated:

$$\log(w_{ijct}) = \beta \log\left(\frac{V_{ijct}}{L_{ijct}}\right) + X_i \gamma + \delta_j + \delta_{ct} + \epsilon_{ijct} \tag{1}$$

where w_{ijct} is the log monthly average wage paid by firm i, in industry j, in city c, in year t; V_{ijct} is the value added of the firm, and that is, the difference between sales revenue of firm i and C_{ijct}, the firm's nonlabor input costs; L_{ijct} is a firm's raw labor input[9]; X_i is a set of firm level characteristics, generally fraction male and the log of the value of the capital stock; δ_j are a set of industry fixed effects; δ_{ct} are a set of city × year fixed effects; and ε_{ijct} is a firm-specific error term.

In table 14.2, column 1, one can see that within a city × year cell, higher value added firms pay higher wages than lower value added firms: we estimate that a 10 percent increase in a firm's value added translates into a 2.3 percent increase in monthly wages. In column 2, we estimate a model nearly identical to equation (1), but adding controls for log capital and the fraction of a firm's workforce who are adult men, as well as industry fixed effects. In column 3, we estimate the specification from table 14.2, column 1, but now include a full set of city × industry × year fixed effects to account for cross-industry (within city × year) variation in wages (note that all specifications in table 14.2 are restricted to city × industry × year cells with at least four firms). Column 4 shows the same specification as column 3, but restricted to cities with at least ten firms (i.e., "urban" labor markets). In table 14.2, column 5, we add to the specification with city × industry × year

Table 14.2 Correlations between Log Wages and Log Value Added

Dependent Variable: Log Average Wage

	(1)	(2)	(3)	(4)	(5)	(6)	(7)
Log (Value added/Labor)	0.234	0.204	0.243	0.327	0.210	0.289	0.147
	(0.015)	(0.014)	(0.019)	(0.041)	(0.016)	(0.021)	(0.074)
Fraction men		0.589			0.582	0.360	
		(0.053)			(0.056)	(0.087)	
Log capital		0.051			0.049	0.068	
		(0.007)			(0.007)	(0.013)	
Skill premium						−0.018	
						(0.018)	
City x year FE	Yes	Yes	No	No	No	No	Yes
City x industry x year FE	No	No	Yes	Yes	Yes	No	No
Industry FE	No	Yes	No	No	No	No	Yes
City x industry FE	No	No	No	No	No	Yes	No
Sample	All	All	All	Urban	All	1880	1850–1870
Observations	8,305	8,263	8,305	1,709	8,305	2,710	3,506
R2	0.39	0.43	0.50	0.60	0.51	0.52	0.16
First stage F							44.53

Notes: Outcome variable is the log average wage in all columns. Robust standard errors, clustered at the city x year level, in parentheses. Columns 1–6 show estimated coefficients from OLS regressions of a firm's log average wage on its value added per worker, plus controls indicated in the table. Column 7 shows estimated coefficients from the second stage of a 2SLS analysis in which a firm's value added per worker is instrumented for using the price of the firm's primary output. Sample restricted to industries in cities (including rural areas) with more than three firms, except for the "Urban" sample, which drops rural firms and those in cities with fewer than ten firms.

fixed effects controls for log capital and for the fraction of a firm's workforce who are adult men. Next, in table 14.2, column 6, we examine whether wage differences across firms simply reflect different skill premiums paid in high value added firms. We do so by controlling for the ratio of a firm's skilled wages to its unskilled wages. Our results across specifications are qualitatively similar to those in column 1: firms in the same city, in the same industry, paid their workers different wages associated with the firms' value added.

A concern with the analysis thus far is that unobserved firm characteristics could be behind both greater value added and higher wages. We next try to isolate the relationship between wages and plausibly exogenous variation in firm value added, using the price of a firm's primary output as an instrument for its value added. The logic behind this instrumental variable analysis is that each firm takes its output price as given, and movements in the output price can generate variation in a firm's value added.[10] Note that output price data are not available for 1880, so this analysis is limited to the 1850–1870 censuses. In table 14.2, column 7, we present second-stage results from a two-stage least squares estimate in which the price of the primary output product of firm i in year t is an instrument for the value added of firm i in year t.[11] The coefficient on the firm's value added in the second stage is smaller than in the OLS regressions; however, variation in value added driven by firm output prices (plausibly exogenous with respect to a single firm) remains positively associated with firm wages (the coefficient's magnitude is consistent with Card et al. 2016).[12] In sum, these regressions show that even within labor markets, defined either as cities or city × industry cells, firm value added is significantly correlated with firm wages. This suggests the existence of firm-specific rents that are not competed away. The data do not allow us to identify particular sources of rents; possibilities include firm-specific human capital, adverse selection, moral hazard, search frictions, norms of fairness, or intrafirm bargaining. Each of these sources, however, is consistent with the existence of rents to be bargained over between employers and employees.

Of course, there are other possible explanations for the observed correlation between wages and value added. For example, high wages at high value-added firms may be compensating differentials for a firm-specific disamenity. It is also possible that our results are driven by sorting of skilled workers into highly productive firms. These two alternative hypotheses would be addressed by our instrumental variables analysis if neither disamenities nor employee sorting varied with a firm's output prices. Controls for firm characteristics (such as the skill premium) should also help. However, the possibility cannot be entirely ruled out that there exists some unobserved firm characteristic that is associated with both wage levels and value added.

Further evidence of rents in the nineteenth-century labor market is the pervasiveness of costly rent-seeking behavior. This was not limited to market interactions or lobbying for state policy, but also took the form of bloody conflicts between workers and employers (and replacement workers) as well as violent state repression. The next section provides evidence of costly conflict over rents in the nineteenth-century labor market.

LABOR CONFLICT

The late nineteenth century saw the rise of the labor union as an economic, social, and political force. Still, the rapid increase in union membership in the late nineteenth century was built on a small base; relatively low union density meant that bargaining in the absence of formal unions was often necessary.[13] The low level of formal union membership is one reason to emphasize (sometimes firm-specific) strikes over unions in collective bargaining; moreover, the existence of labor market frictions meant that worker organizations did not need to control an entire labor market in order to increase wages—withholding labor from the firm could impose severe costs on employers. Importantly, strikers' leverage stemmed from their ability to prevent employers from using replacement workers. But strikers had little *de jure* power: the law did not prevent the hiring of replacements. While scarce skilled workers had high replacement costs, unskilled workers did not. Thus, for the threat of a strike to have bite, strikers often relied on the use of coercion (or at least the *threat* of coercion off the equilibrium path). Coercive action by workers included picketing, social pressure, political dealing, and sometimes violence to restrict the hiring of replacement labor. On the other side of the bargaining process, employers would do whatever they could to induce striking workers to return to their employment, or to force in replacement workers. While the majority of labor conflicts were nonviolent, bargaining over rents in the labor contract was at the root of increasingly violent confrontations between workers and employers in the late nineteenth century.

While strikes were rare events, their increasing frequency and ferocity in the late nineteenth century led to widespread public concern, prompting several government investigations, and spurring the creation of the Bureau of Labor Statistics in 1884. Figure 14.4 presents evidence of increasing labor conflict in three time series. First, it shows the count of strikes, from the *Historical Statistics of the United States* (HSUS). One can see a rise in the late nineteenth century, and large spikes in the early twentieth century. It also shows the number of labor conflict events, and the number of deaths that occurred in labor conflicts, both from Turchin.[14] One can again see evidence of increased conflict in the second half of the nineteenth century, and peaks in the early twentieth century.

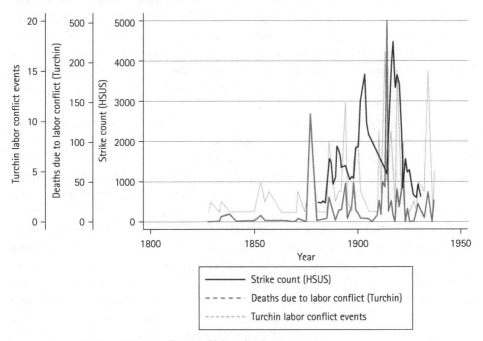

FIGURE 14.4. Strikes, labor conflicts and labor deaths, 1828–1937

Note and sources: Figure shows time series data on the number of work stoppages in the United States (series Ba4954 from the *Historical Statistics of the United States*), the number of violent labor conflicts (from Turchin 2012) and the number of deaths occurring in labor conflicts (also from Turchin 2012).

Table 14.3 Summary Statistics: Firm Characteristics and Strike
          Activity in the Weeks Report

Variable	Mean	SD	n
Log daily wage	0.269	0.267	5,059
Experienced a major strike	−0.178	0.611	5,059
Hot blast technology	0.045	0.206	5,049
Manager reports high labor efficiency	−0.195	0.745	5,059
Fraction female	0.004	0.063	5,059
Fraction child	0.006	0.077	5,059
Fraction black	0.002	0.042	5,059
Fraction Asian	0.005	0.065	5,059

Sources: The original data source is *Weeks Report* (1886), with the sample restricted to post-1865 years. Data downloaded from http://econterms.net/weeksreport/weeks.doc.htm, courtesy of Peter Meyers (last accessed November 17, 2015).

Were strikes successful in raising workers' wages? Strong causal claims are difficult to make due to the endogeneity of strikes: for example, workers may choose to strike disproportionately at firms that pay high wages. Still, it can be informative to examine the association between strikes and wages. We do so using data from the Weeks Report (1886).[15] Table 14.3 first presents summary statistics for the Weeks Report data. The strike measure is either −1, if no strike was known to have occurred, 0 if it was unknown whether a strike had occurred, and 1 if it was known that a strike had occurred. We next regress firm wages on the experience of a strike.

In table 14.4, column 1, one can see that there is, indeed, a positive and statistically significant relationship between strikes and wages. Because in some cases we do not know if there was a strike or not, in table 14.4, column 2, we limit the analysis to those observations in which there was clearly a strike or no strike. One can see that examining only these strikes, there remains a positive relationship between the experience of a strike and wages.

Of course, strikes may occur in particular industries, places, and times that would be associated with higher wages even in the absence of a strike. In table 14.4, column 3, we thus add industry and year fixed effects, which capture many dimensions of a firm's environment that may be associated with both strikes and wages. One can see that the coefficient on the experience of a strike falls, but strikes remain associated with a higher wage. In table 14.4, columns 4–5, we add to the specification in column 3 controls for the composition of a firm's workforce and state fixed effects. Strikes are positively associated with wages in both specifications.

Next, in table 14.4, column 6, we control for workforce composition, as well as industry, state, and year fixed effects. We also include controls for firm characteristics that

Table 14.4 Daily Wages and the Experience of Strikes

Dependent Variable: Log Average Wage

	(1)	(2)	(3)	(4)	(5)	(6)	(7)
Experienced a major	0.039	0.048	0.036	0.035	0.025	0.021	0.029
strike	(0.017)	(0.016)	(0.015)	(0.015)	(0.013)	(0.012)	(0.014)
Hot blast technology						0.212	−0.440
						(0.069)	(0.053)
Manager reports high						−0.025	−0.015
labor efficiency						(0.011)	(0.014)
Composition controls	No	No	No	Yes	No	Yes	Yes
Year FE	No	No	Yes	Yes	Yes	Yes	Yes
Industry FE	No	No	Yes	Yes	Yes	Yes	Yes
State FE	No	No	No	No	Yes	Yes	Yes
Only known	No	Yes	No	No	No	No	Yes
Observations	5,059	2,052	5,059	5,059	5,059	5,049	2,052
R2	0.01	0.03	0.27	0.30	0.48	0.55	0.57

Sources: The original data source is Weeks (1886), with the sample restricted to post-1865 years. Data downloaded from http://econterms.net/weeksreport/weeks.doc.htm, courtesy of Peter Meyers (last accessed November 17, 2015).
Notes: Regressions show the relationship between establishment characteristics—in particular, the experience of a strike—and wages. Standard errors clustered at the establishment level. "High Labor Efficiency" was reported by the establishment manager. Composition controls are fraction black, female, Asian, and fraction child workers.

may be associated with both strikes and wage rates: the use of hot blast technology and manager reports that labor is used highly efficiently. Again we find a positive association between strikes and wages. Finally, we repeat the specification from table 14.4, column 6, but limiting the analysis to observations in which there was clearly a strike or no strike. In table 14.4, column 7, one can again see a positive association between strikes and wages.

We next explore the determinants of strike success, using data collected in Reports issued by the Commissioner of Labor.[16] Here we build on much prior work on the empirical determinants of strike outcomes.[17] For example, Card and Olson, also using data from the Commissioner of Labor Reports, find that

> [s]trikes ordered by a labor organization, strikes with fewer female workers, strikes initiated prior to the wave of unrest following the Haymarket incident in May 1886, strikes in the building trades and the shoe industry, and strikes involving a larger fraction of the firm's workforce were more likely to succeed. Interestingly, all of these factors raise the wage conditional on a successful strike. We interpret this finding as

evidence that employers with greater potential rents had higher costs during a work stoppage. (Card and Olson 1995)

The present authors focus on the role of replacement workers in determining the outcomes of strikes. A sizable economics literature has documented the importance of high replacement costs for strike success, and we undertake an empirical analysis in this spirit here (Cramton and Tracy 2003). We begin by regressing a "successful strike" dummy variable on city and year fixed effects, as well as the log of employment at the firm in question.[18] We then plot the residuals from this regression against the (residualized) fraction of replacement workers hired during the strike. One can see in the left panel of figure 14.5 that there is a strong negative relationship between the success of a strike and the use of replacement workers. In the right panel of figure 14.5, one can see that the hiring of replacement workers also translated into smaller wage gains resulting from a strike.[19]

Different from the regulated strike environment created under the New Deal, nineteenth-century strikes were often borderline illegal. Striking workers, particularly the unskilled, naturally attempted to prevent the hiring of replacements, often using force.[20] Many workers believed they had "property rights" in their jobs, making the use of force legitimate in their eyes. Organizing and paying for the coercive capacity to prevent employers from hiring replacement workers could be a massive undertaking. For example, Brecher describes the organization of the Amalgamated Association of Iron and Steel Workers during the Homestead strike near Pittsburgh in 1892:

> In preparation for the strike, the Amalgamated had formed an Advisory Committee of five delegates from each of its eight lodges. Since the Amalgamated Association

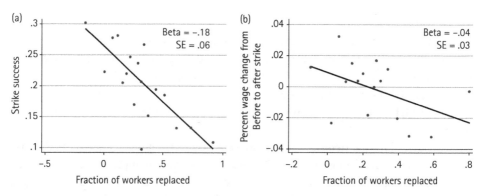

FIGURE 14.5. Replacement workers and strike outcomes for strikes with a positive number of replacement workers

Notes: Replacement workers and strike outcomes, for strikes with a positive number of replacement workers. Left panel plots residualized strike success dummy variable against residualized fraction of replacement workers hired. Right panel plots residualized change in a firm's wage bill (post- minus pre-strike) against residualized fraction of replacement workers hired.

Source: Data come from the Third and Tenth Commissioner of Labor Reports (US Commissioner of Labor, 1888 and 1896).

included only 750 of the 3,800 workers at Homestead, the Advisory Committee called on the rest to support the strike. Three thousand workers packed into the Homestead Opera House and voted overwhelmingly that everyone would strike— for the semiskilled and unskilled workers feared that their wages would be reduced as well. The Advisory Committee then circulated the following statement: "The Committee has, after mature deliberation, decided to organize their forces on a truly military basis. The force of four thousand men has been divided into three divisions or watches, each of these divisions is to devote eight hours of the twenty-four to the task of watching the plant. The Commanders of these divisions are to have as assistants eight captains composed of one trusted man from each of the eight local lodges." (Brecher 1997, 72)

Employers responded to striking workers' use of coercion with force of their own. Sometimes this force was privately organized. Voss (1993) shows that employer associations played a crucial role in suppressing the Knights of Labor in New Jersey in the nineteenth century. New York City elites privately organized to limit labor violence (Beckert 2001).[21] Employers also hired the Pinkerton National Detective Agency ("the Pinkertons") to break strikes: Brecher notes that "[the Pinkertons'] 2,000 active agents and 30,000 reserves totaled more than the standing army of the nation" (1997, 72). Pinkertons could infiltrate and sabotage unions, and could also be used in direct physical conflict with strikers, as in the Homestead strike.

More generally, state institutions—political and legal—determined how aggressively strikers could behave, and how forcefully employers could respond to workers' actions. Friedman, analyzing France and United States in the nineteenth century suggests that mass strikes were less effective in the United States than in France because employers were more likely to benefit from government intervention in America (Friedman 1988).[22] Government intervention at its most dramatic took the form of the deployment of both the state militia and federal army regulars (Cooper 1980). Riker (1957) presents data showing that between 1877 and 1892, the *modal* use of American militia was to quell labor unrest (33 of 112 instances, eight times the number of uses in response to natural disasters). In figure 14.6, one can see that states' militia spending was also positively and significantly related to the number of striking workers. Government intervention also took the form of legal injunctions that legitimized the use of force by the state (if necessary). The next section turns to the role of the judiciary in shaping the rules governing conflict in the labor market.

JUDICIAL IDEOLOGY AND THE ROLE OF COURTS

While employers often received the support of sheriffs, governors, and even the president of the United States in labor conflicts, elected officials could not always be relied

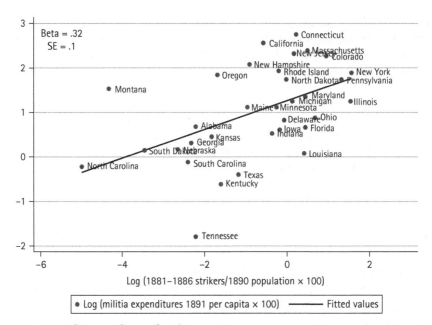

FIGURE 14.6. Militia spending and strikers

Note: Figure plots the log of militia expenditures per capita against the number of striking workers per capita, by state.

Source: Data come from Riker (1957).

on. A labor movement with popular support and sympathy could threaten officials' re-election and thus win pro-labor policies. The historical strike record includes many instances of state sympathy for labor: local police forces or militias might refuse to fight with strikers and instead join them. Governors and legislators, too, sometimes found themselves reluctant to invoke force to break strikes, fearing political repercussions.

However, the most influential institution governing labor conflict in the late nineteenth century was not under electoral contest; it was the body of common law, as interpreted by the courts.[23] The common law of employment, inherited from England, was heavily influenced by the doctrine of Master and Servant, which restricted the ability of most employees to leave their employers.[24] In extreme cases—apprenticeship, indentured servitude, and especially slavery—these restrictions allowed colonial American employers to extract greater labor effort without paying market wages.

Gradually, however, Republican ideology and economic forces eroded the individual coercion available under common law. Differing from Britain, American labor law stayed in the hands of courts in the late nineteenth century: indeed, Forbath (1991) points to the difference between "judicial supremacy" in the United States and "parliamentary supremacy" in Britain as crucial to the diverging labor movements in the two countries.

Horwitz (1977) describes the evolution of American law in the nineteenth century as the "triumph of contract." This overarching ideology enshrined in legal practice, together with the weight of common law, created a bench that was largely opposed to the legislative goals and the direct bargaining tactics of the labor movement. Thus, although American courts recognized unions as legal in *Commonwealth v. Hunt*, this legality was based on the individual's freedom of contract. Because termination of employment was well within the liberal American tradition, striking alone was not illegal.[25] However, the tactics that made strikes succeed in the late nineteenth century often involved persuasion and coercion—for example, attempts to prevent the hiring of potential replacement workers—and were viewed as illegal acts that restricted employers' and replacement workers' freedom of contract.[26] Professional discipline, shaped by bar associations (the American Bar Association was founded in 1878) and respect for precedent, constrained even labor-sympathetic judges. The result was a vigorous defense of individuals' right to contract that severely limited the ability of legislation to intervene in the labor market. Orren (1991) shows that while 11 percent of all antibusiness statutes were ever overturned by the judiciary, 75 percent of labor statutes were.

The institutional innovation that most effectively pacified labor violence was the labor injunction. At the behest of employers, judges issued injunctions ordering employees to return to work and allowing government forces to break up pickets and other activities that prevented replacements from working. In laying the groundwork for the injunction, the judiciary confronted legal dilemmas that were fundamental to the American constitution, pitting rights to property and contract against rights to freedom of association and speech. For example, three powerful tactics for strikers were picketing, the sympathy strike, and the secondary boycott. Judges issued injunctions against all of these tactics, arguing that picketing violated employer property rights, that sympathy strikes constituted enticement, and that secondary boycotts violated the Sherman Act.

Witte describes a series of (failed) attempts to pass federal legislation to limit judicial injunctions as follows:

> For more than a generation organized labor has sought relief through legislation from "government by injunctions." From 1895, when the first anti-injunction bill was introduced, to 1914, this was an important question in every Congress. Three times in 1897, 1902, and 1912—anti-injunction bills passed one house only to fail in the other. President Roosevelt recommended action to curb the "abuse" of injunctions in no less than five of his messages to Congress. Because Republican Congresses refused to pass such a law, the American Federation of Labor launched its nonpartisan political policy and in 1908 and 1912 endorsed the Democratic candidates for president. Finally, when the Democrats gained control of all branches of the government, the Clayton Act was enacted and labor heralded the labor sections of this measure as a combined Magna Carta and Bill of Rights. Within a few years, these sections were construed by the Supreme Court to have made no change in the law except to confer the right of trial by jury in a restricted class of contempt cases. (Witte 1931, 638)

To document the rising use of the injunction as a response to labor disputes, we identified all labor injunction cases in Westlaw and LexisNexis for the time period 1877–1930. Specifically, we searched for "injunction" and (labor OR strike OR workers OR collective bargaining OR combination).[27] Note that many (in fact, most) local court cases that were not appealed are not cataloged in either LexisNexis or Westlaw, so we observe only the tip of the iceberg: still, we find 586 such cases, excluding duplicates (in the sense of reaching multiple court levels).[28]

Figure 14.7 plots the time series of injunctions across time. One can see a steady increase from the mid-1880s, with a sharp spike in the early twentieth century and a high level throughout the period prior to the New Deal. Comparing figures 14.3 and 14.7, one can see that the late nineteenth and early twentieth centuries were a period with *both* the highest levels of violent labor conflict and also the period with the greatest number of injunctions.[29]

Labor conflict continued, despite the limits imposed on strikes, in part because the contract law did not recognize a right for workers to be represented by unions. The labor movement expanded during World War I when the federal government shifted attitudes and began to support collective bargaining in its contracts. The war's end and the federal government's decreased involvement in the economy touched off a series of conflicts over the recognition of unions that led to a decline in unionization during the 1920s. As part of the New Deal, the federal government recognized a right to unionize when more than 50 percent of workers from the same employer voted for unionization under the National Labor Relations Act (NLRA), which was upheld by the *Jones & Laughlin* Supreme Court decision in 1937.[30] The NLRA also moved labor law into the domain of administrative law created by the National Labor Relations

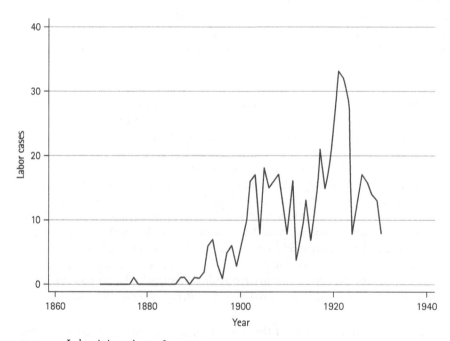

FIGURE 14.7. Labor injunctions, 1870–1930

Source: Figure shows counts from Lexis-Nexis and Westlaw, based on a search for "injunction" and (labor OR strike OR workers OR collective bargaining OR combination), and reading of cases to ensure that injunctions were issued in response to labor disputes.

Board (NLRB). The result was an increase in union membership that carried through the war. The more than 100 million man-days lost to strikes in 1946 and the postwar weakening of the New Deal Democrat coalition led to the passage of the Taft-Hartley Act in 1947, which put more restrictions on strikes and collective bargaining.[31] The share of private-sector workers in unions peaked in the 1950s and has generally declined since that time.

CONCLUSION

This chapter has documented characteristics of late nineteenth-century labor markets in the Northern United States, pointing to the important role played by labor market institutions in determining wages and the distribution of income, even in a context of limited formal regulation. First, it provided evidence of substantial frictions, which generated rents even in urban labor markets. This created a space for bargaining and conflict between workers and firms. Indeed, the second fact documented here is the presence of substantial labor market conflict. The chapter further shows that strikes were associated with higher wages and that a major determinant of a successful strike was the ability to restrict the use of replacement workers. Thus, physical coercion by workers (preventing the hiring of their replacements) was a critical aspect of strikes— one which invited a forceful response by employers, and the state acting on employers' behalf. Finally, the chapter showed that the judicial system played an important role in legitimizing the use of state coercion to end strikes in the nineteenth and early twentieth centuries.

By focusing here on conflict over rents in the labor market, we do not wish to diminish the importance of many other features of the nineteenth-century labor market.[32] We chose to focus on conflict both because it has been relatively neglected in economists' research on labor markets (relative to the attention received from other social scientists), and because we believe that there exist exciting paths forward for synthesizing the recent literature on the political economy of conflict with economic history research on labor markets.

For example, at a macroeconomic level, the role of conflict in building state capacity has long been observed by scholars (Besley and Persson 2009). It is interesting to note that military and law enforcement institutions of the United States, in particular the Army, the National Guard, and the FBI, can trace their origins to the federal troops, state militias, and private Pinkertons deployed in nineteenth-century labor conflicts (see Laurie and Cole 1997; Morn 1982; Skowronek 1982).

At a microeconomic level, currently, no comprehensive, disaggregated, data set on strikes exists, but we believe that exploiting natural language processing techniques, it is only a matter of time (and some effort) to put together far more complete data than are currently available. With vast swaths of nineteenth-century newspapers digitized (reporting on strikes and labor unrest more generally) and the 3rd and 10th Commissioner of Labor reports as training data, text classification methods and hand coding could conceivably be deployed to fill in the gaps in the Commissioner of Labor report data. Such methods could also be used to construct a data set measuring a variety of additional outcomes of interest. For example, newspaper descriptions of strikes often mentioned violations of civil rights, violence, or deaths.[33] Rich, disaggregated strike data could, among other things, be linked to available asset price data for the nineteenth century to examine the impact of strikes on listed firms' values.[34]

Finally, little of the literature estimating the effects of strikes (or labor market institutions) has exploited exogenous variation in strikes' incidence. Given the numerous sources of political variation (e.g., electoral regression discontinuities), weather variation (rainfall, heat, etc.), and sharp policy changes (either judicial or legislative), there seems to be ample scope for hypothesis testing regarding strikes' causes, and for empirical analyses of strikes' causal effects.

We close with some thoughts on the relevance of the past to our understanding of the present. Inequality has risen in recent decades to levels last seen in the early twentieth century. While very different from the violent strikes of 125 years ago, contemporary labor movements continue to wield de facto political power to try to increase their share of the pie. Recent worker mobilizations in the United States have won local minimum wage mandates, and have pressured firms to raise wages independently of legislation. Paralleling the restrictive role of nineteenth-century law and courts are binding arbitration clauses in union contracts, continued judicial injunctions, and NLRB restrictions on unionization drives, which have restricted the tactics available to unions and would-be unions. Inequality and conflict over the distribution of wealth and income thus remain relevant more than a century after the Gilded Age. A better understanding of the causes and consequences of conflicts in the past may reduce the costs of such conflicts in the future.

NOTES

1. See Goldin (2000) for a discussion of labor market institutions in the twentieth century, including the important changes of the New Deal era.
2. The occurrence of strikes could also have long-run effects on labor market outcomes. Hanes (1993) shows that industries in which firms experienced more strikes in the early 1880s were less likely to cut wages during the downturn in 1893. He argues that the fear of strikes, and the resulting increase in workers' bargaining power, generated wage rigidity even in the absence of legally binding contracts.
3. Currie and Ferrie (2000) find that changes in the laws governing labor conflict in the late nineteenth century did not typically have the effects expected by their proponents. In particular, they find no significant effect of labor injunctions on strike outcomes. However, their measure of injunction activity is simply an indicator that an injunction had previously been issued and sustained by a federal or state court in a labor dispute in a particular state. This sort of state × year level variation might be too coarse to capture any effect of injunctions.

4. Fishback (1998, 730–731) writes, "The high degree of mobility of workers offers evidence that workers exercised their opportunities to exit despite the presence of migration and information costs . . .. [Worker] turnover was widely recognized in the historical studies but the view of monopsony and exploitation still prevailed in the historical analysis of the industry. A series of studies offers a quite different picture of the coal industry, one in which the miners' mobility and exit play a substantially more powerful role than previously believed."

5. Ziebarth (2013) presents more general evidence of misallocation in the nineteenth-century United States, despite the relatively laissez-faire institutions. Indeed, he finds that the TFP loss due to distortion is quantitatively similar to that of China and India today.

6. These samples were downloaded from the website of Jeremy Atack; see https://my.vanderbilt.edu/jeremyatack/data-downloads/, last accessed May 2015.

7. Our examination of wage differences across industries and across firms is closely related to work on labor market rents in the twentieth century. See Katz and Summers (1989) for a cross-industry analysis, and Davis and Haltiwanger (1991) for a cross-plant analysis.

8. Atack, Bateman, and Margo (2002) document wage differences between manufacturing plants that operated year-round and those operating for only part of the year. Atack, Bateman, and Margo (2003) estimate the elasticity of output with respect to hours worked, finding a positive coefficient significantly smaller than 1. In Atack, Bateman, and Margo (2008), the authors document that steam power was increasingly used over the nineteenth century, was more likely to be used by larger establishments, and had a positive effect on labor productivity.

9. Atack, Bateman, and Margo (2003) adjust the labor input to reflect workers' composition as follows: adjusted labor = (no. of men) + 0.6*(no. of women) + 0.5*(no. of children). Using labor inputs adjusted this way does not affect our results.

10. Indeed, the instrument is quite strong: as reported in table 14.2, column 7, the F-statistic from the first stage is nearly 45.

11. We do not include city × industry × year fixed effects, as this would absorb nearly all of the variation in value added associated with a firm's output price.

12. In addition, the instrumented value added positively predicts employment, with a significant coefficient of 0.41, further suggesting that firms faced upward-sloping labor supply curves. Indeed, the implied labor supply elasticity facing the firm is 2.8, suggesting substantial monopsony power, with workers paid roughly 65 percent of their marginal product.

13. While it is difficult to identify a causal union wage premium, the available evidence suggests that unions were able to secure wage increases for both unskilled and skilled workers. Paul Douglas, in his 1930 "Real Wages in United States 1890–1926," documented a substantial union premium; Eichengreen (1987), too, finds a union wage premium, using data from Iowa in 1884. Hatton, Boyer, and Bailey (1994) also find a union wage premium in nineteenth-century Britain, which also saw rapid union growth.

14. Turchin (2012) constructs his dataset by combining data from Levy (1991) and Gilje (1996) with information collected from searches of online news databases.

15. The Weeks Report was a study conducted by census agent Joseph Weeks, as part of the 1880 census. Note that it is based on a convenience sample and thus is not perfectly representative of firms. We downloaded the data from http://econterms.net/weeksreport/weeksdoc.htm, courtesy of Peter Meyers (last accessed November 17, 2015).

16. Currie and Ferrie (2000) collected and digitized the reports from the six states (MA, CT, IL, NY, NJ, PA) that accounted for 90 percent of strikes from 1880 to 1894. See also Card

and Olson (1995) and Rosenbloom (1998). Note that Bailey (1991) finds evidence that some strikes were not covered by the reports.

17. See Cramton and Tracy (2003) for a more comprehensive review of the literature on labor disputes.

18. Card and Olson (1995) note that in the last two decades of the nineteenth century, around 80 percent of strikes ended with a clear victory or defeat for the striking workers.

19. Figure 14.5 includes only those strikes in which there was non-zero hiring of replacement workers. The negative relationship between replacement workers and strike success and wage gains is even more striking if strikes without any replacement hires are included.

20. Fishback (1995) describes the use of force on both sides of labor conflicts as a prisoners' dilemma, in which each side was better off arming than not, yet both sides paid the price of the noncooperative equilibrium.

21. Even university students volunteered as strike breakers and enlisted in militia, with Harvard and MIT students used to break the Lawrence Textile strike, Yale students volunteering as replacement workers for railroad workers and team drivers during strikes in 1903 and 1905, and University of Minnesota varsity athletes charging flour mill pickets in Minneapolis (Norwood 2002).

22. Of course, political considerations alone did not determine the prevalence or intensity of strikes. Along with the economic incentives on which we focus here, social factors were certainly important as well. Biggs (2003) argues that there are powerful positive feedback loops, so strikes give rise to further strikes; Biggs (2005) uses a "forest-fire" model to explain the pattern of strikes.

23. We follow Orren (1991) in pointing to the fundamental role played by the courts in governing the American labor market in the nineteenth century. Note that while some American judges were subject to elections, they were more insulated from ballot pressure than other officials.

24. See Tomlins (2004) on the use of Master and Servant law in sixteenth- through nineteenth-century America; Naidu and Yuchtman (2013) for an analysis of the use of Master and Servant law in nineteenth-century Britain; and Naidu (2010) on the use of anti-enticement laws in the postbellum US South.

25. The case is 45 Mass. 111 (1842).

26. Workers did not accept this interpretation of the constitution or the underlying "free labor" ideology. Unions had their own shadow jurisprudence and vision of what the constitution allowed. For example, some unions interpreted the Thirteenth Amendment as guaranteeing the right to strike. Interestingly, Gourevitch (2014) shows that the underlying Republican labor ideology also articulated many of the labor market imperfections that economists would recognize.

27. Cases were read to ensure that injunctions issued were in response to labor disputes.

28. Note also that observed injunctions are an imperfect indicator of injunctions' impact on bargaining over rents, as they may have been important as a threat off the equilibrium path.

29. This might be puzzling at first: one might expect that when the technology of repressing strikes improves, the most violent strikes and most costly conflicts would decline. However, in contest models with asymmetric payoffs (e.g., Nti 1999), the effect of extra repression on wasteful effort is ambiguous. A fall in unions' valuation of winning a strike (due to greater repression) may actually *increase* employer mobilization. This (or simply other variables) may explain why the highest levels of conflict occur at the same time as greater number of legal injunctions.

30. The case is *National Labor Relations Board v. Jones & Laughlin Steel Corporation*, 301 U.S. 1 (1937).
31. The CIO's "Operation Dixie" to organize Southern labor was launched in 1946, generating hostility from Southern Democrats (Katznelson 2013).
32. As noted earlier, changes in the levels of human capital, technological change, and the rise of mass migration dramatically affected the American labor market in the late nineteenth century (see, e.g., Abramitzky, Boustan, and Eriksson 2012, and Goldin and Katz 2008). Race also played a crucial role in determining labor market outcomes (see Hornbeck and Naidu 2014).
33. Automated and computer-assisted coding methods have been used to produce useful datasets on violence in contemporary data-poor environments, such as India (Fetzer 2014).
34. Baker, Frydman, and Hilt (2014) use the asset price data to examine the effect of (pro-business) McKinley's assassination by an anarchist labor radical, and the accession to power of (reformer) Teddy Roosevelt, on stock prices of firms vulnerable to antitrust prosecution. DiNardo and Hallock (2002) link strikes to firm values in the early twentieth century.

BIBLIOGRAPHY

Abramitzky, Ran, Leah Platt Boustan, and Katherine Eriksson. (2012). "Europe's Tired, Poor, Huddled Masses: Self-Selection and Economic Outcomes in the Age of Mass Migration." *American Economic Review* 102(5): 1832–1856.

Atack, Jeremy, Fred Bateman, and Robert A. Margo. (2002). "Part Year Operation in Nineteenth Century Manufacturing: Evidence from the 1870 and 1880 Censuses." *Journal of Economic History* 62(3): 792–809.

Atack, Jeremy, Fred Bateman, and Robert A. Margo. (2003). "Productivity in Manufacturing and the Length of the Working Day: Evidence from the 1880 Census of Manufactures." *Explorations in Economic History* 40: 170–194.

Atack, Jeremy, Fred Bateman, and Robert A. Margo. (2004). "Skill Intensity and Rising Wage Dispersion in Nineteenth Century American Manufacturing." *Journal of Economic History* 64(1): 172–192.

Atack, Jeremy, Fred Bateman, and Robert A. Margo. (2008). "Steam Power, Establishment Size, and Labor Productivity Growth in Nineteenth Century American Manufacturing." *Explorations in Economic History* 45: 185–198.

Bailey, Gary L. (1991). "The Commissioner of Labor's Strikes and Lockouts: A Cautionary Note." *Labor History* 32: 432–440.

Baker, Richard B., Carola Frydman, and Eric Hilt. (2014). "From Plutocracy to Progressivism? The Assassination of President McKinley as a Turning Point in American History." Boston University Working Paper.

Beckert, Sven. (2001). *The Monied Metropolis*. Cambridge: Cambridge University Press.

Besley, Timothy, and Torsten Persson. (2009). "The Origins of State Capacity: Property Rights, Taxation, and Politics." *American Economic Review* 99(4): 1218–1244.

Biggs, Michael. (2003). "Positive Feedback in Collective Mobilization: The American Strike Wave of 1886." *Theory and Society* 32: 217–254.

Biggs, Michael. (2005). "Strikes as Forest Fires: Chicago and Paris in the Late Nineteenth Century." *American Journal of Sociology* 110(6): 1684–1714.

Boal, William M. (1995). "Testing for Employer Monopsony in Turn-of-the-Century Coal Mining." *Rand Journal of Economics* 26(3): 519–536.

Bowles, Samuel, and Arjun Jayadev. (2006). "Guard Labor." *Journal of Development Economics* 79(2): 328–348.

Brecher, Jeremy. (1997). *Strike!* Cambridge, MA: South End Press.

Brody, David. (1960). *Steelworkers in America: The Nonunion Era*. Cambridge, MA: Harvard University Press.

Card, David, Ana Rute Cardoso, Jörg Heining, and Patrick Kline. (2016). "Firms and Labor Market Inequality: Evidence and Some Theory." University of California–Berkeley Working Paper.

Card, David, and Craig Olson. (1995). "Bargaining Power, Strike Durations, and Wage Outcomes: An Analysis of Strikes in the 1880s." *Journal of Labor Economics* 13(1): 32–61.

Carter, Susan B., and Elizabeth Savoca. (1990). "Labor Mobility and Lengthy Jobs in Nineteenth-Century America." *Journal of Economic History* 50(1): 1–16.

Chandler, Alfred D., Jr. (1977). *The Visible Hand: The Managerial Revolution in American Business*. Cambridge, MA: Harvard University Press.

Cramton, Peter, and Joseph Tracy. (2003). "Unions, Bargaining and Strikes." In *International Handbook of Trade Unions*, edited by John T. Addison and Claus Schnabel, Chapter 4, 86–117. Cheltenham, UK: Edward Elgar.

Commons, John R. (1918). *History of Labour in the United States*. New York: Macmillan.

Cooper, Jerry. (1980). *The Army and Civil Disorder: Federal Military Intervention in Labor Disputes, 1877–1900*. Westport, CT: Greenwood Press.

Currie, Janet, and Joseph Ferrie. (2000). "The Law and Labor Strife in the U.S., 1881–1894." *Journal of Economic History* 60(1): 42–66.

Davis, Steve J., and John Haltiwanger. (1991). "Wage Dispersion between and within US Manufacturing Plants, 1963–86." *Brookings Papers on Economic Activity: Microeconomics*, 115–200.

Dinardo, John, and Kevin F. Hallock. (2002). "When Unions 'Mattered': The Impact of Strikes on Financial Markets, 1925–1937." *Industrial and Labor Relations Review* 55(2): 219–233.

Douglas, Paul H. (1930). *Real Wages in the United States, 1890–1926*. Boston: Houghton Mifflin.

Eichengreen, Barry J. (1987). "The Impact of Late Nineteenth Century Unions on Labor Earnings and Hours: Iowa in 1894." *Industrial and Labor Relations Review* 40: 501–515.

Esteban, Joan, and Debra J. Ray. (2011). "Linking Conflict to Inequality and Polarization." *American Economic Review* 101(4): 1345–1374.

Fetzer, Thiemo. (2014). "Social Insurance and Conflict: Evidence from India." Warwick University Working Paper.

Fishback, Price V. (1992). "The Economics of Company Housing: Theoretical and Historical Perspectives from the Coal Fields." *Journal of Law, Economics, and Organization* 8: 346–365.

Fishback, Price V. (1995). "An Alternative View of Violence in Strikes: The Bituminous Coal Industry, 1890–1930." *Labor History* 36: 426–456.

Fishback, Price V. (1998). "Operations of 'Unfettered' Labor Markets: Exit and Voice in American Labor Markets at the Turn of the Century." *Journal of Economic Literature* 36: 722–765.

Friedman, Gerald. (1988). "Strike Success and Union Ideology: The United States and France, 1880–1914." *Journal of Economic History* 48(1): 1–25.

Forbath, William E. (1991). "Courts, Constitutions, and Labor Politics in England and America: A Study of the Constitutive Power of Law." *Law & Social Inquiry* 16(1): 1–34.

Gilje, Paul A. (1996). *Rioting in America*. Bloomington: Indiana University Press.

Goldin, Claudia. (2000). "Labor Markets in the Twentieth Century." In *The Cambridge Economic History of the United States*, edited by Stanley L. Engerman and Robert E. Gallman, Vol. III, 549–624. Cambridge: Cambridge University Press.

Goldin, Claudia, and Lawrence F. Katz. (1998). "The Origins of Technology-Skill Complementarity." *Quarterly Journal of Economics* 113: 693–732.

Goldin, Claudia, and Lawrence F. Katz. (2008). *The Race between Education and Technology*. Cambridge, MA: The Belknap Press of Harvard University Press.

Gourevitch, Alexander. (2014). *From Slavery to the Cooperative Commonwealth: Labor and Republican Liberty in the Nineteenth Century*. New York: Cambridge University Press.

Hanes, Christopher. (1993). "The Development of Nominal Wage Rigidity in the Late 19th Century." *American Economic Review* 83(4): 732–756.

Hatton, Timothy J., George R. Boyer, and Roy E. Bailey. (1994). "The Union Wage Effect in Late Nineteenth Century Britain." *Economica* 61(4): 435–456.

Historical Statistics of the United States. (2006). Edited by Susan B. Carter, Scott Sigmund Gartner, Michael R. Haines, Alan L. Olmstead, Richard Sutch, and Gavin Wright. Cambridge: Cambridge University Press.

Hornbeck, Richard, and Suresh Naidu. (2014). "When the Levee Breaks: Black Migration and Economic Development in the American South." *American Economic Review* 104(3): 963–990.

Horwitz, Morton J. (1977). *The Transformation of American Law, 1780–1860*. Cambridge, MA: Harvard University Press.

Jacoby, Sanford, and Sunil Sharma. (1992). "Employment Duration and Industrial Labor Mobility in the United States 1880–1980." *Journal of Economic History* 52(1): 161–179.

Jäger, Simon. (2016). "How Substitutable are Workers? Evidence from Worker Deaths." Harvard University Working Paper.

Katz, Lawrence F., and Robert A. Margo. (2014). "Technical Change and the Relative Demand for Skilled Labor: The United States in Historical Perspective." In *Human Capital in History*, edited by Leah Platt Boustan, Carola Frydman, and Robert A. Margo, 15–58. Chicago: University of Chicago Press.

Katz, Lawrence F., and Lawrence H. Summers. (1989). "Industry Rents: Evidence and Implications." *Brookings Papers on Economic Activity, Microeconomics*, 209–290.

Katznelson, Ira. (2013). *Fear Itself*. New York: W. W. Norton.

Laurie, Clayton D., and Ronald H. Cole. (1997). *The Role of Federal Military Forces in Domestic Disorders, 1877–1945*. Washington, DC: Center of Military History, US Army.

Levy, Sheldon G. (1991). *Political Violence in the United States, 1819–1968*. Ann Arbor, MI: Inter-University Consortium for Political and Social Research.

Montgomery, David. (1987). *The Fall of the House of Labor: The Workplace, the State, and American Labor Activism, 1865–1925*. Cambridge: Cambridge University Press.

Morn, Frank. (1982). *"The Eye That Never Sleeps": A History of the Pinkerton National Detective Agency*. Bloomington: Indiana University Press.

Naidu, Suresh. (2010). "Recruitment Restrictions and Labor Market Outcomes, Evidence from the Post-Bellum South." *Journal of Labor Economics* 28(2): 413–445.

Naidu, Suresh, and Noam Yuchtman. (2013). "Coercive Contract Enforcement: Law and the Labor Market in Nineteenth Century Industrial Britain." *American Economic Review* 103(1): 107–144.

Norwood, Stephen H. (2002). *Strikebreaking and Intimidation: Mercenaries and Masculinity in Twentieth-Century America*. Chapel Hill: University of North Carolina Press.

Nti, Kofi O. (1999). "Rent-Seeking with Asymmetric Valuations." *Public Choice* 98(3/4): 415–430.

Orren, Karen. (1991). *Belated Feudalism: Labor, the Law, and Liberal Development in the United States*. Cambridge: Cambridge University Press.

Piketty, Thomas. (2014). *Capital in the Twenty-first Century*. Cambridge, MA: The Belknap Press of Harvard University Press.

Piketty, Thomas, and Gabriel Zucman. (2014). "Capital Is Back: Wealth-Income Ratios in Rich Countries, 1700–2010." *Quarterly Journal of Economics* 129(3): 1255–1310.

Riker, William H. (1957). *Soldiers of the States; The Role of the National Guard in American Democracy*. Washington, DC: Public Affairs Press.

Roine, Jesper, and Daniel Waldenström. (2015). "Long Run Trends in the Distribution of Income and Wealth." In *Handbook in Income Distribution*, edited by A. B. Atkinson and F. Bourguignon, Vol. 2, 469–592. Amsterdam: North-Holland.

Rosenbloom, Joshua L. (1996). "Was There a National Labor Market at the End of the Nineteenth Century? New Evidence on Earnings in Manufacturing." *Journal of Economic History* 56: 626–656.

Rosenbloom, Joshua L. (1998). "Strikebreaking and the Labor Market in the United States, 1881–1894." *Journal of Economic History* 58: 183–205.

Saez, Emmanuel, and Gabriel Zucman. (2016). "Wealth Inequality in the United States since 1913: Evidence from Capitalized Income Tax Data." *Quarterly Journal of Economics* 131(1): 519–578.

Skowronek, Stephen. (1982). *Building a New American State: The Expansion of National Administrative Capacities, 1877–1920*. Cambridge: Cambridge University Press.

Sundstrom, William A. (1988). "Internal Labor Markets before World War I: On-the-Job Training and Employee Promotion." *Explorations in Economic History* 25(4): 424–445.

Tomlins, Christopher. (2004). "Early British America, 1585–1875: Freedom Bound." In *Masters, Servants and Magistrates in Britain and the Empire 1562–1955*, edited by Douglas Hay and Paul Craven, 117–152. Chapel Hill: University of North Carolina Press.

Turchin, Peter. (2012). "Dynamics of Political Instability in the United States, 1780–2010." *Journal of Peace Research* 49(4): 577–591.

US Commissioner of Labor. (1888). *Third Annual Report*. Washington, DC: Government Printing Office.

US Commissioner of Labor. (1896). *Tenth Annual Report*. Washington, DC: Government Printing Office.

Vedder, Richard K., Lowell E. Gallaway, and David Klingaman. (1978). "Discrimination and Exploitation in Antebellum American Cotton Textile Manufacturing." *Research in Economic History* 3: 217–262.

Voss, Kim. (1993). *The Making of American Exceptionalism: The Knights of Labor and Class Formation in the Nineteenth Century*. Ithaca, NY: Cornell University Press.

Weeks, Joseph D. (1886). *Report on the Statistics of Wages in Manufacturing Industries with Supplementary Reports*. Washington, DC: Government Printing Office.

Witte, Edwin E. (1931). "The Federal Anti-Injunction Act." *Minnesota Law Review* 16: 638.

Zevin, Robert B. (1975). *The Growth of Manufacturing in Early Nineteenth Century New England*. New York: Arno Press.

Ziebarth, Nicolas L. (2013). "Are China and India Backward? Evidence from the 19th Century. U.S. Census of Manufactures." *Review of Economic Dynamics* 16: 86–99.

CHAPTER 15

....

RETIREMENT AND PENSIONS IN AMERICAN ECONOMIC HISTORY

....

ROBERT L. CLARK AND LEE A. CRAIG

ECONOMIC historians have defined retirement as the "withdrawal from paid labor, and entering retirement is often thought of as an abrupt change in the life an elderly person" (Costa 1998, 6). By this definition, retirees no longer receive wages or salaries. Thus to continue consuming goods and services, they require other sources of income, such as personal assets, a publicly funded retirement program (in the United States, the largest of which is the Social Security system), or an employer-provided pension.

The Social Security system was created in 1935 as part of the New Deal, but employer-provided pensions have a much longer history, especially in the public sector. Although in the past the term "pension" referred to a wide range of payments in addition to retirement income, including survivor's (i.e., "widows and orphans") benefits and disability payments, today the term typically refers to a stream of payments received by a worker following retirement. Defined in this relatively narrow way, pensions are a fairly recent phenomenon in the private sector, dating from the late nineteenth century; however, public-sector pensions date back at least two millennia in Western history. From the Roman Empire to the rise of the early-modern nation-state, Western governments have provided pensions for their workers. Prior to the nineteenth century, public-sector pensions were primarily, though not exclusively, received by military personnel. The United States followed other early-modern Western countries and began offering pensions to its soldiers and seamen from the outset of the American Revolution.

In the nineteenth century, the US government began granting pensions to federal civil servants, but these were typically approved on a case-by-case basis through individual acts of Congress; except for military personnel, prior to the creation of the federal employees retirement plan in 1920, the federal government maintained no retirement *plan* with well-defined rules establishing the terms under which an employee would receive a pension, nor were there any regulations concerning employer or employee contributions, plan funding, and so forth, at any level of government until the late nine-teenth century. Prior to the 1850s, no state or local government maintained a pension plan. Starting with the New York City police department in 1857, a few US municipalities began offering plans, but prior to 1900 the vast majority of (nonmilitary) public-sector workers had no formal pension plan. In the early decades of the twentieth century, this situation changed, as both the number of plans and workers covered by a plan expanded rapidly. At the local level, teachers, firefighters, and police officers were typically the first to receive a retirement plan as part of their compensation, and at the state level, teachers usually preceded other state workers (Clark, Craig, and Wilson 2003; Clark, Craig, and Sabelhaus 2011; Craig 2003). Still, the majority of public-sector workers remained un-covered by a pension plan.

By 1930 that situation had changed dramatically. Pensions in the public sector were relatively widespread in the United States, with all federal workers being covered by a plan and an increasing share of state and local employees covered. In contrast, pension coverage remained much lower in the private sector, in the neighborhood of 10 percent of the labor force. Even today, pension coverage is much higher in the public sector than it is in the private sector.

RETIREMENT

In the United States, the proportion of the population that survives to retirement age has increased over time. The expectation of life at birth has nearly doubled since 1850, and retirement has changed dramatically as well (Haines 2000, 308). In the second half of the nineteenth century, more than 75 percent of US males aged sixty-five and older remained in the labor force; today the figure is below 25 percent, which suggests a dra-matic increase in the incidence of retirement among the elderly.

While the upward trend in the share of the population that retires is not disputed, the exact path through time is. Ransom and Sutch (1986) argue that the 75 percent figure re-ported above is too high. For older workers, they defined retirement as being out of the labor force for six or more months during a year, which puts downward pressure on (and thus flattens the trend of) the labor force participation rate prior to 1935 and the advent of Social Security. However, Margo (1993) argues that many, perhaps most, of the older workers whom Ransom and Sutch classify as retired were simply unemployed, rather than retired. Using the stricter definition of retirement, the labor force participation rate of those sixty-five and older declines by roughly 30 percent even before the creation of the Social Security system, which leads Costa to conclude that there is "no evidence that the institution of Social Security affected the trend in retirement" (1998, 20).

Rather, Costa argues that the decrease in labor force participation among the elderly is primarily the result of an increase in retirement incomes, a process that was underway even before Social Security. Evidence supporting this position includes the incidence of home ownership among the elderly, which increased from just over 30 percent in

1900 to 45 percent by 1930, and is more than 75 percent today (Costa 1998, 15–16, 32–59). The increase in wealth at older ages before 1930 suggests that retirement income also increased, an observation supported by Haber and Gratton (1994), who show that, in 1870, only about 20 percent of males sixty-five and older could have afforded to purchase a ten-year annuity of $231 (in 1917 dollars); whereas by the 1920s, between 40 and 50 percent of that population could have purchased a ten-year annuity of $616 (again, in 1917 dollars). It follows that the subsequent increase in the incidence of retirement was related to old-age income, which in turn was related to the evolution of pension plans.

TYPES OF PENSION PLANS

Pension plans represent a contract between employees and the organizations for which they work. In return for their current labor, workers receive deferred compensation, which, under US tax law, is generally not taxed until it is received as income after retirement. Thus, returns to accumulated pension wealth grow tax-free during an employee's working years. Since the income replacement rate (i.e., that ratio of retirement income to pre-retirement income) is typically less than one, and since personal income tax rates are progressive, workers who plan to save for retirement are typically financially better off if they do so through an employer-provided pension plan.

There are two basic types of retirement plans: defined benefit plans and defined contribution plans.[1] Defined benefit plans promise workers a specified benefit at retirement, typically in the form of a life annuity paid in monthly installments. This annuity is commonly based on years of service (subject to a vesting requirement), annual earnings, and a "multiplier" or "generosity factor." Currently, the modal plan for state and local employees in the United States calculates a retiree's monthly pension annuity as follows. Let Y represent the years of an employee's service (subject to an initial five-year vesting period); let S be the average of the highest five consecutive years of salary; and M is the multiplier of 2.0 percent (Clark, Craig, and Sabelhaus 2011, 122–126). The resulting annuity in retirement would be

$$\text{Monthly Annuity} = \frac{(Y \times S \times M)}{12}$$

So, for example, a worker with thirty years of service, whose average salary in her five highest consecutive years was $48,000, would receive, upon retirement, a monthly annuity of $2,400 (30 x $48,000 x 0.02)/12), which would yield an annual income replacement rate of 60 percent ($28,800/$48,000).

Because the age-earnings profile for most workers has a positive slope, for workers with defined benefit pension plans, switching jobs leads to a reduction in pension wealth; therefore defined benefit plans tend to reduce turnover (Allen, Clark, and McDermed 1993). Defined contribution plans do not have that characteristic. In these plans, the employer and/or the worker make periodic contributions to a retirement account, which is then invested. At retirement, the benefit is based on the sum of these contributions and the accrued investment returns. Assuming a retiring employee with a defined contribution plan converted 100 percent of the accrued funds to an annuity, then to generate the same $2,400 monthly benefit received by the worker in the defined benefit pension example above would require an accumulation of approximately $400,000 in the defined contribution account at the time of retirement.[2]

Today, 87 percent of public-sector workers are covered by a retirement plan, whereas, less than two-thirds of the private-sector workforce is covered (fig. 15.1). Historically, most public-sector pension plans have been defined benefit plans, and this remains the case today, with nearly 80 percent of public-sector workers covered by a defined benefit plan. Although in 1975 roughly 70 percent of private-sector workers were also covered by a defined benefit plan, today the figure is only 22 percent, as private-sector employers have increasingly turned to defined contribution plans (BLS 2011a; Clark, Craig, and Sabelhaus 2011, 163–166). Overall, today less than 20 percent of the labor force is covered by a defined benefit plan (fig. 15.2).

Clark and McDermed (1990) and Clark and Schieber (2002) argue that the trends in pension coverage in the private sector are the result of the funding, accounting, and reporting regulations associated with the 1974 Employees Retirement Income Security Act (ERISA), which was created to regulate private-sector pension plans. According to this view, the burdens associated with adhering to the act have caused private-sector employers to forgo the human resources benefits associated with the defined benefit plan (e.g., a reduction in turnover), and turned to the relatively lower cost defined

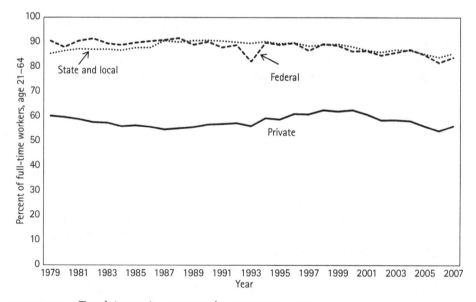

FIGURE 15.1. Trends in pension coverage, by sector, 1979–2007

Source: US Bureau of the Census, March Current Population Survey, from Clark et al. (2011, 166).

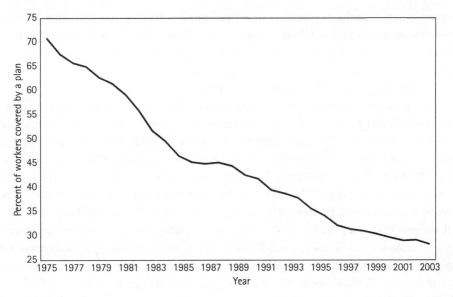

FIGURE 15.2. Trend in proportion of private-sector pension participants enrolled in defined benefit plans

Sources: US Department of Labor, Form 5500 Data Series. For details, see Clark et al. (2011).

contribution plans. In contrast, Munnell, Haverstick, and Soto (2007) argue that the differences in the composition of the public- and private-sector labor forces explain the divergence in types of pensions offered. Public-sector workers are, on average, older, more risk averse, less mobile, and more unionized than their private-sector counterparts, and these characteristics make defined benefit plans more appealing than defined contribution plans.

US MILITARY PENSIONS

As noted earlier, military pensions date back millennia in Western civilization. Clark and his coauthors (2003) argue that this history reflects the fear politicians maintained of disaffected soldiers, in essence binding their soldiers' loyalty to the government by making their future income a liability of the state, a view that is consistent with US policy since the American Revolution.

Shortly after the onset of the Revolution, in 1775, the Continental Congress established a disability pension plan for its naval forces, and one for the Continental Army the following year. Separately from the actions of Congress, the colonies offered disability pensions to their militia, which some of them had been doing since the previous century. Several colonies also maintained navies independent of the Continental Navy, and those colonies also offered pensions to their naval personnel. In 1832, Congress converted the various military disability plans from the Revolution into an old-age retirement plan for surviving veterans, each of whom would receive an annual pension annuity equal to his base pay at the end of the war. This act established a precedent, and, following every subsequent nineteenth-century war, the veterans of that war would receive a federal old-age pension (Clark, Craig, and Wilson 2003, 43–121).

The Continental Navy had been disbanded following the Revolution, but the US Navy was created during George Washington's second administration, and the first disability pension plan for "regular" navy personnel (i.e., uniformed personnel who were not draftees or volunteers of a specific war or campaign) was created in 1799. Under this plan, disabled officers were entitled to receive up to one-half of their base pay for the period of their disability, while the benefit for enlisted personnel and marines could not exceed $5.00 a month. Interestingly, both the Continental Navy disability plan and the subsequent US Navy plan were initially funded by prizes of war—captured enemy ships and contraband. Clark, Craig, and Wilson (1999a, 1999b) argue that this system was created to incentivize the officers and men, whose activities at sea were difficult to monitor in the age of sail. Although the opportunities to capture prizes ebbed and flowed, as the country experienced periods of war and peace, the navy pension fund, which held the proceeds from these activities, continued to pay benefits into the twentieth century.

Other than the disability plan, there was no formal retirement plan for regular naval personnel until 1855, when Congress created a review board of senior officers, which was charged with the task of identifying officers who were no longer fit for sea duty. The board's recommendations for retirement went to the Secretary of the Navy, and with his approval (and the president's), the unfit officers were retired at half-pay. (To pacify the officer corps, whose members were outraged at the imposition of what was in effect mandatory retirement, Congress placed a limit on the number of officers who could be retired in this manner.) With the onset of the Civil War in 1861, to help clear out superannuated officers without having to forcibly retire them, Congress allowed officers to request retirement after forty years of service at 75 percent of their base pay.

The policy of forcibly retiring naval officers fell into disuse until America's war with Spain in 1898. Dissatisfaction with the wartime performance of senior naval personnel led to a reinstatement of the policy. Officers could continue to seek retirement on their own or they could be forcibly retired, receiving 75 percent of the "sea pay" of the next rank above that which they held at the time of retirement.[3] In 1916, Congress imposed a formal "up-or-out" policy in which an officer who achieved a certain age while holding a certain rank was forcibly retired. The discharged officer received a retirement benefit that equaled his base pay at the time of retirement times his years of service times a 0.025 multiplier, up to an income replacement rate of 75 percent (which corresponded with 30 years of service, i.e., 30 x 2.5%). The act also imposed mandatory retirement at age sixty-four (a policy instituted by the army in 1882).

These plans applied to naval officers only. In 1867 Congress authorized the retirement of enlisted seamen and marines who had served twenty or more years and who were formally designated "infirm as a result of old-age." These veterans would receive one-half their base pay for life. In addition, any seaman or marine who, after at least ten years of service, became infirm as a result of his duties could apply to the Secretary of the Navy for a "suitable amount of relief" up to one-half base pay.[4]

As for the army, as the American Revolution approached its successful conclusion, Congress faced a revolt of officers whose pay was hopelessly in arrears. At the personal intervention of George Washington, the officers stood down, and in 1781, Congress created a retirement plan for officers in the Continental Army. The plan called for the payment of a life annuity, equal to one-half base pay, to all officers who remained on active duty until the formal cessation of hostilities. It subsequently became clear that the confederated government's cash flow, as well as any reasonable estimate of its future revenues, was insufficient to honor the promised life annuities, and, in response, Congress converted the life annuities to a fixed-term payment equal to full pay for five years (Chernow 2010; Ferguson 1961; Middlekauf 1982). Even these more limited liabilities went unpaid, and the officers' pension claims were subsequently met by special interest-bearing "commutation certificates." Clark, Craig, and Wilson (2003, 125–127) observe that these securities were nothing more than promissory notes issued against future tax revenues. However, the taxing powers of the Congress were severely constrained under the Articles of Confederation, and it was only after Treasury Secretary Alexander Hamilton reformed the new nation's public finances during the first Washington administration that the government was in a position to honor the Revolutionary debts, including those of its officer corps. Unfortunately, the country's precarious financial situation between the Revolution and Hamilton's reforms had led many embittered officers to sell their bonds in the secondary market at a steep discount, trading them for literally a few pennies on the dollar, and in the end many, perhaps even most, of them received little for their military service.

Congress maintained no retirement plan for the regular army prior to the Civil War.[5] With the onset of the war, however, President Abraham Lincoln pressed Congress to create the first army retirement plan that was not designed for veterans of a specific war or campaign. While the act might have been touted as a reward for long service, Clark, Craig, and Wilson (2003, 137–138) argue that its real objective was to rid the War Department of superannuated officers. Officers became eligible for a pension after forty years of service, and a formal retirement board could retire any officer who had accumulated forty years of service and whom the board deemed incapable of commanding troops in the field (much like the navy had been doing since 1855).[6] The law was amended several times over the next few decades, and ultimately Congress settled on a plan in which thirty years was the minimum service requirement, 75 percent of base pay was the standard income replacement rate, and age sixty-four became the mandatory retirement age. This plan served as the regular army pension plan until 1920, when Congress added an up-or-out policy, similar to that which the navy had adopted earlier. Officers who were not promoted were forcibly retired at the same 75 percent maximum benefit to which naval officers were entitled.[7]

Except for the plans created for the veterans of specific wars and campaigns, the various army retirement plans described above only covered commissioned officers; however, in 1885 Congress created the first retirement plan for enlisted personnel in the

362   ROBERT L. CLARK AND LEE A. CRAIG

regular army. Like the officers' plan, it permitted retirement upon the completion of thirty years of service at 75 percent of base pay.[8] In 1899, Congress extended to the navy the army retirement act of 1885.

The formal merger of the army and navy plans in the 1920s established the foundation of the military pension system offered in the United States today. Although Congress slightly revised the system in 1980 and 1986, the services continue to maintain an up-or-out policy; twenty years of service guarantees a pension based on a percentage of base pay; and with forty years of service, retirees receive, through the 2.5 percent multiplier, 100 percent of their base pay (Military.com 2013).

FEDERAL CIVIL SERVICE PENSIONS

Prior to the passage of the Federal Employees Retirement Act in 1920, the federal government did not offer a civil service pension plan; however, Congress did provide old-age pensions for some retiring civil servants. These were awarded on a case-by-case basis by specific acts of Congress, a process that became increasingly burdensome as government employment expanded. For example, in the year before the federal pension plan went into effect, Congress created 912 new pensions by individual acts, and, also by individual acts, it increased the payments of previously granted pensions for 555 retired civil servants (Clark, Craig, and Wilson 2003; Clark, Craig, and Sabelhaus 2011).

A key to the creation of the federal civil service pension plan was the creation of a federal civil service. With the expansion of the federal government over the course of the nineteenth century, its human resource needs became burdensome. As federal revenues grew from $3 million to over $400 million, the number of post offices, and hence postmasters, grew from 906 to 44,848, and, overall, federal civilian employment went from roughly 1,000 to over 100,000. The vast majority of these workers, as patronage hires, served at the leisure of an elected or appointed official.

Johnson and Libecap (1994) argue that, as a means of more efficiently managing this army of patronage bureaucrats, Congress passed the Pendleton Act in 1883, thereby creating the federal civil service. The act called for the conversion of patronage jobs to civil service jobs; thus it led to the eventual elimination of federal employment as a part of the political spoils system. It also created an enormous set of superannuated federal employees, many of whom refused to retire and most of whom could not be easily discharged.

Once this problem was recognized, Congress, various spokespersons for the executive branch, as well the US Civil Service Commission, and even some employee groups, began the process of inquiry. Craig (1995) describes how this inquiry ultimately resulted in the passage of the Federal Employees Retirement Act in 1920. In the act, all civil service employees qualified for a pension after reaching age seventy and rendering at least fifteen years of service. Mechanics, letter carriers, and post office clerks were eligible for a pension after reaching age sixty-five, and railway clerks qualified at age sixty-two. The ages at which employees qualified were also mandatory retirement ages.[9] All eligible employees were required to contribute 2.5 percent of their earnings toward the payment of pensions. The pension benefit was determined by the number of years of service. Class A employees were those who had served thirty or more years. Their benefit was 60 percent of their average annual salary during the last ten years of service. Benefits were scaled down through Class F employees (at least 15 years but less than 18 years of service), who received 30 percent of their average annual salary during the last ten years of service. (The plan was subsequently revised, and although space constraints prohibit a full accounting of the changes, the current generosity multiplier is a step function: 1.50 percent of pay for the first five years of service; 1.75 for the next five years; and 2.00 percent for years of service beyond ten. Federal employees contribute 7.0 percent of their salaries to the plan, and they are not part of the Social Security system (Hustead and Hustead 2001).

In 1983, Congress created a new plan, the Federal Employees Retirement System (FERS), and roughly 85 percent of current federal employees are covered by the plan,[10] which contains three components: a defined benefit plan, a defined contribution plan, and federal civil servants covered by FERS are also included in the Social Security system. As part of the defined benefit component of the plan, employees contribute 0.8 percent of their salary, and, at retirement, they receive an annual annuity equal to 1.0 percent of the average of the highest three years of salary times the number of years of service.[11] In the defined contribution component, employees may "contribute up to the Internal Revenue Service's maximum contribution rate, and the federal government will match these contributions, up to five percent of salary as follows: one percent regardless of the employee's contribution; three percent to match dollar-for-dollar the employees contribution; and one-half of a percent for the employee's next two percent" (Craig 2014).

It is not difficult to find evidence suggesting that the total compensation of public-sector workers is greater than their private-sector counterparts (see, e.g., Krueger 1988; Poterba and Rueben 1994), and recent empirical work by Gittleman and Pierce (2012) indicates that most of the difference can be explained by the relatively more generous benefit packages enjoyed by public-sector workers. To an extent, workers pay for these benefits. Although US military personnel have never directly contributed to their pensions, since the creation of the federal civil service plan in 1920, nonuniform federal employees have contributed to their retirement plans. Furthermore, economic theory suggests that, as a result of the personal income tax incentives associated with pension plans, workers should be willing to accept a lower wage rate in return for a future pension. If this were the case, then workers pay for at least part of their pensions by direct contributions and lower wage profiles. Craig (1995) shows that, through the combination of worker contributions and lower lifetime earnings profiles, federal civil servants have paid for 35–40 percent of their pensions, on average.

STATE AND LOCAL PENSIONS

In the decades after New York City created a pension plan for its police officers, other large municipalities began offering plans for their police officers, as well as their firefighters and teachers.[12] Overall, the number of plans in place remained small until the twentieth century, when the number of plans expanded relatively rapidly (Clark, Craig, and Sabelhaus 2011). By 1916, 159 municipalities maintained retirement plans either for their police officers, firefighters, or teachers, and more than twenty included civil servants in their plans. Among large cities, coverage was extensive. According to one source, "85 percent of cities with 100,000 or more residents paid some form of police pension; as did 66 percent of those with populations between 50,000 and 100,000; and 50 percent of cities with populations between 30,000 and 50,000 had some pension liability [and] by 1928 . . . all cities with populations of over 400,000 had a pension plan for either police officers or firefighters or both" (Craig 2003). These plans were almost exclusively defined benefit plans.

Relative to the larger US cities, the states were in general slower to create old-age pension plans for their employees. Among state employees, teachers were the first to receive retirement pensions. Between 1900 and 1911, five states (New Jersey, New York, Rhode Island, Virginia, and Wisconsin) created old-age pensions for their public schoolteachers (Clark, Craig, and Sabelhaus 2011, 24). In 1911, Massachusetts created the first state-level retirement plan for (nonteacher) civil servants. By 1930—a date by which all federal employees and almost all police officers, firefighters, and teachers in municipalities of any size were covered by a pension plan—only nine states offered retirement plans to their nonteacher civil servants; however, in the subsequent years, growth was rapid. Six new plans were created in the 1930s, despite the damage done to state finances by the Great Depression, and seventeen more states added plans in the 1940s. Furthermore, the relatively slow growth of the state plans is somewhat misleading, because in 1930, 40 percent of state and local employees were schoolteachers, and by that date twenty-one states offered plans to their teachers. So, a substantial proportion of state workers were covered on the eve of the Great Depression, and by the 1960s nearly all state workers were covered (Clark, Craig, and Sabelhaus 2011, 76–78).

As noted in the previous section, much scholarly works indicates that public-sector workers are overcompensated relative to those in the private sector. Gittleman and Pierce show that, on average, state and local workers earn 40 percent more than private sector workers, and pensions form a substantial proportion of the difference (Gittleman and Pierce 2012, table 2). The absence of competition among public-sector employers generates quasi rents that are manifested in higher worker compensation, including pensions (Mueller 1989). Craig (1995), while not disputing the presence of quasi rents in the public sector, nonetheless argues that pensions represent optimal contracts between workers and employers, and the resulting efficiency gains may be greater than the losses associated with the inherent inefficiencies of the public sector.

PRIVATE-SECTOR PENSIONS

In the United States, retirement pensions for public-sector workers emerged from disability plans, which were initially offered to military personnel. This was not the case in the private sector. Well into the twentieth century, disability pensions or other payments for injuries incurred on the job were primarily paid, to the extent they were paid at all, as a result of the good will of employers. When that proved inadequate, as it often did, the common law of negligence liability was a worker's only recourse. In order to receive a disability payment from an employer, a worker had to demonstrate to the satisfaction of a court that the employer had not exercised "due care" in the workplace and that as a result of the employer's negligence, the disability had occurred. Even when this burden of proof was met, the resulting payments were trifling by any reasonable standard. Prior to the passage of workers' compensation legislation after 1900, the average expected payment to a widow of a worker who died as a result of injuries incurred on the job would have been roughly half a year's earnings. This was a one-time, lump-sum payment, not an annuity (Fishback and Kantor 1998).

Separately from their disability benefits, private-sector employers began establishing retirement pension plans for their employees in the last quarter of the nineteenth century. The American Express Corporation created the first plan in 1875 (Latimer 1932; McGill et al. 2010). By 1900, only twelve private companies had created retirement plans for their employees, and these were concentrated in three industries: railroads, public utilities, and the financial sector. By 1916, there were 117 private pension plans in existence, and the number was roughly 200 ten years later (Costa 1998; Conyngton 1926; Ransom, Sutch, and Williamson 1993). These plans were generally noncontributory, because "private pensions were universally regarded as gratuities from a grateful employer in recognition of long service," and they could be terminated at the discretion of the employer (McGill et al. 2010, 20). In general, the early private-sector plans were not generous by either the standards established by the public-sector plans or subsequently those in the private sector.[13]

The relatively slow expansion of pension coverage among private-sector employees continued throughout the first half of the twentieth century. At most, 12 percent of the nonfarm private labor force was covered by a pension before the Great Depression, and the figure fell into the single digits in the first years of the Depression, as distressed firms found it expedient to simply discard their pension plans and expropriate the pension funds to meet the company's current financial needs. The workers had no protection in these cases.

As the country recovered from the economic crisis towards the end of the 1930s, pension coverage began to expand, and by 1950 roughly 20 percent of the private-sector labor force was covered by a plan. The figure subsequently grew to just over 60 percent in 1980, where it leveled off and remains today. The growth of private-sector plans immediately following the Great Depression resulted from four factors. First, since the permanent establishment of the federal income tax in 1913, pensions received favorable tax treatment. However, since all but the highest earners were exempt from taxation before the wartime revenue acts of the early 1940s, this feature of the tax code had little relevance to most workers before World War II. The combination of higher tax rates on personal income, wage and price controls, and the "bracket creep" resulting from wartime inflation induced workers to welcome deferred compensation in the form of employer-provided pension plans. Second, the wartime wage controls led employers to substitute fringe benefits, mainly pensions, for wage increases. Third, subsequent rulings of the National Labor Relations Board and the federal courts made fringe benefits in general and pensions in particular mandatory bargaining issues during the collective bargaining process. Finally, the creation of the Social Security system was seen by employers as a subsidy for their retirement plans. Instead of being responsible for bearing the full weight of their workers' old-age income, employers could point to future Social Security benefits as a component of their employees' income replacement rate (Clark, Craig, and Sabelhaus 2011; McGill et al. 2010).

Thus in the human resources strategies of private-sector employers, pensions formed a symbiotic relationship with Social Security, and in terms of coverage and generosity, both expanded in the second half of the twentieth century. Despite this growth, employers often continued to consider pensions among the first items to be cut during an economic downturn, and prior to the passage of ERISA, default on pension liabilities were not uncommon. Through the Pension Benefit Guaranty Corporation, ERISA provides workers covered by a plan with a federally guaranteed minimum pension, but the act only covers private-sector plans. As a result, the funding of the public-sector pensions has become one of the most controversial issues in the history of retirement and pensions.

PENSION FUNDING

As noted earlier pensions represent contracts between employers and employees: Employees provide labor today in return for their employers' promise to provide a pension in the future. There are two approaches to meeting the liabilities created by such a contract. A "pay-as-you-go" pension plan is one in which the employer does not maintain a "fund" from which future pension liabilities are paid. With a pay-as-you-go plan, the employer pays current liabilities from current revenues. In contrast, a "funded" pension plan is one in which the employer establishes a fund to hold assets and from which current and future liabilities are paid. Thus an "actuarially sound" pension plan would be one in which the value of the assets in the pension fund is equal to or greater than the present value of expected future pension liabilities. It follows that a "funding ratio"—that is, the ratio of assets to liabilities—greater than or equal to one would be associated with an actuarially sound, or "fully funded," plan. While full funding is a generally accepted goal in pension discourse, it is not clear that a funding ratio of one is necessarily the lower bound for optimal funding (D'Arcy, Dulebohn, and Oh 1999).

Historically, both private- and public-sector employers have struggled to meet their funding obligations, and in attempting to do so they have followed different strategies. For example, from their creation in the eighteenth century, US Army pensions have always been funded on a pay-as-you-go basis; however, initially the navy pension plan was financed with monies from the sale of captured prizes. A fund was established, and the monies were invested in a wide range of assets, including private equities. Although the fund lasted into the twentieth century, it was only actuarially sound for brief periods of time, because whenever it reached soundness, Congress simply increased the benefits paid from the fund. As a result, between 1775 and 1842, it went bankrupt no less than three times, being bailed out by the Treasury each time. During the Civil War, it accumulated an enormous balance, only to have most of that balance confiscated by Congress and turned over to the Treasury. Eventually, as was the case with the army and, later, civil service pensions, navy pensions were paid on a pay-as-you-go basis.

As for the state and municipal plans, there was a great deal of variation in their funding during the period in which the plans were being established, and even today, when all of the defined benefit plans are funded, the extent to which they are actuarially sound varies dramatically across political units. By the late 1920s, employer and employee contributions for at least some plans (including those in New Jersey, Ohio, and Vermont) were being determined based on actuarial calculations (Studenski 1920). However, the methodology was not universally embraced in either the public or the private sector, and many plans were systematically underfunded from their inception. Among the sources of public monies for early municipal pension funds were dog license fees and permits for dancing schools and boxing contests (Clark, Craig, and Wilson 2003).

In the past two decades, demographic changes in many states and cities have worsened the funding status of public-sector plans, as slowing population growth and regional shifts in population have left some states and municipalities with unsustainably low (and often declining) ratios of workers (who contribute to their plans) to beneficiaries. In addition, many public-sector employers have not made the contributions that would have maintained the actuarial soundness of their plans. Currently, state-run retirement plans are collectively underfunded by between $1 trillion and $4 trillion; there are nearly 2,500 local plans that are collectively underfunded by roughly $600 billion; and federal pensions are underfunded by $1.1 trillion (Biggs 2010; Novy-Marx and Rauh 2009, 2010; Pew Center 2010; US Department of Defense 2006). Not surprisingly, many states and municipalities have been revising their pension plans in recent years. Many, like their private-sector counterparts, turned to the defined contribution model; others have reduced the generosity of their traditional defined benefit plans; some have done both (Clark and Craig 2011).

Despite the funding standards required by ERISA, private-sector employers are not immune from the funding crisis that plagues public-sector pensions in the United States. Roughly 20 million private-sector workers are still covered by a defined benefit plan, and these are concentrated in larger (and older) firms. Collectively, the defined benefit plans of the 400 largest companies with such plans are currently underfunded by more than $400 billion (Ramsey and Monga 2013). This underfunding is largely the result of the financial exigencies those firms faced following the financial crisis of 2008. Given this situation, one would reasonably expect the movement toward defined contribution plans to continue in both the public and private sectors.

Direction of Future Research

The history of public- and private-sector pension plans over the past two centuries indicates that during the first seventy-five years of the twentieth century, employer-provided pension plans expanded in number and workers covered, and in general they became increasingly generous. Most pension participants were in defined benefit plans, which have significant economic incentives imbedded in their plan parameters. Seeking to understand how defined benefit plans altered worker behavior, economists have examined the impact of pension coverage on the age of retirement and job turnover. These studies show how employers could encourage younger workers to remain with the firm by penalizing turnover (Allen, Clark, and McDermed 1993; Gustman and Steinmeier 1995; Ippolito 1987), while eventually encouraging retirement for older workers through the structure of their defined benefit pension plans (Kotlikoff and Wise 1989; Lazear and Moore 1988; Quinn, Burkhauser, and Myers 1990).

As noted, ERISA probably contributed to the long-term decline in the incidence of defined benefit plans and the expansion of defined contribution plans, particularly 401(k) plans (named for the section of the Internal Revenue Service code that covers such plans), in the private sector. While providing the opportunity to accumulate wealth for retirement, defined contribution plans tend to be more neutral in their labor market effects than defined benefit plans. Economists continue to attempt to explain employer and employee preferences for alternative types of pension plans. Key factors in the choice of pension plans include who bears the investment risk of retirement savings; whether the plans are portable between employers; and the overall cost and generosity of the plans. Recently, employers have begun to adopt hybrid plans, such as cash balance plans, which have some of the characteristics of both defined benefit and defined contribution plans. The breakdown of long-term labor contracts and the increased mobility of workers have played a role in the movement to the more portable defined contribution plans (Neumark 2000).

The continuing evolution of private-sector retirement plans presents economists with several key questions for future research. With the decline in defined benefit plans and their early retirement incentives, how will employers achieve desired retirement ages? This may become a more important human resource issue if life expectancy continues to increase and results in a substantial proportion of the workforce delaying retirement. The expansion in the coverage of defined contribution plans places increased responsibility on workers to save an adequate amount and to make optimal investment decisions. Workers will need greater financial literacy as individual savings in defined contribution plans become a more important component of overall pension wealth. Other research questions include whether employers can modify their plans in ways to incentivize employees to contribute more to their retirement saving plans and whether enhanced financial literacy will result in greater saving and wiser investment decisions (Allen, Clark, and McDermed 2013; Madrian and Shea 2001).

Although public-sector employers continue to offer defined benefit plans as the dominant form of pension, in recent years, state and local governments have begun to move in the direction of adopting defined contribution and hybrid plans as alternatives to traditional defined benefit plans, and they have adopted a variety of other changes to reduce the future liabilities of their plans. The higher cost of these public-sector retirement plans and the large unfunded liabilities of some plans have been among the factors pushing public employers away from defined benefit plans. Other reforms have included increasing the retirement ages, increasing years for vesting, increasing years used to calculate final average salaries, and increasing employee contributions (Clark and Craig 2011). Policymakers need additional analysis on how these changes will affect their ability to attract, retain, and retire quality workers. Researchers who acquire detailed employer-level data will be able to examine worker preferences when given a choice of retirement plans, and to determine how the selection of a defined benefit or a defined contribution plan affects retirement income.

In the United States, pension plans developed in conjunction with the creation and subsequent expansion of Social Security. All private-sector workers and most public-sector workers are now required to be included in Social Security; thus, workers have the expectation of receiving income in retirement from Social Security, and employees and employers have to pay the payroll tax that finances this program. With this in mind, employers must decide how much more of their workers' total compensation they want to provide in the form of retirement benefits, and workers must decide how much more they want to save for retirement. Confounding the issue is the long-run financing shortfall faced by the Social Security system (SSA Board of Trustees 2013), a problem that, ultimately, Congress will be forced to address by modifying the system. It seems likely that at least some future retirees will pay higher payroll taxes during their working careers and some will receive lower benefits compared to those now promised, while employers will also pay higher payroll taxes. How will firms and workers respond to these changes? For example, if the payroll tax were to be increased by 2 percentage points (1 on employers and 1 on workers) and future benefits are cut, then will employers attempt to make up the lower benefit by increasing their contributions to pension plans, or will they attempt to offset the higher payroll tax by reducing the cost of employee compensation, including cutting their pension contributions? These and related questions offer topics for future research.

Notes

1. In addition, there are so-called hybrid plans, including "cash balance" plans, which contain characteristics of both defined benefit and defined contribution plans.
2. This calculation is based on annuity values in Alchian and Allen (1969, 270), and it is based on the assumption that the worker retires at age sixty-five and has a life expectancy of twenty years beyond retirement.
3. In 1908 the years required for voluntary retirement were reduced to thirty, and after 1912, officers received up to 75 percent of their base pay at the rank they held at the time of retirement, rather than the next highest grade.
4. These monies were to be paid from the navy pension fund, rather than congressional appropriations.
5. The army did maintain a disability plan, and soldiers who were discharged after 1800 were given three months' pay as severance. Officers were initially offered the same severance package as enlisted personnel, but in 1802, officers began receiving one month's pay for each year of service over three years. Hence an officer with thirteen years of service earning $40 a month would receive a lump-sum payment of $400 at the time he resigned his commission (Clark, Craig, and Wilson 2003, 127).
6. The act constrained the number of officers who could be forcibly retired.
7. Although the maximum benefit was temporarily reduced to 60 percent in 1924, it was subsequently increased back to 75 percent (Hustead and Hustead 2001, 66–104).
8. The years-of-service requirement was subsequently reduced to twenty.
9. An employee could, however, be retained for two years beyond the mandatory age if his department head and the head of the Civil Service Commission approved.
10. No federal employees have been added to the older system since the early 1980s (BLS 2011c).
11. For employees who have reached age 62 with twenty or more years of service, the multiplier is 1.1 percent.
12. The New York City plan was solely a disability plan until 1878, when a pension component was added.
13. A multiplier of 1.5 percent was not uncommon, meaning a worker would have to work forty years to replace 60 percent of her pre-employment income.

Bibliography

Alchian, Armen, and William Allen. (1969). *Exchange and Production: Theory in Use*. Belmont, CA: Wadsworth.

Allen, Steven, Robert Clark, Jennifer Maki, and Melinda Morrill. (2013). "Golden Years or Financial Fears: Decision Making after Retirement Seminars." NBER Working Paper No. 19231, July.

Allen, Steven G., Robert L. Clark, and Ann A. McDermed. (1993). "Pensions, Bonding, and Lifetime Jobs." *Journal of Human Resources* 28: 463–481.

Biggs, Andrew. (2010). "An Options Pricing Method for Calculating the Market Price of Public Sector Pension Liabilities." AEI Working Paper, Second Version.

Chernow, Ron. (2010). *George Washington: A Life*. New York: Penguin Group.

Clark, Robert L., and Lee A. Craig. (2011). "State Pension Plans Step Up Efforts to Adapt to 21st Century Financial Pressures." *Pension and Benefits Daily*. Bureau of National Affairs, August 8.

Clark, Robert L., Lee A. Craig, and John Sabelhaus. (2011). *State and Local Retirement Plans in the United States*. Cheltenham, UK: Edward Elgar.

Clark, Robert L., Lee A. Craig, and Jack W. Wilson. (1999a). "Managing a Pension Portfolio in the Nineteenth Century: The U.S. Navy Pension Fund, 1800–1840." *Business and Economic History* 28(Fall): 93–104.

Clark, Robert L., Lee A. Craig, and Jack W. Wilson. (1999b). "Privatization of Public-Sector Pensions: The U.S. Navy Pension Fund, 1800–1842." *Independent Review* 3(Spring): 549–564.

Clark, Robert L., Lee A. Craig, and Jack W. Wilson. (2003). *A History of Public Sector Pensions in the United States*. Philadelphia: University of Pennsylvania Press.

Clark, Robert L., and Elizabeth Ann McDermed. (1990). *The Choice of Pension Plans in a Changing Regulatory Environment*. Washington, DC: American Enterprise Institute.

Clark, Robert L., and Sylvester Schieber. (2002). "Taking the Subsidy Out of Early Retirement: The Story Behind the Conversion to Hybrid Pensions." In *Innovations in Managing the Financial Risks of Retirement*, edited by Olivia S. Mitchell, Zvi Bodie, Brett Hammond, and Steve Seldes, 149–174. Philadelphia: University of Pennsylvania Press.

Conyngton, Mary. (1926). "Industrial Pension for Old Age and Disability." *Monthly Labor Review* 2: 21–56.

Cornwell, Christopher, Stuart Dorsey, and Nasser Mehrzad. (1991). "Opportunistic Behavior of Firms in Implicit Pension Contracts." *Journal of Human Resources* 26: 704–725.

Costa, Dora L. (1998). *The Evolution of Retirement: An American Economic History, 1880–1990*. Chicago: University of Chicago Press.

Craig, Lee A. (1995). "The Political Economy of Public-Private Compensation Differentials: The Case of Federal Pensions." *Journal of Economic History* 55: 304–320.

Craig, Lee A. (2003). "Public Sector Pensions in the United States." *EH.Net Encyclopedia*, edited by Robert Whaples. Available at http://eh.net/encyclopedia/article/craig.pensions.public.us.

Craig, Lee A. (2014). "Pension and Health Benefits for Public-Sector Workers." In *The Oxford Handbook of U.S. Social Policy*, edited by David Beland, Christopher Howard, and Kimberly Morgan, 549–564. New York: Oxford University Press.

D'Arcy, Stephen P., James H. Dulebohn, and Pyungsuk Oh. (1999). "Optimal Funding of State Employee Pension Systems." *Journal of Risk and Insurance* 66: 345–380.

Ferguson, E. James. (1961). *Power of the Purse: A History of American Public Finance*. Chapel Hill: University of North Carolina Press.

Fishback, Price V., and Shawn Everett Kantor. (1998). "The Adoption of Workers Compensation in the United States, 1900–1930." *Journal of Law and Economics* 41: 305–343.

Gittleman, Maury, and Brooks Pierce. (2012). "Compensation of State and Local Government Workers." *Journal of Economic Perspectives* 26: 217–242.

Gustman, Alan, and Thomas Steinmeier. (1995). *Pension Incentives and Job Mobility*. Kalamazoo, MI: W. E. Upjohn Institute for Employment Research.

Haber, Carole, and Brian Gratton. (1994). *Old Age and the Search of Security: An American Social History*. Bloomington: Indiana University Press.

Haines, Michael. (2000). "The White Population of the United States, 1790–1920." In *A Population History of North America*, edited by Michael Haines and Richard Steckel, 305–370. Cambridge: Cambridge University Press.

Hustead, Edwin C., and Toni Hustead. (2001). "Federal Civilian and Military Retirement Systems." In *Pensions in the Public Sector*, edited by Olivia S. Mitchell and Edwin C. Hustead, 66–104. Philadelphia: University of Pennsylvania Press.

Ippolito, Richard. (1987). "Why Federal Workers Don't Quit." *Journal of Human Resources* 22: 281–299.

Johnson, Ronald N., and Gary D. Libecap. (1994). *The Federal Civil Service System and the Problem of Bureaucracy*. Chicago: University of Chicago Press.

Kotlikoff, Laurence, and David Wise. (1989). *The Wage Carrot and the Pension Stick*. Kalamazoo, MI: W. E. Upjohn Institute for Employment Research.

Krueger, Alan B. (1988). "Are Public Sector Workers Paid More than their Alternative Wage? Evidence from Longitudinal Data and Job Queues." In *When Public Sector Workers Unionize*, edited by Richard Freeman and Casey Ichniowski, 217–240. Chicago: University of Chicago Press.

Latimer, Murray Webb. (1932). *Industrial Pension Systems in the United States and Canada*. New York: Industrial Relations Counselors.

Lazear, Edward P., and Robert Moore. (1988). "Pensions and Turnover." In *Pensions in the U.S. Economy*, edited by Zvi Bodie, John B. Shoven, and David A. Wise, 163–188. Chicago: University of Chicago Press.

Madrian, Brigitte, and Dennis Shea. (2001). "The Power of Suggestion: Inertia in 401(k) Participation and Saving Behavior." *Quarterly Journal of Economics* 116: 1149–1187.

Margo, Robert. (1993). "The Labor Force Participation of Older Americans in 1900: Further Results." *Explorations in Economic History* 30: 409–423.

McGill, Dan M., Kyle N. Brown, John J. Haley, Sylvester J. Scheiber, and Mark J. Warshawsky. (2010). *Fundamentals of Private Pensions*. 9th ed. New York: Oxford University Press.

Middlekauff, Robert. (1982). *The Glorious Cause: The American Revolution, 1763–1789*. New York: Oxford University Press.

Military.com. (2013). "The Military Retirement System." Available at http://www.military.com/benefits/military-pay/the-military-retirement-system.html#1.

Mueller, Dennis C. (1989). *Public Choice II*. Cambridge: Cambridge University Press.

Munnell, Alicia, Kelly Haverstick, and Mauricio Soto. (2007). "Why Have Defined Benefit Survived in the Public Sector." Issue Brief No. 2. Center for Retirement Research, Boston College.

Neumark, David, ed. (2000). *On the Job: Is Long-term Employment a Thing of the Past?* New York: Russell Sage Foundation.

Novy-Marx, Robert, and Joshua D. Rauh. (2009). "The Liabilities and Risks of State-Sponsored Pension Plans." *Journal of Economic Perspectives* 23: 191–210.

Novy-Marx, Robert, and Joshua D. Rauh. (2010). "The Crisis in Local Government Pensions in the United States." Unpublished manuscript.

Pew Center on the States. (2010). *The Trillion Dollar Gap*. Washington, DC: The Pew Charitable Trusts.

Poterba, James M., and Kim S. Rueben. (1994). "The Distribution of Public Sector Wage Premia: New Evidence Using Quantile Regression Methods." NBER Working Paper No. 4734.

Quinn, Joseph, Richard Burkhauser, and Daniel Myers. (1990). *Passing the Torch: The Influence of Economic Incentives on Work and Retirement*. Kalamazo, MI: Upjohn Institute for Employment Research.

Ramsey, Mike, and Vipal Monga. (2013). "Low Rates Force Companies to Pour Cash into Pensions." *Wall Street Journal*, February 3.

Ransom, Roger, and Richard Sutch. (1986). "The Labor of Older Americans: Retirement of Men On and Off the Job, 1870–1937." *Journal of Economic History* 46: 1–30.

Ransom, Roger, Richard Sutch, and Samuel Williamson. (1993). "Inventing Pensions: The Origins of the Company-Provided Pension in the United States, 1900–1940." In *Societal Impact on Aging: Historical Perspectives*, edited by K. Warner Shaie and Andrew W. Achenbaum, 1–38. New York: Springer.

Studenski, Paul. (1920). *Teachers' Pension Systems in the United States: A Critical and Descriptive Study*. New York: D. Appleton.

US Bureau of Labor Statistics. (2011a). "Employee Benefits Survey." Available at http://bls.gov/ncs/ebs/benefits/2011/benefits_retirement.htm.

US Bureau of Labor Statistics. (2011b). *The Employment Situation: November 2011*. December 2.

US Bureau of the Labor Statistics. (2011c). *Federal Government Civilian Employment*. Available at http://www.bls.gov/oco/cg/cgs041.htm.

US Department of Defense. (2006). *Military Health System Overview Statement*. Available at http://armed-services.senate.gov/statemnt/2006/April/Chu-Winkenwerder%2004-04-06.pdf.

US Social Security Administration. (2013). *The 2013 Annual Report of the Board of Trustees of the Federal Old-Age and Survivors Insurance and Federal Disability Insurance Trust Funds*. Available at http://www.socialsecurity.gov/OACT/TR/2013/tr2013.pdf.

CHAPTER 16

....

CAPITAL, INCOME GROWTH, IN AMERICAN ECONOMIC HISTORY

....

PAUL W. RHODE

CAPITAL is back.[1] That was the headline of Thomas Piketty's surprise bestseller, *Capital in the Twenty-First Century*. Inequality is rising. The wealth-output ratio is rising. Capital's share of income is rising. Economists, policymakers, and the general public should take note. We are returning to the world captured in nineteenth-century novels, where inherited wealth mattered more than new ideas or hard work (see also Piketty and Zucman 2014).

If capital is back, one wonders where has it been? How long has it been away? An analysis of the role of physical capital formation in American economic growth, in both aggregate and per capita income, shows that economists have downplayed the importance of capital accumulation since the advent of the modern growth theory a half-century ago. In a Solow growth model, increasing the saving rate (the share of income not consumed) could raise the level of income, but it had no effect on long-run growth. Sustained growth depended on technological advance, not capital accumulation. Even the New Growth theorists Charles Jones and Paul Romer (2010, 226) de-emphasize physical capital accumulation, writing, "Ideas, institutions, population, and human capital are now at the center of growth theory. Physical capital has been pushed to the periphery."

In Kold tech can create capital

Citing Kaldor's "stylized facts" (1957, 1961), the standard macro view claims that the US economy has long been on (or near to) a balanced growth path where the following are constant:[2]

1. the rate of capital formation; *NO*
2. the capital-output ratio; *NO*
3. capital's share of income; *NB* *NO*
4. the rate of return on capital; and
5. the growth of per capita output (driven by technological progress). *NO*

These widely espoused claims bear little resemblance to the actual historical record of American income and capital growth: the "stylized" constancies are more myth than reality. The rate of capital formation and capital-output ratio rose dramatically and then fell gradually. Returns to capital decline over extended periods. Trends in the capital's share of income are largely in the eye of the beholder. The history of capital in the United States did not just recently become interesting (again); it has always been interesting.

CAPITAL IN THE AMERICAN ECONOMY

Until the late 1950s, capital accumulation was at the center of economists' understanding of the process of modern economic growth, that is, of the attainment of high, sustained rates of per capita income growth. The countries with high and rising incomes were those that were wealthy and that saved a large share of their income. Adam Smith (1776) entitled his magnum opus *The Wealth of Nations*. In *Das Kapital*, Karl Marx (1867) famously wrote, "Accumulate, accumulate! That is Moses and the prophets!" The great fortunes of America's Gilded Age (roughly 1870–1900) belonged to captains of industry, finance, and transportation who followed this edict. The Great Depression of the 1930s and the Keynesian revolution that it sparked put the investment process at the core of business-cycle analysis. And the early models of long-run growth inspired by Keynesian theory, the so-called Harrod-Domar approach, saw investment in physical capital as the key variable driving income growth (Harrod 1939).[3] In this line of thinking, growth dynamics in rich countries depended critically on the saving rate. And the growth potential of poor countries with little surplus to save depended on foreign investment or aid from rich countries.

It is hardly surprising, then, that Simon Kuznets, one of America's leading economists, devoted his talent and energy in the immediate post–World War II period to a massive study of capital formation. This decade-long endeavor involved defining and estimating capital stocks and formation based on the national income accounts that he had pioneered.[4] Kuznets (1961, 15) wrote, "In a modern society, capital is the stock of means, separable from human beings and legally disposable in economic transactions, intended for use in producing goods and income." (The definitions of capital might differ in different societies, for example, in slave economies.) The physical capital stock is subdivided into structures (or buildings), durables (or equipment), and inventories. It is further divided according to ownership by households, firms, or governmental bodies. The capital stock differs from wealth in that the latter included the value of productive nonreproducible assets (such as land), stocks of monetary metals, and consumer durables. Translating the concepts into accounting practices can be difficult.

Kuznets (1961, 8–11) summarized his key findings of the ambitious *Capital in the American Economy* project:

(a) The share of gross capital formation in gross national product (GNP) measured in current prices was nearly constant (at about 20 percent) between the 1870s and the 1950s.[5]

(b) The capital-output ratio initially rose but then declined. The ratio of the net capital stock to net national product (in constant price) rose from 3.2 in the 1869–1888 period to 3.6 in the 1920s and then declined to 2.5 by 1946–1955.

(c) The price of capital goods rose relative to other goods and services, creating differences between the current and constant price series for the capital formation rate and capital-output ratio.

(d) The investment to cover depreciation (i.e., capital consumption) relative to gross capital formation nearly doubled over the period of study (1869–1955), creating large gaps between the gross and net ratios.[6] The share of capital consumption in GNP rose from 8 percent to almost 18 percent.

(e) Shifts between investments in construction and producer durable equipment helped account for both the post–World War I decline in the capital-output ratio and the rise in the capital consumption rate.

(f) External funding of investment increased modestly in the economy as a whole, with financial intermediaries accounting for a rising share of this activity. The federal government and households financing residential construction accounted for most of the increase. Business, especially nonfinancial corporations, relied increasingly on internal financing.

Kuznets concluded, more speculatively, that limits on the supply of saving, rather than technologically driven changes in the demand for capital, accounted for the (rather slow) rate of capital formation in mid-twentieth-century America. Kuznet's first finding, on the constancy of the rate of capital formation measured in current-price gross flows, was highly influential. It confirmed his earlier finding of a constant average propensity to consume, which had inspired Milton Friedman's permanent-income hypothesis and Franco Modigliani's life-cycle saving model as alternatives to consumption function put forward by John Maynard Keynes. It became one of Kaldor's "stylized facts"; a variant became known as "Denison's Law" (1958). Kuznets (1966, 487) himself concluded that dramatically increasing the rate of capital formation was not a prerequisite for achieving modern economic growth.

Economists paid far less attention to Kuznets's efforts to chart the changing depreciation rate, the shifting composition of investment, fluctuations in relative prices of different types of capital, or the varied channels of finance. Digesting the details of the capstone volume's 134 tables (not to speak of those in the eight subsidiary volumes) proved daunting, indeed overwhelming. Even Kuznets himself had moved on to the new frontier of cross-country comparisons of economic performance before the *Capital* project was complete (Fogel 2013). After gaining a flurry of interest in the early 1960s, this massive scholarly enterprise dropped from view. While Piketty cites the work of Kuznets on income inequality (the Kuznets Curve in which inequality in a given economy rises and then falls as it develops), *Capital in the American Economy* is not mentioned in his bestseller.

Modern Growth Theory

Advances in macroeconomic theory were already taking the keys away from capital accumulation as the driver of the long-run growth process. Robert Solow (1956) offered his path-breaking model relating the growth of per capita income to the saving rate, population growth rate, and rate of technological advance.[7] Solow's success came from creating a model that, unlike its Harrod-Domar predecessor, generated balanced or steady-state growth. In the end, Solow placed technological change in the driver's seat.

It is worthwhile to lay out Solow's model in brief. (Less technically inclined readers can skim this section.) Let Y_t be output and N_t be the population at time t. Assume the number of hours of labor is proportional to the population, which grows at rate n. Output is a function of the capital stock, K_t and labor, N_t, and technology, A_t. The latter will be constant (and suppressed from the notation) for the moment. The production function is

$$Y_t = F(K_t, N_t).$$ (1)

It displays diminishing returns in a single factor—so raising K without changing N increases Y, but at a decreasing rate. There are also constant returns to scale in the two factors taken together—so doubling both N and K exactly doubles Y. Further assuming markets are competitive, a factor's share of output, say capital share is α, measures its marginal contribution to production. These assumptions allow us to rewrite aggregate production function (1) in a per capita form by dividing both sides by N_t. Thus,

$$y_t = \frac{Y_t}{N_t} = \frac{F(K_t, Nt_t)}{N_t} = F\left(\frac{K_t}{Nt_t}, 1\right) = f(k_t),$$ (2)

where y_t is output per capita and $k_t = K_t/N_t$ is the capital-labor ratio.

The capital-labor ratio increases with net additions to the capital stock (gross investment minus depreciation), but decreases with additions to the labor force (growing with the population at rate n). Gross investment is modeled as the fixed saving rate, s, times output, y. Depreciation is modeled as the fixed depreciation rate, d, times the capital stock. Thus, the change in the capital-labor ratio, Δk_t, over time can be written as

$$\Delta k_t = sy_t - (d+n)k_t = sf(k_t) - (d+n)k_t.$$ (3)

That is, the change in the capital-labor ratio is the saving rate times output minus the depreciation and population growth rates times the capital stock.

Given the nature of the production function, the model has a steady-state per capita income, y^*, and capital-labor ratio, k^*, where $\Delta k = 0$. At that point, gross investment (the saving rate times income) exactly equals what's required to keep up with depreciation and population growth (see fig. 16.1). From any starting point, the growth process converges to this equilibrium.[8] Starting at any capital-labor ratio below k^*, gross investment would exceed the levels required to keep up with depreciation and population growth, and k and y would rise to the equilibrium. (Further, the relative return on capital, as captured by the slope of the f(y) curve, will fall.) Starting from any ratio above k^*, gross investment would fall short of the levels required to keep up with depreciation and population growth, and k and y would fall to their equilibrium levels and the return on capital will rise. The equilibrium values of y^* and k^* vary positively with the saving rate, s, and negatively with the population growth rate, n, and depreciation rate, d.

Solow's model recast the growth process. It had been previously thought that a nation stagnated economically because it had little capital; if it saved more, its income would grow. Solow said this is true in comparisons across countries; a nation that saved more (or had more capital) had a higher income level. But it did not have a higher long-run growth rate. If its saving rate increased, a nation would grow temporarily faster as it moved from one steady-state capital-labor ratio to a higher ratio.[9] But this would lead to diminishing returns to capital and would entail greater depreciation. The long-run growth rate would not change. That depended on technological change, not capital accumulation.

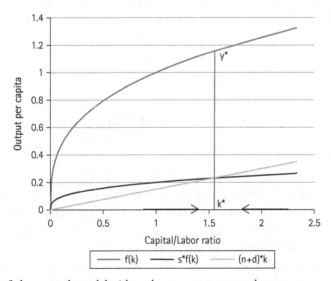

FIGURE 16.1. Solow growth model with $y = k_{1/3}$, $s = 0.2$, $n = 0.03$, $d = 0.12$

Solow incorporated changes in technology, A, into his model, but ensuring the possibility of balanced growth required additional assumptions. One approach was to consider only production functions that can be written as Y = F(K, AN). If technology improved labor efficiency directly, then it fits into this form, which permits the expansion of outcome and capital at equal rates. The model (1–3) can then be rewritten in units of effective labor. A steady-state capital-effective labor ratio will evolve, yielding zero growth in output per effective labor. But output per capita grows now at the rate of labor efficiency. Another approach was to assume the production function took the special Cobb-Douglas form: $Y = AK^{\alpha}N^{1-\alpha}$, which fixes the capital and labor shares independently of economic forces, including A. Under either set of assumptions, exogenously generated technological advance, not capital accumulation, drives sustained growth.

The Solow model inspired the development of modern growth accounting, where the contribution of capital accumulation to income growth for short-run periods could be measured. A little terminology is useful here. An increase in the capital-labor ratio is called capital-deepening. It is contrasted with capital-widening, in which the aggregate capital stock grows merely to keep up with the expanding labor force. Solow attributed the residual—the change in per capita income not explained by capital-deepening—to technological progress. Moses Abramovitz, a contemporary scholar working along the same lines, called the difference instead a "measure of our ignorance." Solow's take on the problem gave economists a plausible way to measure technological progress; what was otherwise an elusive quantity became $\Delta A/A = \Delta y/y - \alpha\,\Delta k/k$. One could compare the contributions of technological change versus capital accumulation—invention versus thrift—in income growth. Examining the American growth record, Solow (1957), Abramovitz (orig. 1956, reprinted in 1989), Kendrick (1961), and Denison (1962) all found that capital-deepening accounted for a small share of per capita income growth during the twentieth century. This finding raised great interest among economic historians and economists (including Nathan Rosenberg, Jacob Schmookler, Kenneth Arrow, and Richard Nelson) who sought to explain the underlying forces shaping the rate and direction of technological change.[10]

NEW GROWTH THEORY

Growth theorists in time became dissatisfied with Solow's treatment of technology as exogenous, falling like manna from heaven. It left the driver of growth unexplained, at least by economic forces. Seeking a new approach, Paul Romer (1986) and Robert Lucas (1988) introduced endogenous growth theory to model sustained growth as a purposeful, economically driven process. One early line, known as AK theory (Rebelo 1991), tried to bring capital accumulation back in by arguing that the social returns to capital were greater than the private returns (as measured by capital's share of income). Solow's model with the conventional capital share fit several facts about the real world poorly. It predicted a faster rate of income convergence (or more precisely, conditional convergence) than was empirically observed. It predicted narrower differences in income levels between rich and poor places than was seen in practice. And it predicted greater differences in the returns to capital than those observed in the real world. Assuming a higher share to capital helped the model fit all these facts better (Mankiw 1995, 281–290). But AK thinking soon ran into theoretical and empirical problems, not unlike those suffered by the Harrod-Domar model, and was abandoned.

A more sustained line of inquiry focuses on the purposeful investments of resources to generate new ideas or add to human capital. Ideas, unlike physical or human capital, are not rivalrous; one person's use of an idea does not prevent another person from using it as well. This added to a dimension of increasing returns or scale effects, in which a given idea was more valuable in a larger economy. Ideas were also often nonexcludible. It could be hard to prevent the spread of one's valuable idea to others and to capture all the benefits of innovative investments. This added a possibility of market failure in the absence of an appropriate intellectual property regime. Another set of models focused on investments in human capital and the allocation of labor resources to research and development.[11] None of the new growth models has achieved the canonical status of the Solow model. A common feature of both the Solow model and the new approach is to deny the importance of the accumulation of physical capital in sustained growth. Indeed, many endogenous growth models leave physical capital out (including only labor and knowledge/human capital) for the sake of analytical convenience.

THE AMERICAN GROWTH RECORD

The standard macro view asserts that the American economy has long grown on a balanced path fitting the five claims listed in the introduction to this chapter. Some macro textbooks point to the near constancy of total income growth since 1790. Others highlight the near constancy of per capita income growth after the 1870s. The series in figure 16.2(a) tells the tale. What stands out in both the total and per capita income series is that growth rebounded from the disaster of the Great Depression. But the two assertions about balanced growth (claim no. 5) are incongruous, because the two series are linked together by a third series (population) that displays profound change. As panel (a) shows, population growth was transitioning from a high rate in the first half of nineteenth century to a far lower rate in the second half of the twentieth century. As panel (b) shows, more of the growth in total income at the beginning of the period was due (mechanically) to population growth; more growth at the end was due to per capita income growth.

As Simon Kuznets knew, the historical record for the US economy was complex and varied. There are many different series on income and capital—aggregate versus per capita; net versus gross; constant versus current price. It may be possible to pick a subset displaying something close to balanced growth. But this is not enough; it is necessary

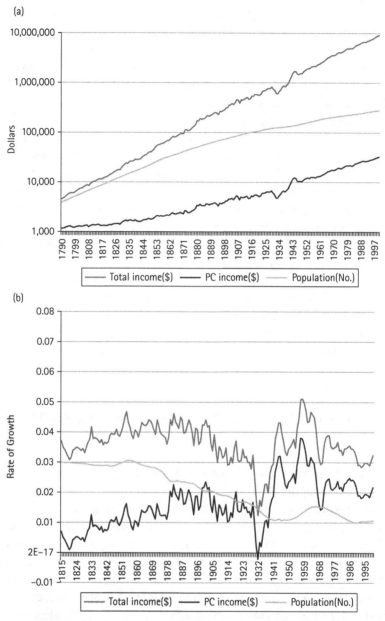

(a)

(b)

FIGURE 16.2. Growth of total income, per capita income, and population, 1790–2000
(a) Levels
(b) Growth rates over the previous twenty-five-year period

Note: In panel (b), the observation for 1814 is the average annual growth rate since 1790, and so on.

Source: Carter et al. (2006, Ca 9, 11), income in 1996 dollars.

but not sufficient.[12] If growth were truly balanced, all conceptually relevant series should display balanced growth—that is, grow at the same rate.

Economic historians understand the American economy differently from macro-economists; they see it as a developmental process involving several important transitions (Abramovitz and David 2001). The first transition, occurring in the early nineteenth century, involved a shift from a process of extensive growth to intensive growth. Extensive growth was characterized by pushing out the frontier and by more people doing the same things—principally farming—as those who came before.[13] Intensive growth was characterized by people doing something new, moving to cities, and working in factories, mines, or offices. A second transition to a knowledge-based economy took hold around the turn of the twentieth century. Per capita income growth continued at a high pace, but now it was driven by increases in the productivity of the factors, by technological and organizational advances, and by investments in human capital. Indeed, Claudia Goldin (2001) has labeled the twentieth century the "human capital century." Americans began to work smarter. This contrasts with the nineteenth century, when they worked harder. In that century, a rising fraction of the population worked, and they worked more hours per year. And they saved a growing share of their current income to invest in raising the capital stock.

Capital in the Nineteenth Century

Historical data on the capital formation rate reveal something fundamentally different from the "stylized facts" assumed by growth theorists. Figure 16.3 plots three series on

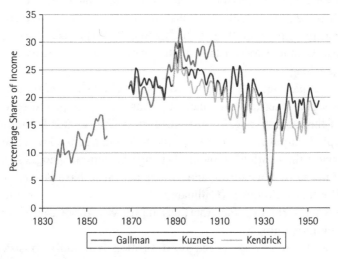

FIGURE 16.3. US capital formation rate, 1834–1955

Sources: Constant Price Series from Gallman (1966); Kuznets (1961); Kendrick (1966).

the US capital formation rate—the share of income withdrawn from current consumption to increase future output—from 1834 to 1955. Despite Kuznets's summary take, his constant-price series showed a rise and then a gradually declining trend. The stability that Kuznets reported reflects the post–World War II rebound of the rate from about 5 percent in 1933 to about 20 percent in the early 1950s. John Kendrick (1961), who reworked the numbers to fit the Department of Commerce definitions, found a similar pattern of a rise and fall.

A different perspective emerged when Robert Gallman (1966, 1986), a student of Kuznets, pushed corrected numbers back into the first half of the nineteenth century. According to Gallman's main series, the share of real gross capital formation in GNP rose from "roughly one-tenth in the late 1830s and early 1840s to about one-quarter" in the 1886–1900 period (Davis and Gallman 1973, 437). The capital formation rate grew by a factor of two or three, claim no. 1 notwithstanding. The largest change occurred during the 1860s, the Civil War decade.[14]

The causes of the nineteenth-century rise of the capital formation rate have been the subject of intense debate among American economic historians. Moses Abramovitz and Paul David (1973) argued that the driving force was increased demand for capital arising from capital-using technological change. They pointed to calculations showing a rise in capital share in output over the late nineteenth century, which if true is at odds with balanced growth claim no. 3. The headaches involved in measuring the capital share during this period are discussed in the following.

Lance Davis and Robert Gallman (1975, 1978) instead attributed the rise in capital formation to shifts in the saving rate. Their position echoed Kuznets's statement in 1961 that saving supply, not technologically driven demand for investment funds, determined the rate of capital formation in the mid-twentieth century. Davis and Gallman (1978, 23) support their claim by noting the general decline in US interest rates from 1840 to 1900. Figure 16.4 graphs interest rates on commercial paper and US government bonds as well as the (3-year centered) inflation rate. The real rate on interest (the nominal rate minus the inflation rate) fell roughly in half. This runs counter to claim no. 4 that the returns to capital are constant and to the view that the returns are little affected by capital-deepening.

Davis and Gallman (1978, 18–21) point to increases in the capital-output ratio in each of the major sectors—agriculture, manufacturing and mining, and services—and in all but one of the subsectors within manufacturing. They contend that the ubiquitous rise in the capital-output ratio was more consistent with a general reduction in the cost of capital services than with technological change. Structural changes such as the shift from agriculture to manufacturing and mining appear to have pushed the economy-wide capital-output ratio down (Gallman and Howle 1971, 32). This finding was due to the somewhat surprising fact that agriculture was more capital-intensive than manufacturing and mining.[15]

Davis and Gallman (1978) argued the transition is broadly consistent with the predictions of a Solow model in response to increase in the saving rate. In terms of figure

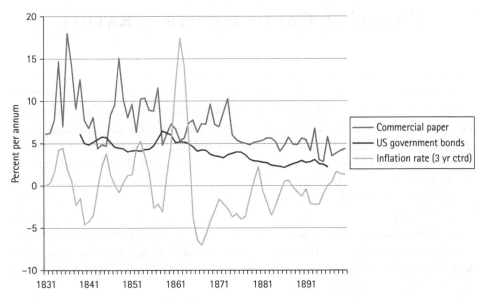

FIGURE 16.4. Interest rates and inflation, 1831–1900

Source: Carter et al. (2006 Ca 13, Cj1192, Cj1223).

16.1, this represents a shift in the sf(k) curve, and rise in the equilibrium levels of k* and y*. (The capital-output ratio, which is equal to k divided by y, rises as f(k) increases.) The growth rate of per capita income temporally picks up during the transition process. Davis and Gallman explained the rise in the saving rate largely as response to improvements in financial intermediation—banks, insurance companies, and securities markets—that linked savers and investors.

Richard Sutch (1991) highlights the emergence of life-cycle saving—investing during the prime-earning years to support one's self in retirement—as a new force raising the saving rate in the late nineteenth century. David (1977) emphasizes the effect of the reductions in childbearing, which he viewed as an unmeasured, unconventional form of saving for old age (in the period before Social Security). Many scholars have pointed to changes in the age structure. Frank Lewis (1983), for example, argues that the falling dependency ratio (the number of dependent children to working adults) accounts for one-quarter of the increase in the saving rate between 1830 and 1900. Shifts in the distribution of income and wealth have also received attention. Williamson (1991, 17–19, 30–32, 74–82), for example, argues that increasing inequality pushed up the saving rate over the long nineteenth century, though the estimated effects were modest compared with the actual increase. Taking a different tack, Ransom and Sutch (1988) assert that the emancipation of slaves as a result of the Civil War led to the jump in saving. (See Davis and Gallman 1994, 208–226, for further details concerning this debate.)

CHANGING CAPITAL-OUTPUT RATIOS

The sharp rise of the capital formation rate over the nineteenth century led to higher capital-output ratios. Similarly, the gradual decline over the first half of the twentieth century led to a falling capital-output ratio (as Kuznets observed). Table 16.1 shows indices on the current-value capital-output ratio. It includes both quantities and prices. The capital figures are from Gallman (1986, 78) and the GDP numbers (and deflator) are from the *Historical Statistics*. Gallman's research focused on the nineteenth century, but the patterns he reports for the twentieth century are broadly consistent with those found by Kuznets, Kendrick, and the Department of Commerce. Gallman found that the capital-output ratio almost doubled between 1800 and 1900. To be precise, the ratio in 1900 was 185 percent of the 1800 figure. Then the ratio began to fall, reaching 82 percent of its 1900 level by 1953. The trend was temporarily interrupted in the 1930s, when depression levels of output caused the ratio to soar. But this was due to business-cycle reasons, rather than to secular forces.

Kaldor was aware of Kuznets's findings about the changes in the US capital-output ratio but paid them little mind. He wrote (1957, 592), "In the United States the capital/ output ratio has shown a slightly rising trend from the decade 1879–1988 to the decade 1909–1918, and a falling trend since, and (ignoring the depression period) is not significantly different now (at around 3.0) than it was sixty years ago." For Kaldor, so long as the ratio ended where it "started," nothing happened. But Gallman's numbers show

Table 16.1 Indices of Capital–Output Ratio

	Capital Stock/ Output	Capital Price/ Output Price
1800	57.5	109.0
1840	68.4	113.1
1850	76.2	118.4
1860	88.5	116.9
1870	79.2	112.9
1880	74.0	123.7
1890	106.0	116.5
1900	106.5	114.1
1929	100.0	100.0
1953	87.5	141.7
1980	100.7	159.8

Sources: Capital stock and price index: Gallman (1986);
GDP and deflator: Carter et al. (2006, Series Ca 9, Ca 13).

that the ascent was steep and began well before the 1880s, undercutting the assertions of claim no. 2.

Table 16.1 also displays price indices. Contrary to the assumptions of one-good models such as Solow's, the price of capital goods is not always the same as that of all other goods. Economic historians have long debated the course and consequences of changes in the price of capital goods relative to price of output. Demand theory predicts that a rise in the present relative prices leads to a decrease in the quantity demanded, but a rise in expected future price (by generating a capital gain) will lead to an increase in the quantity demanded. Supply theory predicts that the price ratio will depend on the relative rates of technological progress in the capital and consumer goods sectors. Government policies can also play a role. Relying on the careful work of Dorothy Brady (1966), Gallman (1986) found a general decline in the relative price of capital goods over the mid-nineteenth century. The patterns were complex because the relative price of manufacturer's produced durables fell very sharply, while those of construction goods (such as buildings) rose. William Collins and Jeffrey Williamson (2001) report similar trends.

Williamson (1974) had attributed the decline in capital goods prices in the mid-nineteenth century to Civil War tariffs. He asserted that the tariff hikes increased the prices of manufactured imports (entering consumption flows) relative to investment goods, which he argued were largely not tradeable. Thereby, Williamson linked changes in the rate of capital formation to debates over national policy enacted during and immediately after the Civil War. J. Bradford DeLong (1998, esp. 369–370), among others, has challenged Williamson's interpretation, arguing that capital goods entered international trade and that the tariff burdens did not differ greatly between the capital and consumer sectors.

In the twentieth century, capital goods prices have generally risen relative to consumer goods (Gordon 1961). This likely contributed to the twentieth-century fall in the capital-output ratio that Kuznets and Kendrick observed (Mayor 1968).

Several scholars have argued that the decline in the measured capital-output ratio was a statistical artifact. One variant belongs to the "no taxation without misrepresentation" school. Paul Anderson (1961) claimed that the enactment of a federal corporate income tax in the 1910s induced American businesses to adopt accounting practices to claim depreciation expenses sooner. This led to higher measured (but not actual) capital consumption and lower measured (but not actual) capital stocks.[16] Another variant argued that official accounts undervalued government-financed investments in plant and equipment during World War II (Gordon 1969).

Other scholars maintain that real structural forces were at work. Alexander Field (1987) points to organizational change as an important force. He argues that modern business enterprise (with its drive for high throughput) was a major capital-saving technology. Another key change, noted by Kuznets, was a decline in investments in structures and a rise (albeit a more modest rise) in investments in equipment. In the period covered in *Capital and the American Economy*, the construction share in gross capital formation fell from two-thirds to about one-half, while the producer durable (or

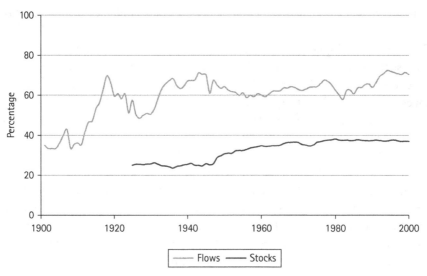

FIGURE 16.5. Equipment as a share of equipment and structures in flows and stocks, 1901–2000

Note: Values in current dollars of private nonresidential investment.

Source: US BEA, Fixed Assets, Series i3ntotlieqoo0; i3ntotl1stoo0; k1ntotlieqoo0; k1ntotl1stoo0.

equipment) share rose from one-fifth to two-fifths (Kuznets 1961, 9). Figure 16.5 shows the changes in the ratio of equipment to the total equipment and structures in the data of the Bureau of Economic Analysis (BEA) of the US Department of Commerce.

Economists and economic historians have debated the causes and consequences of the shift from structures to equipment. One causal claim was that electricity was a capital-saving technology, with differentially large effects on the utilization rate of structures. Electric lighting allowed factories to adopt night work and for stores to be open for longer hours (DuBoff 1966). One of the consequences of the shift from investment in structures to equipment, according to DeLong (1992), has been to stimulate productivity growth. Based on narrative evidence and statistical analysis, he argues that investments in machinery are more protean carriers of new technologies than comparable investments in buildings.

Another less controversial claim is that the shift to equipment drove up capital consumption, much as Kuznets argued in *Capital in the American Economy*. The share of depreciation in GDP rose and the gap between net national product (NNP) and GDP widened as investment shifted from long-lived structures to shorter-lived equipment. In contemporary calculations, the depreciation rate for equipment is typically assumed to be about 10 percent per annum, while that for buildings is 2 percent per annum. Figure 16.6 displays the Department of Commerce (BEA) figures on the GDP shares of gross domestic investment, gross private domestic investment, and capital consumption (depreciation) since 1929. Both measures of the gross capital formation rate were relatively steady in the post–World War II period. But the capital consumption share rose and net capital formation fell. Depreciation is not well understood by economists, but these patterns belie the macro textbook view of the US growth as a balanced process.

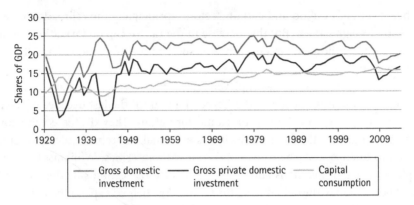

FIGURE 16.6. Gross capital formation and consumption, 1929–2014

Source: BEA, Series W170RC1, A006RC1, A191RC1, A262RC1.

SOURCES OF CAPITAL AND CHANNELS OF FINANCE

Economic historians have sought to chart and explain the changing sources of capital and channels of finance. The historical literature often refers to different periods of capitalism. In the antebellum period, when initial ventures were financed by merchants, the period is sometimes referred to as "merchant capitalism" (Porter and Livesay 1971; see also Lamoreaux 1996). During and after the Civil War, when manufacturers assumed greater control of their own finances, "industrial capitalism" prevailed. Around the turn of the century, when investment banks such as J. P. Morgan rose to prominence, the period is characterized as "finance capitalism." Economic historians have found defining "capitalism" and its different varieties even more elusive than defining "capital."

Developments in the new institutional economics and contract theory have clarified our understanding of why capital generally hires labor (not the other way around) and what limits exist on the use of credit (Williamson 1985). Incentives are better aligned if the decision-maker is the residual claimant on gains or losses. Because potential losses have to be covered and because dedicated capital was subject to holdup and opportunistic behavior, the owner of capital is privileged as the decider. Moreover, the owner of the capitalistic enterprise can borrow a limited fraction of the capital invested. Monitoring becomes a critical problem whenever credit is used.

In addition to documenting the rising rate of capital formation before 1900, Davis and Gallman (1978, 30–54; 2001, 234–334) assembled available statistics to determine the sources of the capital flows. They divided possible sources into three domestic sectors—corporations, government, and private households—and one international sector, foreign investors. They could dispose of the last sector with ease. The United States was a net borrower before 1900 and certain sectors—principally the railroads—relied extensively on foreign capital. But the increase in the rate of capital formation cannot be explained by new inflows of foreign cash. Any such inflows were more than offset by interest payments to service the existing foreign debt.

Davis and Gallman (1978) downplayed the initial role of corporate saving. Such entities carried too little weight in the US economy until the last decades of the nineteenth century to explain the rise in capital formation. They dismissed the government sector, or at least the federal side. It was too small and repaid quickly what it had borrowed to finance war. Their position is not without critics. Williamson (1974), for example, argues that decisions about how to finance the Union side during the Civil War and how to repay the debt during the Gilded Age helped expand the nation's security markets and then to "crowd in" investment for the private economy (see also James 1984). Davis and Gallman (1978, 59–65) concurred about the importance of innovations stimulating the development of financial intermediaries, but they differed on the relative importance of secular trends versus war-related policy changes.

Kuznets (1961) examined the role of financial channels in his monumental investigation of *Capital in the American Economy*. What he found was mixed. Government spending and borrowing grew greatly in size during his period of study. Joining the government in using external (or intermediated) sources of funding were private households financing residential investments. He found that the business sectors, especially those employing the corporate form, did not rely extensively on external sources such as banks or new issues on securities markets. Instead, these businesses invested retained earnings. To the extent that going enterprises engaged in investment largely to make up for capital consumption, use of internal finance is entirely understandable. Paul David and John Scadding (1974) noted that over the 1898–1969 period, corporate saving (and spending on consumer durables) rose to offset the falling personal saving rate and sustain the gross private saving rate.

The changing extent of "financialization" is also of interest. Raymond W. Goldsmith, a pioneer in wealth accounting, charted the share of financial assets in all national assets in twenty developed countries. For the United States (Goldsmith 1985, Table A-22), the fraction rose from 23 percent in 1805 to 30 percent in 1850, then to 40 percent in 1900 and 54 percent in 1929. The fraction remained relatively flat until the late 1970s. The use of high leverage (debt-value) ratios to fund new investment is a recent (post-1980) phenomenon.

NATIONAL WEALTH

National wealth is more comprehensive than capital. It takes the capital stock of reproducible productive assets and adds nonreproducible assets, such as land and natural resources, the value of the stocks of monetary metals, and consumer durables. Scholars such as Thomas Piketty (2014) find this concept more analytically useful than the capital stock as conventionally defined. His choice (and his use of net, after-depreciation measures as opposed to the more conventional gross, pre-depreciation measures of flow variables) led to some recent controversies in which he and his critics talked past one another.

American economic historians analyzing the transition of the American economy from its phase of solely extensive growth to a phase including intensive growth have found it problematic to treat land as strictly a nonreproducible asset. Land in its "raw" state was much less valuable than when cleared, broken, fenced, and drained (or irrigated). Before the twentieth century, large flows of resources were devoted to improving land. Gallman (1986, 1992) added investments in land improvements to his capital stock estimates. (He had always included farm buildings as reproducible capital.) His later work presents one series on capital narrowly defined to match the twentieth-century concept—these are what have been discussed earlier—and another series more broadly defined to match what he considered more representative of the nineteenth-century US development process.

One might note that such investments occurred in Europe, China, and other settled places in the world before their inclusion in national accounts is feasible. To compare like-with-like across countries, using either national wealth everywhere or national reproducible capital everywhere, is more appropriate than including such investments in the US capital stock and excluding them elsewhere (see Piketty and Zucman 2014).

Gallman (1992) found that the US capital stock grew more slowly over the nineteenth century if one used the broad (rather than the narrow) definition. The measured rate of capital formation was higher earlier, but rose more gradually. Much of the early capital formation occurred in a rather mundane manner, with farmers clearing the "bottom 40" acres with family labor during the off-season when the labor would otherwise have been unemployed. The process took place largely outside markets and did not require formal financing. Using the more comprehensive series reduced the magnitude of the changes but did not alter the underlying patterns or the timing of turning points (Davis and Gallman 1994).

The conventional view is that the wealth-to-income ratio in the Unites States is about 3 or 4 to 1. Many economists treat this as a universal constant, applicable to all other places and times. One of the headline findings of Piketty (2014, 116–120) was that the ratio was around 6 or 7 to 1 in Western Europe before World War I. (Kuznets 1966, 75–77, noted the Anglo-American differences.) The higher ratio of wealth-to-income had important social consequences. As Piketty (2014, 53–54, 113–116) observes, the novels of Jane Austen and Honoré de Balzac featured characters seeking to marry into or inherit existing fortunes (landed estates and bond portfolios), rather than generate new riches through hard work, thrift, and invention. Due to the availability of cheap "raw" land in North America, wealth-to-income ratios were lower in the United States and Canada. Commentators on nineteenth-century America marveled at the energetic pursuit of material gain in an expanding economy—"the restlessness, the feverish anxiety to get on"—but saw the drive coming at the expense of other intellectual and social values (Bowen 1859, 122; de Tocqueville 1841, Book 2, Chapter 9).

Capital's Share

A crucial area of contention involves the functional division of output, the split between capital and labor. Alan Krueger (1999) notes that "the empirical determination of factor shares was the proximate cause for the founding of the National Bureau of Economic Research" in 1917. Charles Cobb and Paul Douglas (1928), who introduced their production function a decade later, focused almost exclusively on manufacturing where tasks of measurement were relatively easy and the concepts more applicable. (They set the labor share at ¾ and capital share at ¼.) Generalizing their results has proved problematic.

A key difficulty is that historical accounts are structured as a threefold rather than the classical twofold division between labor and capital (Kravis 1968). The information comes to us as (a) employee compensation; (b) entrepreneurial or proprietors' earnings; and then (c) a combination of interest/dividends plus rents plus corporate profits. This first item clearly belongs in the labor share, and the last set of items belongs in the capital share. The middle item—entrepreneurial or proprietors' earnings—needs to be split between the two. As table 16.2 shows, such earning constituted between one-half and one-quarter of total income in the mid- and late nineteenth century. Over time, as the agricultural sector contracted, this share fell while the employee compensation share rose. The share of income going to proprietors is so great that its treatment largely determines whether one regards the capital share as constant, rising, or falling.

There are many approaches to imputing the labor and capital shares of proprietors' earnings. One is the *asset- (or interest-rate-) based approach*, which assigns to the proprietors' property capital's rate of return prevailing in the rest of the economy; what's left of earnings is attributed to labor. A second method is the *labor-earnings approach*, which assigns to the labor of the proprietor (and family) the wage rates prevailing in the rest of the economy; what's left of earnings is attributed to capital. A problem with each of these approaches is that family businesses are often willing to sacrifice income to remain independent. The high incidence of self-exploitation at family farms and "ma-and-pa" enterprises is well-known. The sum of the measured parts of earnings taken from the first two approaches may exceed total earnings. As Irving Kravis (1968, 137–139) noted, each of these approaches tends to push fluctuations into the residually measured share. A third approach, preferred by Kravis, is the *proportional approach*. The method takes the measured earnings of the total preceding approaches, combines them, and divides the total proprietor earnings according to the proportions that capital and labor comprise of the total. This approach splits the difference. A fourth *economic-wide approach* uses the split from the rest of the economy. This adds no information and unrealistically assumes that capital-labor ratios are the same in proprietor-run and other enterprises. A variant, adopted by D. Gale Johnson (1954), allocates set fraction (two-thirds) to labor and remainder to capital. This is ad hoc but has the virtue of being transparent.

Table 16.2 Factor Shares and Their Imputation (Percent of Income)

	Employee Compensation	Entrepreneurial Income	Interest, Rents, and Profits	Total Property Income			
				Asset Basis	Labor Basis	Prop Basis	1/3 Basis
King							
1850s	36.5	41.6	21.9				35.8
1860s	42.9	35.8	21.3				33.2.
1870s	50.1	26.4	23.5				32.3
1880s	52.5	23.0	24.5				32.3
1890s	50.4	27.3	22.3				31.4
1900s	47.2	28.8	24.0				33.6
Johnson–Kravis							
1900s	55.0	23.7	21.3	30.6	32.2	32.1	20.2
1910s	53.6	23.8	22.6	32.6	35.8	34.8	30.5
1920s	60.8	18.1	21.7	29.2	28.5	28.8	27.7
1930s	67.5	14.8	17.7	22.9	19.8	21.4	22.6
1940s	64.6	17.2	18.3	23.5	25.6	24.0	24.1
1950s	67.3	13.7	18.8	23.0	22.7	23.2	23.4
Commerce							
1930s	67.1	16.4	16.5				22.0
1940s	64.0	17.2	18.9				24.6
1950s	68.0	13.0	18.3				22.6
1960s	71.1	10.0	18.9				22.2

Sources: US Department of Commerce (1957, Series F 61–66; 1976, Series F 187–191); Kravis (1968, 134); Johnson (1954, 179).

Taken as a whole, the evidence in the table 16.2 challenges the notion that factor shares in the United States have been constant. The choice of how to allocate "entrepreneurial income" is quite arbitrary and yet crucial in determining the capital share.

THE CAPITAL-TECHNOLOGY DICHOTOMY

As noted earlier, economists using growth accounting techniques to investigate the performance of the American economy in the first half of the twentieth century found the contributions of capital-deepening were swamped by technology advance (or, more accurately, by the residual). Conducting a similar exercise for the nineteenth century, Abramovitz and David (1973, 430) found that most of the increase in per capita income was explained by increases in the factors of production per capita—more capital per worker and more hours of work per capita. Little was left to be explained by technological progress or investments in human capital.[17]

This finding is at variance with how the nineteenth-century economy was perceived by those living through it. Many contemporaries lauded the period as a great age of invention, with new labor-saving machines playing a starring role. The census in 1850 and again in 1900 was filled with encomia to the marvels of the machine age (Fogel 2013).

Nathan Rosenberg (1982) and Robert Allen (2011) offer a way to reconcile the two views. Standard growth accounting techniques treat technological change and capital accumulation as separate and distinct processes. And they generally treat technological change as a global process. Thinking in terms of figure 16.1 (and assuming a Cobb-Douglas production function), technological change shifts the f(k) curve up by a uniform multiple. Rosenberg (1982) argued that most technological advances were rather local in nature. Producers did not know and had no reason to learn how to produce at every capital-labor ratio; what mattered were those in the range of potential use. Allen (2011, Chapter 4) added to this the notion that technological change principally enabled the productive use of higher capital-labor ratios.

We can put these ideas together in the context of figure 16.1. Instead of thinking f(k) as existing for all k, imagine that given the state of knowledge, there was a threshold capital-labor ratio, $k^{\#}$, at which output per worker becomes fixed. Capital-labor ratios above $k^{\#}$ yielded nothing more than $f(k^{\#})$. As an example, one could add an eleventh shovel to the ten workers digging by hand, but it would just lie idle. In the alternative view, technological change worked to increase the $k^{\#}$ threshold along f(k) relationship; it did not shift the curve so much as extend the range that was feasible to use more capital productively. So in this example, the invention of the steam-shovel would allow a higher capital-labor ratio than was productive before.

This way of stating the alternative view is overly stark. The core idea is that technological change in the nineteenth century (and even later) was not of a factor-neutral or global process. It occurred most rapidly at higher capital-labor ratios. It was generated in the more advanced economies and was directed to solving their problems. Less advanced economies generally were left to use the technologies developed long before and now discarded by the advanced economies. In the alternative view, technological change and factor substitution (replacing labor with capital) are part of the same process, not separate and distinct.[18]

Conclusion

Macro-growth economists have constructed an image of US growth based on "stylized facts" regarding the constancy of the rate of capital formation, capital-output ratio, and

linked

capital share of income. Capital accumulation plays a minor role as driver of long-run growth; knowledge accumulation is the key to growth. The macro-economic school emphasizes the long-run stability of US income growth, at least since the late nineteenth century. The literature concludes that the government policies (taxes, regulations, R&D investments) do not matter in the long run.

Economic historians see things differently. They fully agree on the importance of the growth of knowledge, but do not see technological change and capital accumulation as necessarily distinct and separate processes. Moreover, they tend to see the US growth experience not as a single process along a steady-state path, but rather as a succession of waves or transitions. The presiding image from Schumpeter and Kuznets is of a series of S-shaped growth processes, unfolding one after another. In this succession of waves, physical capital accumulation mattered more in the second two-thirds of the nineteenth century, and knowledge/human capital accumulation mattered more in the twentieth century. And what of the twentieth-first century? By studying capital's history, without blinders, we can more fully appreciate the possibilities.

role crisis as in reduce capital use price and disrupting existing order

NOTES

1. I would like to acknowledge the helpful comments of Hoyt Bleakley, Louis Cain, Price Fishback, Joshua Hausnan, Alan L. Olmstead, and Elyce Rotella, and the time, insights, and research materials that Robert Gallman shared.
2. Kaldor (1961) included two facts involving labor, namely that the capital-labor ratio increased and the real wage grew. His evidence for his "stylized facts" was scanty and related almost entirely to the United Kingdom.
3. The Harrod-Domar model fixed both the (incremental) capital-output ratio and saving rate, making the income growth rate equal to their product minus depreciation. This allowed for unbounded growth with no forces ensuring full employment. Harrod's (1939, 17) "fundamental equation" is closely related to Piketty's (2014, 166) "second fundamental law of capitalism."
4. The accounting scheme of Kuznets differed from that of the US Department of Commerce in the treatment of government expenditures. Kuznets omitted government purchases of goods and services as a separate component of GNP. Instead he added an estimate of government services for consumers to personal consumption expenditures and government capital formation to investment. Some government expenditures (such as expenditures for defense and military purposes) were excluded. The differences were relatively unimportant before 1940.
5. The ratio measured in constant (1929) prices fell modestly. The difference arose because the price of capital goods relative to other goods tended to rise. Economists in this period generally focused on national product (activity by the nation's citizens at home and abroad) as opposed to domestic product (activity within the nation's borders).
6. The share of net capital formation in net national product (NNP) fell from 15 percent in the 1869–1888 period to 7 percent in 1946–1955 period, when measured in constant prices; and from 13 percent to 9 percent in current prices.
7. Trevor Swan (1956) published a similar theory at the same time. In both models, the saving rate is held constant, not made the outcome of optimization decision as in a neoclassical growth model.

8. Stable convergence required additional assumptions about the production function and ruling out borderline cases.
9. The transition phrase to the higher capital-labor ratio could take several decades. In theory, the speed depended on the response of output to capital.
10. Other economists, such as Zvi Griliches and Dale Jorgenson (1966) and John Kendrick (1976), sought to define the capital stock in a more comprehensive way to more fully explain output growth.
11. Another line, unified growth theory, seeks to link income growth and the accumulation of human capital with changes in population growth, hence endogenizing the "n" that Solow takes as given.
12. Evans (2000) found that from 1947 to 1998 the stylized facts held even approximately only in net terms. The depreciation rate, gross returns to capital, gross capital share, and gross rate of capital formation were all rising. But between 1929 and 1946 the capital-output ratio plummeted.
13. Formally speaking, extensive growth is growth of total income; intensive growth is growth of per capita income. Extensive growth includes but is not confined to intensive growth. Informally speaking, extensive growth is used to refer to growth of total income without growth of per capita income (without intensive growth).
14. The rate was likely even lower before the 1830s than after (Davis and Gallman 1994).
15. The overall increase in the capital-output ratio was driven largely by changes in the service sector, specifically the rising importance of the transportation (railroads) and urban housing sectors (Davis and Gallman 1994).
16. Anderson (1961) also questioned why the price of capital goods rose relative to consumer goods. Gordon (1990) picked up the challenge of improving these estimates.
17. Gallman (1972, 29) supported these conclusions. But Gallman (1992, 96–97) found that using more a comprehensive measure for capital (including land clearing) reduces the differences. The measured capital stock is higher in the mid-nineteenth century, its growth slower, and consequently the unexplained residual is larger.
18. See Solow (1957, 316) and Abramovitz (1989). Kuznets argued that depreciation was principally due to obsolesce rather than wear-and-tear, which reinforces this point.

BIBLIOGRAPHY

Abramovitz, Moses. (1989). *Thinking about Growth: And Other Essays about Economic Growth and Wealth*. New York: Cambridge University Press.
Abramovitz, Moses, and Paul A. David. (1973). "Reinterpreting Economic Growth: Parables and Realities." *American Economic Review, Papers and Proceedings* 63(May): 428–439.
Abramovitz, Moses, and Paul A. David. (2001). "Two Centuries of American Macroeconomic Growth: From Exploitation of Resource Abundance to Knowledge-Driven Development." SIEPR Paper No. 01-05.
Allen, Robert C. (2011). *Global Economic History: A Very Short Introduction*. New York: Oxford University Press.
Anderson, Paul S. (1961). "The Apparent Decline in Capital-Output Ratios." *Quarterly Journal of Economics* 75(4): 615–634.
Bowen, Francis. (1859). *Principles of Political Economy*. 2nd ed. Boston: Little-Brown.

Brady, Dorothy. (1966). "Price Deflators for Final Product Estimates." In *Output, Employment, and Productivity in the United States after 1800*, Studies in Income and Wealth, edited by Dorothy S. Brady, Vol. 30, 91–115. New York: Columbia University Press.

Carter, Susan, Scott S. Gartner, Michael R. Haines, Alan L. Olmstead, Richard Sutch, and Gavin Wright. (2006). *Historical Statistics of the United States, Millennial Edition*. New York: Cambridge University Press.

Cobb, Charles W., and Paul H. Douglas. (1928). "A Theory of Production." *American Economic Review: Papers and Proceedings* 18(1): 139–165.

Collins, William J., and Jeffrey G. Williamson. (2001). "Capital-Goods Prices and Investment, 1870–1950." *Journal of Economic History* 61(1): 59–94.

David, Paul A. (1977). "Invention and Accumulation in America's Economic Growth: A Nineteenth Century Parable." In *International Organization, National Policies and Economic Development*, edited by Karl Brunner and Allen H. Meltzer, 179–228. Amsterdam: North-Holland.

David, Paul A., and John Scadding. (1974). "Private Saving, Ultrarationality, Aggregation, and 'Denison's Law.'" *Journal of Political Economy* 82: 225–249.

Davis, Lance E., and Robert E. Gallman. (1973). "The Share of Savings and Investment in Gross National Product during the 19th Century in the U.S.A." In *Fourth International Conference of Economic History, Bloomington 1968*, edited by Frederic C. Lane, 437–466. Paris: Mouton.

Davis, Lance E., and Robert E. Gallman. (1978). "Capital Formation in the United States during the Nineteenth Century." In *Cambridge Economic History of Europe*, Vol. 7: *The Industrial Economies: Capital, Labour and Enterprise*, Pt. 2: *The United States, Japan and Russia*, edited by Peter Mathias and M. M. Postan, 1–69. New York: Cambridge University Press.

Davis, Lance E., and Robert E. Gallman. (1994). "Savings, Investment, and Economic Growth: The United States in the Nineteenth Century." In *Capitalism in Context: Essays on Economic Development and Cultural Change in Honor of R. M. Hartwell*, edited by John A. James and Mark Thomas, 202–229. Chicago: University of Chicago Press.

Davis, Lance E., and Robert E. Gallman. (2001). *Evolving Financial Markets and International Capital Flows*. New York: Cambridge University Press.

DeLong, J. Bradford. (1992). "Productivity Growth and Machinery Investment: A Long-Run Look, 1870–1980." *Journal of Economic History* 52(2): 307–324.

DeLong, J. Bradford. (1998). "Trade Policy and America's Standard of Living: A Historical Perspective." In *Imports, Exports, and the American Worker*, edited by Susan Collins, 349–376. Washington, DC: Brookings Institution Press.

Denison, Edward F. (1958). "A Note on Private Savings." *Review of Economics and Statistics* 40(August): 261–267.

Denison, Edward F. (1962). *The Sources of Economic Growth in the United States and the Alternatives Before Us*. New York: Committee on Economic Development.

De Tocqueville, Alexis. (1841). *Democracy in America*, 2 vols. Boston: Little-Brown.

DuBoff, Richard B. (1966). "Electrification and Capital Productivity: A Suggested Approach." *Review of Economics and Statistics* 48(4): 426–431.

Evans, Paul. (2000). "US Stylized Facts and Their Implications for Growth Theory." Ohio State University Working Paper.

Field, Alexander J. (1987). "Modern Business Enterprise as a Capital-Saving Innovation." *Journal of Economic History* 47(2): 473–485.

Fogel, Robert. (2013). "How Simon Kuznets Codified Modern Economic Growth." *Capital Ideas*, July 1. Available at http://www.chicagobooth.edu/capideas/magazine/summer-2013/simon-kuznets.

Gallman, Robert E. (1966). "Gross National Product in the United States, 1834–1909." In *Output, Employment, and Productivity in the United States after 1800*, Studies in Income and Wealth, edited by Dorothy S. Brady, Vol. 30, 3–90. New York: Columbia University Press.

Gallman, Robert E. (1972). "The Pace and Pattern of American Economic Growth." In *American Economic Growth: An Economist's History of the United States*, edited by Lance Davis et al., 15–60. New York: Harper & Row.

Gallman, Robert E. (1986). "The United States Capital Stock in the Nineteenth Century." In *American Economic Growth and Standard of Living before the Civil War*, edited by Stanley Engerman and Robert E. Gallman, 185–206. Chicago: University of Chicago Press.

Gallman, Robert E. (1992). "American Economic Growth before the Civil War: The Testimony of the Capital Stock Estimates." In *American Economic Growth and Standard of Living before the Civil War*, edited by Robert E. Gallman and Joseph J. Wallis, 79–90. Chicago: University of Chicago Press.

Gallman, Robert E., and Edward S. Howle. (1971). "Trends in the Structure of the American Economy since 1840." In *Reinterpretation of American Economic History*, edited by Robert Fogel and Stanley Engerman, 25–37. New York: Harper & Row.

Goldin, Claudia. (2001). "The Human-Capital Century and American Leadership: Virtues of the Past." *Journal of Economic History* 61(2): 263–293.

Goldsmith, Raymond W. (1985). *Comparative National Balance Sheets: A Study of Twenty Country, 1688–1978*. Chicago: University of Chicago Press.

Gordon, Robert A. (1961). "Differential Changes in the Prices of Consumers' and Capital Goods." *American Economic Review* 51(December): 937–957.

Gordon, Robert J. (1969). "$45 Billion in Private Investment Has Been Mislaid." *American Economic Review* 51(3): 221–238.

Gordon, Robert J. (1990). *The Measurement of Durable Goods Prices*. Chicago: University of Chicago Press.

Griliches, Zvi, and Dale Jorgenson. (1966). "Sources of Measured Productivity Change: Capital Input." *American Economic Review* 56(2): 50–61.

Harrod, R. F. (1939). "Essay in Dynamic Theory." *Economic Journal* 49(193): 14–33.

James, John A. (1984). "Public Debt Management Policy and Nineteenth-Century American Economic Growth." *Explorations in Economic History* 21(2): 192–217.

Johnson, D. Gale. (1954). "The Functional Distribution of Income in the United States, 1850–1952." *Review of Economics and Statistics* 36: 175–182.

Jones, Charles I., and Paul M. Romer. (2010). "The New Kaldor Facts: Ideas, Institutions, Population, and Human Capital." *American Economic Journal: Macroeconomics* 2(1): 224–245.

Kaldor, Nicholas. (1957). "A Model of Economic Growth." *Economic Journal* 67(268): 591–624.

Kaldor, Nicholas. (1961). "Capital Accumulation and Economic Growth." In *The Theory of Capital*, edited by L. A. Lutz and D. C. Hague, 177–222. New York: St. Martins Press.

Kendrick, John W. (assisted by Maude R. Pech). (1961). *Productivity Trends in the United States*. Princeton, NJ: Princeton University Press for NBER.

Kendrick, John W. (1976). *The Formation and Stocks of Total Capital*. New York: Columbia University Press for NBER.

Kravis, Irving B. (1968). "Income Distribution: Functional Distribution." In *International Encyclopedia of the Social Sciences*, edited by David L. Stills and Robert K. Merton, Vol. 7, 132–143. London: Macmillan.

Krueger, Alan B. (1999). "Measuring Labor's Share." *American Economic Review: Papers and Proceedings* 89(2): 45–51.

Kuznets, Simon (assisted by Elizabeth Jenks). (1961). *Capital in the American Economy, Its Formation and Financing.* Princeton, NJ: Princeton University Press for NBER.

Kuznets, Simon. (1966). *Modern Economic Growth: Rate, Structure and Spread.* New Haven, CT: Yale University Press.

Lamoreaux, Naomi R. (1996). *Insider Lending: Banks, Personal Connections, and Economic Development in Industrial New England.* New York: Cambridge University Press.

Lewis, Frank D. (1983). "Fertility and Savings in the United States: 1830–1900." *Journal of Political Economy* 91(5): 825–840.

Lucas, Robert E. (1988). "On the Mechanics of Economic Development." *Journal of Monetary Economics* 22: 3–42.

Mankiw, N. Gregory. (1995). "The Growth of Nations." *Brookings Papers on Economic Activity* 1: 275–310.

Marx, Karl. (1867). *Capital: Critique of Political Economy*, Vol. 1. Moscow: Progress Publishers.

Mayor, Thomas H. (1968). "The Decline in the United States Capital/Output Ratio." *Economic Development and Cultural Change* 16(4): 495–516.

Piketty, Thomas. (2014). *Capital in the Twenty-First Century.* Cambridge, MA: Harvard University Press.

Piketty, Thomas, and Gabriel Zucman. (2014). "Capital Is Back: Wealth-Income Ratios in Rich Countries, 1700–2010." *Quarterly Journal of Economics* 129(3): 1255–1310.

Porter, Glenn, and Harold Livesay C. (1971). *Merchants and Manufacturers: Studies in the Changing Structure of Nineteenth-Century Marketing.* Baltimore, MD: Johns Hopkins University Press.

Ransom, Roger, and Richard Sutch. (1988). "Capitalists Without Capital: The Burden of Slavery and the Impact of Emancipation." *Agricultural History* 62(Summer): 133–160.

Rebelo, Sergio. (1991). "Long-Run Policy Analysis and Long-Run Growth." *Journal of Political Economy* 99(3): 500–521.

Romer, Paul. (1986). "Increasing Returns and Long-Run Growth." *Journal of Political Economy* 94(5): 1002–1038.

Rosenberg, Nathan. (1982). *Inside the Black Box: Technology and Economics.* Cambridge: Cambridge University Press.

Smith, Adam. (1776). *An Inquiry into the Nature and Causes of the Wealth of Nations.* London: Strahan and Cadell.

Solow, Robert M. (1956). "A Contribution to the Theory of Economic Growth." *Quarterly Journal of Economics* 70(1): 65–94.

Solow, Robert M. (1957). "Technical Change and the Aggregate Production Function." *Review of Economics and Statistics* 39(3): 312–320.

Swan, Trevor W. (1956). "Economic Growth and Capital Accumulation." *Economic Record* 32(2): 334–361.

Sutch, Richard. (1991). "All Things Reconsidered: The Life-Cycle Perspective and the Third Task of Economic History." *Journal of Economic History* 51(2): 271–288.

US Department of Commerce. (1957). *Historical Statistics of the United States.* Washington, DC: GPO.

US Department of Commerce. (1976). *Bicentennial Historical Statistics of the United States*. Washington, DC: GPO.

US Department of Commerce, Bureau of Economic Analysis. (2016). "Gross Domestic Product and Fixed Assets Accounts." Available at http://www.bea.gov/.

Williamson, Jeffrey G. (1974). "Watersheds and Turning Points: Conjectures on the Long-Term Impact of Civil War Financing." *Journal of Economic History* 34(4): 636–661.

Williamson, Jeffrey G. (1991). *Inequality, Poverty, and History; The Kuznets Memorial Lectures of the Economic Growth Center, Yale University*. Oxford: Basil Blackwell.

Williamson, Oliver. (1985). *Economic Institutions of Capitalism*. London: Macmillan.

CHAPTER 17

....

EDUCATION AND HUMAN CAPITAL IN AMERICAN ECONOMIC HISTORY

....

JOHN M. PARMAN

THE American economy has been profoundly influenced by the evolution of educational institutions and the American human capital stock. From colonial times to the present, the schooling of Americans not only has helped shape the trajectory of the economy, but also has been shaped by that trajectory in what Goldin and Katz (2009) describe as a race between education and technology. The unique public, decentralized nature of school provision in the United States has set the country apart from other Western nations, allowing the country to be a leader in terms of education for much of its history, while leading to issues of inequality in schooling resources in recent decades. The history of school provision and attendance has taught us much about the sources of regional and racial gaps in socioeconomic outcomes and has highlighted the critical role that educational institutions play in either maintaining or eliminating those gaps. It has also offered evidence of the evolving nature of the household, the complex relationships between childhood health and adult outcomes, and even the nature of the American political process.

While economic historians have exploited the rich educational history of the United States to yield unique insights related to the nature of technological change, political processes, discrimination, household resource allocation, and a variety of other topics, there remain many unanswered questions. New questions are generated from the results of each new study, and new data sources are consistently being unearthed and digitized, allowing economic historians to empirically study both questions about the evolution of the American economy and issues in the modern education, labor, and growth literatures that were previously deemed untestable.

The Evolution of the Human
Capital Stock

A considerable amount of effort has been expended by economic historians to piece together evidence of the growth in the American human capital stock. The task of measuring how the educational attainments and the resulting human capital of Americans has changed over time is aided by the availability of a wide variety of detailed school records dating back to the 1700s, offering a wealth of detailed data relative to other countries. However, these efforts have been hindered by the fragmentary nature of the data. This is an unfortunate side effect of one of the virtues of the American educational system, its decentralization. With schooling decisions decided at a local level, data collection also was typically done at a local or state level, making it difficult to piece together nationally representative education statistics with a consistent interpretation across states.

To get national statistics, researchers have typically focused on the information reported in the federal census and statistics gathered by the Bureau of Education, what would ultimately become today's Department of Education. Questions on literacy and school attendance were first included in the population schedule of the federal census beginning in 1850, offering the first glimpse at the educational levels of the country as a whole. The literacy question would be replaced with an educational attainment question in the 1940 census, marking the first opportunity to consistently measure years of education for the entire US population. The data series from the Bureau of Education date back to 1870 and offer a variety of detailed statistics on the types of schools, enrollment rates, and school quality across the country.

It is important to note that while much of the education literature focuses on these national data sources and is therefore restricted to their limited time span and sets of variables, there are a variety of state-level data sources covering additional years and variables. Given that the schooling system in the United States has been highly decentralized, a substantial amount of data was collected at the county and state level that was never compiled into national data sets. Several economic historians have had success exploiting these additional data sources to expand both the time periods and the detail of schooling and attendance characteristics studied. A prime example is the insights into black-white gaps in schooling gained by looking at district- and county-level schooling data in the work of Fishback (1989), Margo (1991), Fishback and Baskin (1991), Donohue, Heckman, and Todd (2002), and Moehling (2004).

These additional sources, typically in the form of annual reports of states' offices of education, offer largely untapped opportunities to produce a much more detailed account of changes in educational institutions and school attendance over time. Many of them have not been explored—not because they are poor data sources, but simply because they have not been digitized and are restricted to the state level. As more reports are scanned by various projects digitizing the collections of libraries and the costs of transcribing digital documents fall, these data will open up new possibilities for addressing open questions in the education literature.

With the potential of alternate data sources at the state and local level acknowledged, the remainder of this section will focus on national statistics to provide a sense of the overall evolution of the American human capital stock. The available measures of human capital will vary with the time period of focus. In the nineteenth century, the primary measures are actual direct measures of stocks of human capital, namely literacy and numeracy. In the late nineteenth and early twentieth centuries, data on human capital flows in the form of school attendance become increasingly available, allowing for imputations of average educational attainment. From 1940 on, we have the ability to directly measure years of educational attainment. Data on test scores and other measures of cognitive ability begin to appear in the second half of the twentieth century, offering a means to relate the educational attainment of Americans to the level of productive human capital that educational attainment generated.

DIRECT MEASURES OF HUMAN CAPITAL: LITERACY AND NUMERACY

Literacy rates from the 1850 census provide one of the earliest glimpses of America's exceptionalism in terms of educational attainment. This is the first federal census in which enumerators asked whether each adult could both read and write. Under this rather strict definition of literacy, America had already achieved widespread literacy among the white population by 1850, with overall literacy rates among the white population of 90 percent, placing the United States among the most literate nations in the world. Evidence based on the ability to sign documents suggests that America had high literacy rates relative to the rest of the world in the late eighteenth and early nineteenth centuries as well (see Graff 1991 for international comparisons of literacy in the 1700 and 1800s). Table 17.1 shows the trends in literacy from 1850 through 1930, the last year in which literacy was recorded in the federal census. The trends show a steady rise in literacy over this time period for the country as a whole, but also reveal stark variation in human capital across regions and groups within the United States.

The most dramatic difference is the gap in white and black literacy rates over this period. Note that the 1850 and 1860 censuses only recorded literacy for free blacks, accounting for the substantial decline in literacy rates when the calculations include former slaves starting in 1870. While the United States was on average a highly educated society, that did not extend to the black population, which had literacy rates of under 20 percent following the Civil War.

While the black-white gap in literacy rates over time is certainly the most striking, it is not the only gap of note. In particular, there were large differences in literacy across regions that persisted over the nineteenth century into the twentieth century. Most

Table 17.1 Trends in Literacy and Numeracy, 1850–1930

Year	Literacy Rate						Numeracy Rate					
	White	Black	Northern White	Southern White	Native-Born White	Foreign-Born	White	Black	Northern White	Southern White	Native-Born White	Foreign-Born
1850	89.92	57.41	93.35	81.57	90.35	87.98	87.38	70.47	87.95	86.21	89.37	78.28
1860	91.91	63.84	94.05	85.82	92.69	89.62	87.32	68.54	87.68	86.33	90.03	79.37
1870	91.47	17.33	93.96	83.23	92.71	88.20	88.32	65.41	88.80	87.04	90.95	81.42
1880	93.02	28.23	95.24	85.91	93.88	90.44	90.82	70.42	91.20	90.09	92.71	85.21
1900	94.48	52.03	95.74	89.92	96.03	89.50	95.36	83.21	95.47	95.11	96.01	93.27
1910	94.89	66.56	95.47	92.46	97.17	87.80	94.85	86.53	94.87	95.04	95.55	92.70
1920	95.53	74.58	95.89	93.86	97.91	87.04	96.17	88.84	96.09	96.20	96.66	94.44
1930	96.78	82.93	97.22	95.17	98.30	90.38	96.17	87.68	96.26	95.86	96.42	95.12
1940							97.08	91.52	97.20	96.63	97.15	96.68
1950							97.74	94.22	97.67	97.73	97.77	97.48
1960							99.33	98.51	99.55	99.03	99.22	100.00

Notes and sources: Data are from the 1850 through 1960 IPUMS 1 percent samples of the federal census. Samples are restricted to individuals over the age of 19 (Ruggles et al. 2015). The numeracy values given are calculated using the modified Whipple index presented in A'Hearn, Baten, and Crayen (2009).

notably, the North had significantly higher literacy rates than the South. The full 10 percentage point gap in 1870 would take several decades to close. As Collins discusses in Hatton, O'Rourke, and Taylor (2007), the closing of this gap was a product of interregional migration raising levels of human capital in the South and increases in local investments improving the education of native-born Southerners.

A small body of evidence has been uncovered to relate these measures of literacy to enrollment rates, offering some guidance for how to map the literacy rates into educational attainment. From a survey of North Carolina manufacturing workers in the early twentieth century and a survey of adults conducted in 1948 by the Census Bureau, it seems that literacy generally implied that an individual had obtained three or more years of schooling (Collins and Margo 2006; Goldin 2000).

Literacy rates are not the only means of assessing the level of human capital prior to detailed records on educational attainment. Economic historians have recently begun to turn to other measures that can shed light on slightly different dimensions of human capital. In particular, age heaping has begun to gain traction as a means of measuring human capital when data on literacy or educational attainment are either unavailable, unreliable, or incapable of capturing important components of human capital. A'Hearn, Baten, and Crayen (2009) demonstrate the usefulness of this approach, using a measure of age heaping based on the proportion of people that report ages ending in a zero or five (excessive zeros and fives indicate rounding and a lack of numeracy) and showing that this proxy for numeracy is highly correlated with literacy in census data.

These types of numeracy measures have the potential to expand our understanding of the historical evolution of human capital. First and foremost, they require only data on age (or another numerical value where a less numerate individual may tend to round), greatly expanding the number of data sets from which measures of human capital can be derived. Studies that consider earlier time periods or that use documents such as death certificates that contain far more information on individuals than typical census records but lack a measure of educational attainment can potentially incorporate these types of numeracy measures. A second motivation for incorporating numeracy measures into our standard measures of human capital is that even if a data source contains a measure of literacy or school attendance, numeracy may capture elements of human capital relevant to productivity that literacy is not strongly correlated with, namely quantitative cognitive ability.

As a simple demonstration of how looking at numeracy in addition to literacy can affect our interpretation of history, consider the literacy and numeracy trends for foreign-born individuals and native-born whites in table 17.1. Based on literacy alone, it appears that the human capital of immigrants stayed relatively constant over time, while the human capital of native-born whites increased. However, if we instead measure human capital with numeracy, we arrive at a very different conclusion: the human capital of immigrants was rising steadily from 1850 to 1930 and completely converged to the native-born levels. If it is the quantitative skills of these individuals that matter for productivity, relying on literacy may severely underestimate the contribution of immigration to the American economy over the late nineteenth and early twentieth centuries.

Incorporating measures of numeracy, either by looking at age heaping by group within cross-sectional data, or even at the individual level by looking at consistency of age reports across time in longitudinal data, can provide us with a much more complete understanding of the variation in human capital across groups and over time in the decades before we have more detailed educational attainment records.[1]

MEASURES OF SCHOOLING OVER TIME

The first national data available to directly quantify levels of schooling come from school enrollment data from the mid-nineteenth century. By 1850, enrollment rates for white children between the ages of five and nineteen were already over 50 percent and climbed to roughly 80 percent over the next century. As with the literacy and numeracy figures discussed earlier, the statistics for nonwhite children were far different, with enrollment rates at essentially zero in 1850 but converging to white enrollment rates over time. Most of the gap disappeared by the mid-twentieth century. The average educational attainment of cohorts can be estimated from these enrollment rates, as in Margo (1986), but the resulting numbers are difficult to interpret. School attendance or enrollment tells us very little about how much school was attended in a particular year, how students progressed through grades, or how often students had gaps in their educational careers. Furthermore, this approach of constructing an average stock of education from these flow data does not allow researchers to explore the relationship between individual characteristics, educational attainment, and socioeconomic outcomes, limiting the usefulness of enrollment- or attendance-based measures.

More direct measures of educational attainment are first available in the 1940 federal census in which respondents were asked for the highest grade completed, offering a measure of educational attainment comparable to modern schooling variables.[2] Figure 17.1 shows the evolution of years of schooling by race and gender over the twentieth century. The steady gains in literacy and numeracy over the nineteenth century have a clear counterpart in the rapid increase in educational attainment over the twentieth century, with the average educational attainment of white individuals rising roughly three-quarters of a year every decade and the average educational attainment of black individuals rising by a full year per decade. The trends in educational attainment echo some of the disparities demonstrated by the literacy and numeracy data. A substantial black-white gap in educational attainment existed at the beginning of the twentieth century, and while that gap has narrowed over time, it has yet to disappear. Also noteworthy is the male-female gap in education, or rather the absence of a gap. Throughout the twentieth century, the educational attainment of females not only kept pace with that of males but actually exceeded it. The high educational attainment of females relative to males is even more pronounced for the black population.

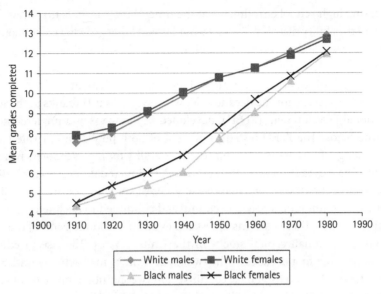

FIGURE 17.1. Educational attainment by race and gender for twenty-five- to thirty-four-year olds, 1910–1980

Sources: Tabulations from IPUMS 1940, 1950, 1960, 1970 and 1980 federal census samples. The 1910, 1920, and 1930 cohort estimates were obtained using the 1940 census (Ruggles et al. 2015).

MEASURING COGNITIVE ABILITY

As the published data on education have improved over time, economic historians have been able to switch from the crude measures of literacy and numeracy to more detailed measures of school attendance and educational attainment. While in most respects this represents a vast improvement in data quality, the switch from direct measures of human capital to a focus on years of education has certain drawbacks. In particular, years of schooling do not perfectly capture an individual's productive human capital, particularly given the variation in quality across schools and over time. Studies focused on recent periods can exploit test scores and direct measures of cognitive ability. Comparable studies are rare historically but do exist.

Fragmentary evidence exists showing a rise in general intellectual achievement (GIA), controlling for level of schooling, over the first half of the twentieth century. These data consist of achievement and IQ tests given to specific grades at a handful of selected schools and show not only a general rise in the overall cognitive abilities of Americans over this period, but also an increase in cognitive ability conditional on years of schooling (Finch 1946; Flynn 1984; Rundquist 1936; Wheeler 1942). In a survey of these studies, Bishop (1989) finds that the cognitive ability of high school students was rising by 1.69 IQ points per decade, impressive in its own right but even more remarkable given the increasing high school enrollments at the time. If high schools first drew from the upper tail of the ability distribution, one would predict that growing enrollments would have been decreasing the average ability of high schoolers. The observed increase of IQ among high schoolers may therefore actually substantially underestimate the growing cognitive abilities of Americans during the high school movement.

Better evidence exists for the decades following World War II thanks to the Iowa Test of Educational Development (ITED), developed in the 1920s and implemented state-wide by the 1940s. The ITED tested 95 percent of both public and private schools in Iowa, providing representative data on cognitive ability for high schoolers from 1942 to the present. These data from Iowa and several other similar data sources for Indiana and Minnesota show that the rising cognitive abilities of students continued until the late 1960s, at which point scores began declining and continued to decline throughout the 1970s (Bishop 1989). These patterns in test scores add a new dimension to the narrative of ever growing human capital stocks in the United States. The rise in educational attainment over the first decades of the twentieth century may actually understate the rise in productive human capital, as cognitive ability conditional on years of schooling was increasing as well. However, the declining test scores later in the twentieth century suggest that more recent advances in educational attainment may have more muted effects on the economy, as the cognitive ability associated with particular levels of schooling actually fell. As more data sources become available, it would be worthwhile for economic historians to explore ways to incorporate more nuanced measures of human capital into their work that can more carefully delineate the relationship between years of education and the cognitive abilities relevant to the workplace.

THE CONTRIBUTION OF HUMAN CAPITAL GROWTH TO ECONOMIC GROWTH

These distinctions between schooling, cognitive ability, and productive human capital become particularly important when assessing the contribution of the tremendous growth of the American human capital stock to overall economic growth over the past two centuries. The ability of schooling to explain differences in economic growth between the United States and other countries, as well as over time within the United States, is still a disputed matter. Some economists have estimated extraordinarily high contributions of education to economic growth; Denison (1962) finds that increases in education accounted for 42 percent of the growth in national income per person employed between 1929 and 1957 and roughly half that from 1909 to 1929. Goldin and Katz (2009) suggest more modest but still large contributions, estimating that the growth in education accounts for 14 percent of the annual increase in labor productivity and 15 percent of the annual growth in real GDP per capita from 1915 to 2005. Care needs to be taken, however, to recognize that it is likely cognitive ability, not simply years of schooling, that is relevant to improved economic performance. Hanushek and Woessmann (2008) demonstrate that for cross-country comparisons of growth rates, models based on test scores directly measuring cognitive ability explain three times the variation in economic growth rates that models based on schooling do. Accurately assessing the historical contribution of human capital to American economic growth requires understanding how the relationship between schooling and cognitive ability has changed over time.

As an example of the importance of distinguishing between these two different variables, Hanushek and Woessmann (2008) note that the United States has maintained favorable growth rates relative to other countries despite its relatively poor performance on achievement tests because of its massive expansion of high school and later college opportunities to a large proportion of its citizens. The United States effectively achieved high growth rates by making up for lower levels of learning per school year with the sheer volume of aggregate school years among its population. Better understanding the historical roles of school quality versus school quantity in accounting for America's growth would offer insights into whether resources are best targeted at increasing years of educational attainment or the quality of those years.

These estimates of the contribution of education to economic growth, whether based on measures of the stock of schooling or the cognitive abilities of the American work-force, pertain to the direct effect of education on productivity, essentially the effect of increasing the level of effective units of labor in a standard production function. However, a potentially more important channel for the effect of education on productivity is its relationship to technology. A more educated workforce can potentially lead to more technological advances and allow for quicker, more successful adoption of new technology. Several growth models have incorporated this notion that educational investments serve to increase the rate of technological change (see, e.g., Jones 1995; Nelson and Phelps 1966; Romer 1990). The possibility that this is the main channel through which schooling influences national economic growth is supported by the finding of Benhabib and Spiegel (1994) that the level of educational attainment, rather than the growth rate of education, explains differences in growth rates across countries. While the direct contributions of a growing human capital stock to America's rising income per capita cited earlier may be modest, the indirect effects through the education's contribution to technological change are likely a critical component of America's success over the past century and an ongoing topic of interest for economic historians.[3]

THE DEVELOPMENT OF EDUCATIONAL INSTITUTIONS

The extraordinary growth of American educational attainments across all segments of society suggests the development of a massive educational system up to the task of providing that schooling. Just as the United States stood out from most of its peers in the nineteenth and early twentieth centuries for the high levels of education across nearly all socioeconomic groups, it also stood out for the way in which that education was provided. The United States developed a system of education that was unique for a variety of reasons: it was largely publicly provided, it catered to the masses, it was highly decentralized, and it developed a focus on practical education that would translate into more productive workers across a wide range of occupations. The American education system was not designed to prepare the children of the elite for college; it was built to provide opportunity to children of all backgrounds and to generate a skilled workforce.[4]

Following the structure described by Goldin and Katz (2009), the history of America's educational institutions can be divided into three major transformations: the rise of common schools and universal elementary education, the high school movement and rise of high school graduates, and finally the rise of mass higher education. The rise in universal elementary schooling was a long process taking place over the nineteenth century and led by the Northern states. By the middle of the nineteenth century, common schools spread throughout the nation. Legislation was passed for tax-supported elementary schools, state school officers were appointed, and rate bills for parents were phased out (see Kaestle 1983 for a history of the development of common schools). The public provision of elementary education was even built into the geographic expansion of the United States at this time, with the Land Ordinance of 1785 reserving a section of each congressional township in the Western Territory for the support of public schools and an amendment in 1850 doubling this allotment. Local governments throughout the country in both urban and rural areas embraced the notion, somewhat radical at the time, that all children should receive a common education.

The next major transformation was the high school movement, occurring during the first half of the twentieth century. As with the expansion of publicly funded common schools, this movement began in the North, with the West North Central region being particularly progressive, and diffused throughout the country. Relative to the rise of common schools, the high school movement was rapid. Figure 17.2 gives a sense of just how rapid the transformation was. The school attendance rates across all age groups demonstrate that the common school transformation was largely complete by 1850, with attendance rates relatively stable from 1850 to 1900 for the white population. The high school movement then led to a rapid increase in attendance rates between 1900 and 1920, with school attendance becoming nearly universal for white children between the ages of six and fourteen, and attendance rates for students of high school age beginning a steady rise. These new high schools maintained the same principles of accessible education for the masses associated with the common schools. Evidence of this can be found in the passage of free tuition laws that enabled students in a district without a high school to attend high school in another district at the expense of the home district rather than the parents. A far more complete history of the high school movement can be found in Goldin (1998).

The third transformation is the rise of higher education. Unlike the expansion of primary and secondary education, the expansion of postsecondary education has always

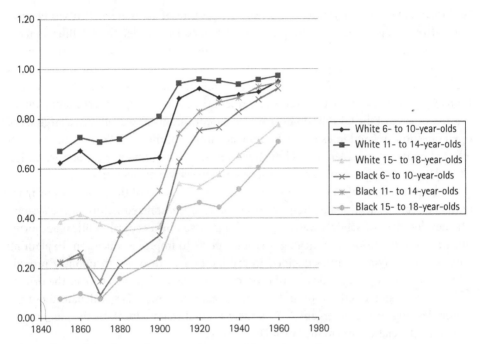

FIGURE 17.2. School attendance rates by race and age, 1850–1960

Sources: Tabulations from IPUMS federal census samples for 1850 through 1960 (Ruggles et al. 2015).

had a large private component. Numerous private colleges and universities, many with a religious affiliation, existed since the earliest decades of the country's history. These private institutions competed for students long before the high school movement created a sizable population of high school graduates ready for college. States began creating public institutions in the early 1800s. The Morrill Act of 1862 further promoted public higher education by establishing federal land grant universities. By the time the high school movement began, a large system of public and private postsecondary institutions was in place and was ready to serve the increasing number of high school graduates. This large number of postsecondary institutions and the mix between private and public control set the United States apart from its peers both historically and to this day.

Mass enrollment in these colleges and universities was triggered by several factors: the large number of high school graduates resulting from the high school movement; technological advances increasing the demand for skills (see Goldin and Katz 1998 and Goldin and Katz 1996 on skill-biased technological change and the demand for skilled workers in the first half of the twentieth century); and a massive but understudied effort of the federal government to support higher education among veterans through the GI Bills. While the American population was on a trajectory of rising college attendance leading up to World War II, the World War II GI Bill and later the Korean War GI Bill would fundamentally alter the accessibility of higher education for millions of

Americans. Stanley (2003) notes that nearly 70 percent of all men who turned twenty-one between 1940 and 1955 were guaranteed free college under the GI Bills. Stanley estimates that the GI Bills increased the postsecondary attainment of men born between 1921 and 1933 by 15 to 20 percent. Bound and Turner (2002) find comparable results focusing on the Korean GI Bill. For such a potentially massive shock to the American human capital stock, these two studies represent the main attempts at estimating quantitative impacts of the GI Bills on postsecondary education. There remains a large set of open questions related to exactly who took advantage of the GI Bills, how the GI Bills affected nonveteran students, and how the promise of federal money to support tuition altered the mix of postsecondary institutions and the way they operated.

As the previous section notes, one of the defining features of the American primary and secondary educational system was the public, decentralized nature of the system. The development of schools was not something driven by a central political authority, but was rather a product of local, grassroots efforts to improve education. Explaining why American communities decided to tax themselves in order to publicly provide education is an ongoing endeavor of economic historians. The debate over the origins of public provision of education in the United States ties into a larger debate about the factors leading to the emergence of publicly funded mass education throughout the world and its relationship to the Great Divergence.

Lindert (2009) provides a series of qualitative international comparisons that highlight that cases of historical underinvestment in education by nations (there are no clear cases of overinvestment) are primarily driven by political decision-making. The United States is somewhat unique in its political will when it came to financing schools. Galor, Moav, and Vollrath (2009) model the potential sources of this political will, arguing that inequality in land ownership was a barrier to passing redistributive policies and creating public schools during the transition from an agricultural to an industrial economy. They cite evidence from the early-twentieth-century United States in support of their model. However, these types of models emphasizing the transition from agriculture to manufacturing fail to fully address several of the important features of American school provision. Public support for common schools arose well before this transition in the United States. Additionally, even when restricting attention to the twentieth century, these types of models emphasizing education's importance to manufacturing fail to capture the US experience of largely agricultural communities leading the high school movement. We are still in search of a formal model of school provision that can fully capture the evolution of American public primary and secondary schools.

Economic historians have begun to use variation in public school funding within the United States to empirically identify the community characteristics correlated with higher levels of support for education and to provide an empirical underpinning for refining models of school provision. Go and Lindert (2010) explain the high levels of support for schooling in the rural North before the Civil War as the product of more affordable schooling (partly due to the low cost of female teachers), more localized voting mechanisms for providing school funding relative to the South, and greater political voice throughout the income distribution. Evidence from the high school movement suggests that in the twentieth century, communities with higher levels of wealth, more evenly distributed wealth, and less manufacturing activity relative to other communities were more likely to invest in public schools (Goldin 1998; Goldin and Katz 2009).

Stoddard (2009) uses these types of stylized facts regarding the provision of public schooling to refine the class of theoretical models of school provision that are consistent with the American experience. Noting that states in which the mean and median wealth were closer together had higher fractions of education revenue from public sources, Stoddard argues that models emphasizing the external benefits of education best explain the United States' public provision of education. This is further supported by evidence that greater public funding of schooling increased attendance of poor children, rather than simply subsidizing the attendance of children from wealthier families. The patterns of school development suggest that increased public spending on schools was not driven by strictly redistributive voter motivations, but rather by the decisive voters realizing benefits from the education of others.

This notion that schools generated positive externalities is a potentially critical element in explaining the causes and consequences of public school expansion that warrants more attention from economic historians. Labor economists have recently begun identifying positive externalities from schooling in modern economies, including improved health of children (Currie Moretti 2003), greater civic participation (Dee 2004; Milligan, Moretti, and Oreopoulos 2004), and reductions in crime (Lochner and Moretti 2004) (an overview of this literature on modern externalities can be found in Moretti 2004). An open question is the extent to which these or other externalities existed in the nineteenth and early twentieth centuries and were taken into consideration by voters or political officials. The notion of education improving the quality of civic participation is certainly referenced in debates about school funding during the expansion of public education, as are arguments that having more educated, productive workers is beneficial to the community.

Direct evidence of positive externalities from the public school system can be found in Iowa, as it led the expansion of public high schools. Parman (2012) finds that farmers in Iowa not only benefited from additional years of their own schooling in the form of higher annual earnings, they also earned higher incomes if their neighbors received more schooling. The return to an additional year of schooling was similar in magnitude whether it was the farmer's own schooling or that of his neighbor. These results provide empirical support to the rhetoric surrounding the social benefits of public school expansion, particularly in agriculture, where farmers can learn from the successes and failures of their neighbors. As individual-level data sources improve, it may be possible to identify similar spillovers in other sectors. These types of spillovers would suggest that the social returns to education were significantly greater than the private returns and that the public investment in education would have led to more socially efficient levels of schooling. Additional work to quantify the various sources of externalities and their association with communities' decisions to increase public funding of schools is still needed.

While there is mounting evidence that the decentralized nature of school pro-vision enabled the United States to be nimble with regard to rising demands for educated workers and led to an egalitarian public school system through the mid-twentieth century, it is worth noting that those very same features have led to dra-matic inequalities in the provision of public education in recent decades, as wealthy school districts have the tax base to support excellent public schools, while students from poor districts have access to far fewer school resources. Further exploration of the evolution of the American school system should consider this transition from local school provision promoting equality of opportunity to increasing the rigidity of the income distribution from one generation to the next. This will be-come increasingly possible with the availability of new data sources, such as the full 1940 federal census manuscripts. With these data, it is possible to link adults and their educational and socioeconomic outcomes to their childhood school districts, as has been done for Iowa in Parman (2011), demonstrating that public school improvements during the high school movement actually initially reduced levels of intergenerational income mobility. Closer examination of variation in and the consequences of school expansion across space and over time in the United States will reveal more about not only why communities chose to increase spending on schools, but also under what conditions that local decision-making led to more or less egalitarian outcomes.

This discussion of the virtues of the egalitarian nature of the American public schools comes with one enormous caveat; black individuals were largely left out of the educa-tional system for much of the history of the country. As noted in the previous section on the rise in educational attainments, school attendance rates and years of schooling for blacks were substantially lower than those for whites throughout the nineteenth cen-tury and well into the twentieth century. This was not simply the product of the political mechanisms described earlier yielding lower levels of school provision in the regions with large black populations; it was largely due to the deliberate denial of schooling re-sources to blacks by local governments.

The exclusion of blacks from the educational system extends back to the time of slavery. Prior to the Civil War, slave owners were concerned that educated slaves would be more likely to rebel and would be more capable of forging passes enabling them to escape the South. To a slave owner, these potential costs reduced the desire to educate slaves, even if an educated slave would be a more productive worker. Further restricting the ability of Southern blacks to receive an education were state laws passed in the 1830s prohibiting teaching slaves to read (see Genovese 1976 for discussion of these constraints on slave literacy). Any education of slaves was certainly not being provided by a progressive public education system. The abolition of slavery did not immediately open up the educational opportunities of whites to Southern blacks. Segregated school systems meant that black children received substantially fewer resources than white children through the first decades of the 1900s, as evidenced by differences in spending per student, average class size, and length of the academic year (Fishback and Baskin 1991; Margo 1991). This highlights one of the chief problems of local control: financing of schools for black students was subject to the local attitudes of voters on race, particularly problematic when blacks were largely disenfranchised.

Improving the quality of schooling for Southern blacks required a solution outside of the localized political process that shaped most of the history of American schools. Donohue, Heckman, and Todd (2002) identify two key factors: private philanthropy from Northern foundations and litigation by the NAACP (National Association for the Advancement of Colored People).[5] The Jeanes Fund, Slater Fund, and, most significantly, the Rosenwald Fund all helped develop and raise the quality of black schools in the South from the late 1800s to the early 1930s.[6] Complementing the efforts of these foundations was civil litigation over teacher salaries by the NAACP that directly led to improvements in school quality inputs.

These litigation efforts ultimately led to *Brown v. Board of Education* and the desegregation of schools. However, even in this victory we can see further evidence of the difficulties presented by the local, adaptable nature of the educational system. The potential positive impacts of desegregation on black schooling outcomes were muted by the geographic mobility of white families in response to desegregation and the availability of private schooling options for these families (Clotfelter 2011; Platt Boustan 2012; Reber 2005). One promising area of future study, highlighted in the conclusions of Collins and Margo (2006), is comparative work relating the narrowing of the racial gaps in schooling for American blacks to the experiences of other historically disadvantaged groups, including former slave populations in other countries and the Native American population within the United States. The evolution of gaps in educational access and achievement under varying political structures and school systems would offer insights into exactly which forces promote or hinder convergence.

INVESTING IN EDUCATION

While American political structures and the potential for large social returns to education can explain much of the rise in American educational institutions, they do little to explain why individuals chose to increase their levels of educational attainment throughout history. Past research has focused on two main reasons that are obvious but whose effects are remarkably difficult to pin down empirically: laws making attendance compulsory, and increased demand for highly skilled workers leading to high returns to education. Recent research has begun to uncover a host of other variables that have influenced the decisions to attend school, including childhood health conditions and the changing structure of the household. Thanks to steady growth in the data available to researchers, our understanding of individual educational investment decisions is growing ever more nuanced.

The most straightforward explanation of increasing investments in education is that there has been a substantial private return to education throughout much of American history. The returns to literacy in the seventeenth and eighteenth centuries are confirmed by a variety of sources. Significantly shorter indenture contracts for literate indentured servants in colonial America offer some of the first evidence of the returns to education in America (Galenson 1981). The data on returns to education from independence up to the high school movement are quite sparse. With no representative samples of individuals containing both income and education (even as proxied by literacy) we lack precise estimates of the value of an additional year of schooling. The best available evidence is in the form of wages of skilled workers relative to unskilled workers, representing the premium to skill presumably obtained through education. This ratio was 1.93 in 1826–1830, 1.99 for 1856–1860, and 2.5 for 1895, suggesting a fairly high return to skill throughout the nineteenth century (calculations from Goldin and Katz 2009, 182, based on wage series from Margo 2000).

The returns to schooling during the high school movement have been estimated using the 1915 Iowa state census, a unique source of individual level earnings and years of schooling data prior to the 1940 federal census. Goldin and Katz (2000) find returns to a year of high school of over 10 percent for employed men between the ages of eighteen and sixty-five. Returns were high for both blue-collar and white-collar occupations. These high returns help explain the eagerness with which Americans attended the newly created high schools. Beginning with the 1940 federal census, we have the educational attainment and income data to estimate standard Mincer regressions and obtain returns to schooling from 1940 to the present. These returns have been consistently high, with the exception of the late 1910s and the 1940s, which saw reductions in the premium for skilled labor and the return to education driven in part by expansions in education, the rise in high school education, and the rise in college attendance, respectively (Goldin and Katz 2009; Goldin and Margo 1992). Even with these periods of wage compression, education has generally always provided a healthy return to individuals.

One needs to be cautious, however, when comparing these historical returns to education to modern estimates. Endogeneity of schooling decisions has been a major concern in the labor and education literatures, and economists have long recognized that conventional returns to education estimates may be biased upward due to selection and other issues of omitted variable bias. Economic historians have rarely had the data required to estimate a standard Mincer regression, let alone tackle these endogeneity issues. When assessing the historical returns to schooling, it is important to note that these endogeneity issues exist and that the resulting biases likely differ over time, as the set of people attending school expanded and the purposes of school in terms of generating productive human capital versus signaling ability changed in relative importance. As more detailed individual level data become available with the release of more census data and the digitization of more administrative records, economic historians will be able to better address these endogeneity issues for a more accurate assessment of the returns to schooling over time and how those returns varied across groups.

While the private returns to education were high enough to induce people to attend, states also passed compulsory schooling laws beginning in the mid-nineteenth century to compel students to attend. These laws became more stringent over time. The evidence is mixed as to whether these compulsory schooling laws were truly binding. Historians of the American educational system have asserted that compulsory schooling laws were increasingly effective at raising school attendance during the high school movement (Troen 1975; Tyack 1974). However, economic historians have estimated far more modest contributions of the compulsory schooling and child labor laws to increases in educational attainment during this period, with Goldin and Katz (2009) finding that they can account for just 5 percent of the overall increase in high school attainment from 1910 to 1938. For roughly the same period, Lleras-Muney (2002) finds that requiring children to attend one additional year of school only increased educational attainment by an average of eighteen days. Recent work by Clay, Lingwall, and Stephens (2012) finds that for the period of 1890 through 1927, laws increased years of schooling by 0.1 years, a modest gain relative to the large overall changes in average educational attainment occurring over that period.

While the average effect of these compulsory schooling laws may have been relatively small, Lleras-Muney (2002) and Clay, Lingwall, and Stephens (2012) suggest that the effects were not uniform across all children. Lleras-Muney finds that the compulsory schooling laws were most binding in the lower percentiles of the education distribution, consistent with Clay, Lingwall, and Stephens (2012) finding that much of the impact of the laws could be seen in sixth grade completion rates. These results suggest that a potentially useful focus of further research into the motivations behind and effects of compulsory schooling laws is the differential impact of these laws across groups and what this did for promoting or hindering equality and intergenerational mobility.[7]

Given that much of the variation in levels of schooling was driven by families deciding to increase educational investments rather than through changes in compulsory schooling laws, a natural question to ask is which families decided to invest. Identifying how individual families responded to changes in access to schools, the returns to schooling, and the occupational opportunities for both children and adults offers an opportunity to provide empirical support to the models of the family and investment in children pioneered by Becker (1991). The available data to undertake such studies are rapidly expanding, particularly with the collection of more administrative data on enrollments and school characteristics and with the release of the complete 1940 federal census and its years of schooling data. The expanding set of administrative data is enabling researchers to better understand how local school, health, and environmental conditions affected the decision to send children to school. The 1940 census data allows for using linking strategies to match adults in 1940 to their childhood households and school districts, providing an opportunity to view the effects of family structure, parental occupations, and school district characteristics on both educational and labor market outcomes across the country and over time.

Evidence based on cross-sectional data of school attendance and retrospective census data has begun to reveal the factors that guide families' decisions to invest in their children. Moehling (2004) considers racial differences in school attendance in the South in 1900 and 1910 and finds that the black-white attendance gap was a function of racial differences in parental literacy, household resources, and local school characteristics. Moehling also finds that the larger number of single-parent households among the black population helps explain the schooling gap; with only a single parent to support the household, children from single parent households were far more likely to enter the labor market at a younger age. This tension between investing in a child's education and having the child work gets at the heart of debates over quantity-quality trade-offs with children, household time and resource allocation, and the roots of the demographic transition. Bleakley and Lange (2009) offer a demonstration of the power of American economic history to shed light on these issues, showing that eradication of hookworm in the South lowered the effective costs of schooling and led to a significant decline in fertility consistent with a quantity-quality framework of fertility.

The work of Bleakley and Lange touches on a rapidly growing literature relating health to educational outcomes. While this topic receives considerable attention in modern labor studies, American economic history has a particularly valuable perspective to add. The American past has instances of enormous shocks to health and a sufficient time span of data to see both the short- and long-term impacts of those shocks on education and labor market outcomes. Examples include not only the eradication of hookworm studied by Bleakley and Lange, but also the eradication of malaria in the South, the influenza pandemic of 1918, the improvement of urban sanitation facilities, and general improvements in medical care. In the case of hookworm and malaria, improved health conditions in the South led to increased school attendance, literacy, and adult earnings (Bleakley 2003, 2007). *In utero* exposure to influenza during the 1918 pandemic led to lower educational attainments and socioeconomic status in adulthood (Almond 2006). These studies suggest a correlation between childhood health and education that is as strong if not stronger than the modern-day correlations concerning economists and policymakers. We still have much to learn about how health impacted human capital, both directly through reduced cognitive abilities and indirectly through the alteration of family resource allocation decisions. Given that the high school movement overlapped with some of the largest changes to the health of the American public, these relationships are central to understanding the development of the American economy and the extent to which improvements in childhood health were a necessary condition for increasing educational attainments and worker productivity.

THE BLACK BOX OF EDUCATION AND THE DIRECTION OF FUTURE RESEARCH

The rise of mass education is certainly a crucial element of the history of the American economy. Extensive work by economic historians has demonstrated critical links between education and technological advance, the role of education in creating or limiting mobility and equality, and the relationships between educational outcomes and household characteristics, school district quality, labor market conditions, and local health and environmental conditions. There is still interesting and important work to be done in all of these areas and an expanding set of data sources to accomplish that work.

However, there is also value in economic historians pursuing a new direction by beginning the herculean task of quantifying how education translates into productive human capital. Exploring the relationship between the actual content of education and the productivity of workers and how that relationship has changed over time would help illuminate the mechanisms underlying all of the various relationships discussed here. We have a variety of data sources at our disposal to begin this task, including the test scores discussed earlier, military test scores for cognitive ability beginning with the Army General Classification Test in World War II, the skill demands of various occupations, detailed records on curricular content and its change over time from state school reports, the subjects taught to teachers at normal schools, and, in many cases, the ability to match individuals and their outcomes to these detailed schooling data. We have a rich history of school systems and occupational distributions with substantial heterogeneity across space and time that can help economic historians open the black box of education and better understand how schooling shaped our economy in the past and how policy reforms will shape our economy in the future.

NOTES

1. This approach of measuring numeracy by comparing consistency in reported age across time in longitudinal data has been used by Long (2006) for nineteenth-century Britain and for Southern households at the time of emancipation by Wanamaker (2009).
2. Some caution is needed when interpreting highest grade completed as equivalent to years of educational attainment. As Collins and Margo (2006) note, individuals educated in the nineteenth and early twentieth centuries were often educated in ungraded schools, particularly in the South. This forced census enumerators to estimate a highest grade completed for individuals that attended ungraded school. Collins and Margo note that this may have overstated educational attainment. This creates some issues in interpreting trends over time as ungraded schools were replaced by graded schools earlier in the North than in the South, causing both regional and racial gaps in schooling to be mismeasured. Goldin (1998) also notes that the 1940 census data likely overstate the number of high school graduates.
3. A second channel for indirect effects of education on growth should be mentioned. Schultz (2002) notes that the education of females is associated with relatively larger benefits for society due to the link between female education and the education, nutrition and health outcomes of children. The unique gender equality in the historical provision of American education may have led to larger impacts of education on economic growth for the United States relative to other countries.
4. By 1933, 17 percent of public school students in grades nine through twelve took typewriting, 21 percent took classes in industrial subjects and 10 percent took bookkeeping (*Historical Statistics of the United States*, Table Bc115–145.)
5. One alternative solution is the presence of group with political power and a vested interest in improving black educational outcomes. Fishback (1989) shows that coal companies in

West Virginia successfully pushed for greater school equality out of a desire to attract black workers in a tight labor market.

6. Recent work by Carruthers and Wanamaker (2013) reveals that the Rosenwald gifts increased contemporaneous spending on schools but did not lead to long run declines in the black-white school quality gap due to funds being diverted or implicitly matched to benefit white schools. However, the funds did help close racial gaps in human capital because of higher marginal returns to schooling expenditures for black students.

7. Note that the politics behind some of the laws suggests that they may have been passed with specific groups in mind such as the children of immigrants. See Eisenberg (1988) for discussion of the politics of compulsory schooling.

BIBLIOGRAPHY

A'Hearn, B., J. Baten, and D. Crayen. (2009). "Quantifying Quantitative Literacy: Age Heaping and the History of Human Capital." *Journal of Economic History* 69(3): 783–808.

Almond, D. (2006). "Is the 1918 Influenza Pandemic Over? Long-Term Effects of in Utero Influenza Exposure in the Post-1940 US Population." *Journal of Political Economy* 114(4): 672–712.

Becker, G. S. (1991). *A Treatise on the Family*. 2nd ed. Cambridge, MA: Harvard University Press.

Benhabib, J., and M. M. Spiegel. (1994). "The Role of Human Capital in Economic Development Evidence from Aggregate Cross-Country Data." *Journal of Monetary Economics* 34(2): 143–173.

Bishop, J. H. (1989). "Is the Test Score Decline Responsible for the Productivity Growth Decline?" *American Economic Review* 79(1): 178–197.

Bleakley, H. (2003). "Disease and Development: Evidence from the American South." *Journal of the European Economic Association* 1(2–3): 376–386.

Bleakley, H. (2007). "Disease and Development: Evidence from Hookworm Eradication in the American South." *Quarterly Journal of Economics* 122(1): 73–117.

Bleakley, H., and F. Lange. (2009). "Chronic Disease Burden and the Interaction of Education, Fertility, and Growth." *Review of Economics and Statistics* 91(1): 52–65.

Bound, J., and S. Turner. (2002). "Going to War and Going to College: Did World War II and the GI Bill Increase Educational Attainment for Returning Veterans?" *Journal of Labor Economics* 20(4): 784–815.

Carruthers, C. K., and M. H. Wanamaker. (2013). "Closing the Gap? The Effect of Private Philanthropy on the Provision of African-American Schooling in the US South." *Journal of Public Economics* 101: 53–67.

Clay, K., J. Lingwall, and M. Stephens, Jr. (2012). "Do Schooling Laws Matter? Evidence from the Introduction of Compulsory Attendance Laws in the United States." Technical Report, National Bureau of Economic Research.

Clotfelter, C. T. (2011). *After Brown: The Rise and Retreat of School Desegregation*. Princeton, NJ: Princeton University Press.

Collins, W. J., and R. A. Margo. (2006). "Historical Perspectives on Racial Differences in Schooling in the United States." In *Handbook of the Economics of Education*, edited by E. Hanushek and F. Welch, Vol. 1, 107–154. Amsterdam: Elsevier.

Currie, J., and E. Moretti. (2003). "Mother's Education and the Intergenerational Transmission of Human Capital: Evidence from College Openings." *Quarterly Journal of Economics* 118(4): 1495–1532.

Dee, T. S. (2004). "Are There Civic Returns to Education?" *Journal of Public Economics* 88(9): 1697–1720.

Denison, E. F. (1962). "Education, Economic Growth, and Gaps in Information." *Journal of Political Economy* 70(5): 124–128.

Donohue, J. J., J. J. Heckman, and P. E. Todd. (2002). "The Schooling of Southern Blacks: The Roles of Legal Activism and Private Philanthropy, 1910–1960." *Quarterly Journal of Economics* 117(1): 225–268.

Eisenberg, M. J. (1988). "Compulsory Attendance Legislation in America, 1870 to 1915." Dissertations available from ProQuest, AAI8824730.

Finch, F. H. (1946). *Enrollment Increases and Changes in the Mental Level of the High-School Population.* Washington, DC: American Psychological Association.

Fishback, P. V. (1989). "Can Competition among Employers Reduce Governmental Discrimination: Coal Companies and Segregated Schools in West Virginia in the Early 1900s." *Journal of Law and Economics* 32: 311.

Fishback, P. V., and J. H. Baskin. (1991). "Narrowing the Black-White Gap in Child Literacy in 1910: The Roles of School Inputs and Family Inputs." *Review of Economics and Statistics* 73(4): 725–728.

Flynn, J. R. (1984). "The Mean IQ of Americans: Massive Gains 1932 to 1978." *Psychological Bulletin* 95(1): 29–51.

Galenson, D. W. (1981). "The Market Evaluation of Human Capital: The Case of Indentured Servitude." *Journal of Political Economy* 89(3): 446–467.

Galor, O., O. Moav, and D. Vollrath. (2009). "Inequality in Landownership, the Emergence of Human-Capital Promoting Institutions, and the Great Divergence." *Review of Economic Studies* 76(1): 143–179.

Genovese, E. D. (1976). *Roll, Jordan, Roll: The World the Slaves Made,* Vol. 652. New York: Vintage.

Go, S., and P. Lindert. (2010). "The Uneven Rise of American Public Schools to 1850." *Journal of Economic History* 70(1): 1–26.

Goldin, C. (1998). "America's Graduation from High School: The Evolution and Spread of Secondary Schooling in the Twentieth Century." *Journal of Economic History* 58: 345–374.

Goldin, C. (2000). *Understanding the Gender Gap: An Economic History of American Women.* New York: Oxford University Press.

Goldin, C., and L. F. Katz. (1996). "Technology, Skill, and the Wage Structure: Insights from the Past." *American Economic Review* 86(2): 252–257.

Goldin, C., and L. F. Katz. (1998). "The Origins of Technology-Skill Complementarity." *Quarterly Journal of Economics* 113(3): 693–732.

Goldin, C., and L. F. Katz. (2000). "Education and Income in the Early Twentieth Century: Evidence from the Prairies." *Journal of Economic History* 60(3): 782–818.

Goldin, C. D., and L. F. Katz. (2009). *The Race between Education and Technology.* Cambridge, MA: Harvard University Press.

Goldin, C., and R. A. Margo. (1992). "The Great Compression: The Wage Structure in the United States at Mid-century." *Quarterly Journal of Economics* 107(1): 1–34.

Graff, H. J. (1991). *The Legacies of Literacy: Continuities and Contradictions in Western Culture and Society,* Vol. 598. Bloomington: Indiana University Press.

Hanushek, E. A., and L. Woessmann. (2008). "The Role of Cognitive Skills in Economic Development." *Journal of Economic Literature* 46(3): 607–668.

Hatton, T. J., K. H. O'Rourke, and A. M. Taylor. (2007). *The New Comparative Economic History: Essays in Honor of Jeffrey G. Williamson.* Cambridge, MA: MIT Press.

Jones, C. I. (1995). "R&D-Based Models of Economic Growth." *Journal of Political Economy* 103(4): 759–784.

Kaestle, C. (1983). *Pillars of the Republic: Common Schools and American Society, 1780–1860.* New York: Hill and Wang.

Lindert, P. H. (2009). "Revealing Failures in the History of School Finance." Technical Report, National Bureau of Economic Research.

Lleras-Muney, A. (2002). "Were Compulsory Attendance and Child Labor Laws Effective? An Analysis from 1915 to 1939." *Journal of Law and Economics* 45(2): 401–437.

Lochner, L., and E. Moretti. (2004). "The Effect of Education on Crime: Evidence from Prison Inmates, Arrests, and Self-Reports." *American Economic Review* 94(1): 155–189.

Long, J. (2006). "The Socioeconomic Return to Primary Schooling in Victorian England." *Journal of Economic History* 66(4): 1026.

Margo, R. A. (1986). "Race, Educational Attainment, and the 1940 Census." *Journal of Economic History* 46(1): 189–198.

Margo, R. A. (1991). *Race and Schooling in the South, 1880–1950: An Economic History.* Chicago: University of Chicago Press.

Margo, R. A. (2000). *Wages and Labor Markets in the United States, 1820–1860.* Chicago: University of Chicago Press.

Milligan, K., E. Moretti, and P. Oreopoulos. (2004). "Does Education Improve Citizenship? Evidence from the United States and the United Kingdom." *Journal of Public Economics* 88(9): 1667–1695.

Moehling, C. M. (2004). "Family Structure, School Attendance, and Child Labor in the American South in 1900 and 1910." *Explorations in Economic History* 41(1): 73–100.

Moretti, E. (2004). "Human Capital Externalities in Cities." *Handbook of Regional and Urban Economics* 4: 2243–2291.

Nelson, R. R., and E. S. Phelps. (1966). "Investment in Humans, Technological Diffusion, and Economic Growth." *American Economic Review* 56(1–2): 69–75.

Parman, J. (2011). "American Mobility and the Expansion of Public Education." *Journal of Economic History* 71(1): 105.

Parman, J. (2012). "Good Schools Make Good Neighbors: Human Capital Spillovers in Early 20th Century Agriculture." *Explorations in Economic History* 49(3): 316–334.

Platt Boustan, L. (2012). "School Desegregation and Urban Change: Evidence from City Boundaries." *American Economic Journal: Applied Economics* 4(1): 85–108.

Reber, S. J. (2005). "Court-Ordered Desegregation Successes and Failures Integrating American Schools since Brown versus Board of Education." *Journal of Human Resources* 40(3): 559–590.

Romer, P. M. (1990). "Endogenous Technological Change." *Journal of Political Economy* 98(5): S71–S102.

Ruggles, Steven, Katie Genadek, Ronald Goeken, Josiah Grover, and Matthew Sobek. (2015). Integrated Public Use Microdata Series: Version 6.0 [data set]. Minneapolis: University of Minnesota. Available at http://doi.org/10.18128/D010.V6.0.

Rundquist, E. A. (1936). "Intelligence Test Scores and School Marks of High School Seniors in 1929 and 1934." *School and Society* 43: 301–304.

Schultz, T. P. (2002). "Why Governments Should Invest More to Educate Girls." *World Development* 30(2): 207–225.

Stanley, M. (2003). "College Education and the Midcentury GI Bills." *Quarterly Journal of Economics* 118(2): 671–708.

Stoddard, C. (2009). "Why Did Education Become Publicly Funded? Evidence from the Nineteenth-Century Growth of Public Primary Schooling in the United States." *Journal of Economic History* 69(1): 172.

Troen, S. K. (1975). *The Public and the Schools: Shaping the St. Louis System, 1838–1920*. Columbia: University of Missouri Press.

Tyack, D. B. (1974). *The One Best System: A History of American Urban Education*. Cambridge, MA: Harvard University Press.

Wanamaker, M. (2009). "Essays in American Fertility." Dissertations available from ProQuest, ISBN: 9781109518559.

Wheeler, L. R. (1942). "A Comparative Study of the Intelligence of East Tennessee Mountain Children." *Journal of Educational Psychology* 33(5): 321.

CHAPTER 18

....

NATURAL RESOURCES IN AMERICAN ECONOMIC HISTORY

....

GAVIN WRIGHT

THE United States has long been rich in natural resources, and this condition of abundance has been central in the country's economic and technological growth. What is perhaps less well appreciated is that American natural resources have a history. The term "natural" may imply that these resources had the character of gifts to the economy, and therefore that the country has been the beneficiary of extraordinary good fortune in its endowments of land, forests, and minerals. Although the United States has indeed been fortunate in many respects, to a very considerable degree its natural resource abundance was man-made, or "socially constructed" in currently fashionable parlance.

The temperate-zone regions of the country were blessed with naturally fertile soils, but expansion of cropland throughout the nineteenth century required an arduous struggle to clear these lands of their forests. Further extensions of farmland in the twentieth century were possible only with the aid of artificial irrigation and other human interventions. Through a combination of new technologies, more enlightened policies, and changing economic incentives, the tide of deforestation began to turn early in the twentieth century, and total forest acreage and production have grown since that time. Thus forests have shifted historically from an extractive to a renewable resource.

Development of the country's mineral resources was no more natural than that of farmland. American world leadership in industrial minerals emerged in historical time, as much a part of the development process as the rise of mechanized agriculture and manufacturing. The centrality of hard-rock minerals to the American economy peaked in the first quarter of the twentieth century. Since then, the country has moved away from its earlier reliance on domestic resources, though important legacies of its resource-based history remain. The change is partly attributable to the depletion of domestic supplies, but it is more fully explained by the decline in transportation costs and other barriers to international trade, the development of mineral deposits around the world, and the rise of science-based technologies not tightly bound to the location of resources. The country's shift to the status of net resource importer is often viewed with alarm, but it does not have decisive economic consequences in the modern world. Environmental issues are now more likely to be an appropriate focus of emerging concern.

unless cutoff

The American Age of Wood

According to E. A. Wrigley (1988), a crucial dimension of the eighteenth-century in-dustrial revolution was the rise of mineral-using technologies, which released industry from the constraints of the "organic economy." So long as energy had to be obtained from vegetable sources such as timber, its supply was either limited to an annual harvest or subject to rising costs as it came from greater and greater distances. The replacement of wood by coal, however, opened for human use a vast inventory of already stored en-ergy, an inventory known to be abundant in England. Allen (2009) elaborates on this interpretation, casting coal in the role of a "backstop" technology capable of providing vast amounts of energy at constant cost. Exploiting that potential through a sequence of technological improvements in steam engines and in iron-making was at the heart of the British industrial revolution.

From the perspective of 1800 North America, however, many of the practices of European settlers represented a step backward. American farmers, with their abundance of land, were indifferent to the intensive, yield-increasing methods that Europeans considered "scientific agriculture." At the same time, North America was not thought to have any significant deposits of useful minerals; the United States relied on imports of British coal until the 1820s. The absence of coal was compensated by an abundance of wood. Timber was not only plentiful, but the growth of supply was accelerated because it was a byproduct of the ongoing process of clearing forests for farmland. Nineteenth-century Americans adapted their technologies and consumption patterns toward wood to an extent unmatched in the world at that time. But relying on wood fuels consigned industries to what were by then outmoded technologies, such as charcoal-using iron foundries. Chandler (1972) maintains that it was not until the opening of the anthracite fields of eastern Pennsylvania that large-scale, steam-powered factories were feasible in the United States. But the diffusion of coke smelting was delayed until the development of the bituminous coal deposits of western Pennsylvania in the latter half of the nine-teenth century.

Although the forests were in principle renewable, from the viewpoint of the settlers the original forestland had the character of a one-time gift of nature. To be sure, even at the time of earliest European arrival, the forests were not really in a "natural" con-dition, because the American Indians engaged extensively in land clearing for agricul-tural purposes and in regular burnings to extend grassland and encourage the growth of plants bearing nuts and berries. To the Europeans, however, the land was much more densely wooded than were the places they had come from; furthermore, the forests stood in the way of their primary means of livelihood, family-farm agriculture. Over the seventeenth through the nineteenth centuries, most of the eastern part of the country was cleared for farming, and during this process, lumber was universally and cheaply available. Sawmills proliferated across the countryside, making lumber the nation's second largest manufacturing industry by value added as of 1860. Indeed, the abundance of wood for buildings and machines was enhanced by technological progress in saws, such as the faster gang and muley saws of the 1840s, followed by the thick-bladed circular saws of the 1850s—albeit at the cost of high rates of kerf, or wastage (Rosenberg 1976).

Cotton #1

Thus nineteenth-century America provides an interesting example of a rapidly industrializing economy, following the technological lead of Great Britain but with a different material base. British engineers visiting in the 1850s were particularly struck by the contrast, as summarized in an 1855 committee report: "In those districts of the United States of America that the Committee have visited the working of wood by machinery in almost every branch of industry is all but universal" (quoted in Hounshell 1984, 125). A notable example was the Blanchard lathe, invented in 1818 for the shaping of gunstocks, but adapted over time for reproducing other irregular shapes such as shoe lasts, hat blocks, spokes of wheels, and oars. Hounshell argues that there was no intrinsic incompatibility between wood and mass-production techniques, as illustrated by the examples of Singer sewing machine cabinets and Studebaker wagons, carriages, and early automobile bodies. A wood-based technology that has endured is newsprint made from wood pulp, which arose in response to an impending rag shortage in the 1860s, and was adopted by nearly all large-circulation newspapers by 1882 (Rutkow 2012).

As timber prices rose, and the coal and iron industries developed, the US economy moved onto a somewhat more "European" technological track across the nineteenth century. But total wood consumption per capita did not peak until the first decade of the twentieth century, when construction of the national rail network was essentially complete (fig. 18.1). In the late nineteenth century, railroads were the largest single consumer, taking between 20 and 25 percent of the annual timber harvest in most years. Between 1900 and 1930, all major demand categories for wood products declined (other than pulp), setting the stage for the rejuvenation of the nation's forests (Williams 1989).

THE DECLINE AND REBIRTH OF AMERICAN FORESTS

Economic theory predicts that a nonrenewable resource will be consumed until exhausted, its price rising at a pace equal to the rate of interest. In contrast, consumption of a renewable resource should tend toward a steady state, in which the annual harvest equals the size of the annual growth, and the stock is maintained. Since American timber was "mined" with little thought of replacement until the twentieth century, this

FIGURE 18.1. US lumber consumption per capita, 1799–2000

Source: Carter et al. (2006, Vol. 4, Table Db423–431).

renewable resource played out a sequence assigned by theory to the nonrenewables. Prices of lumber and forest products show a long-term upward trend over the past two centuries. Berck and Bentley (1997) show that Hotelling's theory of rising *non*renewable prices provides a good fit for the historical record for redwoods, a variety for which the old-growth supply is essentially fixed for all practical purposes.

In contrast to minerals, there were no hidden reserves of timber to be discovered. But lumber companies could expand their reserves by moving their activities westward and southward, and by investing in transport links to carry wood from ever more distant locations to the growing urban markets. Local shortages of firewood and building materials presented serious problems in Eastern cities very early in the nineteenth century. Much the way twenty-first-century Americans cling to their oil-based lifestyles, nineteenth-century Americans maintained their wood-using ways by transporting lumber across previously unheard-of distances—up to one thousand miles by the 1850s.

Why the extractive behavior pattern continued in the industry as long as it did is something of a puzzle for economic historians. One hypothesis argues, by analogy to the common-property or common-pool problem in the case of oil, that property rights in timberland were not clearly enough established because much of the accessible acreage was on the public domain. The forests of the Great Lakes states, however, were thoroughly logged out between 1870 and 1900, despite the fact that most of the land came into private ownership before the cutting. It is true that most forestlands were privatized under agricultural land laws intended to encourage rapid clearing and settlement. Much of the cutover land in the Great Lakes region was resold for farming, but probably more than half, mainly in Wisconsin and Minnesota, was too far north for commercial agriculture and so was abandoned after cutting. An alternative theory is that the price of standing timber in a given location was simply not rising fast enough to cover the anticipated costs of holding the land, including taxes, interest, and the anticipated costs of resale. The risk of forest fires, which were frequent and devastating in the late nineteenth century, added to the motivation for realizing revenue quickly.

Concerns about the disappearance of the nation's forests were central to the rise of the conservationist ethic around the turn of the twentieth century. In 1891 the first legislation was passed permitting the president to set aside public forest reservations. Subsequent laws led to the creation of the Forest Service in 1905, with Gifford Pinchot as its first director. In 1911 the service obtained the right to purchase land for the national forest system, and between 1916 and 1920, nine national forests were established in the Eastern part of the country. These developments reflected a mix of motivations, in which genuine farsighted concern for public welfare blended with the emerging interests of private parties. Much of the land purchased for the national forest was logged-over, burned, and unwanted by its owners. And the Forest Service's program for promoting more sustainable practices found favor with large owners as a way of stabilizing production and keeping prices up.

Eventually, attitudes and practices in the private sector also gravitated toward longer-term sustainability. Even while engaged in "cut out and get out" methods in the Midwest, giants like Weyerhaeuser were planning for the future by buying thousands of forest acres in the South and in the Pacific Northwest. The diffusion of sustainable private-sector practices depended on improvement in the general knowledge base and level of training in forest management, as well as sufficiently long organizational time horizons to make these investments worthwhile. Since the 1950s, the private sector not only has held its inventories for the future, but also has engaged in tree planting on a large scale. Aided by genetic improvements in seedlings, this move toward intensive tree farming has been particularly pronounced in the South, where the period of regeneration is relatively fast. The South now accounts for about three-fourths of US pulpwood and over half of paper and board production (Boyd 2001).

A major factor in this transition was the conquest of forest fires. When the early forest surveys in the 1920s reported surprisingly rapid regeneration, they also found that in roughly half the area surveyed, timber drain exceeded timber growth. The prime culprit was fire, the direct or indirect cause of nearly three-fourths of pine-timber mortality. The problem had a strong regional component, with the South accounting for some 85 percent of all forest fires in the country during the 1920s and 1930s. Roughly 40 percent of these fires were of suspected incendiary origin, reflecting the time-honored tradition of annual woods-burning, practiced in order to improve livestock grazing and eliminate pests. Between the 1920s and 1950s, an ambitious federal-state-voluntary cooperative program worked to transform the regional culture through education and prosecution, and to expand the forest area under federal protection. One consequence was that the Federal Reserve amended its regulations in 1953 to allow financial institutions to make loans on timberland. This step was a significant milestone in the restoration and expansion of the South's forest industries (Boyd 2001). In recent years, many experts have argued that forest fire suppression has gone too far, pointing to the potential benefits of controlled fires for long-term sustainability. From a century-long standpoint, these discussions are only possible because of the prior demise of the uncontrolled fire regime.

In recent decades, debates over forest policies have shifted from the goal of renewability to the broader and more difficult concept of sustainability, encompassing such diverse concerns as biodiversity, ecosystem health, protection of soil and water resources, and socioeconomic benefits. The issues thus no longer turn on the need to conserve timber resources for future generations, but rather on the social value of preserving unique ecosystems that old-growth forests represent, particularly as habitats for unique plant and animal life. As a result of these concerns, timber sales from national forests declined precipitously in the 1990s. But timber sales from privately owned forests, particularly in the South, have largely made up the difference. As a result, the United States has maintained its position as the world's leading producer of industrial wood, accounting for roughly one-quarter of the global total. Extending this leadership to forest sustainability will be a challenge for future generations (Sedjo 2008).

THE RISE OF AMERICAN MINERALS

On the eve of World War I, the United States was the world's leading producer of virtually every one of the major industrial minerals of that era. Other countries may have come close to the lead in one or another mineral, but no other country possessed the depth and range of supplies found in the United States during the early decades of the twentieth century. It is tempting to infer that the country's rise to world economic leadership was propelled by a uniquely favorable geological endowment. When George Otis Smith, director of the US Geological Survey (USGS), wrote in 1919 that "the United States is more richly endowed with mineral wealth than any other country," he expressed the best available scientific knowledge of his day (Smith 1919, 282).

With the advantages of hindsight and modern geological knowledge, however, we can say that this US leadership derived more from early development of its mineral potential than from endowment per se. David and Wright (1997) show that the US share of world mineral production in 1913 was far in excess of its share of world reserves, as estimated in the late twentieth century. For almost all major minerals, new deposits were continually discovered, and production continued to rise, well into the twentieth century—for the country as a whole, if not for every mining area considered separately. To some extent, this growth was a function of the size of the country and its relatively unexplored condition prior to the westward migration of the nineteenth century. But mineral discoveries were not mere byproducts of territorial expansion. Clay and Wright (2012) show that Western settlements following the California gold rush tracked a "mining frontier," driven in turn by active exploratory efforts and advances in geological and metallurgical sciences. Indeed, some of the most dramatic production growth occurred not in the Far West but in older parts of the country: copper in Michigan, coal in Pennsylvania and Illinois, and oil in Pennsylvania, followed by a sequence of states across the Midwest. The rise of minerals was thus an integral part of the broader process of economic development.

The most direct evidence that American mineral abundance was not merely a matter of endowment is that the size and importance of the sector emerged in historical time. In the eighteenth century, both Adam Smith and Benjamin Franklin observed that in North America no mines had been discovered, or "at least none that are at present supposed to be worth the working" (Smith 1937, 531). It was not until the 1820s that the first activities that might qualify as "mining booms" occurred, with the discoveries of gold in Virginia and the Carolinas, the development of lead mining in Missouri and the Galena district (adjoining Illinois, Iowa, and Wisconsin), and the first shipments of anthracite coal from eastern Pennsylvania into Philadelphia. The search for coal soon emerged as the largest and most profitable mineral project during the antebellum era, with strong links to the emerging science of geology. Henry Darwin Rogers, professor of geology and mineralogy at the University of Pennsylvania, estimated in 1858 that Americans had discovered more coal than any other geologists in the world, "twenty times the area [of] all known coal-deposits of Europe" (quoted in Lucier 2008, 106). Figure 18.2 shows that US coal production grew rapidly thereafter, surging past Germany and overtaking the United Kingdom by the 1990s.

Mineral exploration received both encouragement and implicit subsidy in the form of state-sponsored geological surveys, beginning with North Carolina in 1823. By 1860, twenty-nine of the thirty-three states had sponsored surveys at one time or another. These projects served as a form of patronage for the emerging geological profession. Many young scientists practiced "serial surveying," from which they often moved on to consulting positions with private firms (Lucier 2008). Thus the roots of entrepreneurial science go way back in American history. During the Michigan copper boom of the 1840s, the young scientist Josiah Whitney joined the staff of a federal geological survey and soon established himself as a leading industrial consultant: "Making five hundred dollars a month, he remarked in 1853, he could not afford to be a Yale professor" (Bruce 1987, 139–140).

From a quantitative standpoint, the rise of the United States to world mineral leadership was a post–Civil War phenomenon. The California gold rush of the 1850s triggered a massive migration of labor and capital to the West, thereby launching a collective learning process of exploration and technological adaptation, extending well into the twentieth century. Placer miners from California had worked a gulch called Gold Canyon in Nevada for years, until more knowledgeable diggers detected bluish quartz in the gold dust and had it assayed. A newspaper notice of the silver discovery in July 1859 kicked off the Comstock rush, which in turn triggered searches for silver throughout the territories. Nevada became known as the Silver State, but its silver output was soon surpassed by that of Colorado, Montana, and Utah (Smith 1998 [1943]).

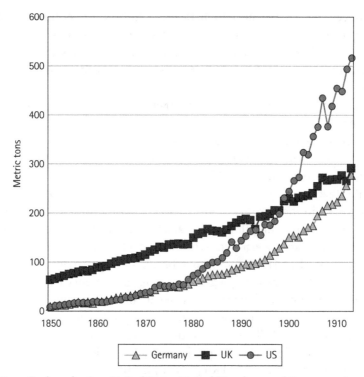

FIGURE 18.2. Coal production: United States, United Kingdom, and Germany, 1850–1913

Sources: International Historical Statistics: Europe (1992, 4416–4421); *International Historical Statistics: The Americas and Australasia* (1975, 399–400).

The linkages did not stop there. Butte, Montana, a gold placer camp from 1864, was nearly deserted until silver was discovered there in 1875. Butte silver was sufficiently promising to induce the Walker Brothers of Salt Lake City to send their associate Marcus Daly to examine and purchase claims. Early indications of copper deposits were neglected at first, as they were elsewhere in the West. Rodman Paul observes, "Just when Daley came to realize that his silver mine was in fact one of the richest copper mines in the world, is not clear" (1963, 147–148). But by 1882 Daly induced a San Francisco group to finance a major investment in mining and smelting copper on a mass-production basis. By 1887 Anaconda was the largest copper mine in the country, propelling the United States into world leadership in copper production.

The rise of American minerals was encouraged by an accommodating legal environment. Mineral law in the United States was novel in that the government claimed no ultimate legal title to the nation's minerals, not even on the public domain. All other major mining systems retained the influence of the ancient legal tradition whereby minerals were the personal property of the lord or ruler, who granted user right concessions if he so chose. This liberality was not entirely intentional. The land ordinance of 1785 did claim for the federal government "one third part of all gold, silver, lead and copper mines" on the public domain, and between 1807 and 1846 a federal leasing system for lead mines was in operation. The system collapsed in the 1830s and 1840s because of noncompliance and fraud, and leasing was discontinued in 1846. Thus, the great California gold rush that began in 1848 took place in a legal vacuum, only partially filled by the rules of local mining districts and the intervention of state courts. Clay and Wright (2005) argue that gold-rush mining districts should not be understood as enforcers of conventional property rights, but rather as institutions for regulating access in a high-turnover setting that approximated open access. Federal mining laws of 1866, 1870, and 1872 largely confirmed what by then was a well-established "free mining" precedent: open access for exploration; exclusive rights to mine a site upon proof of discovery; and the requirement that the claim be worked at some frequency or be subject to forfeit. Although the fuel minerals coal and oil received separate treatment in the twentieth century, for most minerals the Mining Law of 1872 remains the basic mineral law of the country (Mayer and Riley 1985).

This discussion may convey the impression that the rise of US mineral production was an exercise in rapid exhaustion of nonrenewable resources in a common-property setting. Although elements of such a scenario were sometimes on display, resource extraction in the United States was also associated with ongoing processes of learning, investment, technological progress, and cost reduction, generating a manifold expansion rather than a depletion of the nation's resource base. The point is illustrated by the work of the USGS, established in 1879 as the successor to various regional exploration projects. The Survey emerged as the leading scientific bureau and the most productive government research agency of the nineteenth century. It proved highly responsive to the concerns of Western mining interests, and the practical value of its detailed mineral maps gave the USGS, in turn, a powerful constituency in support of its scientific research. The Survey's monograph on Leadville, Colorado, published in 1882, was known for years as "the miner's bible." This thorough geological study of the entire district within a ten-mile radius generated a comprehensive view of the structural conditions affecting the distribution of ores. Although private professional work while on the Survey staff was not permitted, the organization acquired a reputation as an ideal stepping stone toward career success in the mining sector (Spence 1970).

The final element in this expansionary narrative was higher mining education. By the late nineteenth century, the United States emerged as the world's leading trainer of mining engineers and metallurgists. Columbia College in New York City opened what became the country's first successful mining school in 1864. A well-informed 1871 survey declared Columbia "one of the best schools in the world—more scientific than Freiberg, more practical than Paris" (Church 1871, 79). Columbia was dominant for the next quarter-century, but demands arose over time for mining schools in closer proximity to the mining districts. These efforts were an expression of state developmental impulses, combined with the undeniable geographic specificity of much of the relevant knowledge about minerals. The Colorado School of Mines was the first to be set up as a separate institution; it was established by the territorial legislature in 1870 and began instruction in 1873. Mining education at the University of California began in the 1860s, although the first degree was not awarded until 1873. At Berkeley, registration at the mining college grew tenfold between 1893 and 1903, supporting the school's claim to be "without doubt the largest mining college in the world" (Read 1941, 84). The high mobility and professional status of American mining engineers gave them substantial independence, as confirmed by offers of extravagant salaries and bonuses from such faraway locations as South America, Australia, Africa, Siberia, and China. A turning point in Australia's mining history came with the decision in 1886 to recruit highly paid engineers and metallurgists from the Rocky Mountain states, such as William H. Patton from the Comstock Lode, and Herman Schlapp from the smelting towns of Colorado (Blainey 1969; Spence 1970).

TRENDS IN MINERAL SCARCITY
AND SELF-SUFFICIENCY

After having led world production and export of minerals for more than a century, the United States became a net importer of most minerals after World War II. Bauxite became a net import even before the war. Lead, zinc, and copper followed in the late 1940s. Iron ore imports became significant in the 1950s. By the turn of the century, the country was a net importer of most minerals, the only major exceptions being bituminous coal and molybdenum.

During the first decade after World War II, many national leaders viewed this trend with alarm. William L. Batt, administrator of the War Production Board, stated in 1946, "It may hurt our pride, but harden our decision, to ask ourselves if the remarkable combination of assets which enabled this country to develop its fantastic strength may not be gone forever" (quoted in Eckes 1979, 125). Yale geologist Alan M. Bateman wrote in 1952, "The irony is that the more we build our industrial and military power, along with that of other countries, the faster we exhaust the very basis for this power" (Bateman 1952, 27). Concerns such as these led to the appointment of the President's Material Policy Commission (known as the Paley Commission), whose 1952 report was entitled *Resources for Freedom*. The report called for the liberalization of international trade as well as the intensification of domestic resource development. As events unfolded, the ready availability of imports largely allayed fears of impending scarcity, with petroleum an obvious exception (treated separately in the next section).

One factor in the rise of imported minerals was the depletion of domestic mineral supplies, which could be qualitative as well as quantitative. A well-known example is iron ore, where high-grade hematite from the Mesabi Range had largely played out by about 1950, forcing the industry to invest in costly techniques for utilizing the remaining lower-quality taconite ores. Average grades of copper ore also declined, from 2.1 percent metal content in new mines opened between 1910 and 1920, to 0.79 percent in mines opened between 1970 and 1980 (Dale 1984, 258). The fact of depletion is undeniable, yet the deeper causes of the shift are the liberalization of world trade, the fall in transportation costs, and the development of new ore deposits around the world.

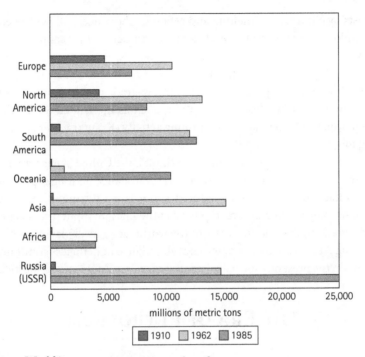

FIGURE 18.3. World iron ore reserves, 1910, 1962, 1985

Sources: International Geological Congress, *The Iron Ore Resources of the World* (1910); United Nations Department of Economic and Social Affairs, *Survey of World Iron Ore Resources* (1970); US Bureau of Mines (1985).

These developments have not been geographically neutral. Figure 18.3 displays three sets of estimates of iron ore reserves by continent, beginning with the survey conducted by the International Geologic Congress in 1910. At that time and well beyond, it was thought that the world's iron ore reserves were overwhelmingly concentrated in Europe and North America. Subsequently, almost all major new additions to reserves were in other parts of the world, notably South America, Oceania, Asia, and Russia. Although the surveys of world iron ore resources were motivated by fears of shortage and rising prices, it is now understood that iron ore remains abundant and widely distributed on the earth's surface. Thus iron ore mining has not yet had to draw upon the more advanced and science-based modes of exploration and refining that have characterized other minerals.

The case of copper is somewhat different. Because of falling world prices and transportation costs, the United States became a net copper importer in the 1940s, even while retaining its status as the world's leading producer. This position was lost to Chile in the 1970s (and subsequently to other nations as well), when the industry was badly hit by import competition. By the mid-1980s, observers such as *Business Week* declared the death of copper mining in the United States, and many mines were indeed shut down. A handful of companies, however, stuck out the hard times and launched a technology-driven revival that was in full swing by the 1990s. The centerpiece of their approach was the solvent extraction-electrowinning (SX-EW) method for refining copper ore, which reduces costs by eliminating smelting and refining. The process allows the economical use of much lower grades of ore, serving as a reminder that this apparent sign of depletion can also be an index of technological progress. Another notable aspect of the SX-EW process is that it tends to favor older mining nations, by providing a way to exploit waste piles of oxide copper materials near low-grade porphyry mines. This feature is especially important in advanced countries, such as the United States, that impose stringent environmental regulations on mining activity (Krautkraemer 2005; Tilton and Landsberg 1999).

The important historical point is that even though the United States remains a formidable player in world mineral supplies, mineral abundance no longer provides a competitive advantage for the country's industries, nor is it a distinguishing feature of its technology. As long as minerals are imported at the margin, input prices are essentially set in world markets, and the countries of the world face a level playing field in this respect. The long American history of mineral abundance nonetheless continues to cast a long shadow on the present, especially in patterns of consumption and lifestyle choices.

THE ERA OF PETROLEUM

World petroleum production was dominated by the United States for nearly a century, from the time of Edwin Drake's first oil strike near Titusville, Pennsylvania, in 1859 until the 1950s. Throughout most of the nineteenth century, petroleum's chief use was as an illuminant, a role claimed by electricity after 1900. In its origins, petroleum was one of several strategies being explored to find an inexpensive substitute for whale oil. The first such effort to achieve some success was a liquid distilled from coal, known as coal oil. The term "Kerosene" was coined in 1850 as the brand name for one type of lamp oil. Sold with a burner that became known as the "Kerosene lamp," the product enjoyed a boom between 1858 and 1860. One of the reasons petroleum was so quickly adopted was that it fit readily into an existing network of refineries, markets, and distribution channels laid out for coal oil, not to mention the lamps themselves. Ultimately, "kerosene" became the generic term for all mineral-based lamp oils, including those made from petroleum (Lucier 2008, 144–161, 233–237).

From Pennsylvania, the oil frontier moved westward and southward, in a series of sporadic jumps, as fears of exhaustion alternated with dramatic breakthroughs in new territories. The oil industry thus displayed the traits of American minerals generally, but in exaggerated fashion. One reason for this tendency to extremes is that oil is fugacious, and once a field was discovered, drillers were in fact pumping from a common pool. Extraction took place under the legal maxim known as the "rule of capture": the owner of the land on which drilling occurred was entitled to claim all of the oil extracted through that channel, regardless of its origins. This dictum had the virtue of simplicity and could be seen as an extension of the "apex" rule in hard-rock mining, allowing those who undertook an investment to pursue a vein wherever it led. In the case of oil, however, the system generated huge inefficiencies in the form of excessive drilling and extraction costs, and saddled the industry with extremes of instability in production and prices. Despite growing misgivings and conservationist concerns, the rule remained in place until the 1930s, when it was displaced by compulsory production controls (Libecap 1986, 1989; Williamson and Daum 1959, 758–766).

It is tempting to entertain the thesis that the history of American petroleum was a gigantic exercise in excessive resource depletion, augmented by the urgency of a race to drain a common nonrenewable pool. Although aspects of such a scenario were at times on display, the record was also characterized by learning, technological improvements, and increasing deployment of advanced scientific knowledge and trained personnel. Replacement of the cable drill by the rotary drill around the turn of the twentieth century was responsible for bringing in the Spindletop gusher of 1901 (Williamson et al. 1963, 29). Employment of petroleum geologists dated from the 1860s, but advances were slow because of resistance from self-educated practitioners, whose views were reflected in such slogans as "oil is where you find it" and "geology never filled an oil tank" (White 1970, 146). The anticlinal theory of the structure of oil-bearing strata was distinctively North American in its origins, and had been developed by scientists over many decades. But the theory had little practical payoff before the 1890s. A pivotal moment in industry history was the discovery in 1912 of the rich Cushing pool in Oklahoma, confirming the theory that anticlines were favorable places to find oil. In 1914 the Oklahoma Geological Survey published a structure-contour map of the Cushing field indicating that the line separating oil from water was parallel to the surface structure contours. For the next fifteen years, most new crude discoveries were based on the surface mapping of anticlines (Frehner 2011, 98–102, 104–140; Williamson et al. 1963, 45–46).

In the twentieth century, oil became the nation's primary source of energy: as fuel oil for industry, heating oil for homes, and gasoline and diesel fuel for transportation. The appearance of the automobile on the American scene was the greatest of these new sources of demand. One of the advantages of oil over coal was its cost, but the primary advantage was transportability, both from the point of origin to the point of use and in moving vehicles themselves. Discoveries in the Los Angeles basin and at Signal Hill near Long Beach made California the leading oil producer between 1900 and 1930, and the state became a symbol of the oil-using, high-mobility lifestyle of the twentieth century. But the contributions of oil-based technologies and products to American lifestyles and living standards went far beyond transportation. The rise of the American chemical industry to world leadership during the 1920s was closely associated with a shift in the basic feedstock for chemical plants from coal to petroleum. Working in close partnership with the Massachusetts Institute of Technology (MIT), New Jersey Standard's research organization in Baton Rouge, Louisiana, produced such important process innovations as hydroforming, fluid flex coking, and fluid catalytic cracking. Petroleum-based pesticides, herbicides, and fertilizers contributed directly and indirectly to unprecedented increases in agricultural yields. The petrochemical industry has generated an astonishing number of new consumer goods: drugs, detergents, synthetic fibers, synthetic glycerine, synthetic rubber, and of course plastics. Pondering the ubiquity of oil-based products leads some social historians to assign cheap oil the prime responsibility for the American ethos of mass consumption and disposability (Black 2012).

These consumption patterns were not disrupted when the United States became a net oil importer in the 1950s and was then surpassed in production by the Middle East in the 1960s (fig. 18.4). But the national commitment to oil proved to be a heavy burden after the oil shocks of 1973 and 1979, brought on by production cutbacks coordinated by the Organization of Petroleum Exporting Countries (OPEC) and subsequently by the Iranian Revolution. A variety of rationing systems intended to restrain consumption led to long lines at gas stations, exacerbating a traumatic decade that featured high levels of both inflation and unemployment. For a time, the anticipation of shortages was self-fulfilling, as producers and suppliers slowed deliveries in hopes of profiting from higher prices in the future. Allowing for lags in adjustment, American consumers displayed remarkable flexibility and responsiveness to changing incentives. Homes and industries moved away from dependence on oil, in favor of natural gas or electricity (mainly generated by coal). Even the gas-guzzling American automobile increased its fuel efficiency, albeit prompted by federal legislation as well as heightened consumer sensitivity to gas mileage. By the early 1980s, under the cumulative effects of demand-side substitution away from oil and supply-side expansion of production capacity in non-OPEC

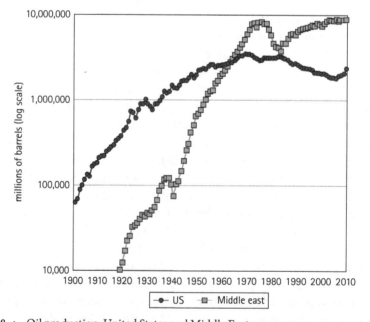

FIGURE 18.4. Oil production, United States and Middle East, 1900–2012

Sources: American Petroleum Institute, Basic Petroleum Data Book 13 (1993); US Energy Information Administration, Petroleum and Other Liquids (2013), https://www.eia.gov/petroleum/, accessed October 21, 2013.

countries, prices began to slip until their collapse in 1986. With the aid of hindsight, the crisis of the 1970s may be seen as a reflection of short-term vulnerability, rather than impending long-term energy scarcity.

It is true that one of the background factors behind the oil crisis of the 1970s was the decline in US oil production after 1970. American reserves peaked in 1971 (when the Alaskan Prudhoe Bay discovery was recorded) and have generally declined since then. This timing was predicted by geologist M. King Hubbert in a famous 1956 paper, which subsequently attained a kind of cult status; "Hubbert's Peak" has become a popular name for forecasts of impending declines in global oil production. But in fact Hubbert's forecasts of US oil production were quite far off, underestimating output as of 2010 by a factor of four (Yergin 2011, 236). Hubbert's predictions for natural gas were equally inaccurate. Driven by new technological developments, US natural gas production has actually been rising since the mid-1980s, rather than experiencing the sustained decline from 1970 that Hubbert forecast (Gorelick 2010, 95).

Perhaps more important than production levels are the reasons for the relative decline in US oil production. As with other minerals, depletion of US reserves is part of the explanation. But as with other minerals, the larger reasons are the discovery and development of oil deposits around the world, and reductions in the cost of transporting oil across long distances. The surge in US oil imports during the 1970s is better explained by the expansion of world supertanker capacity than by the depletion of domestic supplies. As Edward Porter, research manager at the American Petroleum Institute, wrote in 1995,

> The decline in U.S. supply after 1970 did not indicate that the U.S. was "running out" of oil, but rather that the costs associated with much of remaining Lower 48 resources was no longer competitive with imports from lower cost sources worldwide. Consequently the decline in U.S. supply after 1970 represented not a signal of growing resource scarcity, but rather a signal of growing global resource abundance. (quoted in Gorelick 2010, 114)

In retrospect, the century of US leadership in oil production was historically accidental from a geological standpoint. If all of the oil produced in the United States since 1859 were put back in the ground, the exercise would have no more than a marginal effect on world reserves today.

The Twenty-first Century

It is not the role of economic history to forecast the future, and carrying historical analysis into the very recent past often approximates such imprudent forecasting. But new oil and gas technologies developed during the 1980s and 1990s have already had an important impact on production and trade patterns, and their future significance is sufficient to justify including them in this historical survey.

According to a review by the National Research Council, the three most important new oil and gas innovations were horizontal drilling, three-dimensional seismic imaging, and fracturing technology. Improved control capability allowed operators to drill down to a desired depth and then veer at an angle or even sideways, thereby recovering a much higher yield of gas or oil from a given reservoir. Advances in microprocessing enabled geophysicists to analyze vast amounts of data in three dimensions, leading to greatly improved seismic mapping of underground structures and improved success rates in exploration. Hydraulic fracturing refers to a technique in which water is mixed with sand and chemicals, and the mixture is injected into a well bore to create small fractures, along which oil and gas migrate into the well. Although the technique originated as a method for liberating "shale gas" (natural gas trapped within shale formations), after 2000 it began to be applied to the production of "shale oil" (also known as "tight oil") as well. These new techniques, which as in earlier episodes emerged from a combination of public and private research programs, opened up the prospect of commercial development of a vast oil formation known as the Bakken, which sprawls from the Williston Basin in the Dakotas across Montana into Canada. Numerous other shale formations offer oil and gas development prospects in various parts of North America.[1] The short-term result of this technological revolution was a boom in domestic natural gas output in the early twenty-first century, led by production from the Barnett Shale play in northern Texas. Low domestic prices led to extensive substitution of gas for oil, providing immediate environmental benefits as well as a competitive advantage for US manufacturing. The debate over policies to permit and/ or facilitate natural gas exports sharply divides the business community. But the same technologies that fostered the natural gas boom have also generated forecasts that the United States will soon regain its position as the world's leading oil-producing nation. Whether these scenarios are realized will depend on two major factors: the struggle between the industries and environmental advocates over the use of "fracking" and related technologies; and the ease with which these largely American innovations diffuse to other parts of the world. Taken together, these developments confirm the historical generalization that natural resources, even nonrenewables, are not really given by nature, but rather are determined by policy choices and human behavior.

NOTE

1. This summary draws on Yergin (2011, 259–263, 325–332) and Wang and Krupnick (2013).

BIBLIOGRAPHY

Allen, Robert C. (2009). *The British Industrial Revolution in Global Perspective*. Cambridge: Cambridge University Press.

Bateman, Alan M. (1952). "Our Future Dependence on Foreign Minerals." *Annals of the American Academy of Political and Social Science* 281: 25–32.

Berck, Peter, and William R. Bentley. (1997). "Hotelling's Theory, Enhancement, and the Taking of the Redwood National Park." *American Journal of Agricultural Economics* 79: 287–298.

Black, Brian C. (2012). "Oil for Living: Petroleum and American Conspicuous Consumption." *Journal of American History* 99: 40–50.

Blainey, Geoffrey. (1969). *The Rush That Never Ended: A History of Australian Mining.* 2nd ed. Melbourne: Melbourne University Press.

Boyd, William. (2001). "The Forest Is the Future? Industrial Forestry and the Southern Pulp and Paper Complex." In *The Second Wave: Southern Industrialization, 1940–1970s,* edited by Philip Scranton, 168–218. Athens, GA: University of Georgia Press.

Bruce, Robert V. (1987). *The Launching of Modern American Science, 1846–1876.* New York: Knopf.

Carter, S., S. Gartner, M. Haines, A. Olmstead, R. Sutch, and G. Wright, eds. (2006). *Historical Statistics of the United States.* Millennial ed. Cambridge: Cambridge University Press.

Chandler, Alfred D. (1972). "Anthracite Coal and the Beginnings of the Industrial Revolution in the United States." *Business History Review* 46: 141–181.

Church, John A. (1871). "Mining Schools in the United States." *North American Review* 112: 62–81.

Clay, Karen, and Gavin Wright. (2005). "Order without Law? Property Rights during the California Gold Rush." *Explorations in Economic History* 42: 155–183.

Clay, Karen, and Gavin Wright. (2012). "Gold Rush Legacy: American Minerals and the Knowledge Economy." In *Property in Land and Other Resources,* edited by Daniel H. Cole and Elinor Ostrom, 67–97. Cambridge, MA: Lincoln Institute.

Dale, Larry L. (1984). "The Pace of Mineral Depletion in the United States." *Land Economics* 60: 155–267.

David, Paul A., and Gavin Wright. (1997). "Increasing Returns and the Genesis of American Resource Abundance." *Industrial and Corporate Change* 6: 203–245.

Eckes, Alfred E., Jr. (1979). *The United States and the Global Struggle for Minerals.* Austin: University of Texas Press.

Frehner, Brian. (2011). *Finding Oil: The Nature of Petroleum Geology, 1859–1920.* Lincoln: University of Nebraska Press.

Gorelick, Steven M. (2010). *Oil Panic and the Global Crisis.* Chichester, UK: Wiley-Blackwell.

Hounshell, David. (1984). *From the American System to Mass Production, 1800–1932.* Baltimore, MD: Johns Hopkins University Press.

Hubbert, M. King. (1956). "Nuclear Energy and the Fossil Fuels." Presented at the Spring Meeting of the Southern District Division of Production, American Petroleum Institute.

International Geological Congress. (1910). *The Iron-Ore Resources of the World.* Stockholm: IGC.

Krautkraemer, Jeffrey A. (2005). "Economics of Scarcity: The State of the Debate." In *Scarcity and Growth Revisited,* edited by R. David Simpson, Michael A. Toman, and Robert U. Ayres, 54–77. Washington, DC: Resources for the Future.

Libecap, Gary. (1986). "Property Rights in Economic History." *Explorations in Economic History* 23: 227–252.

Libecap, Gary. (1989). *Contracting for Property Rights.* New York: Cambridge University Press.

Lucier, Paul. (2008). *Scientists and Swindlers: Consulting on Coal and Oil in America, 1820–1890.* Baltimore, MD: Johns Hopkins University Press.

Mayer, Carl J., and George A. Riley. (1985). *Public Domain, Private Dominion: A History of Public Mineral Policy in America.* San Francisco, CA: Sierra Club Books.